D1505765

Poetry for Students

Poetry for Students

Presenting Analysis, Context, and Criticism on Commonly Studied Poetry

Volume 12

Jennifer Smith and Elizabeth Thomason, Editors

Foreword by David Kelly, College of Lake County

GALE GROUP

Detroit
New York
San Francisco
London
Boston
Woodbridge, CT

Poetry for Students

Staff

Editors: Jennifer Smith and Elizabeth Thomason.

Contributing Editors: Anne Marie Hacht, Michael L. LaBlanc, Ira Mark Milne.

Managing Editor, Literature Content: Dwayne D. Hayes.

Managing Editor, Literature Product: David Galens.

Publisher, Literature Product: Mark Scott.

Research: Victoria B. Cariappa, *Research Manager.* Cheryl Warnock, *Research Specialist.* Tamara Nott, Tracie A. Richardson, *Research Associates.* Nicodemus Ford, Sarah Genik, Timothy Lehnerer, Ron Morelli, *Research Assistants.*

Permissions: Maria Franklin, *Permissions Manager.* Margaret Chamberlain, *Permissions Specialist.* Jacqueline Jones, *Permissions Assistant.*

Manufacturing: Mary Beth Trimper, *Manager, Composition and Electronic Prepress.* Evi Seoud, *Assistant Manager, Composition Purchasing and Electronic Prepress.* Stacy Melson, *Buyer.*

Imaging and Multimedia Content Team: Barbara Yarrow, *Manager.* Randy Bassett, *Imaging Supervisor.* Robert Duncan, Dan Newell, *Imaging Specialists.* Pamela A. Reed, *Imaging Coordinator.* Leitha Etheridge-Sims, Mary Grimes, David G. Oblender, *Image Catalogers.* Robyn V. Young, *Project Manager.* Dean Dauphinais, *Senior Image Editor.* Kelly A. Quin, *Image Editor.*

Product Design Team: Kenn Zorn, *Product Design Manager.* Pamela A. E. Galbreath, *Senior Art Director.* Michael Logusz, *Graphic Artist.*

Copyright Notice

National Advisory Board

Dale Allender: Teacher, West High School, Iowa City, Iowa.

Dana Gioia: Poet and critic. His books include *The Gods of Winter* and *Can Poetry Matter?* He currently resides in Santa Rosa, CA.

Carol Jago: Teacher, Santa Monica High School, Santa Monica, CA. Member of the California Reading and Literature Project at University of California, Los Angeles.

Bonnie J. Newcomer: English teacher, Beloit Junior-Senior High School, Beloit, Kansas. Editor of KATE UpDate, for the Kansas Association of Teachers of English. Ph.D. candidate in information science, Emporia State University, Kansas.

Katherine Nyberg: English teacher. Coordinator of the language arts department of Farmington Public Schools, Farmington, Michigan.

Nancy Rosenberger: Former English teacher and chair of English department at Conestoga High School, Berwyn, Pennsylvania.

Dorothea M. Susag: English teacher, Simms High School, Simms, Montana. Former president of the Montana Association of Teachers of English Language Arts. Member of the National Council of Teachers of English.

Table of Contents

Just a Few Lines on a Page

I have often thought that poets have the easiest job in the world. A poem, after all, is just a few lines on a page, usually not even extending margin to margin—how long would that take to write, about five minutes? Maybe ten at the most, if you wanted it to rhyme or have a repeating meter. Why, I could start in the morning and produce a book of poetry by dinnertime. But we all know that it isn't that easy. Anyone can come up with enough words, but the poet's job is about writing the *right* ones. The right words will change lives, making people see the world somewhat differently than they saw it just a few minutes earlier. The right words can make a reader who relies on the dictionary for meanings take a greater responsibility for his or her own personal understanding. A poem that is put on the page correctly can bear any amount of analysis, probing, defining, explaining, and interrogating, and something about it will still feel new the next time you read it.

It would be fine with me if I could talk about poetry without using the word "magical," because that word is overused these days to imply "a really good time," often with a certain sweetness about it, and a lot of poetry is neither of these. But if you stop and think about magic—whether it brings to mind sorcery, witchcraft, or bunnies pulled from top hats—it always seems to involve stretching reality to produce a result greater than the sum of its parts and pulling unexpected results out of thin air. This book provides ample cases where a few simple words conjure up whole worlds. We do not ac-

tually travel to different times and different cultures, but the poems get into our minds, they find what little we know about the places they are talking about, and then they make that little bit blossom into a bouquet of someone else's life. Poets make us think we are following simple, specific events, but then they leave ideas in our heads that cannot be found on the printed page. Abracadabra.

Sometimes when you finish a poem it doesn't feel as if it has left any supernatural effect on you, like it did not have any more to say beyond the actual words that it used. This happens to everybody, but most often to inexperienced readers: regardless of what is often said about young people's infinite capacity to be amazed, you have to understand what usually does happen, and what could have happened instead, if you are going to be moved by what someone has accomplished. In those cases in which you finish a poem with a "So what?" attitude, the information provided in *Poetry for Students* comes in handy. Readers can feel assured that the poems included here actually are potent magic, not just because a few (or a hundred or ten thousand) professors of literature say they are: they're significant because they can withstand close inspection and still amaze the very same people who have just finished taking them apart and seeing how they work. Turn them inside out, and they will still be able to come alive, again and again. *Poetry for Students* gives readers of any age good practice in feeling the ways poems relate to both the reality of the time and place the poet lived in and the reality of our emotions. Practice is just another word for being a student. The information given here helps you understand the way to read poetry; what to look for, what to expect.

With all of this in mind, I really don't think I would actually like to have a poet's job at all. There are too many skills involved, including precision, honesty, taste, courage, linguistics, passion, compassion, and the ability to keep all sorts of people entertained at once. And that is just what they do with one hand, while the other hand pulls some sort of trick that most of us will never fully understand. I can't even pack all that I need for a weekend into one suitcase, so what would be my chances of stuffing so much life into a few lines? With all that *Poetry for Students* tells us about each poem, I am impressed that any poet can finish three or four poems a year. Read the inside stories of these poems, and you won't be able to approach any poem in the same way you did before.

David J. Kelly
College of Lake County

Introduction

Purpose of the Book

The purpose of *Poetry for Students* (*PfS*) is to provide readers with a guide to understanding, enjoying, and studying poems by giving them easy access to information about the work. Part of Gale's "For Students" Literature line, *PfS* is specifically designed to meet the curricular needs of high school and undergraduate college students and their teachers, as well as the interests of general readers and researchers considering specific poems. While each volume contains entries on "classic" poems frequently studied in classrooms, there are also entries containing hard-to-find information on contemporary poems, including works by multicultural, international, and women poets.

The information covered in each entry includes an introduction to the poem and the poem's author; the actual poem text; a poem summary, to help readers unravel and understand the meaning of the poem; analysis of important themes in the poem; and an explanation of important literary techniques and movements as they are demonstrated in the poem.

In addition to this material, which helps the readers analyze the poem itself, students are also provided with important information on the literary and historical background informing each work. This includes a historical context essay, a box comparing the time or place the poem was written to modern Western culture, a critical overview essay, and excerpts from critical essays on the poem, when available. A unique feature of *PfS* is a specially commissioned overview essay on each poem by an academic expert, targeted toward the student reader.

To further aid the student in studying and enjoying each poem, information on media adaptations is provided when available, as well as reading suggestions for works of fiction and nonfiction on similar themes and topics. Classroom aids include ideas for research papers and lists of critical sources that provide additional material on the poem.

Selection Criteria

The titles for each volume of *PfS* were selected by surveying numerous sources on teaching literature and analyzing course curricula for various school districts. Some of the sources surveyed included: literature anthologies; *Reading Lists for College-Bound Students: The Books Most Recommended by America's Top Colleges;* textbooks on teaching the poem; a College Board survey of poems commonly studied in high schools; and a National Council of Teachers of English (NCTE) survey of poems commonly studied in high schools.

Input was also solicited from our expert advisory board, as well as educators from various areas. From these discussions, it was determined that each volume should have a mix of "classic" poems (those works commonly taught in literature classes) and contemporary poems for which information is often hard to find. Because of the interest in expanding the canon of literature, an emphasis was also placed on including works by international, multicultural, and women authors. Our advisory board members—current high school and college teachers—helped pare down the list for each volume. If a work was not selected for the present volume, it was often noted as a possibility for a future volume. As always, the editor welcomes suggestions for titles to be included in future volumes.

How Each Entry Is Organized

Each entry, or chapter, in *PfS* focuses on one poem. Each entry heading lists the full name of the poem, the author's name, and the date of the poem's publication. The following elements are contained in each entry:

- **Introduction:** a brief overview of the poem which provides information about its first appearance, its literary standing, any controversies surrounding the work, and major conflicts or themes within the work.

- **Author Biography:** this section includes basic facts about the poet's life, and focuses on events and times in the author's life that inspired the poem in question.

- **Poem Text:** when permission has been granted, the poem is reprinted, allowing for quick reference when reading the explication of the following section.

- **Poem Summary:** a description of the major events in the poem, with interpretation of how these events help articulate the poem's themes. Summaries are broken down with subheads that indicate the lines being discussed.

- **Themes:** a thorough overview of how the major topics, themes, and issues are addressed within the poem. Each theme discussed appears in a separate subhead and is easily accessed through the boldface entries in the Subject/Theme Index.

- **Style:** this section addresses important style elements of the poem, such as form, meter, and rhyme scheme; important literary devices used, such as imagery, foreshadowing, and symbolism; and, if applicable, genres to which the work might have belonged, such as Gothicism or Romanticism. Literary terms are explained within the entry, but can also be found in the Glossary.

- **Historical and Cultural Context:** This section outlines the social, political, and cultural climate *in which the author lived and the poem was created.* This section may include descriptions of related historical events, pertinent aspects of daily life in the culture, and the artistic and literary sensibilities of the time in which the work was written. If the poem is a historical work, information regarding the time in which the poem is set is also included. Each section is broken down with helpful subheads. (Works written after the late 1970s may not have this section.)

- **Critical Overview:** this section provides background on the critical reputation of the poem, including bannings or any other public controversies surrounding the work. For older works, this section includes a history of how poem was first received and how perceptions of it may have changed over the years; for more recent poems, direct quotes from early reviews may also be included.

- **Sources:** an alphabetical list of critical material quoted in the entry, with full bibliographical information.

- **For Further Study:** an alphabetical list of other critical sources which may prove useful for the student. Includes full bibliographical information and a brief annotation.

- **Criticism:** at least one essay commissioned by *PfS* which specifically deals with the poem and is written specifically for the student audience, as well as excerpts from previously published criticism on the work, when available.

In addition, most entries contain the following highlighted sections, set separately from the main text:

- **Media Adaptations:** a list of audio recordings as well as any film or television adaptations of the poem, including source information.

- **Compare and Contrast Box:** an "at-a-glance" comparison of the cultural and historical differences between the author's time and culture and late twentieth-century Western culture. This box includes pertinent parallels between the major scientific, political, and cultural movements of the time or place the poem was written, the time or place the poem was set (if a historical work), and modern Western culture. Works written after the mid-1970s may not have this box.

- **What Do I Read Next?:** a list of works that might complement the featured poem or serve as a contrast to it. This includes works by the same author and others, works of fiction and nonfiction, and works from various genres, cultures, and eras.

- **Study Questions:** a list of potential study questions or research topics dealing with the poem. This section includes questions related to other disciplines the student may be studying, such as American history, world history, science, math, government, business, geography, economics, psychology, etc.

Other Features

PfS includes a foreword by David J. Kelly, an instructor and cofounder of the creative writing periodical of Oakton Community College. This essay provides a straightforward, unpretentious explanation of why poetry should be marveled at and how *Poetry for Students* can help teachers show students how to enrich their own reading experiences.

A Cumulative Author/Title Index lists the authors and titles covered in each volume of the *PfS* series.

A Cumulative Nationality/Ethnicity Index breaks down the authors and titles covered in each volume of the *PfS* series by nationality and ethnicity.

A Subject/Theme Index, specific to each volume, provides easy reference for users who may be studying a particular subject or theme rather than a single work. Significant subjects from events to broad themes are included, and the entries pointing to the specific theme discussions in each entry are indicated in **boldface.**

Illustrations are included with entries when available, including photos of the author and other graphics related to the poem.

Citing Poetry for Students

When writing papers, students who quote directly from any volume of *Poetry for Students* may use the following general forms. These examples are based on MLA style; teachers may request that students adhere to a different style, so the following examples may be adapted as needed.

When citing text from *PfS* that is not attributed to a particular author (i.e., the Themes, Style,

Historical Context sections, etc.), the following format should be used in the bibliography section:

"Angle of Geese." *Poetry for Students*. Eds. Marie Napierkowski and Mary Ruby. Vol. 1. Detroit: Gale, 1997. 8–9.

When quoting the specially commissioned essay from *PfS* (usually the first piece under the "Criticism" subhead), the following format should be used:

Velie, Alan. Essay on "Angle of Geese."*Poetry for Students*. Eds. Marie Napierkowski and Mary Ruby. Vol. 1. Detroit: Gale, 1997. 8–9.

When quoting a journal or newspaper essay that is reprinted in a volume of *PfS,* the following form may be used:

Luscher, Robert M. "An Emersonian Context of Dickinson's 'The Soul Selects Her Own Society.'" *ESQ: A Journal of American Renaissance* 30, No. 2 (Second Quarterl, 1984), 111–16; excerpted and reprinted in *Poetry for Students,* Vol. 2, eds. Marie Napierkowski and Mary Ruby (Detroit: Gale, 1997), pp. 120–34.

When quoting material reprinted from a book that appears in a volume of *PfS,* the following form may be used:

Mootry, Maria K. "'Tell It Slant': Disguise and Discovery as Revisionist Poetic Discourse in 'The Bean Eaters,'" in *A Life Distilled: Gwendolyn Brroks, Her Poetry and Fiction,* edited by Maria K. Mootry and Gary Smith (University of Illinois Press, 1987, 177–80; excerpted and reprinted in *Poetry for Students,* Vol. 1, Eds. Marie Napierkowski and Mary Ruby (Detroit: Gale, 1997), pp. 59–61.

We Welcome Your Suggestions

The editors of *Poetry for Students* welcome your comments and ideas. Readers who wish to suggest poems to appear in future volumes, or who have other suggestions, are cordially invited to contact the editor. You may contact the editors via e-mail at: **ForStudentsEditors@galegroup.com.** Or write to the editor at:

Editor, *Poetry for Students*
The Gale Group
27500 Drake Rd.
Farmington Hills, MI 48331–3535

Literary Chronology

1688: Alexander Pope is born on May 21 in London, England.

1712: Alexander Pope's "The Rape of the Lock" is originally published as *The Rape of the Locke: An Heroi-Comical Poem*. A revised version is published in 1714.

1744: Alexander Pope dies of acute asthma and dropsy on May 30.

1757: William Blake is born in London, England, on May 28.

1789: William Blake's "The Lamb" is published in his collection entitled *Songs of Innocence and Experience*.

1827: William Blake dies on August 12.

1878: Carl Sandburg is born on January 6 in Galesburg, Illinois.

1894: Edward Estlin Cummings, best known as e. e. cummings, is born on October 14 in Cambridge, Massachusetts.

1901: Robert Francis is born in Upland, Pennsylvania, on August 12.

1911: Elizabeth Bishop is born in Worcester, Massachusetts, on February 8.

1912: Irving Layton is born on March 12 in Neamtz, Romania.

1918: Alfred Wellington Purdy is born on December 30 in the small farming town of Wooler, Ontario, Canada.

1921: Richard Wilbur is born on March 1 in New York.

1922: Philip Arthur Larkin is born on August 9 in Coventry, Warwickshire, in the English Midlands.

1926: Francis Russell O'Hara is born in Baltimore, Maryland, on June 27.

1929: John Montague is born in Brooklyn, New York, on February 28.

1933: Alden Nowlan is born on January 25 in a rural area near Windsor, Nova Scotia, in Canada.

1936: Carl Sandburg's "Hope Is a Tattered Flag" first appears in his *The People, Yes*, but is called "16."

1940: Carl Sandburg is awarded his first Pulitzer Prize for his biographical work on Abraham Lincoln.

1944: Eavan Boland is born in Dublin, Ireland, on September 24.

1945: Norman Dubie is born on April 10 in Barre, Vermont.

1948: Robert Francis's "The Base Stealer" is originally published in the *Orb Weaver*.

1949: Teresa Palomo Acosta is born in McGregor, Texas, on March 9.

1950: Carl Sandburg wins his second Pulitzer Prize, this time for poetry.

1957: Richard Wilbur's third volume of poetry, *Things of this World*, wins the Pulitzer Prize and the National Book Award.

1958: e. e. cummings's "maggie and milly and molly and may" is first published in *95 Poems*, cummings' fifteenth collection of verse.

1959: Irving Layton wins the Governor General's Award for Poetry.

1960: Frank O'Hara's "Having a Coke with You" is first published in a small press magazine called *Love*.

1962: e. e. cummings dies on September 3, in North Conway, New Hampshire.

1963: Irving Layton's "A Tall Man Executes a Jig" is published in *Balls for a One-Armed Juggler*, which earns him the Prix Litteraire de Quebec.

1964: Philip Larkin finishes writing "An Arundel Tomb" in 1956, but is not until now that it is published as the final poem in his collection, *The Whitsun Weddings*.

1965: Philip Larkin is awarded the Queen's Gold Medal for Poetry and the Arts.

1965: Elizabeth Bishop's "Filling Station" is published in her third volume, *Questions of Travel*.

1965: Alfred Purdy receives his first Governor General's award.

1966: Frank O'Hara dies on July 25, after being hit by a dune buggy on Fire Island in New York.

1967: Carl Sandburg dies in Flat Rock, North Carolina, on July 22.

1967: Alden Nowlan's "For Jean Vincent d'Abbadie, Baron St.-Castin" is published in the collection entitled *Bread, Wine and Salt* ; the collection wins the Governor General's Award for Poetry.

1968: Alfred Purdy's "Wilderness Gothic" is published in a collection called *Wild Grape Wine*.

1972: John Montague's "A Grafted Tongue" appears in *The Rough Field* but is originally titled "A Severed Head."

1976: Teresa Palomo Acosta's "My Mother Pieced Quilts" is first published in the anthology *Festival de Flor y Canto: An Anthology of Chicano Literature*.

1977: Norman Dubie's "The Czar's Last Christmas Letter. A Barn in the Urals" is published in his collection entitled *The Illustrations*.

1979: Elizabeth Bishop dies suddenly of a cerebral aneurysm on October 6, in Massachusetts.

1980: Eavan Boland's "Anorexic" is published in her collection of poems entitled *In Her Own Image*.

1983: Alden Nowlan dies of pneumonia in Fredericton, New Brunswick, on June 27.

1985: Philip Larkin dies following surgery for throat cancer on December 2, in Hull, England.

1986: Richard Wilbur originally creates "On Freedom's Ground" as the libretto of a cantata which was specifically written for the yearlong celebration of the one hundredth anniversary of the Statue of Liberty, and it premiered on October 28.

1986: Alfred Purdy earns his second Governor General's award.

1987: Robert Francis dies on July 13, in Northampton, Massachusetts.

1987: Richard Wilbur is appointed the second Poet Laureate of the United States.

1988: Richard Wilbur's "On Freedom's Ground" is first published in *New and Collected Poems*, for which he wins his second Pulitzer Prize.

1997: Eavan Boland is awarded the Irish Literature Prize in poetry.

2000: Alfred Purdy dies of lung cancer at his winter home on Vancouver Island on April 21.

Acknowledgments

The editors wish to thank the copyright holders of the excerpted criticism included in this volume and the permissions managers of many book and magazine publishing companies for assisting us in securing reproduction rights. We are also grateful to the staffs of the Detroit Public Library, the Library of Congress, the University of Detroit Mercy Library, Wayne State University Purdy/Kresge Library Complex, and the University of Michigan Libraries for making their resources available to us. Following is a list of the copyright holders who have granted us permission to reproduce material in this volume of *Poetry for Students (PfS)*, Every effort has been made to trace copyright, but if omissions have been made, please let us know.

COPYRIGHTED MATERIAL IN *PfS*, VOLUME 12, WERE REPRODUCED FROM THE FOLLOWING BOOKS:

Acosta, Teresa Palomo. From "My Mother Pieced Quilts," in *Infinite Divisions: An Anthology of Chicana Literature*. Edited by Tey Diana Rebolledo and Eliana S. Rivero. The University of Arizona Press, 1993. Copyright © 1993 Arizona Board of Regents. All rights reserved. Reproduced by permission of the author.—Bishop, Elizabeth. From *The Complete Poems, 1927–1979*. Farrar, Straus & Giroux, Inc., 1983. Copyright © 1979, 1983 by Alice Helen Methfessel. Reproduced by permission of Farrar, Straus & Giroux, LLC.—Boland, Eavan. From "Anorexic," in *An Introduction to Poetry*. Edited by X. J. Kennedy and Dana Gioia. Ninth edition. Longman, 1998. Copyright © 1998 by X. J. Kennedy and Dana Gioia. All rights reserved. Reproduced in North America by permission of W. W. Norton. In the U. K. by permission of Carcanet Press Limited.—cummings, e. e. From "maggie and milly and molly and may," in *Complete Poems: 1904–1962*. Edited George J. Firmage. W. W. Norton & Company, 1983. Copyright © 1956, 1984, 1991 by the Trustees for the E. E. Cummings Trust. Reproduced by permission of Liveright Publishing Corporation.—Dubie, Norman. From "The Czar's Last Christmas Letter: A Barn in the Urals," in *Mercy Seat*. Copyright © 1977, 2001 by Norman Dubie. Reproduced by permission of Copper Canyon Press, P.O. Box 271, Port Townsend, WA 98368–0271.—Francis, Robert. From *The Orb Weaver: Poems*. Wesleyan University Press, 1960. Copyright © 1960 by Robert Francis. Copyright renewed © 1988 by Robert Francis. Reproduced by permission.—Larkin, Philip. From *The Whitsun Weddings*. Faber and Faber, 1964. © 1964 by Philip Larkin. Reproduced in the U. S. by permission of Farrar, Straus & Giroux, Inc. In the rest of the world by Faber & Faber Ltd.—Layton, Irving. From *Balls for a One-Armed Juggler*. McCelland & Stewart, 1963. Reproduced by permission.—Montague, John. From *Selected Poems*. Copyright © John Montague, 1991. Reproduced by permission of Wake Forest University Press in North America. In the rest of the world by Gallery Press.—Nowlan, Alden. From *Selected Poems*. Clarke, Irwin Pub-

Contributors

Emily Archer: Archer holds a Ph.D. in English from Georgia State University, has taught literature and poetry at several colleges, and has published essays, reviews, interviews, and poetry in numerous literary journals. Entry on *Filling Station*.

Bryan Aubrey: Aubrey holds a Ph.D. in English literature from the University of Durham, England. He has worked as editor for Lynn C. Franklin Associates and as a freelance writer and editor. Entries on *An Arundel Tomb, For Jean Vincent d'Abbadie, Baron St.-Castin, A Grafted Tongue,* and *The Lamb*. Original essays on *An Arundel Tomb, For Jean Vincent d'Abbadie, Baron St.-Castin, A Grafted Tongue,* and *The Lamb*.

Jonathan N. Barron: Barron is associate professor of English at the University of Southern Mississippi. He has coedited *Jewish American Poetry, Robert Frost at the Millennium,* as well as a forthcoming collection of essays on the poetic movement, new formalism. He is currently the editor-in-chief of *The Robert Frost Review*. Original essays on *Filling Station* and *Having a Coke with You*.

Liz Brent: Brent has a Ph.D. in American culture, specializing in film studies, from the University of Michigan. She is a freelance writer and teaches courses in the history of American cinema. Original essay on *maggie and milly and molly and may*.

Jennifer Bussey: Bussey holds a master's degree in interdisciplinary studies and a bachelor's degree in English literature. She is an independent writer specializing in literature. Original essays on *Hope Is a Tattered Flag* and *The Lamb*.

Brian Collins: Collins has written on nineteenth-and early-twentieth-century American literature. Entry on *Hope Is a Tattered Flag*. Original essay on *Hope Is a Tattered Flag*.

Michele Drohan: Drohan is a professional editor and writer who specializes in classic and contemporary literature. Entry on *Wilderness Gothic*. Original essay on *Wilderness Gothic*.

Doug Dupler: Dupler is a published writer and critic. Original essays on *For Jean Vincent d'Abbadie, Baron St.-Castin* and *A Grafted Tongue*.

Sheldon Goldfarb: Goldfarb has a Ph.D. in English and has published two books on the Victorian author William Makepeace Thackeray. Original essays on *An Arundel Tomb* and *The Rape of the Lock*.

Joyce Hart: Hart, a former college professor, has lived with Native Americans and studied their traditional ceremonies. Entries on *maggie and milly and molly and may* and *My Mother Pieced Quilts*. Original essays on *Anorexic, maggie and milly and molly and may,* and *My Mother Pieced Quilts*.

Pamela Steed Hill: Hill has had poems published in over 100 journals and has been nominated for a Pushcart Prize three times. Her first collection, *In Praise of Motels*, was published in 1999 by

Blair Mountain Press. She is an associate editor for University Communications at Ohio State University. Entries on *Anorexic* and *A Tall Man Executes a Jig*. Original essays on *Anorexic* and *A Tall Man Executes a Jig*.

Jeannine Johnson: Johnson received her Ph.D. from Yale University and is currently visiting assistant professor of English at Wake Forest University in North Carolina. Original essay on *The Base Stealer*.

David Kelly: Kelly is an instructor of creative writing at several community colleges in Illinois, as well as a fiction writer and playwright. Entry on *The Base Stealer*. Original essay on *The Base Stealer*.

Judi Ketteler: Ketteler has taught literature and English composition and is currently a freelance writer based in Cincinnati, Ohio. Original essay on *My Mother Pieced Quilts*.

Caroline M. Levchuck: Levchuck, a writer and editor, has published articles on literature along with nonfiction essays and children's books. Original essay on *On Freedom's Ground*.

Sarah Madsen Hardy: Madsen Hardy has a doctorate in English literature and is a freelance writer and editor. Original essay on *Filling Station*.

Mary Mahony: Mahony earned an master's in English from the University of Detroit and a master's in library science from Wayne State University. She is an instructor of English at Wayne County Community College in Detroit, Michigan. Entry on *On Freedom's Ground*. Original essays on *Hope Is a Tattered Flag*, *On Freedom's Ground*, and *The Rape of the Lock*.

Daniel Moran: Moran is a secondary-school teacher of English and American literature. He has contributed several entries and essays to the Gale series *Drama for Students*. Entry on *The Rape of the Lock*. Original essay on *The Rape of the Lock*.

Carl Mowery: Mowery has a Ph.D. in writing and literature from Southern Illinois University,

Carbondale, IL. Original essay on *On Freedom's Ground*.

Doreen Piano: Piano is a Ph.D. candidate in English at Bowling Green State University. Original essays on *The Czar's Last Christmas Letter. A Barn in the Urals* and *My Mother Pieced Quilts*.

Sean K. Robisch: Robisch is an assistant professor of ecological and American literature at Purdue University. Original essay on *Wilderness Gothic*.

Cliff Saunders: Saunders teaches writing and literature in the Myrtle Beach, South Carolina, area and has published six chapbooks of poetry. Original essays on *Having a Coke With You* and *maggie and milly and molly and may*.

Chris Semansky: Chris Semansky holds a Ph.D. in English from Stony Brook University and teaches writing and literature at Portland Community College in Portland, Oregon. His collection of poems *Death, But at a Good Price* received the Nicholas Roerich Poetry Prize for 1991 and was published by Story Line Press and the Nicholas Roerich Museum. Semansky's most recent collection, *Blindsided*, has been published by 26 Books of Portland, Oregon. Entries on *The Czar's Last Christmas Letter. A Barn in the Urals* and *Having a Coke with You*. Original essays on *The Czar's Last Christmas Letter. A Barn in the Urals* and *Having a Coke with You*.

Erica Smith: Smith is a writer and editor. Original essays on *Filling Station*, *The Lamb* and *maggie and milly and molly and may*.

Alice Van Wart: Van Wart is an editor who has a Ph.D. in Canadian literature. Original essay on *Wilderness Gothic*.

Cody Walker: Walker teaches courses in poetry and fiction at the University of Washington. Original essay on *The Base Stealer*.

Paul Witcover: Witcover is a novelist and editor in New York City with a master's in creative writing and literature from the City University of New York. Original essay on *Filling Station*.

Anorexic

Eavan Boland
1980

As the title of the poem suggests, "Anorexic" examines the troubling issue of self-inflicted starvation, a topic that some readers (and some poets) consider controversial and out of place in poetry. But that, Eavan Boland would say, is all the more reason to write about it.

Beginning with the publication of *In Her Own Image* in 1980, Boland began to explore and present in her work intimate subjects dealing with all aspects of a woman's life, including her sexuality, her relationship with men, and her relationship with herself. *In Her Own Image* includes poems with such provocative titles as "Menses," "Masturbation," and "Mastectomy," as well as "Anorexic." These poems make public the highly personal thoughts and behaviors of women, and Boland's strong feminist views are the driving force behind their creation. These poems have been both praised and condemned but often by readers who do not fully appreciate their motivations.

"Anorexic" relies heavily on irony to present Boland's disdain for the long-held social practice of judging females by their look or weight. This poem, however, rather than being a straightforward account of a woman's suffering, involves a cynical twist. The speaker imagines herself as the biblical Eve longing to disappear back into Adam's body and become the rib from which she was created. By presenting the woman's body as hideous, with its "sweat and fat and greed," Boland ironically points out the female's desperate desire for independence and an identity separate from an attachment to a man. By using the voice of a woman who believes in society's conception of the perfect female and who is willing to waste away to become it, the poet exposes her outrage that such a conception exists.

Author Biography

Eavan Boland was born in Dublin, Ireland, on September 24, 1944. She was the youngest of five children in a fairly well-to-do and influential family. Her mother was an artist, and her father was a diplomat, serving as an assistant secretary in the Department of Foreign Affairs during World War II.

After the war, tension mounted between Ireland and England, and Ireland finally broke from the Commonwealth in 1948. Not long afterwards, Boland's father was appointed ambassador to England, and he moved his family there. In 1956, he became the Irish ambassador to the United Nations and relocated the family again, this time to New York City.

Although her parents provided a good home for their children and were financially able to take care of their needs, their nomadic lifestyle left Boland feeling, at times, displaced and insecure. In 1959, when she was fifteen years old, Boland returned to Ireland.

Once there, Boland entered Holy Child Convent School. She studied and lived there until 1962 when she was accepted into Trinity College. In 1966, she graduated from Trinity with degrees in Latin and English. At both of these schools, Boland found the solitude, peace, and security that she had missed in her years spent in other countries. She began to write poetry. In 1962, she published her first collection, *23 Poems,* at her own expense. Her following collections were picked up by publishing houses, and the second one, *New Territory,* won her the 1967 Irish Arts Council Macauley Fellowship.

To date, Boland has published twelve volumes of poetry. She has taught at various colleges and workshops in Ireland and the United States. Since 1995, she has directed the creative writing program at Stanford University in California.

Boland's early poetry was heavily influenced by the physical and emotional environments in which she grew up. As a child living in England after World War II, she was witness to the devastation that the cities and countryside had endured,

and she saw firsthand the destruction of both the people and the land. As an Irish child growing up in England, she felt the personal sting of prejudice and hatred that earmarked the relationship between the English and the Irish. As a result, much of her early poetry is political in nature, addressing issues of public and international significance. By 1980, however, with the publication of *In Her Own Image,* Boland's work took a turn toward intensely personal subjects. "Anorexic" is a prime example of that turn.

Poem Text

Flesh is heretic.
My body is a witch.
I am burning it.

Yes I am torching
her curves and paps and wiles.   5
They scorch in my self denials.

How she meshed my head
in the half-truths
of her fevers

till I renounced   10
milk and honey
and the taste of lunch.

I vomited
her hungers.
Now the bitch is burning.   15

I am starved and curveless.
I am skin and bone.
She has learned her lesson.

Thin as a rib
I turn in sleep.   20
My dreams probe

a claustrophobia
a sensuous enclosure.
How warm it was and wide

once by a warm drum,   25
once by the song of his breath
and in his sleeping side.
Only a little more,

only a few more days
sinless, foodless,   30

I will slip
back into him again
as if I had never been away.

Caged so
I will grow   35
angular and holy

past pain,
keeping his heart
such company

40

as will make me forget
in a small space
the fall

into forked dark,
into python needs
heaving to hips and breasts   45
and lips and heat
and sweat and fat and greed.

Poem Summary

Line 1

The first line of "Anorexic" shocks the reader with its bluntness and sets the tone for the entire poem. The word "heretic," meaning something contrary to accepted beliefs, implies a religious theme, since it usually refers to something or someone that opposes the doctrines of Christianity. This subject will return later in the poem when the speaker alludes to Adam and Eve in discussing the relationship among men, women, and anorexia. The word "flesh" is noteworthy because it stresses how anorexia distorts its victims' perception. The speaker does not say that *fat* or any other particular kind of flesh is "heretic"—rather, flesh *in general* is a sin.

Lines 2–3

These lines continue the sharp language and appalling sentiment as the speaker compares her body to a witch condemned to burn at the stake. The separation of the speaker's mental self from her physical self is notable. In the third line, the speaker claims "*I am burning it,*" [italics mine] as though her body is a detached thing her mind can destroy at will. These lines also maintain the religious allusion and the idea of heresy, the sin for which many so-called witches lost their lives.

Lines 4–6

Line 4 not only confirms the speaker's metaphorical act of burning her body, but also intensifies the description of it. Now she is not just "burning" it, but "torching" it. She also becomes more specific about the parts of her body that are on fire, calling attention to the physical features generally attributed to females—"curves and paps [nipples] and wiles." The word "wiles" typically denotes something that entices or seduces, sometimes by trickery and deception. In this case, it likely refers to all parts of a woman's body that men find enticing (the genitalia, in particular, since breasts are mentioned in the same line).

Media Adaptations

- A general search under Eavan Boland's name on the Internet search engine "Yahoo" brings up hundreds of web pages that either feature or mention the poet. The page at http://mmc.arts.uwa.edu.au/chloe/outskirts/archive/VOL2/Feature3.html (January 2001) provides a thorough explanation and review of "Anorexic."

Line 6 introduces another synonym for burning, as the female body parts "scorch" in their starvation. The last three words of this stanza, "my self denials," sum up the position of the anorexic. The disease is based on denying food to the body, but it is notable that Boland does not hyphenate the word "self-denial" as in standard usage. By presenting "self" and "denial" as two separate words, the poet reiterates the idea of a complete division between the anorexic's mind and her body.

Lines 7–9

In these lines, the speaker refers to her body in the third-person as "she" instead of "it," as though her physical being is actually another woman, one she detests. She states that her body "meshed" her head "In the half-truths / Of her fevers," implying that the body attempted to ensnare her mind and lie to it by claiming to hunger for sustenance. The fact that the anorexic calls the need for food a "half-truth" is evidence of her distorted mindset. Line 9 concludes with the word "renounced," which can mean either "gave up" or "rejected." Both work in this case since the speaker is both giving up and rejecting food.

Lines 10–11

These two lines are a clever juxtaposition of phrases, with line 10 having both a literal and a metaphorical meaning. The speaker has "renounced" food, which would include, literally, milk, honey, and anything for lunch. But "milk and honey" is also an allusion to God's description in the Hebrew Bible of a beautiful, peaceful land—the country to which Moses was to lead the Israelites—so lush that it flowed with milk and honey. This line in the poem reiterates the religion and creation mythology allusions, and also implies that the anorexic willfully rejects all that is good, healthy, and plentiful. Contrasting this lofty allusion with "the taste of lunch" causes the poem to drop abruptly into harsh reality.

Lines 12–14

Line 12 presents the same sentiment as appears in lines 9 and 10 but with harsher language and more intensity. "I renounced / Milk and honey" has strengthened into "I vomited / Her hungers." Likewise, the "witch" of line 2 has worsened to the "bitch" who "is burning." Line 14 is the culmination of the speaker's anger and self-hatred, and it occurs just before her emotional turning point.

Lines 15–17

These lines depict a more resigned, melancholy attitude on the part of the speaker. She appears to have become whole again, her mind and body reunited in lines 15 and 16, as she acknowledges, "*I* am starved and curveless / *I* am skin and bone" [italics mine]. Although she reverts to the third person again in line 17, claiming that the body "has learned her lesson," this is the final time in which the third-person reference is made. This is a turning point for the poem and for the speaker, as both become softer and seem to slip into a weakened dream-like state. Just as the physical being loses energy and becomes lethargic as it wastes away in starvation, so do the tone of the anorexic speaker and the poem itself as they parallel the behavior of the disease.

Line 18

The speaker has already described her body as "skin and bone," and now she is specific about the bone she is most like. "Thin as a rib" is a significant line, not only because it stresses how skinny an anorexic becomes, but also because it is thematically important, introducing man's role in the woman's struggle with self-identity and self-hatred. In the biblical story of Adam and Eve, God creates Eve by removing one of Adam's ribs, forming the female body from it. The implication of the tale is that man came first, and that without man, woman would not exist. A woman is essentially a *part* of a man, and as such her role in life is secondary, or diminished, when compared to his. Line 18 of "Anorexic" is pertinent because the speaker is now *becoming* Eve, the perfect representation of women in general.

Lines 19–20

As the speaker sleeps, she dreams she is a rib, her stick-like body able to "probe" the way any long, thin object can.

Lines 21–22

The thing the speaker's dreams probe is not a tangible thing, but "A claustrophobia / A sensuous enclosure." These two items are an odd pair: one connotes a fearful emotional condition and the other a pleasant, comfortable haven. Claustrophobia is an abnormal fear of being in a tight or small space, and it seems as though the speaker has mixed feelings about where her dreams are taking her. At the same time as she tests, or "probe[s]," her fear, she also flirts with the pleasurable, even sexual, solace that being enclosed arouses in her. At this point in the poem, exactly what the "enclosure" is, is not clear. Its connection to the speaker's identifying herself as a "rib," however, soon becomes apparent.

Lines 23–26

These lines reveal what the claustrophobic and sensuous enclosure is: Adam's ribcage. Just as Eve is presumed to represent woman in the poem, so Adam represents man. Here, he is portrayed in a peaceful, yet dominating, position. The speaker, in the form of a rib, recalls what it was like to be inside man's chest, "How warm it was and wide." She remembers lying next to his beating heart, the "warm drum," and listening to the music of his breathing as he slept. This description is quite a turnaround from the anger and hostility that permeated the earlier part of the poem. The resignation in the speaker's dream-voice implies the surrender of her existence as an individual human being, the giving up of womanhood to return to her origin within man.

Lines 27–29

In lines 27 and 28, the reader can almost hear the weak, nearly lifeless voice of the anorexic as she drifts into unconsciousness, waiting for death to end her battle with her physical self. The voice is feeble but hopeful that with "Only a little more" time, in "only a few more days," she will succeed in killing her body, the "witch" she has been burning with starvation. The word "sinless" in line 29 is ironic in that it equates with "foodless." Most people would assume that to starve the body is the real sin, but for the speaker, *eating* is the transgression.

Lines 30–32

Once the speaker's body has died, she will be able to "slip / back into him again." Notably, it is the "I" that will return to Adam's body. It is the "I" who will feel as though she has "never been away," has never become the healthy, fleshy, lustful woman whom the "I" turned into the third-person "she."

Lines 33–34

Brevity and rhyme are conspicuous characteristics of these lines. Irony is also apparent. Something "caged" is not normally associated with growth, yet that is how the speaker sees her return to captivity within Adam. Her prison bars are actually the man's ribcage, and only when she once again takes her place within it will she be able to "grow."

Lines 35–36

The word "angular" in line 35 is a reference to the shape of a rib bone, but it may also imply a phallic symbol since the speaker has relinquished her femininity to reenter the male. This interpretation is reinforced by the inclusion of the word "holy," which sustains the overall irony and cynicism of the poem. Society has not exalted the ribcage as a symbol of power, dominance, and holiness, but the male sex organ has often been afforded these attributes. Because of this, the speaker feels she can grow "past" the "pain" of being a lowly woman only by rejoining the godlike figure of man.

Lines 37–40

These lines present the speaker in her doting role as a rib lying next to the man's heart, keeping it such good company that she will forget the past and her struggles as a woman. Line 40 reiterates the sense of claustrophobia that the speaker initially felt in her dream-like state and that seemed to disappear in her pleasurable musing on how comforting it would be to "slip / back into him again." Calling attention again to the "small space" indicates that not *all* of her fear and discomfort has gone away.

Lines 41–43

These lines can be seen as two separate metaphors, both regarding creation, but one is based on religion and the other on sexual intimacy. The "fall" refers again to the biblical story of Adam and Eve, in which humankind falls from the grace of God by defying His orders and giving in to temp-

tation. Although Eve is warned against eating fruit from the Tree of Knowledge, she is enticed to do so by a snake, and she entices Adam to do the same. In this sense, "the fall / into forked dark" relates to the forked tongue of the snake, and "python needs" is a direct reference to the fierce, deadly reptile. This metaphor maintains the theme of creation and religion within the poem, bringing it full circle from the frenzy of burning heretics to the longing of Eve to slip back into Adam and, finally, to the downfall she brings upon the human race.

But these lines also involve the creation of life through sexual bonding and, in this case, the speaker's own creation as a woman. Although the poet presents the act metaphorically, the language is an example of Boland's move toward explicit and graphic detail. In these lines, woman is created when she falls from her safe place next to man's heart and into the "forked dark" of female genitalia, all at the urgency of the male's sexual needs. Here, "python" is another phallic symbol, and once again it is attributed with power and desire.

Lines 44–46

The final three lines of "Anorexic" consist of a list of human features and characteristics, but the implication is that they are primarily the features of women. But while it is not far-fetched to relate "hips and breasts / and lips and heat" specifically to the female sex, one could reasonably argue that "sweat and fat and greed" apply equally to both sexes. Ending the poem on this ironic point simply reaffirms the speaker's position taken in the beginning—the female body "is a witch" that has grown into a disgusting being with its "greed" for food and the real or imagined "fat" that results.

Themes

Self-Alienation

Anorexia nervosa is a disorder that occurs more often than most people think, yet it is odd in that it is self-inflicted. The "normal" human being would abhor the idea of giving himself or herself cancer, AIDS, or any other serious disease, but many of those same humans withhold proper nutrition from their own bodies for the sake of "dieting" or "getting into shape." But there is a marked difference between individuals who carefully measure their fat grams and count calories and those who simply stop eating. "Anorexic" is not a poem about a woman who falls victim to a bad diet, but

Topics for Further Study

- Write an essay about a physical or psychological disorder that you believe is caused by social pressure. Explain the nature of the pressure, possible reasons for it, and who it affects most often.

- There have been news articles, books, and at least one popular rock song written about the 1972 massacre in Ireland referred to as "Bloody Sunday." Research this event and write an essay describing what happened and why.

- Boland's poem makes metaphorical use of the biblical story of Adam and Eve and is told from Eve's perspective. Write a poem about an emotional stress that is common in males using the same metaphor and told from Adam's perspective.

- Explain how Boland's use of the "anti-lyric" affects the presentation of her poetry in *In Her Own Image* and how the poems would differ if written in traditional lyric style.

an examination of the overwhelming consequences of a female's being so alienated from her own body that she wants to kill it.

From the outset of the work, with its angry tone and violent description, the speaker is engaged in a battle with her own physical being. The alienation from her body that she feels so strongly is stressed by her references to "it" and "her" and "she" instead of "me" or "mine" or "myself." The "self denials" that "scorch" her feminine attributes—"her curves and paps and wiles"—are the result of self-hatred. She is incapable of loving or respecting herself as a woman, and the only solution she sees as viable is to destroy the part that makes her miserable. The "part," unfortunately, happens to be her entire body.

Even when the speaker's body has become so weakened by starvation that "*she* has learned her lesson" [italics mine] and fades into the "I" who sleeps and dreams, the self-alienation is still ap-

parent. Now that the anorexic woman has gotten rid of her physical burden, she imagines that she is Eve and seeks to rejoin her identity with Adam, from whom she originated. By doing so, she can completely obliterate what little personal identity she had and can "grow / angular and holy" within the body of the man, reflecting his physical features. The theme of self-alienation is carried through to the end of the poem, as the speaker claims that closeness to Adam's heart will make her "forget" that she had ever possessed the "hips and breasts / and lips" that made her a female. Instead of respecting those attributes as natural to womanhood, the victim of anorexia equates them with "sweat and fat and greed."

Social Alienation

Boland's poem addresses two types of alienation in its themes. Once the obvious subject of *self*-alienation has been examined, it is equally important to consider the possible causes of it. People who are separated from and disgusted by their own beings may only be reflecting the estrangement and hostility that society has directed toward them. In the case of anorexia, it is most often females, usually teenage girls, who become victims of the disorder. While there have been varying opinions on why teenage girls are more susceptible to this disorder, the most prevalent belief is the one behind the poem "Anorexic"—the pressure to meet cultural expectations, which are unreasonable and unattainable.

The speaker in this poem hates herself. More particularly, she hates her *physical* self, and so she starves her body to punish it for its perceived ugliness. The key word here is "perceived," for the anorexic person distorts the reality that she sees in a mirror. It is society's unattainable perception of the perfect woman that she tries to achieve, inevitably failing, but taking the effort to a deadly extreme. Such cultural standards serve only to alienate females from their own societies. If their flesh cannot be perfect, they reason, then their "Flesh is heretic"—a sin for which the body must burn. But their "heresy" is not a sin against God; rather, it is a transgression against a society that shows no tolerance for imperfect females. "Anorexic" does not directly implicate society, or even mention "society," but the scenario of Eve returning as a rib to Adam's body represents the idea of a female so alienated from her culture that she must destroy her actual self to become a part of it. She must return to "claustrophobia" and the "sensuous enclosure" to please the world. Otherwise, she would be a free, independent woman with whom she equates "sweat and fat and greed."

Creation Mythology

"Anorexic" is neither a "religious" poem nor an "anti-religious" poem, yet its main premise involves the biblical story of Adam and Eve. The poet's personal views on a supreme being do not enter this work because the creation myth is used to provide a comment on human society, not religious doctrine. The speaker, or "Eve," is a symbol of woman and "Adam" is a symbol of both man and society. Adam's role is one of a sleeping, powerful god whose heart is a "warm drum" and whose breath is a "song." Eve is a "starved and curveless" "foodless" rib. She needs to be "caged" within Adam because on her own she cannot measure up to the expectations of her culture. Outside of Adam, she is only a conglomeration of "curves and paps and wiles," "hips and breasts / and lips and heat"— but none of it good enough.

Style

The Anti-Lyric

In general, lyric poetry expresses subjective thoughts and feelings, often deeply personal and emotional ones. The lines are typically drawn out and include regular rhythmic and metrical schemes, giving the work a songlike quality. Before the publication of *In Her Own Image* in 1980, Boland's work had been largely lyrical, and a major influence on her style was the renowned Irish poet William Butler Yeats. As her concerns over the plight of Irish women poets grew, and as she became more involved in the Irish Women's Movement, Boland began to reject the "expected" lyrical poetry and to write what she termed the "anti-lyric." In this style, her lines were very short and the stanzas pared down to pole-like columns. In *Women Creating Women: Contemporary Irish Women Poets,* author and editor Patricia Boyle Haberstroh discusses the poetic style of the collection containing Boland's "Anorexic":

> Boland describes these poems as 'anti-lyric,' her response to the constraints she felt the lyric placed on her as a woman. . . . One of the first things we notice about this volume . . . is the loosening of stanzaic form. Short-line tercets, reminiscent of the American poet Sylvia Plath, appear in half of the poems. Other poems with four-, five-, or ten-line stanzas employ neither regular meter nor rhyme; two of the poems have no fixed stanza. While not unusual in contem-

porary poetry, this loosening of form represents a departure for Boland from those conventional models which had dominated her earlier volumes.

"Anorexic" is a "thin" anti-lyric poem consisting of fourteen stanzas, all but three made up of three lines. The first and fifth stanzas consist of a series of three short sentences, each one blunt and powerful in its message. When read aloud, "Flesh is heretic. / My body is a witch. / I am burning it," has a flat tone, even while the words are horrific. A similar flatness of tone can be heard in "I am starved and curveless. / I am skin and bone. / She has learned her lesson." The eleventh and twelfth stanzas are even briefer, each of the three lines containing only two or three words: "Caged so / I will grow / angular and holy" and "past pain / keeping his heart / such company."

Boland's anti-lyric is actually only "half-anti." While she has chopped the usual flowing lines of lyric verse into blade-like images, she has still maintained—even heightened—the subjectivity and personal expression so prevalent in lyric poetry. The speaker is highly emotional in describing her desire to torch her own sensuous body, and she strongly expresses her anger in stating, "Now the bitch is burning." The language throughout the poem is strongly suggestive and deeply personal, making it lyrical, but the poem is also presented in brief, pared-down lines, making it anti-lyrical.

Rhyme and Alliteration

"Anorexic" is primarily free verse, but it does contain some effective uses of rhyme and alliteration (like-sounding consonants and vowels). Even as the voice is harsh and the message controversial, the work is still "poetic" with such rhymes as "wiles" and "denials," "wide" and "side," and "so" and "grow," as well as the near-rhymes of "needs," "heat," and "greed." The use of alliteration is also impressive, from the abrupt like-consonant sounds of two words—"bitch" and "burning," "sleeping side," "past pain," "forked dark"—to the more strategic and compelling repetition of the "w" sound carried out in "How warm it was and wide / once by a warm drum." In spite of the fierce political and social protest so obvious in this poem, it still retains the grace and style of pure poetry.

Historical Context

The history of Boland's home country is a long and troubled one, from the battles among Celtic tribes

Compare & Contrast

- **1972:** British troops shoot and kill thirteen Roman Catholic protesters in Northern Ireland on a day that becomes known as "Bloody Sunday."

  1998: The Good Friday Accord brings a dubious peace to Northern Ireland after twenty-two months of negotiations and three decades of violence.

- **1979:** The Moral Majority is established and its leader, Jerry Falwell, encourages the effort to block the Equal Rights Amendment for women.

  1995: After a lengthy legal battle, Shannon Faulkner becomes the first woman admitted to the all-male Citadel College.

- **1983:** Pop star Karen Carpenter dies at the age of 32 after an eight-year battle with anorexia nervosa. Although she tried to overcome the disorder for at least two years before her death, the detrimental effects of years of starvation end in heart failure on February 4 of this year.

  1999: A study of 471 college students published in the Fall issue of *Adolescence* finds that twenty percent of the females and ten percent of the males surveyed exhibited anorexic eating patterns. The findings suggest that more males are affected by the disorder than previously thought.

thousands of years ago to the raids on villages and monasteries by the Vikings around 795 A.D. to the takeover by British noblemen 400 years later. Ireland has struggled to maintain its independence since it was first founded, and the hostilities between it and Great Britain still exist today.

Although Boland spent much of her childhood and teenage years outside Ireland, she has lived there most of her adult life except while holding teaching positions in the United States. During the 1970s, when she was writing the poems that would be included in *In Her Own Image,* the country was struck by several terrorist attacks, including the 1976 murder of the British ambassador in Dublin. Even though Ireland, along with Great Britain, joined the European Economic Community (now the European Union) in 1973 to help balance its position in the world community, civil unrest continued to plague the nation and make lasting peace a dim prospect.

Equal rights movements in Ireland were inspired by similar movements all over the world, and many came into being during the 1960s and 1970s. Prior to the Irish Women's Movement, which got into full swing in the 1970s, women already made up the majority of participants in other civil rights actions. As Irish historian Jan Cannavan notes on the web site, "Women's Struggle Liberates Ireland

/ Ireland's Struggle Liberates Women: Feminism and Irish Republicanism":

> In the late 1960s the Northern Ireland Civil Rights Association, inspired by the African-American Civil Rights Movement, waged a non-violent campaign to win equal rights for the Catholic nationalist people of the partitioned Six Counties. Women made up a large proportion of this movement but, except for Bernadette Devlin, the entire leadership was male.

Most of the actions of the Northern Ireland Civil Rights Association (NICRA) involved large marches and demonstrations against British rule. The British-backed police force known as the Royal Ulster Constabulary (RUC) was charged with keeping the marches from getting out of hand and with making arrests when demonstrating turned into rioting. Violent conflicts occurred weekly—if not daily—in Northern Ireland during the late 1960s and early 1970s. Arrests and indefinite internment led to more heated protests by Catholics who supported a Republican Ireland. They constantly found themselves at odds with Protestants who were loyal to the British crown, making trouble in Ireland as much a religious issue as a political one.

Boland was twenty-eight years old in 1972 when tension between Catholic youth and the British Army culminated in one of the worst civil rights movement clashes of the era. No longer able to control the rioting, the RUC had called upon the British Army for help as early as 1969. On January 30, 1972, the NICRA held a massive anti-internment march in Derry County that ended with 13 protesters shot dead by the British Army, most of the victims under the age of 25. This event became known around the world as Bloody Sunday, eventually eulogized in the song "Sunday, Bloody Sunday" by the popular Irish rock band U2. Both sides of the conflict accused the other of lying about the causes. Soldiers claimed they had been fired upon by protesters, as well as by members of the Irish Republican Army who were supposedly among the crowd. Protesters denied the charges. Although the army was exonerated of any wrongdoing in the inquiry that followed, only recently in 1998—nearly 30 years after the tragic event—British Prime Minister Tony Blair announced that there would be a new inquiry into Bloody Sunday.

Obviously, there are many parts of the world in which people of both sexes are subjected to violence, social unrest, harsh physical conditions, and severe emotional distress. Only a small minority turns to self-destructive behavior (such as becoming anorexic) as a means of coping. When Boland turned her poetic attention away from strict political protest and onto issues of feminism, she did so in the wake of a relatively weak women's rights movement in Ireland. Today, not much has changed socially or politically for Irish women in comparison to their counterparts in the United States and other progressive nations around the world. Again according to Cannavan, in Ireland, contraceptives are not easy to come by and abortion is not only illegal but unconstitutional as well. Divorce is also illegal in many states and women are often at the mercy of unscrupulous armed soldiers on the streets. Given these conditions, one is not surprised that an inflaming and accusatory poem such as "Anorexic" found its way onto the pages of a very outspoken female Irish poet's book.

Critical Overview

Before the publication of *In Her Own Image* in 1980, Boland's poetry collections received somewhat mediocre attention in Ireland's poetic circles. The early works were in traditional lyric style, and they exhibited the strong influence of renowned Irish poet William Butler Yeats. Because these characteristics were common to the works of many younger Irish poets, Boland went largely unnoticed

in the poetic world for over a decade. With the release of *In Her Own Image,* however, she sent shock waves throughout the male-dominated network of Irish writers, and the book was predictably condemned by her male counterparts. Women, also predictably, praised the collection for its daring, honest subject matter and its candid presentation. Regardless of the "worthiness" debate, there is no doubt that the collection containing "Anorexic" put Boland on the poetic map.

After 1980, many critics began reviewing Boland's work in terms of "women's writing." Instead of concentrating on her ability as a poet, they became absorbed by her reputation as a feminist. Ironically, the work that appeared to be a breakthrough, not only for Boland, but also for Irish women poets in general, prompted some critics to further pigeonhole her creativity. The subjects of *In Her Own Image* were looked at by some reviewers more as an ostentatious display than as a bold step away from the accepted domain of female poets. The denouncement was not limited to Irish literary criticism.

In an article for the *Michigan Quarterly,* critic Brian Henry states that the poems in this collection

> attempt to shock us with their content—domestic violence, breast cancer, anorexia, menstruation, masturbation. Because these subjects are common material for American poets, these poems carry the extra burden of convincing already skeptical readers. They seldom succeed.

In specific regard to "Anorexic," Henry is a bit more tolerant, calling the poem a "dramatic monologue [that] is faithful to the complexity of this disease." But the overall conclusion of the review reflects an opinion other critics have also voiced: "When Boland can transform her narrators from stock characters to fully realized women, the poems work as verbally taut performances. The too-close resemblances to [Sylvia] Plath's staccato short-line speech acts, however, diminish these poems' long-term significance."

As it turns out, Boland's long-term significance as a poet has not been so easy to dismiss, and *In Her Own Image* was followed by politically-charged collections and works that explored the intricacies of domestic life. Her first overall success in the United States came with the publication of *Outside History* in 1990, and the mainstream American attention helped her win popular acclaim in Ireland as well. Her work is now included in major anthologies and journals in both the United States and Ireland, and in 1997, she was awarded the Irish Literature Prize in poetry.

Criticism

Pamela Steed Hill

Hill has published widely in poetry journals and is the author of a collection entitled In Praise of Motels. *In the following essay, she examines the role of female sexuality in Boland's poem, contending that the poem relies as much on allusions to female sexuality as on the main story of Adam and Eve.*

Anorexia nervosa is a complex disorder with causes that are not completely understood. But what is well documented is the effect on the body that results from the cycle of self-starvation and purging food, such as sallow skin, brittle bones, loss of hair, tooth decay, and, in some cases, heart failure. Females are most susceptible to anorexia, and it is usually adolescent girls or very young women who become victims of this disease. Most recent studies have pointed to a stressful family upbringing as a possible cause for many girls to become anorexic. Research indicates that parents who hold their daughters to high or unreasonable expectations while at the same time discouraging their daughters' independence, create an emotional burden that the young girls cannot resolve. Many turn to self-hatred and, eventually, self-destruction as a form of punishment for not being "good enough."

Eavan Boland's poem "Anorexic" offers a different reason for the existence of this disorder in the lives of women. Instead of placing the blame on parents, the poem points a finger at society in general and at men in particular. The poem is based on the premise that the culture in which a woman lives places undue expectations on her physical appearance, mandating that the "ideal" woman be beautiful and thin. The speaker in the poem is so deeply affected by social pressure that she wants to destroy her "inept" physical self and return spiritually to the inside of a man's perfect body—metaphorically, Eve returning to Adam as the rib from which she came. What is especially interesting about the speaker's obsession with self-annihilation is her focus on destroying the most intimate parts of her body, eradicating her sexuality and all the features particular to a healthy woman. As a result, "Anorexic" is a mixture of allusions to both female sexuality and to the biblical story of creation.

On the web site *WM's Story,* an anonymous woman relates her battle with anorexia nervosa, beginning her story with these words:

Obsession. Hunger. Fraud. Vice. Crutch. Need. Weakness. Selfish. Milk-fed. Stupid. Fat. Worthless. Lazy. Sloth. Me. No matter which word you select, they were all my name at one point or another, yelled at me by that ferocious taskmaster that used to be my conscience.

This grave list of self-loathing words could easily come from the poem's speaker, but she has created a list of her own: "hips and breasts / and lips and heat / and sweat and fat and greed." The lists are similar, and both contain the word "fat," but the anorexic woman in the poem aligns the sexual parts of a woman's body (hips, breasts, and lips) with descriptive words that are both erotic (heat and sweat) and distasteful (fat and greed). She compares female voluptuousness to a sin—in this case, gluttony.

From the beginning of "Anorexic," the speaker spells out the sinfulness of the flesh. Her own "is heretic" and her body "is a witch." From this Puritanical imagery, she goes immediately into a list of the specific body parts that are most heretic, the sensual "curves and paps and wiles." Why would she single out her most intimate features for "torching" with no mention of the more benign fingers, toes, legs, arms, and so forth? Why would she make a point of calling her body "curveless" after she has "vomited / her hungers" and announced that "the bitch is burning"? The answer most likely lies in the second half of the poem, which introduces man, who plays the dual role of savior and destroyer in the woman's life.

The story of human creation through Adam and Eve appears in a variety of similar versions throughout the history of theology and mythology. Typically, it involves a benevolent creator, an opportunity for everlasting happiness, and a "fall" from that happiness through surrendering to temptation. But the study of religion or myth has little, if anything, to do with Boland's "Anorexic." Instead, this poem uses the familiar figures of Adam and Eve to symbolize the difference in society's treatment of men and women. It is a difference, the poet contends, driven by a male-dominated power structure that allows men the freedom to be and to look however they naturally are. That same structure, however, sets up a standard for women to meet, especially when it comes to their personal appearances. In the poem, the speaker despises her own sexuality and the parts of her body that most represent it. As she slips into the identity of Eve, however, she calls Adam's ribcage "a sensuous enclosure," a pleasurable description from the same woman who abhors sensuousness within herself.

She thinks of his heart as a "warm drum," his breath as a "song," and his "sleeping side" as a comforting, safe haven in which she used to exist. Compare these engaging descriptions of the man's physicality to the words the speaker uses to describe her own, and the contradiction is obvious. The point here is that society's inequitable treatment of the two sexes is so all-encompassing that some women themselves begin to accept—even embrace—their lower position.

As the poem moves toward its end, the speaker, now Eve, becomes more and more entrenched in her quest to return to Adam's body. And just as she had targeted the intimate parts of her own body to make suffer, she now alludes to the man's sex organ to praise and to imitate. Back inside his ribcage, she "will grow / angular and holy." Here, sexual imagery is directly associated with religious imagery. The phallic symbol, characterized as "angular," is sacred, and the thinner, more "curveless" she becomes, the more she will resemble it. Eve's need to lose herself inside the male body is evidence of how drastically social pressure has affected her. Her independence as a woman is so weakened that she wants to forfeit her own existence altogether. It is that existence that she refers to as "pain" in saying that she can grow "past pain" by sleeping next to Adam's heart in the form of a rib. Her hope is that by doing so she can "forget / in a small space / the fall" from her secure, yet questionable, sanctuary.

References to the "fall" of humankind from the grace of God have been a very commonplace metaphor in writings of all kinds for hundreds of years. Its usage is trite in most instances, but in "Anorexic" the mixture of creation mythology and sexual imagery provides an interesting twist to an otherwise stale idea. Eve wants to forget that she was ever tempted by a snake, gave in, and, thereby plunged the human race into sin and suffering. She carries the guilt of introducing greed into the world, and her only salvation is to give up her "evil" womanhood and become a safe, benign bone in Adam's body again. The "forked dark" and "python needs" conjure up frightening images of snakes and devils and people falling into bottomless pits. But the final three lines of the poem give new meaning to forked dark and needful pythons.

With the sexually-charged description of "heaving to hips and breasts / and lips and heat / and sweat," the "forked dark" and "python" now become symbols of female and male genitalia. Once again, Boland reverts to sensuous imagery to

> *The speaker in the poem is so deeply affected by social pressure that she wants to destroy her 'inept' physical self and return spiritually to the inside of a man's perfect body—metaphorically, Eve returning to Adam as the rib from which she came."*

emphasize the desire to destroy what is most womanly, what is prominently female. Had the description ended with "sweat," the connotation might not have been so negative. Taken out of context, it might read as an enticing or, at least, expected depiction of human sexuality. But the final two adjectives are "fat and greed"—doleful reminders that the anorexic speaker loathes the idea of intimate pleasure, especially from inside a body she abhors.

Most of the poems collected in *In Her Own Image* are highly emotional and border on extreme responses to women's issues, both personal and social. "Anorexic" is no exception. The language is extreme, the sentiment is extreme, and the speaker's actions are extreme. While one could argue that severe thoughts and behaviors are typical of anorexia victims, a case may also be made for the poem taking things too far. On one level, the poem aptly depicts the distorted mindset of an anorexic woman and does a good job portraying the emaciated effects of starvation. On a deeper level, however, the placement of blame on a society dominated by males appears overdone in the references to sexuality and the destruction of the physical features most commonly associated with sexual behavior. The obvious sarcasm displayed in the annihilation of the female body and the praise of the male body serves only to add unnecessary hysteria to the work. Because the poem relies so heavily on sexual imagery entwined with creation mythology, it is especially important to control the voice to keep the already volatile material from dis-

What Do I Read Next?

- Lori Gottlieb's *Stick Figure: A Diary of My Former Self,* published in 2000, is the candid story of the author's struggle with anorexia, beginning when she was eleven years old. Based on her childhood diaries, the voice is uniquely first-person, sometimes childlike, sometimes adult, and always honest.

- When Nathaniel Hawthorne published *The Scarlet Letter* in 1850, he probably had no idea that the theme of his book would still be a central issue in the lives of many twenty-first-century women. *The Scarlet Letter* examines the social stigma associated with being a female adulterer—the Puritan community of the novel sentences the offender to wear a large red 'A' on her clothing as punishment. Male adulterers did not suffer the same humiliation.

- The 1997 collection entitled *Anorexics on Anorexia,* edited by Rosemary Shelley, provides excellent and chilling insight into the minds of anorexics by allowing victims of the disease to tell their own stories. It is helpful not only for those suffering the disease, but for their loved ones as well.

- Feminist scholar Naomi Wolf takes on the destructive social control of women by the cosmetic, diet, and plastic surgery industries in *The Beauty Myth: How Images of Beauty Are Used Against Women,* published in 1990. Wolf argues that products marketed to women set unrealistic, impossible standards that the "average" woman cannot attain.

- Eavan Boland's *New Territory,* published in 1967, was her first professionally published collection. It reflects her youthfulness as a poet, as well as her serious attention to form. The poems are an interesting contrast to those in *In Her Own Image.*

sipating into baseless emotion. "Anorexic" does not lose total control, but some expressions are over-reaching in the attempt to make a feminist statement. Describing the phallus as "holy" and the female body as everything from a "witch" to a "bitch," for example, is overly obvious sarcasm. In spite of a few lapses, however, Boland's poem achieves its purpose by calling attention to the power of social pressure. Exaggerated or not, the pressure to be thin can result in anorexia nervosa, and the disorder is sometimes fatal. The speaker in the poem may be overwrought in her reasoning, but her battle is very realistic.

Source: Pamela Steed Hill, Critical Essay on "Anorexic," in *Poetry for Students,* The Gale Group, 2001.

Joyce Hart

Hart, a former college professor, is currently a freelance writer and copyeditor. In this essay, she analyzes Boland's poem "Anorexic" in terms of politics, language, and feminist literary theory, with an emphasis on the thoughts of French theorist Helene Cixous.

One of Eavan Boland's most challenging themes, not only in her poetry, but also in her professional life, is that of formulating an authentic identity. By first looking at this challenge in all its aspects, it will be easier to understand the underlying theme in her poem "Anorexic."

In her professional life, Boland has fought for over thirty years the "intensely chauvinistic Irish literary community," as Michael Glover comments in *Independent on Sunday.* In an interview with Eileen Battersby in *The Irish Times,* Boland states that in Ireland "There seems to be no difficulty in being perceived as a woman poet. The trouble appears to lie in being fully accepted as an Irish poet." The traditional Irish poet is male, and it is the male poets who criticize Boland "for her concentration on the domestic" in her poetry, says Battersby. Boland adds that she thinks "there was a hidden struggle over subject matter going on in Irish poetry which I blundered into. I was aware that it was easier to have a political murder as the subject of an Irish poem than a baby or a washing machine."

"'Challenge,'" says Battersby, "is a word which appears frequently in [Boland's] conversation. . . . Few major contemporary Irish writers have been as dismissively treated." Boland adds that "we have a powerful tradition here [in Ireland] of the male poet. Irish poetry was male and bardic in ethos. Historically the woman is the passive object of poetry. We aren't supposed to write poems, we are supposed to be in them." Battersby continues, "'Who is the poet?' and how is that identity constructed are the questions [Boland] seems to be addressing, and what are the issues poetry should explore. . . .she has been marginalised by poets and readers far more prepared to see the heroism in a stolen kiss than to acknowledge the pain which accompanies a mother's realisation that her child no longer needs her." Boland adds to this comment by saying that "so many men . . . sneer at the suburban life and yet it is the very life their wives and their daughters have led and are leading. And not to see through its circumstances to its vision and power and importance seems to be both wrong and illogical."

Irish poetry, with its lack of female voices and female subject matter, shows wide gaps or silences in the woman's exploration of identity. For Boland, says Brian Henry in his article "The Woman as Icon, the Woman as Poet," poetry "becomes a way to usurp those silences, to bring back from an immersion in the collective unconscious, like Dante from his journey, the language that can liberate an oppressed community." That oppressed community is the subject of Boland's poem "Anorexic." It is the community of women, in particular, Irish women, that Boland feels has no voice. Like women who suffer from anorexia, the Irish woman has a distorted image of herself, an image fed to her by male poets who depend on women "as motifs in their poetry," as Boland claims. "The women in their poems were often passive, decorative, raised to emblematic status." Women in traditional Irish poetry are seen only as ornaments. This image matches the psychological image that has been identified in women who suffer from anorexia—women who strive for perfection and are anxious to please. In Irish literature, Boland states, in an *Irish Literary Supplement* interview with Nancy Means Wright and Dennis J. Hannan, "transaction between the male and the female . . . is an active-passive one . . . this community nominates women as the receptors of other people's creativity and not as the initiators of their own." Women are told that their creative "gift is dangerous to [their] tradition of womanhood." If Boland's "creative gift" is substituted for food (for anorexics), Boland's poem takes on a broader meaning.

As stated above by Brian Henry, Boland is searching for a new language, one that will rise from the collective unconscious (a term coined by Carl Jung, referring to a subconscious, mythical awareness by which all human thought processes are connected). This language will hopefully free women. But what is this language? How does one learn to use it? And how does it differ from the language that now exists?

To find a language in which women might liberate themselves, one must first define the language

To find a language in which women might liberate themselves, one must first define the language that confines them."

that confines them. Both of these tasks have been undertaken by French feminist Hélène Cixous. Coincidently, Cixous is also associated with having stressed the relationship between feminine writing and the female body, a relationship that fits very well into an analysis of Boland's "Anorexic."

"What theorists like Cixous . . . are trying to do," says Julie Jasken in her "Introduction to Hélène Cixous," is to "answer the questions that many of us may have personally struggled with." This questioning, Jasken proposes, might find the reasons that women's voices are conspicuously absent in the two thousand-year-long European literary tradition. Cixous, as Jasken presents her, is looking at women's rhetoric to find out if there is a distinct way that women think, speak, and write that is inhibited by the accepted and currently practiced mode of communication.

Cixous has also coined the phrase *l'écriture féminine* which pertains to writing that is located in and authorized by female experience. In other words, Cixous believes that some kinds of writing are specifically gender or biologically determined. Male writing is basically rational and linear, whereas female writing comes more naturally from the subconscious level and flows in a more circular or sensual pattern. (She does not propose, however, that *l'écriture féminine* can be written only by women.) But to understand Cixous (and to analyze Boland's poetry) first it is necessary to understand Cixous's background. And to understand that, it will be necessary to say a little about Jacques Lacan.

Lacan was a French psychoanalyst who based a part of his psychoanalytical thoughts on the ideas articulated in linguistics. Briefly, Lacan believed that from birth to adulthood, humans go through three stages, including the Symbolic stage, in which language is formed. It is also in the Symbolic stage that humans develop a concept of "I" or "self." Another important Lacanian concept is that becoming a speaker in the Symbolic stage requires humans to obey the laws and rules of language. According to Lacan, these rules are paternal. Lacan refers to them as the "Law-of-the-Father" or the "Phallus." The Phallus is the idea of the Father, the patriarchal order, and the position that rules language.

Accepting Lacan's concept that Phallus rules language, Cixous argues that, if this is true, it explains why women find it difficult (if not impossible) to express their feelings and their female sexuality and pleasure in this patriarchal language. In order for women to express themselves according to the rules of the Phallus language, women must do so as the *other,* that is, in the role of women as defined by men: passive and lacking (as in lacking a penis). The only other option open to women in a phallocentric language is to write as a man. The positive side of this Lacanian concept, states Cixous, is that because women are "lacking," they are also less anchored to the phallocentric language and its laws of order and are thus more easily able to communicate in a more fluid or flowing language. This flowing language is found in poetry. Women are more in touch with the imagination and the unconscious, and poetry is the best vehicle to express their imagination. The phallocentric structure of language protects those who occupy the privileged position (the masculine position), and this is why Cixous encourages women to forego logical structure and write from their bodies. The body, for Cixous, is inscribed by everything, every experience of life. "Life becomes text starting out from my body. I am already text," writes Cixous in her article "Coming to Writing." If women write from their bodies, they will expose the logical structure of the phallocentric language. And when it is exposed, it will be seen for what it is—a structure, not the truth. States Cixous in "The Laugh of the Medus," "Woman must write her self: must write about women and bring women to writing, from which they have been driven away as violently as from their bodies."

In her article in *Colby Quarterly,* Jody Allen-Randolph writes that Boland's "Anorexic" is a study of the relationship between "female identity and victimization." The alienation from the female body that Boland presents in this poem is "a symptom of the violence directed toward female identity." Allen-Randolph also states that "Anorexic" shows how a male-dominated culture and the definitions that culture imposes can "impinge tragically upon women, shaping their ideas of them-

selves and their relation to their bodies." For instance, Boland begins the second line of her poem with, "My body is a witch. / I am burning it." With these words, the speaker has already begun to remove herself from her body. She has objectified her body as if it is an entity that is separate from her definition of her self. She does not identify herself with "her curves and paps and wiles." These are the outward signs of woman, the sexual definitions that have been imposed on her—her so-called hourglass figure, the sexuality of her breasts (paps refer to nipples), and her alluring ways of trapping men (this is what is implied by the word "wiles").

In the third stanza, the speaker is totally alienated from her body. She not only has objectified her body, she now refers to herself as "she." It is in this stanza that Boland writes about how women sacrifice their pleasures, using the words "fevers," "milk and honey," and "the taste of lunch." Boland continues with this theme in the next stanza, as she writes, "I vomited / her hungers." As someone who is anorexic, the woman in this poem is now empty. She is devoid not only of food and pleasure, she is also devoid of all passion. In all but vague terms, she no longer exists. "Now the bitch is burning." In this stage of the decomposition of self, the speaker has not only removed herself from her body and identity, but she now finds that which she has removed herself from is repulsive. In the last line of the fifth stanza, the speaker takes on a somewhat phallocentric role as lawmaker and judge as she states: "She has learned her lesson."

This masculine role is defined even more specifically when Boland begins the sixth stanza with the description of the woman who is "thin as a rib." This is a definite phallic symbol that by the end of the stanza is "probing," an action associated with a penis, as the speaker enters "a claustrophobia / a sensuous enclosure / how warm it was and wide." The speaker has now almost completely transformed into the masculine. It is a claustrophobic transformation, but, at the same time, the transformation entices the female with its warmth, the music of the heartbeat, and the song of the masculine breath. She has slipped inside, but she is not quite a part of the masculine. She must still rid herself of the final essence of female by returning to the biblical story of Adam and Eve, returning to the mythical origin of the creation of human beings, returning back so far that she no longer exists except "caged so," as Adam's rib where she will grow "holy / past pain." Only as man will she regain the grace that she lost when she was a woman, the first woman, who enticed man to eat the forbidden fruit.

In the last two stanzas, the speaker has completely denied herself an identity as a woman. Rather, she has diminished herself to the all-consuming role of keeping the man's heart company so that she can "forget / in a small space / the fall." Then, in the very last stanza, Boland introduces the words "python needs," which could refer either to the snake in the Garden of Eden (the tempter), or to the phallic symbol of snake in general (man's sexual needs). It could also be a reference to the mythical Greek god Apollo who slew Python, a large snakelike dragon. It is interesting to note that Apollo was the god of poetry as well as the god who made men aware of their guilt. It also could be that Boland refers to all three symbols and, by using Apollo, gives the last lines a deeper meaning, as man is made aware of his guilt in consuming woman, or worse pushing her into "the forked dark" where he heaves first to her "hips and breasts / and lips and heat" and then slowly descends, as if from heaven to hell, as the concepts move further away from a sexual act to sin, as he heaves to the "sweat and fat and greed."

It is not that Boland commends this female act of self-debasement or annihilation. Rather, she is stating a fact and warning women to find their voice, their language, and their identity. She warns women to not give in to the temptation to withdraw into the phallocentric world where they will lose themselves.

Source: Joyce Hart, Critical Essay on "Anorexic," in *Poetry for Students,* The Gale Group, 2001.

Sources

Allen-Randolph, Jody, "Ecriture Feminine and the Authorship of Self in Eavan Boland's *In Her Own Image,*" in *Colby Quarterly,* Vol. 27, No. 1, March 1991, pp. 48–59.

Amazon, www.amazon.com, (June 2000).

Anorexia Nervosa, http://wellweb.com/INDEX/QANOREX. HTM (August 16, 2000).

Boland, Eavan, *Collected Poems,* Carcanet Press.

"CAIN Project: Bloody Sunday," http://cain.ulst.ac.uk/events/bsunday/bs.htm (October 27, 2000).

Cannavan, Jan, "Women's Struggle Liberates Ireland / Ireland's Struggle Liberates Women: Feminism and Irish Republicanism," http://www.etext.org/Politics/INAC/irish.women (August 8, 2000).

Haberstroh, Patricia Boyle, "Eavan Boland," in *Women Creating Women: Contemporary Irish Women Poets,* Syracuse University Press, pp. 59–90.

Henry, Brian, "The Woman as Icon, the Woman as Poet," in *Michigan Quarterly,* Vol. XXXVI, No. 1, Winter 1997, pp. 188–202.

The History Channel, www.historychannel.com (August 10, 2000).

Irigaray/Cixious, http://social.chass.ncsu.edu/wyrick/debclass/irigar.htm (August 2000).

WM's Story, http://www.angelfire.com/wy/anorexia/WMStory.html (August 16, 2000).

For Further Study

Boland, Eavan, *Object Lessons,* W. W. Norton, 1996.
    Dedicated to her mother, whom she calls "the friend of my lifetime," this is a prose work by Boland that includes autobiographical details as well as her thoughts on women poets in general and women poets in Ireland in particular.

Boland, Eavan, *Outside History: Selected Poems, 1980–1990,* W. W. Norton, 1991.
    This collection provides a good look at Boland's writing in the ten years following *In Her Own Image.* It is interesting to note the subtle changes in her style and subject matter and to understand how these changes helped her gain greater recognition as a poet.

Hoagland, Kathleen, ed., *1000 Years of Irish Poetry: The Gaelic and Anglo-Irish Poets from Pagan Times to the Present,* Welcome Rain, 1999.
    Over 800 pages long, this book is not likely to be read cover to cover, but the comprehensive collection of Irish poetry provides an excellent overview of works from that country.

MacLiammóir, Micheál, and Eavan Boland, *W. B. Yeats and His World,* Viking Press, 1972.
    W. B. Yeats is generally considered to be the most important English-writing poet of his time (late nineteenth to early twentieth centuries), and his work had a great impact on Eavan Boland's early poetry. This is an illustrated biography and an interesting look at Yeats from an Irish perspective.

An Arundel Tomb

Philip Larkin
1964

In January 1956, Philip Larkin took a short vacation on England's south coast, during which he visited Chichester Cathedral. In the cathedral, he saw a monument to the fourteenth-century earl of Arundel and his wife that showed them lying together, hand in hand. This image was the inspiration for "An Arundel Tomb," which Larkin began soon after his return to his job as librarian at Hull University. The poem was finished on February 20, 1956.

Larkin later discovered that the linking of hands that so caught his attention was a detail added long after the original had been completed. It was the work of Edward Richardson, a sculptor who in the 1840s reworked the memorial to repair damage it had suffered during the Reformation and the seventeenth-century civil war. The damage was so extensive that before the repairs, the earl had no arms and the countess' right hand was missing. The two figures were not even lying together, but were placed on separate tombs. The decision to place them in the attitude that struck Larkin as significant was therefore taken over four hundred years after the work was first made, and was not the sculptor's original intention. Larkin later commented with amusement on the historical inaccuracies of his poem, which do not affect the merits of the poem as a work of art.

As the final poem in Larkin's celebrated volume, *The Whitsun Weddings,* (London, 1964), "An Arundel Tomb" has been much admired. By building on the small detail of the earl and the countess holding hands, the poem becomes a meditation on death, the passage of time, and the enduring nature of love. The final statement, "What will survive of us is love," is one of Larkin's most famous lines.

Author Biography

Philip Arthur Larkin was born on August 9, 1922, in Coventry, Warwickshire, in the English Midlands, the son of Sydney Larkin, who was the city treasurer, and Eva Larkin.

Throughout his childhood and adolescence, Larkin read and wrote poetry and prose with enthusiasm and regularity. In 1940, a year after the outbreak of World War II, he entered St. John's College, Oxford. He was excused from military service because of his poor eyesight, and he graduated three years later with a first-class honors degree in English. In the same year, he was appointed librarian of a small public library in Wellington, Shropshire.

In 1945, *The North Ship,* Larkin's first collection of poetry, was published by the Fortune Press. It was heavily influenced by the poetry of W. B. Yeats, W. H. Auden, and Dylan Thomas. In the same year, Larkin was appointed assistant librarian at University College, Leicester, and his first novel, *Jill,* was published by Faber and Faber. A second novel, *A Girl in Winter,* was published in 1947. At that time, Larkin's ambitions focused on becoming a successful novelist, and he regarded poetry as second best. He began a draft of a third and then a fourth novel, neither of which he ever finished. In the late 1940s, Larkin also circulated a poetry collection, titled *In the Grip of Light,* which was rejected by six publishers.

Larkin was on the move again in 1950, when he was appointed sub-librarian at Queen's University in Belfast, in Northern Ireland. While there, he published *XX Poems* at his own expense.

The year 1955 was a momentous one for Larkin. He became librarian of the Brynmor Jones Library at the University of Hull, located 150 miles north of London, a job he was to retain for the rest of his life. In that year also, Marvell Press published *The Less Deceived,* which established Larkin's reputation as a leading British poet of the postwar era. A year later, in 1956, Larkin wrote "An Arundel Tomb."

Larkin was a jazz enthusiast all his life, and in 1961 he began reviewing jazz for the *Daily Tele-*

Philip Larkin

graph, a job he continued to do until 1971. In 1964, *The Whitsun Weddings* was published to great acclaim, enhancing Larkin's standing as a poet of great distinction. His success was confirmed the following year when he was awarded the Queen's Gold Medal for Poetry and the Arts.

In 1973, *The Oxford Book of Twentieth-Century English Verse* was published, edited by Larkin. The selections reflected Larkin's own poetic tastes and provoked considerable controversy. The publication of another volume of poetry, *High Windows,* in 1974, confirmed Larkin's status as the most popular poet in England, appreciated as much by the general reading public as by scholars and academics.

In the last decade of his life, Larkin wrote very little. In 1984 he declined the invitation to become Poet Laureate following the death of John Betjeman.

Larkin died following surgery for throat cancer on December 2, 1985, in Hull, England, at the age of sixty-three.

Poem Text

Side by side, their faces blurred,
The earl and countless lie in stone,

Their proper habits vaguely shown
As jointed armour, stiffened pleat,
And that faint hint of the absurd—
The little dogs under their feet.   5

Such plainness of the pre-baroque
Hardly involves the eye, until
It meets his left-hand gauntlet, still
Clasped empty in the other; and   10
One sees, with a sharp tender shock,
His hand withdrawn, holding her hand.

They would not think to lie so long.
Such faithfulness in effigy
Was just a detail friends would see: 15
A sculptor's sweet commissioned grace
Thrown off in helping to prolong
The Latin names around the base.

They would not guess how early in
Their supine stationary voyage   20
The air would change to soundless damage,
Turn the old tenantry away;
How soon succeeding eyes begin
To look, not read. Rigidly they

Persisted, linked, through lengths and breadths   25
Of time. Snow fell, undated. Light
Each summer thronged the glass. A bright
Litter of birdcalls strewed the same
Bone-riddled ground. And up the paths
The endless altered people came,   30

Washing at their identity.
Now, helpless in the hollow of
An unarmorial age, a trough
Of smoke in slow suspended skeins
Above their scrap of history,   35
Only an attitude remains:

Time has transfigured them into
Untruth. The stone fidelity
They hardly meant has come to be
Their final blazon, and to prove   40
Our almost-instinct almost true:
What will survive of us is love.

Poem Summary

Stanza 1

The first two lines of "An Arundel Tomb" describe the stone effigies of two figures, an earl and a countess, lying side by side on top of their tomb. Their faces are not distinct, and the formal, dignified clothes in which the sculptor has represented them ("their proper habits") are shown only vaguely. One figure, the earl, is dressed in armor, which is assembled in pieces and thus shows "joints"; while the countess' garb is probably some kind of gown that shows "stiffened pleats," stiffened, that is, because the garment is rendered in stone. At the feet of the earl and countess, some small dogs are represented. The speaker of the poem regards this detail as out of place, almost to the point of absurdity, although he gives no reason for this impression.

Stanza 2

At first, the speaker regards the effigies as unremarkable; there appears to be nothing that draws in the spectator's eye. He implies that in their plainness, the effigies are typical of the pre-baroque era from which they come. (Baroque refers to a more ornamental style of art and architecture that flourished from about 1550 to 1750.) But then the speaker points to a small, interesting detail concerning the earl's left gauntlet. (A gauntlet is a long glove, used in medieval armor as a defense for hand and wrist.) The earl clutches the gauntlet in his right hand, and the observer notices that the earl's left hand holds the hand of the countess. This detail surprises the observer and creates a sharp feeling of tenderness in him.

Stanza 3

The speaker suggests that the earl and the countess could never have imagined that their stone forms would have endured for so long. They may have believed that the image of faithfulness between them (the hand-holding) was just a small detail that might attract the attention of friends. The next line suggests that the holding of hands may have been merely an added touch by the sculptor who was commissioned to create the effigies. The creation of the intimate detail was just a casual ("thrown off") addition to his primary task, which was to preserve in Latin the names of the two people around the base of the tomb.

Stanza 4

This stanza continues the idea begun in the previous one, about how the earl and the countess could not have imagined what would happen over time concerning their stone effigies. They would not have guessed that in the "voyage" they take through time while lying motionless ("stationary") on their backs ("supine"), conditions would quickly change. "The air would change to soundless damage," is somewhat obscure. Perhaps the poet means that the constantly changing air, or atmosphere, would accompany the changes that alter the couple's memorial from its original context and intent. There may also be a hint of actual physical damage that exposure to the air over the centuries would cause the monument and the cathedral. The next line refers to the social change that would take place: the old feudal society in which the couple lived would vanish. As social conditions altered and generations passed, visitors to the tomb would no longer read the inscriptions at the base of the tomb but would instead look at the two hands clasped together.

Stanza 5

This stanza describes the passing of time since the effigies were first made. The figures of the earl and the countess persist, unchanging through all the seasons. The snows of winter come. Then the light of the summer sun fills the stained glass windows of the cathedral in which the tomb is situated, and the cheerful sound of birds singing is heard throughout the cathedral grounds, which include a graveyard ("Bone-riddled ground"). Throughout the centuries, endless visitors to the cathedral have walked up the same paths, each generation different in appearance, clothing, and beliefs and attitudes from the one that preceded it.

Stanza 6

The effect of the "endless altered people" as they visit the cathedral over a long period of time is revealed. They erode the original identity of the earl and countess, in the sense that they are no longer understood in the context of the times in which they lived. Instead, the two noble figures now live in an "unarmorial age," which means they have survived in effigy into modern times, far distant from their feudal society, in which knights wore armor in battle, and a coat of arms depicted nobility. Metaphorically speaking, that age has slowly gone up in smoke, and the smoke still lingers in coils ("skeins") over what remains from that bygone era. All that is left of that small portion of history—both the age in which the earl and the countess lived and their personal lives—is an "attitude," by which the poet means the fact that the effigy depicts them holding hands. This detail is all that the modern observer notices.

Stanza 7

The passage of time has altered the couple in the effigy into something that does not reflect the truth of their real-life circumstances. The hand-holding that the speaker believes was of little significance to them has come to be their lasting and final celebration and memorial "blazon" (a coat of arms or shield). The gesture of mutual affection that

Media Adaptations

- An abridged audiocassette version of *The Whitsun Weddings,* including "An Arundel Tomb," is published by Faber and Faber (1971), read by Alan Bennet.

- An audiotape of Larkin himself reading *The Whitsun Weddings* is available from The Marvell Press, 194a Plymstock Road, Oreston, Plymouth, PL9 7LN, England. The Marvell Press also publishes an audiotape of Larkin reading his earlier collection, *The Less Deceived,* for the same price.

the modern observer sees, although not of historical significance, does, however, prove that the instinctive human belief about the significance and enduring nature of love is in fact true: what survives humans when they die is the love they express in their lives.

Themes

Love

The theme of love is first hinted at in the last two lines of the second stanza, in which it is revealed that the earl and his wife are depicted as holding hands. This detail is celebrated twice: the reference to the "sharp, tender shock" that the speaker feels when he first notices it, and the "sweet commissioned grace" that prompted the sculptor (so the poet supposes) to have included it. Both phrases point to the charming quality that the hand-in-hand indication of love possesses.

As the poem progresses, the theme of love develops a much stronger meaning. It transpires that it is the attitude of love in which the two figures are placed that has lasted through the ages. No visitor today can imagine what the reality of living in the "armorial age" might have been like; so many hundreds of years have passed that it is impossible

Topics for Further Study

- Is "An Arundel Tomb" an optimistic or a pessimistic poem?

- Why do humans wish to preserve their names on monuments after their deaths, and why do other human beings choose to visit those monuments?

- Larkin once described religion as a "vast moth-eaten musical brocade / Created to pretend we never die" ("Aubade"). Is "An Arundel Tomb" in any sense a religious poem?

- If you could choose one quality that you have expressed in your life (love, courage, or honesty, for example) to live on after your death, what quality would it be and why?

- Research the relationships that might exist between a nobleman and his wife in medieval times and describe how it might differ from the relationship that a modern couple might have.

to recapture the historical circumstances or the individuality of the man and woman depicted in the effigy. What catches the modern eye are not the names in Latin at the base of the tomb, which is what would have been important to the medieval mind, but the tender gesture of affection that is universal in its significance.

The poet embodies two ironies in this theme of love. First, the tender gesture that gives the monument its lasting significance is not what its subjects would most have valued, and in this sense "Time has transfigured them into / Untruth." But the truth they now seem to embody is perhaps more deeply true than anything they could have said about themselves.

The second irony is that the poet undercuts his final observation, "What will survive of us is love," by stating in the previous line that this instinctual belief about love that humans seem to possess may itself be only "almost true." The poet cannot commit himself unequivocally to this vision of the transcendence of love.

And his final hesitation gives a rich ambiguity to two earlier lines, "The earl and countess lie in stone" and "They would not think to lie so long," since "to lie" may also mean "to deceive." Therefore, both lines can now be seen to express deception, referring either to the fact that the couple did not intend the affectionate gesture to be their lasting memorial, or that the poet's qualified affirmation that what will survive is love is in fact untrue.

Time

Time and the sense of history permeate the poem from the beginning. The subject itself is a sculpture that is nearly five hundred years old; the stone effigy with "jointed armor" suggests a world far removed from the present. Stanzas five to seven, in particular, describe the passage of time and its effects. The fact that time moves in eternal cycles, as well as a linear progression, is made clear in stanza five. Snow falls in winter, "undated," which means it recurs eternally and has nothing to do with the progression of human history. Then, in another season, summer's light shines on the windows of the cathedral, and the chattering of birds is heard. Set against these eternally recurring cycles of the seasons is the linear march of human generations, as suggested by the "bone-riddled" graveyard and the "endless altered people" who over the course of hundreds of years have tramped up the paths to worship in the cathedral or simply visit as tourists.

It is time that erodes the historical identity of the earl and his wife, leaving their effigy "helpless" in the midst of an age so unlike their own. Time has made "scrap" out of their "portion of history." The word scrap also suggests that their historical moment was small and perhaps insignificant—a scrap—when compared to the vast stretch of recorded, or unrecorded, time.

The final stanza reveals that the theme of time is intimately bound up with the theme of love. Time strips away many things, but the poem suggests (if the poet's qualification in the next to the last line is not given undue weight) that what is lost, such as details of historical time and place, is nonessential. The essential quality that the passage of time reveals is love; in fact, time is necessary for this most enduring of all qualities to fully reveal its power.

Art

The poem is also a tribute to the power of art. It is entirely due to the work of the sculptor that the love gesture of the earl and the countess can speak across the ages. It is art that can preserve not only the figures of the past but also the vitality of tender human emotions. It is the skill of the sculptor, rather than any action of a god, that immortalizes the earl and his wife. And perhaps most importantly, art has the power not only to represent a historical moment or historical figure in a realistic manner, but also to shape them imaginatively. In this case, the sculptor of the Arundel tomb has succeeded in creating a form that embodies what humans most desire—the immortality of love—even though that goal may be unattainable in real life.

Style

Rhyme

The poem is rhymed and follows a regular rhyme-scheme of abbcac; that is, line 1 (designated a) rhymes with line 5; line two (designated b) rhymes with line 3; and line 4 (designated c) rhymes with line 6. Most of the rhymes are perfect, or true rhymes, in that the sounds correspond exactly to each other. However, on one occasion, the poet uses a partial rhyme to excellent effect. It comes in lines 4 and 6 in the final stanza, in which "prove" only partially rhymes with "love," since the vowel sound "o" is pronounced differently in each word.

The variation neatly expresses the poet's own ambivalence, since he is making the point that his final statement, "What will survive of us is love," is almost, that is to say, not precisely or completely, true. The partial rhyme conveys and strengthens the hesitation. In spite of the ringing affirmation of the final line, the case for love has not been fully proved.

Enjambment

Enjambment is when a grammatical construction, as well as the sense of a poetic line, carries over into the following line. Larkin uses this device to powerful effect in the transition from stanza four to stanza five.

Referring to the couple in effigy, stanza four ends, "Rigidly they" (which is an incomplete grammatical unit). The following stanza completes the thought: "Persisted, linked, through lengths and breadths / Of time," which illustrates the couple's continuous "stationary voyage" referred to in stanza four. The white space on the printed page between the two stanzas conveys visually the vast stretches of time through which the effigy of the couple has endured, as if they are jumping from one age to the next across a canyon of oblivion. The poet continues to use enjambment throughout stanza five, which serves to express the continuous, unbroken passage of time.

Pun

In poetry today, the pun is used more often in comic than serious verse. But Larkin twice employs the device in this serious poem. The line, "They would not think to lie so long" contains a pun on the word lie. This kind of pun is known as an equivoque, in which the same word is used with different meanings, both of which may be relevant. In this case, lie means "lie down" but also "untruth," a meaning that the last stanza makes clear. The second pun is on the word hardly in "The stone fidelity / They hardly meant" in stanza seven. Hardly means "barely" or "only just," but it is also a pun on the hardness of the stone in which the couple's love is depicted. The effect of this subtle pun, for those who notice it, may be faintly humorous, the secondary meaning tending to diminish the seriousness of the primary one.

Historical Context

The Movement

When Larkin wrote "An Arundel Tomb," in 1956, he was one of a group of young poets in England known as the Movement. The term was first used in an article in the literary magazine *The Spectator* in 1954. Larkin's name was not mentioned, since *The Less Deceived,* the volume that made him widely known, was not published until the following year. But in 1956, poet Robert Conquest produced *New Lines,* an anthology that represented all the Movement poets. Nine poems by Larkin were included. The other poets usually associated with the Movement included Kingsley Amis, John Wain, D. J. Enright, Donald Davie, and Thom Gunn.

The label of the Movement was applied mostly by critics rather than the poets themselves, many of whom, Larkin in particular, were not conscious of belonging to any particular school of poetry. The Movement poets did not all know each other, and Larkin himself was well acquainted only with Amis, his close friend from their Oxford days. There were also differences of style in the work of the Movement poets. However, the label stuck, and although the Movement lasted only a few years,

Compare & Contrast

- **1950s:** In postwar England, food rationing ends, but over the next decade, although consumer prosperity increases, the British economy is often in crisis. Britain is sometimes called "the sick man of Europe" with a habit of looking back at its glorious past rather than to the future.

  Today: Britain enjoys a high economic growth rate, and no longer looks back so nostalgically at what many used to think of as the great days of the British Empire.

- **1950s:** Britons take pride in their long cultural heritage and their pastoral vision of England's "green and pleasant land" that "An Arundel Tomb" obliquely celebrates.

  Today: Environmentalist and preservationists are increasingly concerned about the encroach-

ment of modern society, with its industrial development and its pollution, on what remains of "olde England."

- **1956:** In one of its last attempts to assert itself as a world power, Britain embarks with France on a disastrous military expedition to regain Western control over Egypt's Suez Canal.

  1969: Larkin writes the poem, "Homage to a Government," which criticizes the withdrawal of the last British troops from bases east of Suez, in places that were formerly colonies of the British Empire.

  Today: Britain no longer has the power to act alone in military affairs, but operates in concert with its European and U.S. allies in the North Atlantic Treaty Organization (NATO).

most critics now agree that it did represent certain identifiable trends in English poetry of the mid- and late 1950s.

The Movement was in part a reaction against the obscurity associated with modernism in the arts. The poems of Ezra Pound and the art of Pablo Picasso were favorite targets of Larkin. Simon Petch, in *The Art of Philip Larkin,* quotes Larkin's declaration that modernism amounted to

> irresponsible exploitations of technique in contradiction of human life as we know it. That is my essential criticism of modernism … it helps us neither to enjoy nor endure. It will divert us as long as we are prepared to be mystified or outraged, but maintains its hold only by being more mystifying and more outrageous: it has no lasting power.

In contrast, Movement poets avoided the experimental techniques characteristic of modernism, and returned to more traditional poetic forms. Larkin's formal verse in "An Arundel Tomb," which employs rhyme and meter, is an example typical of this development.

Movement poets also wrote for what they called the Common Reader. The idea was that poetry should be intelligible to everyone, not reserved

only for those who could recognize literary allusions or puzzle out complex or obscure symbolism. This principle remained part of Larkin's approach to poetry all his life, and it enabled him to gain a wide following amongst ordinary readers who did not normally read poetry.

A consequence of writing for ordinary people rather than an intellectual elite was that Movement poets prided themselves on being unpretentious and honest. They tried to use diction that was plain and not self-consciously poetic. Their idea was that poetic diction could also include colloquial language, and this type of language is frequent in Larkin's poetry.

For Movement poets, poetry should express a realistic rather than a romantic attitude to life. In this they were reacting against the neo-romantic poetry written in the 1940s, associated mostly with the names of David Gascoyne, Kathleen Raine, and most importantly, Dylan Thomas. These and other poets of that period made much use of surrealistic imagery, as well as myth and symbol, and they often had a mystical conception of the sacredness of poetry. In contrast, Movement poets wanted to express a truth about life in a clear, down-to-earth way. They valued caution and irony.

England after World War II

This attitude of caution, coupled with emotional reserve, may in part be attributable to the times in which the Movement appeared. Post-World War II England was a time of austerity, and English people were deeply conscious of the diminished wealth of their nation and its loss of influence in world affairs. England seemed smaller, more insular, after the war than it had been before it, and the ambitions of poetry were correspondingly scaled down too. Large, heroic subjects were avoided. The drabness of the period is captured by Larkin in his poem "Mr. Bleaney," written in 1955 and published in *The Whitsun Weddings* in 1964.

On the other hand, the security offered by the post-war welfare state, and the development of what was called at the time "consensus politics," in which the differences between the two major political parties were sharply muted, ensured that the poets of the Movement were not much concerned with politics or questions of social justice, unlike their predecessors in the 1930s.

In the decade from the mid-1950s to the mid-1960s, when "An Arundel Tomb" was published in *The Whitsun Weddings,* England began to become more prosperous. With its references to household gadgets, supermarkets, and billboard advertising, Larkin's poetry of the period reflected the growing consumerism of English society.

By this time, the Movement poets had all developed in different ways. However, Larkin is often regarded as the one who stayed closest to Movement principles throughout his poetic career.

Critical Overview

When "An Arundel Tomb" was first published in *The Whitsun Weddings* in 1964, a number of reviewers singled the poem out for comment. Christopher Ricks, in *The New York Review of Books,* described Larkin as "the best poet England now has," and said of the collection "people will be grateful for its best poems for a long time." Ricks listed "An Arundel Tomb" as one of the six best poems. Praise came also from Joseph L. Featherstone, in *New Republic,* who used the last two lines of the poem to illustrate his point that "[Larkin] is especially good at gathering up the substance of a seemingly slow-paced poem and concentrating it into enormously powerful last lines, lines that echo after they are read." For Louis L. Martz, in *The Yale Review,* "An Arundel Tomb" was a "perfect poem," and like Featherstone he also chose to comment on the last two lines:

> That open utterance of the long-repressed sentiment emerges with an effect of ironic hesitation. Our modern inference from the sculptured hands is only our own simplification of the imagery: for that other age had a broader meaning in its sepulture that we can never apprehend. What remains is our own attitude, based upon the 'almost-instinct' of what we wish come true.

In the years that have elapsed since its publication, "An Arundel Tomb" has come to occupy an important place in Larkin's work. Almost all book-length treatments of Larkin's poetry accord ample space to an analysis of it. Bruce Martin, in *Philip Larkin,* uses the poem as an example of "the preeminence of love in Larkin's scheme of values." Andrew Motion, in his biography of the poet, calls it "one of his most moving evocations of the struggle between time and human tenderness." Roger Bowen, in *Death, Failure, and Survival in the Poetry of Philip Larkin,* argues that "An Arundel Tomb" marks an important transition in the poet's work, in terms of his exploration of the "meaning of death." In his later poems, Larkin begins to express "a view of death in relation to a world which perpetually renews itself. In this latter view . . . a quiet trust is sometimes apparent, a trust in continuity, a belief in something undiminished somewhere . . . which will survive beyond his individual extinction." Seen in this light, "An Arundel Tomb" is "an assertion about the future, a belief in some kind of spiritual survival."

Other critics, however, have not been so ready to read the poem in such a positive light. Particular attention has been paid to the last two lines as the key to interpretation. James Booth, in *Philip Larkin: Writer,* writes, "The sleight of hand whereby the final line *appears* to be a celebration of the transcendence which the whole sentence denies is pathetically ineffective. It is as far as the poet can honestly go." And Andrew Swarbrick, in *Out of Reach: The Poetry of Philip Larkin,* expresses a similar view: "Their joined hands do not represent the triumph of love over time, but our delusory wish that it might be so."

Differences of interpretation notwithstanding, "An Arundel Tomb" has always been a favorite of Larkin readers. A sign of the high esteem in which it is generally held is the fact that it was one of three poems by Larkin that were read aloud at his memorial service held in London's Westminster Abbey in 1986.

Criticism

Bryan Aubrey

Aubrey has published many essays on twentieth-century literature. In the following essay, he focuses on the ambivalence of the final two lines of Larkin's poem.

Larkin's "An Arundel Tomb" is many things—a meditation on death, a tribute to the power of art, a celebration of love, an evocation of England's long traditions and history. It can also be read as a rueful expression of doubt about the conclusions to which it points. The fascination the poem exerts perhaps lies in the tension between these two opposing tendencies: the bold attempt to immortalize the love of the two figures on the tomb, and the half-retreat from that affirmation in the form of equivocation. Both impulses embody readily understandable human attitudes: the desire to believe that something essential and highly prized survives death; the dark fear that it does not. The former is a belief that springs from the human heart; the second is a product of the human mind.

The poem enacts a symbolic journey beyond the small, day-to-day identities with which the human self is normally clothed, into the values of the heart, which are universal. From the outset, it is clear that the earl and countess no longer possess any individuality. Their faces are "blurred"; their clothing only "vaguely" shown. The Latin names around the base of the tomb are no longer what catches the eye of the visitor (who in most cases has not learned or understands Latin). Countless generations of such visitors have long been "washing at their identity."

The word washing suggests two things: erosion—the earl and the countess can no longer be perceived as who they were, in their historical context—and purification, in the sense of having been washed clean. The latter meaning is interesting because it suggests that the movement away from distinct individuality is itself a kind of progress or evolution, a stripping away of the inessential and the impure to reveal, at least through the symbolic mode of art, the essential, enduring nature of life, which is love.

In few, if any, other poems does Larkin make such an explicit statement about the ultimate tri-

umph of love over death. Although in his verse there is sometimes an affirmative impulse that struggles to come out in spite of the weight and oppressiveness of human life, Larkin is usually a poet of misery, disappointment, stoic resignation, bleakness, fear of death, and a refusal to surrender to illusions. It is this side of Larkin's sensibility that is apparent in the qualification that undercuts the ringing affirmation of the last line that "what will survive of us is love."

The qualification occurs in the next-to-final line. The fact that the final attitude of the long-dead earl and his wife is one of love—they are depicted as holding hands—proves "our almost-instinct almost true." Note it is only "almost." The presence of the qualifier, not once but twice, makes the conclusion more problematic. It is not quite the affirmation it appears. But what precisely does "almost true" mean?

The phrase might mean "mostly true," in the sense that a statement may be, say, ninety-nine parts true and one part false. Another possibility is that something may be "almost true" but still miss the mark and be entirely false. This possibility is hinted at in the first line of stanza seven, "Time has transfigured them into / Untruth." The primary meaning of this line is that the earl and the countess did not, in the poet's view, intend the attitude of love, in which they are placed, to be their sole memorial. But a secondary meaning lurks here also, that the message conveyed of the survival of love beyond death is indeed false, an "untruth."

A third possibility is that "almost true" means "probably true," in the sense that it has not been proved conclusively; an element of doubt remains.

A poet's meaning can sometimes be illuminated by following the evolution of the work from early drafts to finished poem. Interestingly, Larkin's notebooks reveal two earlier drafts of the final stanza. Both are quoted by scholar Andrew Swarbrick in his book, *Out of Reach: The Poetry of Philip Larkin.*

The first draft reads as follows:

Time has transfigured them into
Untruth. The stone fidelity
They hardly meant is all that we
Are left of them, as if to prove
Our least accredited instinct true
And what survives of us is love.

A still later version reads:

Time has transfigured them into
Untruth. The stone fidelity
They hardly meant is all that we

Are told, as if thereby they prove
Our first half-hope, half-instinct true,
And what survives of us is love.

In neither draft does the final line contain the qualification added in the final version. There is no "almost." And yet Larkin was dissatisfied with both drafts and wrote a note on the manuscript that read: "Love isn't stronger than death just because statues hold hands for 600 years." In other words, Larkin seemed to feel that he had not proved his case. In terms of the heart-mind dichotomy mentioned earlier, throughout the poem he has followed the direction in which the heart has led, inspired by the touching detail of the clasped hands. The result is an affirmation of the lasting quality of love. But then the discriminating, rational mind reasserts itself, demanding proof. It will always be disappointed because the final statement of principle, "What will survive of us is love," is not something that is susceptible to proof the way the rational mind conceives it; it can only be affirmed by faith, intuition (the "almost-instinct" of the final version), and love itself. The final version of the final stanza shows therefore that the poet cannot quite bring himself to make the same voyage that he has observed and imagined in the stone figures. Unlike them, he cannot dock in the safe harbor of the heart. He must equivocate.

Two factors, however, combine to ensure that the final declaration of love's triumph carries more weight than the ambiguous "almost" might otherwise allow it. The first is that Larkin permits the statement to stand alone, as a complete syntactical unit, as if the doubt or disclaimer is cordoned off from the affirmative vision of the heart. As Andrew Motion writes in his biography of the poet, *Philip Larkin: A Writer's Life,* "The rhetoric of the final line takes charge and establishes it as a separate truth: venerable wisdom arising from a part-medieval, part nineteenth-century monument." It is also significant that this is the line—one of Larkin's most famous—that readers tend to remember and quote. It would appear that the balancing act between tentativeness and certainty, withdrawal and acceptance, that Larkin carefully enacted is shaded in favor of the latter.

The second factor that encourages the transcendent meaning of the final line to overshadow the double "almost" of the previous one is the placement of the poem in *The Whitsun Weddings,* the collection in which it was first published. "An Arundel Tomb" was the last poem in the book, and it serves as a contrast to the first poem, "Here," in which Larkin describes the here-and-now reality of

> " *And yet Larkin was dissatisfied with both drafts and wrote a note on the manuscript that read: 'Love isn't stronger than death just because statues hold hands for 600 years.' "*

the town of Hull and its environs, where he lived and worked.

In "Here" there is no escape from the city's hustle and bustle; only the expansive view from the beach suggests the possibility of "unfenced existence," but such freedom of the spirit is declared, at the end of the poem, to be "out of reach." There is no escape from the pressures of the moment. In contrast, "An Arundel Tomb" looks back to a distant time, and the silence of the stone effigy conveys something beyond the feverish activity of the present. In "Here" everything is in motion but nothing is especially fulfilling or memorable; in "An Arundel Tomb" everything is still (the "stationary voyage" of the earl and the countess through time notwithstanding) and there is one single redeeming value that reaches out beyond the grave.

"An Arundel Tomb" is also in marked contrast to a number of other poems in *The Whitsun Weddings,* the dominant mood of which is the frustration of human hope and the ever-present specter of death. The last four lines of "Dockery and Son" provide a good example:

Life is first boredom, then fear.
Whether or not we use it, it goes,
And leaves what something hidden from us chose,
And age, and then the only end of age.

As a bleak vision of human life, this would be hard to surpass. Death is final and to be dreaded. Generally, in *The Whitsun Weddings,* Larkin sees the possibility of renewal and new life only in the processes of nature, such as the coming of spring in "First Sight." But then finally comes "An Arundel Tomb," with its brave, hand-holding gesture against oblivion, the final declaration of love's immortality reverberating in the reader's mind as he or she closes the volume.

Source: Bryan Aubrey, Critical Essay on "An Arundel Tomb," in *Poetry for Students,* The Gale Group, 2001.

What Do I Read Next?

- Allison Stones maintains a web site, "Images of Medieval Art and Architecture," http://www.pitt.edu/~medart/index.html (January, 2001), that contains photographs of medieval cathedrals in England, including photos of the exterior and interior of Chichester Cathedral, which contains the tomb that inspired Larkin's poem.

- Like "An Arundel Tomb," W. B. Yeats' poem "Sailing to Byzantium" (1927) and John Keats' "Ode on a Grecian Urn" (1819) explore the theme that art can bestow a kind of eternity on human life and passions.

- Thomas Gray's "Elegy Written in a Country Churchyard" (1751) is a traditional graveyard meditation from the point of view of the Christian faith.

- "During Wind and Rain" (1917), by Thomas Hardy, presents a bleak, atheistic view of the cycle of life and death.

- William Shakespeare's Sonnet 116, "Let me not to the marriage of true minds" is an affirmation of the lasting power of love that can triumph over time's destruction.

- Larkin's collection *The Whitsun Weddings* (1964) contains some of his finest poetry, including "Ambulances" and "Dockery and Son," as well as the title poem, "An Arundel Tomb."

- Larkin was invited to edit the prestigious *The Oxford Book of Twentieth-Century English Verse,* (1973), and the result proved controversial. Larkin's selections were considered idiosyncratic, but the book was popular with the public and it gives much insight into the kind of poetry Larkin admired.

- *A Girl in Winter,* (1947), is one of two novels by Larkin, written before he achieved fame as a poet. His young heroine Katherine Lind, a refugee in wartime England, learns that she must leave behind all her imaginative illusions before she can see life clearly.

Sheldon Goldfarb

Goldfarb has a Ph.D. in English and has published two books on the Victorian author William Makepeace Thackeray. In the following essay, he starts with a close reading of one line in Larkin's poem, which leads into a discussion of its portrayal of love, art, and time and a comparison between Larkin's poem and Percy Bysshe Shelley's "Ozymandias."

Perhaps the most puzzling line in "An Arundel Tomb" is the one that begins the third stanza: "They would not think to lie so long." On the surface, it seems to have a simple meaning: the earl and the countess did not think they would lie buried in their tomb for such a long time. But why wouldn't they think that? What did they expect would happen?

Janice Rossen in *Philip Larkin: His Life's Work* answers this question by saying the earl and the countess would have expected "an imminent resurrection." The problem with that answer is that resurrection and a heavenly afterlife, or even religion generally, are not mentioned in the poem and do not seem to have anything to do with its major issues: the passage of time and the love between the earl and the countess, as indicated by their holding hands in the sculpture of them.

Rossen does suggest another reading of the line when she notes that the earl and the countess "are close to lying in the sense of being dishonest." In other words, as in at least one other poem of Larkin's ("Talking in Bed"), there is a pun on the word "lie." The earl and the countess may be telling an untruth in giving the impression, through the sculpture of them holding hands, that they were a loving couple.

There does seem to be something in this second meaning, for much of the poem is about the issue of untruth and whether love (the love between the earl and the countess, and love in general) is true. But if this is the second meaning, what about the first? Why does Larkin say the earl and the countess did not think they would lie in the earth for such a long time? Or does he actually even say that? There is another way of understanding the line, by seeing the word "so" as attached not to "long" but to "lie." Perhaps Larkin is saying the couple would not usually think to "lie so": that is, to lie in this manner, holding hands. They would not usually have held hands like that; they did so in this case just for the sake of the sculpture, the way people today might put their arms around each other for a photograph.

The rest of the third stanza supports this reading. It goes on to say that the "faithfulness in effigy"—that is, the hand-holding, which Larkin describes as a representation of the couple's faithfulness to each other—was just a detail thrown in for friends to see, or perhaps only something to set off the Latin names at the base of the sculpture. The earl and the countess would not think to "lie so" long; they might perhaps hold hands, but it would not be something they would do for an extended period. And yet here they are, centuries later, still holding hands: it is close to a lie, an untruth, as Janice Rossen says, and, therefore, these two readings connect to each other.

So it may not be relevant, in reading the first line of stanza three, to think of lying in the earth at all. Larkin is primarily talking about lying together holding hands: how that is unusual, and thus something of an untruth. And yet the line does conjure up an image of bodies lying in the ground and, in fact, beginning in stanza four, the survival of the earl and the countess in their tomb becomes a central issue:

> . . . Rigidly they
> Persisted, linked, through lengths and breadths
> Of time. . . .

Perhaps writing the line, "They would not think to lie so long," set off a whole new train of thought for Larkin. Even if he originally meant only to be talking about hand-holding, he began thinking about survival. In any case, the last few stanzas of the poem focus on survival and the passage of time. The earl and the countess have survived, the poem tells the readers, but it is a limited sort of survival, a survival into a world they would not know and which does not really know them. The old tenantry (a body of tenants) they would have known have vanished; the modern age is "unarmorial," unlike the one the earl would have known. Modern visitors to the tomb cannot even read the Latin inscription and the general situation is that "altered people" unlike the ones the earl and countess knew come to see their tomb and in the process wash away their identity, leaving them "helpless."

In the end, all that really survives is an "attitude," another punning word, referring both to the hand-holding posture of the earl and the countess and the point of view it is supposed to convey. But the attitude is an untruth. The sculpture seems to say that the earl and countess held hands out of love, but that message of "stone fidelity" is some-

> *Will love survive or not? Is there hope in that gesture of the medieval couple? Or is it a delusion?"*

thing they "hardly meant." The poem, to this point, says that it is a lie—and yet the closing lines of the poem say that this image of the earl and the countess holding hands proves

> Our almost-instinct almost true:
> What will survive of us is love.

The overall effect is thus ambiguous. Will love survive or not? Is there hope in that gesture of the medieval couple? Or is it a delusion? Their hand-holding proves that the hope for love's survival is almost true: not quite true, but almost. Is that a positive or negative conclusion?

Perhaps some light can be shed on the situation by comparing Larkin's poem with another one about an ancient sculpture: Percy Bysshe Shelley's "Ozymandias." In Shelley's poem, a traveler reports on a giant statue of an ancient ruler. On the half-wrecked statue's pedestal is a message from the ruler boasting about his great works, but in fact, aside from the statue, none of the ruler's works have survived. The poem thus mocks the vanity of those who believe they can outwit death and time and survive into another age.

The earl and countess in Larkin's poem do not boast in the manner of Ozymandias and are not mocked as a result. However, Larkin's poem, like Shelley's, does note the victory of death and time, which wash away the identity of the earl and the countess. Two stone effigies of the couple survive, but only "rigidly"; they are not alive in any sense; they are unable to respond to the changing world around them; the real countess and earl are gone.

In Shelley's poem, the one saving grace in the midst of death and destruction is the truth-telling ability of art. The "wrinkled lip, and sneer of cold command" on the statue of Ozymandias "tell that its sculptor well those passions read." Powerful rulers may disappear, according to Shelley's poem, but art will survive and will preserve something important, in this case a true picture of the nature of the ancient ruler, Ozymandias.

In Larkin's poem, even this consolation is denied the reader. The sculptor in this case has lied. His sculpture may not be conveying a true picture of the earl and the countess at all. And yet the poem at the very end suggests that in some way it is true; it is true not to the relationship between the earl and the countess but to the desires of the viewers and of the whole human race: not that the countess and the earl were really in love, but that the human race has an instinctual yearning for love. Of course, even this claim is qualified in the poem; the yearning for love, the belief that love will survive, is only an "almost-instinct."

Still, it is this almost-instinct that is embodied in the sculpture: there may not have been a true love between the earl and countess, but the sculpture reflects the human desire for there to be such a love. Art, then, becomes not an expression of the truth, as it is in Shelley's poem, but as Andrew Swarbrick says in *Out of Reach: The Poetry of Philip Larkin,* an expression of what humans would like to be true: people would like to believe in love, in its reality, in its power, in its survival.

In the end the message of the poem is that people die, societies decay, time and death happens to us all, and even the hope that love somehow provides a means of survival is an illusion or a lie; and yet, how human beings yearn to believe in that illusion.

Source: Sheldon Goldfarb, Critical Essay on "An Arundel Tomb," in *Poetry for Students,* The Gale Group, 2001.

Sources

Booth, James, *Philip Larkin, Writer,* St. Martin's Press, 1992.

Bowen, Roger, "Death, Failure, and Survival in the Poetry of Philip Larkin," in *The Dalhousie Review,* Vol. 58, No. 1, Spring 1978, pp. 79–94.

Featherstone, Joseph L., "A Poetry of Commonplaces," in *New Republic,* March 6, 1965, pp. 27–88.

Graham, W., "'An Arundel Tomb' Restored," in *Phoenix,* Nos. 11–12, Autumn and Winter, 1973–1974.

Larkin, Philip, *Collected Poems,* edited with an introduction by Anthony Thwaite, Farrar, Strauss, Giroux, 1989.

———, *The Whitsun Weddings: Poems by Philip Larkin,* Faber and Faber, 1964.

Martin, Bruce, *Philip Larkin,* Twayne, 1978.

Martz, Louis L., "New Books in Review," in *The Yale Review,* June 1965, pp. 605–608.

Motion, Andrew, *Philip Larkin: A Writer's Life,* Farrar, Strauss, Giroux, 1993.

Petch, Simon, *The Art of Philip Larkin,* Sydney University Press, 1981.

Ricks, Christopher, "A True Poet," in *New York Review of Books,* January 14, 1965, pp. 10–11.

Rossen, Janice, *Philip Larkin: His Life's Work,* University of Iowa Press, 1989.

Shelley, Percy Bysshe, "Ozymandias," in *The Pocket Book of Verse,* edited by M. E. Speare, Washington Square Books, 1940, p.130.

Swarbrick, Andrew, *Out of Reach: The Poetry of Philip Larkin,* St. Martin's Press, 1995.

For Further Study

Day, Roger, *Larkin,* Open University Press, 1987.
An introductory work that encourages the student to develop his or her own opinions about Larkin's work, this book includes study questions on selected poems.

Hassan, Salem K., *Philip Larkin and His Contemporaries: An Air of Authenticity,* Macmillan Press, 1988.
This text is valuable not only for its readings of individual poems but for the chapters Hassan devotes to Larkin's contemporaries, the poets Thomas Gunn, D. J. Enright, Kingsley Amis, and John Wain.

Kuby, Lolette, *An Uncommon Poet for the Common Man: A Study of Philip Larkin's Poetry,* Mouton, 1974.
An illuminating study of the contents and themes of Larkin's poetry, this work contains perceptive readings of individual poems, as well as analyses of Larkin's relationship to other poets, both contemporary and past.

Larkin, Philip, *Required Writing: Miscellaneous Pieces, 1955–1982,* Faber and Faber, 1983.
A collection of Larkin's own writings, including book reviews, essays on jazz and on poetry (other poets' work, mostly, with an emphasis on British twentieth-century poets), as well as two interviews with Larkin.

———, *Selected Letters of Philip Larkin, 1940–1985,* edited with an introduction by Anthony Thwaite, Farrar, Strauss, Giroux, 1993.
More than seven hundred letters reveal Larkin's conflicted inner life. The letters shocked many because of Larkin's reactionary political views and his alleged misogyny, but Larkin's wry humor also makes for entertaining reading.

The Base Stealer

Robert Francis
1948

Robert Francis' "The Base Stealer," a poem about baseball which was published in Francis' 1976 volume *Robert Francis: Collected Poems,* captures a moment poised between two states—an instant of developing action, of leaving one condition and entering another. By describing a base runner, Francis might be describing any experience in which a person is "pulled both ways"; he describes the sense of past and future that enter into such a moment and the heightened sense of life that is felt in the flux of "becoming." The poem's situation is made clear by the title. In baseball, a runner on base is entitled to advance to the next base at his own discretion. This may happen even if the batter does not hit the ball—when the runner tries to "steal" the base. The art of base stealing depends on the runner's ability to perfectly time the pitcher's delivery to the plate. If the runner breaks too soon, the pitcher may catch him, throwing to a fielder instead of to the plate. If the runner breaks too late, the catcher may throw him out at the next base. Thus, the base-stealer's success is determined less by his speed than by his perception, confidence, and cunning. To shorten his route to the next base, the runner takes a "lead" off of the base he currently occupies—that is, he steps away from the base, cheating up the baseline. This is a dangerous place to be: if the pitcher is quick enough, he can "pick off" the runner by throwing to the base the runner is cheating away from. In short, the moment just before base stealing is a tense one, a battle of nerves between the runner and the pitcher. Like many of life's experiences, it is also a battle between the runner and himself, a test of his poise and daring. It is this moment that the poem examines.

Author Biography

Francis was born in Upland, Pennsylvania, on August 12, 1901, to Ebenezer and Ida May Allen Francis. He graduated from Harvard with a bachelor's degree in 1923 and a master's degree in education in 1926. Shortly thereafter he moved to Amherst, Massachusetts, where he taught high school for a year before devoting himself full-time to writing poetry. Francis received his doctorate from the University of Massachusetts in 1970. Among the awards and recognition he received for his work were the Shelley Memorial Award in 1938 and the Brandeis University Creative Arts Award in poetry in 1974. He was a Phi Beta Kappa poet at Tufts University in 1955 and at Harvard University in 1960. He was a Rome Fellow of the Academy of Arts and Letters, 1957–58, and he received a fellowship award from the Academy of American Poets in 1984. Francis died at age 85 on July 13, 1987, in Northampton, Massachusetts. The University of Massachusetts Press established the Juniper Prize for Poetry in Francis' honor in the late 1980s.

Poem Text

Poised between going on and back, pulled
Both ways taut like a tightrope-walker,
Fingertips pointing the opposites,
Now bouncing tiptoe like a dropped ball
Or a kid skipping rope, come on, come on,   5
Running a scattering of steps sidewise,
How he teeters, skitters, tingles, teases,
Taunts them, hovers like an ecstatic bird,
He's only flirting, crowd him, crowd him,
Delicate, delicate, delicate, delicate—now!   10

Poem Summary

Lines 1–3

Both the language and images of the first three lines convey the sense of balance, of being "poised between" two contrary states. When a runner takes his lead away from the base, he enters a dangerous region, a no-man's land between the security of one base and the promise of the next. If the pitcher tries to "pick off" the runner—if he throws to the base

Media Adaptations

- Short stories about baseball are featured on two audiocassettes in the package *Selected Shorts Celebrates Baseball,* recorded live at Symphony Space Center in New York City in 1991. Included on the recording are Robert Francis' "Pitcher" and "The Base Stealer."

- "The Base Stealer" is included on the three-album set from 1973 titled *Readings and Dramatizations for Communicating,* released by D. C. Heath and Co. of Lexington Massachusetts.

- "The Base Stealer" is also included with "Mom's Revenge" on a short audiocassette from Educational Sensory Programming in Jonesboro, Arkansas.

- In 1994, documentary film maker Ken Burns produced a series for the Public Broadcasting System about the history of the sport. Titled simply *Baseball,* it is available as a nine-tape video package from PBS Home Video. It has also been adapted to a four-tape audiocassette package from Random House Audio.

- *Robert Francis Reads His Poems* is available on a record by Folkways, released in 1975.

from which the runner has taken his lead—then the runner must dive back to safety. If the pitcher decides to throw to the plate, then the runner may dash for the next base. In the present state, however, the runner is neither "on base" nor a "base stealer": he is "poised between going on and back." This state is akin to being "pulled both ways taut"—the four consecutive stressed syllables conveying the heightened tension—"like a tightrope walker." The simile implies not only balance and danger but also the runner's physical appearance: his arms stretched at his side, his body in a state of rigid intensity. Similarly, the description of the way he holds his hands offers symbolic meaning as well as a pictorial image: his fingertips point "the opposites," one toward the base he is leaving, one toward the base he is trying to steal.

Lines 4–5

The poet's use of meter here enhances the comparison between the runner and a bouncing ball. Like the ball, he springs on his toes, and the alternating stressed and unstressed syllables in the phrase "bouncing tiptoe" are a sonic imitation of such motion. The second half of the simile—"or like a kid skipping rope"—adjusts the sense of the first. While a bouncing ball unconsciously submits to the forces of nature, each succeeding rebound smaller than the last, the rope-skipper must infuse energy into each jump: a test of will similar to the athlete's. Thus, Francis adds the invocation at the end of Line 5: "come on, come on." Its repetition conveys the internal voice of the runner, his attempt to urge himself (as well as the action of the game) to the climactic moment. Its unstressed-stressed rhythm also echoes the bouncing sound of the previous line.

Lines 6–10

The sideways steps of Line 6 suggest perhaps the movements of a crab. In Line 8, however, the runner is described as hovering "like an ecstatic bird." In either image, the comparison suggests the quick, instinctive motions of an animal. Again, the meter reverts to the stressed-unstressed rhythm of bouncing: "teeters, skitters, tingles, teases, / taunts them, hovers." Now, however, the building momentum is "ecstatic," an embodiment of the surging excitement just before the moment of decision. While the tightrope and rope-skipping metaphors of lines 2 and 5 convey the feeling that danger possesses the upper hand, now it is the runner who has gained control of the situation, taunting and teasing the pitcher. This teasing is part of the base-runner's technique: he hopes that by "flirting" with the pitcher's mind he will force the pitcher into making a mistake. One such mistake would be to "crowd" the batter—that is, to pitch the ball so close to the batter that the catcher's throw to the base would be obstructed. In the final line-and-a-half, the poem descends entirely into the runner's mind. The outer world has dissolved; the runner is merely waiting for the proper moment to make his dash. That wait is conveyed in four consecutive dactyls—"delicate, delicate, delicate, delicate"—followed by a pause, represented by the dash, and the final monosyllabic moment of action: "Now!" Though the reader never learns whether the runner is safe or out, the internal experience is over; the rest is purely a matter of speed. The runner has gone from potential to action, from a would-be base stealer to the actual base stealer of the title.

Themes

Limitations and Opportunity

"The Base Stealer" presents a baseball player who is held suspended by limitations, ready to be thrown out by the pitcher if he wanders the slightest bit too far in either direction. Still, he recognizes the fact that his opportunity to steal the next base will come up at any moment, as it, in fact, does in the last line of the poem. As it is in many of life's circumstances, his limitations pull him in two opposite directions, bringing him to a dead halt in terms of backward or forward motion. He is "poised" almost like an inanimate object. The player knows that his opportunity is coming soon, and this fact is expressed in his up-and-down motion, in the way that he bounces "like a dropped ball, / Or a kid skipping rope," to keep his energy level up so that he will be ready to move fast, as soon as he gets his chance.

The repetition of the word *delicate* in the last line serves to define just how limited the base stealer is and how narrow is his window of opportunity. Each time that the word is used, readers are reminded that he is ready to go, which in turn serves as a reminder of the forces that are stopping him. A base runner waiting for the single right opportunity can be seen as a metaphor for life. People act and react all of the time; but if each decision were weighed with a poet's careful sense of precision, then one could determine that only *one* opportunity for action is the right one. The base runner in this poem shows a sense of humor and a spirit of fun about what he is doing, but, even so, the choice of when to move holds his complete concentration.

Permanence

There is nothing in "The Base Stealer" that would give readers a sense of permanence. The poem is a meditation on the transitory nature of things and on how life's basic, impermanent nature is captured by the rules of the game of baseball. The base runner in this poem has no option to stay where he is but is instead "poised between going on and back" for the brief segment of time that Francis has captured here. The musical words used in line 7—"teeters, shutters, tingles, teases"—have a lively tone to them, implying the runner's kinetic energy. Even though the runner does not take any positive action until the last line of the poem, his action is anticipated in the middle with the impatient "come on, come on" that ends line 5. The whole poem gives readers a sense of anticipation,

Topics for Further Study

- Write a short poem that gives a concentrated description of an athlete or artist performing his or her specific craft.

- This poem repeats the word *delicate* three times at the end to draw out the tension. What other techniques does it use to heighten tension? How successful do you think they are?

- Citing sports experts, explain the statistical odds for or against successful base stealing and why some runners are better at it than others.

- Compile a collection of base stealing anecdotes from various baseball memoirs.

- Robert Francis was a protégé of the great American poet Robert Frost. Choose one of Frost's poems, and find techniques that resemble those Francis used here, developing your own theory about Frost's influence on Francis.

of waiting for the runner to change a situation that cannot be sustained for one second longer.

The pitcher, who is trying to keep the situation stable by keeping the runner motionless, is working for permanence. "Crowd him" is baseball slang for throwing the ball to the base that the runner is supposed to be on, forcing him to stay close to the base so that he will not be able to steal the next one. While baseball is usually thought of as a duel between the pitcher and the batter, this poem reminds readers that, in addition to pitching, pitchers must keep an eye on the base runners to keep them in a stable position. The runners are bound to move eventually, but for the short time that he is in control of the ball the pitcher works to keep the base runners solidly fixed in place.

Time

This poem's success stems from the fact that it not only brings time to a standstill but also makes readers impatient for this standstill to break. From the very start, the base runner is poised, frozen. In some poems, the author will stop action to examine one isolated moment in time to study and savor what is going on. Here, though, the runner's zeal to get time running once more is passed on to the reader.

It is clear from the very first line that the runner is anxious for time to start. He is described as "pulled / Both ways taut," implying that inaction is agony to him. Furthermore, the other nervous motions that he makes clearly indicate that he wants things to move along. In the last line, each use of the word *delicate* serves to pause the action a little longer, letting the poem's static energy build up an almost unbearable pressure before time starts again with a burst of energy, after the dash, with the word now.

Success and Failure

Any sporting competition is about success and failure, but, as an old adage explains, winning and losing are less important than how the game is played. In the example given in this poem, the base runner shows a sense of light-hearted playfulness, even while at some level he is taking his task seriously. Francis describes him as a bird, then, from the point of view of the opposing team, dismisses his abundant energy as "only flirting." In a strictly competitive sense, his action is not at all like flirting but is meant to distract the players on the other team and to assure his confidence in his success and their failure. To see it as flirting is to look at the base stealer's constant motion in a broader scope, as a strategy to get members of the other team to forget the competition involved and to think of the broader entertainment. Even though he seems focused on winning, the base runner does not seem too anxious about the outcome of the game: his flashy, bouncy demonstration seems to have more to do with childish fun than success. The calculated abruptness that he moves with in the end is a clear indication that he has indeed been focused on a successful steal all along, even when his attention seemed to wander.

Style

"The Base Stealer" is written in ten lines of varying length, meter, and sound. While its form might seem erratic and even messy, a close examination reveals the tight control the poet exerts over both the sense and structure of the poem. One measure of this control is Francis' frequent use of lines written in dactylic meter—that is, lines in which the predominant rhythmic unit consists of one stressed followed by two unstressed syllables. For an example of dactylic meter, consider the poem's third line. If we divide the dactyls from one another and mark the unstressed and stressed syllables, the line appears like this:

*Fin*ger tips / *point*ing the / *op*posites

Reading the line naturally, notice the emphasis on the stressed syllables. Dactylic meter gives the poem an energetic, nervous rhythm—the rhythm of an "ecstatic bird" (Line 8)—suggested in the descriptions of the base stealer. This nervousness, however, is balanced by other rhythms that suggest that the runner's energy is also carefully controlled. To see how the poet balances different types of meter, look at the line that follows the one above: "Now bouncing tiptoe like a dropped ball." The first two syllables of it are stressed—a heavier, more controlled meter—but the second, third, and fourth syllables alternate in stress, conveying the bouncing action of a ball.

Historical Context

Postwar America

In 1948, America was just starting to regain its composure and to settle into a routine of life that it had not known for almost two decades. The country had been distracted since the 1920s, first by hard economic times and then by its role in the single greatest global military conflict of the twentieth century. In 1929 there was a stock market crash, with stocks losing more than $50 billion in value in the following two years, causing the worst and longest economic depression in the nation's history. The prolonged period of business failures and high unemployment lasted throughout the 1930s and was only controlled when American production was stepped up to help European allies fight in World War II, which began in 1939. In 1941, with the bombing of Pearl Harbor, the United States was drawn into the war; and the war effort consumed the nation's attention and resources until its end in 1945. The Depression had cost most Americans a sense of economic stability they may have once taken for granted, as they faced levels of poverty that most people would find unthinkable today. The war had depleted the population with its 407,316 deaths and another 607,846 wounded soldiers returning home to their families.

Postwar America was marked by prosperity and leisure. The factories and distribution chains that had been running at full capacity for the war effort switched almost immediately to consumer goods, and, with the spell of the depression broken, Americans had the money to buy the products that were available. Electrical conveniences that became common for the first time in the years after the war included refrigerators, toasters, dishwashers, washing machines, dryers, and televisions. Many of these had existed in the twenties and thirties, but only the wealthiest households could afford them. After the war, however, methods of mass production made them available to members of the growing American middle class. Millions of Americans were suddenly in a position not only to buy more merchandise but also to buy homes where they could keep their new possessions. In the years after World War II, the suburbanization of the United States flourished, with relatively inexpensive houses being built within developments surrounding major cities to accommodate the young men and women who were returning from the war and preparing to start families. This new prosperity gave young families the confidence that they would be able to support large families; and in the years from 1946 to 1960 America experienced one of the greatest increases in population it had ever known, producing the generation that has been dubbed the "Baby Boom."

Baseball and Integration

Because most able-bodied males were pulled into the war effort, major league baseball lagged from 1941 to 1945, getting by with players who had been excluded from military duty because of age or disabilities that left them just barely able to function on the field. The players were in no way equal to the feats of the giants of the game that fans could remember from the 1930s, such as Ty Cobb, Babe Ruth, Lou Gehrig, and Hank Greenberg, but the sport was still the national pastime. The news of the league standings served to raise the patriotic spirits of servicemen overseas who needed reminders of their simple lives back home.

After the war, the quick rise of television ownership helped a new generation of fans to follow games that they were unable to attend. Major league baseball reached new heights, as a slew of seasoned professionals, who had been introduced to fans during their rookie years in the 1930s, all reentered the league at once, giving the pennant races a sudden jolt of excitement. The thrill of seeing old heroes again, such as Stan Musial and Joe DiMaggio, was heightened by the fact that the quality of ball playing suddenly became much better.

Compare & Contrast

- **1948:** Baseball is the national pastime. Businesses slow down when the World Series is being played, as workers and customers are glued to television and radio broadcasts of the games.

  Today: The Super Bowl of football, played on one Sunday in January, draws more millions of television viewers than the World Series, which is spread out across four to seven games.

- **1948:** Baseball great Babe Ruth, retired since 1935, dies. An estimated 75,000 to 100,000 mourners file past his casket at Yankee Stadium to pay their respects.

  Today: Ruth's accomplishments on the field are remembered less than his scandalous personal life.

- **1948:** There are one million U.S. homes with televisions, having increased from five thousand just three years earlier.

  Today: Ninety-eight percent of U.S. homes (96 million total) have at least one color television.

- **1948:** The country is at the start of anti-communist hysteria. In the following years, the fear that communist spies would forward important defense secrets to Russia leads to congressional investigations that cost many public figures in sports and entertainment their jobs, as old associations make fans doubt their patriotism.

  Today: The Soviet Union no longer exists, but there is some worry about military secrets making their way into the hands of communists in China.

- **1948:** Racial segregation is common, especially in the south. President Truman goes before Congress to ask for new laws that will outlaw lynchings and discriminatory practices.

  Today: Discrimination on grounds of race is a crime. Violent acts motivated by race are prosecuted under hate crime laws.

Pitchers were throwing faster, batters were slugging harder, and base runners were more nimble; and they were able to bring youthful energy and cockiness back into the competition.

If baseball seemed renewed, though, there was still one area in which it was mired in the past, and that was in the invisible lines that barred players of color from participating in the all-white major leagues. There had been a Negro league in America since the late nineteenth century, but white audiences knew little of the players who played for them and seldom went out to see them play.

World War II had prepared the way for an integrated league. There were several factors involved that made integration seem inevitable. Though the army had been segregated, black soldiers had been enlisted to serve in black brigades. As a result, more whites had come to know blacks, during the war, better than ever before. They had seen that African Americans did not fit the negative stereotypes that had been circulated about them

and had, in many cases, learned to trust their professionalism. The reverse perspective was also relevant. Black soldiers who had served in Europe had seen societies, such as in France, where race was treated as being hardly important, and that made it hard for them to return to America and accept second-class citizen status. During the war, many blacks who were not in the service had migrated to large cities, where industries needed as many workers as they could get, relaxing the rigid social boundaries that had once prevailed. America was still a segregated country, especially in the south, but the basic fear and distrust that fuelled segregation had been weakened during an era of mutual cooperation. While major league baseball was filled with men excused from military service during the war, it was hard for anyone to deny that the country's most talented players were found in the Negro league.

In 1947, Brooklyn Dodgers' executive Branch Rickey broke the color line by promoting Jackie

Robinson from the minor league to play for his team. It was more than a step in advancing the game; it was a step for human rights across the country. As J. Ronald Oakley explains it in *Baseball's Last Golden Age: 1946-1960,* Rickey prepared Robinson for the task before promoting him, explaining that "good ballplaying would not, in itself, be enough. It would take courage, drive, guts, tolerance, and almost superhuman self-control. He would be the target of beanballs, raised spikes on the base path, curses and racial slurs from opposing players and fans, and other physical and verbal assaults." Robinson was a rare individual in that he could keep his composure even when faced with death threats and insults. He was an outstanding ballplayer, which was necessary of such a groundbreaker: any weakness in his playing ability would have been seized by bigots as proof that blacks were inferior players. He finished his rookie season with a .297 average, 125 runs batted in, and a respectable 12 home runs. He was an aggressive and cunning base runner, leading the league with 29 stolen bases.

Critical Overview

While the reputation of Robert Francis has been overshadowed by that of Robert Frost, the poet with whom he has most often been compared, those critics who have looked closely into Francis' work note the formal care and craftsmanship that often borders on the experimental. Thematically, they observe that Francis' poems often explore extreme internal states such as the one captured in "The Base Stealer." Michael True writes that the core of Francis' poems contain the "inevitability of fate," of "events or lives working themselves out and revealing what has to be." He argues that "Francis is fascinated with human beings … caught at the moment of peak performance, at the height of their powers," a quality found in "the athletes he often writes about and whose superior form he imitates." Howard Nelson comments on Francis' ability to experiment with form without sacrificing more refined elements found in his characteristic "short, clear, meditative, lyrical poem." In Francis' verse, Nelson writes, the reader cannot help notice "the clarity, the subtle lustre of the language. The poems have certainly been polished, but toward a greater transparence and directness rather than glittering effects." While Francis' language is fresh and exact, Nelson argues, "it rarely stops the reader

in his tracks, not for over-cleverness, nor obscurity, nor even a sudden stab of power." Rather, the strength of the poems lies in Francis' unwillingness to "sacrifice the moment of clarity . . . for complicated phrases or images."

Criticism

David Kelly

Kelly is an instructor of creative writing and scriptwriting at Oakton Community College and College of Lake County in Illinois. In the following essay, he examines how Robert Francis uses poetic technique sparingly, so that readers of "The Base Stealer" do not concentrate on style.

Baseball and poetry appear to be made for one another—they both are more entertaining for audiences that have a sly, hypersensitive appreciation of what is going on. Unfortunately, this makes both seem a little boring when compared to other, fast-paced entertainments that are available. The best baseball poetry, like the best pitching, fielding, and baserunning, finesses its audience so calmly that they leave it knowing the facts of what has transpired and experiencing a feeling, but with no real sense of how that feeling came over them.

Usually, poets writing about baseball can rely heavily on the game's natural tension when they want to create an interesting dynamic. The simplest and most obvious example of this is in the most famous baseball poem of all, "Casey at the Bat," which raises the reader's emotional involvement with each pitch thrown, proclaiming the batter's invulnerability right up to the moment that mighty Casey is struck out. "Casey" holds its readers with a good story, but poetry needs more than just a good story.

One of the best baseball poets ever was Robert Francis, who produced his most memorable works on the subject from the 1940s through the 1960s, a time span when the game reached its height of popularity. Francis was a skillful but little-noticed New England writer and teacher. His poetry was often meticulous, the sort of careful, studious work that one expects of a longtime academic. It would be too simple to think it strange to mix poetry and baseball. Only the most snobbish of intellectuals would claim that baseball, being a popular sport, is a surprising choice of subject for educated wordplay. Wrestling and NASCAR racing might be too coarse and obvious to bother writing about care-

> *Poets have no more business drawing attention to themselves than individual players do. Writing about poetry is like being part of the team."*

fully, but baseball, like poetry, becomes more mystifying to people as they mature, and at some point in life the two subjects tend to converge.

Francis' reputation as a fine baseball writer rests firmly on two poems. The one with the most obvious style is "Pitcher," which looks like a poem when it is printed on the page. It is constructed of five couplets, several of them nearly rhyming, and the last one having a solid, definite rhyme. It has an iambic pentameter meter, which is the simplest and most common meter a poet could use. "Pitcher" shows terrific control on the part of the poet and an almost incidental sense of fun. These are, not coincidentally, qualities that befit a good pitcher, making the poem's style appropriate to its subject. Francis' other great baseball poem is "The Base Stealer." This one is less obvious about the craft involved, leading casual readers to think that its appeal might be rooted solely in its subject matter.

"The Base Stealer," in fact, uses techniques so subtle that they are not readily noticed. Its text tells the story of an on-base runner, trying to decide just how much he can lead off the base he is supposed to be on. If he goes far enough, he might be able to steal the next base during the course of the next pitch, especially if the catcher has any trouble controlling the ball. If he leads off too far, though, he can be caught vulnerable between the bases. Like "Casey at the Bat," there is inherent drama that comes from the rules of the game, a situation that could tilt in either direction, toward victory or defeat, within a moment's time.

This life on the edge, with an uncertain result, is the stuff drama is made of; and a mediocre writer could keep readers enthralled with just the facts of the case. Francis imbued the poem with enough style to squeeze more out of the story.

There is no particular poetic meter to "The Base Stealer." The lines are not tightly bound to one particular length but are varied—not wildly, but still they are not standardized enough for easy analysis. The majority of lines are nine syllables, and the dominant meter is the three-syllable dactyl, which has a rhythm of stressed-unstressed-unstressed. Three and nine are significant numbers in baseball: three strikes per out, three outs per inning, nine innings per game, etc. To draw a connection out of this coincidence, though, would be a stretch. Even if the poem had been rigidly, mathematically structured in all threes and nines, readers would still not come away from it with any greater feel for what baseball is all about. The subconscious mind does not process such abstract relationships as numbers; and it is unlikely that the rules of baseball would translate to meaning in a poem in such an obscure way.

What is significant about the dactyl rhythm is not that it happens to occur in groups of three, but that it has the rolling rhythm of tribal drums. The stressed-unstressed-unstressed pattern has a rousing, foot-stamping motion that crowds in huge stadiums sometimes use to stir up excitement and anticipation. In "The Base Stealer," the predominance of dactyls keeps the poem rolling along, while the fact that this rhythm is not absolute, but breaks often, keeps the piece from feeling like a formal presentation where the outcome is predetermined. For instance, the start of the first line follows the dactyl pattern so clearly that its rhythm could be accompanied on a tom-tom drum: "*Poised* be-tween *go*-ing on. . . ." After those first two dactyls, though, the rhythm falls apart, allowing for chance and random occurrence in the poem.

Even without a set, recognizable pattern, rhythm is important to this poem. Rhythm is repetition, usually but not always sustained over a long period of time. Even readers who know almost nothing about poetry can see the repetitions that Francis uses here. Most obvious are the repeated phrases, which take readers, with no prior explanation, into the mind of the base runner. "Delicate," at the end of the poem, draws out the tension, fading as the runner becomes lost in thought, obsessed with just a single idea. Rhythmically, the poem's last line is interesting because it has "delicate" four times instead of three, making it thirteen syllables, significantly longer than the others; the reader's patience is taken to the point of exhaustion and then beyond. The other example of repeated words takes place at the middle of the poem, in line 5: "come on, come on." It, of course, works to stir up the reader's anticipation, to point out the fact that nothing has really yet happened at this point, and to remind readers that they wish something would. With boring poems, readers might notice themselves thinking, "come on, come on," when they reach the middle, but in this case Francis is actually trying to provoke an impatience that is almost similar to boredom.

Those are the cases of repetition that are obvious, because they use the same words over and again. It is in the use of less obvious types of repetition that a poet earns praise or derision. For instance, the list of words in line 7—"teeters, skitters, tingles, teases"—certainly has its own rhythm. The words all share the t sound and have either a hard e or a soft i. Perhaps more important, though, is the sense of the words. They sound silly, made-up. These are not words one uses to describe something with scientific precision; they are words that remind readers of the playfulness of the game.

Throughout the entire poem, Francis uses sound repetition to establish that the poet is in control. It is less obvious than using a rhythmic pattern, which beginning poets are trained to look for. Working with individual sounds puts him on par with scientists who work at the microscopic level. The most obvious sound throughout the piece is the t sound. Since this is one of the most frequently occurring letters in the language, a skeptical reader might think that all of the ts that show up in the poem just happen to be in words that Francis wanted to use. The test is in the words that could easily have been left out, such as "tiptoe," and the conspicuous bunchings, such as "taut like a tightrope-walker." The next most frequent sound is the letter s, as in the phrase "a scattering of steps sideways." These two sounds have opposite effects—t is sharp, s is soft—and neither sound in itself changes readers' sense of what is going on in "The Base Stealer." The overall effect of these repetitions is not what any one technique does, though, but the fact that they exist at all. They serve to remind readers that there is more to this poem than just the story of the base runner; there is also the way in which the story is being told.

A baseball poem should not be very flamboyant. It should be interesting and convey to readers the delicate action of the game. Poets have no more business drawing attention to themselves than individual players do. Writing about poetry is like being part of the team. Robert Francis' "The Base Stealer" is subdued and careful, with no need to insist that readers pay attention to its control of the situation. In telling its story so carefully and well, the poem takes readers into the situation it is describing, giving them a trip to the ballpark in the course of ten short lines.

What Do I Read Next?

- Perhaps one of the most famous baseball poems is Ernest Lawrence Thayer's 1888 piece "Casey at the Bat." It has been published with illustrations by Barry Moser in a deluxe 1999 edition by David R. Godine publishers.

- *The Collected Poems of Robert Francis, 1936–1976* is available in a reprint edition from the University of Massachusetts Press, 1986.

- Red Smith was one of the greatest sports writers of all time, with a career that spanned from 1941 to 1981. No less than 167 of his columns about the national pastime, written with insight and grace, are collected in *Red Smith on Baseball.*

- Francis was a great friend of the poet Robert Frost. A series of interviews between the two men was published in 1972 under the title *Frost: A Time to Talk; Conversations and Indiscretions Recorded by Robert Francis,* by the University of Massachusetts Press.

- One of the best recent anthologies of baseball poetry is *Hummers, Knucklers, and Slow Curves: Contemporary Baseball Poetry,* edited by Don Johnson, with an introduction by W. P. Kinsella, who writes frequently about baseball.

Source: David Kelly, Critical Essay on "The Base Stealer," in *Poetry for Students,* The Gale Group, 2001.

Cody Walker

Walker teaches courses in poetry and fiction at the University of Washington. In the following essay, he considers the feet of "The Base Stealer."

When baseball enthusiasts talk about a "great at-bat," they usually mean that the batter has fought off a number of tough pitches. He may have been jammed on a fastball, fooled on a slider, but he's managed to foul each away, extending his stay at the plate. Finally he finds a pitch he likes—a breaking ball, say, that does not quite break—and he lines it into the left-field seats. The length of the

> *So the poet is able to give readers the slight sense that time is being extended, without breaking the poem's rhythm or throwing off its balance. And balance is everything, whether someone is a poet, a base stealer, a tightrope walker, or a kid skipping rope. It allows a person to stay on his feet, to stay alert to the untowardness of things."*

at-bat has depended on the batter's resourcefulness. As it is with baseball, so it may be with poetry. In "The Base Stealer," Francis keeps the reader in a state of anticipation—pushing the poem to the right, to the left—before allowing the work (a single sentence, containing sixty-four words and nineteen commas) to blast forward.

In the Introduction to his *Collected Poems,* Francis calls some of his later works "positively frisky." A glance at *The Orb Weaver,* Francis' fifth volume of poetry (published in 1960, just before the poet's sixtieth birthday), bears out this judgment. In this book, "The Base Stealer" is bracketed by two poems, "Pitcher" and "Catch." In each poem, the game of baseball serves as a stand-in for the game of poetry. The pitcher's "art is eccentricity"; his passion, like the poet's, is "how to avoid the obvious." Two boys playing catch represent the poet and the reader; the poet keeps the reader off-balance by tossing the poem "overhand, underhand, backhand, sleight of hand, every hand." (And if the phrase "every hand" sounds odd, consider the following passage from Francis' autobiography, *The Trouble with Francis.* Railing against those who see life as a series of black-and-white choices, the poet asks, "Which hand do I choose? I choose both.

Or, I choose neither. I choose a third hand whose very existence you are ignorant of and would deny were possible." These poems are frisky because language, at its best, is frisky. It moves like a base stealer; it "teeters, skitters, tingles, teases."

"The Base Stealer" is a free verse poem; it follows no fixed metrical pattern. But Francis is playing a different game. He uses tumbling rhythms and quick cuts, rather than rhyme and meter, to give his poem tension and momentum. Consider the third line: "Fingertips pointing the opposites." The line can be broken into three rhythmic units (Fingertips / pointing the / opposites), with the first syllable of each unit, or foot, emphasized. In metric verse, these feet are called dactyls. The dactyls in line three cause the poem to lunge forward; but the base stealer is not yet ready to take off, so Francis reins him in with a word that delays forward movement: "opposites." The dactyls reappear in line six ("Running a / scattering") and, most strikingly, in the final line ("Delicate, / delicate, / delicate, / delicate"), where the surge of energy, the rush of fleet feet, finally causes the poem to pop.

In "Juniper," a poem from an earlier volume, Francis writes, "Poets / Are rich in points of view if they are rich / In anything." Twice in "The Base Stealer," Francis shifts the point of view mid-line: first in line five ("come on, come on"), and again in line nine ("crowd him, crowd him"). These interruptions increase the reader's sense of anticipation: something is about to happen, is even being *urged* to happen, but the reader must hang on a bit longer. After the poem has been read several times, the second interruption begins to appear inevitable; those whip-crack hard c sounds link the phrases together. "The Base Stealer" is full of sonic echoes: "poised" leads to "pointing"; "kid" leads to "skipping"; "teeters" leads to "teases"; "bird" leads to "flirting." The lines may not rhyme, but they're intensely musical. Consider lines six and seven: "Running a scattering of steps sidewise, / How he teeters, skitters, tingles, teases." In these lines, slithering s sounds meet staccato t sounds—the s sounds urge the action forward, the t sounds counter with stops and starts. The passage vibrates with controlled energy. Francis earned his living, for fifteen years, as a violin teacher; he understands how to draw out a note.

In her essay collection *Broken English,* poet Heather McHugh writes, "A poem is untoward." Literally, she's saying that a poem is difficult to manage, which is true enough. But she's also claiming something for poetry that Francis would agree with: that it looks in two directions, thinks with two minds. For Francis, a poem is always "going on and back," as meanings and directions multiply and reverse. "The Base Stealer" pulls its readers in two directions from the start. In fact, the word "pulled," by its position at the end of the first line, is almost isolated, given special status: a comma frames one side of it, and white space frames the other. The entire poem, until the final word, pulses with potential energy, as the base runner (not yet a base "stealer") hovers between two possible poles. In the phrase "crowd him, crowd him," the word "crowd" performs a bit of linguistic hovering. It appears at first to be a verb—part of a player's exhortation, similar to "come on, come on." But blink, and it becomes a noun; suddenly the flirting is taking place not only between the pitcher and the base runner but also between the base runner and the crowd. The crowd wants to see some action; the base runner is going to stretch the moment out just a bit longer. Substitute the poet for the base runner, and the readers for the crowd, and part of Francis' game becomes clear: It is the poet as much as the base runner who holds his spectators in suspense.

It's often said that baseball is a game of inches. A line drive past first base lands just inside of the foul line; an inning-ending third strike catches the edge of the plate. A great base stealer—a Lou Brock, a Rickey Henderson—knows how large a lead he can take: too much, and he's picked off; too little, and he's forced to stay put. The poet's predicament is similar. He wants to compress language when possible (for *opposite directions,* Francis writes "opposites"); he wants, at other times, to push language's boundaries. At the end of "The Base Stealer," Francis repeats *delicate* four times. It's a spree of sorts, but one that's perfectly controlled. The poem's first nine lines are all nine or ten syllables long; suddenly, in the final line, Francis stretches the syllable count to thirteen. But the last line is visually no longer than the others, and, like the majority of the poem's lines, it has only five accented syllables (called "beats"). So the poet is able to give readers the slight sense that time is being extended, without breaking the poem's rhythm or throwing off its balance. And balance is everything, whether someone is a poet, a base stealer, a tightrope walker, or a kid skipping rope. It allows a person to stay on his feet, to stay alert to the untowardness of things.

Still, every great at-bat, every pitching masterpiece, every base-stealing battle must come to an end. Francis releases the poem's power at the very last moment—potential energy becomes kinetic, the spring is sprung. "Delicate, delicate, del-

icate, delicate—now!" Francis writes; and the dash as punctuation mark precedes the dash to the base. Baseball fans know that a game can end that quickly—in a dash or a flash—and the losing players are left cursing beneath their caps. But "The Base Stealer," in one sense, does not come to an end; Francis stops the action before the runner is called "safe" or "out." The poem ultimately is not about success or failure on the base paths. It's about playfulness, improvisation, the act of shifting forward, and the act of shifting back. After Frost died, Francis wrote an elegy for his friend that ends, "He worshipped the Great God of Flow / By holding on and letting go." It's in the simultaneity of those expressions, the holding on and the letting go, that poetry lives.

Source: Cody Walker, Critical Essay on "The Base Stealer," in *Poetry for Students,* The Gale Group, 2001.

Jeannine Johnson

Johnson received her Ph.D. in English from Yale University and currently teaches at Harvard. In the following essay, she examines the ways in which the actions of Francis' poem and those of the poet are alike.

Robert Francis' poems often depict figures that are at once still and in motion. As a result, there is a palpable and usually positive tension in many of them. In "The Base Stealer," first published in book form in the 1960 collection *The Orb Weaver,* Francis portrays the multiple, intricate actions of a baseball player as he takes a lead from one base and prepares to steal the next. Though the title implies action, the poem itself is almost exclusively concerned with the instants before the central event, when the base stealer prepares himself to execute his duty but does not yet act. With the exception of the final word "now!" the entire work is dedicated to reproducing the increasing sense of expectancy associated with this episode in a ball game. The poem consists of a single sentence contained in one block stanza, and as this sentence lengthens and winds its way through the piece, the poet builds expectation and then thwarts it, only to build it again. The poet starts and stops his poem in tandem with his descriptions of the base runner's starts and stops, suggesting a meaningful kinship between these two performers.

Mirroring the motions of its subject, "The Base Stealer" advances and retreats with deliberate movements. The first word of the poem is "Poised," a term whose sound and meaning check the poem's momentum just as it is getting started. As a verb,

> *The rhythm and sound of these lines imitates those of the ballplayer as he constantly adjusts the length of his lead from the base. The multiple syllables in 'running,' 'scattering,' and 'sidewise' appropriately accelerate the pace of the line that is describing sudden movements."*

poised signals action, and yet the man who is *poised* does not, in fact, move. With this single word, Francis introduces the delicate tension that will characterize the entire piece: even its sound is full and unhurried, further slowing the progress of the line.

The poem then begins to proceed smoothly, only to be interrupted again just before the end of the line and again at its close:

Poised between going on and back, pulled. . . .

The comma after "back" delays the poetic line and represents a pause in the player's movement. However, the comma does not mark a final stop but a momentary rest, and thus it simultaneously retards the poem and prepares it to continue. After the comma, the base stealer is then "pulled" slowly into the next line. This last word echoes the first, and this similarity draws the ear and the eye back to the beginning of the poem, once more impeding its flow. In addition, the action is suspended by the enjambment in the first line: the end of the poetic line does not coincide with a natural grammatical pause, as it does, for instance, in the second line. This discord between the sense of the words and their arrangement causes a brief lull before the first line tumbles into the second.

As the poem continues, Francis finds other ways to mimic in his verse the actions of the base runner. For instance, the poet writes, "Running a scattering of steps sidewise, / How he teeters, skitters, tingles, teases, / Taunts them. . . ." The rhythm

and sound of these lines imitates those of the ballplayer as he constantly adjusts the length of his lead from the base. The multiple syllables in "running," "scattering," and "sidewise" appropriately accelerate the pace of the line that is describing sudden movements. However, the pace is more regular and predictable in the next line in which the runner "teeters, skitters, tingles, teases. . . ." In this string of two-syllable words, the strong stress is on the first syllable, and the recurrent *t* sounds and the commas punctuate the emphasized beats of the line as they alternate with the weak syllables. This rocking rhythm parallels the rocking motion of the base stealer as he leans one way and then the next, trying to distract the pitcher. Francis also uses alliteration to capture the noises of the scene. The *s* and *t* sounds are repeated to produce the sound of the base stealer's feet shuffling along and scraping the infield dirt, as they would when he "steps sidewise."

Even the number of syllables in each line is significant and contributes to Francis' goal of mimicking in his verse the actions of the runner. There are nine syllables in each of the first four lines of the poem, ten in lines 5–8, nine in line 9, and thirteen in line 10. This pattern is important because the line length reflects the action that is being described. The poem opens with a nine-beat line, one syllable short of the most common poetic line in formal English verse. As a result, the number of beats in these nine-syllable lines seems curtailed, perhaps symbolizing the careful, clipped motions of the base stealer. In the fifth line of the poem, the line length is extended slightly to the more traditional ten beats to accommodate the growing intensity of the situation. The runner grows impatient, thinking "come on, come on" and silently urging the pitcher to throw toward home plate. In the next few lines, the base stealer gathers confidence and moves further away from the base. Here, the poetic line remains at the longer ten syllables to represent the greater distance between the player and the safe base. However, the line shrinks slightly to nine syllables in line 9 as the runner gathers himself in one more time before exploding toward the next base in the extended final line of thirteen syllables.

While the base stealer and the poet may be largely in control of their respective performances, their movements mean nothing without the presence and interaction of others. The base runner with his arms outstretched "hovers like an ecstatic bird," but he does not actually leave the ground or abandon the field of play. Likewise, the poet and his ideas may momentarily float over the heads of his readers, but in the end he does not want to lose touch with his audience. Francis characterizes the experience of poetry, in his *Pot Shots at Poetry,* this way:

> Poetry at its best is a highly skilled game a poet plays with life and language, a game that the reader can follow play by play, able to distinguish the brilliant shots from the merely good ones, and the good ones from the poor ones, if any.

According to Francis, poetry is a sport in which at least two people have an impact on the outcome: the poet, who athletically manipulates language and ideas, and the reader, who observes his agility and power. The reader's role is critical since it is the reader who admires the poet's talent and who confirms the poet's ability to place his words efficiently and well.

Few people may think of poetry as a spectator sport, but, by associating the reader with a sports fan, Francis reveals that he sees poetry as an active experience. In all poems, including "The Base Stealer," there are not merely letters clustered on a page but balls that are "bouncing" and "kid[s] skipping rope." There is much for an outsider to observe and to cheer. As Francis contends in the prose piece "Two Words," in poetry words are involved in "intensive interplay," and, when put together, they "strike sparks" and "breed wonders." While there may be certain rules and bounds within which it plays itself out, poetry, like sport, can produce the unexpected and the awe-inspiring.

Athletes of several kinds appear in many of Francis' poems, especially those in *The Orb Weaver* and *Come Out into the Sun.* In these works, he explores sports as varied as baseball, running, swimming, diving, wrestling, gymnastics, sailing, and boxing. Although Francis is fond of sports metaphors, themes related to nature are even more common in his poetry. He cherishes the outdoors and shows his devotion by writing about the wind, the moon, meadows, birds, trees, flowers, and other inhabitants of the natural world. But whether writing about waxwings or baseball players, Francis is able to compose poems that are contemplative without being abstract. He confirms that this is his intention in an interview: "My poems confront the actual, recognizable world that we share with one another. However imaginative and original my vision and interpretation of that world, I do not want to lose connection with it." Francis believes that his link to other people through poetry will be stronger if that connection is rooted in the common, real world.

Like nature, sports are part of the "actual, recognizable world" and therefore make a worthy subject for poetry. But even if Francis wants to be certain that his readers find something familiar in his work, he does not promise to make the reader's task simple. As he puts it in the poem "Pitcher," which can be found in *The Orb Weaver,* he and this baseball player share a "passion how to avoid the obvious." In "The Base Stealer," too, Francis depicts an athlete who depends in part upon deception, and the poet himself engages in evasions and offers only partial revelations.

One piece of information that the poet declines to provide is the identity of the base this player is attempting to steal. Stealing second is the most common steal in baseball, but, given that the player has so much freedom of movement and seems able to take a walking lead, it is more likely that he is on second or third and less likely that he is on first. Stealing home is certainly more dramatic, and more difficult, than stealing third, and it would make sense if this base stealer were attempting just that, since stealing home might be the sports equivalent of the "sparks" and "wonders" that Francis trusts poetry to make. Also, when the base runner tells himself to "crowd him, crowd him," he may be indicating that he is moving physically closer to the pitcher and further into his line of sight, both of which would happen were the pitcher right-handed and were the runner moving down the third base line toward home. Ultimately, however, it is not clear which base the player is aiming for, yet this uncertainty is also fitting: though Francis wants to make his poems intelligible, he does not go so far as to strip his poem of all its mystery. Like any good poet, he prefers, as he writes in "Pitcher," "to be a moment misunderstood" and to allow ambiguities to remain unresolved.

Perhaps the most compelling information that Francis withholds is the outcome of the play: even though the title would suggest that the runner is successful in his attempt to steal a base, the poet offers no description of the end of the play and presents no confirmation that the player is indeed safe. In the last lines of the poem, Francis loads and then releases a powerful spring: "He's only flirting, crowd him, crowd him, / Delicate, delicate, delicate, delicate—now!" The base stealer takes one last look at the pitcher and decides that he is "only flirting"; in other words, the pitcher is bluffing and does not intend to throw over to the base runner's bag. Once the runner has made this determination, he edges away from the base for the last time. He tries to quietly encourage himself as he repeats the word *delicate* four times. The repetition of this three-syllable word creates a drumroll of anticipation that increases in intensity until it culminates in the runner's burst toward the next base on the cue, "now!" This final exclamation marks the first moment of a new episode in which the base stealer runs down the line and slides into the base; but Francis has reserved the description of this incident for another time and perhaps for another poem.

Source: Jeannine Johnson, Critical Essay on "The Base Stealer," in *Poetry for Students,* The Gale Group, 2001.

Sources

Francis, Robert, *Collected Poems 1936–1976,* University of Massachusetts Press, 1976.

———, *Frost: A Time to Talk,* University of Massachusetts Press, 1972.

———, *The Orb Weaver,* Wesleyan University Press, 1960.

———, *Pot Shots at Poetry,* University of Michigan Press, 1980.

———, *The Trouble with Francis,* University of Massachusetts Press, 1971.

McHugh, Heather, *Broken English,* Wesleyan University Press, 1993.

Nelson, Howard, "Moving Unnoticed: Notes on Robert Francis' Poetry," in *The Hollins Critic,* Vol. XIV, No. 4, October 1977, pp. 1–12.

Oakley, J. Ronald, *Baseball's Last Golden Age: 1946–1960,* McFarland & Co., 1994, p. 27.

True, Michael, "Books: Collected Poems," in *Commonweal,* Vol. CIV, No. 14, July 8, 1977, pp. 441–442.

For Further Study

Conlon, Charles M., *Baseball's Golden Age: The Photographs of Charles M. Conlon,* Neil McCabe and Constance McCabe, contributors, Abradale Press, 1997.
Conlon's photographs make it easy for modern readers to envision what the sport was like when Francis was writing.

Francis, Robert, *The Trouble With Francis,* University of Massachusetts Press, 1971.
The author's autobiography highlights his teaching career and his associations with famous writers.

Meyers, Jeffrey, *Robert Frost: A Biography,* Houghton Mifflin Co., 1996.
Francis' writing is often linked with Frost, his friend and mentor. This is one of the most recent and most comprehensive biographies of Frost.

Wallace, Joseph E., et al., *Baseball: 100 Classic Moments in the History of the Game,* D. K. Publishing, 2000.
Printed under the supervision of the Baseball Hall of Fame, this book gives readers background information about baseball's history, in an interesting format.

The Czar's Last Christmas Letter. A Barn in the Urals

Norman Dubie
1977

"The Czar's Last Christmas Letter. A Barn in the Urals" appears in Norman Dubie's 1977 collection *The Illustrations*. Many of the poems in the collection are told from the point of view of artists or historical figures or are about them. The "Czar" in the title is Nicholas II, Russia's last czar, who abdicated the throne in 1917 and was assassinated with his family by Bolshevik revolutionaries in 1918. Dubie's poem is in the form of a letter from Nicholas to his mother, Maria Fyodorovna Romanova, formerly Dagmar, princess of Denmark, and is written in thirty unrhymed couplets. Traditionally, Christmas letters fill in the person addressed with details of the writer's life over the last year, and this is the approach that Dubie takes. Nicholas tells his mother what his life has been like during his time in captivity in the Ural Mountains. He recounts stories about his servant, Illya, and his wife and daughters.

The tone of the poem is intimate. At the same time the letter intimates death. It is this relationship between intimacy and intimation that makes the poem intriguing because readers realize that the letter is Nicholas' last Christmas letter, whereas he does not. In addition to intimations of death, the poem implicitly addresses the changes in Russia at the time, its movement from monarchy to communism, and the effect that this change has on the country's former czar and those opposed to him and the idea of monarchy. These changes are symbolized in the details that Nicholas provides about his family, and the simple joys he writes that they find

Norman Dubie

in their daily lives, even though they are prisoners. Readers can infer from the details that Nicholas and his mother write to each other often, and that the Czar is as concerned with not upsetting his mother as he is with telling the truth about his situation.

Author Biography

In an age of poetry dominated by the confessional lyric, Norman Dubie's poetry stands out for its exploration of the lives of others. In addition to Russia's last czar, Nicholas II, Dubie has written poems about or from the point of view of Madam Blavatsky, Queen Elizabeth I, Proust, Chekhov, Ingmar Bergman, and Rodin, among others. His poetry is one of America's best-kept secrets. Known for his deep knowledge, allusiveness, and sophistication, Dubie is a "poets's poet," meaning that he has yet to achieve the popular acclaim of others less deserving and less talented. Born on April 10, 1945, in Barre, Vermont, to Norman Dubie, an insurance-claims adjuster and theological student in a progressive congregational church, and Doris Dubie, a registered nurse, Dubie began writing poems when he was eleven years old. Dubie cultivated his distinctive style under poets Barry and Lorraine Goldensohn at progressive Goddard College, where he received his B.A. in 1969. In 1971, he

finished his M.F.A. at the University of Iowa, studying under George Starbuck and Marvin Bell.

Dubie has held a number of academic posts, teaching at the University of Iowa, Ohio University, and the University of Arizona, where he helped found the creative writing program and has taught since 1975 and is now Regents' Professor of English. Few contemporary poets have demonstrated his poetic range or have been more prolific. In addition to being awarded numerous grants and prizes for his poetry, including fellowships from the National Endowment for the Arts, the Guggenheim Foundation, and the Ingram-Merrill Foundation, Dubie has published nearly twenty volumes of poems. These include *Alehouse Sonnets* (1971), *The Illustrations* (1977), which includes "The Czar's Last Christmas Letter. A Barn in the Urals," *The City of the Olesha Fruit* (1979), *Selected and New Poems* (1983), and *Groom Falconer* (1989). His *Collected and New Poems* will be published in 2001. Dubie lives with his wife, the poet Jeannine Savard, and his daughter Hannah in Tempe, Arizona.

Poem Text

You were never told, Mother, how old Illya was drunk
That last holiday, for five days and nights

He stumbled through Petersburg forming
A choir of mutes, he dressed them in pink
    ascension gowns

And, then, sold Father's Tirietz stallion so to rent   5
A hall for his Christmas recital: the audience

Was rowdy but Illya in his black robes turned on them
And gave them that look of his; the hall fell silent

And violently he threw his hair to the side and up
Went the baton, the recital ended exactly one hour   10

Later when Illya suddenly turned and bowed
And his mutes bowed, and what applause and
    hollering

Followed.
All of his cronies were there!

Illya told us later that he thought the voices   15
Of mutes combine in a sound

Like wind passing through big, winter pines.
Mother, if for no other reason I regret the war

With Japan for, you must now be told,
It took the servant, Illya, from us. *It was*   20
    confirmed.

He would sit on the rocks by the water and with
    his stiletto
Open clams and pop the raw meats into his mouth

And drool and laugh at us children.
We hear guns often, now, down near the village.

Don't think me a coward, Mother, but it is   25
    comfortable
Now that I am no longer Czar. I can take pleasure

From just a cup of clear water. I hear Illya's choir
    often.
I teach the children about decreasing fractions, that
    is

A lesson best taught by the father.
Alexandra conducts the French and singing lessons.   30

Mother, we are again a physical couple.
I brush out her hair for her at night.

She thinks that we'll be rowing outside Geneva
By the spring. I hope she won't be disappointed.

Yesterday morning while bread was frying   35
In one corner, she in another washed all of her legs

Right in front of the children. I think
We became sad at her beauty. She has a purple
    bruise

On an ankle.
Like Illya I made her chew on mint.   40

Our Christmas will be in this excellent barn.
The guards flirt with your granddaughters and I
    see . . .

I see nothing wrong with it. Your little one, who is
Now a woman, made one soldier pose for her, she
    did

Him in charcoal, but as a bold nude. He was   45
Such an obvious virgin about it; he was wonderful!

Today, that same young man found us an
    enormous azure
And pearl samovar. Once, he called me Great
    Father.

And got confused
He refused to let me touch him.   50

I know they keep your letters from us. But,
    Mother,
The day they finally put them in my hands

I'll know that possessing them I am condemned
And possibly even my wife, and my children

We will drink mint tea this evening.   55
Will each of us be increased by death?

With fractions as the bottom integer gets bigger,
    Mother, it
Represents less. That's the feeling I have about

This letter. I am at your request. The Czar.
And I am Nicholas.   60

Poem Summary

Lines 1–4

In the first line of "The Czar's Last Christmas Letter. A Barn in the Urals" the speaker, Nicholas II, addresses his mother, Maria Fyodorovna Romanova, formerly Dagmar, princess of Denmark, who was married to Czar Alexander Alexandrovich Romanov. Nicholas II was born in 1868, married Alexandra Feodorovna, formerly Alix of Hesse-Darmastadt, and assumed emperorship of Russia in 1894 when his father died. He was Russia's last czar. If this fictional letter were true, Nicholas would have written the letter in 1917 when the czar and his family were being held by Bolshevik revolutionaries in the city of Tobolsk in west central Russia.

According to Dubie, Illya is not a real person, but a device that allowed the poet to inhabit the persona of the czar more fully. Nicholas is recounting an episode that happened years before. He had never told his mother about this incident and readers can infer that it is because of his dire circumstances that he "confesses" the details of it to her. "That last holiday" is Ascension Day, which commemorates Christ's ascension into heaven. Saint Petersburg, through which Illya stumbles, is the second largest city in Russia and a place of great architectural and natural beauty. From 1712 to 1917 Saint Petersburg was the capital of the Russian empire. Illya's assembling a "choir of mutes" and dressing them in pink ascension gowns suggests both decadence and desperation. The phrase "choir of mutes" itself is an oxymoron. An oxymoron is a paradox reduced to two words, and is used to emphasize incongruities or contradictions.

Lines 5–17

In these lines, Nicholas continues the story of Illya during Ascension Day. Dubie characterizes Nicholas by the way in which he has the Czar tell the story. He does not interfere with Illya's wild behavior but merely observes it, even when Illya sold a stallion belonging to Nicholas' father to finance his absurd plan. Illya's aggressive behavior and the relative ease with which he was able to put on a recital illustrate the privilege and power of those connected with the Romanov family. The very idea of a recital by mutes is a ridiculous one but full of symbolism. The early twentieth century was a chaotic time for Russia. Revolutionaries constantly tried to overthrow the government, almost succeeding in 1905 before finally succeeding in 1917. Russia lost millions of people during World War I, and toward the end of the war, bombings, assassinations, looting, and general mayhem were widespread. During his last year in power, Nicholas was largely ineffectual and powerless in the face of this chaos. The image of a "choir of mutes" embodies this idea of powerlessness. Lines 15–17 con-

Media Adaptations

- Books on Tape released the audiocassette *Romanovs: The Final Chapter,* by Robert K. Massie in 1995. The book is read by Geoffrey Howard.

- Twentieth-Century Fox released *Anastasia* in 1997. This cartoon musical is a fictional story about the daughter of Czar Nicholas II and his wife Alexandra. Anastasia was rumored to have survived the family's 1918 massacre. Meg Ryan plays the voice of Anastasia.

- In the 1986 television drama *Anastasia,* Amy Irving plays the Russian princess who reappears in Berlin in 1923 after supposedly having been murdered five years before.

- The Academy of American Poets sponsors a webpage on Dubie at http://www.poets.org/poets/poets.cfm?prmID=175 (January 2001) with links to other relevant sites.

tain a simile. Like "the voices / Of mutes," the sound of "wind passing through big winter pines" does not so much suggest sound as it suggests an ominous and ghostly silence.

Lines 18–23

Nicholas finishes his story about Illya. Nicholas regrets Russia's war with Japan—in which Russia was soundly defeated—not because so many lives were lost but because Illya was lost to the family. How he was lost is unclear. On the one hand, he might have been a participant in the war and have died. On the other hand, he might have lost his mind during this time. Evidence of this is Illya's drooling and laughing at the children while eating clams in lines 21–23. By telling his mother how he feels about the loss of Illya, Nicholas is humanizing himself for the reader, making him seem more of a regular person than a royal.

Lines 24–40

Nicholas notes the pleasures he takes in his life after he is no longer czar, even while noting the

closeness of danger. On March 3, 1917, with popular uprisings increasing daily and mounting citizen anger at his inability to institute reforms or to address the rampant poverty of the country and the chaos it had fallen into, Nicholas abdicated the throne to his younger brother, the Grand Duke Mikhail Alexandrovitch. The grand duke himself renounced the throne the next day, effectively ending the three-century-old Romanov dynasty. The sound of Illya's chorus haunts Nicholas; symbolically, it is the sound of imminent death. Lines 27–29 underscore the presence of death in Nicholas' thinking. Teaching his children "decreasing fractions" suggests he is teaching them to expect less.

In line 30, Nicholas mentions Alexandra, his wife, the czarina. The two had been estranged for a time in 1917 in part because of his wife's religious obsessions, but were now reunited. Dubie emphasizes Nicholas' tender qualities and his love for his wife, but it is a bittersweet and melancholic love. He is both touched and saddened by her beauty, as line 38 suggests.

Lines 41–50

On March 8, 1917, Alexandra and her family were placed under arrest at the czar's winter palace at Tsarskoye Selo, outside of Saint Petersburg. Riots, bloodshed, and general chaos had engulfed the streets of the capital during February and March, as Bolsheviks staged a major offensive against counterrevolutionaries. The imperial family stayed there until August when the Bolsheviks, unsure of what to do, shipped them to Tobolsk, the capital of Siberia. The czar and his wife made the best of their situation, and these lines emphasize Nicholas's hope and despair. The conflicted feelings of the revolutionaries themselves are highlighted when one of the soldiers calls Nicholas "Great Father," one of the czar's titles. The samovar that the soldier finds is an urn used for boiling tea.

Lines 51–60

Nicholas expresses his fear that when the soldiers give him letters from his mother, which they have been withholding, it will be a sign that he and his family will be executed. He returns to the metaphor of the fraction, comparing the increasing possibility of his death to the way that the bottom integer of a fraction increases the smaller the fraction becomes. Nicholas ends the letter formally, yet affectionately. That he repeats his name at the end shows his own diminishing sense of self in the wake of all that has passed.

Themes

Class Conflict

"The Czar's Last Christmas Letter. A Barn in the Urals" shows how the idea of class is as much a psychological as a social structure and how people's perception of class is ingrained in their behavior. This idea is evident in the relationships that Nicholas describes to his mother. Those of a privileged class, such as royalty, or even the servants of royalty, have a sense of entitlement that others do not. Illya exhibits this when he organizes an absurd recital for Ascension Day featuring a "choir of mutes." A peasant could not have gotten away with this in Russia during this time. Nicholas, on the other hand, is caught between a sense of entitlement, which comes with position, and the realization that he is no longer as entitled as he was before he abdicated the throne and became a prisoner.

Being in this state of "class limbo" means that types of behavior that would previously not have been tolerated, now are. For example, the guards flirt with the czar's daughters and the czar sees "nothing wrong with it." The guards are also caught in a psychologically conflicted position in relation to their duty. On the one hand, as members of the Bolshevik revolution, they are in an adversarial position to the czar and his family, yet on the other hand they still retain a deep respect and admiration for the czar, whose family has ruled Russia for the last three centuries. This conflict is evident when a soldier calls the czar "Great Father," a title of respect and deep reverence, but then refuses to let the czar touch him. Such confusion of class-based affection and affinity is conventionally more common for prisoners than for captors. Its appearance in this poem illustrates the concrete changes that occur when the social order of a country shifts.

Death

"The Czar's Last Christmas Letter. A Barn in the Urals" explores how the possibility of death colors human beings' waking life, and how that possibility floats between the conscious and the unconscious mind. The things that Nicholas tells his mother not only have the feel of a confession, but they also sound like someone's last words. Illya's story is itself like a dream, and Nicholas tells it by way of saying that the loss of his servant was a great emotional blow to him. The tone of the poem, the subtle but ominous images, and readers' own awareness that the czar and his family have only six months more to live all make readers doubt Nicholas' intimations that being czar was more a

Topics for Further Study

- Write a poem to a clearly identified audience from the point of view of a well-known historical figure. Try to locate this poem in time. For example, you might want to imagine what President Clinton might have written to his brother during the president's impeachment hearings.

- Russia has changed a great deal since the Bolshevik Revolution of 1917. Research and report on the ways in which that revolution succeeded and the ways it failed.

- Nicholas mentions mint twice in the poem, once in line 40 and once in line 55. What is its significance?

- Read Dubie's "The Piano," a poem included in *The Illustrations*, then reread "The Czar's Last Christmas Letter. A Barn in the Urals." How does your reading of "The Piano" change your response to the czar's letter?

- Write a letter from the point of view of the czar's mother, answering her son's letter.

burden than a pleasure. If Nicholas were still the czar, his chances for living would be greater.

Ultimately, it is what Nicholas does and not what he says that makes this poem about death. The love that he expresses for his children, his wife, and even his former subjects (the soldiers and guards) all point to a mind in the act of reflection, of combing over the significance of one's life in the face of death. The consolation that he attempts to give himself, that somehow he and his family will be "increased by death," does not ring true, as he himself admits. For Nicholas, this letter is therapeutic; it's a way of grappling with the inevitability of death and of finding a place for it in his daily life.

Style

Epistolary Verse

An epistolary poem is a poem written in the form of a letter. The name comes from the word *epistle*, which means letter. Epistolary novels were popular in the eighteenth century, but epistolary poems have become popular only in recent times. Poems in the form of letters allow for a high degree of intimacy and self-reflection while simultaneously following the formal conventions of a letter. They are often written on a specific occasion for a particular reason. Dubie shapes his poem using free-verse couplets, that is, couplets that do not rhyme and have no set meter. Some of the lines are end-stopped and some of them are an enjambment (the running over of one sentence in a couplet into another). By using end stops or an enjambment, he counterbalances the conversational quality of the letter/poem with a formality befitting someone of Nicholas' rank. Readers can infer from the manner in which Nicholas addresses his mother and the details that he provides that he is fearful and unsure of what is going to happen to him and his family. Other poets who have composed epistolary poems include Ezra Pound, Richard Hugo, and William Carlos Williams.

Historical Context

In 1917 when Nicholas II would have written this letter to his mother (if this were a real letter), Russia was in a state of virtual anarchy. Nicholas had abdicated the throne in March after months of rioting and demonstrations, and the provisional government presided over by Prince Lvov passed a resolution putting the czar and his family under house arrest. The government's intention was to allow the Romanovs to emigrate to England, but the Petrograd Soviet (the Revolutionary Worker's and Soldiers' Council) objected.

In August, as popular sentiment turned more violent against the czar, the imperial family was moved to Tobolsk, the capital of Siberia, where they were housed in the governor's mansion. Home to descendents of political prisoners who had been sent there by Nicholas' own ancestors, Tobolsk nonetheless welcomed the Czar and his family.

In October a wave of revolution and counterrevolution swept Russia again, with Vladimir Ilich Lenin and the Bolsheviks seizing power on November 17th from Alexander Kerensky's government. The Whites, those loyal to the Romanovs or just hostile to the revolutionaries, battled against them. Since Tobolsk is isolated and its rivers are frozen during the winter, the only way to get to the city was by horse. Consequently, news about the

Bolsheviks' victory did not arrive until late November. Nicholas was surprised and dejected by the news, as Lenin made no secret of his contempt for the imperial family. The mood at the mansion darkened considerably. Historian Peter Kurth writes that in December

> Christmas came, and with it the last resemblance of 'useful' activity in the governor's mansion. According to custom, the imperial family gave presents to all of their servants, down to the last footman, and this year a number of the soldiers also received gifts of knitted scarves, gloves, and caps.

In March 1918, Bolshevik Russia signed the Treaty of Brest-Litovsk with Germany, renouncing its sovereignty over Finland, Estonia, Poland, Latvia, and Lithuania, and over the Ukraine in the south. Armenia, Georgia, and Azerbaijan declared their independence as well. The Bolsheviks hoped this would allow them to consolidate their power and institute sweeping social reforms. Instead, the counterrevolution intensified, as the Allies swept into former Soviet strongholds and helped anti-Bolshevik forces. During this time, the Bolsheviks renamed themselves the Communist Party, and moved the country's capital from Petrograd to Moscow. In May 1918, the imperial family was moved one last time, to Yekaterinburg, a dark and lawless diamond-mining town in the Ural Mountains, where they were held in the home of an engineer named Ipatiev. Residents of Yekaterinburg despised the imperial family, jeering at them and spitting on them as they arrived. With anti-Bolshevik forces approaching the town, a decision was made to kill the royal family. Around midnight on July 16, Nicholas and his family were ordered out of bed and into the basement of the house, where they were told they were to be moved again. Instead, they were lined up and shot to death. Their bodies were then run over by trucks, dismembered, burned, and dumped in a mine.

Historians debate whether or not Lenin ordered the killings. Those who claim he did point to Lenin's hatred of Nicholas, and the fact that Lenin's brother, also a revolutionary, had been ordered executed years before under Nicholas' orders. Out of fifty-three Romanovs alive in 1918, the Bolsheviks killed seventeen. The rest escaped the country by 1920. The Dowager Empress Marie Feodorovna, Czar Nicholas' mother, emigrated to Britain to live with her sister, the Queen Mother, Alexandra of Britain.

In 1977, when "The Czar's Last Christmas Letter. A Barn in the Urals" was written, Leonid Brezhnev was head of the Soviet Union. Histori-

Compare & Contrast

- **1917–1918:** Czar Nicholas II abdicates the throne to his brother, who renounces the throne the next day. More than three centuries of Romanov family rule end. The Bolshevik Party changes its name to the Communist Party, and is led by Vladimir Ilich Lenin.

- **1985–1991:** General Secretary of the Communist Party Mikhail Gorbachev announces the programs of *perestroika* (economic and governmental reform) and *glasnost* (openness), which unleashes international political forces that help lead to the fall of the Berlin Wall in November 1989. In 1991 the Soviet Union dissolves. The Communist Party loses power in a failed coup against Gorbachev, and fifteen formerly Soviet republics declare their independence.

- **Today:** Vladimir Putin, former head of the Federal Security Service (FSB), one of the successor bodies of the Soviet-era Secret Police (KGB), is named Russian prime minister and elected president.

- **1917–1918:** Czar Nicholas II and his family are imprisoned and massacred by Bolshevik revolutionaries.

  1991: DNA tests confirm that the bodies found in 1979 are indeed those of the czar and his family.

  1998: Nicholas II and his family are given an official burial in Saint Petersburg eighty years to the day after he and his family were executed. Russian President Boris Yeltsin calls the Czar's murder "one of the most shameful pages in our history."

ans refer to the 1970s in Russia as the "period of stagnation," because few real reforms or changes occurred. The Cold War between the United States and the Soviet Union had thawed a bit, and the two superpowers negotiated a number of strategic arms limitation agreements. In 1979 those relations became tense again, as the Soviets stepped up internal repression of dissidents and invaded Afghanistan. In this same year, the remains of the Romanov family and household were discovered by Dr. Alexander Avdonin. However, due to political conditions, researchers were forbidden to exhume them until 1991, when DNA tests confirmed their identities.

Critical Overview

Critics often note Dubie's ability to internalize the experience of others in his poems. Calling the tone of "The Czar's Last Christmas Letter. A Barn in the Urals" "choric and valedictory," critic Christopher Baker writes that "Dubie's relationship with those who have spoken, written, and painted creates a gallery of alter egos." In the foreword to *The Illustrations,* in which the poem appears, Richard Howard asks if the poet's life is "a world of derived identities?" Howard observes that in writing from the point of view of such figures as Nicholas II "it is always the experience which has the root of *peril* in it, the ripple of danger which enlivens the seemingly lovely surfaces, the 'ordinary' existence." Howard continues, pointing out Dubie's propensity for mixing fact and fiction: "We are not to know what is given and what is taken, what is 'real' and what is 'made up.'"

In their introduction to Dubie's poems, anthologists Richard Ellmann and Robert O'Clair praise Dubie's willingness to tackle historical subjects, noting that he writes "in a period when narrative verse is in disfavor, and specific times and places tend to be avoided." Other critics have not been as kind. Reviewing *The Illustrations,* Lawrence Raab writes that

> even when most (if not all) of the facts of a given poem are clear . . . and the writing is sharp, controlled and engaging, the poem can seem to be talking to itself, and the reader may feel that he has blundered into the middle of a fascinating story the significance of which he can never hope to fathom.

Criticism

Chris Semansky

Semansky's poetry, fiction, and essays appear regularly in literary magazines and journals. In the following essay, he considers how to read Dubie's poem inferentially.

In an interview with critic and reviewer James Green in *American Poetry Review,* Norman Dubie gives this advice about reading his poems:

> I think if you're sitting behind a woman and a girl on a bus and you're listening to them talk and you suddenly are certain that this is a mother and daughter, and that today the daughter visited a friend that the mother doesn't approve of, and then you conclude that the friend has a romantic attachment to the daughter and that the mother has been divorced twice and that her third husband died on a highway in Poughkeepsie. . . . You see what I mean. If the kind of effort that we make out of natural curiosity, eavesdropping in a restaurant or on a bus, was brought to the poem, we would understand the . . . poem.

This advice—to explore a poem through its inferences by "eavesdropping"—fits Dubie's poems well, for they are often communications between two identifiable people and are often packed with historical references and information about those people. Dubie, however, suggests that one need not be versed in this information to understand the *emotional* truth of a poem, that readers can glean enough from the information provided. A close look at his poem "The Czar's Last Christmas Letter: A Barn in the Urals" bears this out.

Readers are first drawn to the poem because it is written in letter form. Everyone has written a letter at one point or another. Because letters are most often a communication between two people, the speaker and the audience are clearly defined. Poems may speak in a universal voice to an undefined or generic audience, but letters do not. They are written on a specific occasion and for a particular purpose. The occasion here is Christmas, the holidays. Often the purpose of Christmas letters is to send greetings to someone with whom the writer has been out of contact and to fill them in on what happened during the last year. This letter/poem begins with the narrator, Russian Czar Nicholas II, confessing something to his mother. Readers do not initially know who Illya is and, indeed, do not have to know to appreciate the gesture of telling someone something that has been kept from them for some time. Nicholas' story of Illya is engaging, not because it is so bizarre (although it is) but because Nicholas imbues it with such significance. What is

a "choir of mutes" and what does Nicholas' choosing to tell this story to his mother tell the readers about their relationship? The joy of eavesdropping is that it places readers/listeners in the position of doing something forbidden, that is, being privy to information not meant for them. They are witnesses to an emotional outpouring not meant for them. This aspect both titillates and intrigues readers, and they want to know more.

What readers learn about Nicholas' character through his letter to his mother is that he is more concerned with personal relationships than world affairs. In lines 18–20 Nicholas writes:

> Mother, if for no other reason I regret the war
>
> With Japan for, you must now be told,
> It took the servant, Illya, from us. It was
>   confirmed.

Russia lost the war with Japan (1904–1905), many soldiers, and a good deal of political capital, yet Nicholas regretted the war because he lost a servant. A personal letter is the only conceivable context in which an internationally known leader of a major country could make such a statement. If Nicholas were to have made this statement in public, he would have been forced to abdicate even sooner than he was. Nicholas continues his "confession" in line 26:

> Don't think me a coward, Mother, but it is
>   comfortable
> Now that I am no longer Czar. I can take pleasure
>
> From just a cup of clear water. I hear Illya's choir
>   often.
> I teach the children about decreasing fractions, that is
>
> A lesson best taught by the father.
> Alexandra conducts the French and singing lessons.
>
> Mother, we are again a physical couple.
> I brush out her hair for her at night.

The images in these lines symbolize simplicity and tenderness. The "clear water," the "mute choir," even the "decreasing fractions" all point to an emptying out of thought and emotional clutter. Nicholas' fear that his mother might think him a "coward" is natural for someone whose image has been built upon his reputation for strength and leadership. But this was precisely the image that Nicholas did not have. He was largely considered to be weak and ineffectual as Russia's leader. These lines rather speak to Nicholas' image of how the czar *ought* to be considered and how he thought his mother thought of him. By admitting that he takes pleasure in simple, often domestic acts now, Nicholas reveals his relief at no longer having to be czar, and the joy he takes in family life.

The last five couplets of the poem spell out Nicholas' fear of death. Whereas, the previous fifty lines detailed events from the distant past (Illya's story) and the recent past (developments in his family), these lines express what was only previously implied.

> I know they keep your letters from us. But, Mother,
> The day they finally put them in my hands
>
> I'll know that possessing them I am condemned
> And possibly even my wife, and my children.
>
> We will drink mint tea this evening.
> Will each of us be increased by death?
>
> With fractions as the bottom integer gets bigger, Mother, it
> Represents less. That's the feeling I have about
>
> This letter. I am at your request, The Czar.
> And I am Nicholas.

Nicholas repeats his mother's name four times during the letter and twice in these lines. This gesture is a convention used to develop a deeper intimacy between the writer and the addressed. Readers see this and empathize with Nicholas because they already know the ending of his story. Adding to the pathos is the way in which Nicholas jumps between surface detail (what they will drink in the evening) and his sense of foreboding. He describes his fear ingeniously, by comparing death to decreasing fractions, thereby continuing an image introduced earlier in the poem. His diminished role in Russia, his imprisonment, and his uncertainty about the future all "add up" to less, as does the letter he has just finished. Fittingly he signs off as both "The Czar" and Nicholas, identities his mother obviously knows. This gesture, however, is more for Nicholas himself, who inhabits the netherworld between these identities and between the past and the future.

John Keats called the process of imagining one's self in a situation one has not necessarily experienced "negative capability." Dubie has made a career out of his capacity to imagine himself in the skin of another and to generate poetry out of that imagining. Some poets, such as Robert Browning, engage in this practice through dramatic monologues, where the mode of expression is written speech. "My Last Duchess," in which Browning writes from the point of view of a diabolical duke discussing the fate of his last wife is one such example. Dubie's mode of expression, however, is writing itself, and the conventions and expectations that letters embody. Whereas speech is immediate, as the addressee typically occupies the same space

> *John Keats called the process of imagining one's self in a situation one has not necessarily experienced 'negative capability.' Dubie has made a career out of his capacity to imagine himself in the skin of another and to generate poetry out of that imagining."*

and time as the speaker, letter writing is, at least theoretically, more reflective. The writer can read over his words and change them. Also, with letters, the intended audience (in this case, the czar's mother) is reading the letter at a later time and in a different place than where the letter was written.

What distinguishes Dubie's monologues and letters from others is that they are always at least partially true. Nicholas and his mother did write to each other often, and they did have a very close relationship. Indeed their correspondence has been published, as have Nicholas' diaries, which he kept every day he was in power. The details that Dubie presents about life at Tobolsk where the Czar and his family were imprisoned *could* have happened. But what's most important is that the details he provides aim at establishing a kind of psychological and emotional truth, which for Dubie transcends the truth of any fact.

Source: Chris Semansky, Critical Essay on "The Czar's Last Christmas Letter. A Barn in the Urals," in *Poetry for Students,* The Gale Group, 2001.

Doreen Piano

Piano is a third-year graduate student in English at Bowling Green State University. In the following essay, she explores how Dubie's poem reveals Czar Nicholas as a once powerful man who, humbled by imprisonment, now focuses on living life as if each day were his last.

In the summer of 1918, Czar Nicholas and his family were executed in the Ural Mountains of east-

What Do I Read Next?

- Dubie's 1989 collection of poems *Groom Falconer* has been widely praised as one of his best collections. In this collection, Dubie continues his practice of writing about historical figures. Some of these figures include Edgar Alan Poe, Sigmund Freud, and Jacques Derrida.

- Dubie's *Selected & New Poems* was published in 1983 and contains poems from all of his previous books, including the ones that are out of print.

- Richard Pipes's 1995 study, *A Concise History of the Russian Revolution,* offers a conservative interpretation of the events leading up to and immediately following the Russian Revolution. Pipes's book is one of the most popular studies on the subject.

- Russian historian and playwright Edvard Radzinsky's 1992 book, *Last Tsar: The Life and Death of Nicholas II,* tells the story of the last days of Russia's last royal family using diaries, letters, and eyewitness accounts from Nicholas and others.

---

ern Russia by the Bolshevik army, the ruling party of the newly founded Soviet Union. As the last Russian monarch to rule before the revolution of 1917, Nicholas was against more democracy in government, but he was never an effective leader. Thus, his rule was rife with mismanaged social and economic affairs that resulted in a number of popular uprisings. Peasants as well as intellectuals organized demonstrations and strikes to oppose Nicholas' totalitarian regime. In addition, what made the royal family even more open to criticism were their elaborate displays of wealth and their intimate relationship with a mystic monk, Rasputin, who at times seemed to be running the country more than the royal couple. Not long after the 1917 revolution, Nicholas and his family were arrested and sent to the Ural Mountains where they lived until they were executed.

Despite reports from a handful of witnesses and the royal family's own letters and diaries, the circumstances of the royal family's life and death under house arrest are still largely undetermined. Thus, this event in Russian history has produced some interesting speculation not only by historians but also by writers such as the poet Norman Dubie. In the poem "The Czar's Last Christmas Letter: A Barn in the Urals," Dubie takes imaginative liberties by writing from the point of view of Czar Nicholas during the last year of his life. What is most striking about this poem is its portrayal of the czar not as a selfish and arrogant despot, the predominant image of him, but as a man humbled by the present conditions of his life. Confined to living on the estate of a former royal member, Nicholas obviously had much time for reflection. It is this more intimate aspect of his life that Dubie probes in his poem. Though often historical in setting, Dubie's poems "exist at the juncture of several 'realities,' sometimes historical and sometimes personal" as the poet David St. John claims in his essay "A Generous Salvation: The Poetry of Norman Dubie." In "The Czar's Last Christmas Letter: A Barn in the Urals," Dubie uses the form of a letter written by Nicholas to his mother to reveal how the historical and personal are deeply entwined.

Dubie relies on the poetic form of the dramatic monologue to create a complex character of the now-dethroned czar. A dramatic monologue is a type of lyric poem characterized by several features. First, it takes on the "persona" or "voice" of a well-known and/or historic person to reveal his or her particular temperament. For example, in the poem "Ulysses," Alfred Tennyson writes from the perspective of the Homeric hero Ulysses to reveal his constant need to wander even after he has returned home from the Trojan War. Secondly, the dramatic monologue has a specific audience or addressee that is part of the poem's content. One of the most popular dramatic monologues, "My Last Duchess" by Robert Browning, has the Duke cavalierly revealing to an emissary that he sentenced his wife to death. Lastly, the poem is recited at a critical moment in the speaker's life. In Dubie's poem, the czar knows that he is nearing the end of his life; his tone then reveals some misgivings about the decisions that he has made and the personal toll they have taken. By analyzing the poem through the particular features of the dramatic monologue, one can get an idea of the complexity of the poem's subject matter and form without having to understand all of the historical references that may or may not be historically accurate.

Contrary to the dominant historical portrayal of him as tyrannical and arrogant, Dubie's czar appears as a sensitive and compassionate man dedicated to keeping his family's spirit buoyed during their imprisonment. Instead of being focused on maintaining his power, the czar in Dubie's poem is a ruler who no longer rules "the masses" and is relieved to do so. "Don't think me a coward, Mother, but it is comfortable / Now that I am no longer Czar. I can take pleasure / From just a cup of clear water. . . ." Dubie creates images of the czar's family participating in ordinary activities such as frying bread, studying math and French, or sketching to reveal how the czar's world view has changed. Everyday activities that he may have overlooked as a world leader are now the sole focus of life. Thus, his daughters' flirtations with the guards, his wife's washing of her legs in front of the family, and a soldier's gift of "an enormous azure / And pearl samovar" are aspects of life that now take on greater meaning as the czar realizes that death is imminent.

Ground-swelling events such as the Russo-Japanese war in 1904–1905, the First World War, and the Russian Revolution of 1917 no longer preoccupy his time. Dubie reveals the change in the czar's perspective by recasting a major conflict that occurred during his rule, the war between Russia and Japan, as being a personal rather than political matter. Rather than viewing the war as a mistake that leads to economic and social upheaval, as many Russians did, the czar focuses on his personal regret for involving Russia in the war when he writes:

> Mother, if for no other reason I regret the war
>
> With Japan for, you must now be told,
> It took the servant, Illya, from us. It was
>   confirmed.

Here, Dubie's czar is far more concerned with telling his mother, as delicately as possible, the truth about a servant of the royal family who died in the war than with the consequences the war had on the Russian economy. However, by admitting his personal regret, he also obliquely appears to take responsibility for his actions as a ruler.

Throughout the poem, the former czar's mother is the recipient of his confessions and observations. The letter starts on a personal note, a recollection of a childhood memory, "You were never told, Mother, how old Illya was drunk / That last holiday, for five days and nights. . . ." Although this appears to be an odd way for such a powerful man to begin a letter, the tone establishes an intimate moment, one that is offstage of the interna-

> *What is most striking about this poem is its portrayal of the czar not as a selfish and arrogant despot, the predominant image of him, but as a man humbled by the present conditions of his life."*

tional political arena. Confessing a childhood secret that Nicholas has kept from his mother reveals the ruler as being vulnerable and honest. His confession suggests that Nicholas did not, like many children, tell his parents everything and that despite his mother's leading role as an adviser to him on foreign and domestic affairs, the czar managed to keep certain kinds of information from her. In Dubie's rendering of their relationship, Nicholas is not seeking counsel but is confessing some very intense truths, probably with the knowledge that he will never see her again.

That Nicholas is writing to his mother is significant as he is trying to tell her, the former czarina of Russia, that the days of the monarchy are over and a new order has arrived. Nicholas uses the image of Illya, a family servant, to describe to his mother the "new man" of Russia, one whose roots are in the peasant class and who is not afraid to be among the people. The power demonstrated by the servant Illya and his "choir of mutes" is representative of the Russian people under the newly formed Soviet Union. Nicholas is aware of this change of power when he writes:

> . . . the audience
>
> Was rowdy but Illya in his black robes turned on
>   them
> And gave them that look of his; the hall fell silent

By describing Illya as a powerful figure who can silence people with a look, Nicholas indirectly acknowledges that the royal family has fallen out of power and that people like Illya have taken their place.

Not only does the czar tell his mother of changes in Russian rule, but he also explains that there is no hope of seeing each other again as when he writes, "The day they finally put them [his mother's letters] in my hands / I'll know that possessing them I am condemned." Throughout the poem, Dubie uses images to convey both the newfound powerlessness of the czar as well as the political and personal dimensions of his relationship with his mother. For example, the last two lines show Nicholas as occupying two roles—both a czar, as when he writes "at your request, The Czar" and also a son, as when he adds "And I am Nicholas." It is possible that only at the end of his life can he allow himself to be intimate and informal with his mother by using his first name, yet this honesty ultimately redeems Nicholas and elicits the reader's sympathy.

What is particularly poignant about this poem is how Dubie renders the royal family as living as normally as they can under such uncertain circumstances. The strain of being confined to a house and having little power over their future is conveyed most acutely by descriptions of Alexandra, who seems especially bereft by their circumstances. Nicholas realizes this when he writes, "We became sad at her beauty. She has a purple bruise." Yet life goes on as "the guards flirt with your granddaughters. . . ." and "Alexandra conducts the French and singing lessons." Even under extreme circumstances, Nicholas and his family continue to conduct the business of everyday life. In fact, with their future as yet unknown and their glories behind them, it is their focus on ordinary everyday events that is their only salvation.

In his essay, "My Dubious Calculus," the writer William Slattery states "Norman Dubie makes images that suggest stories . . . stories in which people, alive with idiosyncrasy and trapped in desperate situations, transfer highly charged bits of their experience to the reader." Regardless of how much he knew of the czar's actual life and death, Dubie renders a complex portrait of the czar and his family's final months of life by using highly descriptive images that makes the royal family's fate tragic, compassionate, and illuminating.

Source: Doreen Piano, Critical Essay on "The Czar's Last Christmas Letter. A Barn in the Urals," in *Poetry for Students,* The Gale Group, 2001.

Sources

Baker, Christopher, "Norman Dubie," in *Dictionary of Literary Biography,* Vol. 120: *American Poets Since World War II,* edited by R. S. Gwynn, Third Series, Gale, 1992, pp. 52–60.

Dubie, Norman, *The Illustrations,* Braziller, 1977.

Ellmann, Richard, and Robert O'Clair, eds., *The Norton Anthology Of Modern Poetry,* 2d ed., Norton, 1988.

Garber, Frederick, "On Dubie and Seidel," in *The American Poetry Review,* May–June 1982, pp. 44–47.

Green, James, "Norman Dubie: 'Groom Falconer,'" in *The American Poetry Review,* November–December 1989.

Horowitz, David A., Peter N. Carroll, and David D. Lee, eds., *On the Edge: A New History of 20th-Century America,* Thomson Learning, 1990.

Howard, Richard, *Alone with America,* Atheneum, 1961.

Kurth, Peter, *Anastasia: The Riddle of Anna Anderson,* Little Brown & Co., 1985.

———, *The Lost World of Nicholas and Alexandra,* Little Brown & Co., 1995.

Raab, Lawrence, Review in *American Poetry Review,* July–August 1978.

Radzinsky, Edvard, *Last Tsar,* Doubleday, 1992.

Slattery, William, "My Dubious Calculus," in *Antioch Review,* Vol. 52, No. 1, Winter 1994.

St. John, David, "A Generous Salvation: The Poetry of Norman Dubie," in *Conversant Essays: Contemporary Poets on Poetry,* edited by James McCorkle, Wayne State University Press, 1990.

For Further Study

Howard, Richard, *Alone with America,* Atheneum, 1980.
    This collection of essays by one of America's finest literary critics of poetry contains reviews of the work of Dubie's contemporaries.

Kurth, Peter, *Anastasia: The Riddle of Anna Anderson,* Little Brown & Co., 1985.
    This book is a comprehensive collection of information on Anna Anderson, the woman who claimed to be Grand Duchess Anastasia, Nicholas II's daughter. Anderson claimed to have survived the July 17, 1918, massacre of her family.

Perry, John Curtis, and Constantine V. Pleshakov, *The Flight of the Romanovs,* Basic Books, 1999.
    Perry and Pleshakov use interviews and unpublished diaries to tell the story of the Romanov family. This text is an authoritative account and one of the most comprehensive to date.

Youssoupoff, Felix, *Rasputin,* The Dial Press, 1928.
    Rasputin was a peasant, a mystic, a rascal, and a confidant of Alexandra. His influence over the royal family is widely debated by historians.

Filling Station

Elizabeth Bishop
1965

"Filling Station" was published in Elizabeth Bishop's third volume, *Questions of Travel,* (1965), most of which was written in Brazil. The book is divided into two parts: "Brazil" and "Elsewhere." "Filling Station" and the poems in "Elsewhere" evoke the geographies, both physical and emotional, of Bishop's childhood.

Even though Bishop traveled extensively in her life, it was not the grand view that interested her. As one can see in "Filling Station," she was more inclined to focus on the details of ordinary life. Once she thanked a friend who had sent her a pair of binoculars: "The world has wonderful details if you can get it just a little closer than usual." "Filling Station" shows what can happen when someone takes the time to look closer than usual and see beyond the surface of things.

"Filling Station" recreates the scene, in keenly observed visual and tactile detail, of a family-run gas station. It is not typical subject matter for a poem. Everything is startlingly "dirty" and "oil-permeated" in this little cosmos, from the father's work clothes to the embroidered doily. After observing the "overall black translucency" of this place, the poem's speaker begins to ask questions: "Do they live in the station?" After all, there is a dirty dog lying "comfy" on the greasy wicker sofa and comic books are on a taboret, or wicker stand. "Why these things?" the voice asks. The question is not answered directly or immediately. Despite the grime of it all, the poem continues, "somebody" cares: "Somebody waters the plant, / or oils it, maybe."

Elizabeth Bishop

From the embroidered daisy-like flowers to the arrangement of softly chanting cans, it finally concludes there is evidence "somebody loves us all."

Author Biography

Elizabeth Bishop was born in Worcester, Massachusetts, on February 8, 1911, the only child of William Thomas Bishop and Gertrude May Boomer Bishop. Unlike the vaguely poor family in "Filling Station," Bishop's family was prosperous, but the circumstances sad. When she was only eight months old, her father died of a kidney disorder. Distraught over her husband's death, Gertrude Bishop drifted in and out of mental hospitals. In 1916 she was permanently institutionalized. Elizabeth, age five, never saw her mother again. Bishop's life was rootless from then on. For a brief happy year, she lived in rural Nova Scotia with her mother's parents, but then her wealthy Bishop relatives demanded she move back to Boston. There, Elizabeth quickly became depressed, asthmatic, and prone to debilitating allergies.

After nine terrible months, Elizabeth was "rescued" by her Aunt Maud Boomer Shepherdson, who brought her home to her poor neighborhood in Revere, Massachusetts. Aunt Maud nursed the

sick child, and introduced her not only to poetry, but to a place, Bishop remembers, where "we were almost all aliens, dreamers, drunkards." The setting and inhabitants of "Filling Station" were typical of Bishop's surroundings in those years. Bishop never knew any truly grounding sense of home except, perhaps, in the words of poems, stories, and songs. As she grew older, her love of literature was soon matched by an ability to write. At the Walnut Hill School for Girls in Natick, she dominated the pages of *The Blue Pencil.*

Bishop entered Vassar College in 1930 and found herself in the company of other gifted writers. But she also found herself falling in love with other women and drinking heavily. Her academic performance was brilliant at times, yet inconsistent. She fell into periods of extreme withdrawal and depression as she attempted to hide her passions and habits. In her last year at Vassar, Bishop met the eccentric poet Marianne Moore, who became not only a great friend, but her most important mentor. Bishop wandered after college from New York City to Europe to Key West, Florida, writing the poems that would comprise the manuscript of her first book, *North & South* (1946). In 1947, she met the poet Robert Lowell, and the two became close friends. Through Lowell's strong literary connections, Bishop gained recognition and support for her work.

In 1951, Bishop traveled to Brazil and stayed there, having fallen in love with the countryside and with Lota Soares, whom she had met in New York in 1942. It was in Brazil that Bishop wrote "Filling Station" and the other poems of *Questions of Travel* (1965). The ten years she lived with Soares in Samambaia were Bishop's happiest. In 1961 Lota Soares moved the household to Rio. Bishop disliked the crowded city with its noise, heat, and threats of revolution, so she left Brazil in 1966 and took a teaching post at the University of Washington in Seattle. There she fell in love again, and her relationship with Soares and Brazil began to disintegrate.

Against doctors' orders, the mentally and physically exhausted Soares flew to New York to visit Bishop on September 19, 1967. During the night, Soares took an overdose of tranquilizers, and died five days later. A distraught Bishop drank ever more heavily, compounding her depression and asthma. Despite the turmoil, her literary reputation continued to rise, helped in large part by filling Robert Lowell's sabbatical post at Harvard, giving her new visibility and greater courage to do readings. Bishop's *Complete Poems* (1969) drew much acclaim, as did the prize-winning *Geography III*

(1976) which, with characteristic restraint, maps the terrain of her many personal losses. This theme is captured profoundly in her poem "One Art" and its refrain: "The art of losing isn't hard to master."

On October 6, 1979, just before she was to give a reading at Harvard's Sanders Theatre, Bishop died suddenly of a cerebral aneurysm. She was sixty-eight.

Poem Text

> Oh, but it is dirty!
> —this little filling station,
> oil-soaked, oil-permeated
> to a disturbing, over-all
> black translucency.   5
> Be careful with that match!
>
> Father wears a dirty,
> oil-soaked monkey suit
> that cuts him under the arms,
> and several quick and saucy   10
> and greasy sons assist him
> (it's a family filling station),
> all quite thoroughly dirty.
>
> Do they live in the station?
> It has a cement porch   15
> behind the pumps, and on it
> a set of crushed and grease-
> impregnated wickerwork;
> on the wicker sofa
> a dirty dog, quite comfy.   20
>
> Some comic books provide
> the only note of color—
> of certain color. They lie upon a big dim doily
> draping a taboret
> (part of the set), beside   25
> a big hirsute begonia.
>
> Why the extraneous plant?
> Why the taboret?
> Why, oh why, the doily?
> (Embroidered in daisy stitch   30
> with marguerites, I think,
> and heavy with gray crochet.)
>
> Somebody embroidered the doily.
> Somebody waters the plant,
> or oils it, maybe. Somebody   35
> arranges the rows of cans
> so that they softly say:
> ESSO—SO—SO—SO
> to high-strung automobiles.
> Somebody loves us all.   40

Poem Summary

Lines 1–6

The first line of "Filling Station" is an exclamation: "Oh, but it is dirty!" The last line of that stanza also exclaims, in an imperative warning: "Be careful with that match!" Between those lines, this world is described as black and greasy. And that "overall black translucency" is "disturbing," not because it is unclean, but because it is altogether fragile. With a single match, it could all go up in flames. The voice that exclaims "it is dirty!" is more caring and maternal than judgmental.

Lines 7–13

Particular features of the "little" station begin to emerge in the second stanza. This is a family-run business (as was that of Bishop's father), and everyone shares the same patina of grease. At the helm is "Father" in his "oil-soaked monkey suit," which is obviously too small for him. It "cuts him under the arms," suggesting both that Father is large, and may be too poor to afford work clothes that fit him well. His many unnamed sons, described as "thoroughly dirty," don't emerge as individuals; they all seem to be the same—"quick and saucy / and greasy"—as they assist their father in servicing the automobiles. The lines of this stanza have settled from exclamation into clear-eyed declaratives, statements of observation.

Lines 14–20

Stanza three begins with a question: "Do they live in the station?" In these lines, the presence of domestic features—a porch with its wicker furniture and lazy dog—suggests the possibility. "Quite comfy" specifically describes the dog, but also the general atmosphere of the place, despite its pervasive dirtiness. The speaker notes there is little distance from the pumps to the porch, which is also "impregnated" by grease.

Lines 21–27

The question that begins stanza three continues to be answered in stanza four. The eye travels next to a taboret and adjacent begonia. These objects, in all their "unrehearsed reality," are composed within the "frame" of this stanza much like one of Bishop's watercolor paintings. The taboret is adorned with "some comic books" whose contents are unspecified. What is important to the poem is their color, for it is the "only note of color" in this otherwise oil-clouded scene. One is left to imagine the "certain" or bright colors of the comic books, which lie "upon a big dim doily." A doily is a lace or linen cloth, often handmade, used to protect and adorn a piece of furniture. This large doily is "dim" from exposure to the same substance that permeates the family's furniture and clothing. The houseplant, a begonia, is not attractive in the

Media Adaptations

- The American Academy of Poets' online site, http://www.poets.org/poets/poets.cfm?prmID= 7 (January 2001), has an Elizabeth Bishop exhibit that contains a photo, a concise biography, selected bibliography, texts of several poems (including "Filling Station"), and links to other Bishop sites.

- Another excellent web site, "Modern American Poetry," contains portions of published criticism of several Bishop poems, including "Filling Station," "The Fish," "The Armadillo," and "One Art." It also has excerpts of the correspondence between Bishop and Marianne Moore, and six Bishop book jacket designs. Three of them feature her watercolor painting. See http://www. english.uiuc.edu/maps/poets/ (January 2001).

- A special collection of Bishop papers is held at her alma mater, Vassar College. A description of those papers and other library collections can be found at http://iberia.vassar.edu/bishop (January 2001).

- You can hear four contemporary poets read Bishop's "Sonnet" at *Atlantic Monthly's* website, http://www.theatlantic.com/unbound/poetry/ soundings/bishop.htm (January 2001).

- A small selection of Bishop poems can be heard on an audio collection called "Poet's Night: 11 Poets Celebrate," a recording of a poetry reading in New York City in 1996. The tape can be ordered through http://www.audiobooks.com (January 2001).

conventional way. The reader learns nothing of its color or foliage, even though begonias are usually grown for their showy leaves and blooms. This one, instead, is big and "hirsute," or hairy. It seems to have taken on the general masculinity of the family business.

Lines 28–33

The next-to-last stanza moves from observation into questioning—"why?" The plant seems "extraneous," irrelevant or unessential to the practical dirty workaday business of filling gas tanks. So, "why is this plant here?" the poem asks. Likewise, "why" the taboret? It seems its only reason-to-be is to hold comic books. Even calling it a "taboret" seems an exotic gesture on the part of the poem's speaker, where the more inelegant "stand" might have sufficed. And finally, "Why, oh why, the doily?" exclaims the voice, as though such decor merits the question twice. "Why this gratuitous bit of beauty in such a dingy place?" "Why" this once-pretty piece of handwork? As if to probe the mystery, the eye of the poem draws closer to the doily and finds it an odd combination of fresh and stale, both "embroidered in daisy stitch / with marguerites" and "heavy with gray crochet."

Lines 34–41

No reasonable "because" answers arrive to satisfy this series of "whys." Instead, the last stanza registers a change in consciousness, leading from one mystery to another. Just as oil "fills" every surface and opening within reach of the pumps, the mysterious presence of "Somebody" fills the last stanza. Regardless of "why" the doily and plants exist in a filling station, "somebody" brings beauty and care to that unlikely place. Somebody has infused a "useless" loveliness into this small world, even into the arrangement of oil cans, so that the visible letters seem to chant; " . . . they softly say: / ESSO—SO—SO / to high-strung automobiles." The only answer to "why" reaches beyond logic and practicality to love. "Somebody loves us all," the poem concludes simply, and profoundly. The journey of perception from first stanza to last has led from surface to depth: from an almost-fussy focus on the dirty aspect of things, to a consciousness of their connection with something deeper, a love that fills the station and beyond.

Themes

Beauty and Aesthetics

An oil-soaked filling station seems an odd subject for a poem. This scene—"Oh, but it is dirty!"— is a stark contrast to those objects of natural and human beauty, which have traditionally inspired poets and artists. An oil-soaked monkey suit, a dirty dog, and a doily heavy with gray crochet would normally avert the eye, not attract it. Bishop's poetics, however, required a certain morality. It was part of her "aesthetic ethic" to be responsible for what she sees, even if what stands before her, like the moose in another poem, is "homely as a house."

Bishop's mentor and friend, Marianne Moore, encouraged Bishop to revere the most ordinary, seemingly ugly things of the world, to see them as worthy of attention and naming. In "The Fish," as in "Filling Station," the poet's patient looking is rewarded in illumination. When she first catches the huge fish, "He hung a grunting weight, / battered and venerable / and homely . . . infested / with tiny white sea-lice," but as the poem proceeds, something else happens: "I stared and stared / and victory filled up / the little rented boat," until at last "everything / was rainbow, rainbow! / And I let the fish go."

As "Filling Station" proceeds stanza by stanza, the reader witnesses a similar process of revelation. The poet's eye lingers on the greasy scene long enough to stir curiosity: "Do they live in the station?" "Why the extraneous plant?" Instead of answers, the questions lead to a different way of seeing. The eye of the poem begins to see a certain harmoniousness and the presence of intentional spots of beauty, even though the surfaces of the scene are uniformly dingy. The eye has looked long enough to penetrate, and go beyond the usual judgments of such things, as unworthy of art or attention. Moreover, this beauty is not an accident: "Somebody embroidered the doily" and "Somebody / arranges the rows of cans." Some unnamed being "waters the plant" and cares for this grimy little cosmos, thus bringing a beauty to it that subverts all poetic cliché. At the end of the poem, beauty finds its source in love, and the poem suddenly opens out to "us all." In doing so, it suggests that no human being, no matter how "thoroughly dirty," is beyond the beautifying power of love.

Masculine and Feminine

"Filling Station" presents the reader with a microcosm, a little world, unified by the pervasive presence of oil, and complete with human and animal, work and rest, order and disorder, masculine and feminine. Feminist critics would be especially interested in the presence of the latter, those "markers" in the poem that indicate a consciousness of gender.

Feminist criticism is one of the most important trends in literary criticism in the last quarter-century. Generally speaking, feminist critics look at the presence, or absence, of a feminine consciousness in works of literature and in the ways works by women are received. They also seek to repair what they view as centuries of exclusion of women writers from a male-dominated Western lit-

Topics for Further Study

- "Filling Station" and other Bishop poems teach readers to look for aesthetic beauty or order in unlikely places. Write a poem that observes in close detail the unexpected "art" of an ordinary place, such as a shoe store, a waiting room (see Bishop's "In the Waiting Room"), a laundromat, a bagel store, or a car wash.

- The family-run business, like that of the gas station in the poem, is an endangered economic species. Research and write a paper that investigates the modern history of family-run business in the United States, and the predictions for its future.

- Create a short documentary film of small businesses in your town or city, a mosaic of brief interviews, snatches of candid conversations, and images. Pay close attention to the presence (or not) of a human "somebody" in the surroundings of the business, dirty or otherwise.

- In stanza three, "Filling Station" asks the question "Do they live in the station?" Many Americans commute hours to their workplaces, even as an increasing number are relocating their work to home offices. Study the impact of home-based work on family, economy, environment, and/or community.

erary canon. Feminist criticism has significantly raised the awareness of gender and sex roles in literature.

The masculinity of "Filling Station" is suggested in rather traditional images. The automobile industry—manufacture, repair, and service—has been largely controlled by men, and this was still certainly the case during the decades from which Bishop draws on her memory. Accordingly, this station is a father and son operation. Moreover, the language of male sexuality is as pervasive as the petroleum. This is, after all, a "filling" station equipped with several "pumps," and the furniture is "impregnated" by grease. The stereotypical dog, "man's best friend," lies on the wicker sofa, just as dirty as his human companions.

However, even though the inhabitants and surfaces of this place are distinctly masculine, there is a feminine consciousness to match it, revealed in the poem's voice and in the traces of a feminine aesthetic in the station. It happens in the first line— "Oh, but it is dirty!"—the fussy tone of a woman for whom cleanliness is a priority. "Be careful with that match!" has the maternal sound of one who is naturally concerned for the safety and health of her household. Beginning in stanza three, the poem questions "why" the presence of a domestic aesthetic amidst this male-dominated place: a begonia, embroidered doily ("daisy stitch"), a wicker taboret, a soothing arrangement of cans. These can be read as feminine markers in the poem, and therefore open to an examination of gender awareness and stereotyping. But the poem never says "she" in the last stanza, leaving the agent of this care and aesthetic open to question. The "somebody" who attends this scene and "loves us all" may be beyond the ascribing of gender.

Style

Free Verse

Because it has no consistent, formal pattern of rhyme or meter, Bishop's "Filling Station" is technically free verse. But even a quick glance at the page reveals that free verse is not free of form; it is not shapeless or undisciplined. As the poet Denise Levertov would say, free verse that is truly poetry is never "spineless"; it is not simply prose with line breaks. Bishop wrote both free verse and in traditional forms, such as the poem she called simply "Sestina," whose formal repetition of lines and images—grandmother, stove, tears, almanac— reveals its ultimate theme, the profound mysteries and losses of Bishop's childhood. Her free verse style is known for its disciplined accuracy of word choice, restrained emotion, and lucid description.

The shapeliness of this free verse poem emerges in part from its well-proportioned six stanzas. Each stanza is composed of six to eight lines, and each of its relatively short lines contains an average of six to seven syllables. This design creates a certain rhythmic and visual tidiness that is in tension with the dirty foreground of the filling station and the bursts of service to those "high-strung automobiles." Yet, "somebody" has clearly arranged the stanzas and lines, and therefore the poem's form

supports its humorous assertion of mystery in the last stanza: that "Somebody / arranges the rows of cans" to chant "ESSO—SO—SO—SO."

The poem's cohesiveness also arises from the repetition of certain words and images. The general idea of "dirtiness" is announced at the beginning, and specified by variations on the reality of "oil": "oil-soaked," "oil-permeated," "black translucency," "greasy," "grease-impregnated." There is also a verbal pun on "doily," a bit of domestic finery that rhymes with "oily." The questions of stanzas three and five also structure the experience of perception, paradoxically opening out into something much larger than the little cosmos of the station. And finally, the repetition of "Somebody" in the last stanza points to mystery. It is *some*body, but the reader does not know whom, who waters and arranges and loves, and at the same time, it is some*body,* not merely some*one,* a presence grounded in the realities of monkey-suits and hot engines.

Historical Context

Elizabeth Bishop was a poet who knew both wealth and poverty intimately. She was born into a wealthy family, but for reasons of health spent several childhood years in her Aunt Maud's tiny tenement in Revere, Massachusetts, and summers in the rural simplicity of Nova Scotia with her grandparents. As an independently wealthy adult she traveled widely, but not extravagantly. Such circumstances helped develop the fruitful tensions in a poem such as "Filling Station." She wrote the poem while living in Brazil in the 1950s, a place and time that spurred memories of her own strangely textured childhood.

Noting Bishop's collection of folk art from Brazil—crudely carved saints and altars-in-bottles—biographer Brett Millier observes that "all her life Elizabeth had a romantic, esthetic appreciation of poor people and the ways in which they 'made do' on limited resources, especially the ways they made art." "Filling Station" clearly shows Bishop's interest in the ways common people bring beauty into their lives from the most ordinary materials and resources at hand. As Bishop was to observe in Brazil, some of the most striking examples of such art come from cultures of the native Americas.

Before its conquest by Spanish explorers in the 1500s, the native people of Mexico and Central America created objects of great beauty from their natural resources. In ancient Mexico, gold, silver,

Compare & Contrast

- **1892:** The first successful gasoline-powered automobile is built and tested by Charles and Frank Duryea in Chicopee, Massachusetts. The brothers are afraid of being ridiculed for their invention, so they test the vehicle indoors. A year later, another model undergoes a trial run in Springfield, Massachusetts.

  1941: As part of the national wartime effort to limit consumption and curb inflation, a gasoline curfew closes filling stations from 7 P.M. to 7 A.M. in seventeen states on the East Coast.

  1973: An oil embargo imposed by OAPEC (the Organization of Arab Petroleum Exporting Countries) creates a serious shortage at U.S. filling stations and temporarily closes oil-dependent factories. In November, President Nixon

calls for nationwide energy conservation measures, including extension of Daylight Savings Time, reduction of highway speed limits, lower temperatures in federal buildings, and a ban on Sunday gasoline sales. The embargo is lifted in March of 1974.

1989: The worst oil spill in U.S. history occurrs on March 24th, when the Exxon supertanker *Valdez* runs aground in Prince William Sound in Alaska and dumps 240,000 barrels of oil into the water, destroying and endangering wildlife for over 730 miles of coastline. Among the fines levied against Exxon over the next five years is an order in August of 1994 for the oil company to pay over $5.2 billion in compensatory and punitive damages.

---

and copper were plentiful and accessible, and from those metals, the Aztec people created masterpieces of jewelry, masks, and sacred objects. However, as the Spaniards conquered the native people, they melted down the beautiful jewelry and sent it back to Europe, dug mines, made slaves of the Aztecs, and forbad them to use precious metals. Of necessity, the Indians turned to tin.

With their skill in metalwork, they soon created beautiful mirror frames, jewelry, ornaments, and candle holders with the shiny, malleable metal. A new form of art thus arose out of political and economic necessity. Much tin work today comes from the city of Oaxaca, home to a very large native Indian population. Among other Oaxacan arts are exquisitely hand carved and brightly painted mythic animals, each of which is individually signed by the artisan who created it.

Like the native people of Mexico, the Kuna Indians of Panama also developed a unique art form, known as *molas* to tell the continuing stories of their culture—the tragedies of Spanish conquest, their retreat into the mountain jungles to survive, the building of the Panama Canal in the early twen-

tieth century, the Kuna revolt in 1925 and subsequent independence in 1930, and today, of their participation in national politics. *Molas* are vibrantly colored, stitched designs that have been created by Kuna women since the late 1800s. Besides historical events, *molas* portray the birds, plants, and animals native to the islands, jungles, and villages where the four groups of Kuna Indians live. In their traditional designs and colors—red, yellow, blue, and black—*molas* resemble much earlier forms of body painting and decoration practiced for centuries by the Kuna Indians.

The largest country in Central America is Nicaragua. It is a country with a history of violence, both natural and political. It is located on the "Ring of Fire," a geographic area so named for its vulnerability to earthquakes, volcanic eruptions, and hurricanes. Hurricane Mitch devastated the population of Nicaragua in 1998, leaving over four thousand dead or missing and over half a million homeless.

Natural upheavals seem to have been matched in recent decades with political ones. Dictators and foreign armies have oppressed the Nicaraguan people for centuries, ever since Columbus claimed Nicaragua for Spain in 1502. The Somoza rule of dictators began in 1937, and after years of resistance, a group of revolutionaries called the Sandinistas came to power and overthrew the government in 1979. This war between the government Contras and the Sandinistas gained worldwide attention in the early 1980s.

During this time, a centuries-old art form known as "the *gigantona* and little Pepe" was used in the Sandinistan resistance to government oppression. *Gigantona,* "the giant one," is an eight-foot tall puppet, a female figure richly dressed and decorated who dances and swings through the streets and villages, accompanied by a puppet called "little Pepe," who jokes, teases, and tells stories. During the Contra-Sandinista war, the Sandinistas used performances of the "Giant One and Little Pepe" frequently to help free political prisoners, accuse those who had betrayed the revolution, and encourage people to remain strong during the violence and upheaval of change.

Elizabeth Bishop also observed phenomena that seemed "larger than life" in Brazil, even while she wrote of the persistence of art among the poorest and least educated. "Manuelzinho," a long poem in *Questions of Travel,* is the portrait of a Brazilian man, "Half squatter, half tenant" who both exasperated Bishop and fascinated her. She calls him "the world's worst gardener since Cain." Yet, artist that he is, he edges "the beds of silver cabbages / with red carnations, and lettuces / mix with alyssum." He brings her "giant ones" from his efforts: "a mystic three-legged carrot, / or a pumpkin 'bigger than the baby.'" At the end of her poetic address to this man, whom she respects in an odd way, Bishop observes, "You paint—heaven knows why—the outside of the crown / and brim of your straw hat. . . . One was gold for a while, / but the gold wore off, like plate." Much like the surprising presence of a begonia in a grease-stricken filling station is this ring of gold around a sweaty straw hat, another testimony by Bishop to the necessity of art.

Critical Overview

According to biographer Brett Millier, Elizabeth Bishop often included "Filling Station" when she gave a reading of her poems, perhaps because it was a signature piece for her; perhaps she simply liked to read it. Although not as often discussed

and anthologized as "Man-Moth," "Armadillo," or "Sestina," "Filling Station" is indeed typical of Bishop's restrained style and acute, nearly child-like observation of ordinary things, places, and people. Critic William Jay Smith notes that "there has always been in Elizabeth Bishop's work a kind of childlike, primitive discovery of relationship" which she establishes through questions: "why?" and "who?" and "what?" And "Filling Station" is certainly typical of that poetic, primitive questioning: "Why the taboret? / Why, oh why the doily?" Critic Bonnie Costello suggests that Bishop's interrogative, or questioning disposition is part of her fundamental desire for wholeness, her search for resolution "without reducing experience to simple answers." In the process of the poet's own genuine change of consciousness, says Costello, the questions somehow "become our own."

In an essay for *American Poetry Review,* Charles Mann describes another important aesthetic habit of Bishop's: her painstaking revisions, her careful shaping of language until the poem carries as perfectly as possible the emotional textures of her observation. "The Moose" took no less than twenty-five years to write. "At the Fishhouses," revised at least seven times, is the focal point of Mann's close reading. In "Filling Station" one can see the result of what Mann identifies as her basic pattern of revising: "a move from the poem being merely a series of intelligent, often prose-like observations, to one that conveys these observations as sensually experienced presences." The movement of "Filling Station," likewise, is from the oily surface of things to the presence behind their "art."

Exactly what that presence is, or whether it exists at all, is open to question for some critics. Robert Dale Parker argues that "Filling Station" is ultimately a poem of supreme irony, established by that unspecified presence, the "somebody" in the last line. Parker suspects that "somebody" could just as easily be "nobody," or, if that somebody is "God," that such a love might "become only a greater irony, if the love of God is no love we expect to know." C. K. Doreski is less troubled by matters of irony than of gender, and believes that the poem's final mystery turns on the "absence of an actual feminine presence."

Other critics are less interested in the poet's work than in the relationship between her life and her art. Donald Stanford, for example, talks about the tensions between Bishop's "undisciplined" life and her always "disciplined" poetry. Despite her "restless, disoriented, and distraught life," he says, Bishop managed to write lucidly crafted, luminous poems. Stanford concludes, "and that is why a few of her poems have gained a permanent place in our literature."

Criticism

Jonathan N. Barron

Barron is an associate professor of English at the University of Southern Mississippi. He has co-edited Jewish American Poetry, *from the University Press of New England, and* Roads Not Taken: Rereading Robert Frost, *forthcoming from the University of Missouri Press, as well as a forthcoming collection of essays on the poetic movement,* New Formalism. *Beginning in 2001, he will be the editor-in-chief of* The Robert Frost Review. *In the following essay, he considers the impact of gender on Bishop's poem.*

The American poet Mary Kinzie believes that no poem worthy of the art can depend only on a mastery of technique and craft. She claims that aesthetic talent alone cannot define a poem. Instead, she argues that "the aesthetic mission is also a moral one." Craft, in other words, must be connected to morality insofar as every poet is responsible for the vision, imagery, tone, and story of the poem. Kinzie adds that "the poet and the poem alike must be held responsible for the nature of their insights."

This is a controversial but necessary position to take with regard to poetry because it implies that the poem communicates information that must be judged in both ethical and moral terms for its insights. Kinzie refuses to ignore the ethical, moral message of a given poem. Whatever its story may be, no matter how ugly, how painful, how potentially upsetting, Kinzie insists that the reader nonetheless make the poet responsible for the story he or she tells. This position is controversial because so many critics prefer only to discuss craft and form. They even prefer to ignore what the poem and the poet say.

This way of discussing poetry was particularly common with regard to the work of Elizabeth Bishop. For most of her life, Bishop's poetry was plagued by a critical failure of insight. Praised for her talent and her craft, her stories were dismissed as minor, unimportant, merely descriptive. She was said to lack vision, depth, grand themes in her work. Critics would praise her imagery, her metrics, her precision, her ability to make a story come to a con-

> *In poetry, every word harkens back to its larger cultural, social, and literary history. In a poem, the word 'station,' when it appears in the story of a journey refers back to that Christian use of the term. And, from that perspective, this poem describes one woman's station on her long journey through the world."*

clusion, but they had very little to say about her themes. Even after her death, critics continued to dismiss the force of Bishop's intellectual depth. Even when they did acknowledge the deeper potential of so many of her poems, they often dismissed what she said as either a cliché or too typically sentimental.

Reacting to "Filling Station" in 1984, for example, the notable literary scholar and Yale professor, David Bromwich, commented that the poem was laden with "awkward condescension." He felt that like so many of her poems its first impact on a reader will "dwindle as one comes to see them more clearly." To Bromwich, in other words, Bishop's poems are too often more flash than fire. On the other hand, Bromwich did do what the poet Mary Kinzie called for: he did take Bishop's story more seriously than most. With regard to "Filling Station," he felt that the poem suffered from a class bias. He felt that in this poem one reads the inner thoughts of an upper-class snob unable socially or emotionally to cope with the poor. Bromwich, therefore, judges the poem as a failure not only for its lack of a deep complex psychological story, but also for its decidedly elitist views.

Bromwich was very much on the right track insofar as he did discuss the poem in terms of the speaker, but he was also very much mistaken in his evaluation of the poem's psychological depths. Re-

What Do I Read Next?

- In 1961, the editors of the *Time/Life* World Library series asked Elizabeth Bishop to write the text for their Brazil volume. She accepted the job, but rapidly grew to hate it. She chafed under pressures of deadlines, and fumed over the editors' insistence on covering topics she was ill prepared to write about, in a tone foreign to her temperament. The first three chapters of Bishop's *Brazil* (1962) are the least "ravaged" by editors and the most indicative of her journalistic style.

- In stark contrast to her distaste for writing the *Time/Life* book was an earlier project Bishop undertook as a "labor of love" in Brazil. Not long after moving there, she discovered the Portuguese diary of a young girl, "Helena Morley" (Dona Alice Brant), whose stories of growing up in the village of Diamantina, Brazil, reminded Bishop in many ways of her own childhood in Great Village, Nova Scotia. Bishop undertook the translation with passionate care, and after five years, it was published as *The Diary of Helena Morley* (1957). Bishop's thirty-five-page introduction to the diary is her longest piece of prose, and her strongest, according to biographer Brett Millier.

- Elizabeth Bishop perpetually felt she was an outsider, no matter where she was living, and many of her poems tell the story of life as a "guest." The *Storyteller* (1989), by Peruvian novelist Mario Vargas Llosa, also tells the story of an outsider and his odyssey among the Machiguenga Indians, a primitive tribe of Amazon peoples. Saul Zuratas, a Peruvian Jew, not only becomes a member of the tribe, but their storyteller, their "voice." In this story about the transforming power of stories, the narrator looks on while the Machiguengas and their odd bard, "ex-Jew, ex-white man, and ex-Westerner," deal with the encroachment of modern commerce and technology upon the Amazon.

- Novelist Joseph Conrad was an "outsider" to the English language. Polish was his first, and French his second language. English, in which he wrote brilliantly, was his third. *Heart of Darkness* (1921), a novel of narrative genius, is a story whose central character is radically unlike that of Mario Vargas Llosa's *The Storyteller*. Kurtz, the protagonist, represents the worst of colonialism in Africa. He silences the voices of the native Congo people in his maniacal thirst for power and dominance. His is the "heart of darkness."

---

turning then to "The Filling Station" with Mary Kinzie's charge in mind, one must acknowledge, as Bromwich does, the gender of the first-person narrator. But to make this assumption that the narrator is a woman, and nothing in the poem argues against that assumption, one also must entertain the gendered vision on which the poem depends. The speaker is a woman, possibly Bishop herself, and given that premise, one must also imagine the psychological complexity of gender relations that would pertain to the scene of the poem. After all, here is a decidedly middle-class woman in a working class, all-male environment. One knows what her class position must be from her language and from what she chooses to describe. Similarly, one

knows that a man and his sons, as she tells us, run this filling station. They are decidedly working-class men who earn their money through hard work and sweat.

Given this scene, this situation, one can only find a class bias and general attitude of condescension by refusing to engage the psychological drama of a respectable woman alone in an entirely male, even aggressively male and slightly disreputable, potentially frightening, place. In short, there really is not much of a class war in this poem if one uncovers and works through the poem's set of complex relations between men and women. With regard to gender relations, this poem holds a great deal of interest.

Turning to the specific gender issues, then, one finds that the title alone begins to make the subtle case for gender as a primary condition of experience. The title, "Filling Station," refers not just to this gas station but also to the larger concept "Station" from the Christian story of the journey of Jesus and the stations of the cross. In poetry, every word harkens back to its larger cultural, social, and literary history. In a poem, the word "station," when it appears in the story of a journey refers back to that Christian use of the term. And, from that perspective, this poem describes one woman's station on her long journey through the world.

One can make this case particularly strong when one considers that this poem appeared in the book, *Questions of Travel* (1965), a book of poems whose major subject is travel and whose principle metaphor is the concept of the journey. Furthermore, "Filling Station" appears in the part of the book titled "Elsewhere," as if to suggest that the moment captured in this poem is but one station of many.

Once the station metaphor is achieved, the full impact of the title can be realized. For in the poem itself Bishop is the one who fills up the site. Rather than depict a simple anecdote where a woman stops to get gas in her car, this poem reverses the logic. Here, a woman stops at a station on her long journey of life. This station is a male zone in a wilderness of neutrality. In the midst of this male environment, Bishop fills up the station with decidedly feminine qualities. Her vision makes of this potentially alienating place a pleasant, feminine atmosphere. What ought to be a trial, a test of her feminine integrity, a typical "station of the cross" in a Christian sense becomes, instead, a site for her particularly powerful transformative power. She makes the strange and alienating place seem, if only for a moment, a little bit more like home when she fills it with domestic, feminine meaning. Such transformations are the work of all great poets.

Turning from the title to the first two stanzas, one sees that the poem begins in dirt. The word "dirty" is repeated three times in two stanzas. Also, it is placed in such a way that every time it is used it forms the final pause at the end of a line and of a sentence. Dirt, in other words, pervades this place, and the reader is forced to notice it.

But what is the speaker's attitude toward dirt? Here, the tone of this poem is particularly tricky. Every good poet knows to use exclamation marks rarely, if at all. This is because they often have the effect of cheapening, even deadening the emphasis one wants them to have. Nonetheless, the first line of the poem uses just such a mark: "Oh, but it is dirty!" How is one to read this? In a tone of horror? Disgust? Given the rest of the poem, one would have to conclude that it is to be read only as mock horror, pretend disgust. A playful, even possibly sarcastic means of noting the obvious and saying, in effect, "well, what did you expect?" A tone of mock horror indicates that Bishop is not really a snob here. Instead, she is far more willing than many might suppose to engage a place so terribly different from her more obviously feminine, clean world.

From the first stanza, she stands for domestic life, cleanliness: traditionally feminine attributes. This place, by contrast, through its dirt, stands for the traditionally masculine attributes of mechanical devices, technology, industry: dirt, sweat, and work. After all, it *is* a gas station! To make the point Bishop adds:

> —this little filling station,
> oil-soaked, oil-permeated
> to a disturbing, over-all
> black translucency.

The color scheme, the texture, the very feel of the dirt is now made even more tangible as a thick coat of oil. But here, too, disgust and horror are not the right tone. Rather one should instead here have that same mocking willingness to say, with a little shrug, "oh well, here I am, how exciting." Bishop concludes: "Be careful with that match!" This use of another exclamation mark only five lines after the first indicates the sort of light, playful detachment she means to convey with her tone.

Given that the scene is utterly alien to a woman like this speaker, one must realize that the playful tone is a brave means of trying to accommodate and cope with the strange. Think of all the ways a woman alone might describe the three men of this place. Of all those ways the least expected and most obviously challenging is to call them "father" and "sons." By commenting on their domestic relationship she not only identifies them in her domestic terms, but she also removes them from the working-class context in which they actually exist. Not workers come to service her car and threaten her sense of decorum and security, but rather a father and his sons.

His sons, the speaker tells us, are "quick and saucy." One can only imagine what specific words, leers, and other typically aggressive gestures gave rise to such descriptions. But rather than focus on what they say and how they behave, the speaker rewrites the boys out of their hyper-masculinity and into a domestic scene. In a parenthesis, Bishop says: "(it's a family filling station)."

By this point in the poem, it is evident that Bishop is in supreme control of the meaning and implication of her punctuation. Her exclamation marks created a mock-heroic tone, and now her parenthesis deflate the cocky aggression of the "saucy" boys. The final line of the third stanza must, therefore, be read as a woman's defensive reaction to the pretense of the men: if they are fathers and sons, if this is a family, then, there must also be, somewhere, a woman. And, if there is a woman, this is not a male zone at all: the three men, from a domestic perspective, exhibit a male pretense, not some genuine male animalistic instinct.

Therefore, in the final line of the stanza, when Bishop declares that "all" is "quite thoroughly dirty" she is saying, implicitly, that these men, as a family, have failed even the most minimal task of creating a healthy environment for themselves. This is not a workspace for men, it is a home for a family. Well, Bishop knows all about homes. And, having declared this place a home she has now given herself the right to judge it on her terms. She can say in no uncertain terms that this home is a mess!

To Bishop's credit the plot of the poem ends with this judgement, just after the third stanza. What follows, however, complicates this plot in fascinating ways. Specifically, Bishop adds four stanzas, each of which depends on a question or series of questions raised by the issue she charted in the first three stanzas. To summarize, in the first three stanzas, Bishop transformed the gas station workspace into a home and, as a home, a familiar place to her, she felt she was able to deal with it, judge it, even be superior to it. While the boys appear to be a threat to her with their "raciness" she can claim a new superiority by denying their premise. If this station is a home, they cannot be men in a male-zone competing for a woman in a Darwinian sexual struggle. Transformed into a domestic scene, they are just a family whose home she can judge as inadequate, filthy.

The final four stanzas of the poem question every aspect of this transformation. By the end of the third stanza, Bishop wonders if it is even true that this is a home? "Do they live in the station?" She asks. And rather than answer her question she offers only a series of speculations based on close observation. She offers abundant detail. Many readers might conclude that these details prove her point, this is a home just as she thought. But stanza five returns to the same question all over again. It must be a home, she decides, for if it is just another male workplace then:

> Why the extraneous plant?
> Why the taboret?
> Why, oh why, the doily?

In other words, the details seem to be convincing but they do not finally convince Bishop. The real issue hiding behind these details is gender, and stanza five reveals gender's importance. According to Bishop, the typical social roles of men and women in the United States suggest that no man, certainly no man in a gas station, would do anything associated with a feminine role. She all but asks, why on earth three men would domesticate their workplace? Why would such rolicking, leering, aggressively male mechanics even consider "plants," "taborets," and, of all things, a "doily?" What she means to say here is that only a woman could possibly have done these things, added these details. And, if there is a woman, then this must be, by definition, a home.

In this stanza, Bishop returns to her light humor, too. Certainly, the "doily" line is funny. When she says, "why, oh why" the exasperation is out of proportion to the problem. But the humor itself speaks to the larger problem of a feminine presence. For, finally, the speaker wants to know if she is the one making this place a home. She wonders if she is the one misinterpreting the facts, the details. She wonders if it really is a place where women already exist.

The poem's final stanza makes another attempt to answer the gender-roll questions of the poem. But now these questions are filled, as is this station, with ambiguity, complexity, and an abundance of meaning.

> Somebody embroidered the doily.
> Somebody waters the plant,
> or oils it, maybe. Somebody
> arranges the rows of cans
> so that they softly say:
> ESSO—SO—SO—SO
> to high-strung automobiles.
> Somebody loves us all.

What Bishop sees cannot be denied. Therefore, somebody, as she says, must have put these typically feminine things there. Does it have to be a woman? Could the men be doing such womanly things themselves?

The joke Bishop makes about oiling the plant refers to the fact that the place is a mess: it is covered in oil. But this also assumes that perhaps the men *are* responsible for whatever domestic touches are to be found. Even the name of the gas station is made to have a gentle, whispering, pleasing, domestic, and feminine quality, "Esso." (This name in fact once stood for Eastern Standard Oil. It tells the reader that this poem is probably taking place in Bishop's favorite New England landscape.) Be that as it may, the oil cans with the gas station's name on them even domesticate the wild "high-strung" cars that are nervously speeding past. This detail means that if even an oil can will soothe a car, if even a filling station like this can have doilies and the like, then the last line might well be true. Somebody really might love us all. There may be a benevolent spirit, a God, on this journey, even here in this strange station. For what is love but concern and compassion for one's own space? Maybe, the poem implies, it is Bishop herself who makes the silly gender assumption that no man would domesticate his own space.

Source: Jonathan N. Barron, Critical Essay on "Filling Station," in *Poetry for Students,* The Gale Group, 2001.

Erica Smith

Smith is a writer and editor. In this essay, she discusses how Bishop's poem reveals the poet's inner struggle of rejection versus acceptance of others, and how she ultimately chooses acceptance.

In "Filling Station" the speaker of the poem describes a gas station whose most prominent outward quality is filth: "Oh, but it is dirty!" she declares in the first line. The reader gains a snapshot view of what the speaker sees: "—this little filling station, / oil-soaked, oil-permeated / to a disturbing, over-all / black translucency." The speaker's derogatory tone turns wry in the final line of the stanza: "Be careful with that match!" she cries, implying that if a match is lit anywhere near the oil-soaked station, the entire place is likely to blow up.

The speaker's distaste likewise extends toward the family that runs the station. "Father wears a dirty, / oil-soaked monkey suit / that cuts him under the arms," she notes. The deliberate choice of the phrase "monkey suit" to describe the man's clothing has the effect of belittling him. The speaker also notes that "several quick and saucy / and greasy sons assist him." The sons, too, seem less than human. Numerous, nameless, and apparently fresh, they too resemble monkeys. Again, the speaker punctuates her horror with a smirk, noting parenthetically that "(it's a family filling station)." Her disdain has decidedly turned into arrogance,

> *These small revelations culminate in the final line of the poem: 'Somebody loves us all.' Even in light of the previous lines reflecting the speaker's change of heart, this statement comes as a shock. It is as if the speaker has flung her arms open wide, forgiven everything that she previously viewed with derision, and come to a place of balance and acceptance."*

and she caps off the stanza by citing again that the scene is "all quite thoroughly dirty."

"Do they live in the station?" the speaker wonders of the family. She then describes the few items of adornment that grace the station. "It has a cement porch / behind the pumps, and on it / a set of crushed and grease; / impregnated wickerwork; / on the wicker sofa / a dirty dog, quite comfy." Like the father and sons who work the station, the dog is oblivious to the filth and disarray that surround him. However, unlike her attitude toward the human residents, the speaker's attitude toward the dog carries a slight feeling of affection. She calls him "comfy," perhaps charmed that the dog seems perfectly happy despite everything.

In the following stanza the speaker continues to survey the scene, noting the available reading material: "Some comic books provide / the only note of color— / of certain color." First, her focus on comic books carries an implicit criticism: remember, the speaker is conveying her thoughts through poetry; comic books may seem repellent and low-class to her. The fact that the comics provide the only "certain color" is probably even more depressing to her, for comics are usually more garish-looking than pleasing to the eye. One can imagine that they too are probably stained with oil.

The additional efforts to gentrify the filling station meet with the speaker's disapproval: the comic books "lie / upon a big dim doily / draping a taboret (part of the set)." The mention of a "set" echoes an exclamation that would normally be heard at an upper-class bridal shower. In this context, however, the overall effect of the speaker's comment is sarcastic. What's more, even the flowering plants are offensive to the speaker; beside the stool she notices a "hirsute begonia." As the word "hirsute" normally refers to individuals who are extremely (and unattractively) hairy, the reader may presume that the begonia is also unattractive, wild, and untrimmed.

The scene is presented as a collage of dirty, untamed, and garish elements, and their collective effect is overwhelming and seemingly senseless to the speaker. Finally she demands, "Why the extraneous plant?" / "Why the taboret?" / "Why, oh why, the doily?" In other words, why even try to add touches of beauty and class to such a clearly dismal place?

Yet, as the speaker's attention focuses on the doily, her rhetorical, somewhat prudish outrage pulls back. She looks at the doily closely, and the reader gets a detailed description of the piece, "Embroidered in daisy stitch / with marguerites, I think, / and heavy with gray crochet." This is the first time the speaker has afforded any item more than a brief mention. There is clearly something about the detail of the doily that affects the speaker.

The speaker's recognition of the doily and her attempts to recall the name of a stitch from her memory lead the reader to think that the speaker is reminded of a past episode in her own life. She may have been taught how to crochet by her mother or a beloved aunt, for example. This suddenly infuses the poem with a feeling of wistfulness that had been completely absent beforehand.

Just as suddenly as the doily becomes the speaker's focus of attention, the speaker's contempt gives way to reconciliation. "Somebody embroidered the doily," she recognizes. Even in this place of filth and disarray, a person took the time to make something beautiful. "Somebody waters the plant," she says; and in a bemused tone she adds, "or oils it, maybe." She is slowly gaining humor and perspective on a scene that horrified her just moments ago.

Ultimately, she notes that some details of the filling station even have a kind of order to them:

"Somebody / arranges the rows of cans / so that they softly say: / ESSO—SO—SO—SO / to high-strung automobiles." ("ESSO" is the name of the company that owns the station. Although it is defunct now, its name was very recognizable in the past, as one would recognize Exxon or Shell today.) The repetition of the "SO—SO—SO" of ESSO is a melodic echo, perhaps mirroring the echoes that have been triggered in the speaker's memory.

These small revelations culminate in the final line of the poem: "Somebody loves us all." Even in light of the previous lines reflecting the speaker's change of heart, this statement comes as a shock. It is as if the speaker has flung her arms open wide, forgiven everything that she previously viewed with derision, and come to a place of balance and acceptance.

This conclusion of the poem represents a kind of triumph. Foremost, it is a triumph of love within the speaker's own heart. It takes a great deal of energy to find beauty amid ruins, or redemption amid poverty. At first the speaker chooses to scorn everything that is unpleasant to her. However, once she finds an image that is meaningful for her—in this case, the doily—her own past seems to unlock. Most likely reminded of family relationships she had in the past, she is able to look at the family running the filling station through more sympathetic eyes. In the end, she is able to appreciate how even a dismal filling station can have a degree of nobility.

The sense of triumph is even more acute when the poem is considered in the context of the volume of work in which it appears. Bishop's *Questions of Travel* (1965) is divided into two parts—"Brazil" and "Elsewhere"—with "Filling Station" appearing in the "Elsewhere" section. One of the essential elements of travel writing, or in this case, travel poetry, is the consideration of habits and customs that are unfamiliar. Because they are so different, these habits and customs have an especially powerful ability to disgust, delight, and shock. In her deliberate and undoubtedly hierarchical division of the book (Brazil is preeminent; everything else is just "elsewhere") the poet knows what delights her and what decidedly does not. While an armadillo in Brazil may enchant her, do the proprietors of a dirty filling station? One can look back upon the speaker's initial, horrified tone of voice as carrying perhaps a touch of self-teasing. This underlying feeling comes out in full bloom at the end of the poem, as the poet muses to herself over oiling the plant.

The overall structure of the volume *Questions of Travel* has yet another implication. Some of the poems in the "Elsewhere" section are considerations of places from the poet's past, particularly her childhood, such as in "First Death in Nova Scotia." (In later volumes the poet can even imagine herself as a child and reevaluate her perceptions of adults. Of course, in the case of one of her most famous poems, "In the Waiting Room," the adult poet agrees with her seven-year-old self, affirming that her Aunt Consuelo was indeed a "foolish, timid woman." But throughout her work the poet does offer relentless examinations of experiences, despite their being positive or negative.)

In the case of "Filling Station" one may imagine the station as a place from the poet's youth, which she is now revisiting as an adult. It is not uncommon for people to harbor contempt for the place in which they were raised. If this is the case in "Filling Station," the poet is able to come to terms with her distaste for the undereducated and most likely economically depressed, find a source of connection, and come to a more mature understanding of people's complex lives.

"Filling Station" presents a picture that is deceptively simple, yet speaks of the poet's inner conflicts. In this case, humor and acceptance prevail over disgust and distancing. With an open heart the poet chooses love.

Source: Erica Smith, Critical Essay on "Filling Station," in *Poetry for Students,* The Gale Group, 2001.

Paul Witcover

Witcover's fiction and critical essays appear regularly in magazines and online. In the following essay, he looks at Bishop's subtle use of phrasing, voice, and meter.

"Filling Station," like so many of the poems of Elizabeth Bishop, creeps up on readers. At its best, as here, Bishop's language is so smooth, assured, and precise—one might even go so far as to call it achingly ordinary in places—that her poetic effects percolate below the reader's consciousness until the instant when, with a carefully prepared but still surprising word or line, Bishop detonates her depth charge. Like another poet of deceptively polished surfaces, Robert Frost, Bishop in such poems as "Filling Station" and "At the Fishhouses" combines an extraordinary eye for detail and description with an ear alert to the most subtle nuances of phrasing, voice, and meter. Joined to these abundant gifts is a sly and subversive wit, both playful and ironic, and above all a penetrating yet com-

> *Just as the speaker of the poem both trembles and takes solace at evidence of Bishop's organizing presence outside the poem, so, too, does Bishop tremble and take solace in the presence of something beyond the boundaries of her perceptions."*

passionate intellect driven not only to accurately record what it sees but to question the implications of what is seen—and what is not seen. An important consideration here is that the category of things not seen includes ones that do not exist or ones that human beings lack the senses or instruments to perceive.

The tension between what is seen and not seen, what tangibly exists and what may or may not exist beyond the tangible, knowable, limited world of human perception and experience, is the engine at the heart of much, if not all, poetry. That tension is what elevates the assemblage of specific "dirty" and "oil-soaked" objects constituting the grubby reality of Bishop's "family filling station" into something transcendent, even prayerful. But the poet does not forget for one instant the grime in which she is kneeling nor the central absence in herself, the world, or in both. Her prayer, her poem, like a child's question about the afterlife, is an attempt, at once hopeful and despairing, to fill.

Critic Bonnie Costello, in an essay entitled "The Impersonal and the Interrogative in the Poetry of Elizabeth Bishop," appearing in *Elizabeth Bishop and Her Art,* edited by Lloyd Schwartz and Sybil P. Estess, writes that "[F]or Bishop, questions are assertions. However open-endedly, they structure experience and self-awareness. Like compasses, they point to something absolute we can neither see nor get to; yet in their pointing, they show us where we are." To this should be appended the corollary that for Bishop, answers are merely questions in disguise. Bishop never outgrew the love of questions and the instinctive recognition of, and contempt for, pat answers so characteristic of childhood (often annoyingly so!).

"Filling Station" appeared in Bishop's 1965 collection, *Questions of Travel,* a book whose very title indicates as plainly as possible the centrality of questions and questioning in her poetry (and the centrality of travel as well, but that's another essay). The poem can be read as a series of seemingly casual, sometimes quite charming and amusing observations that build to a climax of questions, each one apparently innocent, yet combining with the others to devastating effect.

The answers Bishop goes on to provide are, if anything, more devastating still, because upon closer examination they answer nothing and instead only raise the same unanswerable questions all over again, this time with a troubling universality that has been implicit in the poem from the first but never stated explicitly until its end, when the poem is turned inside out with a metaphysical flourish, and the reader gets taken along for the ride. There is a clear technical debt here to the metaphysical poetry of the seventeenth century written by poets such as John Donne and George Herbert; in fact, Herbert was not only a major influence on the young Elizabeth Bishop, but she retained a lifelong fondness for his verse. But while Bishop may have learned a measure of craft from Herbert, a wealthy English aristocrat who became a humble and devout country parson, his certainty of religious faith was foreign to her. In her book *Inscrutable Houses: Metaphors of the Body in the Poems of Elizabeth Bishop,* critic Anne Colwell calls attention to the way in which Bishop's poems "refuse to resolve into a decision, or even into one question, but instead gain power through force of opposition, acquire ambiguity and resonance through their ever-multiplying questions."

The poem is set in a gas, or filling, station. The title is meant to be a pun, one that will become less obvious, however, and increasingly multifaceted and affecting, as the poem's words slowly fill up the page, and its levels of meaning and ambiguity similarly filter into the minds of attentive readers. Bishop cannot help but write poems that are in some way about the process of writing and reading poetry; that is certainly the case here. Every poem is a kind of filling station at which readers pull in to refuel their souls: sometimes successfully, sometimes not. But such simplified explanations really illuminate very little of interest; it should be remembered that the "self-referentiality" of

Bishop's poetry is itself complicated and ambiguous and always placed in the service of the poem's larger purpose. Let's watch the slow and permeating and oh-so-skillfully orchestrated seep of that purpose through the six stanzas of "Filling Station."

To begin with, it's dirty. "Oh, but it is dirty!" the speaker of the first line exclaims. Who is this speaker? Is it Elizabeth Bishop? Yes and no. The voice of the speaker is the voice Bishop has chosen to employ in addressing her readers. Perhaps, it's best just to say that the speaker is a poet like Bishop, and that what one is reading is a record, a transcription, of the creative processes of the poet as a poem is being born in, well, wherever it is that poems are born! That poem is probably not "Filling Station," however. Why not? Quite simply, because "Filling Station" is Bishop's poem, not the speaker's: it is a finished work of art whose subject, on one level, is the germination, rather than the cultivation and completion, of a poem. That may seem like a rather fine, even empty, distinction, but such distinctions are extremely important in poetry, especially in the poetry of Elizabeth Bishop.

The speaker is struck by the dirtiness of the filling station. In the first three stanzas, the word "dirty" appears four times. The word "oil" appears three times in those same stanzas, and "greasy" (or a variation thereof) appears twice. Together these words and images—the "oil-soaked," "oil-permeated," "dirty, / oil-soaked monkey suit" worn by Father, the "set of crushed and grease-impregnated wickerwork," and the "dirty dog" lying "quite comfy"—contribute to the sense of being somewhere, as "quite thoroughly dirty." Far from being repelled by all this dirt and grime, however, the speaker seems to revel in it, even cracking a playfully teasing joke—"Be careful with that match!"—as if the station is so drenched in oil that the slightest spark might set off a conflagration. This is no fastidious clean freak, or repressed control freak, for that matter. The speaker delights in the physicality of all the surrounding filth, though to be sure there's superiority in her interest, a sense of slumming among less civilized humans, if not members of another, lesser species altogether.

In the first half of the poem—that is, in the first three stanzas—the repetitiveness of the language, the lulling rhythm of one- and two-syllable words, especially adjectives, with their simple stresses—"little filling station," "black translucency," "greasy sons," "cement porch"— and the masterful use of alliteration, most notably in the spreading ooze of "s" sounds throughout the second stanza in a remarkably subtle case of poetic foreshadowing, all work to convey the oiliness of the place as well as the stimulating effects of that dirt and oiliness on the poet's creative faculties. She is like a child playing with mud pies. Note also the use of a language almost debased in its generality, a quality normally the enemy of vivid poetry— "several . . . sons," "quite thoroughly dirty," "quite comfy." Only a poet in complete command of her talents can take such bland language and make it sing. Here it's the very ability to make poetry out of the most seemingly unpoetic fodder of everyday language that is important to Bishop's developing theme.

In the first two stanzas, the speaker is both describing the filling station for the reader and, indirectly, revealing things about herself (her sense of humor, for example, as well as her sense of social superiority). She informs the reader of certain facts that she has observed or that she somehow knows. How does she know the assistants are all the sons of the father? How does she know it is a "family filling station?" Readers must take her word for it. Either she has privileged information or she is putting forward as facts conjectures based on observation. She could easily keep this up for the whole poem (in which case it would be a very different poem), but she does not. Suddenly, out of the blue, at the beginning of the third stanza, the speaker poses her first question: "Do they live in the station?" What could be more casual and innocuous? It seems more a rhetorical than an actual question, for the following lines provide ample evidence of domesticity, with the "cement porch," the "grease- / impregnated wickerwork," and the "dirty dog, quite comfy."

But something has changed nonetheless. This change, from a kind of passive reporting to a more active questioning, from observer to participant, will become more pronounced over the final half of the poem, that is, in the concluding three stanzas. The fourth stanza nearly overwhelms the reader with an avalanche of new material qualitatively different from what has gone before. Gone are the repetitions of words like "dirty" and "oil" so integral to the structure of the first three stanzas. Instead one finds "comic books" that provide "the only note of color."

Prior to this, both the poem and the filling station have been colorless, with only an "over-all / black translucency." Here a hint of color, "of certain color," bleeds through the oily sheen. And then comes the wonderful, the amazing "big dim doily." This takes the idea of color a step further, for now, in addition to the beauty and variation of color, the reader has something created: a handmade work of art, however humble. But what is truly a stroke of genius here is how ordinary and unobjectionable the presence of the doily seems in the scene. So there's a doily, so what? Why shouldn't there be a doily? In fact, the doily is derived from the two words most prevalent in the first three stanzas of the poem: "dirty" and "oil." Rather than disappearing from the poem, what has actually happened to these words is something more mysterious and marvelous: Bishop has noted the occurrence and repetition of these words and artfully combined them. If the wickerwork is indeed impregnated with grease, this doily is its offspring! There is a subversive yet playful quality to this linguistic trick reminiscent of Lewis Carroll's ingenious word play in poems like *"Jabberwocky,"* as well as a touch of Vladimir Nabokov's equally ingenious, if less innocent, literary puzzles.

The following lines show the doily "draping a taboret / (part of the set), beside / a big hirsute begonia." The word "taboret" has a variety of meanings. Here, because of the parenthetical "(part of the set)," which refers back to the wickerwork, readers can probably assume that the intended meaning is a piece of furniture: specifically, to quote from *Webster's New Twentieth Century Unabridged Dictionary,* "a stool; a seat without a back or arms." It is possible that Bishop intends a different meaning, however. *Webster's* lists three alternative definitions, each contextually plausible, though perhaps not equally so: "an embroidery frame," "a low ornamental stand," and "a small tabor," or drum. It is hard to know whether Bishop, in composing her poem, intentionally introduced this bit of ambiguity. Again, that is another essay! Here it is simply noted that it *is* ambiguous and move on to something less so: the "big hirsute begonia." The adjective "big" links this plant back to the doily, while the word "hirsute," meaning hairy, links the reader further back in both sound and sense to the "monkey suit" worn by Father. Further, note that the begonia is a living thing, a plant, and, what's more, a colorful plant. But what do all these things *mean?*

The speaker asks the same question in the fifth stanza: "Why the extraneous plant? / Why the taboret? / Why, oh why, the doily?" Beneath the speaker's tone of baffled amusement at such an incomprehensible sense of decor, there is real panic in these questions, tumbling out one after the other. The speaker bravely maintains her characteristic sense of humor and habitual attention to detail in spite of it, describing in a long parenthetical exactly how the doily is embroidered. Yet such a description does not really answer the question of why. These questions are existential. The arbitrariness of the objects themselves, the inexplicability of their presence here (why this and not something, anything else or, for that matter, why not nothing at all) shatters the speaker's rather smug belief that she can reflect in her art an underlying order, or impose order through her art. And not only that, a belief that she has a right to do so based upon her status as someone above and beyond the reality she is describing.

It is the doily that vexes the speaker above all. "Why, oh why, the doily?" Her poet's ear has heard and identified the derivation of "doily" from "dirty" and "oily," but her conscious mind has not registered it. It is therefore profoundly disturbing, but in a way she can't quite put a finger on, even though it has put its finger on her, so to speak. Or, put another way, Elizabeth Bishop has reached into her own poem to send a message to the speaker of that poem, a message the speaker cannot or does not register directly but which nevertheless impinges deeply upon her. But what is that message?

In the final stanza, the speaker attempts to find it or impose it. It is debatable how successful this attempt turns out to be, but it is a brave attempt and a sincere one. The speaker takes solace at first in the idea that "[s]omebody embroidered the doily. / Somebody waters the plant, / or oils it, maybe. Somebody / arranges the rows of cans . . ." Who is this mysterious somebody?

It is surely no accident that the structure of these stanzas suggests the Catechism, the question-and-answer methodology by which the Catholic Church communicates its precepts to young people and converts. The speaker tells herself, tries to convince herself, rather, that things are not random or haphazard, that there is order, beneficent order, in the world. "Somebody loves us all," she concludes in the last line of the poem, including herself for the first time in the world she is describing. But who is this somebody? Is it God? Is it, perhaps, the missing mother whose presence the reader can only infer in the "family filling station" from the evidence of artful arrangement, however idiosyncratic? To know that when Bishop was five years old, her mother was permanently committed to a mental institution and was ever after absent from her daughter's life surely adds something to one's appreciation of this stanza, but such purely biographical detail, while of indisputable interest, is of limited value in explicating a work of art, which, if successful, is always more than the sum of its parts.

The key image of the final stanza occurs in the rows of ESSO (for the Eastern States Standard Oil Company, now Exxon Corporation) cans that "softly say: / ESSO—SO—SO—SO / to high-strung automobiles." It is helpful, but not indispensable to know, that the "SO—SO—SO" was meant by Bishop to suggest the sounds made to soothe horses. The soothing aspect is clear from the context. But working against this soothing by "somebody"—and note the return of the "s" sounds from the second stanza—is the idea that "SO—SO—SO" can be read as a stammer or stutter as well, as if the word "somebody" is describing a thing so frightening that it simply cannot come out. The speaker of the poem feels legitimately soothed by the idea that there is somebody watching over her. But, the experience of being touched by that somebody, which she has perceived only indirectly, in the word "doily," and now in the arrangement of the oil cans, has been far from soothing. It has been terrifying, in fact, launching a series of questions that have no single, authoritative answer. The speaker has been filled indeed, but there is torment as well as satisfaction in the filling. The reader cannot help but think of certain Old Testament prophets who discovered divine contact to be a decidedly double-edged sword.

So, too, Bishop suggests, is poetry when properly written and read: that is, with an alertness to an inexplicable organizing force or principle able to reach into one's life, one's mind, from one knows not where, to arrange, rearrange, or disarrange everything in an instant for reasons one cannot discern, if indeed they even exist. Just as the speaker of the poem both trembles and takes solace at evidence of Bishop's organizing presence outside the poem, so, too, does Bishop tremble and take solace in the presence of something beyond the boundaries of her perceptions. "Somebody loves us all," yes, but how do they love us? As lovers love each other? As a parent loves a child? As a child loves a toy? Or with a love entirely unimaginable? The conflicted and paradoxical embrace of an unknown and unknowable love is characteristic of every art form, especially the dirtiest, most oil-permeated and fertile art of all, life.

Source: Paul Witcover, Critical Essay on "Filling Station," in *Poetry for Students,* The Gale Group, 2001.

Sarah Madsen Hardy

Madsen Hardy has a doctorate in English literature and is a freelance writer and editor. In the following essay, she discusses the unconventional idea of home put forth in Bishop's poem.

Elizabeth Bishop's "Filling Station" is a poem about a filthy gas station, inspired by some place the poet presumably stopped to refuel her car in the course of her many travels. The poem's speaker is a traveler who finds nothing less than universal love—evidence that "somebody loves us all"—in a row of carefully arranged oil cans at the filling station. Thus the word "filling" in the title comes to stand for much more than filling the gas tank up at the pump. Rather, the filling station is a place of emotional replenishment and fulfillment. Through her description, Bishop transforms the mundane experience of stopping for gas into one that evokes the simple and yet profound comfort of home found in an unexpected place. This essay will explore how Bishop uses her position of traveler to redefine the most fundamental concepts of home.

"Filling Station" first appeared in *Questions of Travel,* a 1965 collection that focused largely on Bishop's experiences traveling in Brazil. In the collection's title poem, Bishop poses a series of questions, a self-interrogation about her motivations for wandering the world.

> Where should we be today?
> Is it right to be watching strangers in a play
> in this strangest of theaters?
> What childishness is it that while there's a breath
>   of life
> in our bodies, we are determined to rush
> to see the sun the other way around?

She concludes the poem by juxtaposing these questions of travel with a question about travel's opposite, staying home: "Should we have stayed at home, wherever that may be?" By adding the phrase "wherever that may be?" Bishop opens up the issue of exactly what home means and where one can find it.

In a number of poems in *Questions of Travel,* Bishop seeks to answer a final question—what *is* home anyway? A close reading of the poems reveals that being away from her own home offered Bishop a release from conventional ideas of domesticity that were largely oppressive of women. Bishop rejects these conventional ideas in favor of freer, more open and hopeful ones. This is a form

> " *Just as she breaks down other dichotomies fundamental to the idea of home, she breaks down that between 'us' and 'them'— the traditional family and the strange, diverse people who populate the wide world.*"

of seeing anew—"seeing the sun the other way around"—that travel allows.

As one might guess, Bishop's relationship with her own first home was a troubled one. Her autobiographical story, *In the Village,* offers a glimpse into this poet's childhood, spent with a widowed and mentally ill mother. It also expresses a deep ambivalence about the forever-lost Nova Scotia home from which she was taken at age six, when her mother was institutionalized. Bishop was then taken to Worcester, Massachusetts, to be raised by her grandparents. She spent most of her adult life traveling and through her writing about strange and foreign places, she sought to find the home that she had lost. ("I lost my mother's watch. And look! My last, or / next-to-last, of three loved houses went," she writes in "One Art," a poem about the "art of losing.")

Home is not just something that Bishop has loved and lost, however. Her relationship with the idea of home is further complicated by the fact that she was such a quietly unconventional woman. Bishop was an independent, intellectual lesbian in an era of social conservatism, when the idea of home was inextricably tied to a woman's role as wife and mother. Her refusal of these roles is evident in her depiction of the home presented in "Filling Station" and other poems. Furthermore, there is a long tradition amongst American women poets of writing sentimental poetry about the pleasures of hearth and home; the literary establishment has not taken that poetry seriously. Bishop writes unsentimentally and critically about the concepts held dear in this earlier tradition. The redefined concept of home Bishop generates in her poetry challenges both literary and social conventions.

One of the most fundamental, commonly held ideas of home is that it is what separates indoors from outdoors, and, by extension, culture from nature, and humans from animals. Against this common conception, Bishop often seeks instead to blur the distinction between indoors and out. In her poem, "Squatter's Children," which also appears in *Questions of Travel,* she envisions a home in the torrents of rain that engulf two dirt-poor children who refuse to answer their mother's call to come in out of the storm. The transcendent grandeur of the "rooms of falling rain" contrasts with their desolate human environment. The home provided by nature offers them rights and agency, despite their lowly status as "squatters," people who do not own or rent their own homes: "wet and beguiled, you stand among / the mansions you may choose." In "Song for the Rainy Season," she describes a house that merges with its environment.

> Hidden, oh hidden
> in the high fog . . .
> beneath the magnetic rock . . .
> where blood-black
> bromelias, lichens,
> owls, and the lint of waterfalls cling.

She celebrates the moist natural life forms that invade this house in the rainy season as a testament to its loving inclusiveness.

> House, open house . . .
> to the membership of silver fish, mouse,
> bookworms,
> big moths; with a wall
> for the mildew's ignorant map.

Closely associated with the distinction between indoors and outdoors is that between cleanliness and dirt. Conventionally, home is idealized as a place of cleanliness, a shelter where one can leave the mess of the outside world behind, both literally and figuratively. However, Bishop instead associates the particular loving and welcoming quality of home with being dirty.

In "Song for the Rainy Season," she writes of a house "darkened and tarnished / by the warm touch / of the warm breath / maculate, cherished." In "Filling Station," she makes this point even more emphatically. "Oh, but it is dirty!" the poem begins. Throughout this poem Bishop stresses the filth of the place: "oil-soaked, oil-permeated / to a disturbing, over-all / black translucency." The proprietor, referred to as "Father," "wears a dirty, / oil-soaked monkey suit," and the sons are "greasy."

While the speaker professes a conventional feeling of disturbance at this mess, the imagery of the poem suggests that the oil is the medium that binds the scene's disparate elements into a loving harmony. The "dirty dog" is "quite comfy" on a wicker sofa—a homey term for a domestic image of mixing and mingling. And the wicker itself is "impregnated" with grease. The filling station is not a place of separation, but of happy and productive union between elements conventionally best thought kept separate.

In "Squatter's Children" and "Song for the Rainy Season," Bishop blurs the distinction between a home and the outdoors, but in "Filling Station" she makes the even more unusual move of blurring the distinction between a home and place of commerce. Commerce, with its goal of making money, is often conceived of as "dirty" and heartless. It is also traditionally considered a man's realm. This was especially true in the early 1960s when Bishop wrote the poems in *Questions of Travel.* It was the woman's job to create a home as a place of comfort and refuge for her man at the end of a working day. The filling station is a refuge of sorts, but who has created it? A father and his sons run the station, which seems, on the surface, to be a place of business. "Do they live at the station?" the speaker wonders, noting domestic touches such as a doily draped on a taboret and a begonia. This seems like something that a woman might do.

Perhaps Bishop sees here, through the imagined woman's physical absence, the specter of her own lost mother. But Bishop is careful to leave the question open as to whether this family station includes a mother. While a home is conventionally a woman's realm (and she is the one responsible for keeping it clean), in "Filling Station" an explicitly masculine space is imbued with a loving and beautifying touch that may or may *not* be that of a woman. "Somebody embroidered the doily. / Somebody waters the plant, / or oils it, maybe. Somebody / arranges the rows of cans . . ." Her repetition of the gender-neutral word "somebody" emphasizes the prospect of release from the traditional idea of women's domestic role. It is possible that the father and sons imbued the place with its atmosphere of nourishing, nurturing dirtiness— and, for Bishop, this is a liberating possibility.

Indeed, as Bishop blurs the boundaries between inside and outside, nature and culture, commerce and home, she also blurs that between masculine and feminine. In "Filling Station," she celebrates traditionally feminine qualities—the loving, supportive, and aesthetic touch—in a context that completely defies traditional notions of femininity—a filthy gas station. What she emphasizes is the warm touch itself, not the gender of the person creating it. This touch messily blurs and connects, like the oil that is everywhere. In the poem she envisions the filling station as a kind of home that is free of roles that constrict behavior along the lines of gender, but where the role usually occupied by wife and mother, that of loving nurturer, is still preserved and valued.

"Filling Station" shares with "Squatter's Children" and "Song for the Rainy Season" the value of openness. Instead of portraying homes where people are safely closed in from the world, Bishop imagines homes where the world comes in and is embraced. This is how the nurturing love suggested by the embroidered marguerites on the dingy doily and the cans lined up to say "ESSO—SO—SO—SO" come to transcend the bounds of the family that runs the filling station and touch the heart of a random traveler stopping to buy gas.

Bishop sees these nurturing touches as evidence not that someone loves her family, but that "somebody loves us all." Just as she breaks down other dichotomies fundamental to the idea of home, she breaks down that between "us" and "them"—the traditional family and the strange, diverse people who populate the wide world. The fact that a traveler can happen upon a new kind of home at a filling station is reason enough not to just stay home—wherever that may be.

Source: Sarah Madsen Hardy, Critical Essay on "Filling Station," in *Poetry for Students,* The Gale Group, 2001.

Sources

Bishop, Elizabeth, *Questions of Travel,* Farrar, Straus and Giroux, 1965.

Bromwich, David, "Elizabeth Bishop's Dream Houses," in *Raritan,* Vol. 4, Summer 1984, pp. 77–94.

Carruth, Gorton, *What Happened When: A Chronology of Life and Events in America,* revised ed., Harper Collins, 1996.

Colwell, Anne, *Inscrutable Houses: Metaphors of the Body in the Poems of Elizabeth Bishop,* The University of Alabama Press, 1997, p. 5.

Costello, Bonnie, "The Impersonal and the Interrogative in the Poetry of Elizabeth Bishop," in *Elizabeth Bishop and Her Art,* edited by Lloyd Schwartz and Sybil P. Estess, The University of Michigan Press, 1983, pp. 109–32.

Doreski, C. K., *Elizabeth Bishop: The Restraints of Language,* Oxford University Press, 1993.

Franklin, Sharon, *Artisans Around the World: Mexico and Central America,* Steck-Vaughan Co., 2000.

Kinzie, Mary, *The Cure of Poetry in an Age of Prose,* University of Chicago Press, 1994.

Mann, Charles Edward, "Elizabeth Bishop and Revision: A Spiritual Act," in *American Poetry Review,* Vol. 25, No. 2, March–April 1996, pp. 43–50.

Millier, Brett C., "Elizabeth Bishop," in *Dictionary of Literary Biography,* Vol. 169: *American Poets Since World War II,* 5th Series, Gale Research, 1996, pp. 35–53.

——, *Elizabeth Bishop: Life and the Memory of It,* University of California Press, 1993.

Moss, Howard, "The Canada–Brazil Connection," in *World Literature Today,* Vol. 51, No. 1, Winter 1977, pp.29–33.

Parker, Robert Dale, *The Unbeliever: The Poetry of Elizabeth Bishop,* University of Illinois Press, 1988.

Scott, Nathan A., Jr., "Elizabeth Bishop: Poet Without Myth," in *The Virginia Quarterly Review,* Vol. 60, No. 2, Spring 1984, pp. 255–75.

Smith, William J., "The Hollins Critic," in *Contemporary Literary Criticism,* http://www.galenet.com (February 1977).

Stanford, Donald. E., "The Harried Life of Elizabeth Bishop," in *Sewanee Review,* Vol. 102, No. 1, Winter 1994, pp. 161–63.

Webster's New Twentieth Century Dictionary of the English Language, Unabridged, 2d ed., William Collins Publishers, Inc., 1980.

For Further Study

Bishop, Elizabeth, *The Complete Poems, 1927–1979,* Farrar, Straus and Giroux, 1983.

Not only are all of Bishop's published poems reprinted in this collection, but also her uncollected work and translations of Portuguese, French, and Spanish poets. As in any "complete" volume, this one offers a chance to explore the writer's development over a long period of time.

——, *Exchanging Hats: Paintings,* edited by William Benton, Farrar, Straus and Giroux, 1996.

Besides poetry, the other art form that engaged Elizabeth Bishop was painting. *Exchanging Hats* is a slender volume of reproductions of Bishop watercolors and drawings, along with her comments concerning art. Bishop never studied painting formally, and her technique is somewhat childlike. Her subjects are often plants, the ordinary interiors of houses, and facades of buildings. The watercolor and ink painting she called "Merida from the Roof" appears as the cover illustration for *The Complete Poems.*

Giroux, Robert, ed., *One Art: Elizabeth Bishop,* Farrar, Straus and Giroux, 1994.

Bishop was a prolific letter writer. This collection of her letters constitutes a kind of biography in itself, revealing much about the poet through her relationship with Marianne Moore, Robert Lowell, Lota Soares, and others. Editor Robert Giroux took the title from a late poem, "One Art," which seemed to capture the theme of her personal life: "The art of losing isn't hard to master."

Mann, Charles Edward, "Elizabeth Bishop and Revision: A Spiritual Act," in *American Poetry Review,* Vol. 25, No. 2, March–April 1996, pp. 43–50.

Using papers and drafts of Bishop poems from a special collection, Charles Mann explores the poet's habits of revision and the aesthetic it reveals. In the process, he discovers a spiritual dimension in Bishop's work that bears some comparison to the poems of George Herbert and Gerard Manley Hopkins.

Millier, Brett C., *Elizabeth Bishop: Life and the Memory of It,* University of California Press, 1993.

This biography of Bishop is highly readable. Without critical jargon, Brett Millier fulfills the task she sets about in the preface: "to explain as best I could, using the evidence I had, how Elizabeth Bishop's poems got written and why they turned out the way they did." Millier's way of writing about Bishop's difficult personal life is clear-eyed but compassionate, and she wisely does not interpret the poems solely through that lens.

For Jean Vincent D'abbadie, Baron St.-Castin

Alden Nowlan
1967

The poem, "For Jean Vincent D'abbadie, Baron St.-Castin," is dedicated and addressed to a French noble who played a crucial role in the seventeenth-century struggle between the French, the English, and the Indians for possession of New England. Jean-Vincent D'abbadie first came to the area as an officer on a French expedition to Penobscot Bay, in what is now Maine. While there, he befriended the local Abenaki Indians and eventually married Pidianske, the daughter of Madokawando, chief of the Abenakis in the Penobscot area. Baron St. Castin was instrumental in persuading the Abenakis to join the French side, and he participated in the Franco-Indian expedition against the English settlement at Casco in 1690. He also played a large part in the capture of Fort Pemequid in 1698. St. Castin's loyalty to the Indians and his decision to spend most of his life with them made him almost a legendary figure at the time, and he remains one of the most colorful figures in the history of colonial Maine.

The poem is a celebration of the exploits of this swashbuckling Baron, written from the standpoint of the twentieth century. Nowlan evokes the French noble as a man who straddled two cultures, the French and the Indian, and he raises him to an almost mythic stature. As a representative of the Indian way of experiencing the world, St. Castin represents all that is still foreign to the Anglo-Saxon Protestants of Maine, and their descendents still fear it, three hundred years after the Abenaki warriors descended on their fortresses. "For Jean

Vincent D'abbadie, Baron St.-Castin" is one of many poems by Nowlan that conveys a sense of the mystery of experiencing life in a more primeval, instinctive, and sacramental manner than is customary in rational Western culture.

Author Biography

Alden Nowlan was born to Freeman and Grace (Reese) Nowlan on January 25, 1933, in a rural area near Windsor, Nova Scotia, in Canada. He left school at the age of twelve and worked in a series of unskilled laboring jobs. The job he liked best was that of night watchman at a sawmill, because it gave him time to read. Although Nowlan lacked formal education, he had an intensely curious mind and an active imagination. He wrote poetry and read voraciously at the regional library on any subject that caught his interest.

In 1952, Nowlan became news editor at the *Hartland Observer* in New Brunswick. About that time, he began submitting his poetry to literary magazines. It was not long before his poems started appearing in print. This led to the publication in 1958 of two slim volumes, *A Darkness in the Earth* and *The Rose and the Puritan.* Three more volumes of poetry followed within the next four years, including *Wind in a Rocky Country* (1960) and *The Things Which Are* (1962). His success, together with a small grant from the Canada Council, encouraged Nowlan to leave his newspaper job and devote himself to full-time writing. In 1964 he married Claudine Orser. In the same year, unable to find a publisher for the novel he had written, Nowlan took a job as night editor for a newspaper in New Brunswick. In 1967, he published his most acclaimed book, *Bread, Wine and Salt,* which won a Governor-General's Award for Poetry. This volume includes the poem, "For Jean Vincent D'abbadie, Baron St.-Castin." Also in 1967, Nowlan was awarded a Guggenheim Fellowship.

Nowlan's career was interrupted by his struggle with throat cancer in the mid-1960s. He recovered, against all odds, and in 1969 became writer-in-residence at the University of New Brunswick. That year saw the publication of another volume of poems, *The Mysterious Naked Man.* He later published *I'm a Stranger Here Myself* (1974). In addition to poetry, for which he is best known, Nowlan wrote short stories, including *Miracle at Indian River: Stories* (1968); a novel, *Various Per-*

sons Named Kevin O'Brien: A Fictional Memoir (1973); plays, a collection of essays, and a book of local history.

Nowlan died of pneumonia in Fredericton, New Brunswick, on June 27, 1983.

Poem Text

Take heart, monsieur, four-fifths of this province
Is still much as you left it: forest, swamp and
    barren.
Even now, after three hundred years, your enemies
Fear ambush, huddle by coasts and rivers,
The dark woods at their backs.   5

Oh, you'd laugh to see
How old Increase Mather and his ghastly Calvinists
Patrol the palisades, how they bury their money
Under the floors of their hideous churches
Lest you come again in the night   10
With the red ochre mark of the sun god
On your forehead, you exile from the Pyrenees,
You baron of France and Navarre,
You squaw man, you Latin poet,
You war chief of Penobscot   15
And of Kennebec and of Maliseet!

At the winter solstice
Your enemies cry out in their sleep
And the great trees throw back their heads and
    shout
Nabujcol!   20
Take heart, monsieur,
Even the premier, even the archbishop,
Even the poor gnome-like slaves
At the all-night diner and the service station
Will hear you chant   25
The Song of Roland
As you cross yourself
And reach for your scalping knife.

Poem Summary

Lines 1–5

In the first line of "For Jean Vincent D'abbadie, Baron St.-Castin," the poet addresses the Baron as though he is encouraging him. Although the Indians were eventually defeated in the New England wars, the poet assures St. Castin that he did not live in vain. St. Castin's French origins are made clear by addressing him as "monsieur." The reason for the comfort the poet offers is that although D'abbadie lived three hundred years ago, little has changed since that time. Four-fifths of "this province," by which the poet means Maine, is still covered by forests and swamps. It is still uncultivated, barren land. Then the poet explains that something else remains unchanged too. The local inhabitants, whose English ancestors were, during D'abbadie's lifetime, his enemies, still have not conquered the region or overcome their fear. They live huddled in the coastal regions, or by the rivers, still fearing ambush, with "the dark woods at their backs." This phrase is to be understood both literally and symbolically. The poet does not mean that the citizens of present-day Maine fear attacks from Indians in the woods. The "dark woods" symbolize the unknown, instinctual, subconscious life on which the inhabitants, with their cold, rationalistic religion, have denied and turned their backs.

Lines 6–10

Continuing the address to D'abbadie, the poet tells him that he would laugh if he could see how the descendents of his enemies behave in exactly the same way as their forbears. He mentions Increase Mather (1639–1723), a Puritan minister known for his part in prosecuting the Salem witchcraft trials, in which hysteria about witchcraft resulted in many innocent people being put to death. Mather published "An Essay for the Recording of Illustrious Providence," in which he claimed that the Indian wars had been brought upon the English settlers because of their sins. The emphasis on sin, and the rejection of sexuality, which Increase and his son Cotton Mather both associated with witchcraft, were typical of the Puritan religion.

The poet makes no attempt to disguise his dislike of this attitude. He describes the Calvinists as "ghastly" and their churches "hideous." (The Puritans derived their theology from the teachings of the Protestant reformer, John Calvin. The word Calvinist is sometimes used in a negative sense to refer to anyone who sticks rigidly to a dogmatic point of view.) In the poem, modern-day Calvinists still patrol their "palisades," fences consisting of a row of stakes, sharpened at the top, as a defense against attack. They still bury their money under the floors of their churches because they fear another Indian attack in the night. Once again, the poet is not speaking literally. He is referring to a characteristic way of thinking and of experiencing the world. This might be described as defensive, materialistic, obsessed with wealth, fearful of the unknown, or of anything that lies beyond the immediate realm of experience.

Lines 11–16

These lines are an extended and admiring characterization of Jean-Vincent D'abbadie. He is seen

Media Adaptations

- "The Alden Nowlan Interviews," http://www.unb.ca/qwerte/nowlan/nowlan.htm (January 2001). This website contains audio recordings of Nowlan taken from interviews conducted by Canadian filmmaker Jon Pederson in 1982, one year before Nowlan's death. Nowlan reads some of his poems, and also discusses writing and the topic, "on place."

- "Alden Nowlan," http://www.vix.com/menmag/nowlan.htm (January 2001). This website includes eight poems by Nowlan read by Robert Bly and Thomas Smith in 1994 at Macalester College in St. Paul, Minnesota. It also includes Bly speaking about what he admires in Nowlan's poetry.

to carry the mark of the Indian warrior, the "red ochre mark of the sun god," painted on his forehead. Ochre is a yellow or reddish-brown earthy clay, and the reference to the sun god is a reminder that Indian spirituality took a form very different from that of the European Christian settlers. The poet then evokes the Baron's birthplace in the Pyrenees, a mountain range that separates France from Spain. He follows this with a double reference to D'abbadie's status as a French nobleman from the region known as Navarre, in southwest France. Next, the Baron is described as a "squaw man," a reference to his marriage to an Indian woman ("squaw"), and "Latin poet," which ascribes literary achievements to him, although the historical Baron was not known as a poet. Finally, D'abbadie is described as a war leader of the Indian tribes of Penobscot, Kennebec, and Maliseet, all of whom were involved in the struggle against the English. However, the poet does not mention the Abenakis, with whom the historical D'abbadie was principally associated.

Lines 17–19

Building on his evocation of the powerful figure of the Baron, and the way in which he embodies two distinct cultures, the poet now turns the focus back to the Baron's enemies. As he has done earlier in the poem, the poet refers to the modern-day descendants of the English settlers. At the darkest night of the year (the winter solstice), they still cry out in their sleep at night, perhaps dreaming nightmares of the unknown demons that haunt their lives. Outside, the trees respond to the cries, and the poet pictures them throwing back their heads and shouting out in the Alonquin dialect, the language spoken by the Abenaki.

Lines 20–27

In these final lines, the poet returns to where he began. He assures the baron, who is once more referred to as "monsieur," that no one in present-day Maine can avoid being influenced by what he, the Baron, represents. His reach extends to both the political and religious realms (conveyed by the references to "premier" and "archbishop") and to the impoverished workers at the all-night diner or the service station.

The final threefold image reemphasizes, as lines 11–16 had done earlier, the dual cultural heritage associated with the Baron. The Baron is portrayed chanting *The Song of Roland,* a chivalric romance (adventure narrative) that dates from twelfth-century France. It is used here as a symbol of the height of European culture. As he chants, the Baron makes the sign of the cross, acknowledging the Christian Trinity of Father, Son, and Holy Spirit. The act is a sign of the Catholic faith to which the historical Baron belonged. The third part of the tripartite image with which the poem ends shows St. Castin in the role of Indian warrior. At the very moment he crosses himself, he reaches for his "scalping knife," the weapon with which the Indian warrior mutilated his defeated foe. It is not known whether the historical baron ever actually scalped any of the Puritan English, but the image serves the poet well: the unusual amalgam in the Baron of French Catholic and Indian cultures, both of which possess theologies and world-views different from those of the Puritans and their descendents, has power to annihilate the safe, yet small and impoverished, certainties of their day-to-day life.

Themes

Culture Clash

The poem takes as its inspiration the conflict in seventeenth-century New England between the English settlers on one side, and, on the other, the

Indian tribes in alliance with the French. The dominant theme is the contrast between the world views of the Puritans and the Indians, and how that conflict still continues today, internalized within the minds of the present-day inhabitants of New England.

The clash of cultures is seen from the point of view of the Puritans, who fear what they do not know or understand. Nowlan makes no attempt to be evenhanded or neutral in this fight. The English settlers are equated with the intolerance and religious fanaticism of Increase Mather, who is pointedly referred to as "old." The suggestion that Puritan culture and religion are feeble and in decline is reinforced throughout the poem. The Puritans and their modern-day descendents are fearful; they "huddle" together and turn their backs on life. They cry out at the winter solstice, the darkest point in the year. Everything in their world is dark; they cannot let light in. What they value most are material things. But they cannot enjoy even those. They bury their money under their churches, which suggests that their materialism is bound up in their religion; that Puritanism is as lifeless as money. This enslavement to money continues to the present time, in the form of the "poor gnome-like slaves" who labor for small reward at the diners and service stations of New England. The expression "gnome-like" suggests that they are stunted in their growth; not quite what they are designed to be, not fully human.

The portrait Nowlan creates is hardly a flattering one. It is far more than an indictment of seventeenth century Puritanism; his target is the impoverished rationalistic Western culture of his own time, which according to this poem had cut itself off from the real springs of life.

In clear contrast to this stands the Baron. He belongs to the night, but his world is very different from the dark, fearful night that the Puritans inhabit. When applied to the Baron, night suggests a world of instinct and mystery, filled with secret life. The life that his world honors is conveyed by the red ochre mark of the sun god that he carries on his forehead. There could hardly be a more striking symbol of the vast difference between the two cultures. In Puritan theology, a distant God sits somewhere beyond the skies and judges men and women. And nature is merely a collection of inanimate objects, wholly separate from the mind of man. But for the Indians, all things in the natural world share in the divine energy. The sun is a god; the earth is a god, everything is a god. The Puri-

Topics for Further Study

- Write a poem in free verse about a heroic figure from American history whom you admire. Try to make the poem illustrate at least two qualities that make the person a hero.

- Explain why people throughout history have often hated and feared those who come from a different culture. Why are cultural differences such a potent source of discord? What can be done to minimize cultural conflict?

- Has the American government done enough to compensate Native Americans for seizing their lands? What more could the government do? Should more be done to improve the quality of life for Native Americans?

- Should Native-American reservations be entirely independent, or should they be under the jurisdiction of the federal government?

tans thought such views blasphemous, and indeed the early Puritans regarded the Indians as primitive devil-worshippers.

The vivid picture Nowlan creates of the Baron is a youthful and virile warrior, embodying the divine spirit, rising up out of the mysterious night to tower over the puny settlers. The poet mythologizes the Baron in this way precisely because St. Castin has done what the Puritans cannot. They hate and fear the Indians as a threat to their lives and culture, but the Baron has managed to straddle both cultures. He is at home in two worlds.

This feeling is richly conveyed in lines 12–16 of the second stanza, which begins with three references to the Baron's origins (Pyrenees, France, Navarre). Then in line 14, the two sides of his nature are condensed into one line: "you squaw man, you Latin poet"; the Baron is at once primitive Indian and refined European. Lines 15–16 round out this admiring address by naming three tribes, the Penobscot, Kennebec and Maliseet, that connect the Baron to the Indians. The symmetry of the whole passage is perfect; it suggests a psychic wholeness to the Baron that has eluded the Puri-

tans. And once more, Nowlan is clearly on the Baron's side. The tone in these lines is affectionate and familiar.

The clash of cultures is also conveyed in the dramatic contrast in lines 18–19 between the sleeping Puritans and the great swaying trees outside. The Puritans are unconscious, afraid, crying out involuntarily, symbolically withdrawing from life. But the trees possess consciousness (more, it seems, than the sleeping Puritans) when they are seen in the light of the Indian ability to commune with everything in creation. The Puritans, knowing the value only of dead things like money, cannot penetrate the way of seeing that enables trees to exult and shout out in the language of those who understand them.

It is one of the subtleties of this poem that the Indians, who were eventually defeated by the Puritan English, are presented as the true victors. What they symbolize, a more holistic mode of experience, cannot be defeated. But to those who fear this other, "dark" side of the psyche, it appears like something to be chased away or suppressed—a skulking thing in the night woods.

Style

The poem is written in unrhymed free verse, and is divided into three stanzas of uneven length. A conversational tone is adopted at the beginning, which is reinforced by the colloquial exclamation ("Oh") followed by the contraction ("you'd") in line 6. The entire line, "Oh, you'd laugh to see" gives the impression that the poet is talking to an old friend. This conversational effect is balanced by the formality of addressing the subject as "monsieur," which upholds his dignity and prepares for the laudatory descriptions of him in the second stanza.

The eleven lines that make up stanza two form only one sentence. Lines 6–9 and line 11 are run-on lines, in which the syntactical or grammatical unit carries over to the next line without a natural pause. (This technique is also known as enjambment.) There is only the minimum of punctuation. The effect of the run-on lines is to speed up the verse. In lines 12–16, however, there is a change. With the use of mostly end-stopped lines (the opposite of run-on lines, in which the end of the grammatical unit coincides with the end of the line), the repetition of an initial word ("you"), and of the structure of five short phrases (beginning with "you exile from the Pyrenees"), the verse slows down considerably. The poet achieves a pleasing cadence made up of a rising rhythm. This serves to elevate the Baron and make him seem a larger than life figure.

The poet's manipulation of cadence (measured, rhythmical effects) is apparent also in the final stanza. After the poet repeats in line 20 the statement with which the poem began—"Take heart, monsieur"—the triple repetition of the word "even," in "even the premier, even the archbishop, / even the poor gnome-like slaves," creates a rising rhythm that is a suitable accompaniment to the evocation of the wide scope of the Baron's reach. The rhythm falls with the line that follows: "at the all-night diner and the service station." The slowly rising and falling cadence creates an expectation in the reader's mind of what is to come, thus paving the way for the final image of the baron crossing himself and preparing to kill.

One final stylistic device should be noted. Line 19, "and the great trees throw back their heads and shout nabujcol" is an example of personification, in which an inanimate object is referred to as if it possessed human form or qualities. The effect in this poem is to create the impression that nature responds to human thoughts and feelings.

Historical Context

During the early part of Nowlan's life, the question of the status of Indians in Canadian society was being pushed to the forefront of the national agenda. During the decades up to the end of World War II, Indians had been almost an "invisible" people in Canada. The federal government maintained control over all aspects of life on Indian reservations, and there was massive neglect. But beginning in the late 1940s and continuing into the 1950s and 1960s, this control began to change. Public awareness of the lack of adequate health care and education for the Indian population grew. At the same time, Indian leaders began to organize and campaign energetically to regain their independence and preserve their endangered culture. By 1960, improvements had been made in social and economic conditions. In the same year, the right to vote in Canadian federal elections was extended to Indians.

Nowlan was no doubt aware of these events, and they must have contributed to his interest in Indian culture and history. This interest is evident not only in his book *Campobello: The Outer Island* (1975), which is a volume of local history, but also in *Nine Micmac Legends* (1983), a compilation of Micmac stories. The Micmac tribe is one of the largest Indian groups in Canada.

Nowlan's sympathy with the Indian cause, and their alienation from the dominant culture that is expressed in "For Jean Vincent D'abbadie, Baron St.-Castin," may also have its roots in some of the circumstances of Nowlan's life. He was born and raised during the Depression, in an isolated area of Nova Scotia where the soil was too poor to farm. He grew up in a house that lacked all modern amenities.

Nowlan's difficult early life and gradual climb from poverty gave him an ability to empathize with the underdog. In his poem "Long Long Ago" he remembers with warmth the visits made to the family home by an Indian woman selling her wares. Many of his early poems draw on his own background and reveal how he admired courage and despised intolerance and ill-treatment of the weak or vulnerable.

When Nowlan moved to Saint John in New Brunswick in 1962, it was the first time he had lived in an urban environment. For a while he experienced life there as a not always sympathetic outsider. In "Britain Street," for example, he writes of how the entire street seems as if it is perpetually quarreling: "I have lived here nine months / and in all that time / have never once heard / a gentle word spoken."

All these elements must have contributed to the sympathy that Nowlan felt towards Indians and also the figure of the Baron, as the champion of a threatened people.

St. Castin's War

As Nowlan read in the history of the period, he would have come across many accounts of the Indian wars. As in many wars, atrocities were committed on both sides. In 1688, for example, the Abenaki Indians sent a war party to destroy the English fort at Pemaquid. A contemporary account tells of how the Abenaki, "in full war dress and with terrifying screams, hurled themselves into the village, breaking down doors and killing all they found." Historian Aline S. Taylor, who quotes this passage in her book, *The French Baron of Penagouet* (1998), also notes that the presence of St. Castin usually held the Indians in check, although

Compare & Contrast

- **1675–1760:** During the wars with the English, many Abenaki migrate to Quebec, Canada, where the greatest number can be found today.

  Today: After centuries of cultural assimilation, the Abenaki have banded together as a people and are demanding their rights, their lands, and federal recognition of their tribe. Today's Abenaki in the United States are known as the Western Abenaki (Vermont and New Hampshire) and the Eastern Abenaki (Maine).

- **1800s:** Folktales abound in the villages of New England about the exploits of the Baron St. Castin.

  1967: Nowlan's *Bread, Wine and Salt,* which contains "For Jean Vincent D'abbadie, Baron St.-Castin" is published.

  Today: A monument to Baron St. Castin stands on the site of an old French fort in the town of Castine, Maine, which is named after him.

- **1954:** Native Americans in Maine gain the right to vote in national elections.

1967: Native Americans in Maine gain the right to vote in state elections.

1970s: Scholarly research in New England shows that many of the property deeds through which land changed hands from Indians to English were forgeries. The Indians were often cheated out of land they believed they were sharing.

1980: In the Maine Indian Land Claims Settlement, the Penobscots and Passamoqoddies win their case against the state of Maine after a ten-year court battle. As compensation for land they claimed had been stolen from them, the two tribes receive eighty million dollars and the right to purchase 300,000 acres of woodland.

Today: The status of the Native American people across the United States is still a subject of debate. Indian leaders are involved in jurisdiction claims against states over gambling rights on reservation lands.

---

on this occasion, many English were killed in violation of the terms of their surrender.

On other occasions there was ample provocation from the English side. During 1690, the English insisted on settling in fertile valleys that had been cultivated by the Abenaki for hundreds of years. Throughout the summer and fall of that year, Abenaki revenge attacks terrified the English settlers. Then the English went on a rampage of their own, led by the notoriously brutal Colonel Church. Marching on the Indian villages of the Androscoggin and Kennebec rivers, the English ruthlessly killed men, women, and children.

During this period, Jean-Vincent D'abbadie was such a key figure that the conflict was known as "St. Castin's War." The Baron was a target of English threats, attempted bribery, and a kidnap attempt. Treading a fine diplomatic line, he was also involved in negotiations between English, French,

and Indians, and he acted as a go-between in trade between the English and the Abenaki. Both loathed and admired, it was this romantic, larger than life figure that inspired Nowlan, several hundred years later, to pay him tribute.

Critical Overview

"For Jean-Vincent D'abbadie, Baron St.-Castin" has attracted little or no direct critical appraisal, although it has proved popular enough to be reprinted in at least one anthology of modern Canadian verse. The poem first appeared in Nowlan's volume, *Bread, Wine and Salt* (1967), which critics usually regard as the book that first marked Nowlan's emergence as a poet of distinction. For example, reviewer Fred Cogswell admired "the transparent fluidity of [Nowlan's] presentation. Whether he writes of the inhabitants of Hainesville (Hartland), for whom he feels such ambivalence, his friends, or his own personal feelings and predicament, thought and form merge and change so beautifully and organically that one is not conscious of a seam between them."

Although Nowlan is regarded as one of the most important Canadian poets of the last forty years, he is not well known in the United States. However, the poet Robert Bly, who wrote an introduction to Nowlan's selected poems in 1974, has taken the lead in championing Nowlan's cause. Bly argued that Nowlan was one of the small group of poets who were prepared to tear apart the comforting layer of reassurance that humans create for themselves as a barrier against the chaotic and frightening nature of life as it really is. Nowlan was not afraid to face fear, Bly argued, and bring it to the surface. Although Bly did not mention "For Jean Vincent D'abbadie, Baron St.-Castin," the poem embodies exactly this attitude. The inhabitants of New England who so fear the explosion of unfamiliar, alien life into their midst are an example of the human tendency to construct a life that does not face up to the totality of human experience.

Nowlan also has a reputation as a regional poet, frequently evoking the places and people of his native Nova Scotia and New Brunswick. "For Jean Vincent D'abbadie, Baron St.-Castin" extends that range by a few miles into Maine, and it is strongly rooted in the topography and history of the area.

Criticism

Bryan Aubrey

Aubrey holds a Ph.D in English and has published many essays on twentieth-century literature. In this essay, he approaches Nowlan's poem from the point of view of Jungian psychology.

Nowlan's "For Jean Vincent D'Abbadie, Baron St.-Castin" works at a number of different levels. First, it alludes to the historical situation in New England during the conflict between Indian tribes and English settlers in the seventeenth century. But Nowlan cleverly transposes the conflict into modern times by interpreting it in psychological terms, and this adds another dimension to the poem. This level of meaning can be illuminated by the psychological theories of one of the great thinkers of the twentieth century, Carl Jung.

What is so noticeable about "For Jean Vincent" is not only how the figures that populate it are so starkly split into two opposing sides, but how the poet's sympathy is placed entirely on one side, that of the Baron. The Puritans and their modern-day descendents are presented as truly pitiable. Fearful, huddled together for safety, obsessed with a materialism that is also reflected in their Calvinist religious faith, and tormented in their sleep by nightmares, they are completely overshadowed and dominated by the magnificent figure of the Baron. Nowlan has elevated this historical figure, the French nobleman who married an Indian woman and took up the Indian cause against the English, into a gigantic, almost mythic figure. He is an inhabitant of the dark woods; he blends two very different cultures and traditions; he is a man of refinement and learning and yet also a feared warrior who leads no less than three Indian tribes; and he is a mysterious figure who carries the mark of the sun god worshiped by the Indians upon his forehead. His charisma and power is so great that even the great trees seem to be on his side.

The Baron is thus presented as an almost superhuman figure. Everyone else mentioned in the poem is small by comparison; even the premier and the archbishop, figures of status and power in their society, are given not a single adjective to enhance their standing. Everyone is dwarfed by the Baron, and the poet reinforces this effect with his cunning use of rhythm, cadence, and repetition to describe the hero.

It is clear that on a psychological level, what is being presented in this poem is a radical split in the human psyche. From the point of view of the Puritans, the Baron embodies everything they fear, reject and do not understand. In terms of Jungian psychology, the Baron embodies what Jung calls the "shadow." The shadow is the dark side of the personality that is unacknowledged and repressed, and it is often projected onto others—people of other cultures, for example, or experienced in dreams. The shadow often embodies the qualities that a person dislikes when he or she encounters them in other people.

This is plainly what is happening in the poem. The Baron, who represents not only the Indian cause in war but also its culture and religion, embodies everything that the rational Puritans, with their Calvinist God, have denied. The two opposing camps—the Puritans and the Baron—represent two conflicting world views (corresponding to different aspects of the psyche). One represents rationality, self-control, order, discipline, material progress and conquest of nature, while the other represents instinct, emotion, natural impulse, communion with nature, and communication with the gods who inhabit nature.

Jung believed that the unconscious, repressed aspects of the psyche often found expression in dreams. In his memoir, *Memories, Dreams, Reflections,* Jung, who was Swiss, wrote of a visit he made to North Africa. He noted how people thought and behaved in the Arab cultures that were quite a contrast to his own European background. In a dream Jung had while in North Africa, he encountered an Arab man who attacked him. Jung fought back and the two of them wrestled, each trying to immerse the other's head in water and drown him. As Jung reflected on the dream (of which the battle with the Arab was only a part) he decided that the Arab embodied the shadow side of the personality that had been pushed out of consciousness but was now trying to find a way back in. Jung wrote:

> The predominantly rationalistic European finds much that is human alien to him, and he prides himself on this without realising that this rationality is won at the expense of his vitality, and that the primitive part of his personality is consequently condemned to a more or less underground existence.

Here is the underlying psychology of Nowlan's "For Jean Vincent." The "primitive" part of the personality is embodied in the Baron, a man regarded as alien by the Puritans, who have, as Jung writes, lost the vitality that an integrated rather than fragmented psyche would possess. Like Jung dreaming of being attacked by an Arab, they dream of the Baron and his cohorts and fear an attack from the unknown, "the dark woods at their back." As Jungian scholar M. L. von Franz, writing in *Man and His Symbols,* states, "Through dreams one becomes acquainted with aspects of one's own personality that for various reasons one has preferred not to look at too closely."

It should be noted, however, that the shadow is not in itself a negative or evil force. According to von Franz, "The shadow becomes hostile only when he is ignored or misunderstood." Also, the shadow often contains values that need to be integrated into consciousness. This explains the poet's presentation of the Baron in such a positive light. Only the Puritans see the Baron as evil. For the poet, the Baron represents a higher level of integration than the narrow Puritans are able to comprehend. He symbolizes not the shadow, but the whole psyche that contains opposites and is able to

For the poet, the Baron represents a higher level of integration than the narrow Puritans are able to comprehend. He symbolizes not the shadow, but the whole psyche that contains opposites and is able to integrate them into a powerful whole."

integrate them into a powerful whole. The psychic wholeness of the Baron is made clear by the fact that he is at home in two cultures. Not only is he an Indian war leader, married to an Indian woman (and thus a "squaw man") he also embodies the flower of European culture. He is presented as a Latin poet and as a man who recites the medieval romance, *The Song of Roland.*

It is because of the range of associations that the figure of the Baron calls up that the poet presents him as living on in the present, still threatening his enemies. Everyone will hear from the Baron because he will always represent the Jungian shadow to those who fear him and an integrated psyche to those who perceive him from the broader perspective of the poet. As an ever-present reality in the human psyche, the voice of the Baron cannot forever be drowned out, not by orthodox religion (the archbishop) political action (the premier), or the daily drudgery of work ("the gnome-like slaves" who work in the diners and service stations). As to what effect his voice will have on those who hear him, von Franz points out that "whether the shadow becomes our friend or enemy depends largely upon ourselves."

The shadow, in the Jungian sense, appears in another poem by Nowlan, "He continues to try to avoid being caught," which was published in his 1974 collection, *I'm a Stranger Here Myself.* The entire poem is only four lines, and it shows the difficulty that the conscious part of the personality may have in acknowledging whatever it is that the shadow is trying to communicate:

What Do I Read Next?

- Nowlan's *Selected Poems* (1996), edited by Patrick Lane and Lorna Crozier, was compiled thirteen years after his death. This volume contains some of his most popular and well-formed poems and reflects how well his poems stand the test of time.

- Besides being a poet, Nowlan also wrote short stories. His collection, *Miracle at Indian River: Stories* (1968), has attracted praise for his ability to see into the core of his characters.

- The poet Robert Bly has praised Nowlan, and the volume of poems that Bly edited and introduced, *News of the Universe: Poems of Twofold Consciousness* (San Francisco: Sierra Club Books 1980), illuminates the clash between two ways of seeing the world that is the theme of "For Jean Vincent D'abbadie, Baron St.-Castin." One view sees human consciousness as separate from the world; the other finds consciousness in everything.

- *The Plumed Serpent* (1926), by the English novelist D. H. Lawrence, also explores the clash of two cultures. One of these is modern American culture, which for Lawrence represents the civilization of money. The other is represented by the old Indian religions of Mexico. Many of the issues that Nowlan tackles in miniature in his poem about Baron St. Castin are explored on the much larger canvas of this novel. Like Nowlan, Lawrence is clearly on the side of the Indians.

- *Rooted Like the Ash Trees,* edited by Richard Carlson (Eagle Wing Press, 1987), is a collection of writings by members of the New England Indian tribes. It includes a sampling of legends, crafts, recipes, research and information on the present-day land struggles of the Micmac and Penobscots of Maine, the Paugusset of Connecticut and the Abenakis of Vermont.

A memo to myself: Don't tell
anyone that a fiend from hell
bent over you last night and grinned.
Ask why you whimpered, blame the wind.

Here, in miniature, is "For Jean Vincent D'Abbadie, Baron St.-Castin" once again. The sleeping, or sleepless, poet is like the descendents of the Calvinist Puritans who cry out in their sleep in fear; and the grinning "fiend from hell" is another version of their nightmare vision of the Baron.

The nightmare vision is of course self-created. As Hamlet puts it in Shakespeare's play: "For there is nothing either good or bad but thinking makes it so"; the shadow takes on such a frightening form only because the conscious mind has exerted great effort in fighting it or simply denying its existence. And when an image of this nature does finally well up from the depths of the subconscious, the conscious mind will often go to great lengths to dismiss it or rationalize it away, as the poet does in this example, rather than confront it.

The shadow makes another appearance in Nowlan's poem, "Footsteps in the Dark," which was published in *Bread, Wine and Salt,* the same volume in which "For Jean Vincent D'Abbadie, Baron St.-Castin" appeared.

In "Footsteps in the Dark," the poet hears footsteps, belonging to an unidentified "he," approaching in the dark every night. The footsteps then retreat into the "boundless, teeming / darkness of the blind" as the poet strains to hear. He knows that one day the footsteps will reach him and something of great power will be unleashed upon him but he cannot imagine what that might be. All he knows is that when it happens

It will be loud and quick, though you know he will
   come
like Christ with his bleeding hands to the disciples,
who backed away, half-crazed with fear, or like
   Jack the Ripper
falling upon a whore in Whitechapel.

The phrase "you know he will come" recalls the similar fear of the Puritans in "For Jean Vincent": "lest you come again in the night." Whatever the ominous footsteps represent, they cannot forever be escaped, for they exist in the mind itself. What they bring may be negative or positive—a mysterious, primal force that destroys, or the transformative experience of the numinous, that is, the awe that comes upon a person in the presence of some divine power or revelation.

What this poem suggests, as does "For Jean Vincent," is that there is a lot more to human consciousness than a person's everyday experience might suggest. Nowlan explores this idea in other poems in *Bread, Wine and Salt.* He is particularly interested in moments when a person is swept up into states of consciousness that are beyond the normal, and which yield moments of ecstasy or freedom. Sometimes this comes close to a mystical vision, as when in "I, Icarus," the poet imagines he is flying, and his vision of the freed human soul, floating beyond all the restrictions that normally hedge it in, combines the image of an Aeolian harp—which produces music when the wind blows upon it—with a suggestion of the ancient idea of the music of the spheres:

> Outside, I rose higher and higher, above the pasture
>   fence,
> above the clothesline, above the dark, haunted trees
> beyond the pasture.
> And, all the time, I heard the music of flutes.
> It seemed the wind made this music.
> And sometimes there were voices singing.

In similar fashion, "Daughter of Zion" starts with a description of a very ordinary, sad, beaten-down woman who would merit a second look from no one. It ends with a vision of this same woman the previous night, when, under a tent by a river,

> God himself, the Old One, seized her in his arms
>   and
> lifted her up
> and danced with her,
> * * *
> and the Holy Ghost
> went into her body and spoke through her mouth
> the language they speak in heaven!

Perhaps this is a reminder that, as the poet Walt Whitman wrote in "Song of Myself," "All truths wait in all things." It is the task of the poet to squeeze out those truths, and to do so he must delve deep into his own psyche, where all possibilities dwell. As Nowlan points out in "On names and misnomers," in a conclusion that is very apt for the divided consciousness that is at the heart of "For Jean Vincent D'Abbadie, Baron St.-Castin":

> Each of us contains multitudes,
> every one of whose
> personalities is split.

Source: Bryan Aubrey, Critical Essay on "For Jean Vincent d'Abbadie, Baron St.-Castin," in *Poetry for Students,* The Gale Group, 2001.

Douglas Dupler

Dupler is a published writer and critic. In the following essay, he considers how a poet enhances his powers of description.

Alden Nowlan is a poet who is very skilled at describing a sense of place in his poetry. His manner of description has undoubtedly been affected by the rough and cold landscape of his native Canada. In many poems, he has described places where the forces of nature have the capacity to overwhelm the human inhabitants. "For Jean Vincent d'Abbadie, Baron St.-Castin," is no exception to this sort of description of the natural world. This poem is a wonderful example of how a poet can rely on several techniques to provide a compelling description of a place, to paint a vivid and complex landscape. Alden Nowlan uses many tools of the poet's trade, including diction, imagery, texture, tone, structure, and allusion.

Nowlan began writing poetry in Canada in a period that critics called "cultural nationalism," which began in the 1950s and continued through the 1960s. As the poet and novelist Margaret Atwood described it in *The New Oxford Book of Canadian Verse in English,* "cultural nationalism was merely a determination on the part of writers to stay in their own country . . . and to write about what they knew and saw around them." In "For Jean Vincent," Nowlan describes a landscape that he knows intimately. Nowlan also shows that properly describing a landscape must take into account the culture and history.

The poet and critic Robert Bly writing in *Canadian Writers and their Works: Poetry Series* once praised Alden Nowlan for his powers of description, noting that "[Nowlan's] details are fantastically clear. His clear direct language is not a transformative language—it's not about one thing changing into another—but a descriptive language, about the way things *are.*" For Nowlan, this detailing of "the way things are" is not always so easy, because the present moment is deeper than the reader first expects. In the present moment, there are also connections with the past and future. If "For Jean Vincent" is a descriptive poem of the present state of a particular place, then this poem is

If 'For Jean Vincent' is a descriptive poem of the present state of a particular place, then this poem is also forced to deal with the many layers that make up the present."

also forced to deal with the many layers that make up the present.

From its title, the poem leads readers to presume that they are about to read an ode to an historical figure. An ode is a poem that is dedicated to a person or object and can be enthusiastic or ironic in tone. However, in the first stanza of the poem, the landscape and setting immediately overshadow the person to whom the poem was dedicated. Nowlan uses very particular diction and imagery to establish a sense of place right away. Note the nouns that Nowlan places in the first stanza: forest, swamp, enemies, ambush, coasts, and rivers. These words and images present the landscape and lend an ominous texture to the poem. In this first stanza, Nowlan also uses the verbs "fear" and "huddle," and the adjectives "barren" and "dark." All of these word choices contribute to the poem's texture. Indeed, from the beginning, the reader senses that a forbidding and powerful landscape pervades the poem. If human beings are present in this place, they must take care to watch for things that might creep up "at their backs," a warning issued in the final words of the first stanza.

In the second stanza, the diction and imagery continue to reinforce the eerie and dark texture of the first stanza. Other historical figures are mentioned besides the man of the title, and these people are "ghastly" and "old." The reader can almost visualize the ghosts who "patrol the palisades." When they "bury their money" in "their hideous churches," the imagery is of darkness and of the underground. The churches and the palisades the building blocks of the culture itself, are still haunted by disturbing figures who have long been gone. The past is reaching up into the description of the present.

Midway through the second stanza, Nowlan keeps piling up haunting images and words that have weight. A warning is issued that even the ghosts must fear something that can "come again in the night." The next line, in a single stroke, lifts the poem from darkness into the light, presenting an image of the "red ochre mark of the sun god." Now the poem begins to celebrate and exalt its subject with several lines that describe with repetition. Even though the stanza ends with a jubilant exclamation point, the poem retains its texture by using mysterious and potent names such as Pyrenees, Navarre, Penobscot, Kennebec, and Maliseet.

The third stanza begins with an image that pulls the reader right back into the dark. The "winter solstice" is the darkest day of the year, and even sleep is not safe in the next line that again contains "enemies." The third line of the stanza reinforces that nature is dangerous, as the trees seem to be on the side of the assassin. The line, "the great trees throw back their heads and shout," is an example of anthromorphism, or giving human qualities to non-human objects. Even the trees contribute to the dark atmosphere of the poem, by shouting a strange word, *nabujcol*, into the night. The poem ends with a sentence that repetitively lists other figures that make up the landscape, from the highest government official to the lowest workers. All walks of life subconsciously fear the final image, the "scalping knife."

The tone that a poet uses can also affect the meaning of a poem, can provide descriptive details. In the first line, with the phrase, "Take heart, monsieur," the voice of the poem seems to be speaking intimately and sympathetically to its subject. This tone may serve a purpose. When the voice of the poem is sympathetic with this historical figure, it places the poem in a position to describe the present day against the backdrop of history. Furthermore, a voice that is intimate with history builds the ethos, or credibility, of the poem as well. After the lighthearted entrance, the first stanza lists darker images, and then the tone seems to change again with the first line of the second stanza: "Oh, you'd laugh to see . . ." Again, the tone becomes light and ironic. Later in this same stanza, the tone celebrates the persona of Baron St.-Castin. In the third stanza, the tone alternates between being ironic, when it provides imagery of trees shouting, and being sympathetic, when it repeats the line, "Take heart, monsieur." This ambiguity and shifting of tone may serve to keep the reader as alert as those who fear the "scalping knife" at the poem's conclusion.

The structure of the poem also contributes to its meaning. If the poem aims to describe a world that is deep and chaotic, then a structure that is free and variable in form can contribute to this purpose. One of Nowlan's influences was the modern American poet William Carlos Williams, who frequently used the "triadic stanza" form, or three separate stanzas that vary in form. Williams also relied upon variable sentence structures and changing rhythms in his poems, as Nowlan's poem does. The effectiveness of variable sentence structures and rhythms is illustrated by the second sentence of the first stanza:

> Even now, after three hundred years, your enemies
> fear ambush, huddle by coasts and rivers,
> the dark woods at their backs.

In the first line of this sentence, the rhythm enables the reader to practically hear something sneaking up in ambush. In the second and third lines, Nowlan uses *caesuras,* or pauses, to emphasize the images of those who "huddle" and of the "dark woods." Nowlan once stated in an interview in *Canadian Writers and Their Works: Poetry Series* that he relied upon irregularities and pauses in his sentence structures because "sometimes the break adds an additional level of meaning." Nowlan also strives to write in a manner that imitates how people speak. Another of Nowlan's influences, T. S. Eliot, stated in *A Poetry Handbook* that, "poetry must not stray too far from the ordinary everyday language which we use and hear." In "For Jean Vincent," Nowlan writes in a conversational tone, varying his sentences and rhythms as people would speak naturally. There is none of the rhyming or alliteration that more formal poems contain. They would detract from the deep texture for which Nowlan seems to be striving.

"For Jean Vincent" speaks in figurative language, using bold images and statements that are not meant to be taken literally. For instance, in the third stanza, trees cannot really throw back their heads and shout, and people cannot actually hear songs chanted by a long deceased warrior. Figurative language gives meaning not by what it says, but by how it stimulates the imagination. William Carlos Williams, writing in *Canadian Writers and Their Works: Poetry Series* penned the famous creed for modern poetry of "no ideas but in things." In other words, images of things can be more effective at getting across meaning than explanations with words. In "For Jean Vincent," Nowlan follows this theory, using images instead of ideas.

Nowlan uses allusion quite effectively in this poem as well. Alluding to historical figures adds an extra degree of description. The title of the poem alludes to a historical figure, Baron St. Castin, a French nobleman who went to Canada in the 1600s. This Baron created controversy by marrying a Native American woman and fighting with Indians against English settlers. The allusion in the title creates other connections from the past because the Baron St. Castin was written about by the American poet Longfellow. Another effective allusion occurs in the second stanza. Increase Mather is mentioned in the description of the "ghastly Calvinists" who haunt offices. The reader who is knowledgeable of history will recognize that Increase Mather was a man who was closely connected with the Salem witchcraft trials, a detail which makes the figures even more ghastly.

Allusions can be made to works of art as well as to people. In the final stanza, an allusion to *The Song of Roland* is made. This is an old epic French poem, and mentioning it establishes another connection between modern Canada and the Old World. This allusion also speaks of the power of poetry: words that are centuries old are just under the surface of things, are still present in the way people react to the world.

Source: Douglas Dupler, Critical Essay on "For Jean Vincent d'Abbadie, Baron St.-Castin," in *Poetry for Students,* The Gale Group, 2001.

Sources

Atwood, Margaret, ed., *The New Oxford Book of Canadian Verse in English,* Oxford University Press, 1982, pp. i–37.

Jung, Carl G., and M. L. von Franz, Joseph L. Henderson, Jolande Jacobi, and Aniela Jaffé, *Man and His Symbols,* Picador, 1978.

———, *Memories, Dreams, Reflections,* Collins, 1967.

Lecker, David, and Ellen Quigley, ed., *Canadian Writers and their Works: Poetry Series,* Vol. 7, ECW, 1990, pp. 87, 94, 96, 116.

Nowlan, Alden, *Bread, Wine and Salt,* Clarke, Irwin and Co., 1967.

———, *I'm a Stranger Here Myself,* Clarke, Irwin and Co., 1974.

———, *Playing the Jesus Game; Selected Poems,* with an introduction by Robert Bly, The Crossing Press, 1973.

Oliver, Mary, *A Poetry Handbook,* Harcourt Brace, 1994, p. 68.

Steele, Apollonia, and Jean F. Tener, eds., *The Alden Nowlan Papers: An Inventory of the Archive at the University of Calgary Libraries,* with Biocritical Essay by Robert Gibbs, University of Calgary Press, 1992.

Taylor, Aline S., *The French Baron of Pentagouet: Baron St. Castin and the Struggle for Empire in Early New England,* Picton Press, 1998.

Whitman, Walt, *Leaves of Grass,* The New American Library, 1958, p. 72.

For Further Study

Oliver, Michael Brian, *Poet's Progress: The Development of Alden Nowlan's Poetry,* Fiddlehead, 1978.

This is the most extensive (forty-eight pages) treatment of Nowlan's poetry to date. It traces the development of his verse from his earliest published poems to the work of his maturity.

Taylor, Aline S., *The French Baron of Pentagouet: Baron St. Castin and the Struggle for Empire in Early New England,* Picton Press, 1998.

This text is useful because it supplies the historical background to Nowlan's poem. Taylor describes the dramatic events in St.-Castin's life, ranging from escaping assassination attempts to leading Indian tribes into battle.

Toner, Patrick, *If I Could Turn and See Myself: The Life of Alden Nowlan,* Goose Lane Editions, 2000.

This text is the only full-length biography of Nowlan and sheds light on the relationship between his poetry and his life.

A Grafted Tongue

John Montague
1972

When "A Grafted Tongue" was first published in Montague's *The Rough Field* (1972), it did not bear the same title, which was supplied only when the poem was reprinted in Montague's *Selected Poems* in 1982. *The Rough Field* was intended as one long epic poem, and what is now known as "A Grafted Tongue" appeared as part five of a section entitled "A Severed Head," which was itself part four of *The Rough Field*. It was the old Gaelic rhyme that forms the epigraph to "A Severed Head" that provided the phrase that later became the title of the poem: "And who ever heard / such a sight unsung / As a severed head / With a grafted tongue?"

"A Grafted Tongue" is a terse, powerful poem that conveys a great deal in just ten short stanzas. It shows the disruption and suffering caused when one culture imposes its ways upon another. In this case, the English, who conquered Ireland in the seventeenth century, are in the process of enforcing the teaching of English in Irish schools. The result is that Gaelic, the native Irish language, is rapidly dying out, and with the loss of the language comes the loss of an entire culture. The poem implies that personal identity is bound up with the language of one's birth, the suppression of which produces a crisis in personal identity.

As part of *The Rough Field*, "A Grafted Tongue" marked a development in Montague's poetry in which he began to deal more directly with political topics related to Ireland. "A Grafted Tongue" draws inspiration from Ireland's past; and *The Rough Field* as a whole also includes material

John Montague

drawn from the turbulent situation that occurred in Northern Ireland during the 1960s and 1970s.

Author Biography

John Montague was born in Brooklyn, New York, on February 28, 1929, the third son of James Montague and Mary (Carney) Montague. The family was Irish, Montague's father having immigrated to New York in 1925.

Times were hard in Brooklyn during the depression years, and, in 1933, Montague was sent with his brothers to rural Garvaghey in County Tyrone, Northern Ireland, to live with his aunts on their farm. In 1940 he won a scholarship to St. Patrick's College, Armagh, from which he graduated in 1946. With the help of another scholarship, Montague attended University College, Dublin, from which he was awarded a B.A. in English and history in 1949 and an M.A. in Anglo-Irish literature in 1952.

The following year, Montague attended Yale Graduate School on a Fulbright Scholarship. Over the next three years, he studied at the University of Iowa Writer's Workshop and at the University of California, Berkeley, before returning to Ireland in 1956, where he settled in Dublin, working as an

editor at Bord Failte (Irish Tourist Board). Montague's first volume of poetry, *Forms of Exile,* was published in 1958.

In 1961 Montague moved to Paris and became Paris correspondent of *The Irish Times.* His second poetry collection, *Poisoned Lands,* was published in the same year. During the 1960s, as he returned to visit the places where he grew up, Montague began working on the poems that would later be published as *The Rough Field,* the book that contains "A Grafted Tongue." He also published the first of three volumes of short stories, *Death of a Chieftain, and Other Stories* in 1964, and two more volumes of poetry, *A Chosen Light* in 1967 and *Tides* in 1970.

After teaching at University College, Dublin, from 1968 to 1971, Montague took a position at University College, Cork, where he remained until 1988. During this period, he continued to publish frequently, including the poems in *A Slow Dance* (1975), and literary honors came his way. He was awarded the first Marten Toonder Award in 1977 and the Alice Hunt Bartlett Award from the Poetry Society of Great Britain in 1978 for *The Great Cloak.* A Guggenheim award from 1979 to 1980 enabled Montague to complete his *Selected Poems* (1982) and the long poem, *The Dead Kingdom* (1984).

Since 1989, Montague has regularly taught fiction workshops at the State University of New York at Albany. His recent publications include the short stories in *An Occasion of Sin* (1992), *The Love Poems* (1992), *Time in Armagh* (1993), and *Collected Poems* (1995).

Montague has two daughters by his second wife, Evelyn Robson, whom he married in 1973.

Poem Text

(Dumb,
bloodied, the severed
head now chokes to
speak another tongue:—

   As in   5
a long suppressed dream,
some stuttering garb-
led ordeal of my own)

   An Irish
child weeps at school   10
repeating its English.
After each mistake

   The master
gouges another mark

                15

on the tally stick
hung about its neck

   Like a bell
on a cow, a hobble
on a straying goat.
To slur and stumble   20

   In shame
the altered syllables
of your own name:
to stray sadly home

   and find   25
the turf cured width
of your parents' hearth
growing slowly alien:

   In cabin
and field, they still   30
speak the old tongue.
You may greet no one.

   To grow
a second tongue, as
harsh a humiliation   35
as twice to be born.

   Decades later
that child's grandchild's
speech stumbles over lost
syllables of an old order.   40

Poem Summary

Stanza 1

The first eight lines of "A Grafted Tongue" are enclosed in parentheses, separating them from the main body of the poem. Line 1, consisting of just one word, "Dumb," succinctly announces one of the poem's themes: the inability to communicate through a language that has been forcibly imposed on one's native tongue. Line 2 and the first part of line 3 reveal metaphorically the condition of a culture cut off from its own source of strength: it is a bloody, severed head. The head "chokes" as it tries to speak in another language; the language is indigestible.

Stanza 2

This verse expands metaphorically on the previous one, as the speaker addresses his reader directly. The severed head choking while it struggles to speak a foreign language is likened to a dream the poet had, the memory of which he suppressed for a long time. The dream refers to an upsetting experience of his own in which he was unable to speak properly because of a stutter. The implication is that this incident was more than a dream and refers to a real event in the speaker's life.

Stanza 3

These lines begin the story that forms the main substance of the poem. They can be read in a more literal way than the opening two stanzas. An Irish child at a rural school in Ireland, probably in the nineteenth century, weeps as he is forced against his will and in spite of his poor performance to learn English. Ireland at the time was ruled by England. The stanza ends ominously with the phrase "After each mistake," which suggests that dire punishment is in store for the child because of his lack of facility with the language. Although the gender of the child is unspecified, it is likely to be a boy, since education for girls during this time period was minimal.

Stanza 4

This stanza reveals that a stick, on which the schoolmaster makes ("gouges") a mark each time the child fails to perform a task successfully, is hung around the neck of the child. The use of the harsh word "gouge" suggests the aggression and violence of the act. The stick is called a "tally stick" because tally means to count or keep a record of (as in "tally sheet"). The child therefore carries in humiliating fashion the constant reminder of his failures.

Stanza 5

The tally stick is likened to a bell hung around the neck of a cow or a restraint ("hobble") attached to a straying goat. The last line refers to the experience of the child, who is unable to do more than "slur and stumble" as he tries to learn the unfamiliar words.

Stanza 6

The first line continues the incomplete sentence that ended the previous stanza. The child is enveloped in shame as he tries to pronounce his own name in the altered form of a different language. A Gaelic name sounds very different when it is transliterated into English, so the phrase "altered syllables" is meant literally.

The last line begins another phase of the story that the poem tells. The child returns home, dispirited and saddened by his day at school. The use of the word "stray" to describe his walk home hints that what he is being forced to learn at school alienates him from his own home. He is becoming a stray, without a real home. The verb "to stray" also means to deviate from what is right (that is, in learning an alien language), although this is not the child's fault. The description of the homecoming is not completed until the following stanza.

Stanza 7

In this stanza, the child returns home but finds that he is no longer comfortable there. Slowly his "parent's hearth" becomes alien to him. The phrase "parent's hearth" refers not only to the fireplace in the home; it also has a wider, metaphorical meaning, as the center of family life. The "turf cured width" of the hearth refers to the practice amongst the Irish in former times of using peat to heat their homes. Peat consists of dried blocks of decaying plant material, which is used for fuel. The word "peat" comes from the Medieval Latin "peta," meaning "piece of turf." The word "cured" is used in the sense of "hardened," that is, hardened by many years of burning peat.

Stanza 8

The child's family, as well as other local people, whether in "cabin" or "field," still speak Gaelic, the language of Ireland. But the boy can no longer communicate with them ("You may greet no one"). Perhaps this is because he is not permitted to speak to any of his neighbors in Gaelic, which may be the only language some of them understand.

Stanza 9

This stanza describes the momentous significance of being forced to speak in a language other than one's own. The poet refers to this as growing a "second tongue" and regards it as a great humiliation. Because language is so fundamental to personal identity, being forced to speak a language other than that of one's birth is like being born a second time. It fundamentally alters everything, in all areas of a person's life.

Stanza 10

This stanza provides an ironic twist to the poem. Decades after his experience in school, the child has grown into a man and has become a grandfather, too. The man's grandchild now faces a problem that is at once similar and yet opposite to the one faced by his grandfather in school. The grandson's speech "stumbles," just as his grandfather's did, over an unfamiliar language ("lost syllables"), but this time that language is Gaelic, not English. It must be assumed that English has be-

come completely dominant and that anyone who now tries to learn Gaelic must approach it as a difficult foreign language. And just as the language has been virtually lost in the span of only two generations, so has the ancient culture of Ireland ("an old order"), which was inextricably bound up in that language.

Themes

Culture Clash

The theme of a clash between two cultures is first made explicit in the third stanza, in which an Irish child is being forced to learn English. Much that can be implied here lies below the surface of the actual words of the poem. The two cultures involved—Irish and English—both have a long history, and in the nineteenth century, they were fundamentally incompatible. In terms of religion, Protestant England differed from Catholic Ireland; in terms of language, although both Gaelic and English are considered to be members of the Indo-European family of languages, they belong to widely separate subgroups and are only very remotely connected to each other. And in terms of geographic size and economic and military power, there was also a wide disparity between the two countries.

When two cultures clash, a lot more is involved for the vulnerable culture than the mere imposition of a foreign language. As the last line of the poem makes clear, the extinction of a native language leads to the loss of an entire culture, since language is the means through which culture is transmitted from one generation to the next. The phrase "an old order" conjures up that complex of elements, including language, religion, art, folklore, and a sense of a shared history, that together make up the culture of a nation—the way people view the world and their place in it. Since culture transmitted over generations makes up the body of the community, the loss of it leads metaphorically to the bloody "severed head" described in the poem. The violent image suggests the extreme difficulty and unnaturalness of having to learn the language of an alien culture. The individual who is forced to do so finds the language will not take root in the heart of his being, which remains attached to the native tradition. He becomes divided against himself. Over time, however, if the colonial power continues to suppress the native language, the original culture is entirely forgotten. This is forcefully implied in the ironic reversal in the final stanza, in which the Gaelic language, and with it the whole culture of which it is an expression, is perceived simply as a collection of syllables, not even as a coherent language. This is what Montague refers to in *The Rough Field* as "shards of a lost tradition."

Education

Although it is not central to its meaning, the poem does give an unflattering snapshot of the methods of education in nineteenth century Ireland. First, it suggests an inflexible system of rote learning. Second, although much is left to the imagination, it is fair to surmise that the stick tied around the child's neck is used not only as a humiliating punishment in itself but as a record for the assessment of future punishment. Third, it is apparent that the child is treated with no respect for his dignity as a human being or for his intelligence. He is regarded as no better than a cow, the stick is likened to a bell placed on a cow or to a device to reign in a straying goat. This suggests that, as far as schooling was concerned, children were regarded in the same light as animals and were trained in much the same way. It also suggests the contempt with which the English regarded the Irish, viewing them as savages little better than dumb animals. The fact that the gender of the child is not stated, and is therefore referred to by the impersonal pronoun "it," adds to this dehumanizing effect.

Language and Identity

The poem suggests that being compelled to learn the language of an occupying colonial power, as well as being denied the right to speak one's own language, is so fundamentally destructive that it annihilates one's sense of personal identity. It severs a person in two, as the image of the severed head in the first stanza implies. Stanza six, which shows the child stumbling over the pronunciation of its own name in the unfamiliar tongue, makes it clear how deep the wound goes. His name now appears to him as no more than a jumble of "altered syllables," and this cuts to the heart of who he understands himself to be. The following two stanzas, which show him becoming alienated from his own family, demonstrate this. The theme is continued in stanza nine, where, in a grotesque image, acquiring the new language is compared to growing a second tongue. This "grafted tongue" of the title suggests that the new tongue is unnatural; it has to be added from foreign material; it does not grow organically from the body of the person who must now employ it in the act of speech.

Topics for Further Study

- Research the subject of endangered languages and describe the measures being taken to save one such language.

- What are the arguments for and against bilingual education in the United States?

- Supporters of Esperanto (an artificial language invented in 1887 and developed for international use) say it would be better if everyone in the world spoke only one language. Do you agree?

- As of the year 2000, 58 percent of the 257.5 million people who use the Internet use it in English. The next biggest groups are Japanese (18 percent), German (13 percent), Spanish (11 percent), and French, Chinese, and Italian (11 percent each). Is it a good or a bad trend that the Internet is dominated by English-language sites and that English may be becoming the world language?

Style

Structure

The poem is constructed to reflect the pain and awkwardness of the child's reluctant attempt to learn English. All the stanzas begin with a short line, usually of two words only and consisting of no more than four syllables. This gives the impression of hesitancy or lack of fluency, as if someone is reading aloud something unfamiliar and therefore has to read in small doses, regardless of the length of the grammatical unit. The short lines, generally of only two feet (a metrical foot consists of two or three syllables), continue this choppy effect throughout the poem. The use of run-on lines (also known as enjambment) in which the unit of meaning carries over into the following line also contributes to this effect. It is easy to imagine from the poem the reluctant schoolchild reading line by line with little sense of the grammatical structure or meaning of each sentence.

In stanza two, the hyphenation of the word "garbled" and the fact that it is spread over two lines ("garb-/ led ordeal") creates a strong sense of the jagged, broken manner in which the language is being spoken.

Rhyme

As might be expected in a poem that records extreme discomfort with language, the poet makes little use of the pleasing effect of end rhyme (rhyme which occurs at the end of each line). However, on the one occasion that such a rhyme is used, it is done with great effect. In lines one and three in stanza six, "shame" rhymes with "name," which reinforces the idea that the forced learning of an alien language cuts to the roots of the child's sense of self; he can no longer recognize or clearly speak his own name, and this causes him shame at the deepest level of his self-awareness.

Alliteration

The alliteration (repetition of initial consonants) apparent in stanzas five and six, in which "slur," "stumble," "shame," "stray," and "sadly" occur within the space of five lines, conveys the full import of the distress caused to the child by his painful lessons in an alien language. The alliteration of "harsh" and "humiliation" in stanza nine has a similar effect.

Meter

The use of a trochaic foot (a heavily stressed syllable followed by a lightly stressed one) at the beginning of stanza four, line two ("gouges"), reinforces the harshness of the scene in the schoolroom. Two lines later, a similar effect is achieved by the use of a dactylic foot (a stressed syllable followed by two unstressed ones) in the phrase "hung about." Another example of a trochee placed at the beginning of a line for emphasis occurs in line three, stanza nine: "harsh a humiliation."

Historical Context

Conflict Between Ireland and England

The involvement of England in the affairs of Ireland goes back over eight hundred years, beginning in 1171 when the English king Henry II invaded the country. But for centuries, the Irish language continued to flourish. Irish culture was so strong that many English settlers became, it was said, more Irish than the Irish. This can be seen from the Statutes of Kilhenny in 1366, passed by the English authorities, which instructed all Eng-

lishmen in Ireland to retain English surnames and to speak English. At the end of the fifteenth century, another English king, Henry VII, attempted to make English the only language spoken in Ireland, but this measure met with little success. As late as the end of the sixteenth century, Irish Gaelic flourished in spite of the English presence.

This started to change in the seventeenth century, when England began to take over Ireland completely. English power was finally consolidated in 1690, when an Irish Catholic army was defeated at the Battle of the Boyne by a Protestant English force led by William of Orange.

Decline of Gaelic

Harsh laws against Catholics passed by the English parliament in the eighteenth century made it difficult for Ireland to prosper under English rule. One law stated that Irish Catholics were not allowed to teach in schools. Many illegal schools did spring up, however. Instruction was often in Gaelic, but there was a growing recognition amongst the Irish that English would provide them with more opportunities, since it was the language of politics, law, and commerce. For example, English was the language used by the Irish parliament in the last two decades of the eighteenth century. English became even more dominant after the Act of Union in 1800, under which Ireland was granted one hundred seats in the British House of Commons and twenty-eight seats in the House of Lords.

Historic grievances continued, however, and the nineteenth century saw more conflict between England and Ireland. The introduction by the British government of the National School System in 1831 ensured that the Irish language would go into even more rapid decline. All subjects were to be taught in English.

The great Irish famine of 1845–51, in which over one million people died, further eroded the speaking of Gaelic, since the famine hit hardest in poor, rural, Gaelic-speaking areas. And fear of another famine resulted in Irish parents instructing their children to learn English and emigrate to England, Australia, or the United States.

During this period, the schools in Ireland became even more repressive as far as the speaking of Irish was concerned. In *The Story of English,* Robert McCrum, William Cran, and Robert MacNeil put it this way:

> Gaelic-speaking children were punished with wooden gags, and subjected to mockery and humiliation. Brothers were encouraged to spy on sisters.

Compare & Contrast

- **1860s:** Gaelic is spoken by about thirteen percent of the Irish population; Irish schools teach English exclusively.

  1921: The newly independent Republic of Ireland makes Gaelic the official language of the nation, with English as the second official language, but, in practice, English dominates.

  1971: According to the census, the population of the parts of Ireland recognized as Irish-speaking is 66,840, or 1.4 percent of the total population of Ireland, north and south.

  Today: Although there are fewer Irish Gaelic speakers than in 1971, extensive efforts are made to keep the language alive. In 1996 a national Irish language television station is inaugurated by the Irish government. Gaelic is taught in Irish schools as a second language.

- **1860s–1880s:** The movement for Home Rule (independence) grows in Ireland, associated with the leadership of Charles Parnell (1846–1891).

  1921: Ireland wins independence from Britain, but six northern, Protestant-dominated counties remain under British rule.

  1960s and 1970s: The Catholic minority in Northern Ireland demands civil rights; violence erupts. There are many deaths as the Irish Republican Army targets British troops, and Catholics and Protestants indulge in killing sprees.

  Today: In 1998 a peace agreement is reached, which establishes a Northern Ireland Assembly and provides for more official cooperation between Northern Ireland and the Irish Republic. Ireland gives up its territorial claim on Northern Ireland. Over the next two years, the agreement undergoes many strains.

Under the regime of the tally-sticks, the child would wear a stick on a string round its neck. Every time the child used an Irish Gaelic word, the parents would cut a notch in the wood. At the end of the week, the village schoolmaster would tally up the notches and administer punishment accordingly. There was only one end in view: the eradication of Irish.

By the time in which "A Grafted Tongue" is set (probably around the 1860s or 1870s), only about thirteen percent of the Irish population spoke Gaelic, down from more than fifty percent at the beginning of the nineteenth century. Further decline was inevitable. According to the census figures of 1861, of all children in Ireland between the ages of two and ten, less than two percent spoke Gaelic exclusively.

The 1960s and 1970s: Violence in Ulster

In 1921 Ireland was partitioned. The twenty-six mostly Catholic southern counties of the island became the independent Republic of Ireland. The six predominantly Protestant counties in the north, known as Ulster, remained under British rule.

For nearly fifty years, Northern Ireland was relatively peaceful, but during the 1960s resentment began to build among the Catholic minority, who made up over one-third of the population. Catholics suffered extensive discrimination in jobs, education, and housing. Electoral districts were manipulated so that the Protestants held all the power in the Northern Irish parliament. In the late 1960s, the Catholics began campaigning for civil rights, and there were violent clashes between Catholics and Protestants on the streets of Belfast, the capital city. In 1969 the British government sent troops to Belfast to keep the peace between the two sides.

However, the violence only escalated. The terrorist group, the Irish Republican Army (IRA), took up the Catholic cause. The aim of the IRA was to eject the British by force from Northern Ireland and reunite the Republic of Ireland with the North. In response, Protestant militants, who wanted to retain their link with Britain, formed their own paramilitary groups. The result was an explosion of deadly violence. Atrocities were committed on both sides.

In 1972, the year in which "A Grafted Tongue" was published, 274 people were killed in violence related to the political situation. In the same year, Britain increased the number of its troops in the province to 22,000. In one notorious incident on January 30, 1972, British troops fired on demonstrators after a rally at Londonderry. Thirteen Irish civilians were killed. The tragedy became known as "Bloody Sunday." Two months later, Britain suspended the Northern Irish parliament and imposed direct rule on the province from London.

Critical Overview

When *The Rough Field* was published in 1972, it met with considerable praise from reviewers in literary magazines. Scottish poet Hugh MacDiarmid comments that "The whole thing has the restraint of something profoundly felt, and the movement from section to section evinces a complete grasp and understanding of all the main constituents of Ulster's life and history from the earliest times to the present." In the same review, MacDiarmid quotes Irish poet Seamus Heaney's observation that "The encroachment of the English plantations on the native way of life and the cultural schizophrenia that ensued when the natives are half-subservient to the new law and language provide the starting point for many of the lyrics." Heaney then quotes stanza nine of "A Grafted Tongue" to emphasize his point. Derek Mahon, in *The Malahat Review,* calls *The Rough Field* "a prolonged meditation on a single theme: the death of a culture." For D. E. S. Maxwell, in *Critical Quarterly,* the dominant themes of the long poem are "exile and home," and these themes are made up of elements that include, as "A Grafted Tongue" shows, "a persecuted culture and its language."

Much of *The Rough Field* was reprinted in Montague's *Selected Poems* in 1982, where "A Grafted Tongue" first appears under that title as a complete poem in its own right.

"A Grafted Tongue" seems to be surviving the test of time. R. T. Smith, in a review of Montague's *Collected Poems* (1995) in *The Southern Review,* singles it out for special praise, commenting that "nowhere is the Irish-speaker's dilemma more painfully and memorably reported than in 'A Grafted Tongue.'" Smith quotes the poem in its entirety and offered this analysis:

> The poem's hard consonants and sharp vowels, reinforced by the truncation of syntax across the lines

and the crisp, angling-in rhymes, express anger but not rancor. The master, dominant as a priest or landlord, bells the shamed child like a cow—the animal that once measured Irish tribal wealth. 'Altered' and 'ordeal' underscore the religious and feudal elements of the predicament, but the 'turf-cured' hearth may offer a gleam of hope.

"A Grafted Tongue" is typical of Montague's work because it shows his concern for the cultural and political history of Ulster and because it links that theme to his recurrent interest in the nature of personal identity. As Ben Howard puts it in a review of Montague's *Collected Poems,* "For nearly four decades John Montague has probed the intricacies of history and the enigmas of selfhood. At once a gifted lyric poet and a passionate cultural historian, he has limned the convergences of history and self, taking his own difficult experience as prime example."

Criticism

Bryan Aubrey

Aubrey holds a Ph.D. in English and has published many essays on twentieth-century literature. In this essay, he examines Montague's poem in terms of its mingling of the personal and the political, its relationship to The Rough Field *of which it is a part, and its relevance for today's world.*

In his terse poem "A Grafted Tongue," Montague presents a series of powerful snapshots of the process by which a colonizing power uses language to cement its control over a subject people. It also shows how this process wrenches apart the entire established order of the dispossessed culture and causes great personal suffering.

Like the epic poem *The Rough Field* of which it is a part, "A Grafted Tongue" is a personal poem as well as a political one. The story of the weeping child in nineteenth century rural Ireland, who is forced to unlearn his native Gaelic and replace it with English, is framed by two autobiographical references.

The first of these references occurs in the second stanza, which is part of the parenthetical introduction to the main part of the poem. The poet refers to "some stuttering garb-/ led ordeal of my own." This is the only occurrence in the poem of the first person, and it may well be a reference to the poet's own childhood. At the age of nine, Montague developed a stammer when called upon to recite a poem at his school. For several years, he visited a speech therapist in Belfast. The fact that this ordeal (or some incident similar to it) is referred to as "a long suppressed dream" suggests that it had a lasting, if largely unconscious, effect on the poet. It also serves his purpose by introducing the story that follows, which is set probably seventy or eighty years earlier than the boyhood experience the poet recalls.

The personal reference returns in the final stanza, although it is somewhat veiled. The grandchild of the child in the poem is quite probably the poet himself. Montague records in his essay, "On Translating Irish, Without Speaking It," which appears in his collection *The Figure in the Cave and Other Stories,* that he first learned Irish Gaelic as a boy. This happened after school, when "an enthusiastic priest came to teach us poor northern children our lost heritage." Montague admits that at first he loathed the subject, and it is this early experience that is surely reflected in the closing lines of "A Grafted Tongue," in which the child's speech "stumbles over lost / syllables of an old order." The "lost syllables" are a reference to Irish Gaelic, and the "old order" is the whole culture of which Gaelic was the foundation. Montague reports that he continued to have no interest in Gaelic until he "greeted the last Gaelic speaker in the area after mass one Sunday, and saw the light flood across her face."

The subtle interweaving of the political and the personal, the past and the present, the individual and the collective that underlies "A Grafted Tongue" is present throughout *The Rough Field.* It is Montague's way of bringing into focus over four hundred years of Ulster history by showing its impact on his own relatives and on other people he knew. In fact, it is not possible to fully understand "A Grafted Tongue" without examining the context in which the poem was first published—as one untitled part of a subsection of one long poem.

"A Grafted Tongue" forms the fifth part of section IV of *The Rough Field.* Section IV is entitled "A Severed Head," a phrase that provides an additional explanation for the severed head that is mentioned in stanza one of "A Grafted Tongue." The phrase has three meanings. First, it refers to the violence with which the English conquered Ireland—a woodcut made in 1581 and reprinted in *The Rough Field* shows Elizabethan English soldiers holding up their swords on which are mounted the heads of their defeated Irish foes. Second, the phrase refers to the aftermath of the seventeenth

> *The subtle interweaving of the political and the personal, the past and the present, the individual and the collective that underlies 'A Grafted Tongue' is present throughout The Rough Field. It is Montague's way of bringing into focus over four hundred years of Ulster history...."*

century conquest of Ireland. In 1601 the Ulster Irish, led by Hugh O'Neill, whose ancient family seat in County Tyrone was close to the village where Montague grew up, were defeated at the Battle of Kinsale. O'Neill and other Irish nobles fled into exile in Europe. Hence, Ireland, having lost its leaders, was like a body without a head. It is this defining event in Ulster's history that is referred to in part 4 of "A Severed Head," the last stanza of which reads thus:

Disappearance & death
of a world, as down Lough Swilly
the great ship, encumbered with nobles,
swells its sails for Europe:
The Flight of the Earls.

The "death of a world," the destruction of Irish culture, leads directly into part 5 of "A Severed Head." This is "A Grafted Tongue," which shows the same process going on in the confused and anguished mind of a small child. The image of the severed head now acquires a third meaning as the poet applies it to the level of the individual. The child is metaphorically torn in two; there is no coordination between the head that is being told to speak English and the remainder of the child's being, which has presumably absorbed the Irish Gaelic language in its bloodstream since the cradle. The result is choking, stammering, and slurring and the progressive alienation of the child from everything that has helped to shape his early outlook on the world and his sense of self. One of the

What Do I Read Next?

- Irish writer Brian Friel's play *Translations* (first performed in 1980) deals with the same problem as Montague's "A Grafted Tongue," the erosion of Irish language and culture by the colonizing English. The play is set in rural Ireland in 1833, at a Gaelic-speaking school, where pressure is mounting for instruction to be given in English.

- Besides being a poet, Montague is also a short story writer. Most of the nine stories in *Death of a Chieftain, and Other Stories* (1967) are set in Ulster; five of them focus on childhood and youth.

- *The Penguin Book of Contemporary Irish Poetry* (1990), edited by Peter Fallon and Derek Mahon, is a selection of the best poetry published by Irish poets since the 1950s.

- Like Montague, Irish poet Seamus Heaney, who won the Nobel Prize for Literature in 1995, was raised as a Catholic in Ulster. His *Opened Ground: Selected Poems 1966–1996* (1999) is a representative selection of the work that has made him Ireland's most acclaimed contemporary poet.

- Thomas Cahill's provocatively titled, much-praised *How the Irish Saved Civilization: The Untold Story of Ireland's Heroic Role from the Fall of Rome to the Rise of Medieval Europe* (1995) tells the story of how Irish scribes and scholars, long before Ireland became dominated by England, were instrumental in saving the classical literature of Greece and Rome after the Dark Ages descended on the rest of Europe.

most powerful lines in the whole poem, which is the only line that consists of one complete sentence, is the grim and emphatic, "You may greet no one." The line refers to the child's profound isolation as he wends his way home, cut off from the language of his birth, which is still spoken in the fields and countryside of old Ireland. The distraught child is

literally speechless, exactly as the first, one-word line of the poem dramatically foretells: "Dumb."

It is clear that the poet regards language as absolutely essential to the preservation of a culture. The culture cannot survive if an alien tongue supplants the language upon which it rests. Particularly illuminating in this respect is part 2 of "A Severed Head," in which the poet describes the impressions of his homeland in Ulster, when he returns after an absence of many years. Surveying the landscape and recalling the old Gaelic culture now lost to view, the metaphor that he employs is one of language and of reading:

> The whole landscape a manuscript
> We had lost the skill to read,
> A part of our past disinherited;
> But fumbled, like a blind man,
> Along the fingertips of instinct.

Only fragments, "shards / Of a lost culture," remain, but the poet puts the best possible gloss on them. In part 6, the final part of "A Severed Head," he shows that traces of the lost language can still be found in present-day Ulster, in the form of place names. Many of these are translations of the names first given to them in Gaelic. The poet states that "even English in these airts / Took a lawless turn," and he implies that otherwise there would never be places known by such names as Black Lough, Bloody Brae, or a stream called the Routing Burn.

Some place names go back even further or combine the Scots and Irish heritage:

> And what of stone-age Sess Kill Green
> Tullycorker and Tully glush?
> Names twining braid Scots and Irish,
> Like Fall Brae, springing native
> As a whitethorn bush?

In his essay "On Translating Irish, Without Speaking It," Montague writes, "Like a stream driven underground, Irish still ran under the speech and names of my childhood." He learned that Garvaghey (in Irish Gaelic it is spelled *garbhachaidh*), the village in which he was brought up, meant the Rough Field. It is this that supplied the title of the long poem. The town of Glencull, where Montague went to school, is a Gaelic word meaning "The Glen of the Hazels," and nearby Clogher means "The Golden Stone." Both these are names with which "A Severed Head," part IV of *The Rough Field,* concludes.

Although "A Grafted Tongue" is set mostly in nineteenth century rural Ireland, the story it tells of the gradual erosion of a language and a culture has a continuing relevance for today's world. When

Scottish poet Hugh MacDiarmid reviewed *The Rough Field* in 1973, he describes it as "a long poem of tremendous value at a time when all over the world millions of people are conscious of having been torn away from their roots and trying to re-root themselves in their indigenous languages and traditions." This astute comment, made a generation ago, applies even more urgently to the twenty-first century, wherever two opposing trends jostle together uncomfortably.

Today, the process of language extinction is proceeding at a pace faster than ever before. It is estimated that of the world's current 6,528 languages, half will vanish within the next one hundred years. In earlier times, language suppression was often the result of domination by an economically and militarily superior colonial power. Imperialism, however, went into rapid decline in the second half of the twentieth century, although this has not stopped the oppression of ethnic minorities and their languages within certain nation-states (one example is the struggle of the Kurds in Turkey). But today, the threat to the diversity of the world's languages is caused mostly by the phenomenon of economic globalization, which is accompanied by the steady march of English as the world's dominant language.

On the other hand, there are vigorous movements in many parts of the world, including Ireland, Spain, and the United States, aimed at keeping indigenous languages alive. The struggle is often an uphill one. In the Republic of Ireland, for example, according to the *Unesco Red Book of Endangered Languages,* there may be less than 20,000 speakers of Irish Gaelic. The number that use the language on a daily basis may be even less than that. And in the six counties that make up Northern Ireland, Irish Gaelic is considered by the Unesco report to be extinct—a fact that gives Montague's "A Grafted Tongue" a poignant and even tragic flavor.

Source: Bryan Aubrey, Critical Essay on "A Grafted Tongue," in *Poetry for Students,* The Gale Group, 2001.

Douglas Dupler

Dupler is a published writer and critic. In the following essay he discusses the distinctions between modernism and postmodernism, and how Montague's poem embodies characteristics of both movements.

The movement called postmodernism began not long after World War II. Artists, poets, and writers in this period had grown up on the ideas

> *In the middle of these two world views is John Montague, a minor poet who, like the modernists, believes that poets should find beauty in the older, more traditional ways of life that are disappearing. Montague also strives to 'make it new' by experimenting with forms and styles."*

and works of modernism but were also profoundly shaken by the major changes caused by the Second World War, the Holocaust, the atomic bomb, the Cold War, and other events. Postmodern artists and writers were no longer as idealistic about their works. They were not as confident, as were the modernists, that they had the power in their words and works to change the world. Postmodern artists and writers tended not to be as preoccupied with beauty either, often displaying an ironic acceptance of the changes that modernists saw as ugly and threatening.

Other changes have also influenced postmodern artists and writers, including those changes brought about by technology. The information explosion has changed the way people view the world and the self. The world is changing too fast to keep up with, and the self is becoming "fragmented," or confused and broken up, because people can't make sense of all the different messages. Transportation technology has opened up all parts of the world, and many people are immigrating to new places and living as strangers in new cultures. The increased speed of life makes things superficial instead of deep. Postmodern artists and writers attempt to show all these new conditions in their works. Critics still consider the world to be in the midst of the postmodern period.

In the middle of these two world views is John Montague, a minor poet who, like the modernists, believes that poets should find beauty in the older, more traditional ways of life that are disappearing. Montague also strives to "make it new" by experimenting with forms and styles. Of this he once wrote in an essay that can be found in Garratt's book, "I would hope for a more experimental approach, if [Northern Ireland writers] are to confront the changes in their society." Montague occasionally also tries to make his poetry engage politics, a modernist practice. However, like the postmodernists, Montague deals with accelerating change and a more cosmopolitan view of the world, which shows the immigrant experience of cultures colliding. For Montague, quoted in *Irish Poetry: Politics, History, Negotiation* by Steven Matthews, the "poet should be familiar with the finest work of his contemporaries . . . in other languages." And owing to both movements, Montague knows that the poet must strive to understand the self in the midst of all its influences. He writes that poetry's "real purpose [is] the imaginative and honest expression of the writer's own problems."

Of course, it is hard to deduce all of this from one simple poem like "A Grafted Tongue," but this poem shows evidence of some of the central themes of Montague's work and does so in a very efficient way. It could be argued that the form of the poem is experimental, particularly when taken in context. "A Grafted Tongue" is from a collection of poems called *The Rough Field,* which is an experimental book consisting of a wide variety of forms and techniques, influenced by the modernist penchant for experimentation. "A Grafted Tongue" has a deceptively simple form: ten separate *quatrains,* or stanzas, consisting of four lines each. This structure was used by the modernist poet Ezra Pound. This simple form is a departure from the style of Irish poetry since Yeats, which often consists of long, eloquent sentences.

The rhythm of "A Grafted Tongue" is simple but irregular, serving a purpose toward the poem's meaning. The first line of each stanza generally has one stressed, or strong, syllable, while the other lines tend to be *dimeter lines,* or lines consisting of two stressed syllables. The first stanza of the poem illustrates this:

Dumb,
Bloodied, the severed
head now chokes to
speak another tongue:—

However, this rhythm is not entirely consistent, making it an *irregular rhythm.* This is an example of how form may help reinforce the content

or meaning of a poem. The irregular rhythm of the language has the effect of getting across the difficulty the child experiences when forced to change languages. In the same vein, to illustrate the "stuttering" of the third line in the second stanza, Montague divides the word "garbled" into two lines, a visual stutter to the reader.

The language that Montague uses illustrates how he relies on two differing techniques. Modern poets, like Yeats, loved to make beautiful poetic language full of music and rhyming, while postmodern poets often deliberately avoid using classical poetic language. Montague does both. He uses poetic language such as alliteration and rhyme. To illustrate the "slur and stumble" of the last line of the fifth stanza, Montague uses a nice example of alliteration in the sixth stanza:

In shame
the altered syllables
of your own name;
to stray sadly home

Montague also uses *consonant rhymes,* in which consonant sounds are the same at the end of words instead of at the beginning, as with alliteration. In the fourth stanza, at the end of the second line, "mark," is a consonant rhyme with the end of the fourth line, "neck." This type of rhyme is repeated in following stanzas, with "width" and "hearth," for example. Montague also uses *near rhymes,* such as in the third stanza with "Irish" and "English," and in the fifth stanza with "hobble" and "stumble." These rhymes are called near rhymes because the unstressed syllables of the words are the syllables that rhyme. Full rhymes, where the stressed syllables rhyme, are also present in the poem, as in the sixth stanza, in which "shame" rhymes with "name." Montague also uses *assonance,* or the repetition of vowel sounds, such as in the first stanza, with the words, "Dumb," "bloodied," "another," and "tongue." But none of these rhymes or rhythms is consistent throughout the poem, giving the "garbled" quality of the "grafted tongue." This inconsistency also lends a fragmented quality to the poem's manner of description.

The fragmentation and confusion of the child's sense of self, a postmodern idea, is illustrated with *diction* and *imagery.* A grafted tongue is a sudden change in language where the roots still remain, buried deep. Some words Montague chooses lend a particular *texture* to the poem: "dumb," "bloodied," "chokes," "suppressed," "dream," "weeps," "mistake," and so on. The "severed head" and the "garbled ordeal" are strong images of splitting up, and "the bell on a cow" and the "hobble on a straying goat" are images of confusion and the dismay of being lost. The person in the poem confronts a world that either punishes or causes "shame." The poem never gives a vivid sense of place either, and the subject of the poem, a child, remains vague and anonymous. The child's parents are "growing alien," and the child "may greet no one" in the cold world. This vagueness and anonymity of the individual is what some intellectuals have termed the "postmodern condition." The poem also moves around in time very quickly, starting with a young child in school and ending up far in the future, with the "child's grandchild" still connecting to "an old order" in the poem's final lines.

The politics that the poem engages are subtle but telling. The poem is placed by a passing reference to the "Irish" and "English," but politics actually pervade the poem. The child's problem in the poem is representative of an entire cultural problem; indeed, the cultural problem has overwhelmed and damaged the child, another postmodern theme. Keenly conscious of this cultural problem, Montague writes in *The Figure in the Cave and Other Essays,* "After living abroad for over a decade, I came to the conclusion that . . . it is almost impossible for a poet to change languages. And yet this is what happened to Irish poetry."

Source: Douglas Dupler, Critical Essay on "A Grafted Tongue," in *Poetry for Students,* The Gale Group, 2001.

Sources

Garratt, Robert F., *Modern Irish Poetry,* University of California, 1986, pp. 200, 208.

Howard, Ben, review of *Collected Poems* by John Montague, in *Poetry,* Vol. 171, No. 4, February 1998, pp. 279–282.

MacDiarmid, Hugh, "John Montague's Ulster," in *Agenda,* Vol. 11, Nos. 2–3, Spring–Summer 1973, pp. 109–111.

Mahon, Derek, Review in *The Malahat Review,* No. 27, July 1973, pp. 132–137.

Matthews, Steven, *Irish Poetry: Politics, History, Negotiation,* St. Martin's, 1997, p. 128.

McCrum, Robert, William Cran, and Robert MacNeil, *The Story of English,* Viking Penguin, 1986.

Montague, John, *Collected Poems,* Wake Forest University Press, 1995.

———, *The Figure in the Cave, and Other Essays,* Syracuse University Press, 1989, p. 37.

———, *The Rough Field,* Wake Forest University Press, 1972.

———, *Selected Poems,* Oxford University Press, 1982.

Salminen, Tapani, *Unesco Red Book of Endangered Languages: Europe,* online at http://www.helsinki.fi/~tasalmin/europe_index.html, (September 22, 1999).

Smith, R. T., Review in *The Southern Review,* Vol. 34, No. 1, Winter 1998.

For Further Study

Heaney, Seamus, *Preoccupations: Selected Prose, 1968–1978,* Faber and Faber, 1980.
   Irish poet Heaney discusses Montague's sense of place. There are also essays on Wordsworth, Keats, Hopkins, Yeats, Patrick Kavanagh, and Robert Lowell.

Kernowski, Frank L., *John Montague,* Bucknell University Press, 1975.
   This is the only book-length critical work about Montague; it discusses his poetry and short stories up to and including *The Rough Field.*

MacManus, Seumas, *The Story of the Irish Race,* Devin-Adair, 1972.
   This book presents the story of Irish history from ancient to modern times in a readable way, examining the Irish mind and culture, as well as Ireland's long political struggle.

Mariani, Paul, "John Montague," in *Dictionary of Literary Biography,* Volume 40: *Poets of Great Britain and Ireland Since 1960,* edited by Vincent B. Sherry Jr., Gale, 1985, pp. 380–395.
   This survey of Montague's life and work describes him as "one of the few indispensable voices coming out of Ireland today." Contains an extensive bibliography.

Wallace, Martin, *A Short History of Ireland,* Barnes and Noble, 1996.
   This short (168 page) book examines Irish history with particular emphasis on its difficult relationship with Britain.

Having a Coke with You

Frank O'Hara

1960

Frank O'Hara's love poem, "Having a Coke with You," was first published in a small press magazine called *Love*. O'Hara wrote the poem four days after returning to New York City from a business trip in Spain on April 21, 1960. "Having a Coke with You" is one of many love poems that O'Hara composed during his love affair with Vincent Warren, a dancer with whom O'Hara was madly in love. "Having a Coke with You" expresses O'Hara's idea that poems can be as direct and personal as telephone conversations. It describes the affection O'Hara felt for Warren. By listing the details of his love for Warren, then comparing them to his own activities in Spain, and great works of Western art, O'Hara compares art to the real experience of a lover's company and beauty. O'Hara was an associate curator for the Museum of Modern Art in New York and while in Spain, organized a show called "New Spanish Painting and Sculpture." References to paintings and sculpture, such as Duchamp's *Nude Descending a Staircase* and Marino Marini's *Horse and Rider,* suggests that the artists were not necessarily in love with their subjects. Throughout the poem O'Hara juxtaposes life and art. Life, in O'Hara's interpretation is always the better of the two; it is dynamic and unmediated.

The poem is short, written in long, largely unpunctuated lines, giving it a breathless quality. His use of repetition, detail, and imagery give the poem a cartoonish and hallucinatory sensation.

Author Biography

The first child of Russell J. and Katherine Broderick O'Hara, Francis Russell O'Hara, was born in Baltimore, Maryland, on June 27, 1926. Shortly thereafter, the family moved to Grafton, Massachusetts, where his father managed the family's three farms. Rural life, however, never appealed to O'Hara. He was drawn to the activity and energy of cities. "I can't even enjoy a blade of grass," he once wrote, "unless I know there's a subway handy or a record store or some other sign that people do not totally *regret* life." O'Hara's first love was music. He began taking lessons at the age of seven and later studied piano at the New England Conservatory, nurturing a desire to become a concert pianist. After serving two years as a sonar operator on the destroyer *U.S.S. Nicholas,* O'Hara enrolled at Harvard University under the G.I. Bill of Rights. He first majored in music and then English literature. At Harvard, O'Hara made friends with a number of artists, musicians, and poets, including Edward Gorey, Kenneth Koch, John Ashbery, and James Schuyler. Later, the four were known as members of the New York School of Poets. Encouraged by poet and teacher John Ciardi, O'Hara enrolled at the University of Michigan and won a prestigious Hopwood Award for his poetry. He also received a master of arts degree in literature in 1951.

After graduating from the University of Michigan, O'Hara moved to New York City, working at a number of low-level jobs at the Museum of Modern Art. He began writing reviews for *Art News* before landing a position as special assistant to the director of MOMA's (Museum of Modern Art) International Program. O'Hara befriended many artists and poets in the city. In particular, he became friends with Abstract Expressionist painters such as Jackson Pollock, Larry Rivers, Willem de Kooning, and Franz Kline. His knowledge and passion for the art world directly influenced his poetry. "Sometimes I think I'm in love with painting," he once wrote. O'Hara's reputation as a poet—already established in literary circles—burgeoned in 1957 with the publication of *Meditations in an Emergency,* his first book with a commercial press. That reputation became national in 1960 when Donald Allen published a large group of his poems in the ground-breaking anthology *The New American Poetry, 1945–60,* a book that poet and Beat cultural icon Allen Ginsberg described as "a great blow for liberty." Other O'Hara poetry collections include *Oranges* (1953), *Second Avenue*

Frank O'Hara

(1960), *Odes* (1960), and *Lunch Poems* (1965). *Having a Coke with You* was originally published the same year as *Odes,* appearing in a small press magazine called *Love* and then later in his collection entitled *Love Poems (Tentative Title).*

O'Hara was appointed associate curator for MOMA in 1965 and was in line to be promoted to full curator when, on July 25, 1966, he died after being hit by a dune buggy on Fire Island in New York the day before. *The Collected Poems of Frank O'Hara,* published posthumously and edited by Donald Allen, received the National Book Award in 1971.

Poem Text

Having a Coke with You

is even more fun than going to San Sebastian, Irun,
    Hendaye, Biarritz, Bayonne,
or being sick to my stomach on the Travesera de
    Gracia in Barcelona
partly because in your orange shirt you look like a
    better happier St. Sebastian
partly because of my love for you, partly because   5
    of your love for yoghurt
partly because of the fluorescent orange tulips
    around the birches
partly because of the secrecy our smiles take on
    before people and statuary

it is hard to believe when I'm with you that there
    can be anything as still
as solemn as unpleasantly definitive as statuary
    when right in front of it
in the warm New York 4 o'clock light we are   10
    drifting back and forth
between each other like a tree breathing through its
    spectacles

and the portrait show seems to have no faces in it
    at all, just paint
you suddenly wonder why in the world anyone
    ever did them
    I look
at you and I would rather look at you than all the   15
    portraits in the world

except possibly for the Polish Rider occasionally
    and anyway it's in the Frick
which thank heavens you haven't gone to yet so
    we can go together the first time
and the fact that you move so beautifully more or
    less takes care of Futurism
just as at home I never think of the Nude
    Descending a Staircase or
at a rehearsal a single drawing of Leonardo or   20
    Michelangelo that used to wow me
and what good does all the research of the
    Impressionists do them
when they never got the right person to stand near
    the tree when the sun sank
or for that matter Marino Marini when he didn't
    pick the rider as carefully
as the horse
    it seems they were all cheated of some   25
    marvellous experience
which is not going to go wasted on me which is
    why I'm telling you about it

Poem Summary

Lines 1–10

The first line of "Having a Coke with You" is a predicate to the title. The speaker lists the reasons why he would rather have a Coke with the person he loves. The list of names in the first line refers to the cities in Spain on O'Hara's itinerary. The second line refers to a hangover the author had after a night of food and drink in Barcelona; he had vomited in the gutter of Cuixart's house. Lines three through six provide the details of his adoring love affair. St. Sebastian, referenced to in the third line, was a Roman martyr and is considered to be a protector against the plague. His death is often foreshadowed within the poem by images of arrows piercing his body. The last four lines of the stanza underscore the speaker's belief that being with his lover is a more enjoyable experience than observing art. The speaker compares the dynamics of his feelings for his love to motionless statues: "it is

Media Adaptations

- The Academy of American Poets sponsors a Frank O'Hara page at http://www.poets.org/poets/poets.cfm?prmID=165 (January 2001), with links to articles on the poet.

- A Frank O'Hara website, at http://www.frankohara.com/Pages/MainPage.html (January 2001), incorporates links to other O'Hara websites.

- American Poetry Archives released *Frank O'Hara Second Edition* in 1978. This video features outtakes from the 1966 NET series *USA: Poetry* and shows O'Hara discussing poetry with filmmaker Al Leslie.

- Recycled Video put out a film diary by Jonas Mekas called *Lost, Lost, Lost,* which includes Mekas discussing his friendships with O'Hara and other poets such as Allen Ginsberg and LeRoi Jones.

- New Albion Records released *Three Voices: for Joan La Barbara* in 1989. This compact disc features O'Hara's poem "Wind" set to music by Morton Feldman.

hard to believe when I'm with you there can be anything as still / as solemn as unpleasantly definitive as statuary." The final lines offer a simile. The speaker compares himself and his lover to a "tree breathing through its spectacles." This surreal image joins the qualities of a statue and the qualities of a human being.

Lines 11–23

Lines eleven and twelve refer to an art exhibition O'Hara recently attended. Still caught in the intensity of his feelings for his lover, the speaker cannot appreciate the beauty of the paintings; he wonders why someone would take the trouble to paint them. The speaker continues the comparisons. In the first stanza, he compares his lover to great works of Western art. His lover, for example, far surpasses all art except in the rare case of Rembrandt's *Polish Rider*. The painting, oil on canvas painted in 1655, depicts a writer who was evicted from Poland for publishing a pamphlet in Amsterdam in the defense of free-thinking. The painting expresses the sympathy of the painter for the just cause of free-thinking. O'Hara is drawn to the subject matter and the beauty of the painting. The Frick is a museum in New York City that houses many of the world's art masterpieces. Line seventeen notes how his lover moves "so beautifully" and refers to Warren's life as a dancer. Futurism was an art movement in the early twentieth century that valorized machines, motion, and speed. Art from this movement attempts to depict successful active positions of a subject simultaneously.

O'Hara underscores his obsession with Warren when he suggests that the dancer occupies his entire attention and he does not even think of art that "used to wow me" when he's in the presence of Warren's dancing. He comments on Marcel Duchamp's painting *Nude Descending a Staircase,* and Leonardo DaVinci and Michelangelo, implying that they pale in comparison to Warren's love. In lines 20 through 23, O'Hara extends his thinking by suggesting that all the great painters would have been greater if they focused less on technique and research and focused more on finding passionate subjects. This idea embodied the image of having the "right person to stand near the tree when the sun sank." The meaning behind this verse revolves around the need for painters to play a creative role in their paintings. He repeats this idea when he says that Marino Marini "didn't pick the rider as carefully as the horse." Marino Marini was a twentieth-century Italian sculptor whose work consisted largely of horses and riders. His best known work is *Horseman* (1952), housed in the Walker Art Museum of Minneapolis, Minnesota. The artists were more concerned with representations of beauty than real life beauty. O'Hara concludes, "it seems they were all cheated out of some marvelous experience."

Themes

Art and Experience

"Having a Coke with You" privileges the flux of experience over the static nature of art. Rather than representing a thing, such as a face or a horse and its rider, O'Hara's poem attempts to represent the rush of emotion itself. O'Hara captures the breathless quality of experience by launching into the poem immediately, making the first line a continuation of the title, and then piling up perceptions and thoughts. Beat writers Jack Kerouac and Allen

Topics for Further Study

- In line 20 the speaker asks "what good does all the research of the Impressionists do them[?]" Who were the Impressionists and what role do they play in this poem? Can O'Hara's poem be considered an Impressionist poem? Why or why not?

- O'Hara's poem addresses the relationship between art and life. Using examples from your own experiences, describe the ways in which art can be said to imitate life and vice versa.

- Write a love poem comparing the object of your love to a thing or an activity that you also love. How does your poem compare to O'Hara's poem in terms of relating your two love objects? Do they share a certain tone, style, form, and rhythm?

- O'Hara wrote this poem in 1960, before public professions of love for the same sex became accepted. Rewrite this poem as you think O'Hara might write it today.

Ginsberg wrote in a similar way. They transcribed their thinking as it happened and revised very little. Fellow New York School poets John Ashbery and James Schuyler also practiced this kind of poetic composition.

Love and Passion

It has often been said that love is blind. O'Hara plays with this notion, suggesting that although blindness may perhaps be a consequence of love, it is also pleasurable, desirable, and an emotional state from which people can learn. O'Hara's poem is replete with visual imagery and allusions. The smiles of the speaker and his lover take on a "secrecy"—alluding to the public discretion to which gay couples had to adhere in mid-century America—but, it also enhances the relationship. The speaker describes the way in which their selves mix, as they drift "back and forth / between each other like a tree breathing through its spectacles." Being in love causes the speaker to think about how others can possibly live in the world without love. At an art museum, he sees "no faces . . . just paint," and proclaims to his lover "I would rather look at you than all the portraits in the world." This type of hyperbole is often common to those who are passionately in love and want to express that love to the object of one's feelings. In poetry, this tradition is long. One can think of Andrew Marvell's poem "To His Coy Mistress," for example, in which the speaker uses hyperbolic flattery in an attempt to seduce a woman. O'Hara's goal, however, is not seduction but rather an adequate description of his love. This description also carries with it a lesson for others. That lesson, spelled out in the poem's final two lines, is similar to the argument that Marvell attempts in his poem: life is short; seize the day, and choose love.

Style

Address

"Having a Coke with You" is addressed to a particular reader. This reader, O'Hara's lover Vincent Warren, understands the significance of the references because he is aware of the circumstances. O'Hara named his practice of addressing poems to individuals "Personism," claiming that he could use the telephone instead of writing the poem if he chose. Such a practice puts readers in the position of voyeurs, reading a text ostensibly meant for someone else.

Repetition

As in many of his poems, O'Hara uses lists to create a poetic effect. In the first stanza, he catalogues reasons for why having a Coke with his lover is better than almost anything. The accumulation of details, in addition to developing a rhythm for the poem, creates a sense of intimacy and establishes the authenticity of the speaker's claims. Walt Whitman and Allen Ginsberg are two of the most well-known poets who used lists extensively in their poems.

Punctuation

The absence of end punctuation marks and the lower case beginning of sentences help create the sense that all of the ideas and perceptions in the poem are equal and that the poem is a spontaneous expression of the poet's emotions.

Historical Context

O'Hara wrote "Having a Coke with You" in 1960, the same year that Donald Allen's anthology *The*

New American Poetry: 1945–1960 was published. This anthology gathered together many of the poets, including O'Hara, who were experimenting with form and subject matter and who did not make their living teaching in universities. Allen grouped poets according to schools, such as Black Mountain, New York, San Francisco Renaissance, and Beat Generation, groupings which literary historians and critics still use today. In his introduction, Allen writes "Through their work many are closely allied to modern jazz and abstract expressionist painting, today recognized throughout the world to be America's greatest achievement in contemporary culture." Critic Christopher Benfey questions the connection between abstract expressionist painting and poetry with which it is supposedly "allied," claiming that "one advantage of the label [New York School, in which Allen included O'Hara] was that it asserted a merely geographical common ground between these poets and 'New York School' painters such as Jackson Pollock and Willem de Kooning." Benfey writes that although the poets and painters might share a kind of New York City brashness in their respective arts, "nobody was claiming any specific technical or aesthetic parallels, or implying that these poets were 'Abstract Expressionist' poets, or 'Action' poets, or 'drip' poets."

Pop Art overlapped with and, in many ways, grew out of Abstract Expressionism. The late 1950s and 1960s saw artists such as Larry Rivers and Robert Rauschenberg mix familiar imagery from popular culture, high art, and nostalgic Americana to create paintings and collages that challenged the idealism of Abstract Expressionism. Rivers' painting, *George Washington Crossing the Delaware,* for example, appropriates imagery the famous nineteenth-century painting—George Washington standing on the bow of a boat—into modern context, reinvigorating what had become a pictorial cliché. Jasper Johns, Roy Liechtenstein, and Andy Warhol embodied the fully-flowered spirit of Pop Art in their appropriation of brand names, symbols, and their use of cartoon imagery. Influenced by these artists, O'Hara frequently draws on popular culture in his own writing. Coke, after all, is unquestionably one of the most recognizable consumer brand names. However, O'Hara's contribution to contemporary culture went beyond his own poetry in 1960. The Metropolitan Museum of Art's Spanish exhibition, which O'Hara was organizing and to which he alludes in his poem, opened in July. Many critics in the art community were suspicious of the exhibition, as Fascist Generalissimo Franco was in power in

Compare & Contrast

- **1960:** The Picasso exhibition at Tate Gallery, London, opens.

  Today: Most of Picasso's paintings can now be found online at (http://www.tamu.edu/mocl/picasso/) which is called the On-line Picasso Project.

- **1960:** The American Heart Association issues a report attributing higher death rates among middle-aged men to heavy smoking of cigarettes.

  2000: The tobacco industry is under siege, as individuals and states file suit after suit against cigarette manufacturers. In July, 2000, a Miami, Florida, jury orders big U.S. cigarette companies to pay $145 billion in punitive damages.

- **1960:** Charles Van Doren is among thirteen contestants on the television game show "21" arrested for perjury in testifying that answers to questions were not given to them in advance.

  1994: A major motion picture based on the 1959–1960 "21" scandal is released. *Quiz Show* is directed by Robert Redford and stars Ralph Fiennes, John Turturro, and Rob Morrow.

Spain and they assumed had given his approval for the works to be included in the show.

In general, the circles in which O'Hara moved in the 1960s were bohemian and liberal. The Beat movement of the 1950s gave way to the Civil Rights era, and John F. Kennedy's election in 1960 promised hope and change for America's poor. Martin Luther King, Jr. led sit-in demonstrations against racial discrimination, and in 1961 the Congress of Racial Equality sponsored a series of "freedom rides" to force the federal government to speed up integration of interstate commerce. Though he worked in the rarefied air of museum high culture, O'Hara often embraced the unheralded, the marginal, and the unknown.

Critical Overview

Although O'Hara never hid his homosexuality, he never wrote openly gay poems until he met Vincent Warren. O'Hara critic Alan Feldman notes that "Having a Coke with You" was one of the last love poems O'Hara wrote to Vincent before he began having doubts about him. Feldman writes that "Having a Coke with You" is about "simple joy," and that it "evoke[s], perhaps better than any poem in the language, what might be called a date mood." Feldman explains that "On a date (a really good one, that is) we try to focus on the person we are

with as though to extract the maximum amount of pleasure from even the smallest details and gestures." Biographer Brad Gooch conceptualizes the poem, noting that when O'Hara returned from Spain he became caught up in an exhibit he was working on in his capacity as associate curator and that writing the piece allowed him "to put his work in the proper perspective with life." Gooch also observes that it was one of O'Hara's last love poems to Warren, and notes that one possible reason for their breakup was because shortly after O'Hara returned from Spain he discovered that both he and Warren had syphilis. Warren admits that it was probably he that had given it to O'Hara. George Butterick writes that the love poems O'Hara wrote to Warren, including "Having a Coke with You" "are all affirmative, delicate, precise, poems of frontal immediacy, heartfelt, with feeling no longer hidden behind a bravado of brilliant images and discordant segments." Critic Helen Vendler is forward in her assessment of the poem, claiming that it is "one of the most beautiful of many [of O'Hara's] love poems."

Criticism

Chris Semansky

Semansky publishes poetry, fiction, and essays regularly in literary magazines and journals. In the

> **"** *However, O'Hara, like the other poets with whom he is often linked— John Ashbery, Kenneth Koch, and James Schuyler—was not really a philosopher or even a critic, although he wrote many art reviews and copy for museum catalogues. He was an artist himself and saw words as a kind of paint that captured and created experience."*

following essay, he considers the aesthetics of "Having a Coke with You."

Frank O'Hara's love poem "Having a Coke with You," written to his lover Vincent Warren, takes as its theme the function of aesthetics. Aesthetics is a branch of philosophy that concerns beauty and taste. Questions it attempts to answer include: what makes art, art?; why do we like some kinds of art and not others?; what is the point of art?; and what is the relationship between the beautiful and the good? O'Hara, who worked as a curator for the Museum of Modern Art, literally makes Warren into a work of art within his poem, and suggests that love itself should be considered a criterion when judging a work of art.

Historically critics and writers have judged art by its effect on the viewer. In the early nineteenth century, the word "aesthetics" largely meant the manner in which art was apprehended through the senses, with an emphasis on the visual. Issues such as art's relationship to society didn't become a major concern until the twentieth century. However, O'Hara, like the other poets with whom he is often linked—John Ashbery, Kenneth Koch, and James Schuyler—was not really a philosopher or even a critic, although he wrote many art reviews and copy for museum catalogues. He was an artist

himself and saw words as a kind of paint that captured and created experience. O'Hara critic Alan Feldman notes that O'Hara and the other New York School poets

are not interested in the concept of the soul or the business of the soul. . . . They are not interested in death and violence except in its capacity for energizing language. . . . Their poems never contain a message to help us make some kind of moral order in our lives. They are neither concerned with timeless values, nor with portraying average, everyday reality. Instead they're interested in the colors and textures of life as momentary, isolated phenomena, detached from intellectual, moral or religious pattern.

In treating Warren as an art object himself, O'Hara paints a portrait of the dancer indirectly, by focusing on what makes Warren loveable to him. This is the same tact a painter might take in creating a portrait of a lover, emphasizing the lover's hair, or smile, or eyes. O'Hara emphasizes individual parts of Warren such as his orange shirt and his love for yogurt, but also emphasizes their own relationship, "the secrecy our smiles take on before people and statuary." All of these details are specific to O'Hara's taste and to the relationship itself. That is, another poet writing of Warren would not necessarily even mention these details. By referring to places and incidents about which only Warren would know the significance, O'Hara is practicing "Personism," his own theory of poetry. Ironically, O'Hara does not care if readers get the references in his poems or not. In his essay "Personism," written for fellow poet LeRoi Jones' magazine *Yugen,* O'Hara writes:

But how can your really care if anybody gets it [the poem], or gets what it means, or if it improves them. Improves them for what? For death? Why hurry them along? Too many poets act like a middle-aged mother trying to get her kids to eat too much cooked meat, and potatoes with dripping (tears). I don't give a damn whether they eat or not. Forced feeding leads to excessive thinness (effete). Nobody should experience anything they don't need to, if they don't need poetry bully for them.

This attitude towards poetry and by extension to art itself is populist in sentiment. That is, although himself a student of art and someone responsible for acquiring art for MOMA's many exhibitions, O'Hara implicitly expresses a disdain for art that might be technically and formally brilliant but lacking in passion and feeling. The feeling in "Having a Coke with You" is as much the feeling of frivolity and fun. The very title suggests as much. Having a drink with someone is often what people do on dates. That the drink is a Coke, as opposed to say, a scotch and water, emphasizes the

What Do I Read Next?

- John Ashbery was a close friend of O'Hara's whose poetry helped to define the New York School style of writing. His long poem, *Self-Portrait in a Convex Mirror,* published in 1975, won the Pulitzer Prize, The National Book Award, and The National Book Critics Circle Award.

- John Gruen's 1972 *The Party's Over Now: Reminiscences of the Fifities–New York's Artists, Writers, Musicians, and Their Friends* includes a chapter on O'Hara's focusing of his own activities as a lyric writer for musicals.

- John Bernard Myers edited the anthology *The Poets of the New York School,* which includes O'Hara's work. This anthology contains a useful introduction by O'Hara's first publisher, who provides a history of the New York School and how it came to be.

- Rosanna Warren is a poet who, like O'Hara, has been deeply influenced by painting. Her poems, however, are less colloquial than O'Hara's poems and more conventionally formal. Her collection *Each Leaf Shines Separate* offers many poems about art.

- Richard Howard's *Alone with America: Essays on the Art of Poetry in the United States Since 1950* is a veritable encyclopedia of Howard's reviews and assorted essays on some of the twentieth century's most influential poets, including O'Hara.

- Alexander Smith Jr.'s *Frank O'Hara: A Comprehensive Bibliography,* published in 1979, provides a thorough list of criticism on O'Hara through 1978.

- Donald Allen edited *The Collected Poems of Frank O'Hara,* published in 1971. Allen, an anthologist and critic, is one of the foremost authorities on mid-century American poetry.

- In the October 1998 issue of *New Criterion,* John Simon reviews David Lehman's book *The Last Avant-Garde: The Making of the New York School of Poets,* arguing that O'Hara, Ashbery, Schuyler, and Koch have never "written what I would call a single poem of any importance."

---

lightness of the occasion. O'Hara juxtaposes this feeling of lightness with references to some very "heavy" people, artists, and paintings. St. Sebastian, for example, who O'Hara says Warren looks like a "better happier" version, is a Christian martyr who died for his beliefs. Da Vinci and Michelangelo are two of the world's most famous artists and known for the profundity and gravity of their art, and Marcel Duchamp's *Nude Descending a Staircase* is considered a masterpiece of modern perspective, are compared as well. By preferring having a Coke with Warren to any of these, O'Hara privileges the immediate and the popular and suggests that the true value of art is not in surviving time but in being *in* time. He underscores the distinction between art, life, the past, and the present when he writes "it is hard to believe when I'm with you that there can be anything as still / as solemn

as unpleasantly definitive as statuary when right in front of it." Viewing museum art, which has been judged "great" by critics, history, and collected and exhibited, can never approach the experience of being in love, O'Hara suggests. Feldman sees this focus on the present as an attempt, conscious or not, to ignore the possibility that the relationship might not last. Feldman writes:

> Explaining Vincent's beauty, or even describing it, would be as tedious and unnecessary as explaining why a sunny spring day is lovely. But such blithe joy is, however, too carefree to last. This is not mentioned, yet perhaps O'Hara is signaling such an awareness by deliberately confining his admiration for Vincent to aesthetics. The question of whether Vincent is or is not the "right person" seems to be irrelevant to O'Hara as the identity of the person standing "near the tree" is to an impressionist painter whose only concern, after all, is points of light.

In poetry there is a tradition that takes as its subject other poems or works of art. These types of poems are called *ekphrasis;* they are representations of representations or mirrors of a sort. By treating Warren as a work of art and comparing him to other works of art, O'Hara is saying that Warren himself has representational meaning. For O'Hara, this meaning resides in the idea that rather than imitating art, life *betters* art. Ironically, however, O'Hara uses an art form, the poem, to make this claim. He achieves verisimilitude—the notion that art can create the illusion of reality—by explicitly criticizing the shortcomings of other art that, to him, has not achieved his standard of reality, which is based in a more psychological rather than empirical version of experience. At the heart of O'Hara's poem, then, is the idea that art the world praises is emotionally cold because it concentrates too much on the illusion of appearance rather than feeling. O'Hara, on the other hand, approximates reality through the illusion of spontaneity. His poem has the feel of a diary entry jotted down in the heat of the moment, as opposed to the obviously well planned and meticulously detailed paintings to which he refers. Tradition, O'Hara suggests, can blunt the emotions and lead to cold art, if followed for the sake of tradition itself. He writes "and what good does all the research of the Impressionists do them / when they never got the right person to stand near the tree when the sun sank." Rather than studying the masters, O'Hara suggests that poets "just go on your nerve," something readers cannot help but think he would like painters to do as well. When he writes that "it seems they were all cheated out of some marvelous experience / which is not going to go wasted on me which is why I'm telling you about it," O'Hara is saying that the great painters and artists of the past concentrated too much on their art and not what their art was about.

O'Hara wrote scores of poems about his affair with Warren detailing the emotional ups and downs of the relationship, the doubts, the fears, and the jealousies. These poems, written in 1960–1961 during the eighteenth months of their relationship, were addressed to Warren and serve as a chronicle of the inner life of the affair. Their appeal is that although readers might not understand the references, they do understand the tone of the poems because they deal with the universal and familiar subject of love. So while readers might not know that the Spanish cities O'Hara lists in the first line of "Having a Coke with You," the readers do not need to know that the cities he visited were efforts to recruit artists for a show at MOMA. And while readers might not be familiar with Duchamp's or Rembrandt's paintings or futurism, they do not need to. Readers can infer the speaker's passion for his lover through the familiar gesture he makes of naming the small things he loves about him and by his comparing him to other objects of beauty. For O'Hara, beauty is love.

Source: Chris Semansky, Critical Essay on "Having a Coke with You," in *Poetry for Students,* The Gale Group, 2001.

Cliff Saunders

Saunders teaches writing and literature in the Myrtle Beach, South Carolina, area and has published six chapbooks of poetry. In the following essay, he praises "Having a Coke with You" as a vibrant, kinetic poem in which O'Hara celebrates the experience of new love while also, somewhat ironically, revealing his preference for ongoing life (i.e., process) over finished art (i.e., product).

Although O'Hara spent many years in the service of art, both as a critic and as an associate curator for the Museum of Modern Art in New York City, he clearly prized life more than art. This preference comes through loud and clear in much of his poetry, and it is the overriding theme of "Having a Coke with You." Written during his most fertile period of poetic production (1959–1960) and later published as part of *Love Poems (Tentative Title)* in 1965, "Having a Coke with You" is widely considered one of O'Hara's most successful love poems. According to noted literary critic Helen Vendler, it is one of O'Hara's "most beautiful . . . love poems." Other boosters of the poem are George F. Butterick and Robert J. Bertholf, who, in their entry on O'Hara in the *Dictionary of Literary Biography,* call it an "affirmative, delicate, precise" poem "of frontal immediacy." And in his terrific study *Frank O'Hara,* author Alan Feldman contends that "Having a Coke" "evoke[s], perhaps better than any poem in the language, what might be called a date mood," noting that the poem "*is* fun and *is* marvelous for the very reason that it lacks full awareness of the possibility of pain and sadness in love, or even of mixed feelings." High praise indeed.

"Having a Coke" displays a number of O'Hara's stylistic attributes: his unflinching honesty in expressing his feelings, his delightful wit, his breezy and engaging conversational tone, his gift for capturing movement on the page. Also present in the poem are those elements that O'Hara's detractors have railed against: the numerous "hip insider" references, the lack of verbal compression, the "unmitigated gall" to think that every little thought and perception he possess, constitutes "art," and is worthy of inclusion in a poem, which, of course, is what O'Hara's poetry is all about: sheer gutsiness and passion for life. He said himself in his "Personism: A Manifesto": "I don't even like rhythm, assonance, all that stuff. You just go on your nerve."

Sometimes, poetry needs a swift kick to the butt in order to get it *moving* again, to recharge it, to dislodge it from convention and stasis, and, today, O'Hara is widely admired for injecting new life and vitality into American poetry during a time (the ultraconservative 1950s and early 1960s) when it sorely needed a shot in the heart. O'Hara loved life and the twists and turns of human relationships in all their glorious messiness, and the unpredictability, and if the reader comes away with anything from his poetry, it is his intense passion for life. As Feldman points out so insightfully, O'Hara's poems "try to record the instant at which experience is gathering itself into something that deserves the artist's attention, a confluence of feeling and perception that is suffused with a sense of its own passing away." The key, of course, is to trust the validity of one's own experience, no matter how minor or insignificant the details, and to communicate that experience authentically on the page. Frequently, O'Hara succeeds in doing so, but not always. Some of his longer poems get bogged down with excessive chatter, as if O'Hara could not restrain himself even though he surely knew better. When O'Hara *does* restrain himself and adheres to organic selectivity in the details, great things happen in his poetry. Case in point: "Having a Coke with You."

That the poem is addressed to O'Hara's homosexual lover at the time, dancer Vincent Warren, may be of biographical interest but ultimately is not of thematic concern. The poem is about that joyous state *anyone* feels when first falling love, and it celebrates the newness, the freshness, of that universal experience, though not in any traditional sense. Rather than rhapsodize about his love in an overtly poetical way, O'Hara expresses his feelings casually and dispassionately, trusting that a faithful recording of his thoughts and feelings that day will get to the heart of the matter. And what exactly *is* the heart of the matter? Simply stated, it is O'Hara's realization that ongoing life (i.e., process) is preferable to finished art (i.e., product). To O'Hara, "all the portraits in the world" cannot hold

> *Also present in the poem are those elements that O'Hara's detractors have railed against: the numerous 'hip insider' references, the lack of verbal compression, the 'unmitigated gall' to think that every little thought and perception he possess, constitutes 'art,' and is worthy of inclusion in a poem, which, of course, is what O'Hara's poetry is all about: sheer gutsiness and passion for life."*

a candle to the active beauty of a living, breathing human face. Notice in line 8 how O'Hara criticizes statuary as being "solemn" and "unpleasantly definitive." Later, in lines 10 and 11, he expresses equal dissatisfaction with the portrait show he and his lover are attending, accusing it of having "no faces in it at all, just paint." Art, O'Hara seems to be suggesting in this poem, sucks the life out of life itself.

In typical O'Hara irony, he says he might like to see one painting, Rembrandt's *Polish Rider,* as often as the face of his lover, but toward the end of the poem, he accuses twentieth-century Italian sculptor Marino Marini of failing to "pick the rider as carefully / as the horse." He also has uncomplimentary things to say about the Impressionist painters ("they never got the right person to stand near the tree when the sun sank"), and even the Great Masters Leonardo da Vinci and Michelangelo do not thrill him much any more. To be sure, many of O'Hara's criticisms in the poem are tongue in cheek, for how could an art critic and museum curator like O'Hara *not* love art? Still, one gets the sense that if he had to make a choice, "messy" life would win out over "perfect" art every time.

O'Hara knows that art is an indispensable facet of life and worthy of love and respect, but statuary and paintings are static (i.e., rigid and immobile), and O'Hara prizes movement, speed, and kinetic energy. Throughout his poetry, O'Hara shows a clear preference for action over stasis. In fact, as Scott Giantvalley notes in his entry on O'Hara for the *Critical Survey of Poetry* series, O'Hara was much enamored of "action painting, a style indigenous to New York and led by Jackson Pollock," a style whose "random quality, abstractness, and emphasis on the process of painting rather than the static permanence demonstrated in a still life or a portrait all have their correspondences in O'Hara's poetry." These elements are all present in "Having a Coke with You," giving the poem a quick-moving, almost scattershot feel to it. One could even call "Having a Coke" an "action poem," a term used by Butterick and Bertholf in reference to another O'Hara poem.

Along with the random quality of the poem's observations (what, for example, do "the fluorescent orange tulips around the birches" in line 5 have to do with anything) and the poem's overall abstractly kaleidoscopic effect, this quality of action (i.e., speed and movement) is forcefully communicated in a number of formalistic and stylistic choices made by O'Hara. For example, the way in which O'Hara runs the poem's title into the first line immediately establishes a brisk pace, almost as though O'Hara cannot wait to get on with it. Notice also that the poem has no periods—or, for that matter, any kind of end-stop punctuation. Such punctuation implies fixity and stasis, running counter to the poem's message. Periods, question marks, and semicolons would only make readers pause, slowing them down, and O'Hara cannot have that. This is New York City he's describing, after all, where everything is *go go go,* where thoughts, observations, and sensory perceptions are scarcely made before others are crowding to take their place.

Even the poem's long lines and the way sentences are extended and fused throughout those lines give the impression that words are pouring out of O'Hara almost faster than he can commit them to paper. Thus, even though the only action in the poem concerns two people walking through an art show, the style of writing is very action-oriented in terms of its liveliness and rapid movement from one observation to the next. This style directly mirrors the poem's point that life (i.e., kinetic energy, ongoing change, *process*) may be chaotic and

disjointed at times, but it sure beats any portrait or statue that drains the vitality and volatility of life in a quest for static perfection. Life is too short for exercises in representational flawlessness, O'Hara seems to be saying. Unlike those artsy-fartsy Impressionists, I'm going to live my life as fully as possible right now, for I won't be "cheated of some marvelous experience."

And he was not, of course, though his sudden death at age 40 in 1966 certainly cheated his readers of an untold number of poetic experiences. In his scant forty years, O'Hara lived more passionately, more intensely, and more fully than most people who live twice as long. He was so busy living, in fact, that he could hardly be bothered with something as mundane as submitting poems to journals for publication and organizing his poems into collections. Others had to do this for him, for O'Hara was notoriously casual about forging a career out of his unique poetic talent. Perhaps O'Hara felt that poetry books, like certain portraits and statuary, are too "solemn" and "unpleasantly definitive." A poetry collection, after all, is presumably a finished work of art, a product, and O'Hara disliked completion. Rather, he preferred the journey *toward* completion, the process of life in motion, what Feldman calls "the self that is always becoming." The circumstance of O'Hara's death—he was struck and killed by a dune buggy on Fire Island—is often mentioned by poetry lovers as one of the strangest ways a poet has ever died. When you think about it, though, it makes perfect sense in O'Hara's case. He was constantly on the go, barely stopping for a second, so he was bound to collide hard with something somewhere along the way.

Source: Cliff Saunders, Critical Essay on "Having a Coke with You," in *Poetry for Students,* The Gale Group, 2001.

Jonathan N. Barron

Barron is an associate professor of English at the University of Southern Mississippi. He has co-edited Jewish American Poetry *(from the University Press of New England), and* Roads Not Taken: Rereading Robert Frost, *(forthcoming from the University of Missouri Press) as well as a forthcoming collection of essays on the poetic movement,* New Formalism. *Beginning in 2001, he will be the editor in chief of* The Robert Frost Review. *In the following essay, he considers the impact of postmodernism on O'Hara's poem.*

Reading a Frank O'Hara poem is like being thrown into the middle of a party with some stranger's intimate friends. One has to do one's best to make sense of all the inside references, names, places, and things that one would have no reasonable reason to know. For many, this whirlwind of proper names can, depending on who these people are, be a most exhilarating experience. Cast without a net into the sophisticated, funny, and urbane world of Frank O'Hara's 1960s New York, many never want to leave. For other readers, by contrast, the door cannot be found quickly enough. After the first bombardment of proper names, few experiences could be more annoying. In a discussion of O'Hara's poetry, the literary critic, George Butterick, wrote "the language of the poems is ripe with in-talk of the 1960s; these qualities are indeed dominant in O'Hara's poems from the start. They also happen to be the reason for their great success. This essay discusses the attraction so many have to O'Hara's poetry, an attraction due to its refusal to use a generic name, a generalization, or a universal noun where a specific one can be found.

Postmodernism best explains why readers are so often compelled to enter the party that is Frank O'Hara's poetry. Postmodernism, in other words, explains not only how to read a poem like "Having a Coke With You" but it also explains why its limited, even private poetic style is now one of the favorite forms of post World War II American poetry, a form called the New York School. Without rehearsing the many terms and definitions of either the New York School or of postmodernism, it is enough to know that, at its most simple, postmodernism defines an attitude towards the world and particularly towards language, and that the poetry of the New York School most often expresses that attitude in poetry. At its most basic, postmodernism is the name assigned to a radical skepticism about the existence of fundamental, deep, certain, and final truths. Is there one grand truth, one spiritual, even scientific meaning to life? The postmodernist rejects this possibility and, in so doing, refuses to believe that language, especially poetry, can be a vessel, or container of some grand truth. If there is no truth to begin with, how can one expect poetry to reveal it? And, even if there is a grand truth "out there," even if there is a God, or a final scientific explanation for the meaning of life, no postmodernist would believe that language has the capacity to reveal it. Like a microscope, language, at best, is just an instrument. It can only allow us to see material facts in this world. To suggest that language has the power to do more than that, they argue, is to traffic in the impossible. If there is some Being, whether God or truth, the postmodernist is

> *Is there one grand truth, one spiritual, even scientific meaning to life? The postmodernist rejects this possibility and, in so doing, refuses to believe that language, especially poetry, can be a vessel, or container of some grand truth. If there is no truth to begin with, how can one expect poetry to reveal it?"*

convinced that no word, no mere language could possibly express, let alone contain it.

According to numerous literary scholars, the New York School in general and Frank O'Hara in particular manifest just this postmodern attitude. Perhaps the one scholar to discuss this dimension most is Mutlu Konuk Blasing. She, however, does not discuss "Having a Coke With You," a poem surprisingly neglected in O'Hara scholarship. Taking Blasing's reading of O'Hara's postmodernism as a given, then, it would be a mistake to read "Having a Coke With You" as a simple code that, once cracked, will reveal a deeper, universal truth. Instead, with a postmodern perspective in mind, one must accept that each detail, each proper noun, each name stands for itself no more and no less. The great American poet, Walt Whitman, in a preface to his always-expanding collection of poems, *Leaves of Grass,* wrote: "I will have nothing hang in the way, not the richest curtains. What I tell I tell for precisely what it is." Such is also the case in Frank O'Hara's poetry. "The naked truth," for O'Hara, as for Whitman, is that which one can see. That is to say, one can only recognize truth, meaning, even something as profound as love, through the things that make it possible. Is there love? Well, then, there must be a person one loves. Unlike O'Hara, however, Walt Whitman, as a romantic, still depicts a dualism between the material and the spiritual worlds in his poetry. To put an end to that dualism, the early twentieth-century modernist poet, William Carlos Williams, a mentor of sorts to Frank O'Hara, declared: "no ideas but in things." In effect, Williams, through this bold claim, further refined Whitman's use of things in poetry. According to Williams, poets would have to banish all abstract language in ways even Whitman would not have been able to do. According to Williams, it is impossible to discuss any idea, any abstraction, and any quality at all, without also, at the same time, depicting the thing that gave rise to it. Williams, therefore, meant to be even more naked, more close to the things of the world than Whitman. With the poetry of Frank O'Hara, the war against abstract language reaches a kind of climax.

In "Having a Coke With You," it is as if O'Hara had transformed Williams' "No ideas but in things" to the even more radical "everything an idea!" Even Williams refused to go that far. In his poetry, not all things necessarily lead to deep meaning. Rather, deep meaning can only be discovered in terms of something that gave rise to it. For Williams, as for the great theorist of psychology, Sigmund Freud, sometimes a cigar was just a cigar. O'Hara, by contrast, insists, in his poetry, that everything on this earth from a Coke bottle to his lover's face has equal meaning, even profound meaning. His relentless insistence on the meaningfulness of every thing is particularly postmodern because it refuses to distinguish (as Williams did) between a realm of important highbrow things on the one hand and unimportant lowbrow things on the other. In O'Hara's universe all things are equal because all things mean.

To show what happens when all things in a poem carry equally important, equally meaningful weight, one must begin examining the first stanza of "Having a Coke With You." The poem appeared in *Love Poems (Tentative Title)* (1965), a collection published out of a New York art gallery, Tibor De Nagy. When the book was published, O'Hara was a well-established figure in the New York art world working at the Museum of Modern Art. And, thanks to O'Hara's biographer, Brad Gooch, the specific context that gave rise to the poem is also now generally available. But even with this knowledge one must resist the temptation to see the poem as a personal code to crack in order to yield a larger, more universal meaning. In keeping with the postmodern attitude towards truth and language that this poem engages, the biographical details should be read not as a key to some other story in the poem but rather as the total story itself. In other words, the details matter so much in their own right as themselves that one mis-

takes the very meaning of the poem if one tries to make them mean something else.

Turning then to the poem, O'Hara's biographer, Brad Gooch, explains that O'Hara wrote it on April 21, 1960, five years before it was published in book form. When he wrote the poem, O'Hara was deeply in love with a dancer, Vincent Warren. The poem was written to celebrate their relationship after a brief time apart. Specifically, on March 23, 1960, O'Hara left his home in New York City for Madrid where he was to gather material for a show on Spanish painting. His place of work, the Museum of Modern Art (MOMA) in New York, a major cultural institution in the United States, planned to open the show as a major production celebrating the recent work of Spain. After its New York debut, it was to travel throughout the United States. O'Hara's job, therefore, was fundamental to this production; he would be in large part responsible for making the show possible. These facts, then, explain why there are so many allusions to art in "Having a Coke with You." Art, particularly Spanish art, was all-consuming in the month he spent apart from Warren, the period depicted in this poem. After his month away, O'Hara came back to New York. He wrote this poem as if it were his own conversation with Warren while, quite literally, having a Coke with him.

Not quite a prose poem, certainly not a metrical or traditional poem, "Having a Coke with You" is divided into two stanzas of long lines. Each stanza is full to the brim with details of the trip to Spain. Looking just at the title and first stanza will indicate why the use of such detail matters so much to the poem, and why such use is best understood in a postmodern context. In the stanza's ten lines, O'Hara declares his love for Warren by contrasting his time without him to his time, now that he is back in New York, with him. The very first line follows from the title as part of a sentence that the title begins: "Having a Coke With You / is even more fun than going to San Sebastian, Irun, Hendaye, Biarritz, Bayonne." According to O'Hara's biographer, Gooch, these cities are, in fact, O'Hara's "itinerary after Madrid." In other words, O'Hara does not say: "Being with you is better than any exotic place I might have gone." Instead, using specific nouns, he contrasts a simple, everyday and, for 1960, a very American experience, having a Coke with his lover in New York, with the European experience of business travel just concluded. A simple Coke, a regular, everyday American encounter, says O'Hara, far exceeds the experience of travel even to exotic locales. Does it matter that these are in fact cities O'Hara actually visited? Does it matter that they are named in the order he visited them? Yes and no. Yes, because the facts rather than some made up fantasy make his love seem all the more sincere. He went to these places and he still loves the Coke with Warren better. The names, on the other hand, do not matter because whatever Spanish cities or sites he might have named would have made the same point: what matters is the specific contrast between travel in Spain and a Coke in New York. O'Hara, in other words, connects the seemingly irrelevant, unimportant, lowly, even trivial event of a Coke with the seemingly more important, more meaningful event of travel in Spain. Not only is a Coke equal to that event, it is, says O'Hara, more important! Here, then, O'Hara has reversed the typical poetic logic that reads one kind of cultural experience, European travel, as superior to the popular cultural experience of drinking soda.

In the second line, O'Hara back-peddles. Now that he has delivered the emotional heart of the poem, he backs away from the potential Hallmark card version of sentimentality that any declaration of love risks. The second line, therefore, undercuts the romantic, sentimental tendency of the poem's opening line. Just as with the first line, the details of the second matter for exactly what they say. Aware that he is sounding too mushy after his first line O'Hara next claims that having a Coke with Warren is more fun than "being sick to my stomach on the Travesera de Gracia in Barcelona." This cynical and funny line is his way of saying that compared to vomiting in Spain, this Coke in New York really *is* more fun. But to attack, as this line does, the emotional revelation of the first line is, also, an insult to Warren. On the one hand, it saves O'Hara from seeming to be too sentimental but on the other it risks saying, "I don't really love you, I just prefer you to being sick." And so, the poem, in line three, begins a new topic. Rather than merely announce his love of and preference for Warren, O'Hara, from line three to the end of the stanza, tries to understand why he loves this man and why he prefers him. He establishes a rhythm whereby he declares his love, then makes a cynical comment undercutting it, then declares it again.

This rhythm has the effect of making O'Hara's love for Warren sincere without being sentimental. It also takes O'Hara into a new and more profound dimension because, after line three, he begins to investigate the cause and origin of his love for this man. Rather than investigate his love in abstract language, however, O'Hara always stays on the

surface. It is as if line three had said, "Why is having a Coke with Warren so wonderful, really?" To answer that implicit question, there follow four lines that begin with the word, "partly." Four reasons, four partial explanations, account for his love of this man. Returning in a witty way to the first line's mention of the town of St. Sebastian, O'Hara now compares Warren to the actual saint, a figure familiar to art history for the many depictions of his martyrdom. O'Hara says, "in your orange shirt you look like a better happier St. Sebastian." This allusion is not just to a well-known Catholic Saint from the days of ancient Rome but also to the many famous paintings of St. Sebastian, particularly those from the Renaissance. In the typical painting, Saint Sebastian's martyrdom, his torture by being pierced through his chest with arrows, is the dominant scene. For O'Hara to say his lover looks better than that gruesome depiction, then, is a way to mock that familiar artistic image's seriousness. At once profound and silly, the line asks the reader to see Warren as a swarthy, thin, bearded man, like St Sebastian in so many paintings, but no martyr. Warren is just a healthy American in an orange shirt. What a postmodern line! For here, O'Hara alludes to a profound moment in Christianity and art history even as he strips that moment of its profundity. But in removing the deeper, high cultural meaning, he does not remove the emotional power or personal truth of the image. While Warren is certainly no martyr, he is, nonetheless, magical and important to O'Hara. Who is to say if he is not, finally, as important as the real Saint Sebastian? After all, O'Hara does love him. The stanza ends by celebrating a real man's love for another and contrasting that felt experience with the idealism, abstraction, and allegories of art.

While there is not the space to discuss the second half of the poem in detail, it is enough to say that it raises the question asked in the first stanza; only it does so in an even higher pitch. The first stanza asks, where does my love come from? It then answers that question by looking at the beloved; love comes from the very person sitting before the poet and it does not come from an ideal. The second stanza asks a more serious question still, if the felt experience of people and things matters so much what does one say about Western culture's claim that genuine meaning is to be found not in life but rather in high art or in religious ideals? O'Hara asks how it is that this man before him matters more than the art he just spent a month reviewing in Spain? In the second half of his poem, O'Hara asks if art can ever be as important as "having a Coke with you." Can art be a place for real meaning? Ironically, he answers his question in the negative. Art cannot hold a candle to the reality of everyday life. In the poem's second stanza, O'Hara notes that in "the portrait show" the paintings "have no faces." He contrasts this artistic lack of interest in people with the reality of Warren's actual face.

By the end of the poem, then, O'Hara concludes with a postmodern defense of the particular. He defends the world of objects, places, and people over and against the abstract, ideal, and unreal generalities of art: "it seems they [the various artists] were all cheated of some marvelous experience / which is not going to go wasted on me which is why I'm telling you about it."

Source: Jonathan N. Barron, Critical Essay on "Having a Coke with You," in *Poetry for Students,* The Gale Group, 2001.

Sources

Benfey, Christopher, "The Limits of Fun," in *The New Republic,* January 4, 1999, pp. 37–42

Blasing, Multu Konuk, *Politics and Form in Postmodern Poetry: O'Hara, Bishop, Ashbery, and Merrill,* Cambridge University Press, 1995.

Breslin, James E. B., *From Modern to Contemporary: American Poetry 1945–1960,* University of Chicago Press, 1984.

Butterick, George F., "Frank O'Hara," in *Dictionary of Literary Biography,* Vol. 193: *American Poets Since World War II,* edited by Joseph Conte, Sixth Series, Gale Research, 1998, pp. 213–26.

Elledge, Jim, ed., *Frank O'Hara: To Be True to a City,* University of Michigan Press, 1990.

Feldman, Alan, *Frank O'Hara,* Twayne, 1979.

Giantvalley, Scott, "Frank O'Hara," in *Critical Survey of Poetry,* revised edition, edited by Frank Magill, Salem Press, 1992, pp. 2475–76.

Gooch, Brad, *City Poet: The Life and Times of Frank O'Hara,* Random, 1993, pp. 346–54.

Howard, Richard, *Alone with America: Essays on the Art of Poetry in the United States Since 1950,* Atheneum, 1969.

O'Hara, Frank, *The Collected Poems of Frank O'Hara,* edited by Donald Allen, Knopf, 1971.

———, *Lunch Poems,* City Light Books, 1964.

———, *Meditations in an Emergency,* Grove, 1957.

———, "Personism: A Manifesto," in *The Selected Poems of Frank O'Hara,* edited by Donald Allen, Vintage Books, 1974, p. xiii.

Prestianni, Vincent, "Frank O'Hara: An Analytic Bibliography of Bibliographies," in *Sagetrieb,* Spring 1993, pp. 129–30.

Smith, Alexander, Jr., *Frank O'Hara: A Comprehensive Bibliography,* Garland, 1979.

Vendler, Helen, "The Virtues of the Alterable," in *Parnassus: Poetry in Review,* Fall–Winter 1972, pp. 5–20.

Whitman, Walt, *Leaves of Grass: The First (1855) Edition,* edited by Malcolm Cowley, Penguin, 1959, p. 13.

Williams, William Carlos, *Paterson,* New Directions, 1963, p. 6.

For Further Study

Gooch, Brad, *City Poet: The Life and Times of Frank O'Hara,* Knopf, 1993.
　　Gooch's text is an informative and in-depth study of O'Hara and his relationship to poetry and art. Gooch's biography is successful because he describes O'Hara's life without being psychological.

Lehman, David, *The Last Avant-Garde: The Making of the New York School of Poets,* Anchor Books, 1999.
　　O'Hara is considered a poet from the New York School of poets, a loose group of writers including Ashbery, Frank O'Hara, Kenneth Koch, and James Schuyler. Lehman claims that the four constituted the last true avant-garde movement in American poetry.

McClatchey, J. D., ed., *Poets on Painters: Essays on the Art of Painting by Twentieth-Century Poets,* University of California Press, 1990.
　　O'Hara was an art critic as well as a poet. This collection presents reviews and essays by well-known poets on painters.

Perloff, Marjorie, *Frank O'Hara: Poet Among Painters,* Braziller, 1977.
　　Perloff emphasizes the influences of art on O'Hara's poetry, weaving useful information from a number of interviews and letters into her study.

Hope Is a Tattered Flag

Carl Sandburg

1936

Bearing only the numerical title, "16," "Hope Is a Tattered Flag" first appeared in 1936 in Carl Sandburg's *The People, Yes,* a three-hundred-page celebration of the American spirit, with an emphasis on folksy tales, wit, and wisdom. Always a very socially minded writer, Sandburg penned *The People, Yes* to help rally a nation deflated by the Great Depression.

"Hope Is a Tattered Flag" is written in free verse; the rhythm of the language is more like that of speech than the much more regular patterns of traditional poetry. This more natural structure reflects the writer's belief that poetry ought to be spontaneous and accessible. Sandburg's strong preference for the image as a poetic device is also very apparent in this piece. A clear, precise image was thought to be able to convey a wealth of ideas and emotions.

In one sense, at least, "Hope Is a Tattered Flag" is a very simple poem: a string of images twenty lines long. But the images are all different, and the whole work can be viewed as a kind of collage, where the composite picture of hope that the poet presents is actually quite intricate. There is, however, a dominant theme, an idea that the poem returns to again and again, that the feeling one calls "hope" is very well founded, that life will improve is guaranteed by the laws of the universe. The poet also hints that an increase of hope in humanity could well hasten the coming of better days.

Carl Sandburg

Author Biography

Sandburg was born on January 6, 1878, in Galesburg, Illinois, to Clare and August Sandburg, both Swedish immigrants. August was a railroad worker, who could read but not write, while Clare, a hotel chambermaid, was slightly more literate. Carl, by contrast, learned to read and write with his young schoolmates and soon demonstrated quite a strong interest in books. Unfortunately, he would only advance as far as the eighth grade, when he had to go to work to help his father support the family. After a variety of short-term jobs, Sandburg left home at eighteen to ride the freight trains west, mixing with hoboes and supporting himself with more temporary work along the way.

With the outbreak of the Spanish-American War in 1898, he enlisted in the army and sailed off to fight in Cuba, but hostilities ended before his regiment saw any action. Back at home, he entered Lombard College, only to leave school again prematurely, having failed some graduation requirements. The experience had been a valuable one, however; it was at Lombard that he discovered the satisfaction of seeing his writing in print—in college publications—and where he met Philip Green Wright, a distinguished teacher who would help print Sandburg's first three volumes of poetry in

1904 and 1905. After leaving Lombard, he worked as a journalist for some Chicago magazines, helped to organize Wisconsin workers for the Social Democratic party, and then married and settled in Milwaukee, where he became the private secretary for the city's socialist mayor. Sandburg was still writing poetry during this period but earned no credit for that endeavor until *Poetry* published some of his pieces in 1914. The best known of these poems, "Chicago," stirred up enough controversy to make him a leading figure within what was to become known as the Chicago renaissance: on one side of the controversy, critics celebrated the poem's colloquial style and free verse for their freshness and originality; more traditionally minded reviewers were skeptical about these innovations.

After four volumes of poetry, a book of children's stories, and a collection of his articles on the Chicago race riots, Sandburg began work on his landmark biography of Abraham Lincoln. Published in 1926, this extraordinarily successful book brought the writer financial security, allowing him to put aside all writing but that which most interested him. He would devote the rest of his career to American history (four more volumes on Lincoln; a book on the great president's wife, Mary; and *Remembrance Rock,* a novel that traces the fortunes of one American family from the seventeenth century to World War II), and several volumes of poetry. His work on Lincoln earned him the Pulitzer Prize in 1940, and his poetry the same honor in 1950. Sandburg died in Flat Rock, North Carolina, on July 22, 1967, at the age of 89. Though the literary establishment never embraced the folksy poet and he was passed over for the Nobel Prize, his popularity with the American people far surpassed all other writers of his day.

Poem Text

Hope is a tattered flag and a dream out of time.
Hope is a heartspun word, the rainbow, the
    shadblow in white,
The evening star inviolable over the coal mines,
The shimmer of northern lights across a bitter
    winter night,
The Blue hills beyond the smoke of the steel   5
    works,
The birds who go on singing to their mates in
    peace, war, peace,
The ten-cent crocus bulb blooming in a used-car
    salesroom,
The horseshoe over the door, the luckpiece in the
    pocket,
The kiss and the comforting laugh and resolve
Hope is an echo, hope ties itself yonder, yonder.   10

The spring grass showing itself where least
    expected,
The rolling fluff of white clouds on a changeable
    sky,
The broadcast of strings from Japan, bells from
    Moscow,
Of the voice of the prime minister of Sweden
    carried
Across the sea in behalf of a world family of   15
    nations
And children singing chorals of the Christ child
And Bach being broadcast from Bethlehem,
    Pennsylvania
And tall skyscrapers practically empty of tenants
And the hands of strong men groping for
    handholds
And the Salvation Army singing God loves us....   20

Poem Summary

Lines 1–2

The first few words, "Hope is a tattered flag," provide an interpretive key for the entire poem: the true nature of hope can be best understood by contemplating its effects, just as one might learn more about the wind by studying the shape of a weather-beaten rock. The rest of the poem simply catalogs such phenomena. The images, of course, are all carefully chosen; it's a very particular concept that Sandburg wants to convey. Virtually all of the items on the poet's list fall into one of two categories, the natural or the social. "The tattered flag" of line 1 and the "heartspun word" of line 2 belong to the latter group, flags and other cultural icons, along with shared languages, being the stuff of group solidarity. Writing during a period of unprecedented conflict, Sandburg is searching for signs of a basic impulse in humans to unite. It is true that group identity was also partly responsible for the cataclysmic wars of the early twentieth century (hence the *tattered* flag), but later in the poem Sandburg reconciles this contradiction.

Lines 3–4

With the rainbow and the shadblow (a flowering bush; line 2), the poem turns from social causes for hope to natural ones. Together with the evening star and northern lights of lines 3 and 4, these images highlight the order, purity, and beauty that are intrinsic to the universe. Sandburg is not forgetting the chaos, decay, and terrifying strain in nature—the rainbow follows the squall, the shadblow bush blooms at winter's end, the evening star (Mercury) ushers in darkness, and the northern lights flicker across a frozen landscape—but bad and good in all

Media Adaptations

- *Carl Sandburg: Echoes and Silences,* a docudrama produced for the Corporation for Public Broadcasting, is available on videotape. Contains actual footage of Sandburg.

- Sandburg's appearance on the television show *On the Go* (March 2, 1960) is available on videotape.

- Sandburg reads selections from his autobiography, *Always the Young Strangers,* on cassette from Caedmon.

- *Carl Sandburg Reads Grammy Nominee, Fog, The People Yes, and Other Poems* is also on a Caedmon audiocassette.

- *More Carl Sandburg Reads,* from Caedmon, includes selections from his novel *Remembrance Rock,* and *American Songbag,* a compilation of folk lyrics.

- *Carl Sandburg the Poet Reads Windy City, Wilderness and Wind Song* is on audiocassette from the Listening Library.

of these images point to a fundamental balance in creation as a whole.

Lines 5–6

Sandburg juxtaposes natural and social images in lines 3, 5, and 6. The thrust of all of these lines is clearest in the phrase, "The birds who go on singing to their mates in peace, war, peace": the unifying impulse alluded to above sometimes deserts humanity but in nature it is ever present, as persistent as the song of the birds, as dependable as the "inviolable" motion of the evening star. Why society swings back and forth between good and bad is hinted at in the images of "coal mines" and "the smoke of the steel works." Industrial society by definition is cut off from nature and its magnificent equilibrium.

Lines 7–8

To dispel the gloom of lines 5 and 6, the poet conjures more cheerful images in lines 7 and 8—

the crocus, the horseshoe, and the luckpiece in the pocket. In civilization, Sandburg points out, the good sometimes fades, but tokens of its subterranean existence remain evident, albeit faintly, as in the diminutive crocus blooming at the car lot or the humble lucky charm.

Lines 9–10

"The kiss and comforting laugh," expressions of love and empathy, allude again to an elemental force that draws humans together—at the personal level as well as the collective (as around the tattered flag). At the very heart of the poem flashes what may be the most illuminating of Sandburg's many analogies: hope is to the aforementioned unifying energy as an echo is to sound. Hope, in other words, may sometimes seem as ephemeral as an echo, but it too originates in something very real. The end of line 11—"hope ties itself yonder, yonder"—harkens back to line 1 and the idea that "hope is . . . a dream out of time." Recall that Sandburg sees good and bad in balance in nature, civilization swinging back and forth between the two. These shifting conditions are what give rise to the idea of time, in the poet's view. Time, in other words, only exists where the good comes and goes.

Lines 11–12

In lines 11 and 12, the poem turns once again to the characteristic balance in nature between good and bad, life and death, creation and destruction.

Lines 13–15

"The broadcast of strings from Japan, bells from Moscow" belong to a world made much smaller by radio and other technological advances of the twentieth century. Lines 14 and 15 hint that such developments might allow one to transcend the national and ethnic conflicts of the past and finally unite as a "world family." In casting the Swedish prime minister as the prophet of global unity, Sandburg pays tribute to Per Albin Hansson, best known internationally for his advocacy of disarmament and neutrality.

Lines 16–17

The melodies of line 13 swell in 16 and 17, with a choir of innocents singing Christmas songs and the strains of Johann Sebastian Bach, all of it ushering in the peace foreseen in lines 14 and 15. The emphasis on Christian music here recalls the traditional representation of Christ as the Prince of Peace. The city of Bethlehem, Pennsylvania, has long been the site of a world-famous Bach festival.

Topics for Further Study

- Choose a feeling like fear or joy and write a poem composed of a series of evocative images like the one Sandburg uses to celebrate hope.

- Ask your reference librarian to help you find materials on the psychology of hope. Prepare a short presentation to share what you learn.

- Read one of the personal narratives in *Hard Times*, Stud Terkel's well-known oral history of the Great Depression. Write a brief reaction to your excerpt, focusing on the psychological or emotional challenges of the period.

Lines 18–20

The years between World Wars I and II were the Age of the Skyscraper, climaxing in 1931 with the completion of the Empire State Building, the tallest structure in the world for more than twenty years. As the poem indicates, the Great Depression emptied many of these structures, but the federal government and its Works Progress Administration revived large-scale construction projects. Such efforts were unmistakable signs for Sandburg of social revival, of a nation of "strong men" regaining control. The Salvation Army, an "army" for charity, highlights the conversion of bad to good.

Themes

Time

The monstrous social crises of the first half of the twentieth century (the world wars and the Great Depression) shook to its foundation the modern conviction that civilization was moving steadily toward a state of perfection—technological, artistic, ethical, and political. Indeed, since the turn of the century, there was a growing conviction that all of human advancements were merely allowing human destructive impulses to wreak havoc on a greater scale. When the United States dropped an atomic bomb on Hiroshima in 1945, it was hard not to conclude that civilization was in its last days. In "Hope Is a Tattered Flag," Sandburg offers a very different interpretation of this very troubled period: difficult times, the poem suggests, are merely one phase of an historical cycle that will one day restore peace and prosperity to the world. So hope is less wishful thinking than the disposition of hearts that are in tune with this age-old rhythm.

Nature

Sandburg's social optimism is rooted in his vision of the universe as a whole, a system in which order and chaos, life and death, good and bad are in perfect balance. If society appears to lack this equilibrium, it is because it has become increasingly cut off from nature, ruled more and more by unnatural imperatives (commercial, technological, etc.) that force it off course. Over time, however, even civilization conforms to the basic laws of the cosmos; a nation that swerves toward destruction will at some point revive itself and enjoy a period of peace and prosperity. The poet offers hope during troubled times by pointing to nature where signs of this regenerative cycle are everywhere. In his vision of nature as a unity of opposites (order and chaos, etc.) and as a source of fundamental truth for the human heart, Sandburg resembles transcendentalist writers like Emerson and Thoreau.

Modernism

Though he celebrates nature and is ambivalent about civilization, Sandburg is not a primitivist. He is not suggesting humans would fare better if they returned to a more natural mode of existence. The problem is not civilization *per se,* but merely its excesses. Indeed, as lines 13–18 indicate, the poet sees much that is positive in the twentieth century, an outlook that is characteristic of modernist art more generally. Not just in birdsong does he detect a great unifying spirit at work but also in radio, as it draws the world together to form a great family of nations. And like the "spring grass showing itself where least expected," the "tall skyscrapers" (another icon of the modern) are tokens of a creative energy that cannot be suppressed. As gloomy as the 1930s might have looked to some, Sandburg hints that civilization's greatest days are just ahead.

Style

Free Verse

"Hope Is a Tattered Flag" is written in free verse—the rhythm is closer to that of speech than the more regular metrical patterns of traditional poetry. Among American poets, Walt Whitman is the best-known pioneer of this style, a writer whose pro-

found influence on Sandburg can be discerned at many levels of this poem. Strictly speaking, however, the term "free verse" applies to the work of later poets like T. S. Eliot, Ezra Pound, and Marianne Moore, all contemporaries of Sandburg. The reasons of these writers for preferring this style were, of course, very different. Sandburg's own choice reflects his commitment to a poetry that was more spontaneous than deliberately crafted, more of feeling than of intellect, and directed more at the common person than at an erudite literary readership.

Parataxis

For all of its rhythmical freedom, "Hope Is a Tattered Flag" still has very strong formal regularity. Virtually every line of the poem follows the same syntactical pattern: the words, "hope is," followed by a series of images like "a heartspun word, the rainbow, the shadblow in white." This use of similarly structured, or parallel, clauses is called parataxis. So simple is the basic structure in this particular poem, and so closely does the poet adhere to it, that it has a litany-like tone. (A litany is a prayer composed of parallel invocations like "Lord, have mercy on us. Christ, have mercy on us," etc., which are each echoed by the congregation.) The form reflects Sandburg's conception of the poet as an agent for spiritual renewal.

Imagism

Sandburg and contemporaries like Ezra Pound, William Carlos Williams, and Amy Lowell, taking their cues in part from Asian art and forms like the haiku, showed a special preference for the image as a poetic device, convinced that a well-wrought word "picture" could convey an unusual depth of meaning. "Hope Is a Tattered Flag," little more than a series of images, focuses in large part on the natural world, in which it was thought the most essential truths about the world disclosed themselves, unobstructed as they are by the shambles of civilization. Like free verse, the image also appealed to Sandburg's democratic instincts as a poet: relating as it does to sensory experience of the most basic kind, the image requires neither literary expertise nor extraordinary intellectual exertion. First and foremost, Sandburg thought of himself as a writer of the people.

Historical Context

The Great Depression

Hope is certainly a subject with timeless interest, but Sandburg's poem, along with the whole of *The People, Yes* (the book in which this piece first

Compare & Contrast

- **1936:** German troops occupy the Rhine land; Hitler and Mussolini proclaim the Rome-Berlin axis.

  1999: Fifteen member states of the European Union establish a joint currency.

- **1935:** Under the Social Security Act, the U.S. Congress establishes an old age pension system.

  1998: The First White House Conference on Social Security is held. President Clinton warns that the Social Security Administration will begin to run short of funds in 2013.

- **1936:** BBC London inaugurates television service.

  1996: There are approximately 40 million users connected to the Internet world wide.

appeared), speaks to a very particular historical moment. The Great Depression (1929–1939) was the longest and most severe economic crisis that ever befell the industrialized nations. By 1933 almost half of U.S. banks had failed, and between twenty-five and thirty percent of the country's workforce was unemployed. America was reduced, in the poet's own words, to a nation of "skyscrapers . . . empty of tenants . . . of strong men groping for handholds." Sandburg's allusion to Per Albin Hansson, the Swedish prime minister who was to lead his own country through these dark days, makes it even clearer that the poem reflects upon contemporary social realities. First and foremost, "Hope Is a Tattered Flag" addresses itself to Americans of the Great Depression.

The New Deal

In view of the severity of this social crisis, the poem's optimism might seem unwarranted, but as early as 1932, there were indeed at least some signs that the country was headed in the right direction. It was then that Americans tired of the do-nothing approach of the Hoover administration and rallied behind Franklin D. Roosevelt and his New Deal, a plan for federal government intervention on an unprecedented scale. The economic security of working men and women improved significantly: better workplace conditions were mandated, the beginnings of a social safety net were put in place, and millions of idle Americans were re-employed in massive public works projects. Sandburg himself, already a very popular figure in the United States, was a great admirer of Roosevelt and had used his access to the media to support the president enthusiastically. (This politicking is reputed to have lost

him the friendship of Robert Frost.) In a letter to the president, the great Lincoln biographer insisted that Roosevelt was "the best light of democracy that has occupied the White House" since Honest Abe. As it became increasingly clear that the United States would enter World War II, the parallels between F. D. R. and America's Civil War commander-in-chief became only more vivid.

Sandburg's Populism

Though Sandburg's party affiliation had changed over time, the political sympathies behind "Hope Is a Tattered Flag" go back to his earliest years as a writer, when Sandburg helped to organize workers for the Wisconsin Social Democratic party. Though its opponents tried to paint it as such, the WSD was a far cry from the revolutionary socialist organizations that had sprung up elsewhere. It sought not the overthrow of the capitalist system, but a set of reforms that would protect workers from the worst abuses of big business. Sandburg left the party when it became a vehicle for German chauvinism on the eve of World War I, but he remained heartily committed to the workingman's cause and gravitated quite naturally toward F. D. R., under whom many of the old Social Democratic aims were achieved.

Critical Overview

"Hope Is a Tattered Flag" has not itself received much critical attention, but a sense of its impact on literary culture can be gleaned from reviews of the book in which it first appeared, *The People, Yes,* one of Sandburg's major works. As is always the case with this particular writer, opinion on *The People, Yes* is mixed, with voices at both extremes. Willard Thorp, for example, calls it "one of the great American books," while Mark Van Doren writes it off as "talk, nothing but talk." Many confess admiration for the spirit of the work, a tribute to the common American who had weathered difficult times with quiet dignity. Moreover, it is widely acknowledged that Sandburg succeeds in presenting a very rich image of folk culture. "Not even Whitman," Thorp insists, "knew America as he knew it." But praise for the specifically poetic achievement of *The People, Yes* is more difficult to find, and where it does surface, it is usually qualified. Reviewing the book when it was published, *Time* magazine found great freshness in the language but, in the end, could not offer a more positive judgment than to say it "*just narrowly missed a place with the best of U.S. poetry.*" Much more widespread is the feeling expressed by Peter Jack, writing for the *New York Times Book Review.* Like most, Jack was willing to concede that Sandburg's folkloric work possessed a certain sociological interest but added that "only one tenth is poetically interesting." The poet seemed capable of a potent image here and a fluent line there, but his particularly slack brand of free verse did not have the energy to light up an entire poem. It was, in Jack's words, "a book written by a poet, though no small part of it, taken separately could be called a poem."

In the years since 1936, the weight of critical judgment has not shifted much. To be sure, as literary scholars have become more interested in historical questions, Sandburg has become a more interesting writer. But with those critics who still concern themselves with the complexities of abstract poetic form, he has not made much headway. More recently, for instance, Richard Crowder found in *The People, Yes* "clarity, color . . . suggestion . . . emotional energy . . . [and] melodic variety," but little that would qualify as poetry. Some of these assessments seem too harsh for "Hope Is a Tattered Flag"; Crowder himself thought it one of the better passages in the book. But in the end most readers agree that despite its warm sentiment and homely images, the piece does not stack up formally with the intricate poetry of Sandburg's best-known contemporaries.

Criticism

Brian Collins

Collins has written on nineteenth- and early-twentieth-century American literature. In the fol-

From the Chicago poems with which he first burst upon the literary scene to the Lincoln biography that secured him lasting fame, his writing celebrates a single hero— the common man, whose rugged shoulders, native stoicism, and common sense had seen him through decades of harsh living."

lowing essay, he explores the aims of Sandburg's simple style in his poems.

Like many of Carl Sandburg's poems, "Hope Is a Tattered Flag" is a simple text, little more than a series of images: "Hope is a tattered flag and a dream out of time. Hope is a heartspun word, the rainbow, the shadblow in white," and on and on in this fashion for twenty lines. The critics have never much liked such writing. Bits and pieces please them (the sound of a phrase like "The blue hills beyond the smoke of the steel works" or a memorable picture like "The ten-cent crocus bulb blooming in a used-car salesroom"), but these things are not enough. Reviewing *The People, Yes,* in which "Hope" first appeared, Peter Jack spoke for most critics when he said "[it was] a book written by a poet . . . [but] no small part of it, taken separately could be called a poem."

One does not have to be Sandburg's biggest fan to wonder about pronouncements like Jack's. To be capable of such a judgment, a reviewer must have fixed ideas about the essence of poetry, for centuries a hotly debated topic. Unfortunately, not much is said about this key issue. Perhaps because there is so much agreement among the critics, they do not feel obliged to explain themselves in any detail. To understand what is behind their low opinion of Sandburg, one needs to look at the historical background.

What Do I Read Next?

- *Abraham Lincoln: The Prairie Years* (1926) is the book that first won Sandburg national attention, as well as the work for which he is most often remembered today. And like *The People, Yes,* in which "Hope" first appeared, it is also a tribute to the American spirit.

- The year "Hope" appeared (1936) also saw T. S. Eliot publish his *Collected Poems.* Though Sandburg was the more popular writer at the time, it was Eliot's more intricate, esoteric poetry that would have lasting appeal for increasingly more sophisticated readers.

- Another contemporary of Sandburg was Robert Frost, whose carefully wrought verse was much more like Eliot's than Sandburg's. Frost's *A Further Range* won the Pulitzer Prize in 1937, and he and Sandburg were friends until a falling out over politics.

- John Dos Passos' *U.S.A.* trilogy (1930, 1932, 1936) offers a sweeping fictional treatment of the early twentieth-century milieu in which Sandburg grew up, including vivid passages about the life of common folk in the Midwest and West.

By the time Sandburg began writing in the early twentieth century, literary criticism had become a professional specialty, and the training that was required to work in this field had a profound influence on critical taste. Having studied the literature of the ages (often in more than one language) and having developed sophisticated analytical skills, the professional reviewer quite naturally found most engaging that poetry which exhibited a deep kinship with the literary tradition (through the use of traditional forms, for example) and did so in ways that were complicated enough to allow him to exercise his advanced interpretive powers. Consider the poets whom the critical establishment rated most highly and whose names have since become synonymous with modernist poetry—Eliot, Pound, Frost, to name only the best known—all of them steeped in the cultural tradition and all practitioners of the most intricate art. Small wonder that the homespun rhythms and simple imagery of a poem like "Hope" seemed underdeveloped.

Sandburg's detractors are certainly entitled to their opinion. Given their impressive cultural attainments, it's more than understandable that they prefer Eliot and others, without question superb writers; but they create an impression that Sandburg fails as a poet in some absolute sense, and this is going a bit too far. No, he never penned anything as finely crafted as the verse of the great modernists, but neither was it his intention to do so; indeed, such qualities would have been totally out of place in poetry for Sandburg's ideal reader—the average person during a time when a college education, along with the literary sophistication that it usually brings, was still something of a rarity. It's certainly enlightening to compare him to other poets of his day, but a fair assessment of his writing should also ask whether the assessment was faithful to Sandburg's own conception of art.

If the work of someone as prolific as Sandburg could be summed up in a phrase, it's tempting to borrow one of America's most hallowed: "Of the people, by the people, for the people." From the Chicago poems with which he first burst upon the literary scene to the Lincoln biography that secured him lasting fame, his writing celebrates a single hero—the common man, whose rugged shoulders, native stoicism, and common sense had seen him through decades of harsh living. He was not the only American writer to champion the nation's masses, but none wrote with more firsthand experience than he, this son of semi-literate immigrant laborers, a young man who rode the boxcars and lived among the hoboes. With the people and by the people: both in his subject matter and in his bones, he is a people's writer. But what is even more important to keep in mind in assessing the achievement of a poem like "Hope Is a Tattered Flag" is that it is also for the people. Sandburg hoped that such writing would help the masses crystallize their identity and in doing so come one crucial step closer to controlling their own destiny.

Did Sandburg succeed in making poetry that harmonized with his populism? Does the style of a text like "Hope Is a Tattered Flag" seem an effective one for a people's writer? One of the most distinctive qualities of the poem lies in its "free verse" style: the rhythm is closer to that of speech, more natural than traditional verse with its metronome-like iambs and trochees. Without question, free verse is better suited to Sandburg's purposes. It's not that the effect of metrical poetry would be entirely lost on the unsophisticated—rhythm always has purely sensuous dimension—but good metrical verse distinguishes itself by subtle departures from the root pattern, and such craftiness is really only evident to readers who have both an acquaintance with technical matters like the dactyl and spondee, as well as a habit of very close study of literary texts. Sandburg happily dispenses with these obligations, more or less superfluous in poetry for the common man, and in doing so enjoys the greater liberty of free verse.

The more natural rhythm of "Hope" is also much more in harmony with Sandburg's conception of the poet—someone whose defining qualities set him apart from, but not above, his fellow men. What is unique about him is merely his focus: by choice or personal inclination, the poet is tuned to the universe of essential truths. He is the (spiritual) eyes and voice of the people, just as much a part of them as such faculties are part of the individual. What special powers he possesses flow from the development of capacities all humans have. What should the poetry of such a writer sound like? Should he speak in the tutored rhythms of metrical verse or in a more natural style of an ordinary person opened to the wonders of creation?

Another distinctive feature of "Hope Is a Tattered Flag" is its imagery. As has already been said, there is little else to the poem. Compared with the work of Eliot and Pound, richly textured as it was with an impressive array of poetic devices, Sandburg's minimalism might seem simplistic. But here again, the poet has good reasons for writing the way he does. Like the metrical forms alluded to above, the tropes of the great modernists required a fairly high degree of cultural sophistication to be fully appreciated. Consider their use of classical allusion: In his famous "Sweeney Among the Nightingales," Eliot writes that "Sweeney guards the hornéd gate," but unless the reader is well versed in Greek legend, she/he would not know that only untrue dreams come through that portal. Sandburg too sometimes employs allusion in "Hope" (for example, " . . . the voice of the prime minister of Sweden carried / Across the sea. . . ."), but such references, though obscure to early twenty-first-century readers, would be understood by anyone who read the newspaper in Sandburg's day. In any case, these allusive images are not the poet's mainstay; most of the poem consists of references to nature, familiar to anyone. But it's not just a question of frame of reference. Sandburg also prefers the image because it aims more at feelings than intellect. Compare, for example, a natural image like the

rainbow to a poetic device like the synecdoche. While the meaning of the first is accessible to anyone who has seen a rainbow and felt its magic, the second depends not only on one's being aware that in poetry the part sometimes stands for the whole but also on thinking through the deeper significance of that abstract relation. It's not that Sandburg believes his readers are incapable of thought, but that he knows that aesthetic experience remains largely affective and only becomes intellectual through a kind of training few of his readers have had.

In "Hope Is a Tattered Flag," as in his work more generally, Sandburg gives his vision a form that would have made sense to the average reader of the day, not an uncultivated person, but someone whose frame of reference was more likely to be the oral tradition and the emerging mass culture (newspapers, movies, the radio, and later television) rather than high art as it was then being defined within elite institutions. Some critics have asked whether this strategy actually succeeded. He was very popular with the people, but were they actually reading his poetry or just embracing a celebrity? Surely those who were reading poetry were much more likely to have read Sandburg's than that of any of his contemporaries, but it's worth adding that even if his work were not widely read, it had valuable meaning for his audience in what it represented: in embracing a people's poet, the people were asserting their worthiness of poetry, and this above all else was what the writer hoped to provoke.

Source: Brian Collins, Critical Essay on "Hope Is a Tattered Flag," in *Poetry for Students,* The Gale Group, 2001.

Mary Mahony

Mahony is an English instructor at Wayne County Community College in Detroit, Michigan. In the following essay, she discusses the role of Sandburg's poem in the interconnected themes in his collection The People, Yes.

"Hope Is a Tattered Flag" is one of a series of poems in *The People, Yes* in which Sandburg reminds the American nation of its traditional ability to overcome obstacles. This book, written while much of the United States was still struggling under the devastating hardships of the depression, is a varied collection made up of poems, proverbs, prophecies, folk tales, anecdotes, clichés, conversations, and several other both literary and non-literary categories. Sandburg's intention in this work was to provide a sweeping retrospective portrait of the American past and to reaffirm his positive vision of the American future. Thus, this collection

> *The range of the comments and viewpoints throughout these 107 sections covers the range of hopes and despair, honor and corruption, in the society. In spite of all setbacks, however, Sandburg's ultimate message is that 'the people' will triumph."*

of 107 widely different types of writing creates a patchwork quilt of Americana, complete with glories and failures, wisdom and foolishness. Both the rich and poor, the exploited and the exploiter are portrayed. For example, a poem about the suicide of "Mr. Eastman, the Kodak king of exactly how many millions he wasn't sure" is followed by one about Mildred Klinghofer, wife of "an editor, a lawyer, a grocer, and a retired farmer." Sandburg quotes a meat wholesaler and a restaurant cashier, "an elder Negro," and "a Kansas city girl out of finishing school." In the "Notes for a Preface," which preceded Sandburg's 1950 *Collected Poems,* he describes his desire to make *The People, Yes* an affirmation "of swarming and brawling Democracy."

Sandburg intended *The People, Yes* to be viewed as a whole; therefore, the separate segments repeat, reinforce, and even at times contradict each other, ultimately forming a sum that is greater than any individual part. One indication of this is that no individual piece is given its own title. Each is simply identified by number. Thus, while section 16, "Hope Is a Tattered Flag," may be viewed as an individual poem consisting of a catalogue of definitions, it is also important to see the poem's role in the entire work. Sandburg employs several interconnected themes or ideas that run throughout the book, intensifying one another as they reappear and intertwine. Some of the most prominent are the importance of hopes and dreams, the existence of the family of man, the frequent exploitation of the masses, and the underlying wisdom of the people,

which ultimately overcomes even man's own greed or suffering.

The opening poem, which presents one of the main themes—the unity of all humankind—is set at the biblical Tower of Babel. God, described as a "whimsical fixer," suddenly creates a multitude of languages, causing instant lack of communication. Sandburg, however, indicates that, in spite of the array of different tongues, common bonds in the "family of man" still exist. The poem notes that even though the languages are different, the questions asked are the same: "Who are you?" and "Where do we go from here?" Many of the subsequent sections in the book then present the different faces of America, hoping to provide an answer to the first question. Others deal with the second as they contemplate the past, the present, and the future.

"Hope Is a Tattered Flag" is one of a group of poems that deal with history and the future. The two poems that immediately precede it explain why hope is so necessary and, at times, so fragile. Section 14 restates the theme introduced in the first poem: We are all a part of the family of man: "Everybody is you and me and all the others." However, that same section reminds the reader that humankind is still separated by language and nationality. One result of this is war, and ordinary individuals always pay the cost of war. Sandburg introduces the image of the flag in this section, emphasizing the contradictions that he believes are innate in warfare:

> Two countries with two flags
> are nevertheless one land, one blood, one people–
> can this be so?
> And the earth belongs to the family of man?
> can this be so?

Section 15 continues the description of war, including a brief catalogue of definitions of hate, providing a counterpart to "Hope Is a Tattered Flag." It also notes that inevitably war will wear itself out, since it creates "Hunger and filth and a stink too heavy to stand." However, Sandburg's images of the resulting peace are harsh, reminding the reader that peace does not bring instant happiness and comfort. While it is difficult to rebuild physical structures after the destruction caused by war, it may be even more difficult to erase the hatred which war engenders. Although the poem mentions the "bright new grass" of peacetime, the section concludes with these pictures:

> And the bloated horse carcass points four feet to
>   the sky
> And the tank and caterpillar tractors are buried
>   deep in shell holes

And rust flakes the big guns and time rots the gas masks on skeleton faces.

These images may help to explain why hope's flag is tattered.

"Hope Is a Tattered Flag" provides an emotional contrast to the bitter realities of the previous sections. It also contains a partial answer to the second question that was posed at the beginning of *The People, Yes:* "Where do we go from here?" Sandburg intended that his work provide hope and a vision of the future for a people still dealing with the grim consequences of both the depression and the war. Since hope is an abstract concept, the precise meaning of which changes according to the individual, many metaphors throughout the poem are deliberately ambiguous. Because of this, the lines can encompass many different dreams and desires: the celestial beauty of the northern lights may inspire one person, while another may feel more secure trusting the four-leaf clover tucked inside a pocket. Sandburg begins his catalogue with two images, the "tattered flag" and the "dream out of time," both of which employ emotional appeal rather than specific, concrete details where the comparison in the metaphor is clearly delineated because of the use of commonly understood terms. However, referring to the previous sections illuminates the title image of the tattered flag since it recalls those flags of war, which figured so prominently in the last poems. The adjective "tattered" provides another indication of conflict: thus the opening image portrays hope as a survivor, emerging not unscathed from battle. From this beginning, Sandburg develops the poem using a series of primarily abstract images of hope. Note that these images fall into a variety of categories.

Several of the images present hope as a simple human quality, part of the fabric of daily life. Describing it as "a heartspun word" combines the idea of homespun, meaning simple or plain—part of the lives of ordinary working people—with the image of being woven from the heart's desires. Other images in this category include the "ten-cent crocus bulb blooming in a used-car salesroom." The specific adjectives here highlight the homespun quality, as well as the need for hope, since even when Sandburg wrote these words, buying or selling a used car required a leap of faith. Other lines in this vein contain the horseshoe and the kiss.

Another grouping contrasts a hopeful but distant image with the harsh reality of the present, demonstrating that dreams can flourish even in adversity. The coal mines and steel mills are places of brutal, backbreaking labor, yet even in such places the evening star remains untouched by human grief. The birds sing throughout both war and peace. These untouchable symbols of hope signal the permanence of beauty and speak to man's spirit. However, because these symbols are so remote, they provide a reminder that hope is not a promise that will necessarily be kept. Far-off dreams may prove as unattainable as the northern lights. But in place of a guarantee, hope provides a vision, an answer to the question, Where are we going? Hope gives direction for the future by pointing to a distant ideal. This idea is conveyed most clearly in the category of lines in which hope conveys a promise of a better future as a dream and a vision of "yonder, yonder." A separate category features the kind of hope that bubbles up as a surprise, appearing "where least expected." The final classification, which combines the theme of hope with the theme of the family of man, dominates the poem's final stanza. The lines are filled with visualizations of individuals from all over the world, celebrating the Christmas spirit with bells and Bach and chorales. They carry on with life, in spite of strife and hardship, living in the present, trusting in the future.

Section 19, which opens with the line, "The people, yes, the people," expands this final message of hope. Here Sandburg again uses a catalogue to create a panorama of American life. Many widely different people and situations are presented: the homemaker, the job hunter, the traffic cop, the criminal. The eventual conclusion of this list, however, is that the heroes are ordinary people who "give all they've got and ask no questions and they take what comes and what more do you want?"

It is important to stress that the themes of unity and hope are only one strand in the interwoven themes of *The People, Yes.* Sandburg's work is not blind to the sorrows and miseries of the world. He is extremely critical of those who exploit the ordinary individual. These exploiters range from national leaders who send the masses off to wars to the rich who build empires on the labor of the poor. The poem acknowledges that even hope is often misplaced since advertisers and politicians and gamblers frequently profit by betraying the dreams of the masses.

The range of the comments and viewpoints throughout these 107 sections covers the range of hopes and despair, honor and corruption, in the society. In spite of all setbacks, however, Sandburg's ultimate message is that "the people" will triumph. This is made clear in two separate letters in which he discussed the book. The first, written to Henry

Luce, founder of *Time* magazine warns that the powerful "can't monkey with the public mind as they do without consequences." In the second, to his friend Oliver Barrett, Sandburg summarizes the theme of *The People, Yes:*

> One of my theses, in so far as I have any, in this piece, hovers around the point that the masses of people have gone wrong often in the past and will again in the future—but in the main their direction is right.

That thesis, with its complex, even clouded, message of hope provides the core of section 107, the book's conclusion:

> The people will live on.
> The learning and blundering people will live on.
> They will be tricked and sold and again sold
> And go back to the nourishing earth for rootholds,
> The people are so peculiar in renewal and
>   comeback,
> You can't laugh off their ability to take it. . . .
> In the darkness with a great bundle of grief the
>   people march.
> In the night, and overhead a shovel of stars for
>   keeps, the people march:
> "Where to? what next?"

Throughout his career, Sandburg was perceived as a poet of the people, a spokesman for the common man. He had experienced poverty in his childhood; during his adolescence he traveled the country, working at a variety of jobs as a simple laborer. This background gave him enormous insight into the daily lives of working-class Americans, insights that he turned into poetry celebrating their struggles and their dreams. Nowhere in Sandburg's work is this as apparent as in *The People, Yes* with its vision of hope as "a tattered flag."

Source: Mary Mahony, Critical Essay on "Hope Is a Tattered Flag," in *Poetry for Students,* The Gale Group, 2001.

Jennifer Bussey

Bussey holds a master's degree in interdisciplinary studies and a bachelor's degree in English literature. She is an independent writer specializing in literature. In the following essay, she demonstrates that Sandburg's poem represents a successful union of Sandburg's regionalism and imagism for the purpose of encouraging readers.

Carl Sandburg's poetry is known for its imagery, regionalism, realism, and colloquial language. In many ways, "Hope Is a Tattered Flag" is typical of his work. The language is plain and accessible to everyone, and the poem has a patriotic appeal. It is written in free verse, is rich in imagery, and has a decidedly Midwestern sensibility. What makes "Hope Is a Tattered Flag" memorable is the way Sandburg applies regional images to the theme of hope.

The Midwestern regionalism that characterizes so much of Sandburg's work grows out of the poet's roots in Illinois, where he lived much of his life. As the son of a railroad blacksmith who was a Swedish immigrant, Sandburg was familiar with working-class people and environments. He is often called a poet of the people because he wrote for and about the common man and woman. He also believed in America as a land of opportunity and in Americans as people of strong character. Amid the hardships of the Great Depression, Sandburg sought to comfort and encourage his readers through his poetry. "Hope Is a Tattered Flag" was published in *The People, Yes* in 1936, a time of great struggle and uncertainty. In Illinois, people faced the twin terrors of unemployment and mob violence (especially in Chicago) during Prohibition (1919–1933). Sandburg seems to allude to the joblessness of the depression when he writes, "And tall skyscrapers practically empty of tenants / And the hands of strong men groping for handholds. . . ."

Sandburg is often associated with the imagist poets, and "Hope Is a Tattered Flag" provides an excellent example of this type of poetry. Imagist poets use everyday language and straightforward images to say exactly what they mean. While the language may seem casual and offhand, it is actually quite precise and carefully chosen. Imagist poets also avoid trite expressions; address a wide variety of subject matter, not just romantic or exalted subjects; and craft fresh, concrete images. Many of the images Sandburg uses in "Hope Is a Tattered Flag" do not seem especially poetic outside the context of the poem, but within the poem they are fitting and effective. The result of the straightforward language is that readers easily grasp the structure and main theme of the poem, rather than struggling, line by line, to make sense of it.

Among the best-known imagist poets is Ezra Pound, who explained that the power of an image lies in its ability to depict a complex emotion in a concise way. With "Hope Is a Tattered Flag," Sandburg exemplifies Pound's explanation by offering the reader a series of diverse, compact images unified by the theme of hope. Each image illumines a slightly different facet of the complex emotion of hope. These images include a tattered flag, which flies proudly despite its weathered appearance; a rainbow, which is nature's beautiful ending to storms; ten-cent crocus bulbs, which lie hidden and seemingly lifeless beneath the ground until they emerge in the spring, full of life; a luckpiece, which is nothing more than a small object such as a penny or a rabbit's foot that encourages its owner; and spring grass, whose lush greenery changes the landscape as it heralds the beginning of a fruitful new season. That these are not rare or unusual objects suggests that hope is as commonplace as it is precious. The range of objects represented demonstrates that hope takes many forms. While the symbols are humble, everyday things, readers should note that each has some degree of permanence or regularity; even those that are fleeting (such as rainbows and crocus blooms) can be counted on to return.

Other images of hope include the evening star, the blue hills, and the northern lights, all of which existed in the past and will exist in the future. Similarly, the birds "go on singing" and the spring grass appears "where least expected." The rich beauty of the natural world persists, even through times of poverty and hardship. Sandburg writes, "Hope is an echo, hope ties itself yonder, yonder." Here he ties hope to the past, perhaps alluding to memories of better times, and to the future, when, true to nature's cycles, better times are sure to return.

The images Sandburg chooses for this poem exemplify the regionalism that runs throughout his work. Sandburg's love for and connection to the Midwest is evident in his detailed portrayal. Such details include the "shadblow *a flowering bush* in white," the "blue hills beyond the smoke of the steel works," the "ten-cent crocus bulb blooming in a used-car salesroom," and the "horseshoe over the door." Many of the images are grounded in specific environments. Sandburg writes that hope is "the evening star," which is a compelling vision on its own; but by adding "inviolable over the coal mines," Sandburg sets the evening star in the Midwestern sky. The poem's references to coal mines, "smoke of the steel works," and a "used-car salesroom" create a setting for the poem. This poem is not just about hope; it is mostly about hope in a particular place and for certain people—people who labor in mines and factories, buy used cars, hang horseshoes over their doors, and hear music from distant lands on their radios. By giving many of the images a context (another example: "The shimmer of northern lights across a bitter winter night. . . ."), Sandburg accomplishes two things: he localizes the imagery, and he controls the pace of the poem so that it does not feel hurried or crowded.

This poem, like so many of Sandburg's, swells with patriotism. It is reminiscent of the lyrics of

> *The images Sandburg chooses for this poem exemplify the regionalism that runs throughout his work. Sandburg's love for and connection to the Midwest is evident in his detailed portrayal."*

"America, the Beautiful," which exalt "purple mountains' majesty" and "amber waves of grain." Both the song and Sandburg's poem scan the landscape, glorifying every sight along the way. While the song honors America as a whole, "Hope Is a Tattered Flag" focuses on the region Sandburg loves. The beginning and ending of the poem, however, are broader in scope.

The poem opens with the symbol of a nation portrayed as a symbol of hope: "Hope is a tattered flag and a dream of time." This flag has been beaten around, but not beaten down, and so it represents a nation that has been tried, but not defeated. Later in the poem, Sandburg takes readers abroad as he describes listening to "strings from Japan, bells from Moscow, / . . . the voice of the prime minister of Sweden" on the radio, then returns them to the United States with the mention of "Bach being broadcast from Bethlehem, Pennsylvania." At first, it may seem as if he is taking readers far away to the Middle East, but this Bethlehem is in Pennsylvania. Here Sandburg is referring to the Bach Choir of Bethlehem, a vocal ensemble founded in 1898. With mention of the Bach Choir, the poet brings readers home to the United States.

Lines 13–16 tell the reader that it is Christmas. The Bach Choir is well known for its Christmas performances, Salvation Army Santas are a holiday tradition, and line 16 mentions "children singing chorals for the Christ child." The images borrowed from a Christian holiday that celebrates salvation and renewal end the poem with a crescendo of hope.

The Salvation Army is a fitting organization to mention in the last line because while it is an international organization, founded in London, it is also a fixture of working-class Midwestern communities like those described throughout the poem. The Salvation Army bridges distant lands and local landscapes; its familiar songs bring hope to people everywhere.

With its many and varied images of hope and its references to music, the poem might be interpreted as a chorus of voices, with each line spoken by a different speaker. Rather than a mere list of images that represent hope, the poem seems to offer a community of individuals, each telling what hope means to her or him. Sandburg shows that hope is everywhere and that it is for everyone. Sandburg himself is best able to perceive hope in his native landscape, among the people he knows best, which gives this poem vitality and realism. The images are especially powerful because Sandburg offers them as metaphors rather than similes. The statement that hope *is* the "birds who go on singing to their mates in peace, war, peace. . . ." (rather than the statement that hope is *like* birds who go on singing) makes hope tangible.

In "Hope Is a Tattered Flag," Sandburg takes images from Midwestern geography and Midwestern lives to paint a picture of hope. The poem is a reminder to readers enduring dark times that their familiar surroundings brim with the promise of a better future. For anyone familiar with the sights described, the poem is a sure source of hope.

Source: Jennifer Bussey, Critical Essay on "Hope Is a Tattered Flag," in *Poetry for Students,* The Gale Group, 2001.

Sources

Allen, Gay Wilson, "Carl Sandburg," in *American Writers,* Charles Scribner's Sons, 1974, pp. 575–98.

Crowder, Richard, *Carl Sandburg,* Twayne, 1964.

Hart, James D., "Sandburg, Carl," in *The Oxford Companion to American Literature,* Oxford University, 1995, p. 585.

Hendrick, George, and Willene Hendrick, eds., "Introduction," in *Carl Sandburg: Selected Poems,* Harcourt Brace, 1996, pp. xi–xxix.

Jack, Peter M., "Carl Sandburg Writes in the True Accents of the People," in *New York Times Book Review,* August 23, 1936, p. 3.

"Poets and People," in *Time,* August 31, 1936, p. 47.

Sandburg, Carl, *The Letters of Carl Sandburg,* edited by Herbert Mitgong, Harcourt, Brace, World, 1968.

———, "Notes for a Preface," in *Collected Poems,* Harcourt Brace Jovanovich, 1950, pp. xxiii–xxxi.

———, *The People, Yes,* Harcourt, Brace and Company, 1936.

Thorp, Willard, "The New Poetry," in *Literary History of the United States,* Macmillan, 1963, pp. 1181–84.

For Further Study

Crowder, Richard, *Carl Sandburg,* Twayne, 1964.
    Crowder's clear and concise overview of the writer's life and work remains a valuable introductory text.

Niven, Penelope, *Carl Sandburg: A Biography,* University of Illinois, 1994.
    Of the full-length studies of the poet's life, Niven's is the most meticulous, and includes several photographs of this very visible public figure.

Salwak, Dale, *Carl Sandburg: A Reference Guide,* G. K. Hall, 1988.
    With over 1000 excerpts from the criticism on Sandburg, this volume allows readers to get a sense of the range of opinion without having to page through dozens of literary journals.

Terkel, Studs, *Hard Times: An Oral History of the Great Depression,* Pantheon, 1986.
    One of the most vivid accounts of the period when "Hope" was written is Terkel's compilation of personal narratives, many from ordinary Americans.

Watkins, T. H., *The Great Depression: America in the 1930s,* Little, Brown and Co., 1995.
    Watkin's recent and very readable history of the 1930s is a good place to begin an inquiry into the social and cultural background of Sandburg's work.

The Lamb

William Blake
1789

One of Blake's most celebrated poems from his 1789 collection *Songs of Innocence and of Experience,* "The Lamb" subtly approaches the subject of creativity and creator alike. While on the surface Blake's narrator seems to be speaking of the life of a real, physical lamb, in the end one realizes he is layering meaning with subtext derived from both Christian and classical mythology. The lamb is also a symbol of Jesus Christ, both as a child and as a physical incarnation of the deity. The child is both a creation of God and a lamb, one of God's flock. Blake begins with a simple image and approaches it from differing angles to give the reader a better understanding of his vision of the nature of Divine Creation.

Author Biography

Born in London, England, on November 28, 1757, William Blake was the second of the five children of James and Catherine Blake. Unlike many well-known writers of his day, Blake was born into a family of moderate means. His father was a seller of stockings, gloves, and other apparel. Though he had no formal schooling as a child, Blake was apprenticed at the age of fourteen to engraver James Basire. In 1779, he began studies at the Royal Academy of Arts, but it was as a journeyman engraver that he was to make his living. In 1782, Blake married Catherine Boucher, the illiterate daughter of a

William Blake

vegetable grower. Blake taught her to read and write, and under his tutoring she also became an accomplished draftsman, helping him with the execution of his designs. Throughout his life, booksellers employed Blake to engrave illustrations for a wide variety of publications. This work brought him into contact with many of the radical thinkers of his day, including bookseller Joseph Johnson and fellow artists John Flaxman and Henry Fuseli. Blake drew literary notice at gatherings in the home of the Reverend and Mrs. A. S. Mathew, where he read his poems and occasionally sang them to his own music. In 1783, Flaxman and Mrs. Mathew funded the printing of *Poetical Sketches,* Blake's first collection of verse. Around this time Blake also developed his technique of illuminated printing. His method was to produce the text and illustrations for his books on copper plates, which were then used to print on paper. Final copies of the work were individually colored by hand. This laborious process restricted the number of copies Blake could produce, thus limiting both his income and the spread of his reputation.

At the time of the French Revolution in 1789, Blake was acquainted with a political circle that included such well-known radicals as William Godwin, Mary Wollstonecraft, and Thomas Paine, and the democratic revolutions in America and France

became major themes in much of Blake's poetry. In 1790, Blake and his wife moved to Lambeth, where Blake began developing his own symbolic and literary mythology, which used highly personal images and metaphors to convey his interpretation of history and vision of the universe. This mythology is expressed in such works as *The First Book of Urizen* (1794) and *The Song of Los* (1795). During this time Blake also wrote the poems included in *Songs of Innocence and of Experience* (1794). Very little of Blake's poetry of the 1790s was known to the general public, though he continued to work as an engraver and illustrator.

From 1800 to 1803, Blake and his wife lived at the seaside village of Felpham before moving back to London. Upon his return to London, Blake was met with accusations that he had uttered seditious sentiments while expelling a soldier from his garden at Felpham. He was tried for sedition and acquitted in 1804. In 1809, Blake mounted an exhibition of his paintings that he hoped would publicize his work and help to vindicate his visionary aesthetic. The exhibition caused some interest among the London literati, but was otherwise poorly attended. Blake's later years were distinguished by his completion of *Jerusalem,* his last and longest prophetic book, and by his work on a series of illustrations for the Book of Job, which is now widely regarded as his greatest artistic achievement. The latter work was commissioned in the early 1820s by John Linnell, one of a group of young artists calling themselves "The Ancients" who gathered around Blake and helped support him in his old age. Blake died on August 12, 1827, in London.

Poem Text

Little Lamb, who made thee?
  Dost thou know who made thee;
Gave thee life and bid thee feed
By the stream and o'er the mead;
Gave thee clothing of delight,   5
Softest clothing, wooly, bright;
Gave thee such a tender voice
Making all the vales rejoice?
  Little Lamb, who made thee?
  Dost thou know who made thee?   10

Little Lamb, I'll tell thee,
Little Lamb, I'll tell thee:
He is called by thy name,
For He calls Himself a Lamb.
He is meek and He is mild;   15

He became a little child.
I a child and thou a lamb,
We are called by His name.
   Little Lamb, God bless thee.
   Little Lamb, God bless thee.   20

Poem Summary

Lines 1–2

One of the most famous poems in Blake's collection *Songs of Innocence and of Experience*, "The Lamb" establishes its theme quickly in the first two lines. When the narrator asks the lamb if it knows who created it, it is not calling attention to the biological parents. The narrator specifically asks about the nature of creation in the divine sense. The narrator does not think the creator is a what, but a whom, and this whom has the power to actually create life.

Lines 3–4

The narrator implies much more than eating and drinking and the home of this little lamb with these two lines. The fact that the gift of life is connected to the command to live by natural, instinctual means hints at the nature of Divine Law. These lines suggest that life, the natural life of a lamb, is a divine creation. The landscape reinforces the natural over the urban. The fact that Blake fails to mention any kind of restraint upon the lamb may also be significant.

Lines 5–6

These lines begin to suggest a second layer of meaning pertaining to the image of the lamb. They recall the swaddling cloths of the baby Jesus, and of his hair that was purported to be like "lamb's wool." The brightness of the lamb, and the brightness of Christ, comes from within, and also demonstrates their ability to reflect light. The whitest lamb reflects the most light.

Lines 7–8

The reference to the lamb's voice suggests a double meaning. Of course, the bleating of lambs sounds very "tender," but Blake refers also to the voice of Christ. The words and the speech of Christ are often thought of as "tender" because they acclaim love and "rejoice" in life itself. The "vales" also have an additional meaning. Vales are valleys, and so here the narrator once again asks the reader to think about the concept of landscape, surroundings and how one is influenced by them.

Lines 9–10

With this new repetition, one has a new perspective on the lamb. This repetition emphasizes the largess, the grandeur of creativity. Specifically, one is called upon to contemplate the creation of both a biological lamb and a figurative lamb. One is asked to consider their relationship to each other, and to the Divine.

Lines 11–12

Only now does Blake introduce his narrator in the form of "I." One can guess that this "I" could be Blake, or one could suppose that it is the piper represented in "Introduction to Songs of Innocence." The identity is probably not as important as the idea that this person seems to understand at some level the nature of creation, and is enthusiastic to share with the lamb and with the reader what he or she knows! The repetition hints once again at the double, subtle nature of the lamb as a concept.

Lines 13–14

Now the speaker brings the double definition of the lamb into a more obvious light. There can be no mistake that not only does the narrator refer to a biological lamb, but he also refers to Jesus Christ in the image of the lamb. Since he is writing about the nature of creation itself, then one can begin to draw conclusions about what Blake believes to be true about the spiritual as well as the mundane. Why does Blake use the word "call" twice? Perhaps, it is to illustrate the idea of being "called" into service of the Divine. Since this is a poem about creation, perhaps Blake hints that to be called to creativity is divine. This is a theme that is seen again and again in Blake's poetry.

Lines 15–16

These lines give reference to Christ's message that "the meek shall inherit the world" and the concept that gentleness and love is the ideal way of behaving in the world. Blake's narrator also links the behavior of the Divine to the behavior of a little lamb. Then he makes further connection to the idea that the Creator and the little child are one and the same. One also can guess that Blake sees creativity as a childlike occupation. Furthermore, the fact that the Divine decided to actually come into the world, as any child would, gives one an understanding of one's own nature.

Lines 17–18

Blake has fun with language in these two lines. The mystical relationship between "I" and "thou"

Media Adaptations

- Greg Brown's CD, *Songs of Innocence and Experience* is arranged and sung by Brown, who also plays guitar. Brown is accompanied by bass, violin and mandolin, button accordion, harmonica, and pan pipes. These tuneful, enjoyable songs have a spontaneous quality and the best of them shed new light on the poems. (Red House Records, originally made in 1986, includes sixteen Songs including "The Lamb.")

- English composer Ralph Vaughan Williams set ten Blake poems from the *Songs of Innocence and of Experience,* including "The Lamb," for voice and oboe. They are available on a CD entitled *Vaughan Williams: Ten Blake Songs; Warlock, etc.,* with performers James Bowman and Paul Goodwin, released by Meridian (UK) No. 84158, 1997.

- American poet Allen Ginsberg recorded a videotape, *Ginsberg Sings Blake: 'Songs of Innocence and Experience',* which contains twenty-eight of Blake's *Songs of Innocence and of Experience* including "The Lamb" and "The Tyger." This is an eighty-minute concert/lecture in which Ginsberg accompanies himself at the mini-pump organ and the bells, while guitarist Steven Taylor and Heather Hardy on electric violin also contribute. Available from Arthouse Inc., One Astor Place, Suite 9D, New York, NY 10003, phone: (212) 979-5663.

- Allen Ginsberg's set of four CDs, *Holy Soul Jelly Roll,* Wea/Atlantic/Rhino, 1994 (ASIN: B0000033AN) includes "The Lamb" and many

Blake songs, some of which are previously unreleased.

- British composer Benjamin Britten's settings of *The Songs and Proverbs of William Blake* powerfully evoke Blake's world of "Experience." They can be heard on Britten, Vaughan Williams: Songs (soloists, McMillan, Greer), Marquis Records, Canada, No. 127).

- Dover Publications' *Listen & Read: William Blake's 'Songs of Innocence and Experience'* (1997) is a spoken version on audiotape, which also contains a printed copy of the poems.

- *Glad Day* and *Bright as Fire,* performed by the Mike Westbrook Band, one of Britain's best known jazz ensembles, consist of settings of poems by Blake, including one that combines "The Lamb" and "The Tyger." Many of the songs derive from a musical about Blake staged by England's National Theatre Company in 1971. Westbrook communicates the energy, passion, and variety of Blake's work with conviction and power. Westbrook's web site at (http://www. westbrookjazz.co.uk/westbrook_blake.htm) contains details.

- *The William Blake Archive* at http://www.iath. virginia.edu/blake (January 2001) has crystal-clear electronic reproductions of almost all Blake's work in illuminated printing, and is continually expanding. It also provides transcriptions of the texts, extensive bibliographies and a search engine that can locate words or phrases and even recurring visual images.

---

has often been the very definition of God. The equivalent value of the child and the lamb, suggests a divine connection and comparison between the human being and the Divine, and the higher consciousness and lower unconsciousness. Remember that psychology as it is understood in the twentieth century did not exist in Blake's era. This concept of dual consciousnesses may have surprised Blake's readership. The fact that he emphasizes this

idea with the second of the two lines can only serve to tell the reader that there has been no mistake in interpreting the connection. Both human child and animal child have an equal relationship to the Divine in both name and quality.

Lines 19–20

The repetition here serves to complete this concept with a blessing. The narrator's revelation is now fully revealed. He blesses the lamb, himself, and the Christ with enthusiasm.

Themes

Innocence

When Blake published *Songs of Innocence and of Experience* in 1794, he subtitled the book, "Shewing the Two Contrary States of the Human Soul." The qualities displayed by the child speaker in "The Lamb" are an example of what Blake meant by the state of innocence, which may be found in children but is not confined to them. Perception in the state of innocence is always spontaneous; it does not get bogged down in painful memories of the past or in useless speculation or doubt. It shows an unclouded awareness of the divine spirit that flows through all things.

The speaker of the poem represents this innocent mode of being. He expresses no interest in the difficult, nightmarish, or problematic aspects of life. He only asks questions ("Little Lamb, who made thee?") to which he knows the answer ("Little Lamb I'll tell thee") and he asks only for the joy of explaining what he knows in the simplest of terms.

Because the childlike mind is uncluttered with the mental baggage that adults tend to accumulate in the state of Experience, the child in "The Lamb" is free to experience joy through his senses. He has not learned how to distort his experience into anything less. He enjoys the bleat of the lamb and assumes as a matter of course that everything else in nature ("all the vales") rejoices in it too. He declares the lamb's wool to be "clothing of delight," which can refer either to the delight the child feels when he touches it or the delight he assumes the lamb has in possessing it. It does not take much imagination to suppose that in addition to the child's sense of touch and hearing, his other senses are also finely attuned to the bliss and delight that shape his perception of the world.

The Unity of Creation

The child has an innocent knowledge and perception of the unity between the different levels of creation. The human and animal worlds are linked to each other by their common source in the divine. The child explains this by referring to the image of the lamb, frequently used in the New Testament to symbolize Jesus Christ, whom Christians believe to be the only son of God. In the Gospel of John,

Topics for Further Study

- Who does the lamb think made it? What would be an animal's view of God? Write the lamb's response, in three stanzas, each giving a different aspect of whom it thinks its Maker is.

- Compare this poem to Robert Burns' "To a Mouse, on Turning up Her Nest with the Plough, November, 1785," written at about the same time. In what ways are Burns' attitudes toward the mouse different from Blake's toward the lamb? In what ways are they the same? How do the two poets view a human's place in the world?

- Aside from the seventeenth line, which directly links the lamb with the speaker of the poem, what clues are there to indicate that the speaker is thinking of himself when talking to the lamb?

for example, Jesus is referred to as "The Lamb of God, who takes away the sins of the world." The child uses this "meek" and "mild" aspect of Christ to explain the unity between Christ and his creation. This is apparent in the three lines,

> He became a little child:
> I a child and thou a lamb,
> We are called by his name.

In other words, the universe, at least the way the child experiences it, is a seamless web, and the glue that holds it together is the divine figure of Christ. Because Christ took human form and so "became a little child," the child feels his own connection to the savior. In the child's mind, the Lamb of God is the divine, life-giving power since he created the lamb and defined its nature. The lamb instinctively knows, guided by the creator, where to find food and drink. There is nothing to darken or disturb this harmonious picture of the tender stream of blessings that the Lamb pours down on his creation, represented by lamb and child. Of course for the child, the joy he feels and the sense that he is under divine protection are not religious concepts but simply his experience. No doubt he has received Christian teachings by schoolmaster or parents, but he shows no desire to probe more deeply into the subject. He is happy with what he knows, and in this sense he is complete. He needs nothing more than what he already possesses, quite unlike the speaker in the companion poem, "The Tyger" in *Songs of Innocence and of Experience.* In that poem, the speaker seeks an answer to the question of who made the fierce tiger: "Did he who made the Lamb make thee?" For the child speaker in "The Lamb," safe in the state of innocence, such questions cannot arise.

Style

"The Lamb" consists of two ten-line stanzas which pose a question and give an answer. Each stanza has five pairs of rhyming couplets, where the end word of one line rhymes with the next. Note that Blake often repeats a word to create this rhyme, creating a type of refrain, and twice employs the slant or false rhyme of "lamb" and "name." Most lines have seven syllables, except for the first and last couplets of each stanza, which have only six syllables. In the second stanza, it is worth noting that the word "called" is pronounced with two syllables, so that it is read "call-ed."

Historical Context

Literature for Children

When Blake wrote *Songs of Innocence and of Experience* in the 1780s he was building on a well-established tradition of children's books. However, Blake fundamentally disagreed with the underlying premises of most of these books, which were influenced by Puritan theology. According to this view, which was shared by the Methodists and the Church of England's Evangelical movement, children were born into a state of "original sin." They had to be ruled with a firm hand if they were to overcome their evil tendencies.

Evangelical educator Hannah More, for example, wrote in 1799 (quoted by Zachary Leader) that it was "a fundamental error to consider children as innocent beings, whose little weaknesses may perhaps want some correction, rather than as beings who bring into the world a corrupt nature and evil dispositions, which it should be the great end of education to rectify." In the Methodist schools of the period, play was discouraged; hard work and self-discipline were emphasized. Idleness was considered one of the worst sins. The underlying idea was that

the child's will had to be broken, so he could learn to live in conformity with God's will. These attitudes were reflected in books written for children.

One children's book that was extremely popular in Blake's time was Isaac Watts's *Divine and Moral Songs for Children* (1715). Watts's attitude to children was considerably less harsh than that of many Puritans. He believed that poems for children should be cheerful rather than weighed down with solemn religious instruction.

Blake objected to the emphasis in Watts's poems on hard work, reading and studying, and the absence of childlike play or enjoyment. A number of Blake's *Songs of Innocence* are direct replies to the poems of Watts. None of the children in *Songs of Innocence* go to school or work. They simply enjoy being children.

If Blake diverged from the lyrics that were fashionable in his day, he often followed, as John Holloway has pointed out, the metrics of eighteenth century hymns. "On Another's Sorrow," for example, is identical in meter and rhyme to "Jesu, Lover of My Soul," by the Methodist hymn writer Charles Wesley.

Blake obviously knew Wesley's work well. Heather Glen has pointed out that Blake's "The Lamb" echoes Wesley's hymn for children, "Gentle Jesus, Meek and Mild." The difference is that in the hymn the child has to plead with Jesus, the Lamb of God, to permit him to come close:

> Pity my simplicity,
> Suffer me to come to Thee.

In "The Lamb," the intimacy between Lamb and child is immediately present. The child does not have to plead for it.

The Child in Romantic Literature

Blake was not alone in his belief that childhood was a time of innocent spirituality and joy. Other English Romantic poets, including William Wordsworth, Samuel Taylor Coleridge, Percy Bysshe Shelley, and John Clare shared Blake's belief. In this they were influenced by the writings of the eighteenth century French philosopher Jean-Jacques Rousseau. Rousseau expounded the idea of the "noble savage," the natural goodness of humanity in its primitive condition. He extended this to include the goodness of children.

Inspired by this novel way of thinking, the Romantic poets replaced the Puritan idea that a child was born into original sin with the idea of the child's original goodness. In their spontaneity and

Compare & Contrast

- **1789:** Publication of *Songs of Innocence* coincides with the outbreak of the French Revolution, which proclaims the dignity of the common man and ushers in the modern democratic age. Blake supports the goals of the French revolutionaries.

  Today: Democratic political systems of varying degrees of integrity and efficiency now cover most of the globe.

- **1798:** Wordsworth and Coleridge publish *Lyrical Ballads,* inaugurating the Romantic period, a new era in English literary history.

  Today: Postmodernism tends to scorn the emotional excesses of Romanticism, and unlike the

  Romantics, few postmodern writers believe in the existence of a universal truth or an overall reality.

- **1790s:** Blake is virtually unknown as a poet; few people read *Songs of Innocence and of Experience* or any of Blake's other poems. He is little known as an artist.

  1863: Publication of Alexander Gilchrist's *Life of William Blake,* twenty-seven years after Blake's death, leads to a slow growth of interest in his work.

  Today: Blake is universally acknowledged as one of the greatest of the English Romantic poets.

---

purity of perception, children were close to God and to nature. "Heaven lies about us in our infancy," wrote Wordsworth in the "Ode: Intimations of Immortality from Recollections of Childhood" (1807).

The child's ability to live effortlessly in an imaginative realm made the state of childhood the envy of poets, who regarded it as a rebuke to adult lives that had been reduced to habit, conformity, and dull practicality. Wordsworth in particular praised the child's imaginative power. According to Wordsworth, a child was able to see the divine light; this gave him wisdom beyond his years. Wordsworth mourned the inevitable loss of this gift as the child grew into adulthood.

Most of the Romantic poets wrote in praise of childhood as adults remembering an earlier time in their lives; it was only Blake, in *Songs of Innocence and of Experience,* who wrote poems that captured the voice of childhood itself.

Critical Overview

"The Lamb," has long been one of Blake's most popular and acclaimed lyrics. English poet and

critic Algernon Charles Swinburne notes in his 1906 work *William Blake: A Critical Essay* that the poem is one of the *Songs of Innocence* that has "a very perfect beauty": "All, for the music in them, more like the notes of birds caught up and given back than the modulated measure of human verse. One cannot say, being so slight and seemingly wrong in metrical form, how they come to be so absolutely right; but right even in point of verses and words they assuredly are." Sir Geoffrey Keynes similarly feels that "The Lamb" is "rightly regarded as one of Blake's most triumphant poems," explaining in his 1955 introduction to *Songs of Innocence and of Experience* that "it is also one of his most transparent. The lamb and the child, both symbols of innocence and of religion, converse together, the child properly supplying both question and answer. They are illustrated together in the design, with a cottage to one side and the oak of security in the background. On either side are delicate saplings arching over the scene without any overtones of Experience." Many critics have looked at "The Lamb" within the context of the entire collection of *Songs of Innocence and of Experience.* John Holloway believes that the poem is representative of the *Songs of Innocence and of Experience,* which he sees as a harmonic collection with a distinctive form. In "The Lamb" the critic writes in his 1968 study *Blake: The Lyric Poetry,* "poetic form here merges into explicit statement. The point is that one can virtually assert this poem to have a structure, inasmuch as it has a structure of ideas: and the structure of ideas is a structure of identity, of the merging and inter-fusion which is the ultimate condition of harmonious oneness. In a world of harmony," the critic adds, "the work of the Creator tends simply towards being a duplication and reduplication of himself: until finally, it is oneness which is blessedness." Michele Leiss Stepto likewise observes a directness in the subject of the poem, which she believes "makes explicit the identification of the lamb, type of a sacrificial humanity, with the infant Jesus dear to the Christian church." By contrasting the question of creation posed here with that in "The Tyger" from *Songs of Innocence and of Experience,* Stepto suggests in The Yale Review that "The Lamb" "deals with the origin of the victims of evil": "In calling himself by the name of the lamb, Christ claimed kinship with the suffering victim and promised, by his act of self-sacrifice, to banish both tiger and lamb."

Criticism

Bryan Aubrey

Aubrey holds a Ph.D. in English and has published books and essays on English Romantic poetry. In this essay, Aubrey examines how Blake's poem illustrates his belief in the unity of all life, expressed throughout Songs of Innocence, *and the spiritual perception of children.*

It is easy to dismiss "The Lamb" as a sentimental or naive poem. Simple in its structure and vocabulary, it leaves no difficulties of interpretation. Unlike some of the *Songs of Innocence,* it does not force the reader to consider ironies or ambiguities involved in the state of innocence. The only question the child speaker asks ("Little Lamb, who made thee?") is immediately dissolved, since the child already knows the answer ("Little Lamb, I'll tell thee"). In light of this disarming simplicity, commentators have had little to say about "The Lamb." They have preferred to dwell on the complexities of "The Tyger," Blake's companion poem in *Songs of Experience,* with its unanswered question about the darker side of life: "Did he who made the lamb make thee?"

The real problem in discussing "The Lamb" is not that it lacks depth, but that the kind of depth it possesses demands a visionary leap from the reader, who must attempt to feel the uncommon (for the adult) reality that the child speaker lives so naturally.

For Blake, childhood was a state not of dependency or ignorance but of spiritual vision. In "innocent" perception, everything in creation is embraced by the tenderness of the divine, and there is no separation between the human self, the natural world, and the divine kingdom. Everything is oneness, or unity, which spreads itself through all the phenomena of nature. In "The Lamb," the focal point of this unity, the creator, source, and sustainer of it, is the Lamb. The Lamb is Christ, whose loving generosity flows out endlessly into the world. This generosity is emphasized by the threefold repetition of "gave" or "give" in the first stanza, in reference to the gifts bestowed by the Lamb of God on the lamb, the creature that bears his name. The child is spontaneously aware of all these realities, at all times, and it saturates him with serenity and happiness that he simply wants to express.

As a consequence of the child's innocent wisdom, there is no drama in this poem; it conveys a sense of bliss at play with itself. In play, there are no real questions, since questions are the result of uncertainty or lack. In the world inhabited by the child in "The Lamb," questions are just a playful pretense. The purpose of these questions is to get the knowledge of the nature of life circulating, so it can make "all the vales rejoice."

As another way of putting it, in the state of Innocence, there is no gap between what the soul loves and desires most deeply, and what it experiences, minute by minute, hour by hour, day by day, in the world. Needless to say, this is not the average world in which the average adult lives, which is why, paradoxically, the simple poems in *Songs of Innocence* may sometimes be trickier to fully grasp than *Songs of Experience,* many of which are situated in the gritty, distressed world that people usually think of as being more expressive of the human condition.

But Blake says time and time again that there is no reason why this should be so, since it is the inherent ability of what he later called the "Divine Humanity" to see the "Divine Vision" in everything. For Blake there was no sound reason to believe that there must always be a gap between human desire and human achievement. About the same time as he was writing the *Songs of Innocence,* he wrote in *There is No Natural Religion* (1788): "If any could desire what he is incapable of possessing, despair must be his eternal lot." If there was one thing that Blake believed, it certainly was not the eternity of despair. Despair can only be caused by an error in the perception of the way things truly are, always. As Blake scholar Kathleen Raine, in *Blake and the New Age,* remarked of "Infant Joy," another poem in *Songs of Innocence:* "Being—consciousness—bliss . . . such was Blake's understanding of the essence of life. Joy is not something that happens to the soul, it is the essential nature of every soul."

The joy world that shines out in "The Lamb" is apparent in *Songs of Innocence.* "Every thing that lives is Holy" announced Blake in *The Marriage of Heaven and Hell* (1790-93), and the phrase could almost be a motto for the world depicted in *Songs of Innocence,* in which life is a continuum of delight and everything is under the divine protection. Take the first stanzas of "Night," for example:

Illustration by William Blake for "The Lamb" from his Songs of Innocence.

> The sun descending in the west,
> The evening star does shine;
> The birds are silent in their nest,
> And I must seek for mine.
> The moon like a flower
> In heaven's high bower,
> With silent delight
> Sits and smiles on the night.
>
> Farewell, green fields and happy groves,
> Where flocks have took delight.
> Where lambs have nibbled, silent moves
> The feet of angels bright;
> Unseen they pour blessing
> And joy without ceasing,
> On each bud and blossom,
> And each sleeping bosom.

It should be noted that the moon does not merely shine; it "smiles," it revels in "delight," as do the flocks of sheep in the "happy" groves. Technically these figures of speech are known as the pathetic fallacy, the attribution to inanimate objects of human feelings or qualities. But for Blake they are far more than mere literary ornaments; they are fundamental to his understanding of how bliss, emanating from the divine Lamb, permeates the natural world. Natural processes and cycles are set in motion in order to multiply happiness, just as in "The Lamb," it is the bleating of the lamb that causes the vales to rejoice, to spread joy.

"The Echoing Green" begins with a similar vision: "The sun does arise / And make happy the skies." And in the first stanza of "Laughing Song," human joy interacts with the joy that runs through nature:

> When the green woods laugh with the voice of joy
> And the dimpling stream runs laughing by;

> When the air does laugh with our merry wit.
> And the green hill laughs with the noise of it.

The poem gives the impression that the entire scene is bubbling over with bliss that leaves no corner untouched.

It might be objected that this is merely a child's view, or an attempt to appeal to the naivete of a child. A laughing world is, after all, not the kind of world most adults live in. But to this objection, Blake in effect responded, Why not? He often liked to challenge the limited nature of what "everyone knows," especially as far as perception was concerned, as in the following two lines from *The Marriage of Heaven and Hell:* "How do you know but ev'ry Bird that cuts the airy way, / Is an immense world of delight, clos'd by your senses five?"

In other words, if humans learned to liberate their five senses from the dullness of habit and blunted expectations, they might see the world as it really is, or at least as it is according to Blake. Blake never tired of explaining this, trying to coax his reader into seeing the Divine Vision. In *Europe* (1794), for example, the poet spots a fairy sitting on a tulip, and he asks it a question: "Tell me, what is the material world and is it dead?" The fairy replies, "I'll sing to you to this soft lute; And shew

> *Blake's belief in the validity of visionary, childlike perception that is everywhere present in 'Songs of Innocence' was for him not a theory but a living truth."*

you all alive / The world, when every particle of dust breathes forth its joy."

As has been shown, the *Songs of Innocence* bears ample testimony to this perception of the universe as consciousness alive with joy. And the image of the lamb is central to the vision, since Christ, the Lamb of God, is the source and informing essence of the joy that animates everything in the universe. Lambs appear in other poems in *Songs of Innocence.* The very first poem, "Introduction," features a piper, who is also the poet, who encounters a child. " 'Pipe a song about a Lamb,' " the child asks, and the poet replies: "So I piped with merry chear." At the child's request, he then sings the same song, and the child weeps with joy to hear it.

The merry piper who sings about a lamb is a clear reference to the poem "The Lamb," and the song he sings is the eternal reality of the Lamb who is also a child—the very child who is listening to the song. As in "The Lamb," the poet creates a self-referential loop, in which distinctions of subject and object break down in the fluid intimacy of entwining interrelation.

Seen in this light, another poem in *Songs of Innocence,* "Spring," becomes a celebration not only of the seasonal renewal of life but also of the lamb / Lamb / child intimacy. The last stanza reads:

Little lamb
Here I am.
Come and lick
My white neck:
Let me pull
Your soft Wool.
Let me kiss
Your soft face.
Merrily Merrily we welcome in the Year.

Given that this is the vision that animates *Songs of Innocence,* several details of "The

Lamb" become more significant than they might at first appear. The word "bright," for example, that the child uses to describe the lamb's coat, seems at first a rather odd adjective to use in this context (even though it provides a rhyme for "delight" in the previous line). However, the word occurs very frequently in Blake and is often used to suggest a kind of radiance that Blake associated with heightened perception, or a fully alive, even divine quality, as in "The feet of angels bright" quoted earlier. Wordsworth, another English Romantic poet who celebrated the purity of childhood perception, also used the word "bright" in this context.

Another detail concerns the illustration to the poem. Since Blake intended his books to be read in the form in which he printed them, in which each poem was accompanied by an illustration, it is always worth examining a poem's visual aspect. The illustration for "The Lamb" shows a child reaching out to touch a lamb, while sheep graze behind them. There is also a cottage, an oak tree and a stream. But what catches the eye are the two saplings on either side of the illustration, both of which are entwined with vines. The saplings reach up to the top of the frame, and then arch over the entire scene, intertwining with each other in what looks like a riot of jubilation. The cooperative interfusing of nature that is part of the theme of the poem thus receives visual representation.

Blake's belief in the validity of visionary, childlike perception that is everywhere present in *Songs of Innocence* was for him not a theory but a living truth. Recent research into childhood gives some support to Blake's view. In *Visions of Innocence: Spiritual and Inspirational Experiences of Childhood* (1993), Edward Hoffman, a psychologist, describes hundreds of accounts of "peak experiences" during childhood, as recollected by adults. These include spontaneous moments of bliss, insights about self-identity, life and death, and startling changes in the way ordinary things are perceived. One woman recalls a vacation at Lake Michigan when she was eight years old:

Open-eyed in the cool water, I lay watching the sunlight reflect and sparkle off the tiny, water-polished stones. I continued gazing and began to notice how the pebbles washed back and forth, right below me, at the shallow edge where the water met the land. . . . Suddenly, I shifted into a state of awareness that was far more acute than usual. I experienced a powerful sense of the beauty of the stones, the sparkling light, the fluid motion of the water, which became so overwhelmingly joyful that I could hardly endure it.

Here, in a real experience, is the joy that underlies "The Lamb" and which Blake called simply "Vision."

Source: Bryan Aubrey, Critical Essay on "The Lamb," in *Poetry for Students,* The Gale Group, 2001.

Erica Smith

Smith is a writer and editor. In the following essay, she looks at Blake's poem and its meditation on nature, youthful idealism, and idealized Christian ethics and compares it to another of his poems, "The Tyger."

> Pipe a song about a Lamb;
> So I piped with merry chear,
> Piper, pipe that song again—
> So I piped, he wept to hear.

These words are spoken by a shepherd piper, who narrates the introduction to *Songs of Innocence.* The shepherd piper had been playing songs for his own amusement; his reverie is interrupted by the appearance of a laughing child-angel, who makes the mentioned request. As a result, the piper becomes something more than just a shepherd amusing himself; he becomes a bard, composing poems for others' enjoyment. The bard is bidden to write in a "book that all may read—." The child-angel vanishes just as quickly and mysteriously as he arrived, and the bard fashions a pen out of a reed and commences to write his songs. Thus the bard, rather than Blake, becomes the dramatic voice through which all the poems within *Songs of Innocence* are rendered.

Despite, or perhaps because of, Blake's creation of a persona to narrate the songs, Blake's moral presence is deeply felt throughout *Songs of Innocence.* Rather than being a direct voice of authority, Blake creates personas and songs to spark a poetic "conversation" on the aspects of innocence. Published by Blake in 1789—nearly all of his works were self-published, and illustrated with magnificent original prints—these "songs of happy chear" celebrate the beauties of nature, youthful idealism, and idealized Christian ethics.

The child-angel's request to hear "a song about a Lamb" has special cultural and religious meaning, for the lamb is a significant image in Christianity. The "Lamb of God" is a common euphemism for Christ. As scholar David Fuller elaborates:

> *Songs of Innocence* accepts what are to Blake the positive aspects of ordinary Christianity, the story of the Incarnation and the idea of Jesus as a child with a child's freshness and vulnerability. The Lamb is a

What Do I Read Next?

- Blake's "The Tyger" in *Songs of Innocence and of Experience* (1794) is a companion poem to "The Lamb." It poses the question of whether the meek and mild God who created the lamb also created the fierceness of the tiger. It is a question the poem does not answer.

- Written a little later than most of the *Songs of Innocence and of Experience,* Blake's *The Marriage of Heaven and Hell* (1790–93) is a rebellious and funny satire that includes the essence of Blakean wisdom in a series of provocative proverbs.

- Peter Ackroyd's *Blake* (1995) is the best biography of the poet. It conveys not only Blake's fierce, lonely determination but also his insecurity and the frustration he felt at his lack of worldly success. Ackroyd also gives a vivid picture of London of the time.

- *London Life in the Eighteenth Century* by M. Dorothy George (1965) is a classic work that gives a sweeping portrait of the city at the time in which Blake grew up there. George emphasizes how much cleaner, healthier, and more orderly London was at the end of the century than at the beginning.

- Like Blake's *Songs of Innocence,* Hans Christian Anderson's story, "The Emperor's New Clothes" (1837), has much to say about the innocent wisdom of children.

- "We Are Seven" by William Wordsworth, published in *Lyrical Ballads* in 1798, contrasts the adult and the child's view of life and death.

- "Fern Hill" (1945) by Welsh poet Dylan Thomas is another poem about the delights of childhood, although unlike "The Lamb," it is written from the point of view of an adult looking back.

crucial symbol: it points to an aspect of Christian myth and ethics which is a real force against violence, which can bring peace in a way that mutual fear and selfish love never will.

> *The poem unfolds in staccato lines and a series of ominous questions. The poet asks of the tiger what makes his eyes burn so brightly, what 'twists the sinews' of its heart."*

"The Lamb," one of the poems of *Songs of Innocence,* elaborates on these symbols and themes. The poem begins with a question: "Little Lamb who made thee / Dost thou know who made thee." The speaker inquires of the lamb as if he is about to deliver a gentle lesson. He goes on to elaborate on the question;

> Gave thee life & bid thee feed.
> By the stream & o'er the mead;
> Gave thee clothing of delight,
> Softest clothing wooly bright;
> Gave thee such a tender voice,
> Making all the vales rejoice!

The sounds of this stanza are soft and inviting. Along with the gentle AA / BB / CC rhyme scheme, the lines themselves have a singsong quality. Also, many of them, when read together, have a kind of calming effect by virtue of the repeated *l* sound (little, lamb, life, delight, woolly, I'll, tell, bless). The words and images presented—stream, mead, delight, softest, tender, and rejoice—are positive and pastoral. One can picture a lamb frolicking in the green grass, wearing a coat of soft wool "clothing." Even the bawling of a lamb has a pleasing quality to the poet. The stanza ends by repeating the opening question: "Little Lamb who made thee / Dost thou know who made thee."

The second stanza answers the question posed in the first stanza. Using lines that are structured in a parallel fashion to those that began the poem, the speaker gently says, "Little lamb I'll tell thee, / Little Lamb I'll tell thee!" The reader pauses in anticipation of his answer of "who made thee":

> He is called by thy name,
> For he calls himself a Lamb:
> He is meek & he is mild,
> He became a little child:
> I a child and thou a lamb,
> We are called by his name.

This is the stanza in which the poem's allusions to Christianity come into full bloom. The speaker notes that the one who made the lamb is called by the same name as the lamb. Indeed, in the Christian tradition, Jesus, known as the Lamb of God, is idealized with the lamb-like qualities of meekness and mildness. These are qualities that are inviting and reassuring to a child. The speaker also aligns himself with the lamb, noting that they share the common name of Jesus. This stanza gives the poem a joyful and reassuring feeling. It is concluded with a benediction: "Little Lamb God bless thee. / Little Lamb God bless thee."

Yet this is not the last word on the image of the lamb. This poem, and the volume in which it appears, takes on more complex meaning when compared to the poems of Blake's companion volume, *Songs of Experience.* Blake had begun working on *Songs of Experience* as soon as he had completed *Songs of Innocence.* Originally Blake intended to pen direct satires of the *Songs of Innocence,* poem for poem. The innocent—perhaps oversimplified—world of the *Songs of Innocence* did need to be tempered. However, the poems that evolved in *Songs of Experience,* while at times correlating to the earlier volume, were often more general in their assertions, and more nuanced, to be direct counterparts. Blake's biographer Peter Ackroyd described the songs: "These are not pure lyrics emanating from one voice but dramatisations of various mental states and attitudes—or, perhaps, dramatisations of the various selves that inhabited Blake."

The vision of the *Songs of Experience* is by its very definition darker and more complex than that of the companion volume. And of the poems in *Songs of Experience,* "The Tyger" is most commonly linked with "The Lamb." There could be no two animals more different: one is known for its meekness and mildness, the other for its ferocity. And "The Tyger" begins not with a singsong question, but with a terrifying assertion:

> Tyger Tyger, burning bright,
> In the forests of the night;
> What immortal hand or eye,
> Could frame thy fearful symmetry?

The poem unfolds in staccato lines and a series of ominous questions. The poet asks of the tiger what makes his eyes burn so brightly, what "twists the sinews" of its heart. The lines are fired off with such speed, even accusation, that the poem takes on the feel of a chant, or a kind of panting. The poem culminates in a final image of violence:

When the stars threw down their spears
And water'd heaven with their tears:
Did he smile his work to see?
Did he who made the Lamb make thee?

These last lines are indeed a shock. The poet imagines a creator smiling at destruction. In a final twist, he spins on his heel and invokes the image of a lamb: the echo of the lamb that had been described so compassionately in the previous volume.

However, the images of this poem do not necessarily negate, or defy, the image of the lamb presented in the *Songs of Innocence.* Rather, the descriptions of the tiger enable the reader to see a more complete picture of the forces inside of all living things. Blake's contrasting visions are hopeful and pious, as well as primal and violent. Perhaps by presenting these themes in companion volumes can one only gain a sense of their true emotional power.

Source: Erica Smith, Critical Essay on "The Lamb," in *Poetry for Students,* The Gale Group, 2001.

Jennifer Bussey

Bussey holds a master's degree in interdisciplinary studies and a bachelor's degree in English literature. She is an independent writer specializing in literature. In the following essay, she interprets Blake's poem as a deeply religious poem appropriate for children.

William Blake's "The Lamb" appears in *Songs of Innocence,* a collection of poems published alongside *Songs of Experience.* These two collections are intended to show the dichotomy of human experience as people move from youth to maturity. In *Songs of Innocence,* Blake depicts childlike, joyful, carefree subjects, while in *Songs of Experience,* he portrays cynical, mistreated, and elusive subjects. Many of the poems in *Songs of Innocence and Experience* are to be read together for contrast. For example, "Little Boy Found" from *Songs of Innocence* was written to complement "Little Boy Lost" from *Songs of Experience.* "The Lamb" considers the nature of divine creation and parallels the dark and mysterious poem "The Tyger." "The Lamb" is often considered representative of *Songs of Innocence* because it celebrates nature and life as created by a loving God.

Most stories and verse written for children during Blake's time were blatantly preachy, as they were created to provide moral instruction for life. During the last part of the eighteenth century, many tracts were published with the intention of guiding

The speaker of the poem is a child—a child who becomes a teacher who explains God to other children in easy-to-understand terms. This technique engages children's imaginations and builds self-confidence. The poem opens with two questions, which reflects a childlike curiosity."

young minds in matters of ethics and propriety. Blake, however, understood how uninterested children are in such heavyhanded messages, and as a result, his writing is lighter and more interesting to children. In fact, when *Songs of Innocence and Experience* was published, it was unconventional and challenged existing children's literature. Today, Blake's influence is still felt in this genre, despite the fact that he never considered himself a writer exclusively for children.

The introductory poem of *Songs of Innocence* tells of the poet happening upon a child on a cloud, who urges the poet to share his songs with everyone. The poem ends with the poet declaring, "And I wrote my happy songs / Every child may joy to hear." Blake is true to his word, as the ensuing poems are lively and optimistic, and many have a singsong quality that is appealing to children. In "The Lamb," he expresses a relatively simple idea that can be understood by children, and he does so in a poem that has a light tone, a tender subject, and a straightforward question-and-answer format. Both the style and the content lend themselves to a young audience.

Readers may suspect that Blake is referring to more than a lamb right from the start, although the broader reference is not made explicit until the second stanza. In the first stanza, the speaker asks the lamb if it knows who made it, setting the stage for the poem's religious musings on the divine creator and the creator's relationship to mortal creatures. As the speaker proceeds to tell the lamb that the same creator who made the lamb also made the lamb's natural surroundings, the reader begins to understand the relationship between the lamb and God. The lamb's creator provides for the animal's needs and expects it to live peacefully in the lush natural environment.

In the second stanza, the poem's Christian symbolism is clearly evident, as, in line fourteen, the speaker tells the lamb that the one who made it is also called a "Lamb." At this point, the reader understands the first stanza in a new light. The lamb is a traditional symbol for Christ. (In John 1:36, the book's author, the apostle John, has John the Baptist saying, "Behold the Lamb of God!" The lamb imagery recurs in Revelation, which is widely believed to have been written by the same author.) The pure white lamb signifies something divine and innocent of sin, and Blake incorporates multiple references to this symbolism. The "softest clothing wooly bright" of line six is not just the spotless lamb's coat (which seems to glow with divine light). This line also recalls the swaddling clothes in which the baby Jesus was wrapped, and refers to God's hair like "pure wool" (Daniel 7:9). Line fifteen ("He is meek and he is mild. . . .") is a clear reference to biblical scripture, which describes Christ as mild and even tempered, even when facing His enemies. Further, among the Beatitudes is the statement that the meek shall inherit the Earth (Matthew 5:5).

Blake then writes that Christ "became a little child," referring to the biblical account of Jesus coming to Earth as an infant and maturing into adulthood just like any other man. The mention of becoming a child also refers to Christ's lesson that people must become like children to enter the Kingdom of Heaven (Mark 10:15 and Luke 18:17). When the speaker tells the lamb, "I a child and thou a lamb, / We are called by his name," Blake creates a powerful image of the divine connection among the child, the lamb, and Christ. The speaker essentially tells the lamb (and the reader) that they, humble mortal creatures, are touched by the divine so intimately that they all share names.

Although the lamb as a symbol of Christ is the most compelling religious symbol in the poem, Blake deftly uses other religious elements to provide thematic depth. The structure of the poem is deceptively strict in its organization. Each stanza begins and ends with repetitive couplets. In the first, the couplets are questions, as this stanza is the ques-

tion section of the poem. In the second, the couplets are statements, as the speaker is answering the question from the first stanza. In the second stanza, when Blake introduces the figure of Christ, the second and fourth couplets each comprise two identical lines, while the center couplet describes Christ as meek and mild, and as a child. The speaker describes Christ in both the past and the present ("He is . . . / He became. . . ."), indicating the timelessness of the subject. This formality in structure is a subtle religious element because the poem, like creation itself, seems on the surface to be spontaneous and unorganized, but in reality has a complex and intentional structure of balanced symmetry.

Other religious elements in the poem are more obvious. The format, with the speaker asking a question and then answering metaphorically, parallels the didactic parables of Jesus as He spoke to His disciples and followers. In line three, the speaker says that the lamb's creator instructs it to feed in the meadows. This is reminiscent of the Last Supper, when Christ instructed the disciples to eat the bread as a symbol of His body. Blake ends the poem with, "Little Lamb God bless thee. Little Lamb God bless thee." These final repetitive lines act as a benediction to the lamb and to the reader, who has come to understand that the Lamb as Christ is closely akin to the figures in the poem and, by extension, to the reader.

Blake's focused and straightforward message is presented to the reader in light verse that is appealing to children and adults alike. Blake wrote poetry with children in mind, but did not consider himself a children's writer. At the same time, much of his poetry was not intended for adult readers only. The result is poems like "The Lamb," which contain profound ideas, yet are written in such a way that they are accessible to a wide range of readers. "The Lamb" is ideal for reading aloud because of its rhythmic composition of short lines and simple words. The subject of a lamb is one to which children are responsive, as it is an adorable, nonthreatening creature often featured in children's stories. The tenderness of the subject is emphasized by the poet's use of soft words throughout the poem, such as "wooly," "lamb," "bless," "tender," and "softest."

The speaker of the poem is a child—a child who becomes a teacher who explains God to other children in easy-to-understand terms. This technique engages children's imaginations and builds self-confidence. The poem opens with two questions, which reflects a childlike curiosity. The child's enthusiasm to answer his own question reflects youthful, innocent excitement at having something interesting to tell. The speaker feels that he has an important insight, and he is eager to share it with anyone, even a lamb. The adult reader knows that the child has only begun to understand the complicated nature of divinity, but the speaker is too young and innocent to grasp this.

For modern-day children, the language may be a bit stilted because of the use of "thee" and "thou," but the sound and subject of the poem are adequate to interest them. Although very young children will not understand the religious significance of the poem, older children will. Still, children will gain a sense that the speaker is talking to a lamb about God, and as they grow older and revisit the poem, it offers them new insights. It is a poem that grows with children, and is able to do so because the form and tone are so engaging to young ears.

Source: Jennifer Bussey, Critical Essay on "The Lamb," in *Poetry for Students,* The Gale Group, 2001.

Sources

Ackroyd, Peter, *Blake: A Biography,* Ballantine Books, 1995.

Blake, William, *Songs of Innocence and of Experience,* with an introduction and commentary by Geoffrey Keynes, Oxford University Press, 1970.

Fuller, David, "*Songs of Innocence and of Experience:* Overview," in *Reference Guide to English Literature,* St. James Press, 1991.

Glen, Heather, *Vision and Disenchantment: Blake's Songs and Wordsworth's Lyrical Ballads,* Cambridge University Press, 1983.

Hirsch, E. D., Jr., *Innocence and of Experience: An Introduction to Blake,* Yale University Press, 1964.

Hoffman, Edward, *Visions of Innocence: Spiritual and Inspirational Experiences of Childhood,* Shambhala, 1993.

Holloway, John, *Blake: The Lyric Poetry,* Edward Arnold, 1968.

Keynes, Sir Geoffrey, *Songs of Innocence and of Experience: Shewing the Two Contrary States of the Human Soul, 1789–1794,* reprinted by Oxford University Press, 1977, Edward Arnold, 1968.

Leader, Zachary, *Reading Blake's Songs,* Routledge and Kegan Paul, 1981.

Raine, Kathleen, *Blake and the New Age,* George Allen & Unwin, 1979.

Reinhart, Charles, "William Blake," in *Dictionary of Literary Biography,* Volume 93: *British Romantic Poets, 1789–1832,* edited by John R. Greenfield, First Series, Gale Research, 1990, pp. 16–58.

Stepto, Michele Leiss, "Mothers and Fathers in Blake's *Songs of Innocence,*" in *The Yale Review,* Vol. LXVII, No. 3, Spring 1978, pp. 357–70.

Swinburne, Algernon Charles, *William Blake: A Critical Essay,* revised edition, Chatto & Windus, 1906.

For Further Study

Adams, Hazard, *William Blake, A Reading of the Shorter Poems,* University of Washington Press, 1963.

Adams reads the *Songs of Innocence and of Experience* in the light of the symbolic system that Blake used in his later, more complex work. The speaker of "The Lamb" may be a child, but the poem is also an "adult poem" that makes the "ultimate statement of the one life of innocence."

Bowra, Maurice, *The Romantic Imagination,* Oxford University Press, 1950.

This contains an illuminating chapter on *Songs of Innocence and of Experience.* Bowra emphasizes how Blake was able to distill complex thought into a few lines, managing at the same time to create the effect of light, melodious song.

Gilham, D. G., *William Blake,* Cambridge University Press, 1973.

Gilham gives detailed readings of many of Blake's *Songs of Innocence and of Experience.* He contrasts the simplicity of "The Lamb" with the complexity of "The Tyger", and argues that the child's perspective is equally valid and true.

Glazer, Myra, "On the Dynamics of Blake's Composite Art," in *William Blake's Songs of Innocence and of Experience,* edited by Harold Bloom, Modern Critical Interpretations, Chelsea House, 1987.

Glazer interprets "The Lamb" in the light of another poem from *Songs of Innocence and of Experience,* "The Little Black Boy," which also connects God, children, and lambs.

Hirsch, E. D., Jr., *Innocence and Experience: An Introduction to Blake,* Yale University Press, 1964.

This is one of the best introductions to *Songs of Innocence and of Experience.* Hirsch likens "The Lamb" to "Infant Joy" and "Nurse's Song," and praises the artfulness of the poem's construction.

Johnson, Mary Lynn, and John E. Grant, eds., *Blake's Poetry and Designs,* W. W. Norton, 1979.

This is one of the best editions of Blake. It has many color and black-and-white illustrations, excellent notes, and includes many of Blake's letters, as well as critical essays by contemporary and modern commentators.

Nurmi, Martin, *William Blake,* Kent State University Press, 1976.

Nurmi argues that the metrical effects and repeated lines in "The Lamb" suggest that Blake intended the poem to be sung.

maggie and milly and molly and may

e. e. cummings

1958

"Maggie and milly and molly and may" was first published in *95 Poems,* cummings's fifteenth collection of verse. Like many of cummings's poems, including "in Just—," "maggie and milly and molly and may" depicts children at play and uses them as a vehicle to arrive at a universal statement about life. Mimicking the singsong tone and style common to childhood nursery rhymes, the speaker presents four children who have gone to the beach to play and describes what each child finds in the process. Maggie finds a shell, milly a starfish, molly a "horrible thing," and may a "smooth round stone." Each of these objects then takes on a larger meaning in the poem; each becomes symbolic of the child who finds it. The poem concludes from these examples that every child, and indeed every person, finds in "the sea" something of themselves. In other words, people receive from the world what they bring to it. If people are friendly, they find friendship; if they are fearful, they find monsters; if they are perceptive, they recognize the transcendent beauty and importance of a single stone. All perceived experience, asserts the poem, is colored by individual predispositions—"Seek and Ye shall find." As well, however, one might argue that the poem also asserts "Find and Ye shall become." In other words, the poem suggests that experience changes who a person is and that by virtue of having new experiences one becomes a new and different person. People are constantly evolving, and with every new experience they cease to be who they were and become who they are.

Author Biography

Born in Cambridge, Massachusetts, on October 14, 1894, cummings spent his childhood in that city, where his father Edward Cummings was a sociology professor at Harvard and a Unitarian clergyman. From an early age cummings showed a strong interest in poetry and art, which was encouraged by his mother Rebecca. Cummings attended Harvard University from 1911 to 1915 and joined the editorial board of the *Harvard Monthly,* a college literary magazine. While in college, he became fascinated by avant-garde art, modernism, and cubism, and he began incorporating elements of these styles into his own poetry and paintings. He received a bachelor's degree in 1915 and a master's degree the following year.

His first published poems appeared in the anthology *Eight Harvard Poets* in 1917. These eight pieces feature the experimental verse forms and the lowercase personal pronoun "i" that were to become his trademark. The copyeditor of the book, however, mistook cummings's intentions as typographical errors and made "corrections." During World War I, cummings volunteered for the French-based Norton-Harjes Ambulance Service. As a result of his disregard of regulations and his attempts to outwit the wartime censors in his letters home, cummings spent four months in an internment camp in Normandy on suspicion of treason. Although he found his detention amusing and even enjoyable, his father made use of his contacts in government to secure his son's release. Cummings returned to New York and pursued painting but was drafted in 1918. He spent about a year at Camp Danvers, Massachusetts, during which time he wrote prolifically. Beginning around this time, cummings, with the knowledge and approval of his friend Schofield Thayer, had an affair with Schofield's wife Elaine. Cummings's daughter Nancy was born in 1919, but she was given Thayer's name. Cummings and Elaine Thayer married in 1924, at which time cummings legally adopted Nancy. During the 1920s and 1930s, he traveled widely in Europe, living alternately in Paris and New York, and developing parallel careers as a poet and a painter. He published his first poetry collection, *Tulips and Chimneys,* in 1923. Politically liberal with leftist leanings, cummings visited the Soviet Union in 1931 to learn about that government's system of art subsidies. He was very disillusioned, however, by the regimentation and lack of personal and artistic freedom he encountered there. As a result, he abandoned his liberal

e. e. cummings

views and became deeply conservative on social and political issues. Cummings continued to write steadily throughout the 1940s and 1950s, reaching his greatest popularity during this period and winning a number of honors, including the Shelley Memorial Award for poetry in 1944, the Charles Eliot Norton Professorship at Harvard for the academic year 1952–1953, and the Bollingen Prize for Poetry in 1958. Despite such successes, however, he never achieved a steady income. Cummings continued to give poetry readings to college audiences across the United States until his death on September 3, 1962, in North Conway, New Hampshire.

Poem Text

maggie and milly and molly and may
went down to the beach(to play one day)

and maggie discovered a shell that sang
so sweetly she couldn't remember her troubles, and

milly befriended a stranded star   5
whose rays five languid fingers were;

and molly was chased by a horrible thing
which raced sideways while blowing bubbles: and
may came home with a smooth round stone
as small as a world and as large as alone.   10

For whatever we lose(like a you or a me)
it's always ourselves we find in the sea

Poem Summary

Line 1

Here the speaker of the poem introduces the four characters. Notice how the repetition of the "m" sound in each of the girls' names gives this line a musical quality, like a melody, and makes it sound like a nursery rhyme. Such repetition of consonant sounds at the beginnings of words is called alliteration and serves to create among each of the alliterated words an especially musical relationship. In essence, each of the girls' names shares this "m" quality, and it is implied, at least on some level, that each of the girls is the same or similar. The names blend together and do not distinguish themselves from one another, and each girl's character and personality is similarly undistinguished. cummings commonly took liberties with basic stylistic conventions and does so here with each of the characters' names, which he does not capitalize. Capitalization is traditionally used to denote proper names and to signify respect for the individual, it is arguable that by not capitalizing names here cummings is suggesting that each character is not wholly an individual. Nevertheless, the rest of the poem, as the reader will see, serves to distinguish each of the characters from one another and to give the reader a clearer picture of how they are each individual and unique.

Line 2

This line then sets the scene. The reader is told that all four of the characters have gone to the beach ostensibly to "play." Notice how cummings uses parentheses to set apart "to play one day." Parentheses traditionally serve to set apart information that is not vital to the central meaning of a sentence, and in this sense the speaker of the poem is telling the reader that the reasons why the girls went is not particularly important. More important, when one notes that the word "day" rhymes with "may" in the first line, one might argue that the parentheses serve to separate this ornament from the more important thematic material of the poem. In other words, the parentheses point out that the end of this line serves only to complete the poetic structure and that, in a sense, this poetic structure is not particularly important. This is important when one recognizes how the poem diverges almost completely from this rhyme scheme in later stanzas.

Lines 3–4

Here the reader learns that one of the characters, maggie, finds a shell while she is playing. As is done with shells, she places it to her ear and hears the sound it makes, the sound of the ocean. This sound is so pleasingly musical that she becomes engrossed and forgets herself and all her worries and "troubles." Notice how the word "troubles" does not rhyme with "sang" and thus disrupts the rhyme scheme begun in the couplet. The reader expects the speaker to tell him/her that maggie was so taken with the shell's song that "she couldn't remember her *name*." This would at least create a slant rhyme between "sang" and "name." Instead, having set up in the reader an expectation as to how the poem will play out, cummings diverges from the expected in order to upset the reader's sense of order. One expects the poem to continue its nursery-rhyme-like rhyme scheme, but instead cummings undercuts this expectation with impunity. One gets "troubles." The effect is that maggie, as an individual, is characterized not by her "name" but by her concerns and worries, by what she cares about. What these worries might concern is left unsaid, but what one learns is that "playing" for maggie means getting away from such concerns and being enveloped in the sensory experience of the ocean and the beach: it means losing herself.

Lines 5–6

This couplet depicts the second character, milly, and describes what she finds while playing. Note that she "befriends" the star, presumably a starfish "stranded" on the beach at low tide. In other words, play for milly consists of finding and/or building friendships. In this case, however, the friend she finds, the star, has "five languid fingers." Languid means inert or sluggish or spiritless or lifeless, and it is implied that milly has struck up a friendship with a spiritless, lifeless creature. This then is presumably less than ideal, or at the very least one-sided. One could argue even that this suggests how desperate milly is for friendship and say that she herself is, in this sense, "languid." That is to say she is somehow lifeless or incapable of creating a friendship with something that is itself alive. Note how the slant rhyme of "star" and "were," brings the poem back to the original rhyme scheme begun in the stanza. As well, these lines follow exactly the pattern established in the first stanza: the first line of the couplet consisting of three anapests with an extra single stressed syllable at the end of the line, and the second line consisting of an iamb followed by an anapest followed by two more iambs. In this sense cummings reintroduces the nursery rhyme quality of the poem.

Lines 7–8

In this couplet one sees the third character, molly, and learns that unlike the other two characters described so far, she has found neither solace in music or a friend, but rather has found a "horrible thing," a sort of monster. That it races "sideways" and blows "bubbles" suggest it is most likely some kind of crab, but more important is the fact that it "chases" her away. This crab calls to mind the spider in the nursery rhyme about Miss Muffett. Like her, molly is frightened away by what is essentially a harmless creature. In other words, it is not the crab which menaces molly, but rather her fear of it, this unknown, unnamed thing. In this sense, the "horrible thing," symbolizes the unknown and molly's response to it embodies a particular world view in which the unknown is something to be feared and avoided. For molly, play is defined according to what it is not for her. In other words, for molly play does not include encountering new things or ideas, for when she does, she runs away. Note how the meter and rhyme of the poem once again diverge from the expectations the reader has for nursery rhymes. The effect here is to cast a sort of darkness over the scene. The light-hearted rhythm gives way to something more grinding and full of anxiety and worry. As well, despite the obvious "-ing" rhyme of "blowing" and "thing," the end-line rhyme scheme is disrupted with the addition of "bubbles: and" in line 8, once again downplaying the poem's nursery rhyme feel.

Lines 9–10

In this couplet, one finally sees the last of the four characters, may, and learns what she has found while playing on the beach. Unlike the other characters, who are all described as they are seen on the beach (with the things they discover), may, the reader is told, takes her "smooth round stone" home. This suggests that her experience is somehow more lasting, that it is somehow more important and worthwhile. And yet what she has found is merely a stone. Line 10 suggests, however, that this stone is more important than it may first appear. Indeed, it is "as small as a world and as large as alone." What does this line mean? One explanation is that cummings is making an allusion to the commonly known metaphysical conceit which says that one can see the world in a grain of sand. In other words, the most minute thing is significant and is a world unto itself. Similarly, the last half

Media Adaptations

- An audiocassette titled "E. E. Cummings Reads Kaipe/One Times One and 50 Poems." cummings was well-received as a reader of his own poems. Even though "maggie and milly and molly and may" is not included on this tape, listening to the poet reading his own work would add depth to the poems.

- An electronic magazine (e-zine) titled "Spring" is located at www.gvsu.edu/english/Cummings/Index.htm (January 2001). It offers notes on cummings's works, a bibliography, links to other websites focused on cummings, as well as some of his poems.

- "The Poets' Corner" offers an extensive collection of cummings poems at http://www.geocities.com/~spanoudi/poems/cumming1.html (January, 2001).

- A website titled "Hippies, Hindus and Transcendentalists" written by Arthur Paul Patterson, who discusses Ermerson's essay "The Transcendentalist," can be found at http://www.watershed.winnipeg.mb.ca/literature/Emerson/Emersonheroes.html (January 2001).

of line 10 celebrates being alone and suggests that while humans tend to be extremely gregarious beings and tend therefore to think of "being alone" as a negative circumstance, "being alone" has its value. Ultimately these lines suggest that may recognizes the value and worth of an otherwise common stone. If this stone is reflective of may's personality, of her character, then one might conclude that she is extremely perceptive, slightly intellectual, and possesses a definite sense of self-worth.

Lines 11–12

These lines assert the central theme or message the speaker would have the reader take from this poem. Simply put, these lines build upon the examples given in the previous stanzas and conclude that "it's always ourselves we find in the sea."

Line 11 is particularly interesting because it suggests that even if one loses oneself, one is also discovering oneself. In other words, the poem's message is two-sided. First it suggests that whatever one finds at "the sea" or in the world is somehow symbolic of who one is. That is to say that one's personality and preconceptions will determine how one views what one finds and in what light one looks upon it. For example, molly is frightened by a harmless crab. This would seem to imply that she is a timid person full of fear. If she weren't, she might simply look upon this unknown creature as a curiosity. On the other hand, the poem is also suggesting that while one might lose one's sense of identity when one encounters new experiences in the world, the sum of that experience is who that person is. In other words, what one finds will eventually become a part of who one is, a part of one's memory and experience. In this sense, every experience one has makes one into a different person than one was before he/she had those experiences; one simultaneously loses a self and gains a new self. That is to say, one is constantly evolving and developing as an individual, and one's experiences inform who one is and how one interacts with and views the world around oneself.

Themes

The poem "maggie and milly and molly and may" represents one of e. e. cummings's experiments with rhymed couplets. True to his disregard for formal rules of writing, cummings does not rhyme every couplet in this poem. It is also a perfect and, on the surface, simplistic expression of his belief that the outer self is a reflection of the inner self.

Identity and Self

The characters represented in this poem, maggie, milly, molly, and may, could very well stand for four young girls. However, it would be a strange coincidence to have four young girls come together who had such similar names. The fact that all the names begin with the letter *m* could be a clue that these girls each symbolize an aspect of *me*. In other words, each represents an aspect of the self, a subject that cummings often reflects on.

Whether the characters are looked at individually or as aspects of the self, the main theme of the poem is a search for the self or identity. Each young girl, or each aspect of the self, is marked by different characteristics. Each one finds something at the sea that is quite unlike what the others find.

Also, each experience is unique and, thus, each lesson learned is very personal.

Maggie, in the second couplet, discovers a shell that sings. The music that she hears is so sweet that "she couldn't remember her troubles." Maggie is the thinker, the contemplative one, the one who ponders the troubles of the world (much like cummings). She carries her thoughts around with her, and they have become a burden. But at the sea, she is reminded that art, in this case music, helps one to forget one's worries, temporarily transporting the self to a place beyond the ordinary. Or to look at it in another way, art (or music) brings one back to the purest state of self, to the uncontaminated present where worries of the past do not exist and troubles of the future are not yet discovered.

In the third couplet, there is milly, who befriends a "stranded star." Milly is the sensitive one, the one tuned in to the needs of others. She gives a helping hand to someone in need, in this case a starfish. Through the aspect of milly, cummings might be saying that one finds oneself through helping others. Taken on a more personal level, as a reflection on self, cummings might also be saying that when one feels stranded, one need only look as far as one's own hands for help. The clue to this thought can be found in the word *languid* which means relaxed (or limp) but can also mean lazy.

Next comes molly who "was chased by a horrible thing." Molly is the innocent one (the word *chased* sounding very similar to the word *chaste*). She is naive concerning the ways of the world, unfamiliar with the unusual. She is both frightened and fascinated by horrible things, as she also notices that this crab is "blowing bubbles"—a joyful, childhood pastime. The fact that molly thinks the crab is horrible based merely on its appearance and manner of walking "sideways," attests to molly's easily aroused prejudices for things that do not fit into her narrow definitions of beauty and pleasantness.

May comes home, in the fifth couplet, with a "smooth round stone" in which she finds a complexity. May is a dreamer, a person who can imagine things that are not always visible to the ordinary way of thinking. In the stone that she brings home, she finds that the world is small but in spite of this she, like the stone, feels quite alone. Like cummings, who often had disdain for ordinary thinking, molly realizes that not everyone thinks like she does. Not everyone treasures a small, round stone enough to bring it home from the sea as a souvenir. Not everyone comprehends that one finds one's identity in the things that are found outside of one-

Topics for Further Study

- Describe a place, as this poem does with the beach, where three or four friends might independently pick up things related to their lives. What does this place tell you about the world we live in? What does it tell you about the friendship between your characters?

- The last stanza brings up the idea of loss, for the first time in the poem. Colleen McElroy's "A Pièd" is all about the loss of an object as seemingly insignificant as this poem's shells and stones. In what way does this poem offer an antidote to all of the loss described in "A Pièd"? Is it significant that one poem takes place at the seashore and the other on the highway?

- Why do the second and fourth stanzas have different rhyme schemes from the others? Is it significant that they match each other, while the others rhyme in self-contained couplets? How does this structure relate to the poem's message?

self. Then, to make sure that the reader understands that this is exactly what cummings is trying to say, he states these sentiments in the last couplet.

"For whatever we lose (like a you or a me) / it's always ourselves we find in the sea," are the last lines of this poem, a perfectly rhyming couplet. Also in these lines are the first mention of a "you or a me," the first time the poet steps away from the young girls and brings the poem home to the speaker as well as the reader, uniting them both in the search for a more universal self, the step that follows the definition of the more ordinary and individual identity.

Transcendentalism

The cummings collection called *95 Poems*, from which this particular poem was taken, has been referred to as a collection that continues along the lines of the Transcendental tradition. Transcendentalism was a nineteen-century movement of writers, most of them living in New England, who believed in the power of insight or intuition, often regarding them with greater respect than the intellect or rational mind. It is through intuition, the Transcendentalists believed, that the deepest truths about human nature were revealed.

Highly individualist people such as Ralph Waldo Emerson, Henry David Thoreau, and Walt Whitman are examples of writers who were attracted to this philosophy. Many reviewers of cummings's work have included him in this group.

Transcendentalism celebrates the belief that all the knowledge that a person needs in life is inherent, residing inside of them until experience brings the remembering of this knowledge to the conscious mind. There is also a great respect for the organic or natural world as opposed to the man-made or synthetic world. These beliefs are reflected in his poem "maggie and milly and molly and may" in the way that cummings uses the natural world (the beach, starfish, shells, crabs, and stones) as triggers that stimulate reflection. The self-knowledge of the young girls is already known to them. But the memory of that knowledge and the awareness of themselves is reinforced when they reflect upon the things and the experiences that they find at the sea.

Style

"Maggie and milly and molly and may" is written in the tone and style of a nursery rhyme and is marked by both its skillful use of alliteration and its complex end-line and internal rhymes.

Nursery rhymes do not all share a single poetic form or meter, but they are generally marked by their use of end-line rhyme and for their bouncy rhythms. In "maggie and milly and molly and may" these traditional elements serve to heighten the memorable quality of the poem and also to lend tension to the piece. Strictly speaking, the poem does not duplicate the rhythmic pattern expected in nursery rhymes. Instead, the first couplet sets up an expectation in the reader's mind. The reader expects the poem to continue in this vein, to continue using end-line stressed rhyme and the lines to continue being metrically symmetrical. Instead, cummings takes liberties with both rhythm and rhyme, in order to keep the reader slightly on edge.

The first couplet is written in dactyls, anapests and iambs. Each of these three is a kind of metric foot: a metric foot is a unit of measure to describe a measured pattern in verse. A given type of metric foot (in English verse) is distinguished by a fixed combination of accented and unnaccented syllables. A dactylic foot consists of three syllables, with the stress on the first syllable and the second two syllables unstressed. An anapestic foot consists also of three syllables, but the first two syllables are unstressed and the last is stressed. An iambic foot consists of two syllables, with the first syllable unstressed and second stressed.

> mag gie and / mil lie and mol ly and / may / went
> down / to the beach / to play / one day

These lines exhibit all the qualities of nursery rhyme verse, including the jingly rhythm created by the three syllable feet, and the stressed end-line rhyme of "may" and "day." In contrast, the second stanza breaks with this pattern of rhythm and rhyme:

> and mag gie / dis cov ered / a shell that / sang / so
> sweet ly / she could n't / re mem ber / her trou bles

Notice how these metrical feet disrupt the pattern begun in the first couplet, and how the poem diverges from the end-line rhyme scheme. Instead of dactyls, one suddenly gets amphibrachs, three syllable feet in which the second syllable is stressed and the other two are unstressed. Notice as well how the poem diverges from the rhyme scheme begun in the first stanza. Where one might expect the word "name" to complete the rhyme, one gets "troubles." In this manner, cummings dismisses one's expectations and forces the reader to adjust to the unexpected. This is a particularly interesting strategy when one realizes that thematically the poem is essentially about how one's expectations affect how one views the world.

Finally, cummings makes masterful use of alliteration and slant rhyme in this poem. Alliteration refers to repetitions of consonant sounds at the beginnings of words within a line. For example, if one looks at the first line of the poem, one sees that the "m's" in each of the girls' names are alliterative and give a musical quality to the poem, which contributes to its nursery rhyme feel. Slant rhyme refers to rhymes that are not perfect rhymes (such as white/bite) but are instead partial rhymes, as "star" and "were" are in the third stanza of this poem. Slant rhyme in this poem serves to undercut the nursery rhyme flavor of the poem while not breaking completely with rhyme altogether.

Historical Context

According to cummings's biography, the poet was writing for most of his life. From the time he was four, barely big enough to hold on to a pencil, until his death, he wrote poems. His serious writing career spanned almost fifty years, taking him through two world wars, the Great Depression, and into the 1960s' years of civil protest.

Having been raised in a loving but conservative middle class family in a conventional New England environment, cummings found all the rules and regulations surrounding his proper upbringing somewhat stifling in terms of his creativity. Much of his early poetry reflects his disapproval of the formality of his New England heritage. His poems were full of satire whose purpose was to make fun of the decorum and respectability of the people who embraced the proprieties of the Puritan ethic. Robert E. Wegner in his essay "The Poetry and Prose of E. E. Cummings," states that cummings believed that he had to go beyond his community to gain an education as a poet.

Besides literature, cummings studied art in both New York and Paris. Through his love of art, he became familiar with Pablo Picasso and his cubist paintings. Cubism was a visual arts style that began early in the twentieth century in Paris. It was a style that emphasized a flat, two-dimensional picture, rejecting the traditional concepts of perspective as well as the theories of art as the imitation of nature. Picasso's cubist paintings were fragmentations of bodies, still life, and geometric objects. Picasso was a very strong influence on cummings's early art forms as well as on his writing, as were writers Gertrude Stein and Ezra Pound, all of whom were looking for new ways to express their art.

Cummings's education in the visual arts made him very conscious of the way his poems lay on a page. "This training had its most noticeable effect on the typographical and visual appearance of his poems," says Wegner. Some poems "are designed to be read vertically on the page ... one poem looks like a football standing on end."

In these early years, according to Norman Friedman in his essay "E. E. Cummings and His Critics," cummings's poetry reflects his concern with the technical aspects of his poetry. "Cummings is viewed as a seeker after new forms for expressing the new sensibility of the age." Friedman continues: "Those [critics] who favor him praise his ... originality. ... Those who disfavor him say the technical hijinks don't work."

Cummings's "technical hijinks" included more than just an unusual arrangement of words upon a

Compare & Contrast

- **1913:** Charlie Chaplin's first film opens. Chaplin, who has been called a natural comedian or a comedic genius, plays a character in silent films who always finds the brighter side in life, believing (similar to transcendentalists) that all human beings are good at their core.

  1977: The movie *Star Wars: Episode IV* is released. The concept of a special force inside each person is one of the major themes of this movie.

  1999: *The Matrix* opens in theaters around the United States and presents a new vision of reality based on computerized virtual reality.

- **1909:** Pablo Picasso works together with French painter Georges Barque to create a completely new way of depicting form on the canvas. Their style of painting is referred to as Analytical Cubism—a break from the traditional form of Renaissance painting.

  1913: Russian composer Igor Stravinsky's first performance of "Rite of Spring," a striking departure from the conventions of traditional classical music, is greeted with riots in the streets of Paris. Stravinsky has been credited with starting the modernist movement in music.

  1914: Gertrude Stein publishes her book of poems *Tender Buttons,* which is highly influenced by Picasso's cubism. Her innovative writing emphasizes not so much the meaning behind her words but rather the sounds of the words themselves. In her attempt to break from the traditional form of writing, her writing often becomes difficult to comprehend.

  2000: New York mayor Rudolph Giuliani withdraws funds from the Brooklyn Museum of Art after the directors refuse to remove a work by Cris Ofili. The artist, in an attempt to break from traditionally used artistic materials, utilized excrement in some of his works. The mayor found Ofili's work objectionable.

---

page. He also experimented with punctuation, words that ran together, dislocated syntax, capitalization (and decapitalization) and the misuse of parts of speech.

In the thirties, in between World War I and World War II, cummings's poetry took on a political air. It is during this period that "Cummings is no longer seen merely as a poet of sensations rather than thoughts, and the problem of individualism becomes central," states Friedman. To help define cummings's emphasis on the individual, Wegner states that "throughout his career Cummings insisted that the artist must maintain fidelity to himself. . . . It's you . . . who determines your destiny. . . . Nobody else can be alive for you; nor can you be alive for anybody else. . . . There's the artists' responsibility; and the most awful responsibility on earth."

During the 1930s, critics were still quick to disparage cummings's poetry, calling his style immature, eccentric, and self-indulgent; and his themes boring and showing no sign of growth from his earlier collections. Some critics, says Friedman, regretted the fact that "a good poet [cummings] is being spoiled by lack of growth in social issues."

It was in the 1940s that the mature poet emerged, and critics began to consider him a serious poet. It was also during this period that his poetry took on a metaphysical or Transcendental tone. His works became lighter in tone, often described in terms of joyfulness. This does not mean that all critics appreciated his work. There still were many who could not get over cummings's use of untraditional typography, punctuation, and syntax—tricks, as the critics called them.

It was in 1958 that cummings's *95 Poems* was published. This is the volume in which the poem "maggie and millie and molly and may" appears. Norman Friedman in the book *e. e. cummings: The Growth of a Writer* calls this volume of poetry a "remarkable book . . . for the windows of perception have been cleansed, and the satirical vision has been practically replaced by crystal-clear impressions of nature and a consistently maturing transcendentalism." In respect to the specific poem, Friedman says that in it cummings "reveals a developed sense of how the transcendental world is involved in the ordinary world as well as a maturing grasp of poetic style and technique." *95 Poems* was the last book that cummings would see published. He died in 1962. His last book of poetry was published posthumously.

Critical Overview

Cummings's work has always encountered divergent criticisms. On one end of the spectrum are those critics who deem him one of the most creative and exciting poets of the twentieth century, while others have downplayed his significance arguing that his poems lack anything akin to an intellectual philosophy. Cummings's work is generally noteworthy for the refreshing ways that it incorporates otherwise common language and for its unique visual style. In most cases, the reader simply needs to look at cummings's poem to know he authored it. Cummings's adept use of typographical symbols distinguishes almost all of his poems, and his visual training as a painter made him critically aware of how each poem should look on the page. Nevertheless, many critics argue that such visual treatments are merely ornamental and that cummings's poems lack original subjects. "Maggie and milly and molly and may" exemplifies this philosophical lacking: arguing that the idea that one gets from experience what one brings to it, and that experience shapes one's sense of self, is on the whole a rather trite and worn out idea.

One example of this sort of divergent criticism can be found in R. P. Blackmur's article published in 1931 in *The Hound and the Horn*. Blackmur asserts "how wonderfully individual, characteristic, original, all [cummings's] poems are . . . full of perceptions pure as those in dreams, effects of wonderful delicacy and exactness." In addition, Blackmur argues that "cummings has a fine talent for using unfamiliar, even almost dead words, in such a context as to make them suddenly impervious to every ordinary sense; they become unable to speak, but with a great air of being bursting with something very important to say." In other words, cummings is able to take common language and

make the reader see it in new and interesting ways. Nevertheless, Blackmur also argues that cummings's poems lack proper subject matter. "Soon as we take it seriously," he argues, "we see how little material there is in this poetry except the assurance, made with continuous gusto, that the material exists. . . . Sometimes one word, in itself vague and cloudy, is made to take on the work of an entire philosophy." In short, Blackmur concludes that "there is a great big moral vacuum at the heart of e. e. cummings's poetry."

In a similarly double-edged fashion, G. S. Fraser, in an article published in *Partisan Review* argues that a "general characteristic" of cummings's poetry is "its steadily sustained youthful strident energy, of which the dark shadow is its almost complete failure to mature." Fraser also concludes that cummings's poems exhibit some merit: "There is some of the matter of life here; there is an extraordinary technical dexterity; there is an urbane wit of a very savagely effective sort; a disturbing gift for evoking sexual situations below head-level; one of the most notable talents for direct simple lyrical utterance of this century." Yet he argues vehemently that "there is something which, however narrow and callow, has been held to obstinately enough to deserve the honorary title of 'a philosophy of life.' It is the philosophy . . . of the adolescent who wants the moon down out of the sky, but wants it to stay up there and shine on him, too."

In response to these two critics, William Heyen, in an article published in *Southern Humanities Review* argues that cummings's seemingly anti-intellectual philosophy is simply an extension of Emersonian transcendentalist philosophy. Transcendentalism refers to a school of thought that revered the world of the mind over the world of matter and believed in the power of intuition to lead to Truth. Heyen ultimately argues that "To talk about a 'philosophy' or system of thought in regard to a poet who refuses all but illimitable Being is beside the point. Cummings has been speaking a different language from the one so many of his critics have been wanting to yoke him with."

Criticism

Joyce Hart

Hart, a former college professor, is currently a freelance writer and copyeditor. In this essay, she considers the transcendentalist background of e. e.

cummings's poem and then compares the poem to Anne Morrow Lindbergh's collection of essays Gift from the Sea.

Critics seemed unable to pigeonhole e. e. cummings. He was a man of many moods—some caustic and full of ridicule, others quiet and contemplative. The themes of his poetry were just as likely to be influenced by politics and social affairs as by sexuality and love. But one recurring theme that cummings seems to have always come back to, from the beginning of his career to the end, was his search for self. And in his search, his poetry appears to have been most heavily influenced by the philosophy of transcendentalism.

It was during the 1940s, says Norman Friedman in his essay "E. E. Cummings and His Critics," that critics started to take cummings's poetry more seriously, recognizing that cummings had begun to state a more definite view of life in his poetry, and they could see that his "main issue [was] metaphysical." Critics during this time were "beginning to see the central transcendental vision in cummings' work." This does not mean that cummings did not have transcendental leanings before this time, but only that his critics were beginning to appreciate his poetry more; they were able to see past cummings's unusual attempts at defying the standard rules of grammar, punctuation, and syntax. They were starting to get over their dislike of cummings's literary hijinks (as one critic called them) and were finding deeper meanings hidden in cummings's words.

In the 1950s, when *95 Poems* (the collection that included the poem "maggie and milly and molly and may") was published, critics became even more excited about cummings's work, now stating that his view of life, as displayed in his poetry, not only encompassed transcendentalism but also mysticism. It was as if cummings's had moved up another rung of the ladder. He became more legitimate, not just a "romantic individualist," says Friedman, but a mature poet. In particular, the poem "maggie and milly and molly and may," says Friedman in another essay in *e. e. cummings, The Growth of a Writer,* revealed not only a "developed sense of how the transcendental world is involved in the ordinary world" but also that cummings had secured a "grasp of poetic style and technique." So even though there still remained a lot of controversy about cummings's poetry, there was a consensus of critical opinion that cummings had tapped a transcendental root. But what is transcendentalism? And how is it reflected in cummings's poetry?

> *It is the individual that transcendentalists celebrate—the individual with the indwelling god, the individual with all knowledge contained, the individual for whom Nature provides symbolic answers. Or as cummings sums it up: 'For whatever we lose (like a you or a me) / it's always ourselves we find in the sea.'"*

One dictionary definition of transcendental is: an adjective that describes something that is beyond ordinary or common experience. But the term transcendentalism became popular in the eighteenth century due to German philosopher Immanuel Kant who believed that the mind contained very important ideas that were not learned by the senses through experience but rather were innate in every human being. He believed that every human was born with an all-encompassing knowledge that was contained, in what Kant called transcendental form, in the human faculty referred to as intuition. From then on in popular culture, things related to intuition were referred to as transcendental.

But it was in the nineteenth century in America that the philosophical and literary movement referred to as transcendentalism was created. The most prominent authors associated with this movement were Ralph Waldo Emerson and Henry David Thoreau. Begun as a reform movement in the Unitarian Church, transcendentalism stressed the dwelling of God (in the form of inspiration or intuition) in everyone. In addition, the soul of each individual was believed to be identical with the soul of the world. It contained everything that the world contained. Taking this belief to a deeper level, transcendentalists believed that every natural fact was a symbol of some spiritual fact. They believed that children were possibly more intuitive than adults

What Do I Read Next?

- Any one of the following books by Ralph Waldo Emerson will offer a comprehensive understanding of the transcendentalist movement in America: *Self-Reliance* (1841), *Introductory Lecture on the Times* (1841), and *Nature* (1844).

- Books by Henry David Thoreau will exemplify the transcendentalist movement put into practice. Thoreau's most famous book is *Walden* (1854).

- Modern transcendentalist/modernists include Ezra Pound, an author of prose and poetry. Pound turned his transcendentalist/modernist energy toward the Asian culture, studying Buddhism, Chinese poetry, and Japanese drama. Pound wrote *Cathay,* which was inspired by the poetry of a contemporary Chinese man, Li Po. Pound also edited a book titled *Confucius to cummings: An Anthology of Poetry.*

- Gertrude Stein was a contemporary of cummings. She lived for many years in Paris, and her house became a gathering place of many influential artists and authors of the time, including cummings. Her most famous book is a thinly veiled autobiography written as a novel and called *The Autobiography of Alice B. Toklas.*

- Walt Whitman's *Leaves of Grass* is a collection of his poetry. His major themes are an attempt to identify the American individual as well as the collective group of Americans who possess united souls. One of the most famous poems in this collection is "Song of Myself."

because culture had a tendency to corrupt people, as they grew older. Intuition or insight was held superior to both logical thought and experience in regard to the revelation of the deepest truths.

Transcendentalists also believed that the external world and the interior world of humans were one and the same. What is outside first exists inside human beings in their intuition. But sometimes people are not aware of this intuitive knowledge and must be reminded of it. And that is where nature comes in. Nature is a living mystery, full of symbolic signs that humans can read. With this concept, the transcendentalists believed that knowing oneself and studying nature were the same thing. Nature mirrored human psyche. "All that you call the world is the shadow of that substance which you are," wrote Emerson in his essay "The Transcendentalist."

A deeper interpretation of cummings's "maggie and milly and molly and may" can be easily missed because the poem is very short and is written in a rather uncomplicated couplet form with simple rhyming patterns. But with an understanding of transcendental philosophy in mind, cummings's poem takes on deeper meaning. Because of the brevity of the poem, it might be interesting to reinforce the transcendental elements of the poem by comparing cummings's work with another piece of literature that was published in the same time period. Anne Morrow Lindbergh's *Gift from the Sea* is a collection of essays that expresses a theme similar to cummings's poem and was published in 1955 (some years before the 1958 publication of cummings's collection of poems that contains "maggie and milly and molly and may"). Lindbergh wrote the essays while vacationing at the beach, and she uses the nature that she finds there for self-reflection.

Cummings begins "maggie and milly and molly and may" with straightforward writing: four young girls go down to the beach one day to play. This first couplet paints a lovely picture using very uncomplicated words. The image of four young girls playing along the shore on a warm summer morning is a gentle image to conjure in one's imagination. The fact that these four young girls all have names beginning with the letter *m* could be seen, at first, as a cute way to begin a poem, making the poem read almost like a nursery rhyme. The names are fun to say, one after the other as the sounds skip over the tongue just as the girls might have skipped across the sandy shore. But the chances of four young friends (or even four young siblings) having such repetitive-sounding names might make the more-than-casual reader a little suspicious. The emphasis on the letter *m* might give a clue that cummings is suggesting something—possibly substituting individual names for the pronoun *me.* This is, after all, a poem about self-discovery. "For Cummings," writes Robert E. Wegner in *The Poetry and Prose of E. E. Cummings,* "self-discovery was supremely important and the only valid motive for writing a poem."

Lindbergh begins her book *Gift from the Sea* in a similar way. The first chapter is a short, simple explanation about her setting: where she is, why she is there, and what she hopes to find there. The setting is, of course, the beach, and she is looking for answers in the form of self-reflection.

Back to cummings poem, the second couplet introduces maggie. "Maggie," says Rushworth M. Kidder in *E. E. Cummings: An Introduction to the Poetry,* is the " 'sweetly' troubled one." If cummings is talking through maggie, looking at himself through her eyes, he is saying that when he is troubled, he turns to nature, as transcendentalists do, to find consolation. Maggie not only finds nature, she also finds art in the form of music. The shell sings to her. It is through the shell and its song that maggie (or cummings) loses the troubles of self. And it is in the losing, cummings later states in the last couplet, that one finds oneself.

In the second chapter of her book, Lindbergh also finds a shell. It is an empty shell that has been abandoned twice—once by the snail-like creature that created the shell, and then by a hermit crab that used it as temporary housing. It is through this abandoned shell that Lindbergh realizes that she, too, has abandoned her shell: her roles as mother and wife. She, like maggie in cummings's poem, has brought her troubles to the sea, but the shell is reminding her to abandon them, if only for this week of vacation, in order that she might reconnect with herself.

Milly is next to be spotlighted in cummings's poem. "Milly, 'languid' and friendly," says Kidder, "takes pity on a 'stranded' starfish." Here there is the possibility that cummings is saying that sometimes he feels stranded and alone. The "languid" fingers of the starfish could be his own hand that might sometimes seem incapable of writing another poem. Through milly and the starfish, cummings might see that self-discovery requires making friends with oneself. He could be looking at the five-fingered ray as an objective part of himself—the public part, the man as opposed to the artist. And he might be feeling that one part has been stranded from the other. As Wegner states in his analysis of cummings's play called *Him,* "the artist is the man; the man is the artist. Neither, by himself, could achieve individuality and recognition of self, for the artist without the man would be sterile and lifeless, and the man without the artist would misinterpret what he perceives." This also goes back to the transcendentalist's premise that what is inside and what is outside work together, one feed-

ing the other in an attempt to create a balanced life. Wegner goes further in his statement: "Without the qualifying temperament of the artist, the man would have little resistance to stereotyped beliefs. With the artist and his inner recognition of truth, beauty, and harmony, the man through his senses perceives the manifestations of these in the world around him, and learns to distinguish between what is genuine and what is sham and hypocrisy."

In the third chapter of her book, Lindbergh writes about having found a moon shell. This shell, by its name, reminds Lindbergh of solitude. As the moon is alone, so are all individuals alone in their journey toward self-discovery. By reflecting on the shell she comes to appreciate her solitude. It is in solitude that the artist meditates and creates. And it is through those meditations and creations that the artist befriends herself and then, just as milly befriends the starfish, the artist is capable of befriending others.

Now molly, in the fourth couplet in cummings's poem, is "chased by a horrible thing" and realizes her fears as she is frightened by a strange looking crab walking sideways. Molly most definitely represents the nightmares in cummings's life, or possibly just the challenges that he must face in searching for self-identity. Cummings might be saying that looking into the mirror of self-reflection is not always pleasant. There are parts of oneself that are not always comfortable to look at. And these uncomfortable parts are one's fears.

Lindbergh faces fears at the beach also. She talks about relationships and how they work after her sister comes to share one day with her. She watches as they perform a kind of silent dance throughout the day, knowing each other so perfectly that they do not intrude into one another's silences, do not bump into one another as they prepare their meals in a tiny kitchen. She also talks about what destroys relationships. And that is fear. "It is fear . . . that makes one cling nostalgically to the last moment or clutch greedily toward the next." Clinging and clutching are, coincidentally, strangely familiar tactics of molly's crab.

In cummings's poem, "May is the dreamer," states Kidder, "who in her 'smooth round stone' comes upon a symbol resisting simple categorization . . . this poem suggests the two sides of loneliness: 'alone' is a quality that looms large in may's experience, yet, being large, it is hardly a confining and stiffling place." These thoughts come from the fifth couplet of cummings's poem where may discovers that the stone she has found is "as small as a world and as large as alone." Cummings deals with the concept of loneliness in many of his poems. In looking at loneliness, cummings has often stated that there were two sides to being alone. One was loneliness, but the other was the contemplative state from which creation is borne. Immediately following his statement about may and her discoveries about loneliness, cummings starts the last couplet with the word *for,* which in this case stands for the word *because.* As if to explain the reasons for being alone, cummings ends this poem with his thematic statement.

One of the first sentences in the last chapter of Lindbergh's book starts with the words: "the search for outward simplicity, for inner integrity . . ." As if to emphasize the transcendental nature of her own words (which links this collection of essays to cummings's poem), Lindbergh looks out across the beach and the sea and finds the simplicity that she knows she needs to bring inside of her in order to find unity and peace. "We are now ready for a true appreciation of the value of the here and the now and the individual," she continues. "They are the drops that make up the stream. They are the essence of life itself. When we start at the center of ourselves, we discover something worthwhile extending toward the periphery of the circle." It is the individual that transcendentalists celebrate—the individual with the indwelling god, the individual with all knowledge contained, the individual for whom Nature provides symbolic answers. Or as cummings sums it up: "For whatever we lose (like a you or a me) / it's always ourselves we find in the sea."

Source: Joyce Hart, Critical Essay on "maggie and milly and molly and may," in *Poetry for Students,* The Gale Group, 2001.

Cliff Saunders

Saunders teaches writing and literature in the Myrtle Beach, South Carolina area and has published six chapbooks of poetry. In the following essay, he examines three elements that help make cummings's poem such a memorable poem: its deft lyricism, its selective use of unusual diction and syntax, and its powerful and imaginative figures of speech.

In 1958, when cummings published *95 Poems* (his twelfth and final volume), many critics suggested that the author's creative powers were coming perilously close to being tapped out. In his review of *95 Poems,* John Berryman, a fine poet in his own right, noted that not a single poem in the volume reaches "the standard of [cummings's] finest work." Berryman also took cummings to task for being "extremely sentimental" and for writing in such a way that "some of his deepest feelings scarcely emerge." Another critic, Edward M. Hood, complained in his review of *95 Poems* that "Cummings is so determined to freshen language (and, thereby, perception) by flouting its conventions that he ends by destroying convention, language, and perception itself." Hood also asserted that there is a "vacuum of thought and feeling within" *95 Poems.* Hood, however, named "maggie and milly and molly and may" as one of the collection's more successful poems, and over time, the critical body of thought on cummings's oeuvre has come to see "maggie and milly and molly and may" as one of his finest poems ever.

Indeed, the poem *does* stand out within a collection (i.e., *95 Poems*) of all-too-many undeveloped and tossed-off poems. But why? What makes the poem successful for so many readers, even critics who have had more unflattering things to say about cummings's poetry than complimentary ones? Surely it's not the poem's content, which, when you think about it, seems commonplace and almost trite. The situation described in the poem— four girls at the beach and what they find there— barely warrants mention, let alone any in-depth discussion. No, it isn't so much *what* the poem says as *how* it is said that makes "maggie and milly and molly and may" so successful. For this, the reader must duly acknowledge cummings's gift for lyricism, his selective use of unusual diction and syntax, and his flare for imaginative figures of speech.

Immediately the reader is captivated by the sounds and rhythms in cummings's poem. With its pronounced (some might even say heavyhanded) alliteration of repeated "m" consonants and its regular dactylic meter (i.e., one long stress followed by two shorts, as exemplified by the word *wonderful*), the poem's first line establishes a musical cadence of strong appeal to the reader's ear. In fact, the poem's first stanza is reminiscent of the kind of schoolyard chant one might hear coming from a coterie of young girls playing jumprope at recess; the rhythm is that strong. The strength of this rhythm, bolstered by the full *aa* rhyme scheme of the first stanza, pays off twofold. First, the rhythm can't help but grab one's attention, regardless of the reader's preference for closed form or free verse. After all, every reader was a child at one time and presumably has the cadences of nursery rhymes and playground chants ingrained within their psyche. Second, the formal strategy employed by cummings in the first stanza reinforces the poem's theme (and a common one that runs throughout cummings's canon): the purity and innocence of childhood. Like William Blake before him, cummings viewed childhood as a coveted time before the onset of adulthood corrupts and impairs the individual soul. What better way to introduce this theme than with a nursery-rhyme-like couplet?

But this is cummings we're talking about—the rulebreaker, the grand "violator" of every accepted standard of poetical and grammatical structure—so you can be sure that cummings will seek to undermine any regular pattern of rhythm in his poems at some point. Sure enough, cummings does so in stanza 2, where he veers off not only from the *aa* rhyme scheme of the first stanza but also, in line 4, from the dactylic tetrameter (i.e., four-beat line) structure that had so firmly thrust the poem forward from the start. The switch in rhythmic emphasis is subtle and temporary, though, because cummings roughly maintains a tetrameter pattern throughout the poem's entirety, a pattern that merges both iambic (as in line 6) and dactylic (as in line 7) metrical feet. (An iambic foot is one in which a short stress is followed by a long stress, as exemplified by the word *before*.)

Toward the end of the poem, especially in the last three lines, a strong dactylic meter reemerges, establishing a forceful cadence that harks back to the poem's first three lines. This, of course, constitutes a nice balance, and those who generally find cummings's poetry "sloppy" and "chaotic" would do well to heed this clever, subtle attention to form. It's also interesting to note that the *aa* end rhyme on display in stanza 1 also returns in the last two stanzas. The more emphatic rhyming in the poem's beginning and concluding stanzas seems appropriate in terms of its top and bottom placement, where emphasis is needed most.

Even in the poem's interior stanzas, where both meter and rhyme seemingly stray furthest from the stricter patterns of the top and bottom stanzas, cummings never strays *too* far from formal considerations. In the case of end rhyme, some deceptively subtle and highly effective maneuvering is going on. When first reading the poem, one gets the sense that the rigid formal pattern established in the first stanza totally breaks down, but upon closer inspection, one sees that a rhyme scheme, albeit a less emphatic one, is maintained by cummings. It's easy to see and hear the full end rhymes of stanza 1 (may/day), stanza 5 (stone/alone), and

> *But this is cummings we're talking about—the rulebreaker, the grand 'violator' of every accepted standard of poetical and grammatical structure—so you can be sure that cummings will seek to undermine any regular pattern of rhythm in his poems at some point."*

stanza 6 (me/sea), whereas the end rhyme in stanzas 2, 3, and 4 is less overt but nevertheless still present. Notice how lines 4 and 8 contain full end rhyme (troubles, and / bubbles: and).

As for the other lines, cummings makes masterful use of what is known as *slant* rhyme, in which words don't sound *exactly* alike but still produce echoes of each other. Thus, lines 3 and 7 "rhyme" in a sense (sang/thing), as do lines 5 and 6 (star/were). Slant rhyme is often produced via vowel tonalities (e.g., screen/dream), but in this case, the trick is performed through consonant sounds (the "ng" in sang and thing and the "r" in star and were). Cummings's clever use of slant rhyme in "maggie and milly and molly and may" allows him the illusion of seemingly breaking free of the formal pattern while all the time maintaining it.

Cummings often attracted the ire and exasperation of critics whenever he strayed too far and too often from the rules of poetic engagement. In pushing the boundaries of acceptable diction, syntax, grammar, and punctuation, cummings stepped over the line more often than even a cummings's booster might care to admit. Sometimes, unfortunately, cummings failed to restrain himself in displaying his cleverness, leaving readers feeling, like the aforementioned Edward M. Hood, that cummings reduces language and meaning instead of expanding them as he intented. This is not the case in "maggie and milly and molly and may," a poem in which cummings shows remarkable restraint and selectivity with regard to unusual word and punctuation usage and syntax. In fact, this careful selectivity helps make the few unusual examples of diction and syntax he does employ in the poem stand out.

For example, the reversed word order in line 6, where cummings says "whose rays five languid fingers were" instead of the more grammatically standard "whose rays were five languid fingers," is a stroke of genius. The unusual syntax gives the beautiful image of the starfish more power, emphasizing the human connection (i.e., "fingers") with the sea, which is what the poem is all about.

Cummings also gets great effect from a few (and highly select) odd word choices toward the end of the poem. These include "alone" in line 10 and "you" and "me" in line 11. Each choice violates conventional usage, but each is so wonderfully appropriate within the context of the poem. In the case of the adverb "alone," cummings alludes to how one individual (and especially a *young* individual) normally feels in proximity to something as immense and eternal as the sea. Such an experience is likely to heighten a child's understanding of his/her own mortality and sense of aloneness. The sea tends to do that to people, no matter how many others are around, and for a child this feeling of aloneness often gets amplified, given his/her small stature. The phrase "as large as alone," then, produces appropriate reverberations in the context of the poem despite (or is it because of?) its unconventional usage.

Similarly, cummings's decision to use pronouns in such an unorthodox way (i.e., "a you or a me") perfectly fits the poem's context and subject. On the one hand, the poem deals with children, who are apt to demonstrate verbal inventiveness while playing (at the sea or elsewhere) and could conceivably say something like "I'm a you and you're a me." A more important point to make here, though, is what the pronouns suggest by way of personal identity. Cummings may be suggesting in the poem's final couplet that although individual life is temporal and finite (i.e., the loss of "a you or a me"), the sea is a constant source of solace in that it reminds a person of eternity and the potential for an afterlife.

Given cummings's transcendental views—in which, as noted by author Norman Friedman in his probing book *E. E. Cummings,* "eternal forms are embodied in the phenomenal universe and . . . are embodied as process rather than result"—such an interpretation has much to recommend it. Tran-

scendentalism is a philosophy whose followers value the spiritual and transcendental over the material and empirical. However, cummings may also be implying that one's personal identity correlates directly with childhood, that when one grows older, "a you or a me" (i.e., one's personal identity) gets lost but that the seashore allows a person to recapture memories of his or her youth, granting each one the chance to find that original self again. This interpretation also carries some validity, since it ties in with cummings's belief that childhood represents the spiritual apex of life, the time of true identity that aging, with its attendant social, political, and cultural imperatives, destroys.

Seen in this light, then, the poem ends on a hopeful note with its suggestion that the sea is always there for each person as a source of spiritual purification and renewal, regardless of how old he or she is. But whichever interpretation holds the most "water," cummings's unusual use of pronouns in the last stanza of "maggie and milly and molly and may" is not mere cleverness for its own sake; rather, it draws attention in a most imaginative way to cummings's exploration of the temporal and the eternal.

Along with his extraordinary lyrical abilities and unusual choices in diction/syntax, cummings's facility for striking figures of speech also contributes to the success of "maggie and milly and molly and may." Virtually every figure of speech in the poetic arsenal is on display in the poem. There's metaphor in line 3 ("a shell that sang"), metaphor and personification in lines 5 and 6 ("a stranded star / whose rays five languid fingers were"), and simile and paradox in line 10 ("as small as a world and as large as alone"). Each is wonderfully imaginative in its own right, but cummings seems to outdo himself with each subsequent figure. The metaphor in line 5 comparing a shell to a living creature that can vocalize tonalities (e.g., an opera singer or a warbler) is insightful and perceptive but not all that remarkable. The use of metaphor and personification in lines 5 and 6, where a starfish is compared to a star with "rays" and to a human hand with "fingers," is superbly unique, expressive, and imaginative. In fact, this figure of speech is arguably the most beautiful and memorable description of a starfish ever incorporated into a poem.

Yet cummings manages to top even this brilliant metaphor with his astounding synthesis of simile and paradox in line 10. It would have been effective enough to have compared may's "smooth round stone" to a planet and to the human state of aloneness, but cummings truly gets the reader thinking by reversing expectation and sensibility through his use of paradox, which is a statement that is ostensibly contradictory or nonsensical but nevertheless contains some truth. Worlds are normally considered large and an individual's state of aloneness small in the overall scheme of things, but by reversing these properties, cummings achieves one of the poet's key missions: using language to transform a reader's perception of the world and to heighten awareness of the intrinsic connectedness of all things. By articulating our connectedness to the sea via shells that sing, starfish with fingers, and stones the size of a person's sense of aloneness, cummings brings the readers that much closer to knowing themselves as well as the world around them.

Source: Cliff Saunders, Critical Essay on "maggie and milly and molly and may," in *Poetry for Students,* The Gale Group, 2001.

Erica Smith

Smith is a writer and editor. In this essay, she will examine how within the poem, which is a description of children at the seashore, cummings considers innocence, identity, and timelessness.

"Maggie and milly and molly and may" is a poem by e. e. cummings from the volume *95 Poems.* Published only four years before cummings's death, it carries only a hint of cummings's stylistic hallmarks such as idiosyncratic syntax, capitalization, and punctuation. Nor does the poem touch on many of the thematic concerns—scathing satire of hypocrisy, glorification of love and nature, and praise of individual freedom—that defined the poet as early as his first volume, *Tulips and Chimneys* (1923). Instead, "maggie and milly and molly and may" is a more meditative consideration of a couple of cummings's other prevalent themes: the possibilities of imagination, and the innocence of childhood. In this context, the poem also considers questions of identity and timelessness.

The four major characters of the poem, maggie and milly and molly and may, are described in the first two lines as going "down to the beach (to play one day)." Because they are going out to play, the characters appear to be children. The singsong timbre of the lines, the simple AA / BB / CC rhyme, and the conventional, story-like beginning of the poem also echo childhood nursery rhymes. The one instance of unconventional punctuation—the compressed space before the parenthetical "(to play one day)"—gently alludes to the impressionism of a

> *It is as if the children of the poem, and cummings too, are able to distill their surroundings to their essence. In doing so, they are able to understand them simply and completely."*

child's mind and unsophisticated grammar of a child's speech.

The poem then focuses on each of the children in turn. Maggie discovers "a shell that sang / so sweetly she couldn't remember her troubles." The reader may picture the child holding a large conch shell up to her ear, and listening to the filtered sounds within the shell's inner cavern. The sound inside a conch, which is often said to resemble the sound of the sea, has a lulling effect on maggie. She is able to drift away from her troubles. The reader may be left to ponder what troubles, in fact, would weigh so heavily on the heart of a child.

In the following stanza, milly also is carried away into a new world. She "befriend[s] a stranded star / whose rays five languid fingers were." One can imagine the child picking up a coarse, five-pointed starfish, perhaps "stranded" in sand as the tide pulled in, and bringing it nearer to the water. Yet the line also suggests the other kind of star: a star in the night sky.

The relationship between a child and a star is explored throughout children's literature, most famously in the nursery rhymes "Twinkle Twinkle, Little Star" and "Star Light, Star Bright." In these popular poems, stars are associated with wonder ("twinkle, twinkle, little star / how I wonder what you are"), mystery ("far above the world so high / like a diamond in the sky"), and wishes ("I wish I may, I wish I might / have this wish I wish tonight"). The star is a touchstone for the imagination. In this poem, these meanings are augmented by the suggestion of a humanlike quality of the starfish; its rays are described as "languid fingers." One can almost imagine milly befriending the star, holding it as if it were a hand.

In the couplet that follows, the adventures of molly are described. Unlike milly's dreamy exploration of her environment, molly is caught in a sinister psychological drama. She is "chased by a horrible thing / which raced sideways while blowing bubbles." Most children are mortally afraid of being chased by monsters, beasts, or creatures. In this case, a creature, most likely a scuttling crab, is beastly enough to send molly away screaming.

This stanza attests to the other side of the imagination—the side that can see the sinister as well as the divine in the ordinary. This can be interpreted as cummings's subtle comment on the human psyche. It is complex and flexible enough to consider beautiful possibilities in a star up in the sky and assign poignant humanlike qualities to a starfish, but it also can see danger and sinister qualities in ordinary objects. Cummings's presentation of these stanzas side by side perhaps implies that both of these aspects of the universe—the divine and the horrible—are legitimate. In both cases, the children bring out these aspects in impartial nonhuman objects and creatures.

May's experiences and interactions with the world around her have a poignant effect. In may's case, she contemplates a stone: "She came home with a smooth round stone / as small as a world and as large as alone." She apparently has been collecting rocks on the shoreline. Like the other children, may has a special relationship with the object she finds. The smooth round stone is almost literally a blank, almost featureless object. Yet its smallness and roundness comes to represent nothing less than the world itself. Characteristically, cummings represents the concepts in this stanza as a kind of inverted equation. The world is described as small, when one would expect that the world would appear huge to a child. Likewise, the feeling of aloneness is often thought of as a feeling of being small or diminished; in cummings's case, he describes it as being large, perhaps overwhelmingly so.

Cummings's paradoxes in this stanza serve the poem well, for their spontaneity capture the fresh and unique qualities of a child's perception. Furthermore, in this poem, the world is indeed small: all of the objects that the children consider, such as shells and stars, are easily graspable and meaningful for them. It is as if the children of the poem, and cummings too, are able to distill their surroundings to their essence. In doing so, they are able to understand them simply and completely.

The last stanza of the poem reveals the voice of the omniscient narrator shining through, offering a homily: "For whatever we lose (like a you or a me) / it's always ourselves we find in the sea." Here, cummings acknowledges how one can lose "a you or a me"—one's sense of self or relationship with others. Even children, whose self is characteristically strong and forging, can sometimes feel empty and unconnected to other people. By coming to the sea, they are able to experience the natural world, and the natural world is able to quietly fill their needs.

In this case, the ocean allows the children to see themselves more clearly. Maggie is able to find something to listen to other than the troubled voice inside her head; milly is able to make a friend; molly is able to come face-to-face with demons (posing as a scuttling crab); may sees the smallness of the world, and the hugeness of herself, in the image of a smooth stone. Each of the children is transformed by what she sees.

Furthermore, cummings's words in the final stanza are addressed not only to the children in the poem but to the reader. His is an invitation to join the children in finding aspects of oneself that may have been lost or obscured. Clearly, at this late stage in life, cummings is still asking these questions of himself and trying to stay close to the essence of nature and of his own self. As critic Rushworth M. Kidder notes, regarding *95 Poems,*

> It is a volume full of praise for human goodness and wonder at nature's marvels . . . As such, it is Cummings' most risky volume. . . . [A]fter years of distinguishing the merely sentimental from the genuinely affirmative, [cummings] had learned his balance well. [He has refused] to give over his skills at organization, his ear for nuance, and his fertile metaphoric imagination.

At the end of a long life of poetry, cummings is able to deliver needed lessons with skill and grace.

Source: Erica Smith, Critical Essay on "maggie and milly and molly and may," in *Poetry for Students,* The Gale Group, 2001.

Liz Brent

Brent has a Ph.D. in American Culture, specializing in film studies, from the University of Michigan. She is a freelance writer and teaches courses in the history of American cinema. In the following essay, Brent discusses tone and the process of rereading in cummings's poem.

"Maggie and milly and molly and may," by e. e. cummings, is structured in such a way that the use of tone can only be fully appreciated upon rereading the poem. While it begins playfully in the first stanza, the final stanza introduces a serious, perhaps tragic, tone that invites the reader to reinterpret the entire piece in a new light. The reader is thus invited to reread the entire poem, with the final stanza in mind, to interpret the playful, childlike words of the first stanza through the lens of the more serious adult tone introduced in the last stanza.

The first stanza reads:

maggie and milly and molly and may
went down to the beach (to play one day)

Like much of cummings's poetry, this poem begins with a very playful and childlike tone. The use of alliteration—a series of words all beginning with the same letter—in the opening line, "maggie and milly and molly and may," creates a lyrical, singsong tone, reminiscent of a nursery rhyme. The rhythm of emphasis throughout the line is evocative of the rhythm of skipping—calling to mind the manner in which little girls might skip joyfully down to the beach to play.

As is also characteristic of cummings's writing, the first letters of the names of the four girls are in lower case, rather than the grammatically correct upper case. This unconventional choice on the part of the writer serves several functions in creating a playful tone throughout the first stanza. The lack of capitalization allows the reader's tongue (or mind's ear) to slide effortlessly over the first seven words of the poem. It also calls to mind the writing style of a young child, whose lack of sophistication may lead her to forgo capitalization of her own name.

The second line of the first stanza reads:

went down to the beach(to play one day)

In this line, cummings breaks with convention by adding a parenthetical phrase after the word "beach," without a space between the end of the word and the first parenthesis mark. Cummings often played with unconventional word, letter, and punctuation spacing in his poetry. Furthermore, placing the phrase "to play one day" in parenthesis at first seems idiosyncratic in this poem. The sentence more conventionally written could have read well without the parenthesis around this phrase.

What is the effect of these choices on the meaning of the poem? Jamming the word "beach" right up to the opening parenthesis without a space continues the tone of excitement established in the first line—as if the children are so eager to get to

> *The beloved person is thus grammatically reduced to the status of an animal or inanimate object, such as one whimsically finds on the beach. And yet the loss of a loved one is infinitely more tragic than that of a found object."*

the beach that they are nearly tripping over their own feet in their hurry to arrive. The tone of the line mirrors this feeling in the sense that the writer seems so eager to reach the end of the line of poetry that he can't wait for even the length of a space between words to reach his destination—the end of the line of poetry, and, by implication, the beach, where the playing can begin.

While at the beach, the four girls discover items that lend themselves to their childish imaginations. Maggie finds a seashell which, when held up to her ear, sounds as if it is singing "sweetly." Milly "befriends" a starfish. Molly is chased by some sort of crab, which is described as a "horrible thing," but one which blows bubbles; thus, the reader is invited to imagine that molly is not truly frightened by the sea creature, but only playing make-believe that it is some "horrible" and threatening monster. May finds "a smooth round stone," which is "as small as the world and as large as alone"; that a small stone could represent the entire world suggests the vast capacity of a child's imagination, which can create entire worlds out of the smallest object.

Only with the final phrase of the fifth stanza does a serious tone creep into the poem for the first time. The stone that may finds is "as large as alone." While even the "horrible thing" that chases molly down the beach is presented as a playful imaginary game in which the child engages in pure fun, the small stone which is "as large as alone" presents the reader with a decidedly somber and adult tone. The word "alone," which ends the stanza, not only rhymes with "stone," but creates a heavy, plodding sound which seems to weigh down both the singsong, nursery-rhyme sounds which precede it and the emotional tone of the entire poem. The word "alone" sinks like a stone in the reader's heart. This word causes a shift in the tone of the poem, from childlike and playful to adult and, to use an expression suggested by the stone, "heavy." While children certainly experience loneliness, some perhaps more tragically and completely than an adult ever could, it is a general sentiment that childhood is a time of joy, insulated from the depths of aloneness experienced by many adults.

The sixth and final stanza of the poem delves further into this theme of aloneness, maintaining the somber, adult tone first introduced by the word "alone" which ends the fifth stanza. The final stanza reads:

> For whatever we lose(like a you or a me)
> it's always ourselves we find in the sea

The first line of this stanza is striking in part because it is the first (and only) instance in the poem in which capitalization is used. After the playful, eager, informal tone of the poem up to this point, in part created by the lack of capitalization, the introduction of a capitalized word suggests a grown-up, serious tone. Furthermore, beginning the sentence with the word "For" implies that a logical conclusion is about to be reached; this is in stark contrast to the imaginative, joyful, frolicking tone of the poem up to this point. Cummings mirrors the second line of the poem in the structure of this line: the final phrase appears in parenthesis, and the opening parenthetical mark is jammed up against the preceding word, without the conventional space separating them: "For whatever we lose(like a you or a me)."

It is by way of the words within these parentheses that the tone of the poem strikes its heaviest blow to the reader. The reader has been clued in by the word "alone" (which ends the fifth stanza) that the poem has taken on a more serious and somber tone. But the idea that "whatever we lose" could include "a you or a me" suddenly introduces the idea of the loss of a loved one, either by death or via the dissolution of a romantic relationship. The phrasing of "a you or a me" introduces the lost loved one as an object, paralleling the description of the objects found on the beach, "a shell," "a stranded star," "a horrible thing," and "a smooth round stone." The beloved person is thus grammatically reduced to the status of an animal or inanimate object, such as one whimsically finds on the beach. And yet the loss of a loved one is infinitely more tragic than that of a found object. The final line, "its always ourselves we find in the sea," calls to mind the idea of aloneness mentioned in the previous stanza with the image of a stone "as large as alone." Having lost a loved one, the "we" of the poem is always left "alone," and there is only "ourselves" to reckon with.

Source: Liz Brent, Critical Essay on "maggie and milly and molly and may," in *Poetry for Students,* The Gale Group, 2001.

Sources

Berryman, John, Review of *95 Poems,* in *Critical Essays on E. E. Cummings,* G. K. Hall, 1984, p. 91.

Blackmur, R. P., "Notes on E. E. Cummings' Language," in *The Hound & Horn,* Vol. IV, No. 2, 1931, pp. 163–192.

"Criticism: 'maggie and milly and molly and may' by e. e. cummings," in *EXPLORING Poetry,* Gale Research, 1998.

cummings, e. e., "maggie and milly and molly and may," in *E. E. Cummings, Selected Poems,* Liveright Publishing Corporation, 1994.

Friedman, Norman, *E. E. Cummings,* Southern University Press, 1964, p. 168.

——, "E. E. Cummings and His Critics," in *Valuing Cummings: Further Essays on the Poet, 1962–1993,* University Press of Florida, 1996.

——, "Xiape, 95 Poems," in *e. e. cummings The Growth of a Writer,* Southern Illinois University Press, 1964, pp. 162–173.

Hood, Edward M., Review of *95 Poems,* in *Critical Essays on E. E. Cummings,* G. K. Hall, 1984, pp. 93–95.

Kidder, Rushworth M., *E. E. Cummings: An Introduction to the Poetry,* Columbia University Press, 1979.

——, "95 Poems," in *E. E. Cummings, An Introduction to the Poetry,* edited by John Unterecher, Columbia University Press, 1979, pp. 197–218.

Lindbergh, Anne Morrow, *Gift from the Sea,* Pantheon Books, 1955.

Wegner, Robert E., "Identity of the Artist," in *The Poetry and Prose of E. E. Cummings,* Harcourt, Brace & World, Inc, 1963, pp. 12–37.

For Further Study

"American Transcendentalism" at www.gonzaga.edu/faculty/campbell/enl311/amtrans.htm (January, 2001).
This site is a great reference website of literary movements. It offers an overview of American transcendentalism as well as quotes from some of the most influential people involved in it.

cummings, e. e., *E. E. Cummings: Complete Poems 1904–1962,* edited by George J. Firmage, Liveright, 1994.

This collection of cummings's poems was reissued in honor of cummings's centennial year. The anthology includes all of the poet's works published to date.

————, *may i feel said he,* Welcome Enterprises, 1995.

This is an exciting collection of some of cummings's love poems combined with twenty-one of Chagall's color prints. The illustrations complement the poetry completely.

cummings, e. e., with John Eaton, Illustrator, *Fairy Tales,* Harcourt Brace, 1987.

This is a rare collection of four stories for children, "The Old Man Who Said 'Why,'" "The Elephant and the Butterfly," "The House That Ate Mosquito Pie," and "The Little Girl Named I." These are very imaginative and touching stories, giving the reader a look at another side of cummings.

Dumas, Bethany K., *E. E. Cummings: A Remembrance of Miracles,* Harper & Row, Publishers, Inc., 1974.

Dumas's text is an overview of cummings's works with specific reference to the poem "maggie and milly and molly and may" and a linguistic analysis of the wording.

"e. e. cummings" at www.empirezine.com/spotlight/cummings/cummings.htm (January, 2001).

This site is a wonderful introduction to cummings's work and provides a brief biography of the poet. It also provides commentary on several of his publications as well as critical opinions.

"Modern American Poetry" at http://www.english.uiuc.edu/maps/poets/a_f/cummings/commentary.htm (January, 2001).

This website offers in-depth coverage of cummings's quotes, critical reviews, background, and historical information about the poet and his life.

"PAL: Perspectives in American Literature" at www.csustan.edu/english/reuben/pal/chap4/4intro.html (January, 2001).

This website offers an introduction to early nineteenth-century American transcendentalists. It gives a definition of the movement, several pieces of literature that explain the movement, as well as the names of the most famous authors involved in the movement.

"The Transcendentalist," a lecture by Emerson, at http://www.vcu.edu/engweb/transweb/tdlist.htm (January, 2001).

This site contains a full transcript of Emerson's "The Transcendentalist," a speech that he delivered at the Masonic Temple in Boston in 1842 defining his concepts of what the American transcendentalist movement was all about.

My Mother Pieced Quilts

Teresa Palomo Acosta

1976

"My Mother Pieced Quilts," first published in 1976 in the anthology *Festival de Flor y Canto: An Anthology of Chicano Literature,* is a meditation poem using a mother's handmade quilt as means to access and explore the poet's childhood memories. As in a quilt, which is made from many different scraps of material sewn together by a single hand, the poem pieces together memories in order to show the reader a complete picture of the speaker's childhood and her mother's strong influence. The poet uses many vivid images throughout to help contrast the good memories with the unpleasant, weaving them together into the larger framework of the poem. Through her close observation and careful description of detail, by the end of the poem Acosta is able to place her mother's hobby of piecing quilts in a much larger context, transforming the everyday day practice of quilting into a ritual closer to song and prayer: the quilts themselves are described as "armed / ready / shouting / celebrating."

Author Biography

Born in McGregor, Texas, on March 9, 1949, Acosta is the daughter of parents who migrated to Texas during the Great Depression of the 1930s. After earning a bachelor's degree in ethnic studies at the University of Texas at Austin, Acosta attended the Columbia University School of Journalism, where she received a master's degree in

1977. One of the leading poetic voices of multi-culturalism in America, Acosta has commented that she writes "partly to re-envision and re-tell stories about [myself], [my] family, and the Chicana/Tejana experience." In 1993 Acosta was honored with the Voertman's poetry Award, and in 1995 was a Poetry Fellow at the Virginia Center for the Creative Arts.

Poem Text

they were just meant as covers
in winters
as weapons
against pounding january winds

but it was just that every morning I awoke to these   5
october ripened canvases
passed my hand across their cloth faces
and began to wonder how you pieced
all these together
these strips of gentle communion cotton and   10
    flannel nightgowns
wedding organdies
dime-store velvets

how you shaped patterns square and oblong and
    round
positioned
balanced   15
then cemented them
with your thread
a steel needle

how the thread darted in and out   20
galloping along the frayed edges, tucking them in
as you did us at night
oh how you stretched and turned and rearranged
your michigan spring faded curtain pieces
my father's santa fe workshirt   25
the summer denims, the tweeds of fall

in the evening you sat at your canvas
—our cracked linoleum floor the drawing board
me lounging on your arm
and you staking out the plan: 30
whether to put the lilac purple of easter against the
red plaid of winter-going-into-spring
whether to mix a yellow with a blue and white and
    paint
the corpus christi noon when my father held your
    hand
whether to shape a five-point star from the   35
somber black silk you wore to grandmother's
    funeral

you were the river current
carrying the roaring notes

forming them into pictures of a little boy reclining
a swallow flying   40
you were the caravan master at the reins
driving your threaded needle artillery across the
    mosaic cloth bridges
delivering yourself in separate testimonies

oh mother you plunged me sobbing and laughing
into our past   45
into the river crossing at five
into the spinach fields
into the plainview cotton rows
into tuberculosis wards
into braids and muslin dresses   50
sewn hard and taut to withstand the thrashings of
    twenty-five years

stretched out they lay
armed / ready / shouting / celebrating

knotted with love
the quilts sing on   55

Poem Summary

Lines 1–4

Acosta begins the poem at the most literal level, introducing the quilts and how they were used: for warmth against winter chill. Using a metaphor, she describes the quilts as "weapons" against "pounding january winds," perhaps the way a young child would imagine them during the coldest of winter nights.

Lines 5–7

Here the speaker of the poem explains the daily routine of waking up as a child under the colorful quilts. By describing them as "october ripened," Acosta might be referring to those colors most associated with autumn—red, brown, and orange. The speaker begins to remember how the cloth felt under hand; the sense of touch is one of the strongest triggers for memory. Note the word "faces" to describe the individual frames of cloth, the speaker is beginning to personify, or "give life" to, the inanimate quilt.

Lines 8–12

Once the speaker of the poem remembers touching the covers, she also remembers wondering how the mother was able to make the quilt, a single fabric woven of many smaller pieces. These loose strips of fabric came from many different sources, each with its own nostalgic significance—communion dresses, wedding gowns, nightclothes and "dime store velvets." On a literal level, the quilt is sewn together from these many separate strips. Metaphorically, the speaker of the poem begins to suggest that the memories of those events are woven into the fabric as well.

Lines 13–15

Lines 13–15 focus on the difficult process the mother took trying to take many mismatched and oddly shaped pieces and arrange them in a coherent pattern, much like a puzzle. Note the way the poem's speaker describes how the mother "positioned / balanced" each piece, and Acosta herself uses one-word lines like individual pieces constructing a longer sentence, each line "balanced" atop the other.

Lines 16–19

Once the pieces were arranged, the mother wove them together with needle and thread, a thimble over her finger to avoid sticking herself. The verb-choice "cemented" perhaps adds a sense of permanence to the image that another, weaker, verb would not have.

Lines 20–22

Here the speaker focuses the details even further until the reader can see the individual thread being woven, the needle's action reminding the speaker of a horse "galloping." By remembering how the loose edges of fabric were tucked in by the mother's careful needle, the speaker also remembers how the mother would tuck in the kids before bed.

Lines 23–26

Lines 23–26 return to specific descriptions of the individual fabric pieces, the mother working hard to make them fit together. Every scrap seems to tell its own story, from curtains in a house in Michigan, to a "santa fe work shirt." Each piece even reminds the speaker of the season he or she wore them. By relating these associations, the speaker might be commenting on how memory itself is pieced together, ragged scraps arranged together.

Lines 27–30

Here the mother is compared to a painter at a canvas, using the square patterns of the kitchen floor as a model. For the first time the reader sees the speaker as a child "lounging" on the mother's arm, watching the slow weaving. The young child is perhaps too young to sew, but the mother is still instructing him or her, "staking out the plan." This

scene's example perhaps emphasizes the importance of mother-daughter bonding from the poet's own childhood.

Lines 31–32

With so many scraps of fabric to choose from, the mother had to decide not only what colors might fit well together, but the seasons and events with which each piece is associated as well. The Easter purple might clash with the red plaid, but the holiday fits well with the "winter-going-into-spring" season, for example.

Lines 33–34

In each square of fabric, it seems, the mother would even paint tiny scenes, the quilt a combination of many colors and shapes. "Corpus Christi" is Latin for "body of Christ"; the Roman Catholic holy day of Corpus Christi occurs in late May or early June, several weeks after Easter. The mother has to decide whether to include a patch in honor of some occasion associated with that time of year—perhaps her wedding day. (The stress being placed on a simple event—"my father held your hand"—suggests that it has some greater significance; the gesture, the time of year, and the religious associations all subtly imply a marriage ceremony.)

Lines 35–36

In contrast to the fairly pleasant memories introduced thus far, in these lines the mother has to decide whether to include a scrap of a funeral dress in the quilt as well, shaping it into a black star. By mentioning the good memories as well as the painful, perhaps the speaker is reminding the reader that all memory and experience is a combined weaving of lights and darks, good times and bad.

Lines 37–40

Here the speaker moves from close description of the quilting process to more figurative language, helping lift the mother from her everyday hobby to something greater. The speaker calls the mother "the river current," comparing her to a great force of nature able to shape mountains and valleys with its roaring water. Note, too, how the previous scenes that the mother sewed, though fairly simple in construction, are now quite intricate and difficult to craft: a boy reclining, a flying swallow. This implies the mother was very good at what she did, spending many hours perfecting her art.

Lines 41–45

Continuing to invent analogies for the mother, in these lines the speaker describes her as the master of an army of needles, charging across the cloth battlefield with her hands at the reins. Images like this perhaps help give power to a woman who really just made quilts in her kitchen, perhaps looked upon by many as just a simple hobby. To the child who grew up to be the speaker of the poem, though, this was a wonderful and important task, equal to that of masters and generals. A "mosaic," as mentioned in line 44, is a design composed of many smaller pieces, much like a quilt.

Lines 46–50

Here the speaker's tone seems to turn, the emotion almost overflowing. The speaker tells the mother how those quilts evoke so many painful and joyous occasions. The speaker lists many specific memories. The "list" form that the poem takes here is close to that of litany or prayer, a repeated word "into" contrasted by varying details—"spinach fields," "cotton rows," "tuberculosis wards," etc. Notice, again, the wide variety of memories, each a mere fragment or scrap of a larger whole experience, each ranging in emotional impact.

Line 51

After listing six or more disjointed memory fragments, here the speaker "ties them together" with this single line, the way the mother would sew together individual fabric scraps into a quilt with such careful threading it could withstand the "thrashings of twenty-five years." This is the first time that the speaker gives the reader a sense of how much time has passed between those childhood memories and the present. By taking so much time to describe the process of quilt-making throughout the poem, perhaps the speaker is emphasizing how even the weakest shred of clothes, if woven carefully by skilled hands, can help create a complete and lasting whole quilt.

Lines 52–53

Here the perspective changes, the speaker seeming to "pan the camera back" until the reader can see several quilts laid out. Listing several adjectives in order to describe them, the speaker uses words normally reserved to describe people—in this way, the quilts are charged with life, making them "ready" for whatever bad might happen, making them celebrate the good. As each smaller patch of the quilt might tell its own story, the entire cover seems to be "shouting" with so many voices talk-

Media Adaptations

- A website that gives a basic overview of Chicana feminism is located at http://chicanas.com/whowhat.html#What (January 2001).

- National Public Radio's web site provides a transcript from its show *"All Things Considered,"* dated June 12, 1994, on which host Jackie Lyden discusses the topic "A Resurgence of the Chicano Movement of the 1960s" with reporter Mandalit DelBarco. See http://www.npr.org (January 2001).

- A transcript of host Liane Hansen's interview with Ana Castillo can be found at the National Public Radio's website under *"Weekend Edition-Sunday,"* September 25, 1994 (http://www.npr.org). Castillo discusses her essays defining "Chicanisma," a word Castillo invented to refer to the social implications of being of Mexican heritage and being American.

ing at once. Note the odd slashes between words, the punctuation itself perhaps reminding the reader of cross-stitching.

Lines 54–55

In these last lines, the reader learns what's holding all these scattered memories and fabric scraps together: love. Much like the speaker of the poem describing the mother's careful craft throughout in order to lift her from the mundane "hobbyist" to the powerful and wide-ranging force of a river current or army general, by the end of the poem, the quilts themselves "sing on" in their chorus of voices and experiences.

Themes

Kinship/Motherhood

Teresa Palomo Acosta's poem "My Mother Pieced Quilts" stitches together pieces of memory, history, and tradition to create a poem, much as her

Topics for Further Study

- Think of a common household chore that can be seen in a metaphorical sense, and write a poem about it. Be sure to include many of the small, seemingly insignificant details that are involved, and try to indicate what they might symbolize.

- Compare this poem with Edward Taylor's "Huswifery," written more than 250 years earlier. What does each poem compare sewing to? How are their subjects the same? What is different about them? Explain.

- What does the river symbolize in this poem? Why do you think this is significant to the speaker?

---

mother once stitched together pieces of old dresses, work clothes, and nightgowns to create a quilt.

In the poem "My Mother Pieced Quilts," the speaker reflects on images of her mother, as she runs her hand and her eyes over the individual pieces of material that her mother used to create the quilt. The speaker's first thought is to wonder how her mother made all those random pieces fit together so neatly, how she created such an attractive pattern out of such tiny pieces of worn out cloth. Memories of those individual pieces of cloth—one piece from a white Communion dress, another piece from a black dress worn at a funeral—race through the speaker's mind along with images of her mother sitting on the floor sewing. In the creation of the quilt, the speaker's mother has become an intricate part of the quilt.

The images of the speaker's mother are not limited to her using a needle and thread. Here, sewing is used as a metaphor: the speaker remembers how her mother used to tuck her into bed, just as her mother tucked the edges of the material under when sewing the pieces of the quilt together. The speaker also uses her mother's sewing skills to reflect on how adept her mother was at keeping the family together, as if her mother had sewn the family, with all its random needs and wants, into a recognizable as well as utilitarian pattern.

The speaker also reflects on her mother as an artist with her quilt as a canvas, comparing her skill with materials, colors, and patterns to an artist's with paint. The speaker also sees the mother as a "river current" and a "caravan master." Both these images suggest a strong woman who led the family through very tough times, who was not afraid of challenges. The patterns in the quilt conjure up images for the speaker—the mother's hand is seen in the strong stitches and her needle is the "artillery," or sword.

By the end of the poem, the speaker is laughing at the pleasant memories that the quilt has inspired but also "sobbing" when the quilt reminds her of the sadness in both their lives. It is not clear in the poem whether or not the mother is still alive, but it is evident that the quilt will forever remind the speaker of the relationship she shared with her mother. The quilt, like the poem itself, is "knotted with love"—a love that inspired the mother to make the quilt for her daughter and with the deep love the daughter feels for her mother.

Simplicity and Complexity

Just as a quilt is made out of simple materials—thread and remnants of old clothing, curtains, and other household materials—so is Acosta's poem made out of simple things. From the simplicity of her words, to the simplicity of the form and the images, the poem reads, at first glance, like a simple remembrance of a simple act: a mother sewing a quilt. It is only upon closer inspection and reflection that the complexity of Acosta's poem comes to light.

The poem begins with the speaker looking at a quilt that her mother gave to her. "They were just meant as covers" begins the poem. Quilts are something utilitarian, something that keeps a family warm in cold weather. The speaker may have used the quilt for a long period of time, thinking of it only as blanket, but eventually the speaker looks at the quilt in a different way. Finally the speaker begins to appreciate something in the quilt; a quality that has been hidden from her for a long time. The poem seems to be a tribute to that something that the speaker finally sees. It is this new awareness of the simple quilt that makes this simple poem take on complexity.

The quilt for the speaker becomes not only a work of art but also a kind of family album. Pictures of each house that the family lived in, each city where the family worked, each illness and death that the family suffered, all of these complex family photographs are stored in the simple pieces of cloth. Just as the mother took the simple materials of thread and old, faded cloth and worked them into complex patterns, into fantastic images of "a swallow flying," a "little boy reclining," "corpus christi noon," so does Acosta take simple words and create a complex range of emotions as the poem collects power, going from a simple realization of a quilt to the full understanding of her love for her mother.

Transformation

The most obvious transformation in this poem is that which takes place at the mother's hands as she transforms the pieces of collected material into a quilt. But there are other transformations going on in the poem. First there is the transformation that is occurring in the speaker as she realizes the "canvas" of her mother's work. This is the transformation of a daughter who suddenly sees her mother as more than a mother. She sees her mother as a woman, a woman who had to struggle. She also sees her mother as an artist.

There is also the transformation of nature in Acosta's poem, as she mentions "october ripened canvas," "january winds," "summer denims," and the "tweeds of fall." The seasonal transformations reflect back to the transformations that occurred in the family as the family moved from one city to another, from one job to another, as the family grew and aged.

Transforming sorrow into something pretty is also another transformation as the speaker comments on how the mother took the "somber black silk you wore to grandmother's funeral" and turned it into a beautiful "five-point star." There is also the curious line, "delivering yourself in separate testimonies," insinuating that the speaker's mother transformed herself, possibly by demonstrating different strengths, different talents that may have been hidden or overlooked until the occasion called for them. And then there is the final transformation as the speaker's emotion changes from tears to laughter as she recalls the transitions that the family experienced as they passed from one stage to another in their lives.

Style

"My Mother Pieced Quilts" is written in free verse, its line lengths ranging widely from one to fifteen words, depending on the mood or subject matter expressed. Unlike that of formal verse, which has a set number of beats per line or an interlocking rhyme scheme, this poem's shape varies according to its changing content and emotion. In places where Acosta is describing a very specific detail, or expressing how carefully her mother stitched, she uses short lines—sometimes one word each—in order to help slow down the action and reflect the mood of the scene.

The poem also lacks any formal punctuation. The reader doesn't have to pause for any periods or commas, which helps emphasize and remind the reader of the mother's continuous and uninterrupted stitching.

Historical Context

When Teresa Palomo Acosta first started writing poetry at the age of sixteen, she had read only European and early American poets like Lord Tennyson and Emily Dickinson. Several years passed before she read contemporary African-American and Chicano poets. This was not due to a lack of interest, but rather that in the 1960s it was difficult to find poetry written by African Americans and Mexican Americans. It was even more difficult to find poetry written by women of color.

The Chicano Movement of the late 1960s and 1970s changed all that. And it was during this gentle explosion of Chicana literature that Acosta's poem "My Mother Pieced Quilts" was published. So much of the Chicana poetry that Acosta read was written by her peers—Mexican-American women who were published about the same time that Acosta was published.

The Chicano Movement spread across the United States during the same period that there was much civil unrest involving a variety of issues. At the same time, students were rebelling against the war in Vietnam, women were marching for equal rights, and the civil rights movement was underway. There were labor strikes and food boycotts against unfair practices with regard to migrant workers, and Mexican-American students were boycotting schools, protesting against a lack of cultural studies programs available to them. During this era, the United States saw the creation of the Black Panthers, a militant organization that fought for civil rights for African Americans, and the Brown Berets, an organization that fought for better living conditions and educational opportunities for Mexican Americans. All this unrest in the country emphasized a need for change. And that change was felt in many different areas, not the least of which was seen in colleges throughout the nation and in the publishing industry.

Compare & Contrast

- **Early 1960s:** Cesar Chavez becomes the head of the United Farmworkers Organizing Committee, which later becomes the United Farm Workers, AFL-CIO. In the years that follow, Chavez organizes several history-making strikes and national boycotts of agricultural products to bring attention to the poor living and health conditions of migrant workers.

  1970s: Because of Chavez's efforts, the California legislature passes the California Labor Relations Act, which helps improve wage, health, and housing conditions for farm workers.

  Today: Cesar Chavez died in 1993, and many skeptics declared the union dead with him. In 1994, however, son-in-law Arturo S. Rodriguez took over the union. Cesar's family and the officers of the UFW created the Cesar E. Chavez Foundation to inspire current and future generations, and the union continues their work today.

- **Early 1960s:** The Chicana feminist movement begins. It is during this time that the term Chicana is adopted by a generation of activists to signify their uniquely Mexican-American identity.

  1970s: The Chicana voice is being heard. It is during this decade that many writings by Mexican-American women are being published. This includes Teresa Palomo Acosta's poem, "My Mother Pieced Quilts."

  Today: Chicana culture, arts, and social movements continue to strengthen, in part from the presence of feminist studies in academia and in part from the growth of the internet. More effort is being made to recognize and include Chicana writers and artists in anthologies and publications (for example, Pat Mora and Ana Castillo), and women are creating their own presence on the internet to produce, display, and discuss their art and ideas.

Courses on both the community college and the university levels were created to accommodate the growing awareness and interest in a wider variety of subjects. Thus a student could study fiction written by an African-American author (which prior to these movements was practically nonexistent), essays written by women, and poetry written by Mexican Americans.

This was also the time that the word Chicano, and later the word Chicana (the feminine version), were elevated from their pejorative usage (which implied a fixed, hierarchal status in America with immigrants [such as Mexican Americans] being placed on a lower rung) to an embraced status that implied something unique, something very special about being born a Mexican American. By embracing their culture, young Mexican Americans became more interested in studying their past, retaining their language and customs, and reflecting on how and why they differed from their white European-American and black African-American friends and neighbors. They became aware of how

hard their parents and grandparents had tried to assimilate into the American culture, and they rebelled. Some of this rebellion showed up in the form of their support of strikes and boycotts, like those led by Cesar Chavez against poor health and working conditions in agricultural fields. Some of this rebellion also showed up in the Chicano, a literature that was suddenly finding acceptance in the publishing industry. It was in this era that Acosta was first published.

Her writing, Acosta has said, comes from her point of view as a Chicana and as a woman. The ideas expressed in her writing are derived from her feelings about everyday life. Another important theme in Acosta's writing is her family, especially the females in her family. Her writing is also noted for its celebration of working-class culture. All these elements find their way into her poem "My Mother Pieced Quilts."

Another important element that bears mention is the tradition behind the art of quilting, since it is upon this element that the structure of the poem is created. The history of quilting is one that speaks louder than the voices of women throughout the ages. For some women, it was the only way that their voices and thoughts were carried from one generation to another. As Angeline Godwin Dvorak states in her essay *"Piecing It,"* it is

> as though pulling the tension of the needle through the fabric, the tension in the history that is pieced into the quilter's art form is the universal oppressions of women that have forwarded a patriarchal history, and left diminished or neglected the voice, role, and impact of women in world societies.

Then specifically in reference to Acosta's poem, Dvorak adds, "The mother quilter, as artist and historian, ultimately gives a voice to the quilts, they then become the storytellers . . . the mother translates and preserves her history as a woman as well as the history of their culture."

The history that is represented in a quilt is not the history of presidents or queens. It is the history of every day occurrences, every day people. It is a history that would normally be overlooked. But a quilt is more than just a preservation of history and culture. It is also an art, an art that is created out of waste. Sometimes the making of a quilt was the only way that a woman could express her creativity. Quilting, in some ways, is like writing a poem or painting a picture. Quilting says Christina Walkley in her *"Quilting the Rocky Road"* was also a way of "turning a bare shanty into a home, satisfying the women's hunger for beauty and civilization." In quilting women "found emotional consolation for a harsh and demanding daily life." Quilting, says Walkley, was "turning the seemingly negligible, with skill, patience, and above all with vision, into something of lasting beauty and worth."

It is with this collection of elements, like the small bits of material with which her mother made a quilt, that Acosta wrote her poem.

Critical Overview

Critics have observed a strong sense of family and Chicano culture in Acosta's poetry. Yvonne Yarbro-Bejarano, in her essay "Cultural Influences: Chicana," writes, "Strong ties among females is a recurrent theme in Chicana poetry. . . . 'My Mother Pieced Quilts' is a moving testimonial to the mother's weaving covers from their life's experience, the bonding point of diversity, as well as a celebration of working-class women's culture." Tey Diana Rebolledo and Eliana S. Rivero agree, writing for their anthology *Infinite Divisions: An*

Anthology of Chicana Literature, which they co-edited. In the chapter "Self and Others," they comment on the roles of women in Chicano society and the importance of the mother figure in Acosta's poetry. "Mothers," they write, "are admired for patient ways, for survival skills, for homesteading virtues, and for crafts. They are seen as makers, doers, as women who did not have the opportunity to speak up, or even less to write, but who leave an indelible print on their children's lives."

Criticism

Joyce Hart

Hart, a former college professor, is currently a freelance writer and copyeditor. In this essay, she looks at the similarities between Teresa Palomo Acosta and the images that she portrays of her mother as she creates her poem.

The poem "My Mother Pieced Quilts" was published in 1976 at the beginning of a renaissance of Mexican-American (also referred to as *Chicana* [for female authors]) literary creativity. This renaissance did not reflect the female authors' sudden burst of creativity, for there always were women writing, but rather it reflects the sudden willingness on the part of the publishing industry to put Chicana literary expressions into print. The public appetite for multicultural material as well as the demand for writing by women provided the stimulus, and Teresa Palomo Acosta was one of the women who was ready and willing to provide the material.

This time period (as well as the previous decade) was also a time of reflection. At times it seemed that every established construct that had preceded these two decades was then in question. Young men, in general, were questioning why they should go to war. Young Mexican-American men, in particular, were questioning why such disproportionate numbers of their peers were being sent to Vietnam. Women, in general, were questioning why they should accept the same societal restrictions on their lives that their mothers had tolerated. Mexican-American women were questioning their mothers' complete subjugation to enculturation into the white European-American society that demanded they sacrifice their language and ancestral traditions. These were times of turmoil and public outcry, but they were also times of self-reflection. Out in the streets, voices shouted. But inside the houses, people were quietly reflecting on a more personal search for new answers to such questions

> *In her poem 'My Mother Pieced Quilts,' she looks back with fresh vision at her mother. But in the act of looking back as well as in the act of writing the poem, Acosta also reflects on her definitions of self.*

as: Who am I? Where did I come from? and Where am I going? It was out of these questions, these personal redefinitions of a newly emerging self that much of the Chicana poetry arose.

It was during these times, in the midst of these questions and self-reflection that Acosta wrote "My Mother Pieced Quilts." She wrote without having role models with whom she could identify in the literary field. Men created almost all of the Mexican-American literary works at that time. Very few women had been published before Acosta's poem saw print. But this "does not belie the fact that Chicanas were writing during this early period," say Tey Diana Rebolledo and Eliana S. Rivero in their introduction to their anthology of Chicana literature *Infinite Divisions*. "They were writing, but, having been silenced for long periods of time, the authors found breaking that silence into a public act difficult." In other words, Mexican-American women had become accustomed to their silence. Breaking it was almost like breaking a law, transgressing a taboo.

But once that silence had been broken, first in the second half of the 1970s and then even more proficiently in the 1980s, Chicana literature began to flourish. And "as the numbers of published texts increased," state Rebolledo and Rivero, "critics began to analyze their contents."

That analysis demonstrated that the major themes of these Chicana writers were: "Who am I? How did I become the person that I am? What are my historical and cultural antecedents, my racial characteristics, and how do these factors define my place in society?" One other significant theme that ran through much of the Chicana literature during

that time was the concern of these female poets and authors in defining the influence that their mothers had on them. Acosta's poetry was one of the forerunners of many of these themes. In her poem "My Mother Pieced Quilts," she looks back with fresh vision at her mother. But in the act of looking back as well as in the act of writing the poem, Acosta also reflects on her definitions of self.

The first thing that is interesting to note in Acosta's poem is the fact that in piecing together all the images that must have run through her mind as she wrote this poem, Acosta was, in many ways, mimicking her mother's actions of piecing together material to make a quilt. She, like her mother, was piecing together memories, creating stories, and gathering images from her Mexican heritage. According to Rebolledo and Rivero,

> The Chicana writer like the *curandera* or the *bruja,* is the keeper of the culture, keeper of the memories, the rituals, the stories. . . . She is also the one who changes the culture, the one who breeds . . . new dreams . . . making . . . a new legacy for those who have still to squeeze into legitimacy as . . . American citizens. The writer and the quilter have these characteristics in common. They both preserve the culture and the family stories through their artistic expression as created in words for one; as created in cloth for the other. In the keeping of the culture and the stories, they both inspire new dreams; and in doing so, they both, in their separate ways, help push the next generation forward.

Acosta expresses herself through poetry, making random, and sometimes worn out, phrases (like old pieces of material) fit into a pattern that will, on the whole, make sense. Like her mother, Acosta is picking through the pieces of material, looking at each image and remembering its significance. I remember this image from when I was younger. I remember this other image from when there was a death in the family. I remember another one from when we lived in another town. It is through these remembrances that both Acosta and her mother reflect on their identity, past and present. It is through these remembered incidents that they face certain challenges, and in meeting those challenges, they grow stronger. In remembering the "gentle communion cotton," Acosta might have been reminded of her own innocence as a child. Likewise as her mother sewed that particular piece of material into the quilt, she might have remembered not only the young child who once wore the Communion dress, but also remembered her own innocence as a young mother. In other words, the quilt was just a blanket for Acosta, who used it to keep warm. "They were just meant as covers / in winter. . . ." It was not until she "began to wonder how you pieced / all these together . . ." that Acosta begins to create her poem. It is in the wondering that suddenly the quilt is broken down, in her mind, into small pieces, small memories that create images. And it is through these images that her words and phrases are formed. Thus, the mother who gathered the pieces of material to create the quilt is now inspiring the daughter who is gathering images to create the poem.

In the fourth stanza of her poem, the speaker refers to the craft of sewing a quilt. "How the thread darted in and out / galloping along the frayed edges . . . / oh how you stretched and turned and rearranged. . . ." These skills are also required of the writer: the craftsmanship of sewing words together, rewriting, editing, or in Acosta's words, stretching, turning, and rearranging. More than likely, it is not only that Acosta remembers her mother sewing the quilt, but that she also relates to her mother as an artist, understanding the patience, the clear vision, the determination that is required in finding just the right piece of material, just as she herself must find the right word to make the image convey the exact meaning that is intended. As a writer, she relates to her mother's "staking out the plan. . . ." She understands what is necessary in creating a new form.

"It can be argued . . . that art and literature have as their primary goal the exploration of human identity," state Rebolledo and Rivero. And so it is with both Acosta and her mother. If one asks what might have motivated the mother to make quilts, a quick answer could be that she needed to provide warmth for her family. But if that was the only incentive, then she could have done so by stitching rags together without concern for form. But this mother creates pictures like the "swallow flying." She thinks about how to mix colors, "whether to put the lilac purple of easter against the / red plaid of winter-going-into-spring. . . ." The mother of Acosta's poem is no less an artist than Acosta herself, the writer of the poem. And both women, as artists, are in their own ways looking for definitions of themselves.

"Chicana identity is multiple, a reflection on circular mirrors," write Rebolledo and Rivero. That identity includes not only what they think of themselves but also what others think of them. That definition is sometimes hard to grasp as they are living in the middle of two cultures. When women search for a model to emulate, a model that will help them identify themselves, they first look to their families, to their female kin. The woman they most often turn to is their mother. "Mothers are admired for patient ways, for survival skills, for homesteading virtues, and for crafts," continue Rebolledo

What Do I Read Next?

- Ana Castillo is one of the more famous contemporary Chicana poets. The main themes of her writing revolve around race and gender issues. Although known for her poetry, her book *Massacre of the Dreamers: Essays on Xicanisma* (1992) is a collection of creative nonfiction essays. In these essays, Castillo explores the struggles of "Brown women" who live in a "racially polarized" United States. She also gives an overview of the Chicana feminist movement of the 1970s, as well as her thoughts on where the movement is heading.

- After winning the Lila Wallace–Reader's Digest Foundation Writers Award, Lorna Dee Cervantes became a widely known author. Her two most famous collections of poetry are *Emplumada* (1981) and *From the Cables of Genocide: Poems on Love and Hunger* (1991). Her writing is blunt and deals with social issues, especially the class status of women.

- Pat Mora is a prolific writer. She has won numerous awards for her poetry, which include the collections *Chants* (1984) and *Borders* (1986). Elements of her homeland of southwest Arizona as well as the traditions of her Mexican-American background filter through her writing. A work of fiction, *House of Houses* (1997), tells a generational story of her family.

- Recently, Sandra Cisneros, a writer and poet, won the distinguished MacArthur grant, awarded to people who show great genius in their work. Her poetry collections include the titles *My Wicked Wicked Ways* (1992) and *Loose Woman* (1995).

- Gloria Velasquez is a poet and teaches Spanish at California Polytech San Luis Obispo. She has written a collection of poems entitled, *I Used To Be a Superwoman* (1997). She has also published several stories for children and teens that deal with issues that face children of color as they grow up in the United States.

and Rivero. "They are seen as makers, doers, as women who did not have the opportunity to speak up, or even less to write, but who leave an indelible print on their children." How the mother in this poem identified herself can only be guessed at. But the fact that her daughter, the author of the poem, sees her as the one who "cemented them" suggests that it was the mother who kept the family together, just as she kept the patterns of her quilt together. The poem also suggests that the quilts were used as "weapons / against pounding january winds. . . ." The mother in this image is portrayed as not only the provider, but also the one who guards and protects. This mother may have learned these qualities from her mother. Just as the tradition of making quilts was handed down, so might the character traits of fortitude and stability have been. As the daughter reflects on these characteristics, she senses pride. Her pride decorates her poem and may stimulate a desire to emulate those character traits in herself. Putting these feelings about her mother into her poem will allow the generation of women that follow Acosta to read the poem, much as Acosta has "read" the quilt. And the characteristics of both the mother and the daughter will be handed down. The "indelible print" carries the tradition forward.

"It is part of the writers' routine and compulsion," state Rebolledo and Rivero, "[to] walk around their streets, their well-known towns or neighborhoods, searching for raw materials . . . and getting it from the ordinary, the familiar, the trivial." This is how Rebolledo and Rivero define Chicano writers, but it could easily be transformed to define how the quilter works—looking for raw materials in the neighborhoods, collecting the ordinary and the familiar. Rebolledo and Rivero continue their descriptions by stating that the writing of Chicano women is about "putting down in graphic signs what ordinary life events signify . . . it is the art of cultural preservation by means of capturing the flow of time and people in their lives." How close these definitions align with the craft of quilting. "You were the river current / carrying the roaring notes . . .," writes Acosta in her poem. The music of life floats on the mother through her quilts, just as the music of life flows through Acosta's poem. She continues by describing her mother in the next few lines as having delivered herself "in separate testimonies." With this reference to separate stories, Acosta might be making reference to the separate quilts that the mother made. Or it might be referring to the separate panels on one quilt, separate images through which the mother inscribes a picture of herself through her work. Just as a poet-

ess leaves the mark of herself in her writing, no matter what story she is telling, so too has the mother left her fingerprints on the quilt.

In the final stanzas of the poem, the speaker confesses her emotions. "Oh mother you plunged me sobbing and laughing / into our past . . . " It is the speaker's emotions, but the history is shared between mother and daughter. It is "our past," not my past or your past. It is a past that has been recorded first in the quilt, then seconded in the poem. If Acosta should ever give birth to a daughter, there will be a more complex reading of the past: first through the visual representation of the quilt, then through the literal representation of the poem. The history will echo in the next generation more richly because the tradition, the stories have been recorded and handed down. The quilter and the poet are mirror images, one enhancing the other, and one reflecting the other. And the reflections are multiple: mother seeing herself in her quilt; daughter seeing mother in the quilt; daughter seeing herself in the poem about the quilt; and in the end, both the poem and the quilt, the mother and the daughter, are "knotted with love / the quilts sing on."

Source: Joyce Hart, Critical Essay on "My Mother Pieced Quilts," in *Poetry for Students,* The Gale Group, 2001.

Doreen Piano

Piano is a Ph.D. candidate in English at Bowling Green State University. In the following essay, she explores how the making of quilts are metaphors for the creation of family history in Acosta's poem.

Quilts, in Teresa Palomo Acosta's poem, are not just everyday items, something to sleep under when it is cold out or to wrap around you while watching television. Although they are functional, acting "as weapons / against pounding january winds," quilts carry a much richer meaning in this poem. They are chronicles of family history, revealing physical wear and tear as they age as well as containing memories, which are physically represented by the fabrics found in the quilts. Thus, "my father's santa fe workshirt / the summer denims, the tweeds of fall" refer to specific moments in time when they were worn. Acosta sees family history as not being chronological, a series of events that have taken place in the past, but as continuous, created by the binding of fragments of cloth, or, metaphorically, fragments of memories. Thus, it is through the narrator's understanding of her mother's artistic and physical effort in piecing together scraps of cloth that she begins to understand her mother's role in forming their family history. Acosta uses the act of quilt-making, what is often seen as an everyday, ordinary activity, as a metaphor for the creation of family history and cultural heritage.

Because Acosta is a Mexican-American, or *Chicana* poet (defined by Alvina Quintana, in *Home Girls: Chicana Literary Voices* as a term that "signifies a specific ethnic or political identity or both"), it is important to read the poem within a specific cultural and political context, one that considers both gender and ethnicity as primary concerns of Chicana writers. Questions that many Chicana writers probe in their writing are: What does it mean to be a woman in Chicana culture? And, what does it mean to be a Chicana in mainstream society? The answers to these two questions are often at odds with each other and create complex and conflicted narratives about Chicana identity.

Thus, to reveal their complex "cultural make-up," many Chicana writers write from a specific position, one that Gloria Anzaldua describes in her introduction to *Infinite Divisions: An Anthology of Chicana Literature* as *la frontera* (the borderlands). This concept represents both the geographical location that separates the United States and Mexico, and, when used with an upper case B, a metaphorical space that positions many Chicanas within and among two different cultures. This tension plays itself out in the way that language is used. For example, many Chicana writers use their bicultural backgrounds in their writing, switching from English to Spanish to demonstrate their position as being located within and outside of both Mexican and American culture. In this way, innovative language use forges new cultural, or "hybrid," identities that combine and reject aspects of both cultures. On the other hand, some Chicana writers may use English in one poem and Spanish in another depending on who their intended audience is.

Although Acosta's poem is written in English, she makes frequent references to her bicultural background through her use of a phrase such as "corpus christi noon" to refer to a Roman Catholic wedding and her allusions to migrant farm work that employs a high number of working-class Mexican and Mexican-American families. In one of the final stanzas of the poem, the narrator provides a strong image of migrant work and its repetitious and backbreaking labor by repeating the preposition "into" as in:

> into the river crossing at five
> into the spinach fields

> *The quilts, similar to the poem, become a material symbol of family history; each fabric contains a story, a memory, that like the quilts which are described as 'october ripened canvases,' may fade with time but remain tangible."*

> into the plainview cotton rows
> into tuberculosis wards.

Yet, at the same time that she recounts this painful image of harsh working conditions, the narrator also uses it to show how the quilts her mother made contain both good and bad memories that are all related to her cultural heritage and cannot be disregarded.

Because women's experiences have been historically overlooked by both the Anglo and Chicano literary canons, many Chicana writers respond to that oversight by emphasizing ordinary and everyday experiences where women play an essential role. Acosta follows this particular tradition in her use of a mother as a central figure. She is the "you" of the poem, the one who is being addressed by the narrator as well as the "quilter" of family history. The editors of *Infinite Divisions: An Anthology of Chicana Literature*, Tey Diana Rebolledo and Eliana S. Rivero, note that "In literature, Chicanas' world perspectives are shaped and determined by their immediate female kin and the values they embody. . . ." Hard work, family ties, community, cultural pride, and a reverence for the past are some of the values that the mother in the poem possesses as well as passes on to her daughter.

The narrator's focus on her mother's quilting reflects the influence her mother has had in creating family ties and recording its history. The mother is the glue that binds the discrete elements of the family and its history. For example, in the lines, "how you shaped patterns square and oblong and round / positioned / balanced / then cemented them," the narrator realizes that her mother has shaped and formed each of the individual family members into a larger unit, a family. Strong family ties do not come without some effort, and the mother has not only been a witness to the events that the varied fabrics symbolize, but her quilting reveals her participation in these events. The mother is the one who has "pieced / all these together / these strips of gentle communion cotton and flannel / nightgowns / wedding organdies / dime-store velvets." The variety of fabrics she names such as "cotton," "flannel," "organdies," "velvets" refer to the many occasions that the family has participated in from the ordinary to the extraordinary. In the quilt, these events come together in a mosaic of memories.

In *Contemporary Chicana Poetry: A Critical Approach to an Emerging Literature,* literary critic Marta Esta Sanchez claims that Chicana writers often "celebrate the history of Chicana women in their families, either by showing what their maternal ancestors had contributed to their personal formation or by documenting these ancestors' experiences as memorable in their own right." In "My Mother Pieced Quilts," Acosta's narrator clearly admires her mother's abilities to create a physical testimony of their family history. The poem can be seen as a series of snapshots that the narrator remembers from her childhood. Each of these images reveal a mother who is engaged in both her quilting and her caretaking. The narrator/child watches.

> how the thread darted in and out
> galloping along the frayed edges, tucking them in
> as you did us at night.

The variety of verbs used in the poem ("shaped," "cemented," "balanced," "positioned," "driving," "delivering") demonstrates the different activities that go into quilting as well as raising a family. Both activities require a tremendous amount of work, and it is the narrator of the poem who captures the tireless and spirited efforts, both physical and mental, of her mother.

For many Chicana writers, Tey Diana Rebollado and Elaina Rivero claim in *Infinite Divisions: An Anthology of Chicana Literature,* mothers "are seen as makers, doers, as women who did not have the opportunity to speak up . . . but who leave an indelible print on their children's lives." Thus, Acosta's use of metaphors to describe the mother, such as "you were the river current" and "you were the caravan master," reveal lasting images that have remained strong and vibrant and that portray the narrator's mother as being a vital part of her childhood. Yet, at the same time that the narrator celebrates her mother's creative force that pulled the

family together, she also reveals the generational differences between her and her mother. The mother's creativity found its expression in the making of quilts, a practical and communal act that is focused on the hearth. In contrast, the daughter's creative energy is in her writing of poetry, an act that is more solitary and intellectual. Yet the poem she writes celebrates the community, both ethnic and family, of her childhood. In a sense, the mother's "writing" of family history is similar to the daughter's writing about her childhood memories; both engage in the act of remembrance.

The quilts, similar to the poem, become a material symbol of family history; each fabric contains a story, a memory, that like the quilts which are described as "october ripened canvases," may fade with time but remain tangible. The memories that her mother has stitched into the quilts have informed the narrator's own identity and inspired her to continue the tradition of family storytelling through poetry writing. The individual fabrics of the quilts create a family history, some of which the narrator did not witness, such as her parents' wedding, "the corpus christi noon when my father held your hand," but that have become part of the family's lore, or oral tradition. Regardless of whether these memories are good or bad, the quilt is a testimony to those times and carries meaning into the present.

By the end of the poem, the quilts become personified, almost human, as they "lay / armed / ready / shouting / celebrating." The narrator realizes that her own identity cannot be separated from her cultural heritage or family history as she exclaims in the last couplet of the poem, "knotted with love / the quilts sing on." Thus, family history is never completely in the past but continues to be recreated from generation to generation. Through the passing of family traditions such as stories and heirlooms, cultural heritage, and family bonds are created and formed. The narrator expresses this concept of a living heritage when she claims "oh mother you plunged me sobbing and laughing / into our past." Similar to Alice Walker's short story "Everyday Use" in which quilts function within an African-American family not just as aesthetic objects or sterile family heirlooms but as a vital link to family history and cultural heritage, the quilts in "My Mother Pieced Quilts" are also deeply entwined with the narrator's family and cultural history, one that is living and breathing and always present.

Source: Doreen Piano, Critical Essay on "My Mother Pieced Quilts," in *Poetry for Students,* The Gale Group, 2001.

Judi Ketteler

Ketteler has taught literature and composition, with a focus on nineteenth-century literature. This essay discusses female creativity in "My Mother Pieced Quilts," Chicana mothers' search for an alternative legacy to pass down to their daughters, and the various levels of meaning embedded in the poem's imagery.

"My Mother Pieced Quilts," by Teresa Palomo Acosta, is a poem about memory and the way it becomes intertwined—quite literally—with threads of fabric. But it is as much a poem about memory as it is about womanhood and female creativity. Acosta traces the line of female creativity by laying out the legacy her mother has passed on through her handmade quilts. "My Mother Pieced Quilts" is a deeply personal poem with larger implications about what it means to be a mother, a daughter, and a woman in Mexican-American culture.

Acosta writes from a distinct literary tradition. She is a *Chicana,* or a Mexican-American woman (a related, although separate tradition from Latina or Hispanic writing). The Chicano movement first became prominent in the 1960s, along with the Civil Rights Movement, the Women's Movement, and the Native American Movement. As a marginalized group, Mexican-Americans shared much in common with other minority groups and faced similar daily prejudices and hardships. Mexican-American men, or Chicanos, were among the first to be published.

Tey Diana Rebolledo and Eliana S. Rivero, authors of *Infinite Divisions: An Anthology of Chicana Literature,* write: "Although some women were included among the first [Mexican-American] writers to be published, it was the male authors who made the initial inroads, were most easily and frequently published, and were the most recognized." Chicanas were certainly writing but were silenced in the publishing world for the most part. Chicana writer and thinker Gloria Anzaldua has remarked that Chicanas were "speaking from cracked spaces—from margins."

In the 1970s and 1990s, Chicana writers began to gain a voice. They wrote about womanhood, sexuality, images and definitions of themselves, and the world around them. Acosta speaks about these things too, and "My Mother Pieced Quilts" is rooted in the Chicana tradition. The tradition carries with it a responsibility, as literary critic Rudolfo Anaya explains in *Growing Up Chicano/a: An Anthology:* "The voice of the Chicana writer in our culture is one of the most influential in helping to shape and change the cultural ways." Acosta lives up to that responsibility in this poem about her mother and the strong legacy her mother has passed down to her.

As the poem begins, Acosta reflects on the quilts her mother made, regarding them as utilitarian objects. At first glance, they appear to be no more than covers for warmth, as the first stanza suggests: "they were just meant as covers / in winters / as weapons / against pounding january winds." As a young child wrapping herself in the quilts, Acosta views them as unremarkable. It isn't until she grows up and relives the moments immortalized in fabric and stitches that the full impact of her mother's art stirs her. The poem is a process of remembering, as well as a process of appreciating the significance of those swatches of fabric, bound together stitch by stitch. Acosta works throughout the poem to personify the quilts, so that they move from being mere objects in the beginning to being alive in the end. They become living memories, ready to share their secrets with the next generation: "knotted with love / the quilts sing on."

Acosta remembers her childhood in pieces, like snapshots from a photo album. The quilts trigger those memories in the snippets of cloth and scraps of old dresses: "these strips of gentle communion cotton and flannel nightgowns / wedding organdies / dime store velvets." The fabric is rich and varied, and her mother shows resourcefulness in her ability to transform the mundane, the outfits of everyday life, into art. The entire process of making quilts is in fact a process of transformation for Acosta's mother. As the matriarch of the family, she is the keeper of the domestic, the preserver of memories. According to Rebolledo and Rivero, Mexican-American culture values mothers for certain sets of skills. They explain: "Mothers are admired for patient ways, for survival skills, for homesteading virtues, and for crafts. They are seen as makers, doers, as women who did not have the opportunity to speak up, or even less to write, but who leave an indelible print on their children's lives." In other words, a women's space is the domestic, and her role as housekeeper and mother defines her. Traditional avenues of artistic expression are not generally open to mothers, who find themselves limited by an unbending identity as a caregiver.

However, women find other methods to express their creativity and to pass their legacy down to their daughters. This requires inventiveness, and it requires women who would be artists to look at "domesticity" in a fresh way, as an avenue of possibility. For Acosta's mother, art becomes inter-

> *However, women find other methods to express their creativity and to pass their legacy down to their daughters."*

twined with her domestic duties, so that the poet remembers "how the thread darted in and out / galloping along the frayed edges, tucking them in / as you did us at night." Her mother is both caretaker and artist in the same moment; she creates as she tends to her children. Her role as a mother is woven into her art and the quilts reflect that duality.

Author and essayist Alice Walker, in her pivotal collection of essays, *In Search of Our Mother's Gardens,* addressed the female line of creativity. She is speaking specifically about the ways African-American women have passed down artistic legacies to their children in a society where they were both stereotyped and silenced, although her argument holds true for other marginalized identities. Walker recalls coming across a beautiful and inspired quilt in the Smithsonian museum that depicted the crucifixion, "made out of bits and pieces of useless rags." Below the quilt, the plaque reads, "Made by an anonymous Black woman in Alabama, a hundred years ago." Walker comments: "And so our mothers and grandmothers have more often than not anonymously handed on the creative spark, the seed of the flower they themselves never hoped to see: or like a sealed letter they could not plainly read." The situation for Acosta and her mother is slightly different in that the quilts are not anonymous; the identity of the artist is known. But female creativity—realized in these beautiful quilts—faces the same kind of culture anonymity in that it is not valued in the way the great male artists' work is valued.

"My Mother Pieced Quilts" is also a poem about work. Organizing a household and caring for children is not easy work. It is constant and demanding. Quilting provides an escape from the monotony, but it also involves its own work. Acosta emphasizes the active nature of quilting in the third stanza, which stands out from the rest of the poem because of its short, choppy phrases. The short phrases build on one another, similar to the way

pieces of fabric build on one another to make a complete picture. It is a stanza about work: "how you shaped patterns square and oblong and round / positioned / balanced / then cemented them / with your thread / a steel needle / a thimble." She uses active verbs and words that denote strength and stability such as cement and steel. Quilting is more than a pastime, it is a medium of expression, requiring as much raw talent and hard work as arts such as sculpting, drawing, painting, or writing.

Furthermore, quilting is not something Acosta's mother just *happens* to do; there is planning and thinking involved. The poet recalls her mother's planning sessions, sprawled out in the domestic space of the kitchen. One can image Acosta's mother, fabric arranged neatly on the floor, picking and choosing colors and themes. "In the evening you sat at your canvas / —our cracked linoleum floor the drawing board." Again, the reader feels a sense of the duality of the mother's life. Her art and her domestic duties are intertwined, literally inhabiting the same spaces. And her children are nearby, watching her, as Acosta remembers, "me lounging at your arm." Images of strength and nurturance are brought together as the cement and steel images float side by side with the image of the young Acosta lounging in her mother's arms.

Throughout the poem, Acosta works to construct a portrait of her mother. She becomes multidimensional: the mother and the artist, performing household duties while she plans her next quilt. She becomes complex, and she becomes an active agent in her own life. In other words, in patriarchal cultures where men are dominant, women's decisions are often made for them, consciously or unconsciously. Acosta's mother finds a way to complicate that through her art. She is the active one, making the decisions, calling the shots, dreaming and envisioning beauty. In each stanza, Acosta's mother takes on more and more urgency, as she makes crucial decisions about her quilts: "whether or not to mix a yellow with blue and white and paint the / corpus christi noon when my father held your hand / whether to shape a five-point star from the / somber black silk you wore to grandmother's funeral."

There is power in Acosta's mother's art. This power is fluid, such as the image of her mother as the "river current" suggests. But Acosta also portrays female power in ways it is not usually imagined; she uses battle imagery and reads her mother as a kind of high commander: "you were the caravan master at the reins / driving your threaded needle artillery across the mosaic cloth / delivering yourself in separate testimonies." Her mother's art allows her to inhabit multiple roles, to transform herself. That is the legacy Acosta finally understands her mother has given her: she can be who and what she sets out to be and define herself in the way she chooses. She can deliver her own testimony as to who she is: she is free.

In a patriarchal tradition, it is men who pass down the name and the property to their sons. Acosta's mother imagines an alternative tradition, a distinctly Chicana tradition, whereby she passes down the legacies of memory and identity. The reader understands by the end of the poem that the quilts are about more than just reminiscing. They are—symbolically—the thing that both connects Acosta with her mother and frees her to define herself in multiple ways. "Oh mother you plunged me sobbing and laughing / into our past." That fall into the past keeps the quilts alive. They have both a history, which has withstood "the thrashings of twenty-five years," and a future. In the same breath that "My Mother Pieced Quilts" recalls the past, it also looks toward the future. The quilts are ready for future battles, for new sets of experiences and challenges. "Stretched out they lay / armed / ready / shouting / celebrating." In the end, the tone is hopeful more than nostalgic. The lessons and struggles of the past are not over; rather they live in the legacy Acosta's mother has passed down, which lays waiting to tackle the obstacles of the next generation Chicana women.

Source: Judi Ketteler, Critical Essay on "My Mother Pieced Quilts" in *Poetry for Students,* The Gale Group, 2001.

Sources

Acosta, Teresa Palomo, "My Mother Pieced Quilts," in *Women Poets of the World,* edited by Joanna Bankier and Deirdre Lashgari, Macmillan, 1983, pp. 393–395.

Anaya, Rudolfo, *Growing Up Chicano/a: An Anthology,* William Morrow and Company, 1993.

Anzaldua, Gloria, *Infinite Divisions: An Anthology of Chicana Literature,* University of Arizona Press, 1993.

Dvorak, Angeline Godwin, "Piecing It: The Mother–Quilter as Artist and Historian in Teresa Palomo Acosta's 'My Mother Pieced Quilts,'" in *Women in Literature and Life Assembly (WILLA),* Vol. 5, The Assembly: National Council of Teachers of English, 1996, pp. 13–17.

Quintana, Alvina E., *Home Girls: Chicana Literary Voices,* Temple University Press, 1996.

Rebolledo, Tey Diana, and Eliana S. Rivero, eds., *Infinite Divisions: An Anthology of Chicana Literature,* University of Arizona Press, 1993.

Sanchez, Marta Ester, *Contemporary Chicana Poetry: A Critical Approach to an Emerging Literature,* University of California Press, 1985.

Walker, Alice, *In Search of Our Mother's Gardens,* Harcourt Brace Jovanovich, 1983.

Walkley, Christina, "Quilting the Rocky Road (Women in a New World)," in *History Today,* Vol. 44, November 1, 1994, pp. 30–37.

Yarbro-Bejarano, Yvonne, "Cultural Influences: Chicano," in *Women Poets of the World,* edited by Joanna Bankier and Deirdre Lashgari, Macmillan, 1983, pp. 343–345.

For Further Study

Acosta, Teresa Palomo, "They are Laying Plans for Me—Those Curanderas," in *Infinite Divisions,* edited by Tey Diana Rebolledo and Eliana S. Rivero, University of Arizona Press, 1993, pp. 296–297.

In this poem, the speaker is looking for a spiritual healing that will lead her back to herself. In other words, Acosta is searching for her roots.

Aida, Hurtado, "'Sitios y lenguas': Chicanas Theorize Feminisms," in *Hypatia,* Vol. 13, March 22, 1998, pp. 134–162.

With extensive coverage of the history and an understanding of Chicana feminism, the article summarizes the works of Chicana feminist scholars, creative authors, and artists in reference to their understanding of Chicana feminism.

Bankier, Joanna, and Deirdre Lashgari, eds., *Women Poets of the World,* MacMillan, 1983.

This extensive collection of poetry includes Acosta's poem "My Mother Pieced Quilts," as well as poems from other women from around the world.

Carlson, Lori, ed., *Cool Salsa: Bilingual Poems on Growing up Latino in the United States,* Juniper, 1995.

This exciting collection of poems deals with the concerns that many young adults must face as they try to bridge the gap between two cultures and two languages. Concepts of bilingualism, prejudice, and Latino culture are presented. Poems are written in both English and Spanish.

Christ, Carol P., *Diving Deep and Surfacing: Women Writers on Spiritual Quest,* Beacon, 1980.

This work presents a study of other women writers whose writings, like Acosta's, focus on a search for self. Authors covered include Kate Chopin, Doris Lessing, Ntozake Shange, and others.

Milligan, Bryce, and Mary Guerrero-Milligan, eds., *Floricanto Si: A Collection of Latina Poetry,* Penguin, 1998.

This work is an extensive collection of newly emerging young poets of the post-Chicano movement. Forty-seven different voices are heard in this collection, coming from all over the United States, Mexico, the Caribbean, and South America.

On Freedom's Ground

Richard Wilbur

1986

Richard Wilbur originally created "On Freedom's Ground" as the libretto of a cantata, which was specifically written for the yearlong celebration of the one-hundredth anniversary of the Statue of Liberty. It premiered on October 28, 1986, at Avery Fisher Hall in New York City, exactly one hundred years after the day on which the statue was first dedicated. After William Schuman, the composer, was unable to find a poem, which he felt would adequately convey the statue's importance, he asked Wilbur to create an original work for the occasion. At first, Wilbur was reluctant. In a *New York Times* article, he explained his hesitation: "Great God! What a wealth of clichés are suggested by this theme. How hard it will be to be the least fresh, the least worthy of the subject." Eventually, however, he accepted the challenge. The poem was later included in his 1988 Pulitzer Prize–winning volume, *New and Collected Poems.*

The poem is divided into five separate sections, each covering a different aspect of the struggle for liberty in the United States. The first describes the land before the arrival of the settlers from Europe. The next focuses on the American Revolution and the friendship between the United States and France during this time. The third section begins with the soldier's sacrifice. It continues, however, by noting how this country has frequently denied that sacrifice when those hard won freedoms were withheld from certain groups. However, the section concludes with hope, stating that the willingness to acknowledge wrongdoing can

lead to change. The fourth section celebrates the different immigrants through their music and dance. Finally, Wilbur categorizes the people of the United States as "immigrants still," bravely voyaging into the future.

Author Biography

Richard Wilbur was born on March 1, 1921, in New York, and spent the first two years of his life in New York City, a period he described as spent on a "fire escape overlooking the Hudson River." His family then moved to a pre-revolutionary war stone house on a farm in North Caldwell, New Jersey. Although it was not far from the city, Wilbur and his brother were fairly isolated from other children and spent much of their time amusing themselves by exploring the nearby woods and fields as well as the farm itself. Wilbur credits those years with developing his interest in the natural world, an interest that later became central to his poetry.

Wilbur attended Amherst College, where he was chairman (editor) of the student newspaper. While in college, he spent two summers hitching rides in cars and freight trains around the country, eventually visiting forty-six of the forty-eight states. It was also during this period that he first became interested in the serious study of poetry, finding himself drawn to writers such as Robert Frost and Marianne Moore. In 1942 Wilbur graduated from Amherst, married Charlotte Ward, and enlisted in the army. He served as a cryptographer in both Italy and Germany. During the war he began to write poetry as "one way of putting the world to rights a little bit."

After Wilbur returned home from the war, he entered Harvard on the G.I. Bill. While he was there, he ran into André du Bouchet, a fellow Amherst student who, as poetry editor for *Foreground* magazine, was looking for "new talent" for the publishing house of Reynal and Hitchcock. After Wilbur's wife informed du Bouchet about the wartime poems that Wilbur had sent her, du Bouchet asked to read them. In an interview in *The Amherst Literary Magazine,* the following quote appears in "Richard Wilbur: An Interview" in the book *Conversations with Richard Wilbur* according to source materials. How does The Amherst Literary Magazine come into play here? Wilbur described du Bouchet's reaction: "With a marvelous display of Gallic fervor, [he]

Richard Wilbur

wrapped his arms around me, kissed me on both cheeks, and declared me a poet." Wilbur's first book, *The Beautiful Changes and Other Poems,* was published in 1947, the same year that he received his master of arts degree. Following the publication of his book, Wilbur spent three years as a Junior Fellow of the Society of Fellows at Harvard University.

Throughout the course of his career, Wilbur produced a wide range of works in addition to poetry. During the 1950s, he began working on translations. The musical *Candide,* a collaborative work with Leonard Bernstein and Lillian Hellman, opened on Broadway in 1957. The first of Wilbur's books for children, *Loudmouse,* was published in 1963. He was active as a critic and editor throughout his career. His talent has been acknowledged with numerous awards through the decades. In 1957, his third volume of poetry, *Things of this World,* won both the Pulitzer Prize and the National Book Award; in 1988 *New and Collected Poems,* which includes "On Freedom's Ground," earned him a second Pulitzer. In 1987 he was appointed the second Poet Laureate of the United States. Wilbur remains a prolific writer and had two new books—a collection of poems and a children's book—published in 2000.

Poem Text

I. Back Then

Back then, before we came
To this calm bay and savage oceanside,
When Bedloe's Island had no English name,
The waves were but the subjects of the tide
And vassals of the harnessed wind, which blew   5
Not as it chose, but as it had to do.

The river had no choice
But to create this basin to the south,
Where every springtime tuned the peeper's voice
And drove the shad-run through its narrow mouth,   10
And the high-hovering sea-birds, even they,
Were slaves to hunger, diving on their prey.

Where was the thought of freedom then?
It came ashore within the minds of men.

II. Our Risen States

It was an English thought   15
That there is no just government
Unless by free consent,
And in that English cause we fought.

Our George defied their George;
Our Continentals would not yield   20
On Saratoga's field,
Or to the snows of Valley Forge.

But Yorktown's fall we owe
Not to ourselves alone, and let
This nation not forget   25
Great Lafayette and rochambeau.

It was our risen states
Which heartened France at least to rise
And beat with angry cries
On Prison doors and palace gates,   30

Till Frenchmen all might say
With us, and by the world be heard,
The sweet and rousing word
Of liberty, of liberté.

III. Like a Great Statue

Mourn for the dead who died for this country,   35
Whose minds went dark at the edge of a field,
In the muck of a trench, on the beachhead sand,
In a blast amidships, a burst in the air.
What did they think of before they forgot us?
In the blink of time before they forgot us?   40
The glare and whiskey of Saturday evening?
The drone or lift of their family voices?
The bend of a trout-stream? A fresh-made bed?
The sound of a lathe, or the scent of sawdust?
The mouth of a woman? A prayer? Who knows?   45
Let us force them to speak in chorus,
These men diverse in their names and faces

Who lived in a land where a life could be chosen.
Say that they mattered, alive and after;
That they gave us time to become what we could.   50

Grieve for the ways in which we betrayed them,
How we robbed their graves of a reason to die:
The tribes pushed west, and the treaties broken,
The image of God on the auction block,
The immigrant scorned, and the striker beaten,   55
The vote denied to liberty's daughters.
From all that has shamed us, what can we salvage?
Be proud at least that we know we were wrong,
That we need not lie, that our books are open.

Praise to this land for our power to change it,   60
To confess our misdoings, to mend what we can,
To learn what we mean and to make it the law,
To become what we said we were going to be.
Praise to our peoples, who came as strangers,
Who more and more have been shaped into one   65
Like a great statue brought over in pieces,
Its hammered cooper bolted together,
Anchored by rods in the continent's rock,
With a core of iron, and a torch atop it.
Praise to this land that it's most oppressed   70
Have marched in peace from the dark of the past
To speak in our time, and in Washington's
        Shadow,
Their invincible hope to be free at last—

Lord God Almighty, free
At last to cast their shackles down,   75
And wear the common crown
Of liberté.

IV. Come Dance

Now in our lady's honor
Come dance on freedom's ground,
And do the waltz or polka,   80
Whatever spins around,

Or let it be the raspa,
The jig or Lindy hop,
Or else the tarantella,
Whatever doesn't stop,   85

The highland fling, the hornpipe,
The schottische or the break,
Or, if you like, the cakewalk,
Whatever takes the cake,

But end it with the John Paul Jones,   90
Invented in this land,
That each of us may circle 'round
And take the other's hand.

V. Immigrants Still

Still, in the same great bay,
Now edged with towers and with piers,   95
Where for a hundred years
Our lady has been holding sway,

The risen tide comes flooding as before
To ramble north a hundred miles or more,
And the same sea-birds rise, though now they   100
    wheel
Above the crossing wakes of barge and keel.

These waters and these wings,
Whatever once they seemed, now wear
A bright, cavorting air,
And have the look of ransomed things: 105

To our free eyes the gulls go weaving now
Loose wreaths of flight about our lady's brow,
And toward her feet the motions of the sea
Leap up like hearts that hasten to be free.

Not that the graves of our dead are quiet,   110
Nor justice done, nor our journey over.
We are immigrants still, who travel in time,
Bound where the thought of America beckons;
But we hold our course, and the wind is with us.

Poem Summary

Line 1

"On Freedom's Ground: A Cantata" was written for the rededication of the Statue of Liberty. It was commissioned as one segment of a yearlong national celebration. Therefore, the speaker in the poem, which was originally the libretto accompanying the music, uses the plural "we," assuming the role of the voice of the American people. The first two words of line one, "back then," serve as the title for the first section of the poem, which describes the land, in particular, the New York Bay harbor, before the European settlers arrived. Wilbur uses alliteration, the repetition of the *b* in back and before, not only to help establish the rhythm of the poem, but also to highlight meaning, since both words refer to the past. Each of the sections is written in a different style. Part I, which contains fourteen lines, is a variation of the sonnet form. The first two stanzas are six lines each: the first and third, second and fourth, fifth and sixth lines in each rhyme. The final rhyming couplet sums up the poem's meaning.

Line 2

Wilbur uses both alliteration and a type of half-rhyme as "calm" is paired with "came" from line one and "bay" reinforces the sounds in "back" and "before." The line includes a contrast in meaning as well, as the "calm bay" is juxtaposed with the "savage oceanside."

Media Adaptations

- A 1985 PBS Home Video, *The Statue of Liberty,* part of a film series by Ken Burns, uses diaries, news accounts, film clips, and a variety of other sources to tell the story of the statue from construction to the present day.

- *Candide,* the musical adaptation of Moliere's play, which combined the talents of Wilbur, Leonard Bernstein and Lillian Hellman, is available in the original 1956 cast recording from Sony and the 1997 Broadway revival from BMG/RCA.

- Richard Wilbur is one of many poets who can be heard reading their own works at http://www.theatlantic.com/unbound/poetry/antholog/aaindx.htm (January, 2001); this is an excellent source for an introduction to contemporary poetry.

Line 3

The Statue of Liberty was built on Bedloe's Island, originally named for its seventeenth-century owner, Isaac Bedloe. When the sculptor of the statue, Frédéric-Auguste Bartholdi saw the island, he immediately selected it as the ideal spot for his monument, describing it as "an admirable spot . . . just opposite the Narrows, which are, so to speak, the gateway to America." In 1956, President Dwight Eisenhower officially changed the island's name to Liberty Island. Wilbur has been criticized because this line, as well as the rest of this section, ignores any mention of the native American names or values.

Lines 4–6

The speaker uses various images to show that nature itself is not free. The waves become "subjects" or "vassals" of the wind. The latter term, in particular, is used to describe European peasants who were tied to the land as property of a feudal lord. This carries a reminder that the ancestors of the early settlers were not themselves free. Even the wind which directs the waves is "harnessed."

The final line of the stanza concludes that nature has a pattern that it must follow. The use of a regular rhythm throughout the section reinforces the sense of pattern which the stanza presents.

Lines 7–8

The second stanza begins by reemphasizing the theme that all nature follows a preordained path. The geography of the land determines that the mighty Hudson River flow south to the sea, in the process creating the upper and lower parts of the New York Bay.

Lines 9–10

Wilbur introduces two of nature's springtime rituals here. The "peeper" refers to tree frogs of the northeastern United States. They are often called spring peepers since their shrill calls announce the spring. Shad are Atlantic Coast saltwater fish, which, like the salmon, swim up the rivers to lay eggs. The shad-run refers to this annual springtime journey to spawn.

Lines 11–12

Traditionally, birds are portrayed as free creatures in song, poetry, and cliché. However, the image in this stanza pictures them trapped by their need for food. Again, Wilbur selects a term of human bondage, one that resonates with a powerful emotional connotation in the United States. The word "slaves" also foreshadows the third section of the poem, which lists freedom's failures.

Lines 13–14

The final couplet proclaims that freedom is not one of nature's guarantees. Instead, it has risen out of humankind's idealism and desire.

Lines 15–18

Part II, titled "Our "Risen States," is written in quatrains, stanzas of four lines each, where the first and fourth and the second and third lines rhyme. The first stanza introduces one of the political theories underlying the colonists' rebellion against England: the right of the governed to have a voice in the government. The speaker describes this as "an English thought." While the rights and duties of the individual were often debated in Greek philosophy and the Romans developed a political system with voting powers for free men, the idea of modern governmental rights is often traced to King John's signing of the Magna Carta in 1215. He was forced to guarantee specific liberties, including several which listed that the governed had to consent to be taxed

and to do military service. These rights applied only to the nobility at first; later they were extended to the majority of men. In 1689 England adopted a Bill of Rights, which served as a model for the rights built into colonial governments. When George III violated these, the revolutionary war began.

Lines 19–22

The army established by the Second Continental Congress to battle the British troops was known as the Continental army. One of its first great victories was at Saratoga. This demonstrated to the world that the revolution could succeed, and convinced the French government to openly supply aid to Washington's army. Valley Forge is another symbolic war site. It was the location of Washington's camp, several miles outside of Philadelphia. Because of the brutal conditions during the winter of 1777–1778, thousands died. It became a symbol of the perseverance and heroism of the troops.

Lines 23–26

The Battle of Yorktown ended the British hopes of retaining the colonies. This stanza pays tribute to the contributions of the French troops and leaders to that victory.

Lines 27–30

This stanza, containing the title for the second part, firmly connects the spirit of liberty in the two countries by noting that the French people, "heartened" by the defeat of the mighty British army, rose up and overthrew the government of Louis XVII in 1789. The words "prison doors" refer to the storming of the Bastille, a prison in Paris that frequently held political prisoners, on July 14, 1789. Today, July 14 is a national holiday throughout France, that nation's independence day.

Lines 31–34

The final stanza again provides a conclusion to the section as the speaker declares that the two countries present a united front in proclaiming to the world their love of liberty. To emphasize the unity, the word is repeated in French: "liberté." This spirit inspired Bartholdi to create the Statue of Liberty as a permanent monument to the friendship between the two nations.

Lines 35–38

Part III, the longest section in the poem, is the most complex, both in style and subject matter. Wilbur uses blank verse, which has meter but no established rhyme scheme at the end of the line. It is divided into three sections: a commemoration of the soldiers who died fighting for freedom, a mournful apology for the nation's denial of freedom to some, and a pledge for the future. Each of the three begins with a stressed verb in the command form highlighting the dominant emotion.

Line 35 requests that the reader or listener mourn for the dead soldiers. The following three lines envision possible circumstances of death during battle. Note that while the subject is clearly the dead of the American Revolution, the descriptions vividly evoke pictures of World War I with the horrors of trench warfare, and the Normandy beachheads and Pacific naval battles of World War II.

Lines 39–40

These lines ponder the last memories of the dead. The use of repetition, rhyme, and alliteration helps to reinforce the mournful tone. While line 39 asks its question simply and directly, line 40 creates additional poignancy with its echo of the previous phrase. "Think of before" is rhymed with "the blink of time before," hinting at the fragility of life; the repetition of "before they forgot us" tells of the permanence of death.

Lines 41–45

Wilbur makes very effective use of the list here, speculating on possible memories of the dying men. The final two words in line 45 note, however, that this is all only speculation. The quiet drama is reinforced by Wilbur's verse technique. The lines are very similar in their structure, each beginning with "the" so that the emphasis on the line falls on the second word These words— "drone," "bend," "sound"—repeat the *n* and *d*, while "mouth" from line 45 is matched with "sound" in an example of assonance.

Lines 46–48

The speaker points out that what these men had in common is the fact that they died in the pursuit of freedom. They have many different backgrounds, occupations, dreams. Since they died asserting that human beings have the right to choose the circumstances of their own lives, no speaker should assume the right to assign final thoughts to their last moments.

Lines 49–50

What is ultimately important is that both their lives and deaths created a future for the United States and its citizens.

Lines 51–52

The second segment of Part III opens with the verb "grieve." The speaker then accuses the country of making the deaths of these men worthless by failing to honor the freedoms for which they sacrificed everything.

Lines 53–57

Wilbur again uses a list, this time cataloguing a series of injustices: to native Americans, to slaves, to immigrants, to workers, to women. Following this sad roster, the speaker poses the question, "What can we salvage?"

Lines 58–59

These two lines provide a partial answer. The nation must admit its sins, not hide them. The speaker emphasizes the honor and potential for healing that becomes possible when the truth is told.

Lines 60–63

These lines open the third section of Part III, where "praise" is the dominant verb. The speaker continues his answer to the question in line 57 as he notes that considerable change has occurred in the United States. The laws that oppressed or neglected the rights of some in the past have been acknowledged and at least in part changed. Freedom has been extended so the society more closely reflects the ideal.

Lines 64–69

The building of the statue is used as a metaphor to describe the merging of immigrants from many lands into one nation. The details of the construction—brought here in many pieces, welded together—also refer to the people of the land. The iron core further develops the metaphor, emphasizing a solid underpinning of values, while the torch emphasizes the nation's role as a beacon of hope and freedom.

Lines 70–73

These lines specifically refer to Martin Luther King Jr. and the civil rights movement. The reference to the nation's "most oppressed" includes both the inhumanity of slavery and the subsequent denial of full citizenship to African Americans in the many years that followed slavery's eradication. Wilbur, speaking of the longing of both present and past generations for freedom and tolerance, incorporates King's voice into the poem. Line 73 concludes with the famous line from King's "I Have a Dream" speech: "free at last."

Lines 74–77

Unlike the rest of Part III, these lines are rhymed; they are also set apart. The first two continue Reverend King's speech; the final two again celebrate the union of France and the United States. This time, however, all citizens wear the "common crown."

Lines 78–93

With its emphasis on dance, this section celebrates the different types of folksong and popular music in the United States. It is composed in four quatrains. As in many folksongs, the second and fourth lines rhyme. The final line in the first three stanzas provides a type of refrain, each six syllables long, beginning with "whatever." This is characteristic of folksong and therefore rhythmically apt for this tribute to folk music.

Wilbur lists dances representing different cultures and nationalities in these stanzas. He concludes his roster with an American dance, named for a revolutionary war naval hero. The dance symbolizes the nation's unity since it is a circle dance where all participants join hands.

Line 78 uses the words "our lady" to describe the Statue of Liberty, providing a religious connotation to the celebrations.

Lines 94–101

Part V is divided into two sections. The first uses the same rhyme scheme as Part II, but the length of the lines and the meter varies. It begins by connecting the present with the past. The bay and tides still exist, but are now surrounded by buildings and graced by the statue. Once again, "our lady" is used to convey the redemptive quality of the statue who promises freedom to the immigrants who pass under her protection.

Lines 102–109

In the first section of the poem, the speaker emphasized that the river and birds were "slaves" to the laws of nature. Now his perception has been altered so that they seem "ransomed." Even nature has become a part of the celebration of freedom. Wilbur uses personification to illustrate this as the birds weave a crown for Lady Liberty. In a simile, the waves are compared to the hearts of immigrants who have come seeking her blessing. The continual use of "our lady" stresses that these immigrants have found a type of salvation.

Lines 110–114

The last five lines shift the poem's mood from celebration to reflection. Lines 110 and 111 warn that there are still injustices that must be corrected. The title of the section, which is taken from line 112, presents a metaphor for the United States and its citizens. It is more than a country of immigrants who have reached a final destination after a journey across land or seas. Collectively, the country is embarked on a journey through time, still seeking a land where everyone will be truly free. The final two lines hold out the promise that this dream is attainable; the journey can have a wondrous conclusion, but only if the country remains true to its dreams.

Themes

Freedom

One of Wilbur's main themes, named specifically in the poem's title, is the idea of the United States as a home for freedom. However, as an abstract concept, freedom is open to a multiplicity of interpretations. According to the *American Heritage Dictionary,* it is a general term meaning an absence of restraint. The dictionary goes on to say that it is frequently equated with liberty, a word that refers to those rights defined and guaranteed by law. In addition, freedom is associated with political independence, with freedom from oppression, with the guarantee of civil rights. During the course of the poem, Wilbur includes most of these aspects in the poem's overall representation of freedom.

In the final couplet of the first section, the speaker directs the reader to speculate about the origin and meaning of this word. Interestingly, in this section Wilbur creates a partial definition of freedom by developing a vivid portrayal of its absence. He describes nature, both animate and inanimate, as ruled by a firm set of immutable laws. Only a cataclysmic event, such as an earthquake, can alter the course of a river. Even then, the river will simply follow a new set of laws. The shad always return to the same river to spawn each year. The laws of nature are far less variable than the laws of man.

Wilbur begins the second section of the poem with an initial definition of freedom, equating it with liberty. The speaker describes freedom as a thought, one that the colonists inherited from England. When the barons rebelled in 1215, demanding that King John grant them certain freedoms and forcing him to sign the Magna Carta at Runnymede, the seed of English freedom was created. That seed was later nurtured when England adopted a Bill of Rights for its citizens. One of these basic rights demanded that a just government can only rule with the consent of the governed. When this guarantee was denied to the colonists, George Washington and the Continental army challenged the might of the British Empire.

The third section of the poem expands the definition of freedom by illuminating its role in the lives of individuals throughout the history of the United States. Wilbur personalizes the soldiers' dreams in his speculations about their final thoughts. The variety of these dreams symbolizes freedom: the right to choose, the right to be different, the right to challenge the forces of nature. Human lives need not be determined by external forces, whether it be the laws of nature or the restrictions of an unjust government. An individual may fight and die for freedom. Unlike the shad who are compelled to return to the same spot, humans can cross the ocean to seek a new life "On Freedom's Ground." Wilbur concludes this section with a line from another dreamer who was seeking the meaning of American freedom. The closing line from Martin Luther King Jr.'s powerful "I Have a Dream" speech adds the voices of those who had long been denied freedom towards the praise of liberty. The final two sections stress the role of the immigrant in this country, those who arrived looking for a new and better life, one centered around freedom.

The Betrayal of Freedom

One of the most powerful themes of the poem is expressed in Part III where Wilbur encourages the reader to examine freedom by witnessing examples of its betrayal, not by individuals, but by governments and their representatives. For many years, both in England and the United States, the contract between the authorities who governed the land and the individuals who inhabited that land was not extended to everyone. The speaker lists those excluded groups, reminding the reader of the nation's sins, sins that both betray liberty and mock those who fought for it. While this section is brief, the details are clear. The tribes were robbed of their land and the treaties made with them repeatedly broken. Women were denied the vote until 1920. Wilbur describes the sale of slaves as "the image of God on the auction block," a phrase that draws attention to both the immorality of slavery and the irony of a country presumably founded by those who sought freedom collaborating in the sale of human beings.

Topics for Further Study

- Find out who else, in addition to Richard Wilbur, has been Poet Laureate of the United States. Write a report on one of these other poets.

- The Internet has many resources on the people who have traveled through Ellis Island. Choose one particular group of immigrants and report on its immigration patterns.

- Select a monument or geographical feature that you feel symbolizes the United States. Explain your reasons in a poem, a song, or an essay.

- Wilbur quotes the phrase "free at last" from a speech that Martin Luther King Jr. gave during the 1963 March on Washington. There has been a long tradition of protest marches to the nation's capital. Investigate this practice.

The Redemptive Quality of Liberty

Part IV, "Come Dance," opens with the line, "Now in our lady's honor." While the lady under discussion is, of course, the Statue of Liberty, Wilbur uses a phrase that holds a religious connotation for many readers, since several Christian denominations refer to Jesus' mother, Mary, as "our lady." The same phrase reappears in the final section of the poem. Lines 106 and 107 describe the seagulls "weaving . . . wreaths . . . about our lady's brow." This image reinforces the religious connotation since traditional religious pictures frequently show Mary wearing such a garland. Thus, in the final sections of the poem, the secular statue assumes a spiritual aspect. Liberty becomes a blessed commodity, and the statue repesents a type of salvation for those who seek her protection.

Style

A major factor that influenced Wilbur's form and structure in "On Freedom's Ground" is the fact that it is the libretto for a cantata. Like a symphony, a cantata is divided into sections, each of which has a different mood and a different tempo or rhythm. Schuman, the composer, and Wilbur, the lyricist, collaborated fully on the joint endeavor from its inception. Thus, since the music of the first part is dramatic and stately, Wilbur chose the sonnet, an elegant poetic form with a regular rhythm, to match the composer's tone. The theme, too, of nature following its inexorable pattern over the years is deliberate and measured like the music. The style and subject of the second section is again fitted to the music, a march. The meter in the section is iambic, having a strong beat where an unstressed syllable is followed by a stressed one. This meter seems to imitate the beat of a drummer. Each first and third line contains six syllables, while the second and fourth contain eight. In the third, musically slower segment, Wilbur adapts the four-stress pattern of the Anglo-Saxon dirge. Blank verse is often thought to add a dignified tone to a work, a tone that fits this somber section. Schuman's music in Part IV utilizes themes from traditional dances in America, and Wilbur's words follow suit. The last section provides a dramatic conclusion in words and music.

Since the earliest stages of his career, Wilbur has had a reputation as a writer of carefully structured and intricately rhymed poetry. Many examples are present in "On Freedom's Ground." Wilbur uses alliteration to build his rhythm throughout the work, from "bay" and "back" in the first two lines to "bound," "beckons," "where," "we," "wind," and "with" in the last two lines. Several lines employ a variety of types of internal rhyme. Notice how most of the words in line 49 are, in some way, connected. "Say" and "they" rhyme. "That" and the first syllable in "mattered" reinforce each other. "Alive" and "after," "that" and "they" use alliteration. In addition, Wilbur uses elaborate imagery to build complex comparisons, such as the one between the building of the Statue of Liberty and the building of the country.

Historical Context

The Statue of Liberty is an amazing tribute designed to celebrate the friendship between two nations, France and the United States. It commemorates the influence that each country had on the other's search for basic freedoms. Without the financial, military, and naval support of the French nation, the thirteen British colonies would have had

little chance of winning their independence from England. Ironically for the French monarchy, the successful rebellion in the United States paved the way for the French Revolution.

This relationship between the two countries had many of its roots in the troubled association between France and England. This began as early as 1066 when William, the Duke of Normandy, which is a province in the north of France today, invaded England. The next major source of conflict came during the twelfth century, when England's Henry II, thanks to his marriage to Eleanor of Aquitaine, assumed control of a large section of land in western France, which ran from the northern coast to the Pyrenees. In fact, he actually controlled more of present-day French territory than the French king. The subsequent series of battles over this disputed territory became known as the Hundred Years War. Although the English dominated the struggles at first, eventually the French forces rallied under the leadership of Joan of Arc and drove the English from French soil, with the exception of a small area around Calais.

The growth of powerful nation states in Europe during the Renaissance also helped to inflame national hostilities as the two states challenged each other. Throughout English history, challengers to the throne frequently launched their rebellions from French soil, often receiving both money and assistance from the French king.

As exploration and colonization developed in North America, the two nations entered a new area of conflict. Britain had established colonies along the coastal areas of the present-day United States, while French explorers and voyageurs had ventured across the territory that is now eastern Canada, eventually traveling through the Great Lakes down the Mississippi. Once again, France and England became involved in a conflict over territory in the first war with battlefields set on two widely separate continents. Eventually France was defeated on both fronts. As a result of the Treaty of Paris in 1763, they were forced to turn over all of their lands in Canada and east of the Mississippi to Britain.

The French were understandably bitter about their defeats. This helped them to sympathize with the colonists' challenge to the authority of George III. They contributed troops and financial support to the fledgling country. The two soldiers whom Wilbur mentions, the Marquis de Lafayette and Count Jean Baptiste Rochambeau, were instrumental in the defeat of the British at Yorktown. Rochambeau led a troop of six thousand soldiers

Compare & Contrast

- **1986:** The United States approves the first tests of genetically altered food.

  Today: Many genetically altered foods are currently available in supermarkets throughout the United States; consumer advocates are upset, however, because no labeling is required to inform consumers if foods have been altered.

- **1986:** Chinese students begin demonstrating for democratic freedoms.

1989: In massive demonstrations in China's Tiananmen Square, students bring in a thirty-three-foot styrofoam replica of the Statue of Liberty, which is later crushed by government tanks.

Today: In the United States Senate and House of Representatives, debate over Chinese-American trade relations introduces the Chinese government's attacks on democracy.

sent by King Louis XVII to help Washington. After the surrender of General Cornwallis and his troops, the revolution was effectively won. A few years later, the French overthrew their monarchy.

Because of this mutual support, many Frenchmen felt a proud kinship with the United States. The inspiration for the Statue of Liberty grew out of this emotion. At a dinner party in France in 1865, Edouard Lefebvre de Laboulaye, a leader of the French Republican forces, called France and the United States "two sisters," wishing that some sort of monument could be devised to commemorate their friendship permanently. This idea fascinated Frédéric-Auguste Bartholdi, a young sculptor in the group, who dreamed of creating such a tribute. Although Bartholdi became involved with other projects and served as an officer in the Franco-Prussian War, neither he nor Laboulaye forgot this idea. After six years the two dreamers decided that Bartholdi should sail to America to see if there would be any interest in such a project. As soon as he arrived in New York harbor, Bartholdi was convinced that Bedloe's Island would be the ideal location. He met with politicians as well as private citizens, showing them sketches and a miniature model of his statue. Although Bartholdi's plans received much enthusiastic comment, there were no promises of financial support from any source. In order to raise money, a Franco-American Union was formed in 1874, and an agreement was reached wherein the United States would erect the pedestal, while France would build the statue itself. Fund-

raising in France was successful, and by the spring of 1885, the statue was ready for transportation to the United States. Unfortunately, little had been done in the United States. Politicians were reluctant to commit government funds to the project. Finally, Joseph Pulitzer, a newspaper editor, began a campaign to raise money from the working individual. His campaign was successful, and on October 28, 1886, the statue was unveiled.

The day was declared a holiday in New York City. French flags lined the streets. A parade of twenty thousand marched in celebration of liberty. When it passed down Wall Street, where the workers had not been allowed to take the day off, office boys leaned out the windows, spiraling down the ticker tape from the stock machines in order to participate in the occasion—and the famous New York City ticker-tape parade was born. Ships of all kinds crowded New York harbor. At a prearranged signal, Bartholdi, who was alone in the statue's head, dropped the French tri-color veil that covered the statue.

In the years that followed, the statue was hailed as a symbol of America and of freedom. In 1903, Emma Lazarus' poem "The New Colossus," which welcomed immigrants to this country, was attached to the base. During World War I, Lady Liberty and her torch were used in fund-raising efforts to sell war bonds. Years later, as her hundredth anniversary approached, it became obvious that some repairs were needed. In 1981 another international alliance, the French-American Committee for the

Restoration of the Statue of Liberty, was formed. Lee Iacocca chaired a committee specifically formed to raise funds for the statue's restoration in preparation for its centennial. In 1986 President Ronald Reagan rededicated the restored statue as 1.5 billion people around the world watched.

Critical Overview

"On Freedom's Ground," like much of Wilbur's work, has received mixed reviews fom the critical establishment. Throughout his career, he has received widespread praise for his technical skill and wordplay. In a review of Wilbur's second book of poetry, however, Randall Jarrell accused him of complacency, of being a bit too satisfied with his elegance, poetic wit, and charm. That criticism has regularly been applied to Wilbur's work since. In his review of *New and Collected Poems,* William Logan sums up that critical perspective: "The complaints against his work are a litany of old virtue: its sweetness, and its polish, and its cordiality, and its complacence—you'd think he were a peaceable kingdom all to himself, a lamb that has devoured all the lions in sight."

Logan goes on to add that many of Wilbur's poems give ammunition to these critics. He feels that in many ways "On Freedom's Ground" is such a poem. Logan particularly finds fault with Part IV, saying that it is an example of the "trivialization" of Wilbur's poetic instincts. Another poet and reviewer, Sam Hazo, echoes Logan's criticism. He, too, feels that Part IV is rather obvious, describing it as verse rather than poetry.

Other critics, however, believe that Wilbur has succeeded admirably with difficult material. Anthony Hecht, in "Master of Metaphor," finds that Wilbur has been very skillful in allowing both readers and listeners to follow his argument while avoiding being too sentimental or unquestioningly patriotic. Rodney Edgecombe, in one of the most detailed analyses of the poem, praises Wilbur's understanding of the special characteristics necessary for poetry to be composed for musical accompaniment. In a section-by-section critique, he points out Wilbur's homage to other poets. On the whole, Edgecombe finds the poem "remarkable for its justice and humanity," with the failure to acknowledge the aboriginal inhabitants of the country as its only false note.

Bruce Michelson also provides a detailed, positive analysis. He notes the echoes of Robert Frost's style and language in the first part of the poem. Stressing the simple, musical quality of Part II, he compares it to a "revised Concord Hymn," noting, however, that the "rhetorical engines intermittently race and drop to an idle." Like many critics, he most admires the third section, where the elegiac overtones contain some of Wilbur's best use of the four-stress alliterative lines from Old English poetry. He does, however, criticize both the poem's conclusion and its ultimate predictability of subject.

Criticism

Mary Mahony

Mahony is an English instructor at Wayne County Community College in Detroit, Michigan. In the following essay, she discusses the effect that its role as a public performance had on the critical reception of "On Freedom's Ground."

Richard Wilbur has often been accused of complacency. In his review of Wilbur's second book, *Ceremony and Other Poems,* the poet Randall Jarrell complained, "I don't blame his readers if they say to him in encouragingly impatient voices: 'Come on, *take a chance!*'" However, Wilbur has taken chances throughout his career by remaining faithful to his own poetic vision. His elegantly rhymed and carefully metrical poems have been both highly regarded and slantingly dismissed as throwbacks to the past. His optimistic stance has sometimes been deemed inappropriate for a world rife with confusion. Yet Wilbur has never pandered to popular or professorial criticism. Such decisions seem the opposite of complacency. "On Freedom's Ground" provides an example of Wilbur's poetic daring.

When Wilbur agreed to accept the task of composing a libretto for the rededication of the Statue of Liberty, he was aware of the snares that lay in wait. First of all, the subject matter was, to a certain extent, predetermined. There was also the danger of falling into triteness or cliché. In his article "Master of Metaphor," Anthony Hecht sums up these hazards: "The task was rife with potential pitfalls. There were the twin perils of jingoism and chauvinistic sentimentality on the one hand, and the symmetrical or compensatory danger of leaning over backward to avoid anything that looked suspiciously like affirmation."

Another element that was bound to figure in the poem's reception was its unique origin as part of a national celebration to honor the Statue of Liberty. Some of the negative response to the poem has, in part, evolved out of that origin. In the last half of the twentieth century, patriotism and poetry have been uneasy allies, and many critics have greeted such alliances with mistrust. In fact, the poetry of protest has been far more fashionable than poetry in praise of country. In the aftermath of the civil rights struggle, Vietnam, Watergate, and the self-absorbed materialism of the 1980s, it has been easier to attack than affirm a national identity.

In addition, there was the factor that however moving and restrained "On Freedom's Ground" proved, it was at least initially attached to a series of television spectaculars, many of which seemed to pander to some of the least sophisticated elements of the national psyche. In *Wilbur's Poetry: Music in a Scattering Time,* Bruce Michelson notes that the cantata was "part of the big show in New York, the multimillion-dollar Reagan–Iacocca–Sinatra main event, which would brim with Las Vegas glitz and corporate vulgarity." Many of the events surrounding the occasion celebrated overwhelming ostentation. On Liberty weekend, television networks broadcast the national extravaganza. There were thousands of musicians and tap dancers. Quantities of costumed ethnic dancers representing the immigrants Wilbur graciously portrayed spiraled their way along in elaborate celebration. In one of the more unique features of the event, over a hundred Elvises serenaded freedom and the cameras in all their rhinestone-studded glory.

While such elements are tangential to the text and theme of the poem, they nonetheless have exerted some influence on its critical reaction. And since the poem was composed for a public performance honoring a national icon, it has received a level of scrutiny not always attached to a single poem in a collection. The fact that Wilbur chose to present the work as the complete libretto in *New and Collected Poems* rather than as a series of separate poems, which he had considered, once again demonstrates his willingness to take chances.

Finally, the fact that the poem's speaker adopts a role as the voice of the people of the United States has also raised certain critical eyebrows. Some critics have used the poem as a forum to question the wisdom of a poet, or any individual, acting as a voice of the nation. William Logan maintains that "On Freedom's Ground" "reminds us how poets suffer when they speak not for themselves but for

> *In the last half of the twentieth century, patriotism and poetry have been uneasy allies, and many critics have greeted such alliances with mistrust. In fact, the poetry of protest has been far more fashionable than poetry in praise of country."*

a country. Taste is the enemy of patriotic sentiment—we would not have to appoint a poet laureate otherwise." In a humorous review of Wilbur's *New and Collected Poems,* Hugh Kenner questions the wisdom of even having a poet laureate, a role he calls "Poet Laureatcy," a pun perhaps on poet lunacy. (Although Wilbur was not laureate when he composed "On Freedom's Ground," he was appointed to the role one year later.) Kenner describes the thankless role as a "grim task," noting that the English Poet Laureate Ted Hughes had been driven to compose fifteen stanzas celebrating the marriage of Prince Andrew to Sarah Ferguson. Although he finds "On Freedom's Ground" less unsettling than Hughes's wedding commemorative, Kenner is wryly skeptical of the entire concept; his initial criticism is not of Wilbur's writing, but of the task he has accepted. "Wilbur confronting august Ms. Liberty was as little himself as Hughes rapt by broad-beamed Fergie." His review ends by stating that Wilbur will not disgrace the role (although Kenner implies that the role is enough of a disgrace in itself), and condescendingly adding that Wilbur is "just the man to be taking decorous notice" of whoever occupies the White House. While criticisms like these specifically center around Wilbur's role as a public poet, they reiterate the long established criticism that has labeled him too hopeful, too agreeable, too quick to reject the idea that despair is the natural voice of the poet.

Because this type of critical reaction may be expected, few poets have taken part in national public events since Robert Frost read "The Gift Outright" at the inauguration of John Fitzgerald

What Do I Read Next?

- Wilbur's 1988 Pulitzer Prize-winning volume, *New and Collected Poems,* gathers together some of the best poems from each of his books.

- Simone Davis's "Checking in the Mirror: Liberty Weekend's Patriotic Spectacle," from the Summer 1996 *Journal of American Culture,* provides a revealing and entertaining description of the extravaganza surrounding the rededication of the Statue of Liberty.

- Robert Frost's "The Gift Outright," which is often compared to "On Freedom's Ground," may be found in his 1962 collection, *In the Clearing.*

- The Fall 1992–Winter 1993 issue of the journal *Renascence* is devoted to the poetry of Richard Wilbur.

- Wilbur's prizewinning translations of *The Misanthrope, Tartuffe, The School for Wives,* and *The Learned Ladies,* published in 1982 under the title *Moliere: Four Comedies,* have been credited with introducing new readers and audiences to the wit and irony of French comedy.

- *Days of the French Revolution* (1999) by Christopher Hibbert provides an interesting narrative account of the French people's quest for liberty.

- The Ellis Island–Statue of Liberty Foundation has published a guidebook, *Ellis Island and the Peopling of America,* which introduces the immigrant experience through personal histories, interviews, census reports, maps, and photographs.

Kennedy. Wilbur was aware of the difficulties that he faced. However, he was willing to undertake the challenge. Wilbur himself is content with his view of the world. He once described himself as a "poet-citizen rather than an alienated artist." In comparing American and Soviet poetry, he pointed out that a kind of political awareness permeates the Soviet experience, and thus is integrated into its art. He adds that American poetry has for the most part focused on "private experience" such as love, nature, sex, religion. Wilbur distinguishes between poetry with a nationalistic view and poetry whose sole purpose is propaganda. "Poetry does best by politics when it acknowledges complexity, tells the whole truth, and authenticates the political by treating it not in isolation but in conjunction with all else that the poet knows of life." These goals are clear in "On Freedom's Ground."

The view of freedom that Wilbur presents is not simplistic. As the poem develops, it becomes clear that liberty is defined by both individuals and governments. The variety of subject and tone in each of the five sections presents this fact in all its complexity. Each section reveals a slightly different aspect. One is a government that establishes a Constitution and Bill of Rights to guarantee freedom to its citizens. A second is the role of the soldier fighting for a fledging nation. Another perspective comes from the immigrant who has journeyed across distances in pursuit of this freedom. Still another voice insists that the faults of the country be revealed so that they can be changed. A final view pulls all these disparate elements together, on a journey to a future where the full potential of freedom may be found. Wilbur combines the reality of the nation's flaws with the expression of hope for a brighter future.

Wilbur's presentation of history for this public occasion, indeed, allows the reader or listener to experience many of the complexities of American history and the American landscape. The beauty of his imagery in the first and fifth sections allows the reader to reevaluate the richness of the land, with its changes over the centuries. The introduction of the role that France has played in United States history serves as a reminder that the French people were inspired to emulate the ideals on which the nation was established. Part III of the poem, in particular, creates a haunting view of the cost and failure of freedom. However, in spite of these virtues, the poem is, at times, uneven, constrained by the circumstances of its creation. It is hard not to agree with Bruce Michelson's evaluation. After noting the positive qualities of the poem, he concluded that "as an official, commemorative work on the Lincoln Center scale, this cantata must telegraph its gestures, must pretty much do what one expects it to do, and in the prescribed order. We open with an Aaron Copeland wilderness, fight the Revolution, mourn the dead and mourn our forgetting, discover or contrive excuses to dance and be happy, celebrate ethnic diversity, and ultimately declare that the American adventure is still beginning—a computer programmed to generate Fourth of July speeches might work in the same pathways." However, given the constraints under which Wilbur labored, it is a noble effort.

Source: Mary Mahony, Critical Essay on "On Freedom's Ground," in *Poetry for Students,* The Gale Group, 2001.

Carl Mowery

Mowery has written many analytical essays for the Gale Group. In the following essay, he examines the celebratory aspects of Wilbur's poem "On Freedom's Ground."

Poetry serves several functions depending on the intent of the author. Sometimes poems are meant to inform, sometimes amuse, sometimes puzzle the reader. Sometimes poems are meant to be statements of national pride or to galvanize support for a political figure or a war, or sometimes they address a domestic crisis. "On Freedom's Ground" by Richard Wilbur, which is included in his collection of works, *New and Collected Poems* (1988), is a poem that celebrates the political history of the United States in conjunction with the one-hundredth anniversary of the Statue of Liberty. What makes this poem even more special is the collaboration with the American composer William Schuman, who set these lines to music as a five-part cantata for baritone soloist, chorus, and orchestra.

Rodney Edgecombe remarks that not all poets who write lyrics to be set to music "have a proper grasp of music and the demands it places on the word." The eighteenth-century English poet and writer William Shenstone once remarked that "a certain flimsiness of poetry" is necessary to allow the music to carry some of the meaning of the piece. Wilbur approached his task paying careful attention to the needs of the composer's melodies, but he has not sacrificed the quality of his poetry. His results are a beautiful set of poems that are equally beautiful as texts for Schuman's cantata.

This work consists of five shorter poems, varying in form and style, each of which celebrates a different facet of the history of life in the United States. Part I, in a sonnet form, begins before there were any European settlers in North America; Part II, using tight rhythmic quatrains of alternately three and four feet per line, concerns the revolutionary war; Part III, the most rhapsodic section, discusses personal sacrifices made over the centuries; Part IV, in dance-like quatrains where the first and third lines use the feminine ending, is a celebration of folk ways; and Part V, employing

> *His recognition of the merits of the United States and of its flaws keeps this work in tune with the kind of country it is: one that continually strives to be better than it has been so all its people may 'wear the common crown of liberté.'*

rhapsodic quatrains, returns to the opening notion that there is an America to be settled and the people to do it will be immigrants.

Each of these five parts may stand alone as an individual poem, with its own set of images and symbols. The first, since it concentrates on the ancient history of the country, uses images of raw nature in action. The accumulation of these images shows symbolically the manner in which the new nation will be formed. It was out of an unruly and sometimes savage past that the United States was established. In this part Wilbur hints at some of the unsavory aspects in U.S. history. The sea birds are "slaves" of their own hunger, and the waves are "vassals" and "subjects" of the wind and tide. These hint at the history of servitude in early colonial days and the slaves of plantation owners in the early days of the nation. The image of the river that "had no choice" but to run its course is symbolic of the progress toward freedom for the people that also "had no choice." In its timeless journey through the landscape, the river carved out "this basin" just as the United States in time will carve out its role in nurturing freedom for all people (a notion that is more fully presented in Part II).

These forces were the result of choiceless urges and motivations. There were the natural cycles of the seasons with their associated life and death struggles. The cycles were buoyed by the hopefulness of "every springtime" that "tuned the peeper's voice," the new song of a returning bird announcing the potential of a new year, symbolic representations of the new nation coming to terms with its role in the world of the nineteenth century.

The first part closes with a rhetorical question that moves it into Part II: "Where was the thought of freedom then?" Wilbur answers that it originated "within the minds of men" who were coming ashore from Europe.

There is an important, and unfortunate, omission in this pre-history of North America: the Native Americans who lived here for thousands of years before the Europeans arrived. Wilbur seems to be saying that these peoples had no concept of freedom nor an ability to name islands. Edgecombe notes that Wilbur's claim that "the thought of liberty" came ashore with the Europeans is a "false note" in an otherwise remarkable poem. The Native American tribes only get a brief mention in Part III, as "the tribes [were] pushed west and the treaties broken." These events were sanctioned by the policy of Manifest Destiny, which stated that the European-Americans had the right to displace the so-called savages from their ancestral lands.

"Our Risen States," the title of the second poem in this cantata, is a celebration of the political conflicts that controlled the history of the last half of the eighteenth century, especially the American Revolution. This second section says that everything derived from "an English thought," which is the Magna Carta, the first document to outline personal freedom for all people. Wilbur notes that the colonists took that English thought and used it against them as the political basis for the American Revolution. These new awakenings in North America were then adopted by the French in their revolution several years later.

In this poem, Wilbur uses several well-known names and places to hint at the American revolutionary war. This process of synecdoche, a literary technique where a part represents the whole, is a clever usage because it allows the poet to cover a great deal of historical ground, sometimes in a single word. For example, the words "Valley Forge" capture the images of harsh weather conditions, an almost hopeless military situation, the resolute nature of the Colonial army and the indefatigable and hardy soldiers.

The last word of Part II, the French word *liberté,* suggests the participation of the French in the struggle against the British. It symbolically ties the names of the French generals together with the important American names. It also reassociates the American Revolution with the beginnings of the French Revolution.

The third poem in this cantata, "Like a Great Statue," is the most somber of them all. In this three-sectioned poem Wilbur celebrates and reflects on the nature of sacrifices made in the name of the country. What is better still, "Say that they mattered, alive and after." He wonders in a litany of disparate images what these men might have thought important in their final moments of life.

The second section opens with confessions of "the ways in which we betrayed them," who lay in their graves. In the name of Country, those of European stock mistreated the Native Americans, who were victims rather than participants in shaping the emerging society, the slave "on the auction block," who was denied freedom, and "liberty's daughters," who were disenfranchised because of sex. At the end of the second section of Part III Wilbur ruminates on the notion that such Americans can "be proud at least that we know we were wrong." At first this may seem like an excuse for past excesses. But it goes on to say, in the next section, that such Americans have the power to change the bad behavior into more appropriate behavior. Wilbur says Americans have the opportunity to become "what we said we were going to be" and to allow everyone to "live a life that could be chosen." The poet says that it is important that all people have the opportunity to speak freely and to choose whatever life they want.

At the close of this part, Wilbur solidifies the ever-present urges of all people to rise up from oppression when he reminds the reader that it is the "invincible hope to be free at last" that drives each person towards freedom. It ends with a reference to the well-known "I Have a Dream" speech of Martin Luther King Jr.

The most important image in this part of the cantata is the construction of the statue itself. This is a symbolic representation of the construction of the country, as each new plate of "hammered copper" is put into place. Similarly, the fabric of the United States is molded by the collective hammering of new immigrants bringing new ideas. The anchor rods and the "core of iron" represent the foundations of the government, its constitution and laws. The many peoples who make up the country "more and more have been shaped into one" through the tempering processes of wars, forming and reforming laws, and by joining together as in the dances of Part IV.

Part IV, "Come Dance," is the liveliest part of the cantata. It is a delightful four-stanza poem that uses a dance-like rhythmic pattern and an *abcb* rhyme scheme. Even in a non-musical reading, it lilts with the rhythms of the dances mentioned within. Each of these dances represents a different ethnic group and symbolizes the diversity of the people of the United States, the polka from Germany, the tarantella from Italy, the Highland fling from Scotland, the Lindy hop from the United States.

The symbolism of the last stanza encourages all to "take the other's hand" and in a harmonious coming together create the nation in the manner of a dance. The image of the circle comes from the last dance, the John Paul Jones, a type of dance that involves concentric circles. All of the folk dances mentioned are those for multiple participants, often eight or more, requiring all members of the dance to work together and to contribute to the dance to make a single event out of many people's efforts. In these dances, the more cooperative each participant becomes, the more freely the dance is performed. Ironically then, out of a highly organized dance comes freedom.

The last part takes the reader (or the listener at a musical performance) into the present (1986), and it asks everyone to celebrate their present condition as "Immigrants Still." Wilbur looks at the river again and sees the birds, still flying "ransomed" and "free," but now over barges and ships.

The cantata ends with a hopeful observation that if Americans as a country hold their course steady, the wind will be with them. Then they will succeed in meeting the promise of their beginnings. From the rough beginnings of the unpopulated continent to the highly mechanized society of the modern world, Wilbur says that Americans can be proud of their progress. They have made errors in the past but with vigilance they are capable of rectifying those errors and living in the future without making similar ones.

The image of the statue girdled by the free-flying gulls combines the two concepts of the natural world and the world of human beings. In this final image not just the gulls are free but one's eyes are free to watch them weave about the statue creating "wreaths of flight." With their special construction of images and patterns freely drawn in the air about the statue, the gulls are no longer slaves to hunger.

Wilbur once said a poem is not a vehicle for communicating a message but it is an object with "its own life" and "individual identity." Wilbur wrote this five-part poem as a celebration of the one-hundredth anniversary of the Statue of Liberty. His celebration is filled with national pride and national images. His recognition of the merits of the United States and of its flaws keeps this work in

tune with the kind of country it is: one that continually strives to be better than it has been so all its people may "wear the common crown of *liberté*." In this recognition, he follows a different poetic philosophy than that outlined above inasmuch as the cantata communicates a very strong and important message.

Source: Carl Mowery, Critical Essay on "On Freedom's Ground," in *Poetry for Students,* The Gale Group, 2001.

Sources

Butts, William, "An Interview with Richard Wilbur," in *Conversations with Richard Wilbur,* edited by William Butts, University Press of Mississippi, 1990.

"A Conversation with Richard Wilbur," in *Image: A Journal of the Arts and Religion,* Winter 1995, pp. 55–72.

Edgecombe, Rodney S., *A Reader's Guide to the Poetry of Richard Wilbur,* University of Alabama Press, 1995.

Frank, Robert, and Stephen Mitchell, "Richard Wilbur: An Interview," in *Conversations with Richard Wilbur,* edited by William Butts, University Press of Mississippi, 1990.

Grey, Paul, "A Testament to Civility," in *Time,* May 9, 1988, p. 84.

Hazo, Samuel, "One Definite Mozart," in *Renascence,* Fall 1992–Winter 1993, pp. 81–96.

Hecht, Anthony, "Master of Metaphor," in *The New Republic,* Vol. 3, No. 826, May 16, 1988, pp. 23–32.

Jarrell, Randall, "A View of Three Poets," in *Richard Wilbur's Creation,* edited by Wendy Salinger, University of Michigan Press, 1983.

Kenner, Hugh, "Whatever Spins Around," in *National Review,* September 2, 1988, pp. 48–49.

Logan, William, "Richard Wilbur's Civil Tongue," in *Parnassus: Poetry in Review,* Vol. 21, No. 1–2, pp. 90–110.

McKnight, Paul, and Gary Houston, "An Interview with Richard Wilbur," in *Conversations with Richard Wilbur,* edited by William Butts, University Press of Mississippi, 1990.

Michelson, Bruce, *Wilbur's Poetry: Music in a Scattering Time,* University of Massachusetts Press, 1991.

Robertson, Nan, "A Musical Collaboration in Homage to America," in *The New York Times,* January 2, 1986, p. C16.

Statue of Liberty—History: The Two Sisters, http://www.americanparknetwork.com/parkinfo/sl/history/liberty.html (2000).

For Further Study

Bixler, Frances, *Richard Wilbur: A Reference Guide,* G. K. Hall & Co., 1991.

This annotated bibliography includes descriptions of articles, reviews, and passages in books, as well as full-length studies. In addition, Bixler provides a valuable summary of the criticism.

Butts, William, ed., *Conversations with Richard Wilbur,* University Press of Mississippi, 1990.

The interviews in this collection, which span the years from 1962 to 1988, give insights into Wilbur's personal and poetic life as he discusses his own work along with the state of poetry in the contemporary world. These interviews reveal Wilbur's wit, charm, and humanity.

Harris, Peter, "Forty Years of Richard Wilbur: The Loving Work of an Equilibrist," in *Virginia Quarterly,* Summer 1990, pp. 412–25.

Harris shows Wilbur's growth as a poet, tracing major themes and analyzing his use of language and traditional poetic forms.

Hill, Donald L., *Richard Wilbur,* Twayne, 1967.

This is a good summary of theme and style in Wilbur's poetry.

Salinger, Wendy, ed., *Richard Wilbur's Creation,* University of Michigan Press, 1983.

This is an excellent collection of essays that presents the critical response to each of Wilbur's collections of poetry.

The Rape of the Lock

Alexander Pope
1714

"The Rape of the Lock," originally published as *The Rape of the Locke: An Heroi-Comical Poem* (1712), is a mock-epic based upon an actual disagreement between two aristocratic English families during the eighteenth century. Lord Petre (the Baron in the poem) surprises the beautiful Arabella Fermor (Belinda) by clipping off a lock of hair. At the suggestion of his friend and with Arabella Fermor's approval, Alexander Pope used imagination, hyperbole, wit, and gentle satire to inflate this trivial social slip-up into an earth-shaking catastrophe of cosmic consequence. The poem is generally described as one of Pope's most brilliant satires.

The poem makes serious demands upon the reader, not only because of its length but also because it requires a background knowledge of epic literature and some understanding of the trappings of upperclass England. "The Rape of the Lock" constantly shifts between mocking silly social conventions of the aristocracy (such as elaborate courtship rituals) and satirizing serious literary conventions of traditional epic literature (such as its lofty style, exhaustive descriptions of warriors readying for battle, and heavy doses of mythology). With many allusions to Homer's *Iliad* and *Odyssey,* Virgil's *Aeneid,* and John Milton's *Paradise Lost,* the speaker compares the loss of Belinda's hair to the great battles of classic epic literature. The speaker describes Belinda applying makeup as if she were a warrior going to battle. While playing a game of cards, the Baron sneaks up behind Belinda and performs the "tragic" snipping of the lock

Alexander Pope

of hair. An army of gnomes and sprites attempts to protect Belinda to no avail. Belinda demands the restoration of her lock and another "battle" ensues. Finally, the lock ascends skyward as a new star to beautify the heavens.

Author Biography

Pope was born on May 21, 1688, in London, England, the son of Alexander Pope, a London linen merchant, and his second wife, Edith Turner. Pope attended two Catholic academies before the family moved from London in 1700 to live in the village of Binfield. A new law, prohibiting Catholics from living within ten miles of the city of London, forced the family to move. The relocation to Binfield enabled Pope to make enduring friendships with other Catholic exiles like himself. Pope's early education was sporadic. He learned to read and write at home and was taught Latin and Greek by priests. By the age of twelve, he was already well versed in Greek, Roman, and English literature, and he diligently emulated the works of his favorite poets. At twelve, Pope contracted Pott's disease, a tuberculosis of the spine, from infected milk. The disease left him with a crooked spine and a severe weakness, which

caused him almost continual headaches for the rest of his life.

Pope's first published work, "Pastorals," a group of lyric poems on rural themes, was published in 1709. Two years later, he published "An Essay on Criticism," a treatise on literary theory written in verse couplets. The impressiveness of this feat caught the attention of English literary society, and with the publication of the first two cantos of *The Rape of the Lock* in 1712 (expanded to five cantos in 1714) Pope was regarded as one of the most prominent poets of the age. He eventually became the first independently wealthy, full-time writer in English history.

Despite such success, Pope suffered throughout his career from recurring attacks against him for his Catholicism, his political sympathies, and his literary criticism, which often raised the anger of the authors he analyzed. Some of these attacks were personal, commenting unfavorably upon his physical appearance. Much of Pope's later satirical writings were aimed at those who had criticized him over the years. Pope's last years were spent revising the body of his writings in preparation for a complete, edited edition of his works. He died on May 30, 1744 of acute asthma and dropsy before the task was completed.

Poem Text

CANTO I

What dire offense from amorous causes springs,
What mighty contests rise from trivial things,
I sing—This verse to Caryll, Muse! is due:
This, even Belinda may vouchsafe to view:
Slight is the subject, but not so the praise,   5
If she inspire, and he approve my lays.
  Say what strange motive, Goddess! could
      compel
A well-bred Lord to assault a gentle belle?
Oh, say what stranger cause, yet unexplored,
Could make a gentle belle reject a lord?   10
In tasks so bold can little men engage,
And in soft bosoms dwells such mighty rage?
  Sol through white curtains shot a timorous ray,
And oped those eyes that must eclipse the day.
Now lap-dogs give themselves the rousing shake,   15
And sleepless lovers just at twelve awake:
Thrice rung the bell, the slipper knocked the
      ground,
And the pressed watch returned a silver sound.
Belinda still her downy pillow pressed,
Her guardian Sylph prolonged the balmy rest: 20
'Twas he had summoned to her silent bed

The morning dream that hovered o'er her head.
A youth more glittering than a birthnight beau
(That even in slumber caused her cheek to glow)
Seemed to her ear his winning lips to lay, 25
And thus in whispers said, or seemed to say:
"Fairest of mortals, thou distinguished care
Of thousand bright inhabitants of air!
If e'er one vision touched thy infant thought,
Of all the nurse and all the priest have taught, 30
Of airy elves by moonlight shadows seen,
The silver token, and the circled green,
Or virgins visited by angel powers,
With golden crowns and wreaths of heavenly
    flowers,
Hear and believe! thy own importance know, 35
Nor bound thy narrow views to things below.
Some secret truths, from learned pride concealed,
To maids alone and children are revealed:
What though no credit doubting wits may give?
The fair and innocent shall still believe. 40
Know, then, unnumbered spirits round thee fly,
The light militia of the lower sky:
These, though unseen, are ever on the wing,
Hang o'er the Box, and hover round the Ring.
Think what an equipage thou hast in air, 45
And view with scorn two pages and a chair.
As now your own, our beings were of old,
And once inclosed in woman's beauteous mold;
Thence, by a soft transition, we repair
From earthly vehicles to these of air. 50
Think not, when woman's transient breath is fled,
That all her vanities at once are dead:
Succeeding vanities she still regards,
And though she plays no more, o'erlooks the cards.
Her joy in gilded chariots, when alive, 55
And love of ombre, after death survive.
For when the Fair in all their pride expire,
To their first elements their souls retire:
The sprites of fiery termagants in flame
Mount up, and take a Salamander's name. 60
Soft yielding minds to water glide away,
And sip, with Nymphs, their elemental tea.
The graver prude sinks downward to a Gnome,
In search of mischief still on earth to roam.
The light coquettes in Sylphs aloft repair, 65
And sport and flutter in the fields of air.
    "Know further yet; whoever fair and chaste
Rejects mankind, is by some Sylph embraced:
For spirits, freed from mortal laws, with ease
Assume what sexes and what shapes they please. 70
What guards the purity of melting maids,
In courtly balls, and midnight masquerades,
Safe from the treacherous friend, the daring spark,
The glance by day, the whisper in the dark,
When kind occasion prompts their warm desires, 75
When music softens, and when dancing fires?
'Tis but their Sylph, the wise Celestials know,
Though Honor is the word with men below.
    "Some nymphs there are, too conscious of their
        face,
For life predestined to the Gnomes' embrace. 80
These swell their prospects and exalt their pride,
When offers are disdained, and love denied:

Then gay ideas crowd the vacant brain,
While peers, and dukes, and all their sweeping
    train,
And garters, stars, and coronets appear, 85
And in soft sounds, 'your Grace' salutes their ear.
'Tis these that early taint the female soul,
Instruct the eyes of young coquettes to roll,
Teach infant cheeks a hidden blush to know,
And little hearts to flutter at a beau. 90
    "Oft, when the world imagine women stray,
The Sylphs through mystic mazes guide their way,
Through all the giddy circle they pursue,
And old impertinence expel by new.
What tender maid but must a victim fall 95
To one man's treat, but for another's ball?
When Florio speaks what virgin could withstand,
If gentle Damon did not squeeze her hand?
With varying vanities, from every part,
They shift the moving toyshop of their heart; 100
Where wigs with wigs, with sword-knots sword-
    knots strive,
Beaux banish beaux, and coaches coaches drive.
This erring mortals levity may call;
Oh, blind to truth! the Sylphs contrive it all.
    "Of these am I, who thy protection claim, 105
A watchful sprite, and Ariel is my name.
Late, as I ranged the crystal wilds of air,
In the clear mirror of thy ruling star
I saw, alas! some dread event impend,
Ere to the main this morning sun descend, 110
But Heaven reveals not what, or how, or where:
Warned by the Sylph, O pious maid, beware!
This to disclose is all thy guardian can:
Beware of all, but most beware of Man!"
    He said; when Shock, who thought she slept too 115
        long,
Leaped up, and waked his mistress with his tongue.
'Twas then, Belinda, if report say true,
Thy eyes first opened on a billet-deux;
Wounds, charms, and ardors were no sooner read,
But all the vision vanished from thy head. 120
    And now, unveiled, the toilet stands displayed,
Each silver vase in mystic order laid.
First, robed in white, the nymph intent adores,
With head uncovered, the cosmetic powers.
A heavenly image in the glass appears; 125
To that she bends, to that her eyes she rears.
The inferior priestess, at her altar's side,
Trembling begins the sacred rites of Pride.
Unnumbered treasures ope at once, and here
The various offerings of the world appear; 130
From each she nicely culls with curious toil,
And decks the goddess with the glittering spoil.
This casket India's glowing gems unlocks,
And all Arabia breathes from yonder box.
The tortoise here and elephant unite, 135
Transformed to combs, the speckled and the white.
Here files of pins extend their shining rows,
Puffs, powders, patches, Bibles, billet-doux.
Now awful Beauty puts on all its arms;
The fair each moment rises in her charms, 140
Repairs her smiles, awakens every grace,
And calls forth all the wonders of her face;

Sees by degrees a purer blush arise,
And keener lightnings quicken in her eyes.
The busy Sylphs surround their darling care,   145
These set the head, and those divide the hair,
Some fold the sleeve, whilst others plait the gown;
And Betty's praised for labors not her own.

CANTO II

Not with more glories, in the ethereal plain,
The sun first rises o'er the purpled main,   150
Than, issuing forth, the rival of his beams
Launched on the bosom of the silver Thames.
Fair nymphs, and well-dressed youths around her
    shone,
But every eye was fixed on her alone.
On her white breast a sparkling cross she wore,   155
Which Jews might kiss, and infidels adore.
Her lively looks a sprightly mind disclose,
Quick as her eyes, and as unfixed as those:
Favors to none, to all she smiles extends;
Oft she rejects, but never once offends.   160
Bright as the sun, her eyes the gazers strike,
And, like the sun, they shine on all alike.
Yet graceful ease, and sweetness void of pride,
Might hide her faults, if belles had faults to hide:
If to her share some female errors fall,   165
Look on her face, and you'll forget 'em all.
    This nymph, to the destruction of mankind,
Nourished two locks which graceful hung behind
In equal curls, and well conspired to deck
With shining ringlets the smooth ivory neck.   170
Love in these labyrinths his slaves detains,
And mighty hearts are held in slender chains.
With hairy springes we the birds betray,
Slight lines of hair surprise the finny prey,
Fair tresses man's imperial race ensnare,   175
And beauty draws us with a single hair.
    The adventurous Baron the bright locks
    admired,
He saw, he wished, and to the prize aspired.
Resolved to win, he meditates the way,
By force to ravish, or by fraud betray;   180
For when success a lover's toil attends,
Few ask if fraud or force attained his ends.
    For this, ere Phoebus rose, he had implored
Propitious Heaven, and every power adored,
But chiefly Love—to Love an altar built,   185
Of twelve vast French romances, neatly gilt.
There lay three garters, half a pair of gloves,
And all the trophies of his former loves.
With tender billet-deux he lights the pyre,
And breathes three amorous sighs to raise the fire.   190
Then prostrate falls, and begs with ardent eyes
Soon to obtain, and long possess the prize:
The powers gave ear, and granted half his prayer,
The rest, the winds dispersed in empty air.
    But now secure the painted vessel glides,   195
The sunbeams trembling on the floatingtides,
While melting music steals upon the sky,
And softened sounds along the waters die.
Smooth flow the waves, the zephyrs gently play,
Belinda smiled, and all the world was gay.   200

All but the Sylph—with careful thoughts
    oppressed,
The impending woe sat heavy on his breast.
He summons strait his denizens of air;
The lucid squadrons round the sails repair:
Soft o'er the shrouds aërial whispers breathe   205
That seemed but zephyrs to the train beneath.
Some to the sun their insect-wings unfold,
Waft on the breeze, or sink in clouds of gold.
Transparent forms, too fine for mortal sight,
Their fluid bodies half dissolved in light,   210
Loose to the wind their airy garments flew,
Thin glittering textures of the filmy dew,
Dipped in the richest tincture of the skies,
Where light disports in ever-mingling dyes,
While every beam new transient colors flings,   215
Colors that change whene'er they wave their
    wings.
Amid the circle, on the gilded mast,
Superior by the head was Ariel placed;
His purple pinions opening to the sun,
He raised his azure wand, and thus begun: 220
    "Ye Sylphs and Sylphids, to your chief give
    ear!
Fays, Fairies, Genii, Elves, and Daemons, hear!
Ye know the spheres and various tasks assigned
By laws eternal to the aërial kind.
Some in the fields of purest ether play,   225
And bask and whiten in the blaze of day.
Some guide the course of wandering orbs on high,
Or roll the planets through the boundless sky.
Some less refined, beneath the moon's pale light
Pursue the stars that shoot athwart the night,   230
Or suck the mists in grosser air below,
Or dip their pinions in the painted bow,
Or brew fierce tempests on the wintry main,
Or o'er the glebe distill the kindly rain.
Others on earth o'er human race preside,   235
Watch all their ways, and all their actions guide:
Of these the chief the care of nations own,
And guard with arms divine the British Throne.
    "Our humbler province is to tend the Fair,
Not a less pleasing, though less glorious care: 240
To save the powder from too rude a gale,
Nor let the imprisoned essences exhale;
To draw fresh colors from the vernal flowers;
To steal from rainbows e'er they drop in showers
A brighter wash; to curl their waving hairs,   245
Assist their blushes, and inspire their airs;
Nay oft, in dreams invention we bestow,
To change a flounce, or add a furbelow.
    "This day black omens threat the brightest fair,
That e'er deserved a watchful spirit's care;   250
Some dire disaster, or by force or slight,
But what, or where, the Fates have wrapped in
    night:
Whether the nymph shall break Diana's law,
Or some frail china jar receive a flaw,
Or stain her honor or her new brocade,   255
Forget her prayers, or miss a masquerade,
Or lose her heart, or necklace, at a ball;
Or whether Heaven has doomed that Shock must
    fall.

Haste, then, ye spirits! to your charge repair:
The fluttering fan be Zephyretta's care;   260
The drops to thee, Brillante, we consign;
And, Momentilla, let the watch be thine;
Do thou, Crispissa, tend her favorite Lock;
Ariel himself shall be the guard of Shock.

    "To fifty chosen Sylphs, of special note,   265
We trust the important charge, the petticoat;
Oft have we known that sevenfold fence to fail,
Though stiff with hoops, and armed with ribs of
    whale.
Form a strong line about the silver bound,
And guard the wide circumference around.   270

    "Whatever spirit, careless of his charge,
His post neglects, or leaves the fair at large,
Shall feel sharp vengeance soon o'ertake his sins,
Be stopped in vials, or transfixed with pins,
Or plunged in lakes of bitter washes lie,   275
Or wedged whole ages in a bodkin's eye:
Gums and pomatums shall his flight restrain,
While clogged he beats his silken wings in vain;
Or alum styptics with contracting power
Shrink his thin essence like a riveled flower: 280
Or, as Ixion fixed, the wretch shall feel
The giddy motion of the whirling mill,
In fumes of burning chocolate shall glow,
And tremble at the sea that froths below!"

    He spoke; the spirits from the sails descend;   285
Some, orb in orb, around the nymph extend;
Some thread the mazy ringlets of her hair;
Some hang upon the pendants of her ear:
With beating hearts the dire event they wait,
Anxious, and trembling for the birth of Fate.   290

CANTO III

    Close by those meads, forever crowned with
    flowers,
Where Thames with pride surveys his rising towers,
There stands a structure of majestic frame,
Which from the neighboring Hampton takes its
    name.
Here Britain's statesmen oft the fall foredoom   295
Of foreign tyrants and of nymphs at home;
Here thou, great Anna! whom three realms obey,
Dost sometimes counsel take—and sometimes tea.

    Hither the heroes and the nymphs resort,
To taste awhile the pleasures of a court;   300
In various talk the instructive hours they passed,
Who gave the ball, or paid the visit last;
One speaks the glory of the British Queen,
And one describes a charming Indian screen;
A third interprets motions, looks, and eyes;   305
At every word a reputation dies.
Snuff, or the fan, supply each pause of chat,
With singing, laughing, ogling, and all that.

    Meanwhile, declining from the noon of day,
The sun obliquely shoots his burning ray;   310
The hungry judges soon the sentence sign,
And wretches hang that jurymen may dine;
The merchant from the Exchange returns in peace,
And the long labors of the toilet cease.
Belinda now, whom thirst of fame invites,   315

Burns to encounter two adventurous knights,
At ombre singly to decide their doom,
And swells her breast with conquests yet to come.
Straight the three bands prepare in arms to join,
Each band the number of the sacred nine.   320
Soon as she spreads her hand, the aërial guard
Descend, and sit on each important card:
First Ariel perched upon a Matadore,
Then each according to the rank they bore;
For Sylphs, yet mindful of their ancient race,   325
Are, as when women, wondrous fond of place.

    Behold, four Kings in majesty revered,
With hoary whiskers and a forky beard;
And four fair Queens whose hands sustain a
    flower,
The expressive emblem of their softer power;   330
Four Knaves in garbs succinct, a trusty band,
Caps on their heads, and halberts in their hand;
And parti-colored troops, a shining train,
Draw forth to combat on the velvet plain.

    The skilful nymph reviews her force with care;   335
"Let Spades be trumps!" she said, and trumps they
    were.
Now move to war her sable Matadores,
In show like leaders of the swarthy Moors.
Spadillio first, unconquerable lord!
Led off two captive trumps, and swept the board.   340
As many more Manillio forced to yield,
And marched a victor from the verdant field.
Him Basto followed, but his fate more hard
Gained but one trump and one plebeian card.
With his broad sabre next, a chief in years,   345
The hoary Majesty of Spades appears,
Puts forth one manly leg, to sight revealed,
The rest, his many-colored robe concealed.
The rebel Knave, who dares his prince engage,
Proves the just victim of his royal rage.   350
Even mighty Pam, that kings and queens o'erthrew
And mowed down armies in the fights of loo,
Sad chance of war! now destitute of aid,
Falls undistinguished by the victor Spade.

    Thus far both armies to Belinda yield;   355
Now to the Baron fate inclines the field.
His warlike amazon her host invades,
The imperial consort of the crown of Spades.
The Club's black tyrant first her victim died,
Spite of his haughty mien, and barbarous pride.   360
What boots the regal circle on his head,
His giant limbs, in state unwieldy spread?
That long behind he trails his pompous robe,
And of all monarchs only grasps the globe?

    The Baron now his Diamonds pours apace;   365
The embroidered King who shows but half his face,
And his refulgent Queen, with powers combined
Of broken troops an easy conquest find.
Clubs, Diamonds, Hearts, in wild disorder seen,
With throngs promiscuous strew the level green.   370
Thus when dispersed a routed army runs,
Of Asia's troops, and Afric's sable sons,
With like confusion different nations fly,
Of various habit, and of various dye,
The pierced battalions disunited fall,   375
In heaps on heaps; one fate o'erwhelms them all.

The Knave of Diamonds tries his wily arts,
And wins (oh, shameful chance!) the Queen of
    Hearts.
At this, the blood the virgin's cheek forsook,
A livid paleness spreads o'er all her look;   380
She sees, and trembles at the approaching ill,
Just in the jaws of ruin, and Codille,
And now (as oft in some distempered state)
On one nice trick depends the general fate.
An Ace of Hearts steps forth: the King unseen   385
Lurked in her hand, and mourned his captive
    Queen.
He springs to vengeance with an eager pace,
And falls like thunder on the prostrate Ace.
The nymph exulting fills with shouts the sky,
The walls, the woods, and long canals reply.   390
    Oh thoughtless mortals! ever blind to fate,
Too soon dejected, and too soon elate:
Sudden these honors shall be snatched away,
And cursed for ever this victorious day.
    For lo! the board with cups and spoons is   395
    crowned,
The berries crackle, and the mill turns round;
On shining altars of Japan they raise
The silver lamp; the fiery spirits blaze:
From silver spouts the grateful liquors glide,
While China's earth receives the smoking tide.   400
At once they gratify their scent and taste,
And frequent cups prolong the rich repast.
Straight hover round the fair her airy band;
Some, as she sipped, the fuming liquor fanned,
Some o'er her lap their careful plumes displayed,   405
Trembling, and conscious of the rich brocade.
Coffee (which makes the politician wise,
And see through all things with his half-shut eyes)
Sent up in vapors to the Baron's brain
New stratagems, the radiant Lock to gain.   410
Ah, cease, rash youth! desist ere 'tis too late,
Fear the just Gods, and think of Scylla's fate!
Changed to a bird, and sent to flit in air,
She dearly pays for Nisus' injured hair!
    But when to mischief mortals bend their will,   415
How soon they find fit instruments of ill!
Just then, Clarissa drew with tempting grace
A two-edged weapon from her shining case:
So ladies in romance assist their knight,
Present the spear, and arm him for the fight.   420
He takes the gift with reverence, and extends
The little engine on his fingers' ends;
This just behind Belinda's neck he spread,
As o'er the fragrant steams she bends her head.
Swift to the Lock a thousand sprites repair,   425
A thousand wings, by turns, blow back the hair,
And thrice they twitched the diamond in her ear,
Thrice she looked back, and thrice the foe drew
    near.
Just in that instant, anxious Ariel sought
The close recesses of the virgin's thought;   430
As on the nosegay in her breast reclined,
He watched the ideas rising in her mind,
Suddenly he viewed, in spite of all her art,
An earthly lover lurking at her heart.
Amazed, confused, he found his power expired,   435

Resigned to fate, and with a sigh retired.
    The Peer now spreads the glittering forfex wide,
To inclose the Lock; now joins it, to divide.
Even then, before the fatal engine closed,
A wretched Sylph too fondly interposed;   440
Fate urged the shears, and cut the Sylph in twain
(But airy substance soon unites again):
The meeting points the sacred hair dissever
From the fair head, forever, and forever!
    Then flashed the living lightning from her eyes, 445
And screams of horror rend the affrighted skies.
Not louder shrieks to pitying heaven are cast,
When husbands, or when lapdogs breathe their last;
Or when rich china vessels fallen from high,
In glittering dust and painted fragments lie!   450
"Let wreaths of triumph now my temples twine,"
The victor cried, "the glorious prize is mine!
While fish in streams, or birds delight in air,
Or in a coach and six the British Fair,
As long as Atalantis shall be read,   455
Or the small pillow grace a lady's bed,
While visits shall be paid on solemn days,
When numerous wax-lights in bright order blaze,
While nymphs take treats, or assignations give,
So long my honor, name, and praise shall live!   460
What Time would spare, from Steel receives its
    date,
And monuments, like men, submit to fate!
Steel could the labor of the Gods destroy,
And strike to dust the imperial towers of Troy;
Steel could the works of mortal pride confound,   465
And hew triumphal arches to the ground.
What wonder then, fair nymph! thy hairs should
    feel,
The conquering force of unresisted Steel?"

CANTO IV

    But anxious cares the pensive nymph
    oppressed,
And secret passions labored in her breast.   470
Not youthful kings in battle seized alive,
Not scornful virgins who their charms survive,
Not ardent lovers robbed of all their bliss,
Not ancient ladies when refused a kiss,
Not tyrants fierce that unrepenting die,   475
Not Cynthia when her manteau's pinned awry,
E'er felt such rage, resentment, and despair,
As thou, sad virgin! for thy ravished hair.
    For, that sad moment, when the Sylphs
    withdrew
And Ariel weeping from Belinda flew,   480
Umbriel, a dusky, melancholy sprite,
As ever sullied the fair face of light,
Down to the central earth, his proper scene,
Repaired to search the gloomy Cave of Spleen.
    Swift on his sooty pinions flits the Gnome,   485
And in a vapor reached the dismal dome.
No cheerful breeze this sullen region knows,
The dreaded east is all the wind that blows.
Here in a grotto, sheltered close from air,
And screened in shades from day's detested glare, 490
She sighs forever on her pensive bed,

Pain at her side, and Megrim at her head.
    Two handmaids wait the throne: alike in place,
But differing far in figure and in face.
Here stood Ill-Nature like an ancient maid,   495
Her wrinkled form in black and white arrayed;
With store of prayers, for mornings, nights, and
    noons,
Her hand is filled; her bosom with lampoons.
    There Affectation, with a sickly mien,
Shows in her cheek the roses of eighteen,   500
Practiced to lisp, and hang the head aside,
Faints into airs, and languishes with pride,
On the rich quilt sinks with becoming woe,
Wrapped in a gown, for sickness, and for show.
The fair ones feel such maladies as these,   505
When each new nightdress gives a new disease.
    A constant vapor o'er the palace flies,
Strange phantoms rising as the mists arise;
Dreadful as hermit's dreams in haunted shades,
Or bright as visions of expiring maids.   510
Now glaring fiends, and snakes on rolling spires,
Pale specters, gaping tombs, and purple fires;
Now lakes of liquid gold, Elysian scenes,
And crystal domes, and angels in machines.
    Unnumbered throngs on every side are seen,   515
Of bodies changed to various forms by Spleen.
Here living teapots stand, one arm held out,
One bent; the handle this, and that the spout:
A pipkin there, like Homer's tripod, walks;
Here sighs a jar, and there a goose pie talks;   520
Men prove with child, as powerful fancy works,
And maids, turned bottles, call aloud for corks.
    Safe passed the Gnome through this fantastic
    band,
A branch of healing spleenwort in his hand.
Then thus addressed the Power: "Hail, wayward   525
    Queen!
Who rule the sex to fifty from fifteen:
Parent of vapors and of female wit,
Who give the hysteric or poetic fit,
On various tempers act by various ways,
Make some take physic, others scribble plays;   530
Who cause the proud their visits to delay,
And send the godly in a pet to pray.
A nymph there is that all thy power disdains,
And thousands more in equal mirth maintains.
But oh! if e'er thy Gnome could spoil a grace,   535
Or raise a pimple on a beauteous face,
Like citron-waters matrons' cheeks inflame,
Or change complexions at a losing game;
If e'er with airy horns I planted heads,
Or rumpled petticoats, or tumbled beds,   540
Or caused suspicion when no soul was rude,
Or discomposed the headdress of a prude,
Or e'er to costive lapdog gave disease,
Which not the tears of brightest eyes could ease,
Hear me, and touch Belinda with chagrin: 545
That single act gives half the world the spleen."
    The Goddess with a discontented air
Seems to reject him though she grants his prayer.
A wondrous bag with both her hands she binds,
Like that where once Ulysses held the winds;   550
There she collects the force of female lungs,

Sighs, sobs, and passions, and the war of tongues.
A vial next she fills with fainting fears,
Soft sorrows, melting griefs, and flowing tears.
The Gnome rejoicing bears her gifts away,   555
Spreads his black wings, and slowly mounts to day.
    Sunk in Thalestris' arms the nymph he found,
Her eyes dejected and her hair unbound.
Full o'er their heads the swelling bag he rent,
And all the Furies issued at the vent.   560
Belinda burns with more than mortal ire,
And fierce Thalestris fans the rising fire.
"Oh wretched maid!" she spread her hands, and
    cried,
(While Hampton's echoes, "Wretched maid!"
    replied),
"Was it for this you took such constant care   565
The bodkin, comb, and essence to prepare?
For this your locks in paper durance bound,
For this with torturing irons wreathed around?
For this with fillets strained your tender head,
And bravely bore the double loads of lead?   570
Gods! shall the ravisher display your hair,
While the fops envy, and the ladies stare!
Honor forbid! at whose unrivaled shrine
Ease, pleasure, virtue, all, our sex resign.
Methinks already I your tears survey,   575
Already hear the horrid things they say,
Already see you a degraded toast,
And all your honor in a whisper lost!
How shall I, then, your helpless fame defend?
'Twill then be infamy to seem your friend!   580
And shall this prize, the inestimable prize,
Exposed through crystal to the gazing eyes,
And heightened by the diamond's circling rays,
On that rapacious hand forever blaze?
Sooner shall grass in Hyde Park Circus grow,   585
And wits take lodgings in the sound of Bow;
Sooner let earth, air, sea, to chaos fall,
Men, monkeys, lapdogs, parrots, perish all!"
    She said; then raging to Sir Plume repairs,
And bids her beau demand the precious hairs   590
(Sir Plume of amber snuffbox justly vain,
And the nice conduct of a clouded cane),
With earnest eyes, and round unthinking face,
He first the snuffbox opened, then the case,
And thus broke out—"My Lord, why, what the   595
    devil!
Z——ds! damn the lock! 'fore Gad, you must be
    civil!
Plague on't! 'tis past a jest—nay prithee, pox!
Give her the hair"—he spoke, and rapped his box.
    "It grieves me much," replied the Peer again,
"Who speaks so well should ever speak in vain.   600
But by this Lock, this sacred Lock I swear
(Which never more shall join its parted hair;
Which never more its honors shall renew,
Clipped from the lovely head where late it
    grew),
That while my nostrils draw the vital air,   605
This hand, which won it, shall forever wear."
He spoke, and speaking, in proud triumph spread
The long-contended honors of her head.
    But Umbriel, hateful Gnome, forbears not so;
      610

He breaks the vial whence the sorrows flow.
Then see! the nymph in beauteous grief appears,
Her eyes half languishing, half drowned in tears;
On her heaved bosom hung her drooping head,
Which with a sigh she raised, and thus she said:
    "Forever cursed be this detested day,   615
Which snatched my best, my favorite curl away!
Happy! ah ten times happy had I been,
If Hampton Court these eyes had never seen!
Yet am not I the first mistaken maid,
By love of courts to numerous ills betrayed.   620
Oh, had I rather unadmired remained
In some lone isle, or distant Northern land;
Where the gilt chariot never marks the way,
Where none learn ombre, none e'er taste bohea!
There kept my charms concealed from mortal eye,   625
Like roses that in deserts bloom and die.
What moved my mind with youthful lords to roam?
Oh, had I stayed, and said my prayers at home!
'Twas this the morning omens seemed to tell,
Thrice from my trembling hand the patch box fell;   630
The tottering china shook without a wind,
Nay, Poll sat mute, and Shock was most unkind!
A Sylph too warned me of the threats of fate,
In mystic visions, now believed too late!
See the poor remnants of these slighted hairs!   635
My hands shall rend what e'en thy rapine spares.
These in two sable ringlets taught to break,
Once gave new beauties to the snowy neck;
The sister lock now sits uncouth, alone,
And in its fellow's fate foresees its own;   640
Uncurled it hangs, the fatal shears demands,
And tempts once more, thy sacrilegious hands.
Oh, hadst thou, cruel! been content to seize
Hairs less in sight, or any hairs but these!"

CANTO V

    She said: the pitying audience melt in tears.   645
But Fate and Jove had stopped the Baron's ears.
In vain Thalestris with reproach assails,
For who can move when fair Belinda fails?
Not half so fixed the Trojan could remain,
While Anna begged and Dido raged in vain.   650
Then grave Clarissa graceful waved her fan;
Silence ensued, and thus the nymph began:
    "Say why are beauties praised and honored
        most,
The wise man's passion, and the vain man's toast?
Why decked with all that land and sea afford,   655
Why angels called, and angel-like adored?
Why round our coaches crowd the white-gloved
        beaux,
Why bows the side box from its inmost rows?
How vain are all these glories, all our pains,
Unless good sense preserve what beauty gains;   660
That men may say when we the front box grace,
'Behold the first in virtue as in face!'
Oh! if to dance all night, and dress all day,
Charmed the smallpox, or chased old age away,
Who would not scorn what housewife's cares   665
        produce,
Or who would learn one earthly thing of use?

To patch, nay ogle, might become a saint,
Nor could it sure be such a sin to paint.
But since, alas! frail beauty must decay,
Curled or uncurled, since locks will turn to gray   670
Since painted, or not painted, all shall fade,
And she who scorns a man must die a maid;
What then remains but well our power to use,
And keep good humor still whate'er we lose?
And trust me, dear, good humor can prevail,   675
When airs, and flights, and screams, and scolding
        fail.
Beauties in vain their pretty eyes may roll;
Charms strike the sight, but merit wins the soul."
    So spoke the dame, but no applause ensued;
Belinda frowned, Thalestris called her prude.   680
"To arms, to arms!" the fierce virago cries,
And swift as lightning to the combat flies.
All side in parties, and begin the attack;
Fans clap, silks rustle, and tough whalebones crack;
Heroes' and heroines' shouts confusedly rise,   685
And bass and treble voices strike the skies.
No common weapons in their hands are found,
Like Gods they fight, nor dread a mortal wound.
    So when bold Homer makes the Gods engage,
And heavenly breasts with human passions rage;   690
'Gainst Pallas, Mars; Latona, Hermes arms;
And all Olympus rings with loud alarms:
Jove's thunder roars, heaven trembles all around,
Blue Neptune storms, the bellowing deeps resound:
Earth shakes her nodding towers, the ground gives   695
        way,
And the pale ghosts start at the flash of day!
    Triumphant Umbriel on a sconce's height
Clapped his glad wings, and sat to view the fight:
Propped on their bodkin spears, the sprites survey
The growing combat, or assist the fray.   700
    While through the press enraged Thalestris
        flies,
And scatters death around from both her eyes,
A beau and witling perished in the throng,
One died in metaphor, and one in song.
"O cruel nymph! a living death I bear,"   705
Cried Dapperwit, and sunk beside his chair.
A mournful glance Sir Fopling upwards cast,
"Those eyes are made so killing"—was his last.
Thus on Maeander's flowery margin lies
The expiring swan, and as he sings he dies   710
    When bold Sir Plume had drawn Clarissa down,
Chloe stepped in, and killed him with a frown;
She smiled to see the doughty hero slain,
But, at her smile, the beau revived again.
    Now Jove suspends his golden scales in air,   715
Weighs the men's wits against the lady's hair;
The doubtful beam long nods from side to side;
At length the wits mount up, the hairs subside.
    See, fierce Belinda on the Baron flies,
With more than usual lightning in her eyes;   720
Nor feared the chief the unequal fight to try,
Who sought no more than on his foe to die.
    But this bold lord with manly strength endued,
She with one finger and a thumb subdued:
Just where the breath of life his nostrils drew,   725
A charge of snuff the wily virgin threw;

The Gnomes direct, to every atom just,
The pungent grains of titillating dust.
Sudden, with starting tears each eye o'erflows,
And the high dome re-echoes to his nose. 730
  "Now meet thy fate," incensed Belinda cried,
And drew a deadly bodkin from her side.
(The same, his ancient personage to deck,
Her great-great-grandsire wore about his neck,
In three seal rings; which after, melted down, 735
Formed a vast buckle for his widow's gown:
Her infant grandame's whistle next it grew,
The bells she jingled, and the whistle blew;
Then in a bodkin graced her mother's hairs,
Which long she wore, and now Belinda wears.) 740
  "Boast not my fall," he cried, "insulting foe!
Thou by some other shalt be laid as low.
Nor think to die dejects my lofty mind:
All that I dread is leaving you behind!
Rather than so, ah, let me still survive, 745
And burn in Cupid's flames—but burn alive."
  "Restore the Lock!" she cries; and all around
"Restore the Lock!" the vaulted roofs rebound.
Not fierce Othello in so loud a strain
Roared for the handkerchief that caused his pain. 750
But see how oft ambitious aims are crossed,
And chiefs contend till all the prize is lost!
The lock, obtained with guilt, and kept with pain,
In every place is sought, but sought in vain:
With such a prize no mortal must be blessed, 755
So Heaven decrees! with Heaven who can contest?
  Some thought it mounted to the lunar sphere,
Since all things lost on earth are treasured there.
There heros' wits are kept in ponderous vases,
And beaux' in snuffboxes and tweezer cases. 760
There broken vows and deathbed alms are found,
And lovers' hearts with ends of riband bound,
The courtier's promises, and sick man's prayers,
The smiles of harlots, and the tears of heirs,
Cages for gnats, and chains to yoke a flea, 765
Dried butterflies, and tomes of casuistry.
  But trust the Muse—she saw it upward rise
Though marked by none but quick, poetic eyes
(So Rome's great founder to the heavens withdrew,
To Proculus alone confessed in view); 770
A sudden star, it shot through liquid air,
And drew behind a radiant trail of hair.
Not Berenice's locks first rose so bright,
The heavens bespangling with disheveled light.
The Sylphs behold it kindling as it flies, 775
And pleased pursue its progress through the skies.
  This the Beau monde shall from the Mall
      survey,
And hail with music its propitious ray,
This the blest lover shall for Venus take,
And send up vows from Rosamonda's Lake. 780
This Partridge soon shall view in cloudless skies,
When next he looks through Galileo's eyes;
And hence the egregious wizard shall foredoom
The fate of Louis, and the fall of Rome.
  Then cease, bright nymph! to mourn thy 785
      ravished hair,
Which adds new glory to the shining sphere!
Not all the tresses that fair head can boast,

Shall draw such envy as the Lock you lost.
For, after all the murders of your eye,
When, after millions slain, yourself shall die: 790
When those fair suns shall set, as set they must,
And all those tresses shall be laid in dust,
This Lock, the Muse shall consecrate to fame,
And 'midst the stars inscribe Belinda's name.

Poem Summary

Lines 1–6

The speaker, in typical epic fashion, invokes his muse to inspire him in his composition. Traditionally, the goddess presiding over epic poetry is Calliope. In this case, Pope's friend John Caryll is the "muse" who suggested the poet attempt a playful satire to cure the family squabble that erupted when Lord Petre cut a lock of hair from Miss Arabella Fermor. The speaker's aim is to raise this insignificant dispute to a "mighty contest."

Lines 7–12

In these three couplets, the speaker poses three questions the mock-epic will attempt to answer: why would a lord assault a gentle maiden?; why would an aristocratic lady reject a lord?; how can "mighty rage" hide in polite society?

Lines 13–26

The speaker uses personification, describing the sun as "Sol" who tries to awaken the poem's heroine, Belinda, and her lapdog, Shock. Pope uses the word "sylph" to mean an imaginary fairy—a creature that inhabits the air.

Lines 27–66

Ariel's speech takes up most of Canto I, continuing to line 114. The speaker introduces an army of supernatural, imaginary creatures because it is one of the conventions of epic poetry being satirized. Homer, Virgil, and Milton made use of classical mythology to puff up the significance of their heroes' exploits. Pope uses characters from Rosicrucian mythology such as Ariel (Canto I), Umbriel (Canto IV), and Thalestris (Canto V). According to Rosicrucian myth and the theories of metaphysical philosopher Paracelsus, all things were believed to have been made of four Aristotelian elements: fire, water, earth, and air. In lines 59–66, the speaker mentions all four elements and the supernatural creatures associated with them: salamanders (fire); nymphs (water); gnomes (earth); and sylphs (air). The intent of this section

Media Adaptations

- A recording of "The Rape of the Lock" is included in the two-cassette set, *Penguin English Verse: The Eighteenth Century: Swift to Crabbe, Volume 3*. The tapes were released in 1996 by Penguin Highbridge Audio.

is to elaborate on the background of the mythological creatures that come and go throughout the course of "The Rape of the Lock." The mythology contributes weight and gravity to an otherwise light social satire. The speaker satirizes the conventions of epic poetry and literary tradition as well as the social vanity of the aristocratic Belinda.

Lines 67–114

Ariel tells Belinda that sylphs embrace all the fair and chaste maidens of society by assuming any shape they want, an allusion to Milton's description of the army of devils in *Paradise Lost*. Ariel issues the vague warning of "some dread event" impending upon her before the day is out, but he does not specify what this dread event may be. Ariel concludes his long speech by saying that Belinda should above all "beware of men," a hint that the impending doom relates to her flirtations with men. Line 101, "where wigs with wigs, with swordknots sword-knots strive" is an allusion to Homer's *Iliad* and his description of the Greek forces readying their weapons to battle the Trojans. Also in this speech, Ariel resembles the angel Raphael, the angel who came to Eve in the Garden of Eden to warn her of Satan's approach, in Milton's *Paradise Lost*.

Lines 115–120

Shock, Belinda's lapdog, thinks that his mistress has slept too long and licks Belinda with his tongue. As Belinda pulls herself out of bed, she sees a "billet-deux" or love-letter on her bed. Reading the charming words of some admirer, Belinda's "vision" or lesson from Ariel disappears from her memory. Belinda forgets Ariel's warning about the need to beware of jealousy, vanity, pride, and impertinent men.

Lines 121–148

Belinda goes to her toilet or cosmetic table to prepare herself for the day to be spent in fashionable society. With the help of her servant Betty, whom the speaker describes as "the inferior priestess," Belinda grooms herself and accumulates intense pride in her beauty. This masterfully written section catalogues the exotic jewelry, pins, powders, perfumes, mirrors, tortoise shell and ivory combs, blushes, and rouges that Belinda uses to heighten her exquisite beauty and egoistic sense of importance. The speaker says in line 139 that "Now awful Beauty puts on all its arms," meaning "awful" as "awe-inspiring" the way the enemy watches the epic hero prepare his battle gear for combat and is awestruck at his weaponry and prowess. Also, the speaker presents Belinda at the "altar" of her beauty as a religious analogy, satirizing Belinda as the high priestess of vanity. The speaker also uses the catalogue of beauty aids as an allusion to the serious epic convention of describing soldiers readying for battle. Thus, Belinda "arms" herself for "battle" with the Baron, about whom Ariel has indirectly warned her.

Lines 149–166

Like many chapters of the *Iliad* or the *Odyssey*, Canto II begins with the sun rising over "the purple main," or sea reddened by dawn to a royal purple. Belinda is presented as the sun's rival because her self-appointed radiance shines as she drifts in a boat upon the river Thames. Surrounded by well-dressed admirers and nymphs, Belinda sails from London to Hampton Court, the royal palace about fifteen miles up the river. Belinda extends her smile to all surrounding courtiers like a true coquette. The speaker says that one look at Belinda's beautiful face would make anyone forget her female faults, if any were to be found.

Lines 167–182

The speaker mentions Belinda's two locks of hair that gracefully hang behind her in "sparkling ringlets," using similes to compare the locks with a labyrinth that enslaves admirers to her love or snares that trap the unsuspecting courtier dazzled by her beauty. The first mention of the Baron comes in line 177 as he admires the radiant locks and resolves to possess one by any fraudulent or deceptive means. So captivated by the beautiful Belinda, the Baron must possess her beauty somehow.

Lines 183–194

The speaker writes that before the sun rose, the Baron had built an altar to the goddess Love and arranged around it all his symbols of success with former mistresses: twelve French romances bound in gold, garters, gloves, "trophies," and love letters. The Baron had thrown himself prostrate before this Love altar, a parallel to Belinda's cosmetic altar, and prayed for powers from the goddess that would allow him to capture the lock and keep it forever. However, Love grants the Baron only half of his prayer that he might acquire the lock but not keep it forever. This line (193) foreshadows the conclusion of the poem.

Lines 195–220

All the sailing company enjoys the leisurely cruise upon the Thames river except the sylph Ariel, who is oppressed with gloom because his warning against vanity was lost upon Belinda. Line 199 demonstrates Pope's use of onomatopoeia because the sound of the words mimics the sense of the gentle ride upon the water. Ariel summons his army of sprites and sylphs—inhabitants of the air whose fluid bodies disappear in transparent forms. Ariel stands tall before the other sylphs just as the typical epic hero—Odysseus, Achilles, or Agamemnon—towers before the troops addressing them before combat.

Lines 221–290

The second long speech by Ariel concludes Canto II. Ariel reminds the sylph army that their humble purpose is to guard the fair maiden Belinda, protecting her beauty from harsh winds and brightening her complexion when she needs it. The impending threat approaches, says Ariel, the "black day" of some dire disaster or threat to Belinda's chastity and beauty. Therefore, special assignments are dealt out by Ariel. Ariel shows special care in assigning duties associated with the sylph's name: Zephyretta (the west wind) protects Belinda's fan; Brilliante protects the diamond earrings; Momentilla protects the watch; Crispissa (a word for curling) protects Belinda's favorite lock of hair. Ariel himself will guard Shock, the lapdog. Fifty sylphs are chosen to guard Belinda's petticoat, associated with her virginity. Though the petticoat is armed with stiff hoops and stout whale rib, danger is still possible, and so the sylphs are needed. Ariel concludes his speech admonishing that any sylph who neglects his watch "shall feel sharp vengeance" and severe physical punishment—like Ixion, who in Greek mythology was punished in the underworld by being bound to an ever-turning wheel. After Ariel's pep talk, the sylphs disperse to their assigned guardian posts, waiting anxiously for the disaster that beats down quickly upon them.

Lines 291–308

Belinda's boat approaches Hampton Court, a royal palace where the Baron lies in wait. Hampton Court is one home of Queen Ann of England. With Britain's noble statesmen, Queen Ann plots the fall of foreign tyrants and then engages in trivial social bantering at teatime. Belinda and her retinue of servants, admirers, and unseen sylphs enter the social scene of the court. Belinda is very much aware that her social reputation depends on how she might hold her fan or chit-chat with nobles and dignitaries.

Lines 309–334

In the afternoon, Belinda desires to play "ombre," a Spanish card game resembling whist or bridge, against two suitors, the Baron and a young man. The speaker describes each card in elaborate detail, its ranking suit and number, along with the invisible sylphs who guard each card. This resembles armies assembling for combat in epic poems such as the *Iliad*. Pope has carefully arranged the cards exactly according to the rules of ombre. The game is played with forty cards, the 10s, 9s, and 8s removed from play. Each player holds nine cards and Belinda's cards are winning at first. Ariel is perched upon a "Matadore," the highest trump cards. The trump cards are the ace of spades (Spadillio), the two of spades (Manillio), and the ace of clubs (Basto). The descending order of kings, queens, and jacks are described as readied for "the velvet plain" (or card table) a term used for the battlefield in epic poetry.

Lines 335–390

In this section, the actual game of ombre is described in astonishing detail. While Belinda is winning at first, the tide of "battle" turns in line 356 when the Baron sends his "warlike amazon" or Queen of spades to win the first of four tricks. The Baron's egoistic pride shows through as he wins the card game/battle. When the "routed army" begins to run away in line 371, confusion sets in. The speaker uses a parody of an epic simile in lines 371–376 to compare the losing cards with a confused army retreating from battle.

Lines 391–414

The speaker foreshadows "the fall" of Belinda's lock of hair in elevated language, comparing it to the fall of Eve in *Paradise Lost*. After the card game is finished and the Baron relishes his victory, coffee is served to the guests. Another convention of epic poetry is parodied, the epic repast or feast wherein warriors refresh themselves after battle or during a long journey. The speaker luxuriates in the lavish detail of the coffee beans, silver pots, lacquered tables, and delicate chinaware of the "feast." However, the strong smell of the coffee travels to the Baron's brain and inspires him to new stratagems to get the lock of hair. The speaker compares the Baron to Scylla in Greek mythology, the daughter of Nisus who was punished and turned into a sea bird because she cut from her father's head the purple lock upon which his safety depended.

Lines 415–436

Suddenly, Clarissa, one of the Baron's assistants—and also the heroine of a famous novel by Samuel Richardson—draws a pair of scissors out of her case. The speaker compares this action with the knight who is presented a battle-axe before a joust. Just as Belinda bends over to smell the fragrant aroma of coffee, a thousand sylphs rush over to guard her hair. They attempt in vain to warn Belinda by blowing back her hair and twitching her earrings. Ariel himself tries to enter into Belinda's thoughts to warn her, but he gives up in vain, resigned to the disastrous fate.

Lines 437–468

The "fatal engine" or the scissors held by the Baron draw close to Belinda's lock; at the last moment, a sylph interposes and gets cut into two. Pope's use of phrases like "fatal engine" for scissors (line 439) or "the finney prey" for fish (line 174) are examples of poetic diction, a highly refined system of words used for exaggeration here but used seriously by lesser eighteenth-century poets. Poetic diction was criticized by later generations of poets and critics who felt that words elevated too far beyond their common usage distorted their meaning. While the sylph's parts can soon come together because he is made of a magical airy substance, as the scissors close, the lock is permanently severed from Belinda's head. Belinda screams as the lock falls into the Baron's hands. The Baron yells "the glorious prize is mine" and praises the scissors, comparing them with the Greek swords that brought down the walled fortress-city of Troy in the *Iliad*. The Baron yells that his honor, name, and praise will live forever because of his great conquering act of snipping the lock of hair—much like Odysseus did as he was leaving the cave of Polyphemus, the Cyclops in the *Odyssey*.

Lines 469–484

Ariel, the guardian sylph, cries bitterly and flies away. Because of the loss of her lock, Belinda

feels more rage, resentment, and despair than all the scorned kings, virgins, and lovers of history—according to the speaker in his typically hyperbolic fashion. A melancholy gnome named Umbriel, whose name suggests shade or darkness, travels to the cave of Spleen. This is a digression or sub-plot and not a part of the main action of the poem. Queen Spleen is the Queen of all bad tempers, ill-nature, affectation, and every negative human quality. This section focusing on Umbriel's journey is a parody of the journey to the underworld that takes place in traditional epics such as Odyssey, *Aeneid*, and *Paradise Lost*.

Lines 485–546

The gnome Umbriel travels through the gloomy recesses of the underworld into the cave sheltered from all sunlight and air. Once Umbriel approaches the throne of Spleen, he notices the Queen's attendants and the languid, sickly atmosphere surrounding the place. Strange specters, phantoms, and snakes arise from the ground. The cave surely seems to be the pits of Hell. Umbriel begins his speech to Spleen in line 525, singing her praises because of her powers. Spleen rules over women with her "vapors" of hypochondria, melancholy, and peevishness. These were actual diagnoses used to describe the maladies of fashionable ladies of Pope's day. Spleen makes women act with inappropriately bad social manners. Umbriel says that Belinda has disdained Spleen's powers on earth because of Belinda's beauty and happiness. Umbriel asks Spleen for some power to touch Belinda with ill humor because if Belinda suffers, half the world will suffer with her (another of many wild exaggerations).

Lines 547–556

The cave goddess Spleen grants the request of Umbriel, giving him a bag filled with terrifying noises such as those expressed by female lungs: sighs, sobs, passions, and complaints typically associated with disappointment in love. This is an allusion to Homer's *Odyssey,* in which Odysseus gets a bag of winds from Aeolus, the god of wind, in order to propel his ship. In a vial, Spleen places fainting fears, sorrows, griefs, and flowing tears. The gnome rejoices and his black wings carry him away, back to earth.

Lines 557–588

Umbriel travels back to earth and finds Belinda in Thalestris' arms. Thalestris, another character from Rosicrucian mythology, is Queen of the Amazons, who are fierce and warlike women. Umbriel pours over Belinda's head the bag of noxious noises given to him by Spleen. Thalestris magnifies Belinda's suffering by chastising her, blaming her "rape" or loss of the lock of hair upon her carelessness; Ariel had attempted to warn Belinda in Canto I about such a catastrophe. Thalestris asks what good the elaborate beauty preparation did when Belinda fell prey to the Baron's scissors? Thalestris complains that fashionable ladies and gentlemen are talking behind Belinda's back about the rape and Belinda's loss of reputation. For someone who so values the pleasantries of social discourse amongst the upper crust, this is a fate worse than death. Meanwhile, the Baron gazes upon his "inestimable prize" of the lock of hair as it is encased in a ring upon his hand. All of Belinda's honor appears to be lost.

Lines 589–608

Thalestris goes to her brother, Sir Plume, and requests that he go to the Baron and demand the return of the lock of Belinda's hair. Sir Plume curses against the loss of the lock and considers the whole episode a worthless waste of time. However, Sir Plume honors Thalestris' request by going to the Baron. The Baron refuses to return his precious prize as long as he lives because he feels he won it for himself. The Baron wants to wear the ring with the lock of hair forever—against the prophecy given by the goddess Love in Canto II.

Lines 609–644

In these lines, Umbriel breaks the vial of sorrows, tears, and griefs over Belinda's head as she continues her intolerable suffering. Canto IV concludes with a long speech of lament by Belinda, in which she cries for the return of happy times. Belinda expresses regret that she ever came to Hampton Court and played ombre with the Baron. Belinda wishes that she had led a simple country life instead of entering into the dangerous affairs of polite society. If Belinda had kept her beauty concealed, she feels that she never would have suffered. Belinda would have dutifully uttered her prayers at home. In line 633, Belinda finally recalls the speech of Ariel, her guardian sylph who had warned her of the disaster. But Belinda did not listen at the time. Now, the other lock of hair sits "uncouth, alone" upon Belinda's head as she suffers in vain. If only she had listened to Ariel!

Lines 645–678

Thalestris' attempt to retrieve the lock through Sir Plume has failed. Clarissa, who had given the Baron the pair of scissors, speculates in a long speech about the vanity of women and the stupidity of the men who court them. All the luxuries of the rich are wasted upon this idle game of courtship, says Clarissa, since beauty must fade with age. These superficial attributes of beauty and charm pale in comparison with lasting qualities. The speech is summarized in the couplet in lines 677–678: "Beauties in vain their pretty eyes may roll; / Charms strike the sight, but merit wins the soul." Clarissa's speech is a parody of a speech given by the Greek warrior Sarpedon to Glaucus in Homer's *Iliad*. Alexander Pope knew the *Iliad* and *Odyssey* so well because he had translated both of them from Greek into English. Today, Pope's translations are still highly regarded.

Lines 679–700

Belinda frowns after Clarissa's speech. Thalestris calls Clarissa a prude for her moralizing tone. Thalestris gets ready an army of sylphs for another epic battle, the concluding action of the poem. Umbriel, sitting on a candlestick holder mounted on the wall, delights at the prospect of another battle, clapping his wings.

Lines 701–756

While the battle between Thalestris and Belinda's enemies, the Baron and Clarissa, rages on, Belinda surprises the Baron by pouncing upon him in line 720. Belinda throws some snuff into the Baron's face to confuse him and to make him sneeze. "Now meet thy fate," Belinda yells to the Baron as she draws a "deadly" weapon from her side—a bodkin or ornamental pin. The speaker compares Belinda's pin with Agamemnon's scepter in lines 733–740 in another parody of an epic simile. Belinda demands restoration of the lock. According to the speaker, Belinda is more fierce than Shakespeare's *Othello* when he screamed for the return of Desdemona's handkerchief. However, confusion reigns supreme and no one can locate the lock of hair. After all this fighting and quarreling, the prize has apparently disappeared.

Lines 757–794

Belinda's precious lock of hair cannot be found. Perhaps the lock has gone to the moon "since all things lost on earth are treasured there" (line 758), apparently a popular belief of the time. The moon is also home of heroes' wits, love letters, broken vows, lovers' hearts, courtiers' promises, and other tokens of tender passions. However, the muse of poetry—either John Caryll or Calliope—saw the lock rise towards heaven and become a star. The speaker compares this ascension of the lock to Romulus of Roman mythology, the legendary founder of Rome who was snatched up to heaven in a storm cloud while he was reviewing his army. Thus, the lock will become visible to astronomers and consecrate Belinda's name to eternity. Belinda has at last achieved her desired honor.

Themes

Pride

"The Rape of the Lock" concerns a teenage coquette whose lock of hair is cut off by a suitor. Ordinarily, such an act would be regarded as bizarre, but certainly not as terrible as the "rape" mentioned in the poem's title. However, to the characters of the poem, the ruin of one's hair is like a rape, since their egos are so all consuming that they think of little besides their own appearance.

The poem's protagonist, Belinda, is one of the most vain creations in English literature. A spoiled and beautiful girl, she begins the poem by awaking from a prophetic dream, the important contents of which she forgets because she opens her eyes on a love letter, which appeals to her vanity and thus causes her to dismiss more important matters. Pope's long description of Belinda's readying herself for her trip to Hampton Court likens the application of her makeup to a religious service: the "sacred rites of pride" that Belinda initiates (with the help of her lady-in-waiting, an "inferior priestess") reveal the great attention she pays to her appearance. Once at Hampton Court, Belinda flirts with "well-dressed youths" to draw attention to herself, and her skill in doing so reflects the degree to which she has perfected her coquettish arts:

> Her lively looks a sprightly mind disclose,
> Quick as her eyes, and as unfixed as those:
> Favors to none, to all she smiles extends;
> Oft she rejects, but never once offends.
> Bright as the sun, her eyes the gazers strike,
> And, like the sun, they shine on all alike.

Belinda knows she is beautiful and uses her beauty as a way to satisfy her desire to be noticed and admired.

Belinda, however, is not the poem's only proud person: the baron, who covets Belinda's beauty and aspires to possess her, has an ego to rival that of Belinda. After being defeated in a card game by Belinda—and thus humiliated at such a prominent

Topics for Further Study

- Write a short story that shows the foolishness of male or female vanity. Set your story in an imaginary land that you have made up just for this occasion.

- Compare Poepe's poem to Samuel Taylor Coleridge's *The Rime of the Ancient Mariner*, which is also extremely lengthy. Which poet's style do you think makes reading a long poem easier? Which story is a reader more likely to become absorbed in? Why?

- Do you agree with the roles of the two sexes as shown in Pope's poem? Refer to specific examples in explaining your thoughts.

social gathering—the Baron cuts Belinda's hair (or "rapes her lock") to assert himself after such a devastating defeat. After snipping and seizing the hair that was Belinda's trademark, the baron exalts his power to the sky and bombastically boasts of his strength:

> "Let wreaths of triumph now my temples twine,"
> The victor cried, "the glorious prize is mine!
> While fish in streams, or birds delight in air,
> Or in a coach and six the British Fair,
> As long as *Atalantis* shall be read,
> Or the small pillow grace a lady's bed,
> While visits shall be paid on solemn days,
> When numerous wax-lights in bright order blaze,
> While nymphs take treats, or assignations give,
> So long my honor, name, and praise shall live!"

Like Belinda, the baron is obsessed with his reputation and status—both of which he assumes will skyrocket with his possession of the lock. In a poem where egos as large as these clash, the reader is invited to examine his or her own ego to see if it ever approaches such ridiculous heights.

Beauty

While Belinda is certainly vain, she also possesses an undeniable beauty. Her very name means "beautiful" in Spanish, suggesting that she is the personification of physical attractiveness. Ariel, her guardian sylph, addresses her as "Fairest of mortals" and tells her that a troop of airy spirits hover round her, always on the lookout to address any lapses in beauty that might occur:

> "Our humbler province is to tend the Fair . . .
> To save the powder from too rude a gale,
> Nor let the imprisoned essences exhale;
> To draw fresh colors from the vernal flowers;
> To steal from rainbows e'er they drop in showers
> A brighter wash; to curl their waving hairs,
> Assist their blushes, and inspire their airs;
> Nay oft, in dreams invention we bestow,
> To change a flounce, or add a furbelow."

Belinda is so "fair" that her invisible army perfects her "powder" and "fresh colors" (makeup), "imprisoned essences" (perfume), and "waving hairs," as well as the ornaments of her dresses ("a flounce" or a "furbelow"). Only the "fairest of mortals" warrants such treatment.

When Belinda arrives at Hampton Court, Pope describes the effects of her beauty on all who see her; calling her "the rival" of the sun, he remarks that "every eye was fixed on her alone." Pope even remarks, "On her white breast a sparkling cross she wore, / Which Jews might kiss, and infidels adore," stressing, in the poem's hyperbolic fashion, the power of Belinda's physical charms. Pope also narrows the reader's focus to Belinda's locks, which epitomize her overall beauty, and its effect on the men who see it:

> Love in these labyrinths his slaves detains,
> And mighty hearts are held in slender chains.
> With hairy springes we the birds betray,
> Slight lines of hair surprise the finny prey,
> Fair tresses man's imperial race ensnare,
> And beauty draws us with a single hair.

Here, Belinda's hair—and, by extension, her beauty—is likened to a trap: as materials like hair are used to catch birds and fish (the "finny prey"), Belinda's hair is so stunning that it "ensnares" all who gaze at it. This, according to the poem, is an unalterable law of nature—a law whose truth is demonstrated in the acts of the baron, who "the bright locks admired" and who "implored / Propitious Heaven" to gain the "prize."

After Belinda's hair is "raped" by the baron, she is naturally upset and laments her newly-marred appearance. However, Pope informs her in the poem's final lines that her lock has become a constellation, forever brightening the night sky like the lock of Bernice, the wife of Ptolemy III whose hair was also enshrined in the stars. The poem's final couplet—"This Lock the Muse shall consecrate to fame, / And 'midst the stars inscribe Belinda's name"—explains that Belinda's beauty will be for-

ever admired, as true beauty has been since people first gazed at the sky. Like the stars themselves, Belinda's beauty is a source of inspiration to all who see her; and it always will be.

Style

"The Rape of the Lock" is the finest example of a mock-epic in English. The poem's 794 lines are divided into five cantos or sections. The word "canto" is derived from the Latin cantus or song; it originally signified a section of a narrative poem sung by a minstrel. "The Rape of the Lock" is written in heroic couplets, lines of iambic pentameter, rhyming aa, bb, cc, and so forth. The description "heroic" was first used in the seventeenth century because of the frequent use of such couplets in epic poems. This couplet style was first used in English by Geoffrey Chaucer in The Canterbury Tales. Pope was the greatest master of the metrical and rhetorical possibilities of the heroic couplet; he turned this concise, restrictive form into a dynamic world of ideas and characters. Pope achieved diversity of style within the couplet by changing the position of the caesura or line break. He expertly balanced the two lines, often using a slight pause at the end of the first line and a heavy stop at the end of the second line. Moreover, he frequently balanced a statement of a thesis and antithesis somewhere within each line, as in these lines from his "Essay on Criticism:"

> Careless of censure, nor too fond of fame; Still pleased to praise, yet not afraid to blame; Averse alike to flatter, or offend; Not free from faults, nor yet too vain to mend.

The caesura moves around within each line, sometimes coming after four syllables and sometimes after seven. Moreover, Pope balances a main idea or thesis within each line with a statement of its opposite or antithesis. He displays great ingenuity and wit in his skillful compression of ideas. The structure of "The Rape of the Lock" roughly corresponds to that of many epics: invocation to a muse (Canto I), conference of the protective gods (Canto II), games and epic banquet (Canto III), the journey into the underworld (Canto IV), and heroic battle and climax (Canto V). Pope both satirizes and honors the elevated style of epic poetry and many of its conventions such as a formal statement of theme, division into cantos, grandiose speeches, challenges, boasts, description of warriors' battle equipment, warfare, epic similes, and supernatural elements. However, the poem ridicules the silly social manners of the aristocracy and deflates the elevated sense of importance in the affairs of wealthy ladies and gentlemen. Yet, the poem also displays some fondness for the grace and beauty of that world. Pope enjoys all the ivory and tortoise shell, cosmetics and diamonds, expensive furniture, silver coffee service, fancy china, and light conversation—this was the world in which he moved attempting to find patronage for his poetry.

Historical Context

The eighteenth century is alternatively known as "The Enlightenment" or "The Age of Reason," two labels indicative of the era and the personality of the time. In the broadest sense, the term *eighteenth-century literature* encompasses writing from the Restoration of Charles II in 1660 to the publication of Wordsworth and Coleridge's collection of Romantic poems, *Lyrical Ballads,* in 1798. Of course, literary periods overlap, and new styles and attitudes do not arrive or disappear as with the flip of a switch. However, one can gain a general understanding of eighteenth-century literary forms and content by examining the ways in which historical events shaped the minds of the writers living through them, as well as reviewing the subjects of some of the era's most notable books.

The seventeenth century saw the outbreak of a terrible civil war, in which Puritan Parliamentary forces clashed with Royalist supporters of King Charles I. Eventually, the Puritans, led by Oliver Cromwell, prevailed, and in 1649 Charles I was tried and beheaded by the victors. A period known as the Interregnum began, where Cromwell led the country as Lord Protector until his death in 1658, when his son, Richard, assumed the title—only to abdicate and set the scene for more national chaos. Eventually, through a series of negotiations, Charles II—the former king's son—was brought out of hiding and returned to London, where the monarchy was restored in 1660. England now yearned for an era of lasting peace, which it mostly enjoyed, although peace was deterred by the outbreak of the bubonic plague in 1665 and the Great Fire of London, which occurred in 1666. Civil unrest and war, therefore, drove the English mind to search for ways in which to establish an ordered understanding of the world, and this search was fueled by the 1662 formation of the Royal Society,

an organization of scientists working to share their findings with each other.

As scientists struggled to cultivate a view of the world based on reason rather than superstition, authors of the time likewise sought to explore their world from an intellectual rather than emotional stance. In 1660, John Locke published his *Essay Concerning Human Understanding,* a philosophical work exploring (among other things) the ways in which the five senses apprehend the world and thereby form one's mind. The year 1726 saw the publication of Jonathan Swift's *Gulliver's Travels,* a satiric look at the ways in which mankind abuses his reasonable faculties. In 1755, Samuel Johnson completed what could be called the most representative eighteenth-century work: his *Dictionary of the English Language.* This first, exhaustive English dictionary reflects the Enlightenment desire for order, for a dictionary's primary purpose is to fix the language at a given point in time. Even recreation was viewed as an orderly activity, as seen in the publication in 1760 of Hoyle's *Rules for Whist and Other Popular Card Games.* Other notable monuments to reason published in this era include the first edition of the *Encyclopedia Britannica* (1768), Goldsmith's *History of the Earth and Animated Nature* (1774), Burke's *Reflections of the Revolution in France* (1760), and Gibbon's *Decline and Fall of the Roman Empire* (1776).

Part of the era's love of reason manifested itself in a renewed interest in heralded classical authors, resulting in the era sometimes being called the Neoclassical Age. Homer's *Iliad* (composed circa 750–650 B.C.) was viewed as the pinnacle of poetry, and when Pope began his translation of this epic in 1715 (completed in 1720), he guaranteed himself financial stability. Because of the great number of readers familiar with Homer's epic, Pope was able to parody it in both "The Rape of the Lock" (1714) and "The Dunciad" (1728). Like many poets of his day, Pope felt that his work, in part, should illuminate the tendencies of humanity as a whole; in this sense, art was thought to be a kind of science, which examined the world as intensely as the Royal Society. Pope's satiric style, keen wit, lofty diction, and strict meter are all qualities associated with Enlightenment poets; his stature as a public figure—rather than a solitary, "tortured" artist—is also indicative of the way writers were perceived by the reading public. However, the publication (and success of) Wordsworth and Coleridge's *Lyrical Ballads* in 1798 took poetry in a new direction, away from the reason-based liter-

Compare & Contrast

- **1687:** Sir Isaac Newton publishes his *Philosophiae Naturalis Principia Mathematica (The Mathematical Principles of Natural Philosophy)*, the revolutionary book containing his work on gravity. The book marks the Enlightenment as a time of great scientific progress.

  1859: Charles Darwin publishes his *Origin of Species*, the work containing his theory of natural selection.

  1921: Albert Einstein publishes *The Meaning of Relativity* in which he explores the workings of the space-time continuum. His mathematical formula for relativity is added to the book in 1950.

- **1755:** Samuel Johnson finishes his monumental *Dictionary of the English Language*, printed in two large folio volumes.

  1884: The *Oxford English Dictionary*, containing the history of every word in the English language, begins publication, which will be complete in 1928.

  1986: The final supplement to the *Oxford English Dictionary* is published.

  Today: The *Oxford English Dictionary* is available on CD-ROM.

- **1720:** Pope publishes the final books of his translation of Homer's *Iliad*, which proves to be very successful. His translation is written in rhyming (or "heroic") couplets of iambic pentameter.

  1990: After a period of years in which the general reading public's interest in Homer has declined, Robert Fagles, a professor at Princeton University, publishes his translation of the *Iliad* to rave reviews and surprisingly high sales. Fagles' translation is written in a looser meter than Pope's.

---

ature of the Enlightenment and into the emotionally charged Romantic era.

Critical Overview

The criticism on a major author like Alexander Pope is so rich that a brief survey cannot adequately account for the diversity and breadth of analysis. However, the following three critics (one each from the eighteenth, nineteenth, and twentieth centuries) agree on Pope's enormous achievement. Samuel Johnson, one of Pope's contemporaries, writes in "Pope" in his *Lives of the English Poets* that "The Rape of the Lock" is "the most attractive of all ludicrous compositions," in which "new things are made familiar, and familiar things made new." According to Johnson, "The Rape of the Lock" exhibits to a high degree the two most engaging powers of an author. Johnson says Pope creates a race of imaginary creatures never witnessed before and presents them in a style in perfect accord with his purpose. Although Johnson says the poem's subject is "below the common incidents in common life," he praises Pope's wit and imagination in carrying off such an excellently silly composition. William Hazlitt wrote in "On Dryden and Pope" in his *Lectures on the English Poets and the English Comic Writers* that he considered "The Rape of the Lock" to be "the most exquisite specimen of filigree work ever invented." Hazlitt praises Pope's ability to lend a decorous beauty to every element in the poem from characters to props to dialogue and description. Hazlitt writes that "a toilette is described with the solemnity of an altar raised to the Goddess of Vanity, and the history of a silver bodkin [a pin] is given with all the pomp of heraldry." According to Hazlitt, the true achievement of the poem is its ability to balance concealed irony and apparent seriousness. Great things are made trivial and trivial things elevated to ridiculous heights, leaving the reader dazzled and uncertain as to whether he or she should laugh or cry. A more recent evaluation by Stanley Edgar Hyman in "English Romanticism" in *Poetry and Criticism: Four Revolutions in Literary Taste* demonstrates several ways of interpreting "The Rape of the Lock." In general, Hyman says it would be a mistake to look for hidden political messages, Marxist yearning for revolution, or mythological renderings of Belinda as the corn maiden "raped" by the Baron in a fertility ritual. However, Hyman goes on to find exactly these types of hidden meanings in the poem because it is so rich and allusive. Hyman believes that perhaps critics have been too easygoing in their reading of the poem, not finding the hidden messages that Pope carefully left behind. Perhaps most appealing to Hyman are the hidden sexual messages: "The poem is one vast comic symbolic defloration. . . . 'Lock' is a pun on Freud's lock that all keys fit. . . . Its rape by the baron is a sex act." Hyman also finds ample evidence for political and mythological interpretive possibilities. "The Rape of the Lock" seems capable of supporting many different kinds of readings.

Criticism

Daniel Moran

Moran is a secondary-school teacher of English and American literature and has contributed to Drama for Students *and* Poetry for Students. *In the following essay, Moran examines the ways in which Pope manipulates the reader's reactions to Belinda's vanity.*

> Satire is a sort of glass, wherein beholders do generally discover everybody's face but their own.
> —Jonathan Swift

The ease with which many readers of "The Rape of the Lock" cultivate a sense of superiority toward Belinda could cause one to assume that such a reaction is both solicited and warranted by Pope. "This silly girl," a reader may invariably argue, "is a fool. Her concerns over her appearance, and her overblown reaction to losing her hair mark her as one of literature's most shallow characters." One may argue that Pope is satirizing people like her—the vain, the pompous, the self-absorbed—and stand correct, for if (according to Hamlet) frailty is the name of woman, then vanity is surely the name of Belinda. But this understandable attitude toward her is more of a critical quick-fix than what Pope actually asks readers to consider, for if the main thrust of the poem is to attack Belinda's lack of substance, surely a poet as deft as Pope could have

done so in less than five cantos. A more satisfying reading of the poem examines the ways in which the poem (to again quote Hamlet) "holds a mirror up to nature." In other words, it is easy to scorn Belinda; but is that all Pope is asking the reader to do? Swift's description of satire, cited above, likens it to a mirror in which one sees the faults of others, but never (because of vanity) those of him or herself; the problem lies not in the glass, but in the gazers. Readers of satire often feel that the joke is on somebody else; but a careful examination of "The Rape of the Lock" reveals that it works in much the same way as Swift's mirror, and ultimately asks the reader if he or she can see his or her own figurative face in Belinda's. In other words, to dismiss Belinda as an egoist and decide that the poem satirizes people like her only accounts for part of the poem's meaning. Ultimately, the poem suggests that there is something worthwhile about Belinda, after all; and that she does possess something, the force of which no reader can deny. The poem works as Swift's satirical glass, gently mocking those who gaze into it and forcing them to see themselves as well as the "Belindas" of the world.

To understand fully how Pope's satiric glass operates, one must first examine the ways in which Pope manipulates the reader's reaction to Belinda and her world. Every work of art presupposes its own world with its own values, assumptions, and laws; and the world of "The Rape of the Lock" is initially one where "normal" human attitudes toward beauty and love are reversed. The opening lines feature three seemingly unanswerable questions:

> Say what strange motive, Goddess! could compel
> A well-bred lord to assault a gentle belle?
> Oh, say what stranger cause, yet unexplored,
> Could make a gentle belle reject a lord?
> In tasks so bold can little men engage,
> And in soft bosoms dwell such mighty rage?

The first question here is a logical one, but the second seems ridiculous: the speaker finds the rejection of a lord more puzzling than the lord's physical assault of a belle. Thus the reader is introduced to the dominant characteristic of the poem's world: it is a place where assault is curious, but rejection is almost unexplainable; and social graces are more important than one's real worth as a human being. This inversion of "normal" assumptions marks the milieu in which Belinda thrives, and Pope is never subtle about this point. His description of Belinda's toilet is a clear example of the way in which Pope invites his reader to laugh at his heroine:

And now, unveiled, the toilet stands displayed,
Each silver vase in mystic order laid.
First, robed in white, the nymph intent adores,
With head uncovered, the cosmetic powers.
A heavenly image in the glass appears;
To that she beds, to that her eyes she rears.
The inferior priestess, at her altar's side,
Trembling begins the sacred rites of Pride.

The emphasis on Belinda's physical vanity (the table where she applies her makeup) suggests a religious devotion to her emotional vanity: words like "mystic order," "robed in white," "powers," "heavenly," "priestess," "trembling," and "sacred rites" all combine to exaggerate the importance Belinda places on her appearance. Her beauty is her religion, and who cannot but laugh at a person so devoted to something so ephemeral and (as the adage goes) skin-deep? "Yes, I care about how I look," the sensible reader says. "But *she* is ridiculous!" Indeed, she is, and the description of her cosmetics' effects again stresses Belinda's lack of depth: her makeup "awakens every grace" by making a "purer blush arise" and "keener lightnings quicken in her eye." Paradoxically, only the addition of something artificial brings "purity" and "grace" to her appearance, as the world of the poem is one in which *seeming* is more important than substance. At this point, the reader sees only the faces of the vain in Pope's satirical mirror.

After thus establishing Belinda's vanity (and soliciting the reader's amused disapproval of it), Pope throws Belinda into Hampton Court, where the inversion of "normal" values is further stressed and established as a rule:

Here Britain's statesmen oft the fall foredoom
Of foreign tyrants and of nymphs at home;
Here thou, great Anna! whom three realms obey,
Does sometimes counsel take—and sometimes tea.

As he does throughout the poem, Pope here employs a *zeugma,* a figure of speech where unlike things are yoked together with a single verb for comedic effect: thus, the problem of "Foreign tyrants" is as terrible as "nymphs at home," and Queen Anne's "counsel" is as important as her "tea." In the world of the poem, local scandal is on a par with international upheaval, in keeping with the overall idea that the seemingly trivial parts of life (beauty, hair) are here regarded as monumental. Pope often employs a zeugma to reinforce the degree to which the values of those in the poem's world are off-kilter. For example, when Ariel runs through the possibilities of what the omen might portend, he considers:

Whether the nymph shall break Diana's law,
Or some frail china jar receive a flaw,

> *In other words, to dismiss Belinda as an egoist and decide that the poem satirizes people like her only accounts for part of the poem's meaning."*

Or stain her honor or her new brocade,
Forget her prayers, or miss a masquerade,
Or lose her heart, or necklace, at a ball;
Or whether Heaven has doomed that Shock must
    fall.

Belinda's losing her virginity ("Diana's law") is on a par with a "frail china jar"; her "new brocade" needs to be defended as thoroughly as her "honor"; forgetting "prayers" is as sinful as forgetting a "masquerade"; her "heart" and "necklace" carry equal weight, as does the fate of Shock, her lapdog. The entire poem hinges on these kinds of comparisons—in this world, losing one's hair elicits reactions like one would find in a poem about an actual rape. This is why, after the baron uses the "fatal engine" to cut the lock, he boasts of his conquest in language that only the most innocent reader could fail to read as smacking of masculine sexual triumph:

What Time would spare, from Steel receives its
    date,
And monuments, like men, submit to fate!
Steel could the labors of the Gods destroy,
And strike to dust the imperial towers of Troy;
Steel could the works of mortal pride confound,
And hew triumphal arches to the ground.
What wonder then, fair nymph! thy hairs should
    feel,
The conquering force of unresisted Steel?"

These words belong more in the mouth of a theatrical Roman soldier, fresh from the ravishing of a virtuous virgin, than that of a spiteful playboy. Of course, that is part of Pope's design: as the words of the title are incongruous and zeugmatic so are the characters' motives and reactions. Both the baron and Belinda respond to the rape with language more suited to an actual act of violence and terror than the cutting of one's hair. Belinda's reaction to her rape sounds like the one Thomas Hardy's Tess Durbeyfield would make almost two-

What Do I Read Next?

- Pope's "An Essay on Criticism" (1711) is a long poem in which he prescribes his rules for good poetry and attacks a number of poetic clichés.

- Like "The Rape of the Lock," Pope's "An Epistle to Dr. Arbuthnot" (1735) is a satirical work; this time, Pope's targets are the amateur poets who constantly seek his approval.

- One of Pope's four *Moral Essays* (1735) is subtitled "Of the Characters of Women;" this poem is an interesting companion piece to "The Rape of the Lock" in the ways that it treats what Pope saw as the concerns and personalities of women.

- Jonathan Swift's poem "The Progress of Beauty" (1719), like "The Rape of the Lock," examines the ways in which cosmetics altar a woman's appearance.

- The American novelist Henry James' second novel, *Roderick Hudson* (1875), concerns a sculptor who, like Pope's baron, is haunted by the beauty of a striking woman.

- Samuel Johnson's series of essays known as *The Rambler* addresses a number of topics; his "Rambler 155" (1751) examines the ways in which one's own vanity prevents him or her from taking advice. This is a good essay to read after considering Clarissa's speech about "good sense."

---

hundred years later, after her literal rape by Alec D'Urberville:

> Happy! ah, ten times happy had I been,
> If Hampton Court these eyes had never seen!
> Yet am I not the first mistaken maid,
> By love of courts to numerous ills betrayed.

But any pity one could have for Belinda is immediately undercut by the fact that she never denies her own beauty—the only thing she seems to have learned is that Hampton Court is a rough place, not that one's appearance is hardly worthy of all this trouble. She describes herself as a vic-

tim of her own beauty, one too perfect for the imperfect world in which her admirers live. So the reader presses on, feeling superior to the superficial Belinda and confident that he or she can laugh at her, rather than with her. As the reader gazes into the glass of satire, he or she still sees only the face of Belinda.

The reader's sense of superiority is heightened when he or she reads the speech of Clarissa in Canto V. Leaping out of the poem as the apparent voice of reason, she admonishes the zeugmatic values of those around her and urges Belinda to consider her virtue instead of her vanity:

> How vain are all these glories, all our pains,
> Unless good sense preserve what beauty gains;
> That men may say when we the front box grace,
> "Behold the first in virtue as in face!" . . .
> Beauties in vain their pretty eyes may roll;
> Charms strike the sight, but merit wins the soul.

This is exactly the kind of "literary moral pill" that many readers like to swallow: it tells the reader what he or she already suspects while simultaneously patting him or her on the back for having suspected it in the first place. It offers sound advice: beauty and charms only please one's senses, but a person's worth is much more important. The inversion of values that has characterized the poem seems momentarily halted, as if Pope is calling a time out before wrapping things up.

However, the question remains: Who is really listening to these words of sense? Surely not Belinda or any of the other characters, who begin their final melee of dirty looks and slanderous accusations without showing any signs of heeding Clarissa's advice. But also deaf to Clarissa's advice is Pope himself, who transforms the lock into a constellation, destined to hover in the heavens forever. The poem's last ten lines, where Pope speaks directly to his heroine, contain the poem's greatest surprise and expand the breadth of Pope's satire:

> Then cease, bright nymph! to mourn thy ravished
>   hair,
> Which adds new glory to the shining sphere!
> Not all the tresses that fair head can boast,
> Shall draw such envy as the Lock you lost.
> For, after all the murders of your eye,
> When, after millions slain, yourself shall die:
> When those fair suns shall set, as set they must,
> And all those tresses shall be laid in dust,
> This Lock the Muse shall consecrate to fame,
> And 'midst the stars inscribe Belinda's name.

These lines force the reader to reevaluate his or her attitude toward Belinda. Pope's attitude toward her seems very much like the reader's: he placates her by appealing to her vanity, telling her that her lock will forever "draw such envy"; she is, in effect, immortalized. However, the question remains of why, if Belinda is so superficial, she is rewarded at the end of the poem with her own constellation? The answer is simple: she is beautiful. Despite what readers may have been taught by their parents and teachers about a person's looks (and locks) being unimportant, despite the reader's mounting his or her high horse throughout the poem, despite Clarissa's sage advice, and despite even Pope's own attempts to portray her as the most shallow of coquettes, Belinda does possess something—like the stars—that is nonetheless inspiring. Merit may "win the soul" (as Clarissa remarks), but beauty ignites it. Only the insensible would deny the powers of beauty, and only the reader looking for an easy moral could read Pope's poem and feel wholly superior to Belinda at its end. Scorning Belinda is effortless, but turning Swift's glass of satire to the readers' own faces—and thus seeing how Belinda's reward is one that cannot be denied her—demands more from a reader solely interested in seeing only Belinda's face in the satirical glass. Part of the overall joke therefore lies in the fact that, because of the reader's own vanity, he or she may have a difficult time seeing him or herself in Belinda. She may be unbearably vain, but only slightly more so than other people—for who will deny that he or she is susceptible to the powers of beauty, whether in the night sky or the face of a fellow human being? Gazing into Swift's mirror and finding other people ridiculous only serves to assuage the very egos that readers might fault Belinda for possessing. Rather, everyone, in a sense, is a "Belinda": a lover of beauty who finds it inspiring and fascinating. If not, why would anyone spend time gazing at the *Mona Lisa,* admiring Michelangelo's *David,* listening to Mozart's symphonies, or reading poems as wonderfully crafted as Pope's? Everyone knows they are supposed to live by Clarissa's words, and, much of the time, they do. But it is impossible to deny that readers are also entranced by the very beauty that they say is so trivial when reading the poem.

At the end of George Orwell's *1984,* Winston Smith is finally brainwashed into submission by the Totalitarian Party; the famous last sentences read, "He had won the victory over himself. He loved Big Brother." Like Winston, Pope's reader may try to rebel against the great concern for beauty shared by the characters—but, in the final analysis, he or she must, like Winston, submit to an undeniable power. Readers do love Belinda, precisely for the

> *Part of the poem's charm, as well as its richness and complexity, lies in the fact that this literary form creates a variety of levels of meaning, frequently challenging the reader's expectations."*

very things they claim to be unimportant as they read the poem. Only after finishing it and stepping back do they see themselves in Swift's glass. "The Rape of the Lock" is therefore not only a satire of people like Belinda, but also of those who would deny the power of her beauty.

Source: Daniel Moran, Critical Essay on "The Rape of the Lock," in *Poetry for Students,* The Gale Group, 2001.

Mary Mahony

Mahony is an English instructor at Wayne County Community College in Detroit, Michigan. In the following essay, she discusses Pope's use of the mock-epic form to create both the humor and the multiple levels of meaning in Pope's poem.

In "The Rape of the Lock," Pope uses the mock epic to present a multi-layered exploration of the foibles of the genteel society of the eighteenth century in a manner that is both satiric and sympathetic. Part of the poem's charm, as well as its richness and complexity, lies in the fact that this literary form creates a variety of levels of meaning, frequently challenging the reader's expectations. Symbols are open to multiple interpretations; words can be seen as innocent or shocking. Issues of importance and triviality are often confused. The title itself provides a clear illustration of this technique as it pairs the harsh, sexually violent connotations of the word *rape* with the delicate use of *lock* to describe the pillaged curl. This word use engages both critics and casual readers in an exploration for meaning. Most critics believe that the exaggeration implicit in the title phrase indicates the extreme foolishness of making such ado about nothing. A few, however, take the rape more seriously, feeling that the poem ultimately admits, given the rules of the society in which it is set, that a violation has actually occurred. "The Rape of the Lock" is filled with a multitude of such contrasts that keep critics debating still.

Pope employs this mock-heroic style to satirically recount the social turmoil that occurred when Lord Petre impulsively snipped off a lock of Arabella Fermor's hair, creating hostility between their two families. The genre seems ideally suited to the topic, since it combines the elegant language and tone of the literary epic with subjects that are more suitable for satire than seriousness. To fully appreciate Pope's handling of this style, however, it is necessary to review some of the history and characteristics of epic poetry. The epic poem has a long tradition in literature. These works recount events of national or historic importance, starring heroes and gods. They employ skillfully polished language and images, enhancing a dramatic presentation of conflicts involving serious moral issues. Homer's classic narratives of the Trojan War and its aftermath, the *Iliad* and the *Odyssey,* are perhaps best known to the modern reader. However, during the seventeenth and eighteenth centuries, the epic form was a mainstay of literature. Homer's classics, along with other works such as Virgil's *Aeneid* and John Milton's *Paradise Lost,* were widely read and analyzed. In fact, since the Renaissance, literary theorists such as Le Bossu, whose work Pope greatly admired, had attempted to codify rules for the epic form. While Pope himself challenged some aspects of the rigid application of a code to the epic form, certain key elements are standard in most epic literature. The mock epic form adapts many of the standard characters and situations of these traditional narratives and presents them in a tone and style that are seemingly inappropriate for such trivial matters. Much of the allure of "The Rape of the Lock" occurs as the epic machinery is deflated from its original stature in a heroic-comical style, presenting contrasts that underscore the poem's humor. These contrasts also endow the work with its various levels of complexity and meaning.

The first epic convention that appears is the "Invocation to the Muse." In the opening six lines of Canto I, Pope acknowledges his muse and friend, John Caryll, who requested that he create a work that might defuse the animosity between the two families by allowing them to see the humor in the incident. This invocation carefully imitates the elevated style of the traditional epic. It also sets up

the poem's theme or proposition, involving the battle between the sexes rather than a war between nations. Readers familiar with the form will immediately appreciate the contrast between style and subject since the theme of sexual bantering is traditionally the province of comedy. Because Pope operates on multiple levels, however, the reader should recognize that the introduction does include a serious purpose, since the poem is, in actuality, an attempt to ameliorate a dispute.

Epics center around a hero or heroes. These are usually warriors who embody a whole series of masculine values: bravery, honor, and wisdom. When Pope introduces the poem's "hero," however, convention is again reversed. Instead of the traditional male champion, the reader meets a female, Belinda, who is still asleep in bed, indulging in a dream. The spirit in this dream first flatters Belinda then tells her of other spirits that surround her. His message ends, however, with a warning:

> I saw, alas! some dread event impend,
> Ere to the main this morning sun descend . . .
> This to disclose is all thy guardian can:
> Beware of all, but most beware of man.

This section illustrates Pope's use of the elevated language of the epic style. It also includes visions, guardian spirits, cryptic warnings—all frequent elements of epic form. The humorous contrast centers around the substitution of the trivial (the dreadful event that is foretold is, after all, only the loss of a piece of hair) for the significant, such as warnings of losses in battle, of betrayal, of the wrath of the gods. Ironically, however, the final warning proves genuine. Belinda is right to beware of man. Several critics also point out the relationship between this incident and Eve's dream in Milton's epic *Paradise Lost.* Like Belinda, Eve is first flattered, then warned in a dream of the danger that lies ahead of her. Both women, of course, ignore the warnings and succumb to their fate. The eighteenth-century reader would recognize an additional level of irony in the juxtaposition of these two falls: the banishment from Paradise and the loss of a lock of hair.

The final lines of Canto I introduce another epic convention. This type of literature frequently dwells on the preparation for battle as the warrior dons both his armor and his virtue. In a parody of these martial displays, Pope presents Belinda's preparation for her foray into the war between the sexes. While the description is filled with ordinary feminine devices such as combs, pins, puffs, and powder, Pope greatly enhances the importance of a simple make-up session. First, he elevates the cosmetics themselves:

> This casket India's glowing gems unlocks
> And all Arabia breathes from yonder box.
> The tortoise here and elephant unite,
> Transformed to combs, the speckled and the white.

In addition, he uses military images to describe Belinda as she dons her beauty to enter the fray: "Now awful Beauty puts on all its arms." Critics differ in their interpretation of this section. Some find the satire caused by the feminization of the warrior's rituals cruelly mocking of Belinda and therefore of women, believing that the poem has a misogynistic undertone. Others, however, believe that in spite of the irony, Pope demonstrates an admiration for Belinda's beauty, an acceptance of her right to do all she can to win the admiration of those who surround her. They feel the poem critiques the values of the society itself, rather than one individual. Thus while Canto II may indicate that Belinda is somewhat shallow, as she smiles graciously on "all alike," it is society that is truly guilty because it allows itself to be blinded to any faults by her beauty: "If to her share some female errors fall, / Look on her face and you'll forget 'em all."

Canto II includes other lines that also deal with the artificial values of this society. In the traditional epic, the warrior is the representative of the noblest ideal of the society; if he is defeated, the entire society is likely to fall. In contrast to this, lines 105–110 list some possible disasters in eighteenth-century society:

> Whether some nymph shall break Diana's law,
> Or some frail china jar receive a flaw,
> Or stain her honor or her new brocade,
> Forget her prayers, or miss a masquerade,
> Or lose her heart, or necklace, at a ball:
> Or whether Heaven has doomed that Shock must
>   fall.

Not only do these "disasters" fall short of the enormous consequences of a true epic, the list indicates a total inability to distinguish the trivial from the meaningful. Thus losing virginity is paired with getting a stain on a new dress.

One of the most ingenious reversals of traditional epic form comes in Canto III where the traditional battle is replaced by a game of cards. Military imagery abounds throughout this section. Belinda's opponents are referred to as "adventurous knights." She is presented as a leader of a powerful army: not only do her spirit guardians descend to assist her, but the cards themselves are given personalities. In true epic fashion, the game rages back and forth, with Belinda winning the early skir-

mishes and eventually the game itself. Pope's detailed description of each separate trick is both humorous and suspenseful. However, it proves only a prelude to the real battle in the Canto, the Baron's assault on Belinda's hair. Pope's description of that momentous snip takes eight extravagantly dramatic lines as the scissors slowly open, then close on both the lock and a Sylph who gallantly tried to intervene. Belinda's reaction is immediate, loud, and out of proportion. Lines 445–450 compare her grief to the shrieks that occur "when husband, or when lapdogs breathe their last." The Canto ends with a reference to Troy, a city that seemed—like Belinda—invincible, until deceit and trickery brought the Greeks inside the city's walls. Given the fact that even mighty Troy could be destroyed, the speaker states it is no wonder that Belinda herself should fall victim to the "conquering force of unresisted Steel." Pope blends the serious and comic elements so skillfully throughout this Canto that, although the game of cards is merely a humorous counterfeit of a true epic battle, it is engaging in its own right. The overblown language of the final sections mocks the incident, the reaction, and the values of the society, yet, to many critics, the overall drama of the Canto makes Belinda, the ultimate loser in the skirmish, a figure who is not entirely unsympathetic.

The epic element in Canto IV involves a descent into the underworld that Pope vividly portrays as a gloomy cave where ill-nature and affectation serve the Goddess Spleen. The word *spleen* was open to multiple interpretations for the eighteenth-century reader, including anger, melancholy, and various sexual and emotional problems that plagued women. In this cave of "strange phantoms" and "expiring maids," the gnome Umbriel successfully begs the Goddess to "touch Belinda with chagrin." As a result, her outrage reaches new heights. Belinda curses the entire day in a long speech, whose final lines contain an example of the sexual double entendres that occur throughout the poem: "Oh, hadst thou, cruel! been content to seize / Hairs less in sight, or any hairs but these." While the phrase may be interpreted as innocent (if poorly phrased) regret, it seems more likely that Belinda would rather lose her virginity than mar her beauty.

Canto V recreates the epic form in a speech by Clarissa who advocates common sense and good humor, concluding that "merit wins the soul." Clarissa's advice is clearly adapted from Sarpedon's noble speech in Book XII of the *Iliad*. Many critics feel it provides the poem's true moral. While

> *This low style to discuss high things is an interesting reversal of the usual practice in the rest of the poem, where a very elevated style, full of heroic and mythic allusions, is used to discuss low things, like a card game or Belinda putting on her make-up."*

the final Canto does not resolve the conflict, Pope's narrative concludes with divine intervention, as the lock ascends to the sky, thus permanently establishing Belinda's role in the firmament.

Pope's portrait of Belinda and her world is remarkably rich and detailed. His use of the mock-epic form invites the reader to explore this world from different perspectives since "The Rape of the Lock" contains a maze of meanings and images. Each journey through the poem can provide new and unexpected revelations.

Source: Mary Mahony, Critical Essay on "The Rape of the Lock," in *Poetry for Students,* The Gale Group, 2001.

Sheldon Goldfarb

Goldfarb has a Ph.D. in English and has published two books on the Victorian author William Makepeace Thackeray. In the following essay, he discusses Clarissa's speech in Pope's poem.

Clarissa's speech stands out in Pope's "Rape of the Lock." As John Trimble puts it, in his essay "Clarissa's Role in 'The Rape of the Lock,'" Clarissa sounds like a grown-up talking to children. Belinda and the other characters in the poem are mostly interested in dancing, flirting, putting on make-up, playing cards, and stealing a lock of hair. Clarissa, in contrast, talks of serious things: aging, disease, and death. For this reason, critics have sometimes taken her for Pope's mouthpiece, as the voice of seriousness in the midst of frivolity. There is even encouragement to do this in a note appended to Clarissa's speech. This note, which first ap-

peared in the 1751 edition of the poem after Pope's death, says that Clarissa was a new character introduced in later editions to "open up more clearly the Moral of the Poem. . . ."

Following the suggestion of the 1751 editor, most critics have accepted the note as being written by Pope, but it is not clear that it was. Even if it was, it is not clear that people should take it seriously: Pope was a master of irony, after all. And even if people are to take the note seriously, what exactly does it mean? That people are to accept Clarissa's attitude to life: that she speaks the moral directly? Or does it perhaps mean something a little more complicated? Perhaps Clarissa opens the moral in spite of herself, revealing something she herself does not understand.

Some critics do simply accept Clarissa's view as being Pope's own. Reuben Brower, in his essay "Am'rous Causes," sees her as "the voice of common sense in the midst of much ado about nothing." Aubrey Williams, in his essay "The 'Fall' of China and 'The Rape of the Lock,'" speaks of "the fundamental validity of Clarissa's attitude."

In contrast, other critics point out that the supposedly virtuous Clarissa who speaks such apparent good sense in Canto V is the same character who earlier helped the baron cut off Belinda's lock. John Trimble sees her speech as her means of continuing a jealous attack on Belinda. Robin Grove, in *The Art of Alexander Pope,* speaks of her "high-minded insincerity." Reuben Brower notes that though she talks of serious things, Clarissa's language is low and common, bordering on burlesque.

This low style to discuss high things is an interesting reversal of the usual practice in the rest of the poem, where a very elevated style, full of heroic and mythic allusions, is used to discuss low things, like a card game or Belinda putting on her make-up. The mock-heroism in the rest of the poem creates a double vision of Belinda's world: the contrast with true heroism and with religion, the fact that Belinda keeps her Bibles with her make-up, and the fact that glittering appearance and reputation matter more in Belinda's world than does true virtue—all these things suggest that her world is superficial and trivial. And yet, as critics such as Cleanth Brooks and J. S. Cunningham have noted, despite the mockery of Belinda's world, there is admiration for it in Pope's poem. Pope makes this world seem attractive, charming, and fun.

But long before Clarissa raises more serious matters in Canto V, Pope lets people know that there is a sterner world beyond Belinda's, a world where "wretches hang that jury-men may dine," an uglier, unfair world, in other words. The baron, in a way, is part of that uglier world. Although he moves in the same circles as Belinda, he functions as something of an intruder or even a marauder. In Belinda's world, there is empty but charming flirtation. She is constantly smiling yet rejecting—but rejecting without giving offence. The baron, however, gives great offence, by cutting off Belinda's lock of hair. In doing so, he breaks the spell surrounding Belinda's world and introduces an ugly note, marked by such words as "force" and "fraud," "ravish" and "betray." This is the ugly outside world breaking into Belinda's fashionable one, as it is no doubt bound to do. One can't live forever in a world of charming glitter: that is one of the points of Clarissa's speech. Smallpox will strike, she says, or old age: "frail beauty must decay," she explains, and even the most charming of locks will turn to grey.

To this extent Clarissa does indeed talk sense. She is quite correct to point out the realities of life (and death). And yet she combines this accurate perception with an approach to life that is not particularly inspiring or heroic. Not only is her language low, as in such phrases as "trust me, dear!" but when examined closely, her message seems rather limited.

At first it seems that Clarissa is criticizing the emptiness of such things as the attentions that "white-glov'd Beaus" pay to beautiful young women. "How vain are all these glories," she says. If one stopped stopped reading there, Clarissa might seem to be advocating a moralistic rejection of the whole notion of women seeking to win men. But in fact Clarissa is not telling Belinda and others to give up the pursuit of men; she is saying she has a better way to pursue them. If people finish the rest of her sentence about the vanity of pursuing men, they find that she is merely saying that it is vain to pursue them if one has no means of holding onto them, and though beauty may attract, only good sense can hold onto what has been attracted:

> How vain are all these glories, all our pains,
> Unless good sense preserve what beauty gains

Clarissa ends up recommending good sense, good humour, and virtue, not as ends in themselves but as ways to hold onto men. It is instructive to compare what she says with what Pope wrote to the real Belinda (Arabella Fermor) when she got married. As reported by Valerie Rumbold, in *Women's Place in Pope's World*, Pope told Arabella that he was sure she would become "a great many better things than a fine Lady; such as an excellent wife, a faithful friend, a tender parent, and at last as a consequence of them all, a saint in heaven."

Pope based Clarissa's speech on his own translation of a heroic speech by Sarpedon in Homer's *Iliad*. Sarpedon spoke of pursuing virtue as an end in itself; Clarissa, sounding much less heroic, speaks of pursuing virtue as a means to hold on to men. One might object that Clarissa cannot possibly match Sarpedon's heroism or virtue because she lives in a non-heroic world; but in his letter to Arabella, Pope showed how one could talk heroically even on a non-heroic scale. Pope could have had Clarissa tell Belinda to look to such serious things as being a good wife and mother; instead, he has her advocate a better way to hold on to a man.

The result is that it is hard to take Clarissa seriously. And yet her speech does help open the moral, though not in the way she intends. Clarissa reminds people that there is a cruel world out there, one they have had glimpses of already: a world of death and decay. Clarissa also warns people that dancing and dressing up will not stave off this death and decay. The real world will eventually destroy the beautiful fantasy world in which Belinda moves, just as the baron destroys the beautiful arrangement of her hair. Clarissa's conclusion, based on these perceptions, is that one should give up the fantasy world and be virtuous, win a man you can hold onto, and settle down as a good housewife.

But is this what Pope is recommending? "The Rape of the Lock," for all its mockery of Belinda's world, essentially celebrates that world. The poem as a whole does not seem in accord with what Clarissa recommends; rather than give up Belinda's glittering world, the poem encourages people to enjoy it and indulge themselves in it. Clarissa may indeed be the grown-up in the poem, but there are pleasures in being a child, and the poem celebrates those.

The point seems to be, and this emerges in part because of Clarissa's speech, that people should value Belinda's world precisely because it is so fragile, because it is transient, because all its charms will eventually decay. Critics like Cleanth Brooks and Aubrey Williams have noted the depiction of fragile China jars in the poem and have suggested that one should see a comparison between the fragile jars and Belinda's chastity, which, in Williams' words, "is somehow rendered more precious . . . by recognition of how easily it can be marred or shattered." This comparison should perhaps be extended to Belinda's whole world: the beau monde as a whole is like a fragile China jar, to be valued all the more for its fragility.

It is instructive to note that Clarissa does not get the last word in the poem. Instead, the ladies reject her advice and return to a flirtatious "war" with the gentlemen, the culmination of which is a cry to "Restore the Lock." Of course, the lock cannot be restored to Belinda's head, but in a way the lock is restored at poem's end: Pope has it elevated to the heavens, where it will be adored long after other locks have turned to dust. Pope's closing lines remind people again, as did Clarissa, that death will come; but in the face of death he seeks to make the lock immortal, the lock that symbolizes Belinda's world of fashion and fantasy. The true moral of the poem, then, is that it is precisely because of life's serious aspects that people must treasure its less serious ones.

Source: Sheldon Goldfarb, Critical Essay on "The Rape of the Lock," in *Poetry for Students,* The Gale Group, 2001.

Sources

Brower, Reuben A., "Am'rous Causes," reprinted in *Twentieth Century Interpretations of "The Rape of the Lock,"* edited by G. S. Rousseau, Prentice-Hall, 1969, pp. 52–68.

Grove, Robin, *The Art of Alexander Pope,* excerpt reprinted in *Alexander Pope's "The Rape of the Lock,"* edited by Harold Bloom, Chelsea House, 1988, pp. 33–65.

Hazlitt, William, "On Dryden and Pope," in *Lectures on the English Poets and the English Comic Writers,* edited by William Carew Hazlitt, George Bell and Sons, 1894, pp. 91–113.

Hyman, Stanley Edgar, "English Romanticism," in *Poetry and Criticism: Four Revolutions in Literary Taste,* Athenaeum, 1961, pp. 85–128.

Johnson, Samuel, "Pope," in *Lives of the English Poets,* Vol. II, Oxford University Press, 1967, pp. 223–344.

Pope, Alexander, "Essay on Criticism," in *English Critical Essays,* edited by Edmund D. Jones, Oxford University Press, 1922.

———, *The Poems of Alexander Pope,* Yale University Press, 1993.

Rumbold, Valerie, *Women's Place in Pope's World,* Cambridge University Press, 1989, p. 80.

Trimble, John, "Clarissa's Role in 'The Rape of the Lock,'" in *Texas Studies in English,* Vol. 15, 1974, pp. 673–691.

Williams, Aubrey, "The 'Fall' of China and 'The Rape of the Lock,'" reprinted in *The Rape of the Lock,* edited by David G. Lougee and Robert W. McHenry Jr., Merrill, 1969, pp. 119–128.

For Further Study

Bernard, John, ed., *Pope: The Critical Heritage,* Routlage & Kegan Paul, 1973.
  This collection features original reviews of Pope's work when it first appeared. It provides some of the very first reactions to "The Rape of the Lock."

Johnson, Samuel, *Rasselas, Poems, and Selected Prose,* Holt, Rinehart and Winston, 1952.
  This anthology of Johnson's writing features his entire *Life of Pope,* which was published in 1781, thirty–seven years after Pope's death.

Mack, Maynard, *Alexander Pope: A Life,* W. W. Norton & Company, 1986.
  Mack's text is an exhaustive and definitive biography of Pope that illuminates his poetry as well as his times.

Rousseau, G. S., ed., *Twentieth Century Interpretations of "The Rape of the Lock,"* Prentice-Hall, 1969.
  These collected critical essays feature examinations of the poem's mock-heroic elements as well as a section of shorter critical passages.

Tillotson, Geoffrey, ed., *Eighteenth Century English Literature,* Harcourt Brace Jovanovich, 1969.
  This brilliantly edited anthology features extensive selections by Pope, copious notes to the allusions in his poems, and a short but comprehensive introductory essay on Enlightenment literature as a whole. This is a valuable source for the student who wants to learn about the literary climate of Pope's day.

A Tall Man Executes a Jig

Irving Layton
1963

"A Tall Man Executes a Jig" is one of Layton's most anthologized poems, as well as one of his most ambitious and difficult. Layton himself would not argue this. In a 1963 review of *Balls for a One-Armed Juggler* by critic A. W. Purdy, reprinted in 1978 in *Irving Layton: The Poet and His Critics,* Purdy likens "A Tall Man Executes a Jig" to a parable written by God for his worshippers. He also recounts what Layton said to him about it: "'Al, in ten years you'll be able to understand this poem. In twenty you might be able to write one as good.'"

While humility may not be one of this poet's virtues, he does make a valid point regarding the complexity and the quality of "A Tall Man Executes a Jig." Like a parable, it does tell a story to illustrate a moral lesson, but that lesson is not as evident or orthodox as those found in common parables. Layton incorporates religious imagery and allusions—both Christian and Hebrew—as well as naturalist, or pagan, principles, taking his persona through encounters with each one only to be disappointed every time. This is a poem about man and his search for the knowledge of existence, the true wisdom of the earth. It is also about his power to create, to destroy, and to choose death as a means to achieve "transformation." Animals typically figure into a Layton poem, and in this one gnats and a snake are central characters. After the tall man tries to find solace first in nature, then in Christianity, and then in Judaism, in the end he decides to lie down beside a dead snake and die too.

The reptile, it seems, is the only one who has been "The manifest of that joyful wisdom."

Author Biography

Born on March 12, 1912, in Neamtz, Romania, Irving Layton immigrated to Canada with his parents the following year. He studied agriculture, economics, and political science in college and earned his master's degree from McGill University in 1946. During the early 1940s, Layton was writing poetry that concentrated on what he thought was an infuriating complacency in typical Canadian life. As a result, he helped found and edit *First Statement,* a literary journal highlighting his own work as well as that of other young Canadian writers who wanted to bring attention to the need for social and political enlightenment in their country. In 1945, Layton published his first book, entitled *Here and Now,* which received very little notice or respect.

For a man whose formal education was in the social sciences and whose early creative efforts were something less than encouraging, Layton became one of the most prolific, highly regarded, and consistently controversial writers of the twentieth century. He holds fervent opinions on countless issues and has never hesitated to voice them publicly. He uses his poetry to lambaste government officials, anti-environmentalists, poetry teachers, and women writers, among others. In letters to newspapers and published articles, Layton has targeted critics who have reviewed his books, and there have been many—over fifty since 1945. A typical rebuttal from Layton involves a direct personal attack on the critic. For instance, in 1964 he wrote a letter to *The Tamarack Review* as a reply to a critique on *Balls for a One-Armed Juggler* (in which "A Tall Man Executes a Jig" first appeared) by critic Gerald Taaffe. Debunking Taaffe's statement that the poems are dedicated to "insulting persons as various as a hose manufacturer," Layton said the critic misled readers "by fusing together two totally unrelated ideas and then planing and slanting them to make a smooth board for Mr. Taaffe's behind so that he can slide easily into the stinkpuddle of his own making." In a letter to *The Montreal Star* that same year, Layton wrote that "There hasn't been a writer of power and originality during the last century who hasn't had to fight his way to acceptance against the educated pipsqueaks hibernating in the universities." He went on to say that "95% of the

teachers of literature in our universities and schools would be more honestly employed cleaning toilets."

Layton biographies are filled with the poet's outrageous proclamations and discussions of his controversial, often sexually explicit poetry. It should also be noted that he received a Canada Council award in 1967, allowing him to travel extensively overseas, and Italy and Korea nominated him for a Nobel Prize in 1981. He was both a high school teacher and professor of English in the 1950s and 1960s (careers that some would call hypocritical), and he has been a poet in residence at several universities in Canada. While these accolades are common among accomplished twentieth-century poets and writers, any kinship Layton has with "typical" personalities ends just about there.

Poem Text

I

So the man spread his blanket on the field
And watched the shafts of light between the tufts
And felt the sin push the grass toward him;
The noise he heard was that of whizzing flies,
The whistlings of some small imprudent birds,   5
And the ambiguous rumbles of cars
That made him look up at the sky, aware
Of the gnats that tilted against the wind
And in the sunlight turned to jigging motes.
Fruitflies he'd call them except there was no fruit   10
About, spoiling the hatch these glitterings,
These nervous dots for which the mind supplied
The closing sentences from Thucydides,
Or from Euclid having a savage nightmare.

II

Jig, jig, jig, jig. Like minuscule black links   15
Of a chain played with by some playful
Unapparent hand or the palpitant
Summer haze bored with the hour's stillness.
He felt the sting and tingle afterwards
Of those leaving their orthodox unrest,   20
Leaving their undulant excitation
To drop upon his sleeveless arm. The grass,
Even the wildflowers became black hairs
And himself a maddened speck among them.
Still the assaults of the small flies made him   25
Glad at last, until he saw purest joy
In their frantic jiggings under a hair,
So changed from those in the unrestraining air.

III

He stood up and felt himself enormous.
Felt as might Donatello over stone,   30

Or Plato, or as a man who has held
A loved and lovely woman in his arms
And feels his forehead touch the emptied sky
Where all antinomies flood into light.
Yet jig jig jig, the haloing black jots   35
Meshed with the wheeling fire of the sun:
Motion without meaning, disquietude
Without sense or purpose, ephermerides
That mottled the resting summer air till
Gusts swept them from his sight like wisps of   40
     smoke.
Yet they returned, bring a bee who, seeing
But a tall man, left him for a marigold.

IV

He doffed his aureole of gnats and moved
Out of the field as the sun sank down,
A dying god upon the blood-red hills.   45
Ambition, pride, the ecstasy of sex,
And all circumstance of delight and grief,
That blood upon the mountain's side, that flood
Washed into a clear incredible pool
Below the ruddied peaks that pierced the sun.   50
He stood still and waited. If ever
The hour of revelation was come
It was now, here on the transfigured steep.
The sky darkened. Some birds chirped. Nothing
     else.
He thought the dying god had gone to sleep: 55
An Indian fakir on his mat of nails.

V

And on the summit of the asphalt road
Which stretched towards the fiery town, the man
Saw one hill raised like a hairy arm, dark
With pines and cedars against the stricken sun   60
—The arm of Moses or of Josha.
He dropped his head and let fall the halo
Of mountains, purpling and silent as time,
To see temptation coiled before his feet:
A violated grass snake that lugged   65
Its intestine like a small red valise.
A cold-eyed skinflint it now was, and not
The manifest of that joyful wisdom,
The mirth and arrogant green flame of life;
Or earth's vivid tongue that flicked in praise of   70
     earth.

VI

And the man wept because pity was useless.
"Your jig's up; the flies come like kites," he said
And watched the grass snake crawl towards the
     hedge,
Convulsing and dragging into the dark
The satchel filled with curses for the earth,   75
For the odours of warm sedge, and the sun,
A blood-red organ in the dying sky.
Backwards it fell into a grassy ditch
Exposing its underside, white as milk,
And mocked by wisps of hay between its jaws;   80

And then it stiffened to its final length.
But though it opened its thin mouth to scream
A last silent scream that shook the black sky,
Adamant and fierce, the tall man did not curse.

VII

Beside the rigid snake the man stretched out   85
In fellowship of death; he lay silent
And stiff in the heavy grass with eyes shut,
Inhaling the moist odours of the night
Through which his mind tunnelled with flicking
     tongue
Backwards to caves, mounds, and sunken ledges   90
And desolate cliffs where come only kites,
And where of perished badgers and racoons
The claws alone remain, gripping the earth.
Meanwhile the green snake crept upon the sky,
Huge, his mailed coat glittering with stars that   95
     made
The night bright, and blowing thin wreaths of
     cloud
Athwart the moon: and as the weary man
Stood up, coiled above his head, transforming all.

Poem Summary

Lines 1–7

The first lines of the poem provide the setting
for the persona's whereabouts. It is a very pastoral
scene, describing a man lying on a blanket in the
grass, feeling the sunlight that seems to "push the
grass towards him." He hears flies buzzing about
and the songs of "small imprudent birds." Although
"imprudent" means unwise or indiscreet, in this
case it probably connotes innocence on the part of
an unwary, harmless animal. The man also hears
cars passing on a nearby roadway, but their sounds
are "ambiguous" and indistinguishable from one
another, implying the persona's boredom with their
"rumbles." With this mixture of natural and unnatural noises all around him, the man casually looks
up at the sky and becomes "aware"—the last word
in line 7 and the first implication of an intellect at
work amid a seemingly lazy and uneventful day.

Lines 8–11

At first it seems that the persona is "aware"
only of the gnats that swarm about and that must
tilt their tiny, almost weightless bodies against the
wind to keep from being swept away. The insects
soon become much more important as the man observes them and begins to imagine the role they
play in the entire realm of nature. In the sunlight,
they appear as "jigging motes," or as little dancing

Media Adaptations

- An audiocassette of *A Wild Peculiar Joy: Selected Poems 1945–89* was released by McClelland and Stewart in 1995. Layton is the reader.

- There are two National Film Board documentaries on Layton available on videocassette. One is called *Poet: Irving Layton Observed* (1 hour) and the other is called *A Tall Man Executes a Jig* (1/2 hour).

- There are many tapes of interviews and poetry readings by Layton available through *A Catalogue of the Letters, Tapes and Photographs in the Irving Layton Collection,* University of Calgary Press, 1993.

specks, and look like the minute flies that are attracted to various fruits, such as bananas. The man is reminded of "fruitflies," but he thinks these creatures must be something different since "there was no fruit / About, spoiling to hatch these glitterings." The last phrase refers to the fact that some fruit flies have larvae that hatch in plant tissue, damaging the crop.

Lines 12–14

From "jigging motes" to "glitterings" and now to "nervous dots," Layton describes the gnats in a variety of creative ways, all designating free, spontaneous, and chaotic movement. There is no evident pattern, plan, or logic in their frenzied motion, and that is the reason for juxtaposing them against the likes of Thucydides, a Greek historian (ca. 460 B.C.), and Euclid, a Greek mathematician (ca. 350 B.C.). Both these men were known for insisting on logical analysis, whether it was in regard to recording history or developing geometry. The poet implies here that the undisciplined, pointless behavior of raw nature would be a "savage nightmare" to Euclid, in particular. Critic Milton Wilson, in "Notebook on Layton" (from *Irving Layton: The Poet and His Critics*) suggests that the gnats "are

like the 'nervous dots' of punctuation which mark the missing 'closing sentences' of Thucydides."

Lines 15–18

These lines are all metaphors for the "Jig, jig, jig, jig" movement of the gnats. They look like a chain being jerked around by an invisible hand or by the summer haze that amuses itself with trembling and shaking to jostle the "miniscule black links" about.

Lines 19–24

In these lines, some of the buzzing gnats spot the man's bare arm and land on it. The "unrest" they leave to land is "orthodox" in the sense that their meaningless movement is actually an accepted standard of gnat behavior. "Undulant excitation" is yet another way of describing the wavering and dancing of their typical state of excitation. The man starts to feel more a part of the natural world as he imagines the grass and the wildflowers as "black hairs." Just as the insects are only tiny, frenzied specks compared to the world around them—including the hairs on the man's arm—he now sees himself as only a "maddened speck" amidst the enormity of nature. At this point in the poem, the persona is beginning to doubt his first attempt to *connect* with the wisdom that he hoped lay in the gnats. As he studies them further, he is uncomfortable with what he discovers.

Lines 25–28

Here, the man confesses to being "made" to feel "Glad at last" by the tiny creatures, even though he considers their flitting about among the hair on his arm as "assaults." But he then confesses to feeling "purest joy" as they writhe and do their "frantic jiggings" under the hair on his arm. This is not the joy and wisdom he was seeking, however, because the pleasure he feels in watching them is at the expense of the gnats now trapped on his arm. Line 28 implies that the flies who left their "orthodox unrest" to land there are "changed from those in the unrestraining air." Since it is obviously not a change for the better, the man must consider that it is likewise not better for him to think of himself as a speck amid the "black hair" of the grass, wildflowers, and all the rest of nature.

Lines 29–32

Line 29 is an apparent contradiction of line 24. In the previous, he felt himself "a maddened speck" and five lines later, "He stood up and felt himself enormous." To emphasize his massiveness, Layton compares the persona to Donatello, the fifteenth-century Italian sculptor who lorded over his works in stone and bronze, and to Plato whose "size" was measured more in brain power and high intellect than in physical stature. The man's feeling of enormity is also likened to that of a lover who has pleased a "lovely woman," implying pride as well as satisfaction. Why would the sudden switch from feeling so small to feeling so big take place in the man's mind? It likely indicates his urgency to forego a transformation into the world of the gnats. His disappointment in seeing how easily the once-free insects became prisoners in his hair makes him rethink the idea of being one with them. Now he chooses the opposite side, wanting to feel not only big again but dominating.

Lines 33–36

Line 33 continues to emphasize the feeling of largeness the tall man experiences—so tall that he "feels his forehead touch the emptied sky." And in the sky, "all antinomies flood into light," meaning that all of life's paradoxes, or all the contradictions between reasonable assumptions, are exposed. The man's finding joy in nature and then finding it in being away from nature is a paradox. He can rationalize good things about both, and yet they contradict each other. These unavoidable "antinomies" continue to weaken his faith in the gnats' wisdom, and he returns his attention to them—the "haloing black jots"—that still swarm around his head like an angelic aura. Even though they continue to "jig jig jig," they have now lost the unique and extraordinary qualities that so amazed and stimulated the man in the first place. Now he sees them simply "Meshed with the wheeling fire of the sun." It is not unusual for the sun to appear as a symbol in Layton's poetry. Often, it carries more than one connotation in the same poem, and in line 36 of "A Tall Man Executes a Jig" it alludes to the continuous flux of the gases that make up the bright star. They constantly whirl about at speeds unrecognizable to the human eye, and the similar movement of the gnats blends well with them.

Lines 37–42

The latter half of the third stanza brings an end to the man's first attempt to find the true knowledge of life on earth and to transform into a being that can reach that level of understanding. The things of nature that move chaotically no longer appear to be caught up in a joyful dance. Now they simply exhibit "Motion without meaning, disquietude / Without sense or purpose." The "ephemerides"—or short-lived insects, such as mayflies—are now accused of having "mottled" (marked with spots) the "resting summer air." Their motion is an aggravation, not an enticement. The beings that once maintained their space by moving "tilted against the wind" have now been "swept" by that same wind from the man's sight "like wisps of smoke." Lines 41 and 42 close out the stanza with a final smack in the tall man's face: the gnats come back with another flying creature in tow, but the bee is so disinterested in human life that it snubs the man for a flower.

Lines 43–45

Just as the insects in the previous stanza cast off the importance of the man, he, in turn, "doffed [removed] his aureole of gnats" and walks away from the field. The sinking sun in these lines symbolizes Christ, the "dying god" whose blood was shed on a hilltop. At this point in the poem, the tall man turns to a second possible route to pure wisdom—Christianity. But just the reference to Jesus as a "dying god" does not imply much enthusiasm or hope that this effort will be any more gratifying than the endeavor with the "natural" gnats—or paganism, as it were.

Lines 46–50

Lines 46 and 47 allude to *human* qualities and behavior. While an argument can be made for both the positives and the negatives regarding ambition, pride, sex, and "all circumstance of delight and grief," most people would agree that these are indeed a part of the lives of men and women. The supreme beings in Christian, Jewish, and other religious faiths are considered above such attributes. The next two lines of the poem refer to the crucifixion of Christ and the metaphor of his blood washing humans clean of their sins. His blood turns into "a clear incredible pool," symbolizing purity and grace. The mountains are "ruddied," or red, in reference to blood, and their peaks have "pierced the sun," in reference to the nails that pierced Christ's flesh on the cross. Line 50 continues the metaphor of the sun equaling a dying god and the dying god equaling Christ.

Lines 51–53

The tall man has now decided to give Christianity a fair chance. He stands at the bottom of the mountain and waits, presumably for a miracle or a sign from God that this is truly the way to pure wisdom. He cannot imagine a better time for it to happen in light of all the Christian imagery that surrounds him, and so he claims that "If ever / the hour of revelation was come / It was now." The description of the steep as "transfigured" refers to the visible change in appearance of Jesus as he stood on the mountaintop surrounded by a radiant light.

Lines 54–56

Line 54 details the disappointment that the tall man once again experiences in his quest. Even though the "sky darkened" and "Some birds chirped," that was it. "Nothing else" happened. He imagines, sarcastically perhaps, that Christ has gone to sleep and neglected his duty to reveal truth. The tall man compares the deity to a "fakir on his mat of nails," or a religious beggar who performs endurance feats for alms. If surviving crucifixion was Christ's endurance feat, the tall man is not satisfied that it was a good enough performance. He has still not been transformed.

Lines 57–61

The fifth stanza is the beginning of the tall man's third attempt to find a method for transformation—this time through Judaism. The "one hill raised like a hairy arm" has at least two references. First, it returns to the idea of the hair on the man's arm that trapped the gnats in the early part of the poem. Secondly, it implies the outstretched arms of the Hebrew prophets Moses and Joshua. At one point in their lives as leaders of the Israelites, each was instructed by God to stretch out his arm as a signal to the people—Moses with a staff in his hand and Joshua with a spear.

Lines 62–66

The tall man's third attempt is short lived. The "mountains" here represent Judaism, and he finds that they are "purpling and silent as time." In other words, they lack the vitality and the enlightening qualities it will take to find the truth about life and death and the core of existence on earth that he seeks. Just as he had "doffed his aureole of gnats," the tall man now "dropped his head and let fall the halo / Of mountains." What he sees when he looks at the ground is the object of his search, and he appears to recognize it immediately. The "temptation coiled before his feet" is, literally, a grass snake and, figuratively, the unashamed and unflagging thirst for knowledge. In the Biblical story, it was a serpent that tempted Eve to taste the fruit of the "tree of knowledge," and snakes have been associated with evil and temptation throughout history. But in this poem, *evil* is not a quality of the animal. Instead, the beast is the one who has been "vi-

olated" and who must drag "Its intestine like a small red valise" to its death.

Lines 67–70

Although the tall man realizes that the grass snake is now "A cold-eyed skinflint" about to die, he also knows that in life it was "The manifest of that joyful wisdom, / the mirth and arrogant green flame of life." In other words, the snake represents the true knowledge of earth—of humankind's place on it and of its glory beyond human existence. The tall man knows that "vivid tongue that flicked in praise of earth" can transform him with its wisdom.

Lines 71–77

Line 71 tells the reader that the man also knows the "vivid tongue" is about to be silenced. Pity cannot restore the snake's life, and so he resigns himself to tell it, " 'Your jig's up,' " an obvious play on words indicating that the creature's time is over just like the dance of the gnats. The "kites" are predatory birds, such as hawks, that will feast on the body of the snake once it's dead. Lines 74–77 describe in pathetic terms the last crawl of the snake. Its guts are once again referred to as burdensome luggage—a "satchel"—which holds curses for those things in nature that once comforted the creature: the earth itself, the smell of the foliage, and the sun are now appearing as a "blood-red organ" are within a body that is dying—in this case, the sky.

Lines 78–81

When the snake falls dead into the ditch, the tall man can see that its belly is "white as milk," implying a hidden purity that is never afforded a serpent. Even in death, it receives no dignity or respect, for it is "mocked by wisps of hay" as its body becomes rigid.

Lines 82–84

The snake's mouth opens as it dies, and the man imagines that it must scream for the injustice of its death, and even the "silent scream" is strong enough to echo throughout the dark sky. Recall that the snake took with it a satchel full of curses, indicating its anger and indignation at its fate. But "the tall man did not curse" because he now understands what he must do, and it is his choice. His own life is within his power to retain or to end, and he will make that decision for himself.

Lines 85–89

The tall man's decision is to die beside the snake, and by positioning himself next to the creature and calling it a "fellowship of death," he has also decided that the snake will be his vehicle to transformation. He will understand the secrets of true knowledge by becoming one with the holder of that knowledge. He closes his eyes and breathes in the odors of nature. Line 89 implies the beginning of the transformation by referring to the man's mind as having a "flicking tongue" with which to travel back into the history of the earth. This, of course, is a metaphor that indicates a direct connection between the tall man and the serpent who also had a flicking tongue.

Lines 90–93

These lines describe a world where there are animals, rock formations, and other natural objects, but there is one noticeable absence: humans. The only remaining evidence of dead badgers and raccoons are their claws that are still "gripping the earth" after death. This symbolizes the need and desperation that pure nature has to hold onto itself—and not to perish at the hands of an unknowledgeable and careless human race.

Lines 94–98

While the man lies beside the snake taking his mind through layers of history and into the thoughts of the creatures who inhabited it, the snake's soul has "crept upon the sky"—or ascended into the heavens—where it appears huge, and the hard, scaly coat that it still wears glitters against the stars. The "thin wreaths of cloud" that blow across the moon may be another religious reference in comparing the wreath to the crown of thorns placed upon Christ's head before his death. For the tall man, the snake itself becomes a wreath or crown of sorts. As he stands up (dead or alive), now weary of his mental journey, the image of the serpent is coiled above his head the same way that the gnats and the mountains had been halos above him. The difference here is that the man does not "let fall the halo" as he did previously. Instead, the snake provides a heavenly crown that he will keep. Through its death, it has transformed the man into a being of true wisdom.

Themes

Creation and Destruction

Irving Layton has been noted for his perceptions on mankind's ability and willingness to be both a creator and a destroyer. Human beings *create* everything from medicine and technology to art and poetry, but they also *destroy* everything from mountains and beaches to each other and themselves. "A Tall Man Executes a Jig" embraces this theme in regard to the earth and its creatures, religious figures, and the man himself.

In his search to understand the meaning of life on earth and to gain the knowledge that can transform him into an enlightened being, the tall man tries to become one with nature—from the field he lies in, the wildflowers, and the gnats to "the moist odours of the night" and the "caves, mounds, and sunken ledges." In this sense, the man is an observer of creation. He believes there is something missing in humans as they were created and that he can find it within the natural world. But the gutted grass snake reminds him of man as a destroyer. While it is true that animals fall victim to their own kind in the wild, the implication in this poem is that the reptile—the holder of true wisdom and joy—has been cut open by a human and is, therefore, a victim of human destruction.

The references to religion in the poem obviously relate to the theme of creation and destruction. While some people believe that God is a human invention, many others hold that God is the creator of human life. Regardless of which side one falls on in this debate, few would argue against the fact that histories of religions contain a story of man as a destroyer of his gods. The fourth stanza in "A Tall Man Executes a Jig" is full of references to the crucifixion of Christ and the "blood upon the mountain's side." The tall man is disappointed that "the hour of revelation" never comes, and so he walks away from an opportunity to find wisdom through religious belief.

The title of this poem contains an ambiguity. The word "Executes" may mean to perform or to carry out, and it may also mean to kill. In the latter sense, the tall man ends up destroying the "jig" that he encountered and enjoyed with the gnats. If the jig represents the frenzied energy of life, then the point Layton makes is that what human beings are initially attracted to may end up destroyed regardless of the attraction. When the man became disillusioned by the jig, he "doffed his aureole of gnats" and walked away. But the most noteworthy reference to man as a destroyer in this poem is in the form of self-destruction. In the end, the tall man makes a conscious decision to join in the "fellowship of death" with the snake. The power of human beings appears limitless, even when it is, ironically, suicidal.

Topics for Further Study

- Explain why Irving Layton said about this poem that it may take ten years to understand it and twenty to write one as good.

- Choose an animal or insect, and write an essay on how the creature has been misperceived by human beings and what effect this has had on its existence.

- Write an essay explaining why Layton chose the Greek mathematician Euclid to make a point about the gnats in the poem.

- Write a response to the tall man's notion that traditional Christianity and Judaism do not satisfy the quest for wisdom but that the grass snake is the "manifest of that joyful wisdom."

Man, Nature, and Religion

In an article titled "A Tall Man Executes a Jig," (published in *Engagements: The Prose of Irving Layton*), Layton made these comments about his poem by the same name:

> More than any other poem of mine, this one fuses feeling and thought in an intense moment of perception. Of truth. Truth for me, of course. That's the way I feel about gnats, and hills, and Christian renunciation, the pride of life and crushed grass-snakes writhing on the King's Highway.

If the man in the poem represents Layton himself, then the theme of man, nature, and religion is in direct correlation to Layton's article. But when the poet says, "That's the way I feel about gnats . . . and crushed grass-snakes . . .," how is it that he actually feels? Some confusion occurs in considering the tall man's responses to the gnats and to the snake. Obviously, both are a part of nature, and yet the gnats become a nuisance while the snake is heralded as the "manifest of that joyful wisdom." What's the difference?

Perhaps the thematic answer lies in religion—in particular, the tall man's perceptions of the role that Christianity and Judaism play in true wisdom and human enlightenment. Gnats have no significance or recognizable symbolism in history,

mythology, or religion. They may be of great interest to entomologists or biologists, but most people consider them pests to shoo away. In the beginning of the poem, the little creatures flirt with an exalted role. They grab the attention of the persona and, for a while, channel his imagination into a very thoughtful, intellectual mode. With their whizzing and jigging and "undulant excitation," they stir up thoughts of Thucydides, Euclid, Donatello, and Plato—a lofty group for such a humble creature to bring to mind. But in the end, they are sent back to their low ground in the animal kingdom when first a breeze sweeps them away and then the tall man rids his head of the aureole they had made.

The snake plays a much greater and long-lasting role. It also has a history—usually bad—within the annals of religion and mythology. Perhaps because the serpent has so often been a symbol of evil and of temptation to do wrong, the tall man (and Layton) finds it an appropriate beast to make the point about mankind's ironic treatment of nature. Human beings are "natural" too, but they consider themselves above everything else that constitutes nature. As it turns out in the poem, however, the lowly, feared snake is the creature that is truly one with the earth. This, of course, is directly opposed to the Old Testament story of the Garden of Eden in which the snake is only a deceitful beast with a big role in the downfall of man. The tall man finds orthodox religions dissatisfying. It is fitting, then, for him to make a godlike figure out of the traditional symbol of evil in those religions.

Style

Quasi-Sonnets

This relatively lengthy poem is actually a collection of seven quasi-sonnets, in that each stanza contains 14 lines—like a sonnet—most which are made up of 10 syllables. Of the poem's 98 lines, 80 contain 10 syllables, 14 contain 11, and nine contain four. There is no strict adherence to end rhyming (except for the couplet that completes the second stanza and rhymes "hair" and "air") although there are many near-rhyme endings and sporadic inside rhyming. Examples of these patterns include the *apparent* rhyme in lines 12 and 13: "supplied" and "Thucydides," although the latter is broken into four syllables and is pronounced thoo-sid'-i-deez; the first two words and the last two words of line 48: "That blood," "that flood"; the a-b-a-b pattern of lines 53–56: "steep"/ "else"/ "sleep"/ "nails"; and the inside near-rhyme of line 84: "Adamant and *fierce,* the tall man did not *curse.*"

Alliteration

"A Tall Man Executes a Jig" is also rich with alliteration (the repetition of initial consonant sounds in two or more neighboring words or syllables). Examples include "whizzing" and "whistlings" in lines 4 and 5; "Motion without meaning" in line 37; the various uses of the "s" sound in "Gusts swept them from his sight like wisps of smoke" (line 40) and in "A last silent scream that shook the black sky" (line 83); and "cliffs" and "kites" in line 91. There are other examples of alliteration in the poem, but these samples make it clear that Layton was fond of using the device. In the article "A Tall Man Executes a Jig," (published in *Engagements: The Prose of Irving Layton*), the poet states, "Formless poems give me the pips. If ideas, I want to see them dance." Clearly, the poem that carries the same title is full of ideas and has a methodical form—as well as the ability to "dance."

Historical Context

The setting for "A Tall Man Executes a Jig" is obvious in place but not time. Even the location is generic, in that it is an open field with mountains around, but it could be a field in Canada, the United States, China, or anywhere else. The point is that Irving Layton was writing a type of parable with an "everyman" character in the leading role, and placing him in a particular political domain during a particular year would not enhance the poem or its intentions. What, then, may have been the historical or cultural influences that played a part in Layton's creating this work? Probably both his own experiences as a Jewish immigrant to Canada and as a Canadian citizen growing up in the early part of the twentieth century, as well as the global events that changed life forever in the form of world war.

Although Layton was only one when he left Romania, his birth there gave him a lasting link to Eastern Europe. His upbringing in Judaism heavily influenced his religious tendencies toward and struggles against orthodox faith, and his life in a rather socially sedate Quebec brought out the political rebel in him. In his forward to *Balls for a One-Armed Juggler,* as reprinted in *Engagements: The Prose of Irving Layton,* the poet is clear about the things of the world that concern him:

Today, poets must teach themselves to imagine the worst. To apprehend the enormity of the filth, irrationality, and evil that washes in on us from the four corners of the earth, they must have the severity to descend from one level of foulness to another and learn what the greatest of them had always known: there is, [of] course, no bottom, no end. . ... What insight does the modern poet give us into the absolute evil of our times? Where is the poet who can make clear for us Belsen? Vorkuta? Hiroshima? The utter wickedness of Nazism and National Communism?. . .

The forward to the book continues for five pages in this fashion. Obviously, "man's inhumanity to man" and religious hypocrisy figure greatly into Layton's concerns. In "A Tall Man Executes a Jig," the persona exemplifies the poet's own dissatisfying encounters with various aspects of human life, as well as his contradictory behavior in regard to creation and destruction. He does not mention the notorious leaders of the world wars by name in the poem, but he alludes to the atrocities that befell—and still befall—helpless beings who are singled out for torture and degradation. In this case, it is "A violated grass-snake" that becomes a victim of some unseen hand, a hand of apparent cruelty and authority. Even the tall man himself appears fickle in his response to the tiny gnats, first showing interest and amazement in their movement and then casting them off in total disregard. His approach to and retreat from Christianity and Judaism may seem blasphemous and arrogant, but it is not necessarily a rejection of a belief in a supreme being. Instead, he questions the authenticity of religions so heavily influenced by human history and human interpretation, especially considering his skepticism about the "nature" of man in the first place.

Critical Overview

Irving Layton's first few poetry collections achieved little success. He published his first book in 1945 and followed it with several others throughout the late 1940s and early 1950s, but it was not until the publication of *A Red Carpet for the Sun* in 1959 that Layton became a popular voice in Canadian poetry. When he did become popular, it was essentially for the same reason that he remained *un*popular with many general readers and critics: his subject matter and language. Layton had no reservations about using graphic imagery and sexually explicit language in his work, nor did he hesitate to rail against social injustices, often offending everyone from government officials to college professors to members of the bourgeois or elite society. But for every critic who labeled this poet a raging egomaniac who filled his volumes with scenes of violence, death, and sex, there were many more who pointed to his unique voice and intriguing examination of the relationship between the spiritual and the physical.

After the publication of *A Red Carpet for the Sun,* which won the Governor General's Award for Poetry in 1959, Layton went on to publish nearly forty more collections, each one meeting with more critical praise than condemnation. Over the years, he received several prestigious awards, including the Prix Litteraire de Quebec in 1963 for *Balls for a One-Armed Juggler* and the Encyclopedia Britannica Life Achievement Award in 1978. Although it is true that Layton's poems demonstrate more love and sympathy for animals than for humans and that he spares no one a tongue-lashing when he believes it is warranted, those targeted have often been the ones to support his work. The general consensus among critics is that however one feels after reading a Layton collection, the guarantee is that he or she will feel *something.*

Criticism

Pamela Steed Hill

Hill has published widely in poetry journals and is the author of a collection entitled In Praise of Motels. *In the following essay, she suggests that the tall man cannot achieve true transformation by nature because of his own human hypocrisy.*

"A Tall Man Executes a Jig" is a somewhat complicated poem in that it is like a parable in telling a story to represent the real meaning. Also like a parable, it can often be more of a riddle that readers must "figure out" to understand and appreciate fully. In this poem, however, Layton adds further complexity by throwing in an apparent contradiction in the persona's thoughts and behavior. As the tall man seeks to find the true wisdom of life on earth, he explores both the natural world and the metaphysical in the form of two different religions. Being dissatisfied with all three encounters, he finally stumbles upon what he has been looking for—a grass snake that has been cruelly victimized by humankind and that the tall man recognizes as the "manifest of that joyful wisdom" he seeks. If the point of the poem is that the nature of man is

a, more or less, sorry one and that only the natural world is the true inheritor of the earth, then it makes sense for the tall man to exalt the serpent and condemn humanized Christianity and Judaism. But where does that leave the gnats? These tiny creatures play a starring role in the first three stanzas but are then readily cast off by the man and not mentioned again. But gnats are a part of the natural world just as snakes are, so why does the tall man exhibit such contradictory behavior toward these two creatures? The most likely answer is that he himself is a part of the mankind that he despises, and his hypocrisy is evidence of it.

To examine this theory, it is best to start at the end of the poem and work backwards. Here, the tall man not only praises the purity, knowledge, and vulnerability of animals and the earth, but he also tries to become a part of it. He is even willing to die beside the snake to be transformed to the level of existence that the creature has attained. So strong is his adulation for it that his "mind tunneled with flicking tongue" back through natural history, allowing his consciousness to take on the characteristics of a serpent and to envision the natural formations of earth: "caves, mounds, and sunken ledges / And desolate cliffs." He recognizes the helplessness of animals and their desperate attempt to hold on to their world in the "perished badgers and raccoons" whose "claws alone remain, gripping the earth." Finally he glorifies the snake that has "crept upon the sky" and coils above his head like a halo or a crown.

In the previous stanza, the man weeps for the snake's horrible condition. The description of it dragging its exposed intestines off to the ditch to die is pathetic, to say the least, and points a strong finger at the savagery of mankind. The snake has been cut open and must

crawl towards the hedge,
Convulsing and dragging into the dark
The satchel filled with curses for the earth.

Its innocence is demonstrated as it falls "into a grassy ditch / Exposing its underside, white as milk, / And mocked by wisps of hay between its jaws." As the tall man witnesses this heart-wrenching scene and looks on as the snake opens it mouth for "A last silent scream that shook the black sky," he is overcome by the knowledge of what he must do. Taking his own human life is the only way to rid himself of the sadistic qualities that are man's alone and to join the world of grace, innocence, and wisdom—the natural world.

Just before the man discovered "temptation coiled before his feet" in the form of the grass snake, he had been mentally wrestling with the pros and cons of religious faith. The fourth and fifth stanzas of the poem contain several allusions to Christian and Hebrew tenets as well as the prominent figures representing those religions—Jesus Christ, Moses, and Joshua. The tall man acknowledges the crucifixion of Christ and considers the possibility of following Christianity as a means to enlightenment. He looks toward the "blood-red hills" and is reminded of the sacrifice made by Christ in "That blood upon the mountain's side, that flood / Washed into a clear incredible pool." Perhaps the tall man thinks that the "clear incredible pool" is the place to find the pure knowledge of life, and so he decides to stand and wait for the moment of revelation to come to him. It doesn't take long for him to surmise that his wait is useless and he decides—cynically, it seems—that "the dying god had gone to sleep" like a beggar who tires of performing duration feats for a living.

Judaism fairs no better in the mind of the tall man. For a moment he thinks one of the hills looks like the arm of Moses or of Joshua in the way it is raised as though positioned by God to do his will. But then he discovers that the hills and mountains are "purpling and silent as time." In other words, they seem old, bruised, and not about to reveal any knowledge they may have once held. When the man "dropped his head and let fall the halo / Of mountains," he was severing his ties completely with the notion of religious faith—at least faith as interpreted and defined by man. Neither the tall man nor Irving Layton is an atheist. The rejection of and dissatisfaction in these two religions do not imply a rejection of God. It is *man* that is the problem, for both the tall man and the poet. Over time, human beings fell from the grace of nature—and, therefore, of God—to the lowest levels of, in Layton's terms, "cruelty, perversion, systematic lying, and monstrous hypocrisy," as he points out in the forward to *Balls for a One-Armed Juggler.* Although the persona in "A Tall Man Executes a Jig" seems to have transcended the treacherous behavior of his own race, he too proves himself a hypocrite.

Initially, readers may assume that the lesson to be learned in this poem is that there is goodness, truth, and wisdom in the world, and if one wants to find it, he or she must look outside the human race. And no one creature in nature has ownership of knowledge and virtue, as evidenced by the tall

> *Had the tall man recognized the same natural beauty in the gnats that he did in the snake, he would not have had to go through the other disappointments that he set himself up for."*

man glorifying everything from snakes, badgers, and raccoons to caves, mounds, ledges, and cliffs. Even the tiniest, arguably most annoying, creatures can hold wisdom far beyond the human mind. In the beginning of the poem, the tall man becomes enthralled by gnats, or those "jigging motes" who seem to represent the frenzied energy of life itself. The gnats are *free*—a quality revered, if not worshipped, by man—and the poem's persona recognizes this as the "glitterings" whiz about his head and fascinate him with their abandonment. In this early part of the poem, the reader does not know how the tall man will end up heralding nature as the keeper of truth and knowledge, and so it does not seem inappropriate for him to begin to change his feelings toward the little flies buzzing all around.

The language of the poem—in particular, the adjectives used to describe the gnats—is a good indicator of the tall man's weakening pleasure in the insects. They quickly dwindle from "jigging motes" and "glitterings" to "nervous dots," "black jots," and, finally, the dry, technical "ephemerides." There is a hint that naturalism, or the belief that religious truths derive from nature as opposed to revelation, may lead to the enlightenment that the man seeks. His attention to the gnats is at first acute, and he contemplates the response of such great thinkers as Thucydides and Euclid to their uncanny energy. But when a few of them drop out of their wild dance in the air to land on his bare arm, the tall man ponders something darker, something disturbing. He wonders what it would feel like to see the world from a gnat's perspective, how *gigantic* everything must seem to them and how insignificant they must reckon themselves to be. He imagines that the grass and the wildflowers in the field where he lies have become huge and that he is only a "maddened

What Do I Read Next?

- Scientist May R. Berenbaum takes an unusual, sometimes humorous look at the insect world in *Ninety-Nine Gnats, Nits, and Nibblers,* published in 1989. The book is for general readers and discusses such topics as eating habits, sex, and death among insects.

- Mary Lou Randour presents an intriguing perspective on human responsibility for animals in *Animal Grace: Entering a Spiritual Relationship With Our Fellow Creatures,* published in 2000. In this book, she addresses the need for a kinship between people and animals and offers many examples of how different creatures have made positive differences in human life.

- In *The Creating Consciousness: Science as the Language of God* by Arne Wyller (1999), the author argues that the theory of evolution and physical science may be accurate, but that there was also a pre-existing consciousness at work during creation. This is a very accessible book for the general reader.

- Irving Layton's 1986 collection entitled *Dance With Desire* contains primarily love poems and is a departure from his more typical ravings on social and religious issues.

speck" among them. This is the same way the gnats must feel "In their frantic jiggings under a hair." They have made prisoners of themselves by "Leaving the undulant excitation" of their "orthodox unrest" to become trapped on the man's arm. He does not consider this very noble or sensible behavior, much less *wise* behavior, and so he loses faith in their ability to transform him.

The third stanza of the poem becomes much more important after the rest of the work is read. This is the point at which the tall man admits "antinomies," or paradoxes and contradictions, but the significance of that is not as clear as it will be later. Not only does the man scoff at the gnats' foolish behavior and minuteness, but he responds by becoming the opposite: "He stood up and felt himself enormous." He goes so far as to compare himself to Donatello, Plato, and a great lover. Now when he considers the "jig jig jig" of the tiny insects, he sees them simply "Meshed with the wheeling fire of the sun," their "Motion without meaning" and their continuous movement "Without sense or purpose." The feeling of disillusionment seems mutual, as the bee—another member of the natural world—is so unimpressed with the human that it "left him for a marigold." It would appear, then, that the break between man and nature is a clean one, allowing the man to turn to theology and philosophical thought for the wisdom he wants to attain.

The reader now knows, however, what happens next and that there is no break with nature for the tall man at all. Instead, he ultimately embraces the natural world, the snake in particular, as a kind of god after all his other encounters have proved disappointing. Given that, how does he justify his attitude toward the insects and the fact that he "doffed his aureole of gnats," presumably as easily as the unknown human had sliced open the belly of the grass snake? The man finds that act a vile crime against nature and further evidence of mankind's violent tendencies. His own similar act, however, does not seem vile to him at all. Actually, he does not even recall the gnats as he exalts other creatures and objects of the earth. People who do not see in themselves the same behavior that they criticize in others are classic hypocrites. The tall man believes he has achieved the supreme and transcendent answers to life on earth as the snake is "coiled above his head, transforming all." But transformation hardly seems complete when hypocrisy and neglect are still a big part of the picture.

Layton's intent in making the persona of this poem a foolish hypocrite was probably not to show how much "better" animals are than people. It may, however, cause one to consider that the road to "joyful wisdom" is not as clear as it seems even if it lies "coiled" at one's feet or above one's head. Had the tall man recognized the same natural beauty in the gnats that he did in the snake, he would not have had to go through the other disappointments that he set himself up for. In the end, man is not the noble creature that he imagines himself to be. He may have gotten closer, but Layton's humans don't usually prove victorious.

Source: Pamela Steed Hill, Critical Essay on "A Tall Man Executes a Jig," in *Poetry for Students,* The Gale Group, 2001.

Sources

amazon.com, www.amazon.com (June 20, 2000).

DISCovering World History, Gale Group, 1999.

The History Channel, www.historychannel.com (June 21, 2000).

Layton, Irving, Forward to *Balls for a One-Armed Juggler,* in *Engagements: The Prose of Irving Layton,* edited by Seymour Mayne, McClelland and Stewart, 1972, pp. 104–105.

———, Letter to *The Montreal Star,* in *Engagements: The Prose of Irving Layton,* edited by Seymour Mayne, McClelland and Stewart, 1972, pp. 188–191.

———, Letter to *Tamarack Review,* in *Engagements: The Prose of Irving Layton,* edited by Seymour Mayne, McClelland and Stewart, 1972, pp. 194–196.

———, "'A Tall Man Executes a Jig,'" in *Engagements: The Prose of Irving Layton,* edited by Seymour Mayne, McClelland and Stewart, 1972, p. 45.

———, *A Wild Peculiar Joy: Selected Poems 1945–1982,* McClelland and Stewart, 1982.

Purdy, A. W., *Irving Layton: The Poet and His Critics,* McGraw-Hill Ryerson, 1978, p. 131.

Wilson, Milton, "Notebook on Layton," in *Irving Layton: The Poet and His Critics,* McGraw-Hill Ryerson, 1978, p. 233.

For Further Study

Layton, David, *Motion Sickness: A Memoir,* MacFarlane Walter and Ross, 2000.

This is an autobiography of Irving Layton's son. It becomes tedious in places, but it does provide interesting insight on growing up with the unconventional poet father.

Layton, Irving, *Fornalutx: Selected Poems 1928–1990,* McGill Queens University Press, 1992.

As the title suggests, this book is a comprehensive look at the poet from the time he was a young man of 16 through the age of 78. Considering he did not publish until the mid 1940s, it is an interesting look at his more youthful efforts.

Layton, Irving, Dennis Lee, and Duncan Campbell Scott, *Annotated Bibliography of Canada's Major's Authors,* E. C. W. Press, 1993.

This book places Irving Layton's work among several other Canadian writers, and it is a good comparison of his poetry with the more mainstream creative artists.

Mansbridge, Francis, *God's Recording Angel,* E. C. W. Press, 1995.

This is a well written and accessible biography of Layton, sometimes shocking but consistently revealing of the poet and the inspiration for his work.

Wilderness Gothic

Al Purdy
1968

"Wilderness Gothic" was published in 1968 in a collection called *Wild Grape Wine* just as Purdy's career was beginning to take shape. In many ways, the poem reflects on the themes of human aspiration and the possibility of failure, which corresponds with Purdy's own struggle to succeed in the literary world. At the start of Purdy's career, he endured criticism of his early works and his lack of formal education, yet he continued to create poetry, a testament to his own commitment to his craft and his unbridled faith in his abilities.

The poem begins in the present time and describes the actions of an ordinary man who is working hard to repair a church spire. The man hangs from a rope and takes a great risk to donate his time and labor to God. The poem then shifts in time and place so as to discuss history. The speaker mentions a Durer landscape, a reference to the artist Albrecht Durer (1471–1528). One of Durer's woodcuts is called *The Fall of Icarus,* which reflects some of the themes of "Wilderness Gothic." According to the myth of Icarus, Icarus and his father, Daedalus, tried to escape imprisonment by flying with wings fashioned of feathers and wax. However, Icarus did not heed his father's warning about flying too close to the sun. Rather, Icarus was so exhilarated by the act of flying that he flew too high and the sun melted the wax in his wings, and Icarus fell to his death. As a result, Icarus has become a symbol of aspiration, yet he also represents the human capacity for failure.

Just as Icarus fell to his death, "Wilderness Gothic" ends with the line "perhaps he will fall." This statement implies that while the man working on the church is willing to take a heroic and noble risk, he is not immune to the consequences of that risk. However, the overall message of the work is that the risk is still worth taking.

Author Biography

Alfred Wellington Purdy was born on December 30, 1918, in the small farming town of Wooler, Ontario, Canada. When Purdy was just a toddler, his father died, prompting him and his mother to move to the nearby town of Trenton. There he enrolled in public school and published his first poem, "Spotlight." Purdy dropped out of school in the ninth grade and never went to college, preferring to ride the rails in and around Vancouver and support himself through several odd jobs. He joined the Royal Canadian Air Force in 1940 and married Eurithe Parkhurst a year later. After World War II, Purdy continued to earn a living with random work, so that he could have the freedom to pursue his poetry. He self-published his first collection, *The Enchanted Echo,* in 1944; however, it would take more than ten years for Purdy to produce another compilation, *The Crafte So Long to Lerne.* Since Purdy was a self-taught poet and had not immersed himself in the work of his peers, critics felt Purdy's early work to be immature and undeveloped. This criticism did not stop Purdy from fully dedicating himself to writing, and he succeeded in creating his own style with his next work *Poems for All the Annettes,* a volume that finally brought him some critical praise and the title of working-class poet.

During the 1960s, Purdy traveled extensively, spending time in Cuba, Mexico, Europe, Japan, and Africa. In 1965, he published *The Cariboo Horses,* a breakthrough compilation that confirmed his reputation in the literary world and earned him a Governor General's Literary Award. At that point, Purdy was able to support himself and his wife with work as a teacher and lecturer at the university level. He also continued his globetrotting and added travel essays to his resume. In 1970, Purdy became a visiting associate professor at the University of Manitoba and the University of Western Ontario, among others.

Purdy continued to produce several volumes of poetry, including *The New Romans, Being Alive,*

Al Purdy

Wild Grape Wine, The Stone Bird, and *The Collected Poems of Al Purdy.* The last work was dedicated to his wife and earned him another Governor General's Literary Award in 1986 as well as the status of one of the most significant Canadian poets of the twentieth century. Late in his life, Purdy published several works that focused on his correspondence with fellow poet Charles Bukowski, and he then tackled his first novel, *A Splinter in the Heart* in 1990. Purdy completed his autobiography *Reaching for the Beaufort Sea* in 1993. For a man with modest means and little education, Purdy enjoyed great success. However, he told critic Peter O'Brien (in *Essays on Canadian Writing*) that "it's an awful cliché to say it, that writing itself is its own reward . . . but it's true. It has to be." Purdy died of lung cancer at his winter home on Vancouver Island on April 21, 2000. He was eighty-one years old.

Poem Text

Across Roblin Lake, two shores away,
they are sheathing the church spire
with new metal. Someone hangs in the sky
over there from a piece of rope,
hammering and fitting God's belly-scratcher, 5

working his way up along the spire
until there's nothing left to nail on—
Perhaps the workman's faith reaches beyond:
touches intangibles, wrestles with Jacob,
replacing rotten timber with pine thews,   10
pounds hard in the blue cave of the sky,
contends heroically with difficult problems of
gravity, sky navigation and mythopeia,
his volunteer time and labor donated to God,
minus sick benefits of course on a non-union job—   15

Fields around are yellowing into harvest,
nestling and fingerling are sky and water borne,
death is yodeling quiet in green woodlots,
and bodies of three young birds have disappeared
in the sub-surface of the new county highway—   20

That picture is incomplete, part left out
that might alter the whole Dürer landscape:
gothic ancestors peer from medieval sky,
dour faces trapped in photograph albums escaping
to clop down iron roads with matched grays: 25
work-sodden wives groping inside their flesh
for what keeps moving and changing and flashing
beyond and past the long frozen Victorian day.
A sign of fire and brimstone? A two-headed calf
born in the barn last night? A sharp female agony?   30
An age and a faith moving into transition,
the dinner cold and new-baked bread a failure,
deep woods shiver and water drops hang pendant,
double yolked eggs and the house creaks a little—
Something is about to happen. Leaves are still.   35
Two shores away, a man hammering in the sky.
Perhaps he will fall.

Poem Summary

Lines 1–7

In the opening stanza, Purdy introduces the narrator who stands on the shore of Roblin Lake, which happens to be near the home of the poet. This implies that Purdy is the one who observes, just two shores away, a crew of workingmen "sheathing the church spire with new metal." Upon closer inspection, Purdy notices a lone man who "hangs in the sky over there from a piece of rope." The man is clearly taking a chance with his life to fix the spire because he is "working his way up along the spire until there's nothing left to nail on." The spire is also described as "God's belly-scratcher," implying that while the man is dedicated to his work, there's a sense that in the grand scheme of things, the act may just be a minor, inconsequential job.

Lines 8–15

In the following lines, Purdy ponders the workman's motivation for his work. He hypothesizes that it is the man's faith that drives him. However, because the work is so dangerous, the man's faith "reaches beyond: touches intangibles, wrestles with Jacob." The mention of Jacob refers to the Book of Genesis in which Jacob has a vision of a stairway that leads to heaven and later builds a pillar in the place which he believes is the gate to heaven. Jacob's experience leads him to believe that God manifests himself and his purpose in times of hardship. Thus, Purdy believes that the man working on the church is not only doing God's work but also thinks his faith in God will protect him from harm. As the man "pounds hard in the blue cave of the sky, [he] contends heroically with difficult problems of gravity, sky navigation and mythopoeia." This last word, *mythopoeia,* means creating a myth. This suggests that the man hanging in the sky might see his work in mythic terms and its value in mythic proportions, which could lead to a struggle with maintaining his humility to avoid an act of hubris that is a sin in God's eyes. If the man hopes to reach heaven's gate through his acts of good will, he must remember that acts alone do not guarantee entry to heaven. Ultimately, it's the man's faith that will redeem him in God's eyes.

The next lines confirm the man's commitment, saying that in addition to contending with the above issues (gravity, mythopoeia), he isn't being paid for his work. Rather, the man is volunteering his time and labor to the church and to God. Purdy refers to the man's labor as a "non-union job" without tangible benefits such as health insurance. This comment is a testament to the sacrifice one makes to God in doing his work; however, it also implies that the compensation is intangible, and, therefore, it has the potential to be more spiritually rewarding.

Lines 16–20

The second stanza moves away from the lone man working on the church. It abandons the shores of Roblin Lake and expands out into the world. Purdy mentions the fields and the woodlots that line the environment and how "death is yodelling quiet" throughout the land. The mention of death silently hovering around the man alludes to the fact that death is a common occurrence; in fact, it has taken the lives of three young birds that were crushed "in the sub-surface of the new county highway." These deaths confirm the idea that death is a necessary part of life, even when great risk is not being taken. In addition, the act of progress, shown in the creation of a new highway, can often result in the sacrifice of innocent victims.

Lines 21–24

The beginning of the third stanza makes a transition from the present time to the past. Purdy states that the "picture is incomplete." He delves into a "Durer landscape," making a reference to the artist Albrecht Durer, who created religious woodcuts in the fifteenth and sixteenth centuries. The Durer landscape adds another dimension to the poem, putting it into a context that involves the myth of Icarus. Icarus and his father, Daedalus, tried to climb to great heights using wings made with feathers and wax to gain their freedom. However, Icarus ignored his father's advice to watch how high he flew. Icarus got too close to the sun, which melted his wings and resulted in his fall and death. Daedalus was devastated as he watched his son's demise, which is reflected in the line, "gothic ancestors peer from medieval sky, dour faces trapped." The dour face is that of Daedalus, who must helplessly watch his only son die because of his noble vice.

Lines 25–31

As the fourth stanza continues, Purdy mentions "work-sodden wives groping inside their flesh for what keeps moving and changing and flashing," and "a two-headed calf born in the barn." These images have religious overtones and hark back to pioneer times, implying that the history of Purdy's landscape must be acknowledged to understand the present. The poem seems to say that, despite the agony and pain that accompanies life, it keeps moving in an unforgiving fashion. Purdy questions the reason behind agony, asking if it is a sign of "fire and brimstone?" He then answers his own question by saying that these acts are, instead, just signs of "an age and a faith moving into transition."

Lines 32–37

The poem comes to a close by returning to the present and engaging the reader in some suspenseful action. Coming back to the man working on the church, Purdy sets up the ending by saying "deep woods shiver and water drops hang pendant, double-yolked eggs and the house creaks a little— something is about to happen." The foreshadowing is clear and alludes to the calm before the storm, as if Purdy is anticipating a tragedy. With the myth of Icarus resonating throughout the poem, Purdy believes that the workingman with the capacity to rise above the earth will eventually return to the earth, just as Icarus did. The final line "perhaps he will fall," confirms the theory, yet it's also an affirmation because with death the man's life and work will not be just a fleeting moment in time, but it will become a part of history and speak to and inspire future generations.

Themes

Religion and Mythology

The themes of religion and mythology are present throughout "Wilderness Gothic." Most prominent is the image of a workingman at the top a church repairing its spire, which is then coupled with a mention of Jacob from the Book of Genesis. This allusion serves to connect the man with the concept of whether good works and acts of faith ensure a rightful place in heaven. As the workingman hangs in the air against the blue sky, it brings to mind Jacob's vision of a ladder that leads directly to Heaven. In addition, the Greek myth of Icarus plays a large part in the poem by exploring the idea of human aspiration and the capacity for failure. Purdy's poem suggests a connection between the workingman's noble ambition and Icarus' attempts to fly. However, Icarus died because he had too much ambition, a vice that may also bring the workingman to his demise. Another association that exists involves the idea that Icarus, because of his folly, became an emblem of aspiration, and so the poem offers the same possibility to the workingman—that death may, ironically, bring him immortality.

Work

Purdy introduces the theme of work immediately with the first few lines of the poem. The first thing the narrator observes is a crew repairing a church two shores away. The focus turns on one man, who is hanging by a rope, "working his way up along the spire." As the poem continues, Purdy announces that the man is doing volunteer work. He will not be paid for his labor nor will he receive the type of benefits that come with other jobs. However, the man is doing God's work, a notion that has in large part disappeared from modern culture. The admiration for the workingman is evident as Purdy refers to his deeds as heroic. Since Purdy was a working-class poet, he understood the inherent value in doing hard labor. He suggests that there's something noble in a hard day's work, a concept that might put Purdy in direct contrast with his intellectual, university-educated peers. By creating a poem that exalts the workingman, Purdy criticizes the values of modern society by compar-

Topics for Further Study

- Critics claim that Purdy is a distinctively Canadian poet. What makes his work Canadian? Explore the relationship between American and Canadian politics and how that relationship may affect and influence Purdy's political poems.

- Read about Jacob in the Book of Genesis, and explore how his relationship with God parallels the plight of the man in "Wilderness Gothic."

- Compare and contrast the work ethic of the Victorian pioneers mentioned in "Wilderness Gothic" with that of today's culture. How do they differ? Why do you think these differences exist?

- Have you ever taken a risk and failed? Explain your encounter, your motivations, and what, if anything, you learned from your experiences.

ing modern people to the people of past centuries, who eagerly sacrificed time and labor for the greater glory of God. The workingman seems to be an exception for his time, having more in common with his medieval counterparts who were not concerned with a wage or whether they had a union job.

Death

The first image of death in "Wilderness Gothic" is a misdirection of sorts. The third and fourth lines of the poem announce that "someone hangs in the sky / over there from a piece of rope." This immediately brings to mind someone who has committed suicide by hanging. However, it is quickly realized that the man in question is not dead, rather he is working to repair the spire on a church. It is made clear in the next few lines that the man is putting his life in danger for the sake of God and putting his fate in God's hands. Since, the man could fall to his death at any time, the narrator believes the man's faith must reach far and wide. As the poem continues, it describes the death of three young birds who meet their demise because

of the construction of a new county highway. Considering that the birds meet their death while the workingman holds his life in the balance, the poem implies that death is present everywhere and can occur randomly and without warning.

The idea of death is continued as the myth of Icarus is mentioned. Icarus met his death while trying to secure his freedom. Consequently, the workingman may lose his own life in the pursuit of a kind of spiritual freedom. Finally, the poem ends with the line, "perhaps he will fall," which predicts the death of the workingman. And while it is not definite that the man will die while working on the church, the line "something is about to happen" implies that the possibility of death hovers heavily in the air. This further confirms the concept that death can come at any time, and is, in fact, a necessary part of a life and a consequence of a world that inevitably moves and progresses over time.

Style

Non-linear Narrative

When Purdy composed "Wilderness Gothic," he departed dramatically from his early dependence on romantic models and delved into a more relaxed, nonlinear form of poetry that boasts a colloquial and contemporary style. As he traveled the Canadian countryside with his contemporaries, reading his poetry to audiences, his construction was liberated and became more relaxed and connected to oral syntax and speech patterns. Essentially, his style accommodates the speaking voice, which highlights run-on sentences, fragments, and mixed tenses, as well as variations in tone and diction. It also infuses Purdy's poetry with a range of emotions, such as humor and anger. In addition, the nonlinear narrative of "Wilderness Gothic" affords Purdy the freedom to express different points of view.

Narrative Lyric

"Wilderness Gothic" can also be considered a narrative lyric, a construction that is characterized by a two-part poem. The first part of the poem is usually some type of anecdote, while the second part offers an investigation and further understanding of that anecdote, then it finishes with a satisfying end. The first part of "Wilderness Gothic" begins with the tale of a workingman repairing a church spire. After the poem introduces this character, it shifts into an investigation of the

Compare & Contrast

- **1928:** Television station WGY, in Schenectady, New York, airs the country's first regularly scheduled television broadcasts.

  1948: One million homes in the United States have televisions, up from five thousand just three years earlier.

  1952: Nearly 17 million homes in the United States have television sets.

  1962: Ninety-eight percent of the households in the United States have at least one television.

  Today: Television screens are seen frequently in public places, including grocery stores, airport terminals, stadiums, and classrooms.

- **1928:** A year after the first commercial talking movie, *The Jazz Singer,* Disney releases the first cartoon with a voice track. Named *Steamboat Willie,* the cartoon introduces the popular character Mickey Mouse.

  1938: Disney releases the world's first full-length animated film, *Snow White and the Seven Dwarfs.*

  1961: *The Flintstones* becomes the first animated television series to be broadcast during the prime-time evening hours.

  Today: Computer artists use graphic simulations to design impressive visual effects for movies and television.

- **1928:** Penicillin is first proven to have bacteria-fighting properties. In following years, a number of antibiotics are developed, changing the face of medicine.

  Today: Researchers are finding antibiotics to be less successful than they were a generation ago. Because of the extensive use of antibiotics, tougher bacteria strains that are resistant to antibiotics have evolved.

subject in relation to the past. Once the investigation ends, the poem comes full circle, back to the workingman. The last few lines serve to provide closure.

Historical Context

When Purdy created "Wilderness Gothic," he was going through a major transformation that reflects the times in which he lived. Purdy had lived through the Depression and World War II, and the style of his early poetry was quite formal, which mirrored the literary and social culture of the 1940s. However, during the 1960s, the United States and Canada were experiencing significant social changes that divided older and younger generations. The younger generations were expelling rigid social constraints and getting involved in a number of political movements, such as the civil rights movement (which fought for equal rights for mi-

nority ethnic groups), the antiwar movement (which promoted civil disobedience against the war in Vietnam), the sexual revolution (which encouraged people to express their sexual desires more freely), and the women's movement (which fought for equal rights for women). In addition, the literary culture was expanding. The Beat poets in America, such as Kerouac and Ginsberg, were changing the literary landscape and redefining and revolutionizing the craft. Since the attitudes in America inevitably permeated its northern neighbor, Canada, these attitudes affected Purdy and his work, as it was at this time that he began to change his old style of writing and expand his horizons.

In addition, during the 1960s, the Canada Council began programs that allowed Purdy to dedicate himself to writing and not to worry about supporting himself with other work. This gave him the freedom to stop doing the menial work that he'd done since he left school as a teenager and to travel extensively during this time, wandering the Canadian countryside with his fellow poets and taking his poetry directly to the people. By reading his work to large audiences and interacting with his peers, Purdy was able to modify his rigid style of poetry in favor of a freer verse. He also began traveling to different countries, such as Cuba, Mexico, Turkey, Greece, and Italy, which exposed Purdy to different people and cultures. During this time, he familiarized himself with the poets Pablo Neruda, Charles Bukowski, and Cesar Vallejo. While he recognized these poets as influences, he explained in *For Openers: Conversations with Twenty-four Canadian Writers,* "I believe that when a poet fixes on one style or method he severely limits his present and future development." This statement serves to prove that Purdy finally set aside his previous inclination of mimicking other poets to the point that his influences were no longer apparent in his work.

While "Wilderness Gothic" is not necessarily set in the 1960s—in fact, it does not have a definite time frame—the subject matter resembles a shift in generational values. Purdy's poem compares and contrasts religious faith and work between the Victorian pioneers and that of more modern people. This idea has its roots in the generational struggles that occurred during the 1960s. Young people were at odds with their parents and the conservative political system over their views about gender, ethnic, and international relations. The 1960s, in some respects, represented a change in the cultural climate toward greater freedom. In this poem, it is Purdy's style and construction that serve to capture the spirit of the freedom of the 1960s.

Critical Overview

When "Wilderness Gothic" was published in the volume *Wild Grape Wine,* Purdy achieved a breakthrough in the literary world. Critics regarded his previous work as generally inferior and immature in comparison to the work of his peers. However, with the collection that included "Wilderness Gothic," Purdy reinvented himself, and the critics noticed that he had finally developed his own unique style. Critic George Woodcock calls it one of "his most completely successful poems," saying "it is one of the poems in which Purdy deftly juxtaposes the different elements of his world." As a result of this work and others he published at the time, Purdy received the Governor General's Literary Award, which significantly advanced his rep-

utation as a poet. At that point in his life, Purdy was able to support himself financially with his writing and began to lecture at prestigious Canadian universities.

Purdy sustained a successful career until his death. While some critics note that his works has a rough, unfinished quality, other critics praise Purdy for continuing to create poems with expanding insight at a late stage in his life. When his *Collected Poems of Al Purdy* was published, critics called it an exceptional accomplishment. Purdy's prolific career is summed up by critic John Bemrose, who says, "a hundred years from now, one of the few Canadian poets whose work will still be read is Al Purdy. . . . A handful of his best poems . . . already have the feel of classics; they are uncannily powerful meditations on fate, landscape, and history."

Criticism

Michele Drohan

Drohan is a professional editor and writer who specializes in classic and contemporary literature. In the following essay, she explores Purdy's working-class background and the idea that his personal beliefs about life and his experiences in the working world find their way into his poems, particularly the ideas that are expressed in his poem.

Purdy's ancestors were Canadian Loyalists who settled in Upper Canada in the 1780s after the Revolutionary War. This family history influenced Purdy's early writing, and he exalted his ancestors' tenacity and courage in his writing. After Purdy's father (a farmer) died, young Purdy moved with his mother to a house that was more than one hundred years old. Purdy described the house in his poem "Morning and It's Summer," saying: "The floors were sagging upstairs and down, as if the house was tired from all these years and couldn't stand properly upright any longer." While Purdy attended public school for a while, he eventually dropped out and spent his teenage years working through the Great Depression. After Purdy joined the Royal Canadian Air Force, he married and moved to Ameliasburgh, Ontario, where he built his own house and continued working in places such as a mattress factory. During all these years, Purdy kept writing poetry. By Purdy's own admission, the poems he writes represent himself. He tells critic Peter O'Brien that he doesn't understand how "anybody could not say that about their poems." Purdy continues, "I'm not saying that everything I write is God's truth or anybody's truth, but it is my kind of truth. It's the truth of the moment." In fact, one of his poems "Piling Blood," discussed his work at a factory where he stacked piles of blood from animal slaughters. Because he does not dissociate himself from his work, Purdy's life inevitably influences his poems. With "Wilderness Gothic," Purdy is making a fierce statement about sacrifice, ambition, aspiration, and faith, while also reflecting on his own strength of character. While Purdy always considered poetry his true calling, the work he did to support himself made him a working-class poet, one who did not receive any formal training and who looked to Canada's history for inspiration. Critic George Woodcock said "Canada—and Loyalist Ontario in particular—is indeed the heart of [Purdy's] world." These factors combined to earn him the title of poet of the people.

Much of Purdy's work is grounded in the Canadian land. Critic George Woodcock believes that Purdy has "an awareness of the brilliant surface of the earth as clear as that of an imagist, and yet at the same time a sense of depths and heights, of super real dimensions, so that common things can suddenly become irradiated and the world swing into ecstasy." This idea is represented fully in "Wilderness Gothic," as Purdy takes a common moment of a man working to fix a church spire and turns it into something greater, a testament to his dedication to God, his heroic work ethic, and his connection to history.

The setting of Purdy's poems are often recognizable as his homeland. His house in Ameliasburgh was close to Roblin Lake, which is the first image presented in "Wilderness Gothic." This implies that the narrator in the poem is Purdy, who stands watching "across Roblin Lake, two shores away." By inserting himself into the poem, Purdy shows that the ideas expressed in the work reflect his own feelings about life. He is writing about the world in which he lives, that of the common man. As "Wilderness Gothic" progresses, Purdy is surprised to see a man hanging in the sky by a rope "working his way up along the spire until there's nothing left to nail on." Purdy's first reaction is that of wonder, and he ponders the man's motivation for working at such a dangerous task. The idea of faith is introduced, as Purdy believes it must be the man's intense faith in God that gives him the strength and desire to risk his own life.

Purdy's curiosity turns to admiration as he describes the man's efforts as brave, pointing out that

As 'Wilderness Gothic' progresses, Purdy is surprised to see a man hanging in the sky by a rope 'working his way up along the spire until there's nothing left to nail on.' Purdy's first reaction is that of wonder, and he ponders the man's motivation for working at such a dangerous task. The idea of faith is introduced...."

the man "contends heroically with difficult problems of gravity, sky navigation and mythopoeia." The next few lines make a strong statement about the times in which Purdy lived: "his volunteer time and labour donated to God, minus sick benefits of course on a non-union job." Upon closer look, this epiphany becomes a declaration about the work ethics of the man in relation to society at large. Purdy lives in a modern time, where most people are concerned with their daily wage and what kind of benefits they are receiving when they do a job. Instead of doing work for the sake of the work, the focus of any job for most people is on tangible compensation. The workingman in the poem stands out as a rare example of doing work for God, a kind of work that is primarily volunteer in nature. The rewards are therefore intangible. The man working on the church reaches noble heights, as he labors for his faith. While his rewards will inevitably be more spiritual, there is no guarantee, in the end, that his good works will ensure his place in heaven. This lack of guarantee makes the work that much more courageous and admirable in Purdy's eyes.

Purdy then shifts in time and introduces what he calls a Durer landscape. Albrecht Durer was an artist in the fifteenth and sixteenth centuries who made religious woodcuts. One of his woodcuts de-

What Do I Read Next?

- *The Bukowski/Purdy Letters, 1964–1974: A Decade of Dialogue* (1983) is a volume of correspondence between the two poets.

- *Dig Up My Heart: Selected Poems 1952–1983* (1994) is a collection by Milton Acorn, a fellow "working class" Canadian poet who was admired by and often compared to Purdy.

- *Poems for All the Annettes* (1962) is Al Purdy's first critically acclaimed collection of poetry.

- *Reaching for the Beaufort Sea: An Autobiography* (1994) by Al Purdy is a comprehensive look into the poet's life and work. It is edited by Alex Widen.

tails the fall of Icarus. Icarus is a mythical Greek figure who died while trying to escape from imprisonment. He had wings attached to his body with wax; however, he flew too close to the sun and fell to his death. Despite Icarus' mistake, his legend became a symbol for human aspiration. By making a reference to the Durer landscape, Purdy suggests a comparison between the workingman in the poem and the myth of Icarus. At first glance, the workingman's dedications might seem naive and foolish; however, Purdy seems to be saying that, like Icarus, the workingman should be admired for his ambition, even if it might result in tragedy.

The poem also makes references to Victorian pioneers and medieval ancestors and how they faced great adversity in their times. Hard work was a way of life back then and it was commonplace to dedicate time and energy to God. Similarly, Purdy was a self-educated man who worked hard to support himself, a sacrifice he made for his creative ambition. Perhaps unlike some of his contemporaries who were university educated, Purdy understood the value in a hard day's work and how it gave him not only the freedom to engage in creative pursuits but a wealth of ideas to use in his poetry. Purdy clearly admires and relates to the work-

ingman in his poem, while also commenting on a society that undervalues the meaning of hard work.

At the end of "Wilderness Gothic," Purdy makes a statement that hints at his own fear of defeat. There is an anticipation of something tragic in the last few lines. By announcing that "something is about to happen," Purdy exposes the anxiety that accompanies any risk—that of fear of failure. Purdy understood failure very well. In his early years as a poet, he received negative criticism about his work, causing him to doubt his own abilities. However, Purdy never stopped writing, an ambition that mirrors the man in the poem who will keep climbing his way up the spire until "there's nothing left to nail on."

The last line of the poem is perhaps the most shocking and most revealing in the whole piece. It also proves to be a bit of a conundrum. By saying "perhaps he will fall," it seems that Purdy is almost willing the tragedy to occur. However, it begs the question, why would Purdy wish for the man he admires to meet his demise? One interpretation is that he is envious of the man's dedication and wishes him to fall and be punished for his naivete. On a second reading, though, the line takes on another meaning. When Purdy says, "perhaps he will fall," he seems to be acknowledging one of life's ironies—that to succeed at anything great, one must be prepared to fail. Considering the fate of Icarus, it was his failure that was captured in legend. Certainly, falling or failing is the risk one takes to achieve such grand ambitions; but, for Purdy, that fate is far more noble than never having taken the risk at all. Purdy's last line then serves to confirm the man's courage, because if there were no risk, the man would never have the opportunity to be a hero. On another level, Purdy is also serving to confirm his own life's work as if to say, because he risked so much himself for the sake of his craft, he too has lived a courageous life, and he too may one day become a legend and, more importantly, a part of Canadian literary history.

Source: Michele Drohan, Critical Essay on "Wilderness Gothic," in *Poetry for Students,* The Gale Group, 2001.

Alice Van Wart

Van Wart is an editor who has a Ph.D. in Canadian literature. In the following essay, she offers a close reading of the poem to show Purdy's development of theme and technique.

In the sixties, Canada experienced a cultural renaissance in its poetry, a phenomenon that started in the fifties. One reason for the rising popularity of poetry was coffeehouse poetry readings that made it possible for a poet to become a public figure and persona. Two flamboyant and well-known Canadian "coffeehouse" poets were Leonard Cohen and Irving Layton. A third was Al Purdy. Purdy was one of a number of poets, along with Alden Nowlan, Milton Acorn, and Patrick Lane, whose roots lay in Canada's working class. These poets turned away from the formal poems favored at the time and wrote an informal poetry based on narrative and anecdote written in a colloquial voice. Their interests were in the rediscovery of their personal history and in bringing to Canadian poetry a sense of its own past.

A prolific poet, who won numerous awards, Purdy began writing poetry in his teens, paying to have his first book published. Though he did not continue his formal education beyond grade ten, Purdy read voraciously and worked diligently at his craft. In his introduction to *The Collected Poems of Al Purdy,* Dennis Lee, speaking of Purdy's long, self-taught apprenticeship, observed that Purdy was one of "the slowest developers in the history of poetry."

Purdy also traveled widely and worked at various casual and manual jobs, often using these experiences for his subject matter. His poetry moved towards an exploration of indigenous myth. He mythologized the landscape of the southeastern end of Lake Ontario, the area where he was born and lived. Human behavior and destiny fascinated Purdy. His unique voice used humor and compassion as it blended the cadences of real speech with elegiac form. Because of his colloquial language, the informality of his tone, and his tendency towards using a long line, Purdy's poems are immediately accessible though they convey complex ideas that express universal values.

"Wilderness Gothic" is typical of Purdy's poetry both in subject and technique. Though located in the particular, the poem reflects complex ideas. The human figure in the poem, the workman re-sheathing the church spire, is in the poet's eyes both literally a tiny dot in the sky and metaphorically a tiny dot at the intersection of historical time. As the poet reflects on what he sees, the changing nature of his perceptions constitutes a complex meditation that moves beyond the temporal and spatial boundaries of the physical to the metaphysical and encompasses the historical. It expresses the idea of life as a continuing process where each new age brings in new ideas and casts off the old.

The poem works through three stanzas of free verse. Each stanza expresses the poet's changing

> *Because of his colloquial language, the informality of his tone, and his tendency towards using a long line, Purdy's poems are immediately accessible though they convey complex ideas that express universal values."*

perspective as he watches a workman contending with the physical problems of "replacing [the] rotten timber" of the church's spire "with pine thews" while being suspended in the sky. In the second stanza, the poet's perceptions broaden as he sees the workman with the framework of the countryside. In the third stanza, the poet sees the scene as a tableau, equating the scene before his eyes with a painter's landscape.

The oxymoron in the poem's title points to poets' strategy of juxtaposing the abstract and the concrete and the past and the present. The wilderness, a land in the new world, is thought of as uninhabited, uncultivated, and uncivilized. Gothic is a term that describes a style of highly evolved and excessively ornate architecture popular in Western Europe from the twelfth to sixteenth centuries. Yoking these terms highlights Purdy's intention of showing the abstract through the concrete, while collapsing the past and the present.

Purdy's poem begins in the particular locale of Roblin Lake with a casual observation. The poet notices across the lake "two shores away / they are sheathing the church spire / with new metal." From the distance, it appears to the poet that the person doing the work "hangs in the sky / . . . from a piece of rope." Both the line's syntax and the break between lines three and four work to isolate the image of the man hanging in the sky, a startling image to the poet and reader, before the poet realizes the worker is suspended by a rope "hammering and fitting God's belly-scratcher." The playful image of the church's spire as God's belly-scratcher returns the poet to the workman "working his way up along the spire / until there's nothing left to nail on."

As the poet casually observes the image before him, he begins to think about the nature of the person working on the spire. He speculates on what the worker is thinking as he works in "the blue cave of the sky." The poet wonders if the worker's religious faith "reaches beyond" the top of the spire, or if he "touches intangibles, wrestles with Jacob." The allusion to Jacob suggests the biblical story of Jacob wrestling with an angel (Genesis 32: 24-29), and unites the concrete, temporal, and physical world of "rotten timber" and "pine thews" to the metaphysical world of abstract speculation concerned with the nature of faith. The last five lines of the stanza reinforce the connection between the concrete and the abstract as the worker "pounds hard in the blue cave of the sky," and contends "heroically with difficult problems of / gravity, sky navigation and mythopoeia." Mythopoeia in this sense refers to the mythology associated with religious thought. In the last line of the first stanza, however, the poet's tone shifts away from the seriousness of his reflections to ironic humor. The poet wonders if the worker has volunteered his time and labor, donating it "to God." In this case, the job is non-union and has no "sick benefits." Considering the danger of his job, the poet implies he may very well need them.

In the second stanza, the poet sees the scene of the man hanging beside the spire in the distance within the framework of the countryside. The sense of the poet's presence and his watching eyes fade as the focus in the stanza turns outward to the impersonal natural world where fields "are yellowing into harvest" and "nestling and fingerling are sky and water borne." The images of the mature birds and fish suggest summer's end and approaching autumn. The symbolic association of fall with death is explicit in the colorful image of death "yodelling quiet in green woodlots." In the last two lines of the stanza, death becomes literal when "the bodies of three young birds [that] have disappeared" are found "in the sub-surface of the new county highway." The death of the birds suggests the inherent dangers in the "new county highway."

By the end of the second stanza, the poet has painted with words a picture of a church in a country landscape where a man is repairing a church spire. In the third stanza, the poet compares the picture in front of him to a Durer landscape. Yet, he is aware that the picture in front of him "is incomplete" and understands that the "part left out / . . . might alter the whole Durer landscape." The allusion to this particular painter is central to the meaning of "Wilderness Gothic." Albrecht Durer, considered the greatest artist of the northern

Renascence, brought the development of Gothic art in northern Europe to its pinnacle. At the same time, he radically altered the Gothic style of earlier German art by bringing to it the new styles of the Italian Renaissance. Durer's art represents a period of intense change when new learning and beliefs and new styles of art were changing the world from medieval to modern.

Behind Durer's new style, however, exist the unseen eyes of his "gothic ancestors" who "peer from medieval sky." The gothic ancestors not only represent the traditions that came before but also the lives of the people. In the same way, the poet sees beyond the "dour faces trapped in photograph albums." Like the gothic ancestors, the poet sees peering from behind Durer's paintings, he sees the dour faces in the photographs "escaping / to clop down iron roads with matched greys: / work-sodden wives groping inside their flesh." The enjambment of lines twenty four and twenty five places the emphasis on the word "escaping," and brings back to the trapped faces a sense of their lives. The photographs could be those of his own Victorian ancestors. Whoever they are, the poet sees what the still images cannot show: "what keeps moving and changing and flashing / beyond and past the long frozen Victorian day." The progressive verbs suggest the nature of life in all its flux and change and work in direct contrast to the words "trapped" and "frozen." What paintings and photographs cannot capture is life with its constant flux and change. The next two lines shift to a series of rhetorical questions that evoke through the poet's use of image something of "the long frozen Victorian day."

The Victorian era, defined by repressive attitudes about sex and matters of the body taught by a grim Presbyterianism, believed in "fire and brimstone" as the consequence of sin. Natural aberrations like the birth of a "two headed cow" or "a sharp female agony" (a miscarriage or natural abortion) would have been seen as signs of sin in an age going wrong. The images evoke an ominous sense of impending disaster often associated with events in a transitional age. The poet clarifies the association of the images with a transitional time when he calls it "an age and a faith moving into transition." The following lines list a series of minor domestic occurrences. Dinner is cold and the "new-baked bread a failure." Outside the "deep woods shiver and water drops hang pendant" while the eggs are "double yolked and the house creaks a little." He concludes with the apocalyptic suggestion that "Something is about to happen."

The shift to the present tense in line thirty one, however, indicates a return to the present time of 1968 when the poem was written. The age and faith that moves into transition refers not only to the transition of the previous time but also to the sixties, a time of radical ideals and changing values. There is a corresponding shift in tone in these lines as the poet's thoughts turn back to the present, to the double yoked egg he has just cracked and the creaking of the house, and to the ominous sense of something about to happen. The shift in tone accompanies the change in the choice of images. A doubled yoked egg is less ominous than a two headed calf, and the failure of baked bread and a cold dinner could not seriously be seen as signs of troubled times. The serious nature of the poet's reflections has turned into playful self-mockery. His seemingly ominous prediction that "something is about to happen" is followed by the ironically portentousness of the "leaves are still." The image deflates the poet's high seriousness as he returns to "a man hammering in the sky" two shores away. The poem turns back to the beginning and the specific moment where "something is about to happen." The wry humor that ended the first stanza concludes the poem with the poet's short and cryptic conclusion that "perhaps he will fall." The line is intentionally bathetic as apocalyptic imaginings are brought back to the moment and the physical reality of the danger of the man's work.

In "Wilderness Gothic," Al Purdy creates seamless shifts in perspectives and voice to transcend spatial and temporal boundaries, to collapse past and present, and to bring together the near and the far, the here. The poem expresses a process that shows the universal in the concrete particulars of place and event.

Source: Alice Van Wart, Critical Essay on "Wilderness Gothic," in *Poetry for Students,* The Gale Group, 2001.

S. K. Robisch

Robisch teaches ecological and American literature at Purdue University. In the following essay, he considers Al Purdy's poem as not only a regional and Canadian poem but as a North American poem.

Al Purdy spent several years and five books of poetry on finding his subject matter, and when he found it, he achieved great success. "Wilderness Gothic" may be the poem that best demonstrates the subject matter he found. His early work followed strict formal conventions; much of it was derivative and unoriginal, but it gave him an education in po-

> *. . . Purdy captured in his work a Canadian sense of vastness, of the land as a presence that prompts Canadians to think in terms of great scale, ancient time, and their position in that place . . . . the Canadian sense exhibited in much contemporary writing is different than the United States' sense of promised land, nature as gift, and revolutionary conquest."*

etry. He did not attend a university, and so he learned poetry by reading, by examining, by meeting other poets, and, finally, by moving to a place that inspired a great change in his language. He is a poet of the school of hard knocks. It is important to know this when reading "Wilderness Gothic," because his strength as a writer and the fame he gained have often been attributed to his strong ties to his region and his nation. One important trait of this particular poem, however, is that it also demonstrates Purdy's sense of history and scope. In an Al Purdy poem, a small place usually points the reader to a much larger and older one.

The poem begins with a reference to Roblin Lake, which is located in Ontario, Canada, where Purdy and his wife bought a house in the mid-1960s. At the lake, Purdy produced a new, more vibrant poetry that looked closely at his surroundings in a rough-hewn voice, a voice like the land around him. The lines in "Wilderness Gothic" are long. The poem is a narrative, full of the life not only of the lake but also of religion and doubt and mythology. The narrator is an observer, as Purdy must have often been, a thinker capable of taking the long view of his subject. This viewpoint is vital to understanding Purdy's work; the change in his poetry from formalist verse to strong observational free verse changed his very heritage as a poet.

"Wilderness Gothic" and other poems from books such as *The Cariboo Horses* and *North of Summer* make him a descendant of the poets of place, those who know that who one is is very often shaped by where and when one is living.

When the reader arrives at the lake, he or she sees the church spire standing against the sky "two shores away." The first stanza of the poem shows a lake and sky, simple in place, epic in scale. The workman on the church steeple is given a religious persona as well—Jacob of the Old Testament, who had a dream about a ladder reaching heaven and who wrestled with an angel. Laced throughout this stanza is Purdy's characteristic roughness, a mild vulgarity, in the way he calls the spire "God's belly scratcher"; in his wry reference to there finally being "nothing left to nail on" (that the spire does not, in fact, reach heaven, and if it does, that there's nothing left there); and in the final line in reference to blue-collar labor with God as the boss. The word *mythopeia* is included as a problem with which the laborer must contend, along with gravity (which becomes important in the final line), and "sky navigation." Mythopeia, or mythmaking, is equated with knowing the stars and with the scientific fact of gravity, so that this church at Roblin Lake points the reader to things of great magnitude, things that the narrator considers without too much faith or too much hope. He focuses instead on the worker, which is another common trait of Al Purdy's poetry.

In the second stanza of the poem, the reader sees a kind of pivot into the voice of the third stanza. The narrator is a skeptic; his view of this job of reaching God is, in some ways, similar to God's own view of the tower of Babel. In the fields around this church, "death is yodelling," and "gothic ancestors peer from a medieval sky." The stanza ends with an odd, augural image of the county highway as a place of disappearance. The accomplishment of human labor, it seems, only provides the reader with another means by which the ancient truths come back again and again. People still have old faiths and repair the church steeple. Where once the wilderness frightened Europeans who came to North America, it has become rural and, in some ways, tamed, but Purdy does not let it remain so. The births and deaths of the natural world go on, but "that picture is incomplete." It requires a closer look at how natural time and human time, when combined, produce a sometimes dark and difficult history.

The connotations of gothic literature surface in those moments of labor throughout "Wilderness Gothic"; hard work is dangerous work and has associated with it something of the sublime and grotesque. The labor of child birth, for example, appears in the middle of the third stanza in connection to all of the elements of the poem: the mythmaking of fire and brimstone, the hard fact of a mutated calf, the juxtaposition of that unfortunate birth with the "sharp female agony," implied to be the agony of the "work-sodden wives," who are dehumanized in the stanza. There are omens in this stanza, indications of something pagan and primordial in the land around Roblin Lake as the laboring man works on the church, and the laboring woman works against a suffering associated with "an age and a faith moving into transition." The medieval reference gives the reader a sense of many centuries of people working on churches, building towns in the wilderness, and trusting the creaks of their houses, divination, and the legacy of the generations who worked before them. In "Wilderness Gothic," Purdy tells the reader through his narrative voice that those mythic invocations have not changed, partly because the land is older than humans, and the fields around Roblin Lake, while cultivated, are the place where young birds still disappear, only now, they disappear into highways.

Purdy gained considerable fame in Canada for bringing its poetry a strong voice—not only for writing strong poems but for writing strong loyalist poems. The voice of Roblin Lake is also, in the canon of poetry, the voice of loyalist Ontario and of Canada, which gave Purdy two Governor General's awards, the highest Canadian literary honor. One of the reasons for this particular acclaim, according to several writers and critics, is that Purdy captured in his work a Canadian sense of vastness, of the land as a presence that prompts Canadians to think in terms of great scale, ancient time, and their position in that place. From British Columbia to Newfoundland, the Canadian sense exhibited in much contemporary writing is different than the United States' sense of promised land, nature as gift, and revolutionary conquest. In poem after poem of Purdy's work, this sense is acute, but in "Wilderness Gothic" something even bigger is happening. This poem reaches even beyond the national impulse and invokes a kind of North American consciousness. Margaret Atwood said of Purdy that his voice "wasn't just focused on personal event. It had a geographic, geological, archaeological scope to it, and it was the way he would connect time and space with the moment."

Two other art works might give the reader some idea of how Purdy's poem achieves a North American scope, Marianne Moore's poem "The Steeple Jack" and Grant Wood's painting "American Gothic." Moore's poem depicts the same scene as Purdy's but in a supposedly quintessential United States venue. Just as Purdy writes in the third stanza of "Wilderness Gothic," "That picture is incomplete, part left out / that might alter the whole Durer landscape." Moore writes, "Durer would have seen a reason for living in a town like this." Albrecht Durer was famous for his detail, for being meticulous at rendering, and so it is with the efficiency of workmanship, such as the repair of the church steeple. The middle of Moore's poem seems to celebrate the wildness of life around the steeple; she lists flowers and describes the flights of birds. Purdy's second stanza does a little of the same. He turns to the fields, to the way nature follows it seasonal course and builds its own mythology, but his is a darker mythology.

While in "The Steeple Jack" the reader sees a sense of celebration and hope, "Wilderness Gothic" forcefully shifts its view to the possibility of danger. "It could not be dangerous to be living," writes Moore in her poem, "in a town like this, of simple people, / who have a steeple-jack placing danger-signs by the church / while he is gilding the solid-pointed star, which on a steeple / stands for hope." For Purdy, this is not the case. His worker, as seen in the last line, "could fall," and the long third stanza leading to it prepares the reader for that possibility, a possibility that pervades the industrious efforts of European North Americans, whether in Canada or in the United States.

But even though Moore and Purdy have different approaches to the subject, the material is the same in many ways. Even Moore acknowledges the risk of approaching God when she calls "the pitch of the church / not true," and says that her steeple jack has a sign on the sidewalk below that reads, "Danger." Moore was a prominent poet, "The Steeple Jack" one of her best-known poems; and Purdy was an ardent reader, so he may have been under some influence. It is almost certain, however, that he knew of "American Gothic." The painter Grant Wood was influenced by German and Flemish painting styles but interpreted those styles into his own vision, a rural American one. His painting gets its title partly from the gothic window of the house behind the two famous figures in the foreground. Wood, who knew Iowa, used his sister and his dentist as models for the work. He brought to his painting a subtle irony, a combination of celebrating the American farmer and looking hard at the dourness of the work. This is precisely Purdy's sense as well.

None of this is said in an attempt to deny the national and regional significance of "Wilderness Gothic." On the contrary, the reader should see the poem as being so precise, so strongly written, that while it focuses acutely on a small place, it invokes a whole continent as well as the history of its working class, those who are often at physical and, in "Wilderness Gothic," spiritual risk when doing their jobs.

The sounds of the lines, the choice of words such as "dour," "clop," "iron," "frozen," and "brimstone"—all in the space of a few lines—casts a long shadow. The wilderness around the steeple is the living indicator that the reader should not be too confident in his or her assumptions about God. When danger is at hand, "woods shiver and water drops hang pendant." When the worker might fall, "leaves are still." Purdy puts no good and evil in the poem. Wilderness is not evil, it is not against people; it is simply what existed before towns and churches and a sense of region and nation. This is another reason that "Wilderness Gothic" has such a wide lens. In the quest for true religion, for the promised land of the New World, the narrator declares that there is failure and potential failure as well as the potential for a fall, and those who build European churches in the North American wilderness ought to take that seriously.

Source: S. K. Robisch, Critical Essay on "Wilderness Gothic," in *Poetry for Students,* The Gale Group, 2001.

Sources

Al Purdy: A Passion for Poetry, http://www.infoculture.cbc.ca/archives/bookswr/bookswr_11221999_purdy.phtml (November, 1999).

Bemrose, John, "A Passionate Voice," in *MacLean's,* May 8, 2000, pp. 366–368.

Brown, Russell, "Perhaps He'll Fall: Rereading the Poetry of Al Purdy," in *Essays on Canadian Writing,* Vol. 49, 1993, pp. 59–84.

Moore, Marianne, *Collected Poems,* Penguin, 1994.

O'Brien, Peter, "An Interview with Al Purdy," in *Essays on Canadian Writing,* Vol. 49, 1993, p. 147–162.

Twigg, Alan, "Al Purdy: One of a Kind," in *For Openers: Conversations with Twenty-four Canadian Writers,* Harbour, 1981, pp. 1–12.

Woodcock, George, *Contemporary Literary Criticism,* Vol. 14, Gale Research, 1980, p. 431.

———, *Dictionary of Literary Biography,* Vol. 88: *Canadian Writers, 1920–1959,* Gale Research, 1989, pp. 246–256.

For Further Study

Bowering, George, *Al Purdy,* Copp Clark, 1970.
    This is a biography of Al Purdy.

Stouck, David, "Al Purdy," in *Major Canadian Authors,* University of Nebraska Press, 1984.
    This work discusses Purdy as part of a critical introduction to Canadian literature.

Woodcock, George, "On the Poetry of Al Purdy," in *The World of Canadian Writing,* Douglas & McIntyre, 1980.
    This discussion of Purdy is found in a collection of essays that critique Canadian writers.

Glossary of Literary Terms

A

Abstract: Used as a noun, the term refers to a short summary or outline of a longer work. As an adjective applied to writing or literary works, abstract refers to words or phrases that name things not knowable through the five senses.

Accent: The emphasis or stress placed on a syllable in poetry. Traditional poetry commonly uses patterns of accented and unaccented syllables (known as feet) that create distinct rhythms. Much modern poetry uses less formal arrangements that create a sense of freedom and spontaneity.

Aestheticism: A literary and artistic movement of the nineteenth century. Followers of the movement believed that art should not be mixed with social, political, or moral teaching. The statement "art for art's sake" is a good summary of aestheticism. The movement had its roots in France, but it gained widespread importance in England in the last half of the nineteenth century, where it helped change the Victorian practice of including moral lessons in literature.

Affective Fallacy: An error in judging the merits or faults of a work of literature. The "error" results from stressing the importance of the work's effect upon the reader—that is, how it makes a reader "feel" emotionally, what it does as a literary work—instead of stressing its inner qualities as a created object, or what it "is."

Age of Johnson: The period in English literature between 1750 and 1798, named after the most prominent literary figure of the age, Samuel Johnson. Works written during this time are noted for their emphasis on "sensibility," or emotional quality. These works formed a transition between the rational works of the Age of Reason, or Neoclassical period, and the emphasis on individual feelings and responses of the Romantic period.

Age of Reason: See *Neoclassicism*

Age of Sensibility: See *Age of Johnson*

Agrarians: A group of Southern American writers of the 1930s and 1940s who fostered an economic and cultural program for the South based on agriculture, in opposition to the industrial society of the North. The term can refer to any group that promotes the value of farm life and agricultural society.

Alexandrine Meter: See *Meter*

Allegory: A narrative technique in which characters representing things or abstract ideas are used to convey a message or teach a lesson. Allegory is typically used to teach moral, ethical, or religious lessons but is sometimes used for satiric or political purposes.

Alliteration: A poetic device where the first consonant sounds or any vowel sounds in words or syllables are repeated.

Allusion: A reference to a familiar literary or historical person or event, used to make an idea more easily understood.

Amerind Literature: The writing and oral traditions of Native Americans. Native American literature was originally passed on by word of mouth, so it consisted largely of stories and events that were easily memorized. Amerind prose is often rhythmic like poetry because it was recited to the beat of a ceremonial drum.

Analogy: A comparison of two things made to explain something unfamiliar through its similarities to something familiar, or to prove one point based on the acceptedness of another. Similes and metaphors are types of analogies.

Anapest: See *Foot*

Angry Young Men: A group of British writers of the 1950s whose work expressed bitterness and disillusionment with society. Common to their work is an antihero who rebels against a corrupt social order and strives for personal integrity.

Anthropomorphism: The presentation of animals or objects in human shape or with human characteristics. The term is derived from the Greek word for "human form."

Antimasque: See *Masque*

Antithesis: The antithesis of something is its direct opposite. In literature, the use of antithesis as a figure of speech results in two statements that show a contrast through the balancing of two opposite ideas. Technically, it is the second portion of the statement that is defined as the "antithesis"; the first portion is the "thesis."

Apocrypha: Writings tentatively attributed to an author but not proven or universally accepted to be their works. The term was originally applied to certain books of the Bible that were not considered inspired and so were not included in the "sacred canon."

Apollonian and Dionysian: The two impulses believed to guide authors of dramatic tragedy. The Apollonian impulse is named after Apollo, the Greek god of light and beauty and the symbol of intellectual order. The Dionysian impulse is named after Dionysus, the Greek god of wine and the symbol of the unrestrained forces of nature. The Apollonian impulse is to create a rational, harmonious world, while the Dionysian is to express the irrational forces of personality.

Apostrophe: A statement, question, or request addressed to an inanimate object or concept or to a nonexistent or absent person.

Archetype: The word archetype is commonly used to describe an original pattern or model from which all other things of the same kind are made. This term was introduced to literary criticism from the psychology of Carl Jung. It expresses Jung's theory that behind every person's "unconscious," or repressed memories of the past, lies the "collective unconscious" of the human race: memories of the countless typical experiences of our ancestors. These memories are said to prompt illogical associations that trigger powerful emotions in the reader. Often, the emotional process is primitive, even primordial. Archetypes are the literary images that grow out of the "collective unconscious." They appear in literature as incidents and plots that repeat basic patterns of life. They may also appear as stereotyped characters.

Argument: The argument of a work is the author's subject matter or principal idea.

Art for Art's Sake: See *Aestheticism*

Assonance: The repetition of similar vowel sounds in poetry.

Audience: The people for whom a piece of literature is written. Authors usually write with a certain audience in mind, for example, children, members of a religious or ethnic group, or colleagues in a professional field. The term "audience" also applies to the people who gather to see or hear any performance, including plays, poetry readings, speeches, and concerts.

Automatic Writing: Writing carried out without a preconceived plan in an effort to capture every random thought. Authors who engage in automatic writing typically do not revise their work, preferring instead to preserve the revealed truth and beauty of spontaneous expression.

***Avant-garde*:** A French term meaning "vanguard." It is used in literary criticism to describe new writing that rejects traditional approaches to literature in favor of innovations in style or content.

B

Ballad: A short poem that tells a simple story and has a repeated refrain. Ballads were originally intended to be sung. Early ballads, known as folk ballads, were passed down through generations, so their authors are often unknown. Later ballads composed by known authors are called literary ballads.

Baroque: A term used in literary criticism to describe literature that is complex or ornate in style or diction. Baroque works typically express tension, anxiety, and violent emotion. The term "Baroque Age" designates a period in Western European literature beginning in the late sixteenth century and ending about one hundred years later.

Works of this period often mirror the qualities of works more generally associated with the label "baroque" and sometimes feature elaborate conceits.

Baroque Age: See *Baroque*

Baroque Period: See *Baroque*

Beat Generation: See *Beat Movement*

Beat Movement: A period featuring a group of American poets and novelists of the 1950s and 1960s—including Jack Kerouac, Allen Ginsberg, Gregory Corso, William S. Burroughs, and Lawrence Ferlinghetti—who rejected established social and literary values. Using such techniques as stream-of-consciousness writing and jazz-influenced free verse and focusing on unusual or abnormal states of mind—generated by religious ecstasy or the use of drugs—the Beat writers aimed to create works that were unconventional in both form and subject matter.

Beat Poets: See *Beat Movement*

Beats, The: See *Beat Movement*

Belles-lettres: A French term meaning "fine letters" or "beautiful writing." It is often used as a synonym for literature, typically referring to imaginative and artistic rather than scientific or expository writing. Current usage sometimes restricts the meaning to light or humorous writing and appreciative essays about literature.

Black Aesthetic Movement: A period of artistic and literary development among African Americans in the 1960s and early 1970s. This was the first major African American artistic movement since the Harlem Renaissance and was closely paralleled by the civil rights and black power movements. The black aesthetic writers attempted to produce works of art that would be meaningful to the black masses. Key figures in black aesthetics included one of its founders, poet and playwright Amiri Baraka, formerly known as LeRoi Jones; poet and essayist Haki R. Madhubuti, formerly Don L. Lee; poet and playwright Sonia Sanchez; and dramatist Ed Bullins.

Black Arts Movement: See *Black Aesthetic Movement*

Black Comedy: See *Black Humor*

Black Humor: Writing that places grotesque elements side by side with humorous ones in an attempt to shock the reader, forcing him or her to laugh at the horrifying reality of a disordered world.

Black Mountain School: Black Mountain College and three of its instructors—Robert Creeley, Robert Duncan, and Charles Olson—were all influential in projective verse. Today poets working in projective verse are referred to as members of the Black Mountain school.

Blank Verse: Loosely, any unrhymed poetry, but more generally, unrhymed iambic pentameter verse (composed of lines of five two-syllable feet with the first syllable accented, the second unaccented). Blank verse has been used by poets since the Renaissance for its flexibility and its graceful, dignified tone.

Bloomsbury Group: A group of English writers, artists, and intellectuals who held informal artistic and philosophical discussions in Bloomsbury, a district of London, from around 1907 to the early 1930s. The Bloomsbury Group held no uniform philosophical beliefs but did commonly express an aversion to moral prudery and a desire for greater social tolerance.

Bon Mot: A French term meaning "good word." A *bon mot* is a witty remark or clever observation.

Breath Verse: See *Projective Verse*

Burlesque: Any literary work that uses exaggeration to make its subject appear ridiculous, either by treating a trivial subject with profound seriousness or by treating a dignified subject frivolously. The word "burlesque" may also be used as an adjective, as in "burlesque show," to mean "striptease act."

C

Cadence: The natural rhythm of language caused by the alternation of accented and unaccented syllables. Much modern poetry—notably free verse—deliberately manipulates cadence to create complex rhythmic effects.

Caesura: A pause in a line of poetry, usually occurring near the middle. It typically corresponds to a break in the natural rhythm or sense of the line but is sometimes shifted to create special meanings or rhythmic effects.

Canzone: A short Italian or Provencal lyric poem, commonly about love and often set to music. The *canzone* has no set form but typically contains five or six stanzas made up of seven to twenty lines of eleven syllables each. A shorter, five- to ten-line "envoy," or concluding stanza, completes the poem.

Carpe Diem: A Latin term meaning "seize the day." This is a traditional theme of poetry, especially lyrics. A *carpe diem* poem advises the reader or the person it addresses to live for today and enjoy the pleasures of the moment.

Catharsis: The release or purging of unwanted emotions—specifically fear and pity—brought about by exposure to art. The term was first used by the Greek philosopher Aristotle in his *Poetics* to refer to the desired effect of tragedy on spectators.

Celtic Renaissance: A period of Irish literary and cultural history at the end of the nineteenth century. Followers of the movement aimed to create a romantic vision of Celtic myth and legend. The most significant works of the Celtic Renaissance typically present a dreamy, unreal world, usually in reaction against the reality of contemporary problems.

Celtic Twilight: See *Celtic Renaissance*

Character: Broadly speaking, a person in a literary work. The actions of characters are what constitute the plot of a story, novel, or poem. There are numerous types of characters, ranging from simple, stereotypical figures to intricate, multifaceted ones. In the techniques of anthropomorphism and personification, animals—and even places or things—can assume aspects of character. "Characterization" is the process by which an author creates vivid, believable characters in a work of art. This may be done in a variety of ways, including (1) direct description of the character by the narrator; (2) the direct presentation of the speech, thoughts, or actions of the character; and (3) the responses of other characters to the character. The term "character" also refers to a form originated by the ancient Greek writer Theophrastus that later became popular in the seventeenth and eighteenth centuries. It is a short essay or sketch of a person who prominently displays a specific attribute or quality, such as miserliness or ambition.

Characterization: See *Character*

Classical: In its strictest definition in literary criticism, classicism refers to works of ancient Greek or Roman literature. The term may also be used to describe a literary work of recognized importance (a "classic") from any time period or literature that exhibits the traits of classicism.

Classicism: A term used in literary criticism to describe critical doctrines that have their roots in ancient Greek and Roman literature, philosophy, and art. Works associated with classicism typically exhibit restraint on the part of the author, unity of design and purpose, clarity, simplicity, logical organization, and respect for tradition.

Colloquialism: A word, phrase, or form of pronunciation that is acceptable in casual conversation but not in formal, written communication. It is considered more acceptable than slang.

Complaint: A lyric poem, popular in the Renaissance, in which the speaker expresses sorrow about his or her condition. Typically, the speaker's sadness is caused by an unresponsive lover, but some complaints cite other sources of unhappiness, such as poverty or fate.

Conceit: A clever and fanciful metaphor, usually expressed through elaborate and extended comparison, that presents a striking parallel between two seemingly dissimilar things—for example, elaborately comparing a beautiful woman to an object like a garden or the sun. The conceit was a popular device throughout the Elizabethan Age and Baroque Age and was the principal technique of the seventeenth-century English metaphysical poets. This usage of the word conceit is unrelated to the best-known definition of conceit as an arrogant attitude or behavior.

Concrete: Concrete is the opposite of abstract, and refers to a thing that actually exists or a description that allows the reader to experience an object or concept with the senses.

Concrete Poetry: Poetry in which visual elements play a large part in the poetic effect. Punctuation marks, letters, or words are arranged on a page to form a visual design: a cross, for example, or a bumblebee.

Confessional Poetry: A form of poetry in which the poet reveals very personal, intimate, sometimes shocking information about himself or herself.

Connotation: The impression that a word gives beyond its defined meaning. Connotations may be universally understood or may be significant only to a certain group.

Consonance: Consonance occurs in poetry when words appearing at the ends of two or more verses have similar final consonant sounds but have final vowel sounds that differ, as with "stuff" and "off."

Convention: Any widely accepted literary device, style, or form.

Corrido: A Mexican ballad.

Couplet: Two lines of poetry with the same rhyme and meter, often expressing a complete and self-contained thought.

Criticism: The systematic study and evaluation of literary works, usually based on a specific method or set of principles. An important part of literary studies since ancient times, the practice of criticism has given rise to numerous theories, methods, and "schools," sometimes producing conflicting, even contradictory, interpretations of literature in general as well as of individual works. Even such basic issues as what constitutes a poem or a novel have been the subject of much criticism over the centuries.

D

Dactyl: See *Foot*

Dadaism: A protest movement in art and literature founded by Tristan Tzara in 1916. Followers of the movement expressed their outrage at the destruction brought about by World War I by revolting against numerous forms of social convention. The Dadaists presented works marked by calculated madness and flamboyant nonsense. They stressed total freedom of expression, commonly through primitive displays of emotion and illogical, often senseless, poetry. The movement ended shortly after the war, when it was replaced by surrealism.

Decadent: See *Decadents*

Decadents: The followers of a nineteenth-century literary movement that had its beginnings in French aestheticism. Decadent literature displays a fascination with perverse and morbid states; a search for novelty and sensation—the "new thrill"; a preoccupation with mysticism; and a belief in the senselessness of human existence. The movement is closely associated with the doctrine Art for Art's Sake. The term "decadence" is sometimes used to denote a decline in the quality of art or literature following a period of greatness.

Deconstruction: A method of literary criticism developed by Jacques Derrida and characterized by multiple conflicting interpretations of a given work. Deconstructionists consider the impact of the language of a work and suggest that the true meaning of the work is not necessarily the meaning that the author intended.

Deduction: The process of reaching a conclusion through reasoning from general premises to a specific premise.

Denotation: The definition of a word, apart from the impressions or feelings it creates in the reader.

Diction: The selection and arrangement of words in a literary work. Either or both may vary depending on the desired effect. There are four general types of diction: "formal," used in scholarly or lofty writing; "informal," used in relaxed but educated conversation; "colloquial," used in everyday speech; and "slang," containing newly coined words and other terms not accepted in formal usage.

Didactic: A term used to describe works of literature that aim to teach some moral, religious, political, or practical lesson. Although didactic elements are often found in artistically pleasing works, the term "didactic" usually refers to literature in which the message is more important than the form. The term may also be used to criticize a work that the critic finds "overly didactic," that is, heavy-handed in its delivery of a lesson.

Dimeter: See *Meter*

Dionysian: See *Apollonian and Dionysian*

Discordia concours: A Latin phrase meaning "discord in harmony." The term was coined by the eighteenth-century English writer Samuel Johnson to describe "a combination of dissimilar images or discovery of occult resemblances in things apparently unlike." Johnson created the expression by reversing a phrase by the Latin poet Horace.

Dissonance: A combination of harsh or jarring sounds, especially in poetry. Although such combinations may be accidental, poets sometimes intentionally make them to achieve particular effects. Dissonance is also sometimes used to refer to close but not identical rhymes. When this is the case, the word functions as a synonym for consonance.

Double Entendre: A corruption of a French phrase meaning "double meaning." The term is used to indicate a word or phrase that is deliberately ambiguous, especially when one of the meanings is risque or improper.

Draft: Any preliminary version of a written work. An author may write dozens of drafts which are revised to form the final work, or he or she may write only one, with few or no revisions.

Dramatic Monologue: See *Monologue*

Dramatic Poetry: Any lyric work that employs elements of drama such as dialogue, conflict, or characterization, but excluding works that are intended for stage presentation.

Dream Allegory: See *Dream Vision*

Dream Vision: A literary convention, chiefly of the Middle Ages. In a dream vision a story is presented as a literal dream of the narrator. This device was commonly used to teach moral and religious lessons.

E

Eclogue: In classical literature, a poem featuring rural themes and structured as a dialogue among shepherds. Eclogues often took specific poetic forms, such as elegies or love poems. Some were written as the soliloquy of a shepherd. In later centuries, "eclogue" came to refer to any poem that was in the pastoral tradition or that had a dialogue or monologue structure.

Edwardian: Describes cultural conventions identified with the period of the reign of Edward VII of England (1901–1910). Writers of the Edwardian Age typically displayed a strong reaction against the propriety and conservatism of the Victorian Age. Their work often exhibits distrust of authority in religion, politics, and art and expresses strong doubts about the soundness of conventional values.

Edwardian Age: See *Edwardian*

Electra Complex: A daughter's amorous obsession with her father.

Elegy: A lyric poem that laments the death of a person or the eventual death of all people. In a conventional elegy, set in a classical world, the poet and subject are spoken of as shepherds. In modern criticism, the word elegy is often used to refer to a poem that is melancholy or mournfully contemplative.

Elizabethan Age: A period of great economic growth, religious controversy, and nationalism closely associated with the reign of Elizabeth I of England (1558–1603). The Elizabethan Age is considered a part of the general renaissance—that is, the flowering of arts and literature—that took place in Europe during the fourteenth through sixteenth centuries. The era is considered the golden age of English literature. The most important dramas in English and a great deal of lyric poetry were produced during this period, and modern English criticism began around this time.

Empathy: A sense of shared experience, including emotional and physical feelings, with someone or something other than oneself. Empathy is often used to describe the response of a reader to a literary character.

English Sonnet: See *Sonnet*

Enjambment: The running over of the sense and structure of a line of verse or a couplet into the following verse or couplet.

Enlightenment, The: An eighteenth-century philosophical movement. It began in France but had a wide impact throughout Europe and America. Thinkers of the Enlightenment valued reason and believed that both the individual and society could achieve a state of perfection. Corresponding to this essentially humanist vision was a resistance to religious authority.

Epic: A long narrative poem about the adventures of a hero of great historic or legendary importance. The setting is vast and the action is often given cosmic significance through the intervention of supernatural forces such as gods, angels, or demons. Epics are typically written in a classical style of grand simplicity with elaborate metaphors and allusions that enhance the symbolic importance of a hero's adventures.

Epic Simile: See *Homeric Simile*

Epigram: A saying that makes the speaker's point quickly and concisely.

Epilogue: A concluding statement or section of a literary work. In dramas, particularly those of the seventeenth and eighteenth centuries, the epilogue is a closing speech, often in verse, delivered by an actor at the end of a play and spoken directly to the audience.

Epiphany: A sudden revelation of truth inspired by a seemingly trivial incident.

Epitaph: An inscription on a tomb or tombstone, or a verse written on the occasion of a person's death. Epitaphs may be serious or humorous.

Epithalamion: A song or poem written to honor and commemorate a marriage ceremony.

Epithalamium: See *Epithalamion*

Epithet: A word or phrase, often disparaging or abusive, that expresses a character trait of someone or something.

Erziehungsroman: See *Bildungsroman*

Essay: A prose composition with a focused subject of discussion. The term was coined by Michel de Montaigne to describe his 1580 collection of brief, informal reflections on himself and on various topics relating to human nature. An essay can also be a long, systematic discourse.

Existentialism: A predominantly twentieth-century philosophy concerned with the nature and perception of human existence. There are two major strains of existentialist thought: atheistic and Christian. Followers of atheistic existentialism believe that the individual is alone in a godless universe and that the basic human condition is one of suffering and loneliness. Nevertheless, because there are no fixed values, individuals can create their own characters—indeed, they can shape themselves—through the exercise of free will. The atheistic strain culminates in and is popularly associated with the works of Jean-Paul Sartre. The Christian existentialists, on the other hand, believe that only in God may people find freedom from life's anguish. The two strains hold certain beliefs in common: that existence cannot be fully understood or described through empirical effort; that anguish is a universal element of life; that individuals must bear responsibility for their actions; and that there is no common standard of behavior or perception for religious and ethical matters.

Expatriates: See *Expatriatism*

Expatriatism: The practice of leaving one's country to live for an extended period in another country.

Exposition: Writing intended to explain the nature of an idea, thing, or theme. Expository writing is often combined with description, narration, or argument. In dramatic writing, the exposition is the introductory material which presents the characters, setting, and tone of the play.

Expressionism: An indistinct literary term, originally used to describe an early twentieth-century school of German painting. The term applies to almost any mode of unconventional, highly subjective writing that distorts reality in some way.

Extended Monologue: See *Monologue*

F

Feet: See *Foot*

Feminine Rhyme: See *Rhyme*

Fiction: Any story that is the product of imagination rather than a documentation of fact. Characters and events in such narratives may be based in real life but their ultimate form and configuration is a creation of the author.

Figurative Language: A technique in writing in which the author temporarily interrupts the order, construction, or meaning of the writing for a particular effect. This interruption takes the form of one or more figures of speech such as hyperbole, irony, or simile. Figurative language is the opposite of literal language, in which every word is truthful, accurate, and free of exaggeration or embellishment.

Figures of Speech: Writing that differs from customary conventions for construction, meaning, order, or significance for the purpose of a special meaning or effect. There are two major types of figures of speech: rhetorical figures, which do not make changes in the meaning of the words; and tropes, which do.

Fin de siecle: A French term meaning "end of the century." The term is used to denote the last decade of the nineteenth century, a transition period when writers and other artists abandoned old conventions and looked for new techniques and objectives.

First Person: See *Point of View*

Folk Ballad: See *Ballad*

Folklore: Traditions and myths preserved in a culture or group of people. Typically, these are passed on by word of mouth in various forms—such as legends, songs, and proverbs—or preserved in customs and ceremonies. This term was first used by W. J. Thoms in 1846.

Folktale: A story originating in oral tradition. Folktales fall into a variety of categories, including legends, ghost stories, fairy tales, fables, and anecdotes based on historical figures and events.

Foot: The smallest unit of rhythm in a line of poetry. In English-language poetry, a foot is typically one accented syllable combined with one or two unaccented syllables.

Form: The pattern or construction of a work which identifies its genre and distinguishes it from other genres.

Formalism: In literary criticism, the belief that literature should follow prescribed rules of construction, such as those that govern the sonnet form.

Fourteener Meter: See *Meter*

Free Verse: Poetry that lacks regular metrical and rhyme patterns but that tries to capture the cadences of everyday speech. The form allows a poet to exploit a variety of rhythmical effects within a single poem.

Futurism: A flamboyant literary and artistic movement that developed in France, Italy, and Russia from 1908 through the 1920s. Futurist theater and poetry abandoned traditional literary forms. In their place, followers of the movement attempted to achieve total freedom of expression through bizarre imagery and deformed or newly invented words. The Futurists were self-consciously modern artists who attempted to incorporate the appearances and sounds of modern life into their work.

G

Genre: A category of literary work. In critical theory, genre may refer to both the content of a given work—tragedy, comedy, pastoral—and to its form, such as poetry, novel, or drama.

Genteel Tradition: A term coined by critic George Santayana to describe the literary practice of certain late nineteenth-century American writers, especially New Englanders. Followers of the Genteel

Tradition emphasized conventionality in social, religious, moral, and literary standards.

Georgian Age: See *Georgian Poets*

Georgian Period: See *Georgian Poets*

Georgian Poets: A loose grouping of English poets during the years 1912–1922. The Georgians reacted against certain literary schools and practices, especially Victorian wordiness, turn-of-the-century aestheticism, and contemporary urban realism. In their place, the Georgians embraced the nineteenth-century poetic practices of William Wordsworth and the other Lake Poets.

Georgic: A poem about farming and the farmer's way of life, named from Virgil's *Georgics*.

Gilded Age: A period in American history during the 1870s characterized by political corruption and materialism. A number of important novels of social and political criticism were written during this time.

Gothic: See *Gothicism*

Gothicism: In literary criticism, works characterized by a taste for the medieval or morbidly attractive. A gothic novel prominently features elements of horror, the supernatural, gloom, and violence: clanking chains, terror, charnel houses, ghosts, medieval castles, and mysteriously slamming doors. The term "gothic novel" is also applied to novels that lack elements of the traditional Gothic setting but that create a similar atmosphere of terror or dread.

Graveyard School: A group of eighteenth-century English poets who wrote long, picturesque meditations on death. Their works were designed to cause the reader to ponder immortality.

Great Chain of Being: The belief that all things and creatures in nature are organized in a hierarchy from inanimate objects at the bottom to God at the top. This system of belief was popular in the seventeenth and eighteenth centuries.

Grotesque: In literary criticism, the subject matter of a work or a style of expression characterized by exaggeration, deformity, freakishness, and disorder. The grotesque often includes an element of comic absurdity.

H

Haiku: The shortest form of Japanese poetry, constructed in three lines of five, seven, and five syllables respectively. The message of a *haiku* poem usually centers on some aspect of spirituality and provokes an emotional response in the reader.

Half Rhyme: See *Consonance*

Harlem Renaissance: The Harlem Renaissance of the 1920s is generally considered the first significant movement of black writers and artists in the United States. During this period, new and established black writers published more fiction and poetry than ever before, the first influential black literary journals were established, and black authors and artists received their first widespread recognition and serious critical appraisal. Among the major writers associated with this period are Claude McKay, Jean Toomer, Countee Cullen, Langston Hughes, Arna Bontemps, Nella Larsen, and Zora Neale Hurston.

Hellenism: Imitation of ancient Greek thought or styles. Also, an approach to life that focuses on the growth and development of the intellect. "Hellenism" is sometimes used to refer to the belief that reason can be applied to examine all human experience.

Heptameter: See *Meter*

Hero/Heroine: The principal sympathetic character (male or female) in a literary work. Heroes and heroines typically exhibit admirable traits: idealism, courage, and integrity, for example.

Heroic Couplet: A rhyming couplet written in iambic pentameter (a verse with five iambic feet).

Heroic Line: The meter and length of a line of verse in epic or heroic poetry. This varies by language and time period.

Heroine: See *Hero/Heroine*

Hexameter: See *Meter*

Historical Criticism: The study of a work based on its impact on the world of the time period in which it was written.

Hokku: See *Haiku*

Holocaust: See *Holocaust Literature*

Holocaust Literature: Literature influenced by or written about the Holocaust of World War II. Such literature includes true stories of survival in concentration camps, escape, and life after the war, as well as fictional works and poetry.

Homeric Simile: An elaborate, detailed comparison written as a simile many lines in length.

Horatian Satire: See *Satire*

Humanism: A philosophy that places faith in the dignity of humankind and rejects the medieval perception of the individual as a weak, fallen creature. "Humanists" typically believe in the perfectibility of human nature and view reason and education as the means to that end.

Humors: Mentions of the humors refer to the ancient Greek theory that a person's health and personality were determined by the balance of four basic fluids in the body: blood, phlegm, yellow bile, and black bile. A dominance of any fluid would cause extremes in behavior. An excess of blood created a sanguine person who was joyful, aggressive, and passionate; a phlegmatic person was shy, fearful, and sluggish; too much yellow bile led to a choleric temperament characterized by impatience, anger, bitterness, and stubbornness; and excessive black bile created melancholy, a state of laziness, gluttony, and lack of motivation.

Humours: See *Humors*

Hyperbole: In literary criticism, deliberate exaggeration used to achieve an effect.

I

Iamb: See *Foot*

Idiom: A word construction or verbal expression closely associated with a given language.

Image: A concrete representation of an object or sensory experience. Typically, such a representation helps evoke the feelings associated with the object or experience itself. Images are either "literal" or "figurative." Literal images are especially concrete and involve little or no extension of the obvious meaning of the words used to express them. Figurative images do not follow the literal meaning of the words exactly. Images in literature are usually visual, but the term "image" can also refer to the representation of any sensory experience.

Imagery: The array of images in a literary work. Also, figurative language.

Imagism: An English and American poetry movement that flourished between 1908 and 1917. The Imagists used precise, clearly presented images in their works. They also used common, everyday speech and aimed for conciseness, concrete imagery, and the creation of new rhythms.

***In medias res*:** A Latin term meaning "in the middle of things." It refers to the technique of beginning a story at its midpoint and then using various flashback devices to reveal previous action.

Induction: The process of reaching a conclusion by reasoning from specific premises to form a general premise. Also, an introductory portion of a work of literature, especially a play.

Intentional Fallacy: The belief that judgments of a literary work based solely on an author's stated or implied intentions are false and misleading. Critics who believe in the concept of the intentional fallacy typically argue that the work itself is sufficient matter for interpretation, even though they may concede that an author's statement of purpose can be useful.

Interior Monologue: A narrative technique in which characters' thoughts are revealed in a way that appears to be uncontrolled by the author. The interior monologue typically aims to reveal the inner self of a character. It portrays emotional experiences as they occur at both a conscious and unconscious level. Images are often used to represent sensations or emotions.

Internal Rhyme: Rhyme that occurs within a single line of verse.

Irish Literary Renaissance: A late nineteenth- and early twentieth-century movement in Irish literature. Members of the movement aimed to reduce the influence of British culture in Ireland and create an Irish national literature.

Irony: In literary criticism, the effect of language in which the intended meaning is the opposite of what is stated.

Italian Sonnet: See *Sonnet*

J

Jacobean Age: The period of the reign of James I of England (1603–1625). The early literature of this period reflected the worldview of the Elizabethan Age, but a darker, more cynical attitude steadily grew in the art and literature of the Jacobean Age. This was an important time for English drama and poetry.

Jargon: Language that is used or understood only by a select group of people. Jargon may refer to terminology used in a certain profession, such as computer jargon, or it may refer to any nonsensical language that is not understood by most people.

Journalism: Writing intended for publication in a newspaper or magazine, or for broadcast on a radio or television program featuring news, sports, entertainment, or other timely material.

K

Knickerbocker Group: A somewhat indistinct group of New York writers of the first half of the nineteenth century. Members of the group were linked only by location and a common theme: New York life.

***Kunstlerroman*:** See *Bildungsroman*

L

Lais: See *Lay*

Lake Poets: See *Lake School*

Lake School: These poets all lived in the Lake District of England at the turn of the nineteenth century. As a group, they followed no single "school" of thought or literary practice, although their works were uniformly disparaged by the *Edinburgh Review.*

Lay: A song or simple narrative poem. The form originated in medieval France. Early French *lais* were often based on the Celtic legends and other tales sung by Breton minstrels—thus the name of the "Breton lay." In fourteenth-century England, the term "lay" was used to describe short narratives written in imitation of the Breton lays.

Leitmotiv: See *Motif*

Literal Language: An author uses literal language when he or she writes without exaggerating or embellishing the subject matter and without any tools of figurative language.

Literary Ballad: See *Ballad*

Literature: Literature is broadly defined as any written or spoken material, but the term most often refers to creative works.

Lost Generation: A term first used by Gertrude Stein to describe the post-World War I generation of American writers: men and women haunted by a sense of betrayal and emptiness brought about by the destructiveness of the war.

Lyric Poetry: A poem expressing the subjective feelings and personal emotions of the poet. Such poetry is melodic, since it was originally accompanied by a lyre in recitals. Most Western poetry in the twentieth century may be classified as lyrical.

M

Mannerism: Exaggerated, artificial adherence to a literary manner or style. Also, a popular style of the visual arts of late sixteenth-century Europe that was marked by elongation of the human form and by intentional spatial distortion. Literary works that are self-consciously high-toned and artistic are often said to be "mannered."

Masculine Rhyme: See *Rhyme*

Measure: The foot, verse, or time sequence used in a literary work, especially a poem. Measure is often used somewhat incorrectly as a synonym for meter.

Metaphor: A figure of speech that expresses an idea through the image of another object. Metaphors suggest the essence of the first object by identifying it with certain qualities of the second object.

Metaphysical Conceit: See *Conceit*

Metaphysical Poetry: The body of poetry produced by a group of seventeenth-century English writers called the "Metaphysical Poets." The group includes John Donne and Andrew Marvell. The Metaphysical Poets made use of everyday speech, intellectual analysis, and unique imagery. They aimed to portray the ordinary conflicts and contradictions of life. Their poems often took the form of an argument, and many of them emphasize physical and religious love as well as the fleeting nature of life. Elaborate conceits are typical in metaphysical poetry.

Metaphysical Poets: See *Metaphysical Poetry*

Meter: In literary criticism, the repetition of sound patterns that creates a rhythm in poetry. The patterns are based on the number of syllables and the presence and absence of accents. The unit of rhythm in a line is called a foot. Types of meter are classified according to the number of feet in a line. These are the standard English lines: Monometer, one foot; Dimeter, two feet; Trimeter, three feet; Tetrameter, four feet; Pentameter, five feet; Hexameter, six feet (also called the Alexandrine); Heptameter, seven feet (also called the "Fourteener" when the feet are iambic).

Modernism: Modern literary practices. Also, the principles of a literary school that lasted from roughly the beginning of the twentieth century until the end of World War II. Modernism is defined by its rejection of the literary conventions of the nineteenth century and by its opposition to conventional morality, taste, traditions, and economic values.

Monologue: A composition, written or oral, by a single individual. More specifically, a speech given by a single individual in a drama or other public entertainment. It has no set length, although it is usually several or more lines long.

Monometer: See *Meter*

Mood: The prevailing emotions of a work or of the author in his or her creation of the work. The mood of a work is not always what might be expected based on its subject matter.

Motif: A theme, character type, image, metaphor, or other verbal element that recurs throughout a single work of literature or occurs in a number of different works over a period of time.

Motiv: See *Motif*

Muckrakers: An early twentieth-century group of American writers. Typically, their works exposed the wrongdoings of big business and government in the United States.

Muses: Nine Greek mythological goddesses, the daughters of Zeus and Mnemosyne (Memory). Each muse patronized a specific area of the liberal arts and sciences. Calliope presided over epic poetry, Clio over history, Erato over love poetry, Euterpe over music or lyric poetry, Melpomene over tragedy, Polyhymnia over hymns to the gods, Terpsichore over dance, Thalia over comedy, and Urania over astronomy. Poets and writers traditionally made appeals to the Muses for inspiration in their work.

Myth: An anonymous tale emerging from the traditional beliefs of a culture or social unit. Myths use supernatural explanations for natural phenomena. They may also explain cosmic issues like creation and death. Collections of myths, known as mythologies, are common to all cultures and nations, but the best-known myths belong to the Norse, Roman, and Greek mythologies.

N

Narration: The telling of a series of events, real or invented. A narration may be either a simple narrative, in which the events are recounted chronologically, or a narrative with a plot, in which the account is given in a style reflecting the author's artistic concept of the story. Narration is sometimes used as a synonym for "storyline."

Narrative: A verse or prose accounting of an event or sequence of events, real or invented. The term is also used as an adjective in the sense "method of narration." For example, in literary criticism, the expression "narrative technique" usually refers to the way the author structures and presents his or her story.

Narrative Poetry: A nondramatic poem in which the author tells a story. Such poems may be of any length or level of complexity.

Narrator: The teller of a story. The narrator may be the author or a character in the story through whom the author speaks.

Naturalism: A literary movement of the late nineteenth and early twentieth centuries. The movement's major theorist, French novelist Emile Zola, envisioned a type of fiction that would examine human life with the objectivity of scientific inquiry. The Naturalists typically viewed human beings as either the products of "biological determinism," ruled by hereditary instincts and engaged in an endless struggle for survival, or as the products of "socioeconomic determinism," ruled by social and economic forces beyond their control. In their works, the Naturalists generally ignored the highest levels of society and focused on degradation: poverty, alcoholism, prostitution, insanity, and disease.

Negritude: A literary movement based on the concept of a shared cultural bond on the part of black Africans, wherever they may be in the world. It traces its origins to the former French colonies of Africa and the Caribbean. Negritude poets, novelists, and essayists generally stress four points in their writings: One, black alienation from traditional African culture can lead to feelings of inferiority. Two, European colonialism and Western education should be resisted. Three, black Africans should seek to affirm and define their own identity. Four, African culture can and should be reclaimed. Many Negritude writers also claim that blacks can make unique contributions to the world, based on a heightened appreciation of nature, rhythm, and human emotions—aspects of life they say are not so highly valued in the materialistic and rationalistic West.

Negro Renaissance: See *Harlem Renaissance*

Neoclassical Period: See *Neoclassicism*

Neoclassicism: In literary criticism, this term refers to the revival of the attitudes and styles of expression of classical literature. It is generally used to describe a period in European history beginning in the late seventeenth century and lasting until about 1800. In its purest form, Neoclassicism marked a return to order, proportion, restraint, logic, accuracy, and decorum. In England, where Neoclassicism perhaps was most popular, it reflected the influence of seventeenth-century French writers, especially dramatists. Neoclassical writers typically reacted against the intensity and enthusiasm of the Renaissance period. They wrote works that appealed to the intellect, using elevated language and classical literary forms such as satire and the ode. Neoclassical works were often governed by the classical goal of instruction.

Neoclassicists: See *Neoclassicism*

New Criticism: A movement in literary criticism, dating from the late 1920s, that stressed close textual analysis in the interpretation of works of literature. The New Critics saw little merit in historical and biographical analysis. Rather, they aimed to examine the text alone, free from the question of how external events—biographical or otherwise—may have helped shape it.

New Journalism: A type of writing in which the journalist presents factual information in a form usually used in fiction. New journalism emphasizes description, narration, and character development to bring readers closer to the human element of the story, and is often used in personality profiles and in-depth feature articles. It is not compatible with "straight" or "hard" newswriting, which is generally composed in a brief, fact-based style.

New Journalists: See *New Journalism*

New Negro Movement: See *Harlem Renaissance*

Noble Savage: The idea that primitive man is noble and good but becomes evil and corrupted as he becomes civilized. The concept of the noble savage originated in the Renaissance period but is more closely identified with such later writers as Jean-Jacques Rousseau and Aphra Behn.

O

Objective Correlative: An outward set of objects, a situation, or a chain of events corresponding to an inward experience and evoking this experience in the reader. The term frequently appears in modern criticism in discussions of authors' intended effects on the emotional responses of readers.

Objectivity: A quality in writing characterized by the absence of the author's opinion or feeling about the subject matter. Objectivity is an important factor in criticism.

Occasional Verse: Poetry written on the occasion of a significant historical or personal event. *Vers de societe* is sometimes called occasional verse although it is of a less serious nature.

Octave: A poem or stanza composed of eight lines. The term octave most often represents the first eight lines of a Petrarchan sonnet.

Ode: Name given to an extended lyric poem characterized by exalted emotion and dignified style. An ode usually concerns a single, serious theme. Most odes, but not all, are addressed to an object or individual. Odes are distinguished from other lyric poetic forms by their complex rhythmic and stanzaic patterns.

Oedipus Complex: A son's amorous obsession with his mother. The phrase is derived from the story of the ancient Theban hero Oedipus, who un-

knowingly killed his father and married his mother.

Omniscience: See *Point of View*

Onomatopoeia: The use of words whose sounds express or suggest their meaning. In its simplest sense, onomatopoeia may be represented by words that mimic the sounds they denote such as "hiss" or "meow." At a more subtle level, the pattern and rhythm of sounds and rhymes of a line or poem may be onomatopoeic.

Oral Tradition: See *Oral Transmission*

Oral Transmission: A process by which songs, ballads, folklore, and other material are transmitted by word of mouth. The tradition of oral transmission predates the written record systems of literate society. Oral transmission preserves material sometimes over generations, although often with variations. Memory plays a large part in the recitation and preservation of orally transmitted material.

Ottava Rima: An eight-line stanza of poetry composed in iambic pentameter (a five-foot line in which each foot consists of an unaccented syllable followed by an accented syllable), following the *abababcc* rhyme scheme.

Oxymoron: A phrase combining two contradictory terms. Oxymorons may be intentional or unintentional.

P

Pantheism: The idea that all things are both a manifestation or revelation of God and a part of God at the same time. Pantheism was a common attitude in the early societies of Egypt, India, and Greece—the term derives from the Greek *pan* meaning "all" and *theos* meaning "deity." It later became a significant part of the Christian faith.

Parable: A story intended to teach a moral lesson or answer an ethical question.

Paradox: A statement that appears illogical or contradictory at first, but may actually point to an underlying truth.

Parallelism: A method of comparison of two ideas in which each is developed in the same grammatical structure.

Parnassianism: A mid nineteenth-century movement in French literature. Followers of the movement stressed adherence to well-defined artistic forms as a reaction against the often chaotic expression of the artist's ego that dominated the work of the Romantics. The Parnassians also rejected the moral, ethical, and social themes exhibited in the works of French Romantics such as Victor Hugo. The aesthetic doctrines of the Parnassians strongly influenced the later symbolist and decadent movements.

Parody: In literary criticism, this term refers to an imitation of a serious literary work or the signature style of a particular author in a ridiculous manner. A typical parody adopts the style of the original and applies it to an inappropriate subject for humorous effect. Parody is a form of satire and could be considered the literary equivalent of a caricature or cartoon.

Pastoral: A term derived from the Latin word "pastor," meaning shepherd. A pastoral is a literary composition on a rural theme. The conventions of the pastoral were originated by the third-century Greek poet Theocritus, who wrote about the experiences, love affairs, and pastimes of Sicilian shepherds. In a pastoral, characters and language of a courtly nature are often placed in a simple setting. The term pastoral is also used to classify dramas, elegies, and lyrics that exhibit the use of country settings and shepherd characters.

Pathetic Fallacy: A term coined by English critic John Ruskin to identify writing that falsely endows nonhuman things with human intentions and feelings, such as "angry clouds" and "sad trees."

Pen Name: See *Pseudonym*

Pentameter: See *Meter*

Persona: A Latin term meaning "mask." *Personae* are the characters in a fictional work of literature. The *persona* generally functions as a mask through which the author tells a story in a voice other than his or her own. A *persona* is usually either a character in a story who acts as a narrator or an "implied author," a voice created by the author to act as the narrator for himself or herself.

Personae: See *Persona*

Personal Point of View: See *Point of View*

Personification: A figure of speech that gives human qualities to abstract ideas, animals, and inanimate objects.

Petrarchan Sonnet: See *Sonnet*

Phenomenology: A method of literary criticism based on the belief that things have no existence outside of human consciousness or awareness. Proponents of this theory believe that art is a process that takes place in the mind of the observer as he or she contemplates an object rather than a quality of the object itself.

Plagiarism: Claiming another person's written material as one's own. Plagiarism can take the form of direct, word-for-word copying or the theft of the substance or idea of the work.

Platonic Criticism: A form of criticism that stresses an artistic work's usefulness as an agent of social engineering rather than any quality or value of the work itself.

Platonism: The embracing of the doctrines of the philosopher Plato, popular among the poets of the Renaissance and the Romantic period. Platonism is more flexible than Aristotelian Criticism and places more emphasis on the supernatural and unknown aspects of life.

Plot: In literary criticism, this term refers to the pattern of events in a narrative or drama. In its simplest sense, the plot guides the author in composing the work and helps the reader follow the work. Typically, plots exhibit causality and unity and have a beginning, a middle, and an end. Sometimes, however, a plot may consist of a series of disconnected events, in which case it is known as an "episodic plot."

Poem: In its broadest sense, a composition utilizing rhyme, meter, concrete detail, and expressive language to create a literary experience with emotional and aesthetic appeal.

Poet: An author who writes poetry or verse. The term is also used to refer to an artist or writer who has an exceptional gift for expression, imagination, and energy in the making of art in any form.

Poete maudit: A term derived from Paul Verlaine's *Les poetes maudits* (*The Accursed Poets*), a collection of essays on the French symbolist writers Stephane Mallarme, Arthur Rimbaud, and Tristan Corbiere. In the sense intended by Verlaine, the poet is "accursed" for choosing to explore extremes of human experience outside of middle-class society.

Poetic Fallacy: See *Pathetic Fallacy*

Poetic Justice: An outcome in a literary work, not necessarily a poem, in which the good are rewarded and the evil are punished, especially in ways that particularly fit their virtues or crimes.

Poetic License: Distortions of fact and literary convention made by a writer—not always a poet—for the sake of the effect gained. Poetic license is closely related to the concept of "artistic freedom."

Poetics: This term has two closely related meanings. It denotes (1) an aesthetic theory in literary criticism about the essence of poetry or (2) rules prescribing the proper methods, content, style, or diction of poetry. The term poetics may also refer to theories about literature in general, not just poetry.

Poetry: In its broadest sense, writing that aims to present ideas and evoke an emotional experience in the reader through the use of meter, imagery, connotative and concrete words, and a carefully constructed structure based on rhythmic patterns. Poetry typically relies on words and expressions that have several layers of meaning. It also makes use of the effects of regular rhythm on the ear and may make a strong appeal to the senses through the use of imagery.

Point of View: The narrative perspective from which a literary work is presented to the reader. There are four traditional points of view. The "third person omniscient" gives the reader a "godlike" perspective, unrestricted by time or place, from which to see actions and look into the minds of characters. This allows the author to comment openly on characters and events in the work. The "third-person" point of view presents the events of the story from outside of any single character's perception, much like the omniscient point of view, but the reader must understand the action as it takes place and without any special insight into characters' minds or motivations. The "first person" or "personal" point of view relates events as they are perceived by a single character. The main character "tells" the story and may offer opinions about the action and characters which differ from those of the author. Much less common than omniscient, third person, and first person is the "second-person" point of view, wherein the author tells the story as if it is happening to the reader.

Polemic: A work in which the author takes a stand on a controversial subject, such as abortion or religion. Such works are often extremely argumentative or provocative.

Pornography: Writing intended to provoke feelings of lust in the reader. Such works are often condemned by critics and teachers, but those which can be shown to have literary value are viewed less harshly.

Post-Aesthetic Movement: An artistic response made by African Americans to the black aesthetic movement of the 1960s and early 1970s. Writers since that time have adopted a somewhat different tone in their work, with less emphasis placed on the disparity between black and white in the United States. In the words of post-aesthetic authors such as Toni Morrison, John Edgar Wideman, and Kristin Hunter, African Americans are portrayed as

looking inward for answers to their own questions, rather than always looking to the outside world.

Postmodernism: Writing from the 1960s forward characterized by experimentation and continuing to apply some of the fundamentals of modernism, which included existentialism and alienation. Postmodernists have gone a step further in the rejection of tradition begun with the modernists by also rejecting traditional forms, preferring the antinovel over the novel and the antihero over the hero.

Pre-Raphaelites: A circle of writers and artists in mid nineteenth-century England. Valuing the pre-Renaissance artistic qualities of religious symbolism, lavish pictorialism, and natural sensuousness, the Pre-Raphaelites cultivated a sense of mystery and melancholy that influenced later writers associated with the Symbolist and Decadent movements.

Primitivism: The belief that primitive peoples were nobler and less flawed than civilized peoples because they had not been subjected to the corrupt influence of society.

Projective Verse: A form of free verse in which the poet's breathing pattern determines the lines of the poem. Poets who advocate projective verse are against all formal structures in writing, including meter and form.

Prologue: An introductory section of a literary work. It often contains information establishing the situation of the characters or presents information about the setting, time period, or action. In drama, the prologue is spoken by a chorus or by one of the principal characters.

Prose: A literary medium that attempts to mirror the language of everyday speech. It is distinguished from poetry by its use of unmetered, unrhymed language consisting of logically related sentences. Prose is usually grouped into paragraphs that form a cohesive whole such as an essay or a novel.

Prosopopoeia: See *Personification*

Protagonist: The central character of a story who serves as a focus for its themes and incidents and as the principal rationale for its development. The protagonist is sometimes referred to in discussions of modern literature as the hero or antihero.

Proverb: A brief, sage saying that expresses a truth about life in a striking manner.

Pseudonym: A name assumed by a writer, most often intended to prevent his or her identification as the author of a work. Two or more authors may work together under one pseudonym, or an author may use a different name for each genre he or she publishes in. Some publishing companies maintain "house pseudonyms," under which any number of authors may write installations in a series. Some authors also choose a pseudonym over their real names the way an actor may use a stage name.

Pun: A play on words that have similar sounds but different meanings.

Pure Poetry: poetry written without instructional intent or moral purpose that aims only to please a reader by its imagery or musical flow. The term pure poetry is used as the antonym of the term "didacticism."

Q

Quatrain: A four-line stanza of a poem or an entire poem consisting of four lines.

R

Realism: A nineteenth-century European literary movement that sought to portray familiar characters, situations, and settings in a realistic manner. This was done primarily by using an objective narrative point of view and through the buildup of accurate detail. The standard for success of any realistic work depends on how faithfully it transfers common experience into fictional forms. The realistic method may be altered or extended, as in stream of consciousness writing, to record highly subjective experience.

Refrain: A phrase repeated at intervals throughout a poem. A refrain may appear at the end of each stanza or at less regular intervals. It may be altered slightly at each appearance.

Renaissance: The period in European history that marked the end of the Middle Ages. It began in Italy in the late fourteenth century. In broad terms, it is usually seen as spanning the fourteenth, fifteenth, and sixteenth centuries, although it did not reach Great Britain, for example, until the 1480s or so. The Renaissance saw an awakening in almost every sphere of human activity, especially science, philosophy, and the arts. The period is best defined by the emergence of a general philosophy that emphasized the importance of the intellect, the individual, and world affairs. It contrasts strongly with the medieval worldview, characterized by the dominant concerns of faith, the social collective, and spiritual salvation.

Repartee: Conversation featuring snappy retorts and witticisms.

Restoration: See *Restoration Age*

Restoration Age: A period in English literature beginning with the crowning of Charles II in 1660 and running to about 1700. The era, which was characterized by a reaction against Puritanism, was the first great age of the comedy of manners. The finest literature of the era is typically witty and urbane, and often lewd.

Rhetoric: In literary criticism, this term denotes the art of ethical persuasion. In its strictest sense, rhetoric adheres to various principles developed since classical times for arranging facts and ideas in a clear, persuasive, appealing manner. The term is also used to refer to effective prose in general and theories of or methods for composing effective prose.

Rhetorical Question: A question intended to provoke thought, but not an expressed answer, in the reader. It is most commonly used in oratory and other persuasive genres.

Rhyme: When used as a noun in literary criticism, this term generally refers to a poem in which words sound identical or very similar and appear in parallel positions in two or more lines. Rhymes are classified into different types according to where they fall in a line or stanza or according to the degree of similarity they exhibit in their spellings and sounds. Some major types of rhyme are "masculine" rhyme, "feminine" rhyme, and "triple" rhyme. In a masculine rhyme, the rhyming sound falls in a single accented syllable, as with "heat" and "eat." Feminine rhyme is a rhyme of two syllables, one stressed and one unstressed, as with "merry" and "tarry." Triple rhyme matches the sound of the accented syllable and the two unaccented syllables that follow: "narrative" and "declarative."

Rhyme Royal: A stanza of seven lines composed in iambic pentameter and rhymed *ababbcc*. The name is said to be a tribute to King James I of Scotland, who made much use of the form in his poetry.

Rhyme Scheme: See *Rhyme*

Rhythm: A regular pattern of sound, time intervals, or events occurring in writing, most often and most discernably in poetry. Regular, reliable rhythm is known to be soothing to humans, while interrupted, unpredictable, or rapidly changing rhythm is disturbing. These effects are known to authors, who use them to produce a desired reaction in the reader.

Rococo: A style of European architecture that flourished in the eighteenth century, especially in

France. The most notable features of *rococo* are its extensive use of ornamentation and its themes of lightness, gaiety, and intimacy. In literary criticism, the term is often used disparagingly to refer to a decadent or overly ornamental style.

Romance:

Romantic Age: See *Romanticism*

Romanticism: This term has two widely accepted meanings. In historical criticism, it refers to a European intellectual and artistic movement of the late eighteenth and early nineteenth centuries that sought greater freedom of personal expression than that allowed by the strict rules of literary form and logic of the eighteenth-century Neoclassicists. The Romantics preferred emotional and imaginative expression to rational analysis. They considered the individual to be at the center of all experience and so placed him or her at the center of their art. The Romantics believed that the creative imagination reveals nobler truths—unique feelings and attitudes—than those that could be discovered by logic or by scientific examination. Both the natural world and the state of childhood were important sources for revelations of "eternal truths." "Romanticism" is also used as a general term to refer to a type of sensibility found in all periods of literary history and usually considered to be in opposition to the principles of classicism. In this sense, Romanticism signifies any work or philosophy in which the exotic or dreamlike figure strongly, or that is devoted to individualistic expression, self-analysis, or a pursuit of a higher realm of knowledge than can be discovered by human reason.

Romantics: See *Romanticism*

Russian Symbolism: A Russian poetic movement, derived from French symbolism, that flourished between 1894 and 1910. While some Russian Symbolists continued in the French tradition, stressing aestheticism and the importance of suggestion above didactic intent, others saw their craft as a form of mystical worship, and themselves as mediators between the supernatural and the mundane.

S

Satire: A work that uses ridicule, humor, and wit to criticize and provoke change in human nature and institutions. There are two major types of satire: "formal" or "direct" satire speaks directly to the reader or to a character in the work; "indirect" satire relies upon the ridiculous behavior of its characters to make its point. Formal satire is further divided into two manners: the "Horatian," which

ridicules gently, and the "Juvenalian," which derides its subjects harshly and bitterly.

Scansion: The analysis or "scanning" of a poem to determine its meter and often its rhyme scheme. The most common system of scansion uses accents (slanted lines drawn above syllables) to show stressed syllables, breves (curved lines drawn above syllables) to show unstressed syllables, and vertical lines to separate each foot.

Second Person: See *Point of View*

Semiotics: The study of how literary forms and conventions affect the meaning of language.

Sestet: Any six-line poem or stanza.

Setting: The time, place, and culture in which the action of a narrative takes place. The elements of setting may include geographic location, characters' physical and mental environments, prevailing cultural attitudes, or the historical time in which the action takes place.

Shakespearean Sonnet: See *Sonnet*

Signifying Monkey: A popular trickster figure in black folklore, with hundreds of tales about this character documented since the nineteenth century.

Simile: A comparison, usually using "like" or "as," of two essentially dissimilar things, as in "coffee as cold as ice" or "He sounded like a broken record."

Slang: A type of informal verbal communication that is generally unacceptable for formal writing. Slang words and phrases are often colorful exaggerations used to emphasize the speaker's point; they may also be shortened versions of an often-used word or phrase.

Slant Rhyme: See *Consonance*

Slave Narrative: Autobiographical accounts of American slave life as told by escaped slaves. These works first appeared during the abolition movement of the 1830s through the 1850s.

Social Realism: See *Socialist Realism*

Socialist Realism: The Socialist Realism school of literary theory was proposed by Maxim Gorky and established as a dogma by the first Soviet Congress of Writers. It demanded adherence to a communist worldview in works of literature. Its doctrines required an objective viewpoint comprehensible to the working classes and themes of social struggle featuring strong proletarian heroes.

Soliloquy: A monologue in a drama used to give the audience information and to develop the speaker's character. It is typically a projection of the speaker's innermost thoughts. Usually delivered while the speaker is alone on stage, a soliloquy is intended to present an illusion of unspoken reflection.

Sonnet: A fourteen-line poem, usually composed in iambic pentameter, employing one of several rhyme schemes. There are three major types of sonnets, upon which all other variations of the form are based: the "Petrarchan" or "Italian" sonnet, the "Shakespearean" or "English" sonnet, and the "Spenserian" sonnet. A Petrarchan sonnet consists of an octave rhymed *abbaabba* and a "sestet" rhymed either *cdecde, cdccdc,* or *cdedce.* The octave poses a question or problem, relates a narrative, or puts forth a proposition; the sestet presents a solution to the problem, comments upon the narrative, or applies the proposition put forth in the octave. The Shakespearean sonnet is divided into three quatrains and a couplet rhymed *abab cdcd efef gg.* The couplet provides an epigrammatic comment on the narrative or problem put forth in the quatrains. The Spenserian sonnet uses three quatrains and a couplet like the Shakespearean, but links their three rhyme schemes in this way: *abab bcbc cdcd ee.* The Spenserian sonnet develops its theme in two parts like the Petrarchan, its final six lines resolving a problem, analyzing a narrative, or applying a proposition put forth in its first eight lines.

Spenserian Sonnet: See *Sonnet*

Spenserian Stanza: A nine-line stanza having eight verses in iambic pentameter, its ninth verse in iambic hexameter, and the rhyme scheme *ababbcbcc.*

Spondee: In poetry meter, a foot consisting of two long or stressed syllables occurring together. This form is quite rare in English verse, and is usually composed of two monosyllabic words.

Sprung Rhythm: Versification using a specific number of accented syllables per line but disregarding the number of unaccented syllables that fall in each line, producing an irregular rhythm in the poem.

Stanza: A subdivision of a poem consisting of lines grouped together, often in recurring patterns of rhyme, line length, and meter. Stanzas may also serve as units of thought in a poem much like paragraphs in prose.

Stereotype: A stereotype was originally the name for a duplication made during the printing process; this led to its modern definition as a person or thing that is (or is assumed to be) the same as all others of its type.

Stream of Consciousness: A narrative technique for rendering the inward experience of a character. This technique is designed to give the impression of an ever-changing series of thoughts, emotions, images, and memories in the spontaneous and seemingly illogical order that they occur in life.

Structuralism: A twentieth-century movement in literary criticism that examines how literary texts arrive at their meanings, rather than the meanings themselves. There are two major types of structuralist analysis: one examines the way patterns of linguistic structures unify a specific text and emphasize certain elements of that text, and the other interprets the way literary forms and conventions affect the meaning of language itself.

Structure: The form taken by a piece of literature. The structure may be made obvious for ease of understanding, as in nonfiction works, or may be obscured for artistic purposes, as in some poetry or seemingly "unstructured" prose.

Sturm und Drang: A German term meaning "storm and stress." It refers to a German literary movement of the 1770s and 1780s that reacted against the order and rationalism of the enlightenment, focusing instead on the intense experience of extraordinary individuals.

Style: A writer's distinctive manner of arranging words to suit his or her ideas and purpose in writing. The unique imprint of the author's personality upon his or her writing, style is the product of an author's way of arranging ideas and his or her use of diction, different sentence structures, rhythm, figures of speech, rhetorical principles, and other elements of composition.

Subject: The person, event, or theme at the center of a work of literature. A work may have one or more subjects of each type, with shorter works tending to have fewer and longer works tending to have more.

Subjectivity: Writing that expresses the author's personal feelings about his subject, and which may or may not include factual information about the subject.

Surrealism: A term introduced to criticism by Guillaume Apollinaire and later adopted by Andre Breton. It refers to a French literary and artistic movement founded in the 1920s. The Surrealists sought to express unconscious thoughts and feelings in their works. The best-known technique used for achieving this aim was automatic writing—transcriptions of spontaneous outpourings from the unconscious. The Surrealists proposed to unify the contrary levels of conscious and unconscious, dream and reality, objectivity and subjectivity into a new level of "super-realism."

Suspense: A literary device in which the author maintains the audience's attention through the buildup of events, the outcome of which will soon be revealed.

Syllogism: A method of presenting a logical argument. In its most basic form, the syllogism consists of a major premise, a minor premise, and a conclusion.

Symbol: Something that suggests or stands for something else without losing its original identity. In literature, symbols combine their literal meaning with the suggestion of an abstract concept. Literary symbols are of two types: those that carry complex associations of meaning no matter what their contexts, and those that derive their suggestive meaning from their functions in specific literary works.

Symbolism: This term has two widely accepted meanings. In historical criticism, it denotes an early modernist literary movement initiated in France during the nineteenth century that reacted against the prevailing standards of realism. Writers in this movement aimed to evoke, indirectly and symbolically, an order of being beyond the material world of the five senses. Poetic expression of personal emotion figured strongly in the movement, typically by means of a private set of symbols uniquely identifiable with the individual poet. The principal aim of the Symbolists was to express in words the highly complex feelings that grew out of everyday contact with the world. In a broader sense, the term "symbolism" refers to the use of one object to represent another.

Symbolist: See *Symbolism*

Symbolist Movement: See *Symbolism*

Sympathetic Fallacy: See *Affective Fallacy*

T

Tanka: A form of Japanese poetry similar to *haiku*. A *tanka* is five lines long, with the lines containing five, seven, five, seven, and seven syllables respectively.

Terza Rima: A three-line stanza form in poetry in which the rhymes are made on the last word of each line in the following manner: the first and third lines of the first stanza, then the second line of the first stanza and the first and third lines of the second stanza, and so on with the middle line of any

stanza rhyming with the first and third lines of the following stanza.

Tetrameter: See *Meter*

Textual Criticism: A branch of literary criticism that seeks to establish the authoritative text of a literary work. Textual critics typically compare all known manuscripts or printings of a single work in order to assess the meanings of differences and revisions. This procedure allows them to arrive at a definitive version that (supposedly) corresponds to the author's original intention.

Theme: The main point of a work of literature. The term is used interchangeably with thesis.

Thesis: A thesis is both an essay and the point argued in the essay. Thesis novels and thesis plays share the quality of containing a thesis which is supported through the action of the story.

Third Person: See *Point of View*

Tone: The author's attitude toward his or her audience may be deduced from the tone of the work. A formal tone may create distance or convey politeness, while an informal tone may encourage a friendly, intimate, or intrusive feeling in the reader. The author's attitude toward his or her subject matter may also be deduced from the tone of the words he or she uses in discussing it.

Tragedy: A drama in prose or poetry about a noble, courageous hero of excellent character who, because of some tragic character flaw or *hamartia*, brings ruin upon him- or herself. Tragedy treats its subjects in a dignified and serious manner, using poetic language to help evoke pity and fear and bring about catharsis, a purging of these emotions. The tragic form was practiced extensively by the ancient Greeks. In the Middle Ages, when classical works were virtually unknown, tragedy came to denote any works about the fall of persons from exalted to low conditions due to any reason: fate, vice, weakness, etc. According to the classical definition of tragedy, such works present the "pathetic"—that which evokes pity—rather than the tragic. The classical form of tragedy was revived in the sixteenth century; it flourished especially on the Elizabethan stage. In modern times, dramatists have attempted to adapt the form to the needs of modern society by drawing their heroes from the ranks of ordinary men and women and defining the nobility of these heroes in terms of spirit rather than exalted social standing.

Tragic Flaw: In a tragedy, the quality within the hero or heroine which leads to his or her downfall.

Transcendentalism: An American philosophical and religious movement, based in New England from around 1835 until the Civil War. Transcendentalism was a form of American romanticism that had its roots abroad in the works of Thomas Carlyle, Samuel Coleridge, and Johann Wolfgang von Goethe. The Transcendentalists stressed the importance of intuition and subjective experience in communication with God. They rejected religious dogma and texts in favor of mysticism and scientific naturalism. They pursued truths that lie beyond the "colorless" realms perceived by reason and the senses and were active social reformers in public education, women's rights, and the abolition of slavery.

Trickster: A character or figure common in Native American and African literature who uses his ingenuity to defeat enemies and escape difficult situations. Tricksters are most often animals, such as the spider, hare, or coyote, although they may take the form of humans as well.

Trimeter: See *Meter*

Triple Rhyme: See *Rhyme*

Trochee: See *Foot*

U

Understatement: See *Irony*

Unities: Strict rules of dramatic structure, formulated by Italian and French critics of the Renaissance and based loosely on the principles of drama discussed by Aristotle in his *Poetics*. Foremost among these rules were the three unities of action, time, and place that compelled a dramatist to: (1) construct a single plot with a beginning, middle, and end that details the causal relationships of action and character; (2) restrict the action to the events of a single day; and (3) limit the scene to a single place or city. The unities were observed faithfully by continental European writers until the Romantic Age, but they were never regularly observed in English drama. Modern dramatists are typically more concerned with a unity of impression or emotional effect than with any of the classical unities.

Urban Realism: A branch of realist writing that attempts to accurately reflect the often harsh facts of modern urban existence.

Utopia: A fictional perfect place, such as "paradise" or "heaven."

Utopian: See *Utopia*

Utopianism: See *Utopia*

V

Verisimilitude: Literally, the appearance of truth. In literary criticism, the term refers to aspects of a work of literature that seem true to the reader.

Vers de societe: See *Occasional Verse*

Vers libre: See *Free Verse*

Verse: A line of metered language, a line of a poem, or any work written in verse.

Versification: The writing of verse. Versification may also refer to the meter, rhyme, and other mechanical components of a poem.

Victorian: Refers broadly to the reign of Queen Victoria of England (1837–1901) and to anything with qualities typical of that era. For example, the qualities of smug narrowmindedness, bourgeois materialism, faith in social progress, and priggish morality are often considered Victorian. This stereotype is contradicted by such dramatic intellectual developments as the theories of Charles Darwin, Karl Marx, and Sigmund Freud (which stirred strong debates in England) and the critical attitudes of serious Victorian writers like Charles Dickens and George Eliot. In literature, the Victorian Period was the great age of the English novel, and the latter part of the era saw the rise of movements such as decadence and symbolism.

Victorian Age: See *Victorian*

Victorian Period: See *Victorian*

W

Weltanschauung: A German term referring to a person's worldview or philosophy.

Weltschmerz: A German term meaning "world pain." It describes a sense of anguish about the nature of existence, usually associated with a melancholy, pessimistic attitude.

Z

Zarzuela: A type of Spanish operetta.

Zeitgeist: A German term meaning "spirit of the time." It refers to the moral and intellectual trends of a given era.

Cumulative Author/Title Index

Cumulative Author/Title Index

Cumulative Nationality/Ethnicity Index

Acoma Pueblo

Ortiz, Simon
  Hunger in New York City: V4

African American

Angelou, Maya
  Harlem Hopscotch: V2
  On the Pulse of Morning: V3
Baraka, Amiri
  In Memory of Radio: V9
Brooks, Gwendolyn
  The Bean Eaters: V2
  The Sonnet-Ballad: V1
  Strong Men, Riding Horses: V4
  We Real Cool: V6
Clifton, Lucille
  Miss Rosie: V1
Cullen, Countee
  Any Human to Another: V3
Dove, Rita
  This Life: V1
Hayden, Robert
  Those Winter Sundays: V1
Hughes, Langston
  Harlem: V1
  Mother to Son: V3
  The Negro Speaks of Rivers: V10
  Theme for English B: V6
Johnson, James Weldon
  The Creation: V1
Komunyakaa, Yusef
  Facing It: V5
Madgett, Naomi Long
  Alabama Centennial: V10
McElroy, Colleen
  A Pièd: V3

Randall, Dudley
  Ballad of Birmingham: V5
Reed, Ishmael
  Beware: Do Not Read This Poem:
    V6

American

Acosta, Teresa Palomo
  My Mother Pieced Quilts: V12
Angelou, Maya
  Harlem Hopscotch: V2
  On the Pulse of Morning: V3
Ashbery, John
  Paradoxes and Oxymorons: V11
Auden, W. H.
  As I Walked Out One Evening:
    V4
  Musée des Beaux Arts: V1
  The Unknown Citizen: V3
Bishop, Elizabeth
  Brazil, January 1, 1502: V6
  Filling Station: V12
Blumenthal, Michael
  Inventors: V7
Bly, Robert
  Come with Me: V6
Bradstreet, Anne
  To My Dear and Loving Husband:
    V6
Brooks, Gwendolyn
  The Bean Eaters: V2
  The Sonnet-Ballad: V1
  Strong Men, Riding Horses: V4
  We Real Cool: V6
Clifton, Lucille
  Miss Rosie: V1

Crane, Stephen
  War Is Kind: V9
Cullen, Countee
  Any Human to Another: V3
cummings, e. e.
  l(a: V1
  *maggie and milly and molly and
    may*: V12
  old age sticks: V3
Dickey, James
  The Heaven of Animals: V6
  The Hospital Window: V11
Dickinson, Emily
  *Because I Could Not Stop for
    Death*: V2
  The Bustle in a House: V10
  *"Hope" Is the Thing with
    Feathers*: V3
  *I Heard a Fly Buzz—When I
    Died—*: V5
  *My Life Closed Twice Before Its
    Close*: V8
  A Narrow Fellow in the Grass:
    V11
  *The Soul Selects Her Own
    Society*: V1
  There's a Certain Slant of Light:
    V6
  This Is My Letter to the World: V4
Dove, Rita
  This Life: V1
Dubie, Norman
  *The Czar's Last Christmas Letter.
    A Barn in the Urals*: V12
Dugan, Alan
  How We Heard the Name: V10
Eliot, T. S.
  Journey of the Magi: V7

Australian

Subject/Theme Index

***Boldface** denotes dicussion in *Themes* section.

Cumulative Index of First Lines

A

A brackish reach of shoal off Madaket,— (The Quaker Graveyard in Nantucket) V6:158

"A cold coming we had of it (Journey of the Magi) V7:110

A narrow Fellow in the grass (A Narrow Fellow in the Grass) V11:127

A poem should be palpable and mute (Ars Poetica) V5:2

A wind is ruffling the tawny pelt (A Far Cry from Africa) V6:60

About me the night moonless wimples the mountains (Vancouver Lights) V8:245

About suffering they were never wrong (Musée des Beaux Arts) V1:148

Across Roblin Lake, two shores away, (Wilderness Gothic) V12:241

After you finish your work (Ballad of Orange and Grape) V10:17

"Ah, are you digging on my grave (Ah, Are You Digging on My Grave?) V4:2

All Greece hates (Helen) V6:92

All night long the hockey pictures (To a Sad Daughter) V8:230

All winter your brute shoulders strained against collars, padding (Names of Horses) V8:141

Anasazi (Anasazi) V9:2

And God stepped out on space (The Creation) V1:19

Animal bones and some mossy tent rings (Lament for the Dorsets) V5:190

As I perceive (The Gold Lily) V5:127

As I walked out one evening (As I Walked Out One Evening) V4:15

At noon in the desert a panting lizard (At the Bomb Testing Site) V8:2

Ay, tear her tattered ensign down! (Old Ironsides) V9:172

As virtuous men pass mildly away (A Valediction: Forbidding Mourning) V11:201

B

Back then, before we came (On Freedom's Ground) V12:186

Bananas ripe and green, and ginger-root (The Tropics in New York) V4:255

Because I could not stop for Death— (Because I Could Not Stop for Death) V2:27

Bent double, like old beggars under slacks, (Dulce et Decorum Est) V10:109

Between my finger and my thumb (Digging) V5:70

Beware of ruins: they have a treacherous charm (Beware of Ruins) V8:43

Bright star! would I were steadfast as thou art— (Bright Star! Would I Were Steadfast as Thou Art) V9:44

By the rude bridge that arched the flood (Concord Hymn) V4:30

C

Come with me into those things that have felt his despair for so long— (Come with Me) V6:31

Composed in the Tower, before his execution ("More Light! More Light!") V6:119

D

Darkened by time, the masters, like our memories, mix (Black Zodiac) V10:46

Death, be not proud, though some have called thee (Holy Sonnet 10) V2:103

Devouring Time, blunt thou the lion's paws (Sonnet 19) V9:210

Do not go gentle into that good night (Do Not Go Gentle into that Good Night) V1:51

Do not weep, maiden, for war is kind (War Is Kind) V9:252

(Dumb, (A Grafted Tongue) V12:92

E

Each day the shadow swings (In the Land of Shinar) V7:83

F

Falling upon earth (Falling Upon Earth) V2:64
Five years have past; five summers, with the length (Tintern Abbey) V2:249
Flesh is heretic. (Anorexic) V12:2
From my mother's sleep I fell into the State (The Death of the Ball Turret Gunner) V2:41

G

Go down, Moses (Go Down, Moses) V11:42
Gray mist wolf (Four Mountain Wolves) V9:131

H

"Had he and I but met (The Man He Killed) V3:167
Had we but world enough, and time (To His Coy Mistress) V5:276
Half a league, half a league (The Charge of the Light Brigade) V1:2
Having a Coke with You (Having a Coke with You) V12:105
He clasps the crag with crooked hands (The Eagle) V11:30
He was found by the Bureau of Statistics to be (The Unknown Citizen) V3:302
Hear the sledges with the bells— (The Bells) V3:46
Her body is not so white as (Queen-Ann's-Lace) V6:179
Her eyes were coins of porter and her West (A Farewell to English) V10:126
Here they are. The soft eyes open (The Heaven of Animals) V6:75
Hog Butcher for the World (Chicago) V3:61
Hope is a tattered flag and a dream out of time. (Hope is a Tattered Flag) V12:120
"Hope" is the thing with feathers— (Hope Is the Thing with Feathers) V3:123
How do I love thee? Let me count the ways (Sonnet 43) V2:236
How shall we adorn (Angle of Geese) V2:2
How would it be if you took yourself off (Landscape with Tractor) V10:182
Hunger crawls into you (Hunger in New York City) V4:79

I

I am not a painter, I am a poet (Why I Am Not a Painter) V8:258
I am silver and exact. I have no preconceptions (Mirror) V1:116
I am trying to pry open your casket (Dear Reader) V10:85
I cannot love the Brothers Wright (Reactionary Essay on Applied Science) V9:199
I have just come down from my father (The Hospital Window) V11:58
I have met them at close of day (Easter 1916) V5:91
I hear America singing, the varied carols I hear (I Hear America Singing) V3:152

I heard a Fly buzz—when I died— (I Heard a Fly Buzz—When I Died—) V5:140
I know that I shall meet my fate (An Irish Airman Foresees His Death) V1:76
I sit in the top of the wood, my eyes closed (Hawk Roosting) V4:55
I'm delighted to see you (The Constellation Orion) V8:53
I've known rivers; (The Negro Speaks of Rivers) V10:197
If ever two were one, then surely we (To My Dear and Loving Husband) V6:228
If I should die, think only this of me (The Soldier) V7:218
"Imagine being the first to say: *surveillance*," (Inventors) V7:97
In China (Lost Sister) V5:216
In ethics class so many years ago (Ethics) V8:88
In Flanders fields the poppies blow (In Flanders Fields) V5:155
In the Shreve High football stadium (Autumn Begins in Martins Ferry, Ohio) V8:17
In Xanadu did Kubla Khan (Kubla Khan) V5:172
Ink runs from the corners of my mouth (Eating Poetry) V9:60
It is an ancient Mariner (The Rime of the Ancient Mariner) V4:127
It little profits that an idle king (Ulysses) V2:278
It looked extremely rocky for the Mudville nine that day (Casey at the Bat) V5:57
It was in and about the Martinmas time (Barbara Allan) V7:10
It was many and many a year ago (Annabel Lee) V9:14
Its quick soft silver bell beating, beating (Auto Wreck) V3:31

J

Januaries, Nature greets our eyes (Brazil, January 1, 1502) V6:15
Just off the highway to Rochester, Minnesota (A Blessing) V7:24

L

l(a (l(a) V1:85
Let me not to the marriage of true minds (Sonnet 116) V3:288
Listen, my children, and you shall hear (Paul Revere's Ride) V2:178
Little Lamb, who made thee? (The Lamb) V12:134
Long long ago when the world was a wild place (Bedtime Story) V8:32

M

maggie and milly and molly and may (maggie & milly & molly & may) V12:149
Mary sat musing on the lamp-flame at the table (The Death of the Hired Man) V4:42
Men with picked voices chant the names (Overture to a Dance of Locomotives) V11:143
"Mother dear, may I go downtown (Ballad of Birmingham) V5:17

Cumulative Index of First Lines

Cumulative Index of Last Lines

A

a man then suddenly stops running (Island of Three Marias) V11:80

a space in the lives of their friends (Beware: Do Not Read This Poem) V6:3

A terrible beauty is born (Easter 1916) V5:91

About my big, new, automatically defrosting refrigerator with the built-in electric eye (Reactionary Essay on Applied Science) V9:199

Across the expedient and wicked stones (Auto Wreck) V3:31

Ah, dear father, graybeard, lonely old courage-teacher, what America did you have when Charon quit poling his ferry and you got out on a smoking bank and stood watching the boat disappear on the black waters of Lethe? (A Supermarket in California) V5:261

All losses are restored and sorrows end (Sonnet 30) V4:192

Amen. Amen (The Creation) V1:20

Anasazi (Anasazi) V9:3

and all beyond saving by children (Ethics) V8:88

And all we need of hell (My Life Closed Twice Before Its Close) V8:127

and changed, back to the class ("Trouble with Math in a One-Room Country School") V9:238

And Death shall be no more: Death, thou shalt die (Holy Sonnet 10) V2:103

And drunk the milk of Paradise (Kubla Khan) V5:172

And gallop terribly against each other's bodies (Autumn Begins in Martins Ferry, Ohio) V8:17

And his own Word (The Phoenix) V10:226

And I am Nicholas. (The Czar's Last Christmas Letter) V12:45

And life for me ain't been no crystal stair (Mother to Son) V3:179

And like a thunderbolt he falls (The Eagle) V11:30

And makes me end where I begun (A Valediction: Forbidding Mourning) V11:202

And 'midst the stars inscribe Belinda's name. (The Rape of the Lock) V12:209

And miles to go before I sleep (Stopping by Woods on a Snowy Evening) V1:272

And not waving but drowning (Not Waving but Drowning) V3:216

And oh, 'tis true, 'tis true (When I Was One-and-Twenty) V4:268

And reach for your scalping knife. (For Jean Vincent D'abbadie, Baron St.-Castin) V12:78

and retreating, always retreating, behind it (Brazil, January 1, 1502) V6:16

And settled upon his eyes in a black soot ("More Light! More Light!") V6:120

And so live ever—or else swoon to death (Bright Star! Would I Were Steadfast as Thou Art) V9:44

and strange and loud was the dingoes' cry (Drought Year) V8:78

and sweat and fat and greed. (Anorexic) V12:3

And that has made all the difference (The Road Not Taken) V2:195

And the deep river ran on (As I Walked Out One Evening) V4:16

And the midnight message of Paul Revere (Paul Revere's Ride) V2:180

And the mome raths outgrabe (Jabberwocky) V11:91

And the Salvation Army singing God loves us. . . . (Hope is a Tattered Flag) V12:120

and these the last verses that I write for her (Tonight I Can Write) V11:187

And those roads in South Dakota that feel around in the darkness ... (Come with Me) V6:31

and to know she will stay in the field till you die? (Landscape with Tractor) V10:183

and two blankets embroidered with smallpox (Meeting the British) V7:138

And would suffice (Fire and Ice) V7:57